This is a major piece of work. It is a complete treatment of medical visualization and certain to become essential reading for any researcher, practitioner, and educator in the field. The book is well written and organized, with nice summaries at the end of each chapter that point to further reading. Some parts of the book have value beyond the field of medicine—for example, the sections on volume visualization, with their clear exposition of the different techniques, will be a useful reference in quite separate fields, such as computational fluid dynamics. The book also covers aspects of virtual reality in medicine, with its chapter on virtual endoscopy, an increasingly important application area. The authors are to be congratulated on a major achievement.

—DR. KEN BRODLIE, Professor of Visualization, School of Computing, University of Leeds, UK

Visualization and medicine are a great combination. In the past, medical images such as X-rays were directly produced as photographs. Today, highly advanced imaging devices such as MRI scanners produce large and complex data sets, which require a large amount of processing to be turned into images useful in medical practice. This book describes the current technology for this visualization process. Medical doctors are enthusiastic, highly-critical users, and many fruitful cooperations with visualization scientists have developed. As a result, medicine has become one of the largest and most successful applications of visualization, and the results have found their way to clinical practice and industrial products. The field has matured to the point that the state of the art needs a book, and I congratulate the authors for recognizing this and creating this impressive volume. The book can serve as a standard reference text for researchers and practitioners, both technical and medical. As new courses and curricula in medical technology are developed and taught around the world, Visualization in Medicine fills the need for a comprehensive text. Theory, practical applications, and advanced topics are all covered in a well-balanced mixture. This book will find its way to research laboratories, classrooms, companies, and hospitals, where it will help to disseminate sound, useful medical visualization technology to support the processes of medical diagnosis and treatment of numerous patients around the world.

—FRITS H. POST, Associate Professor of Visualization, Delft University of Technology, The Netherlands

This significant book helps fill a long-standing gap in textbooks for students in scientific visualization and medical imaging as it successfully bridges the two domains with thorough explanations, vivid examples, and useful references. The visualization community is well-served by the authors' overview of imaging modalities, standard radiological practices, and clinical applications, while the medical imaging community benefits from a coherent exposition of core visualization methods like isosurface extraction, direct volume rendering, and illustrative rendering. The section on volume data exploration demonstrates how visualization requires effective interfaces and quantitative interaction modes to meet clinical needs, and the coverage of more advanced topics exemplifies how knowledge from both the visualization and imaging domains can be leveraged and combined to create insight for medical diagnosis, planning, and education. The authors' backgrounds, in the intersection of visualization research and medical imaging applications, make them ideally suited to explain such a breadth of material in this valuable text.

—DR. GORDON KINDLMANN, Brigham and Women's Hospital, Harvard Medical School

This text will be popular with students of medical visualization data acquisition and analysis. A lot of care and experience have gone into the book. The consistency and effort is impressive. I do not know of a comparable book in scope or relevance. Well done!

—DREW BERRY, The Walter and Eliza Hall Institute of Medical Research, Melbourne, Australia

Primarily this is a book for a computer scientist or engineer, as well as the technically interested physician. A comprehensive book, providing grounding in all of the important techniques currently available for visualization in medicine. Easy to read, timely, current, state-of-the-art, extremely useful. I know of no other text that presents all of this information in one place. There is no real competitor to this book!

—Professor NIGEL W. JOHN, School of Computer Science, University of Wales, Bangor

A good mix of technology and applications, readers will find concepts presented clearly, plentiful illustrations and images, easy to read. The authors' passion and experience for the subject matter show.

—DR. KLAUS MUELLER, Professor, Stony Brook University (SUNY), New York

The authors have accomplished the laudable feat of nicely structuring a quite diverse research field and delivering a comprehensive piece of work that makes an interesting read for experts from varying areas of expertise. The book will be an authoritative guide to medical visualization for years to come.

—from the foreword by DR. EDUARD GRÖLLER, Professor, Vienna University of Technology

THE MORGAN KAUFMANN SERIES IN COMPUTER GRAPHICS

VISUALIZATION IN MEDICINE

THE MORGAN KAUFMANN SERIES IN COMPUTER GRAPHICS

VISUALIZATION IN MEDICINE

THEORY, ALGORITHMS, AND APPLICATIONS

BERNHARD PREIM

DIRK BARTZ

AMSTERDAM • BOSTON • HEIDELBERG • LONDON
NEW YORK • OXFORD • PARIS • SAN DIEGO
SAN FRANCISCO • SINGAPORE • SYDNEY • TOKYO

Morgan Kaufmann Publishers is an imprint of Elsevier

ELSEVIER

MORGAN KAUFMANN PUBLISHERS

Publishing Director: Denise E. M. Penrose
Acquisitions Editor: Tiffany Gasbarrini
Publishing Services Manager: George Morrison
Senior Production Editor: Paul Gottehrer
Assistant Editor: Michele Cronin
Marketing Manager: Misty Bergeron
Out-Source Management: Multiscience Press, Inc.
Composition: diacriTech
Interior printer: Hing Yip
Cover printer: Hing Yip

Morgan Kaufmann Publishers is an imprint of Elsevier.
30 Corporate Drive, Suite 400, Burlington, MA 01803, USA

Library of Congress Cataloging-in-Publication Data
Application submitted

ISBN: 978-0-12-370596-9

For information on all Morgan Kaufmann publications,
visit our Web site at www.mkp.com or www.books.elsevier.com

Printed in China
07 08 09 10 11   5 4 3 2 1

Working together to grow
libraries in developing countries

www.elsevier.com | www.bookaid.org | www.sabre.org

ELSEVIER   BOOK AID International   Sabre Foundation

BERNHARD PREIM is Professor of Visualization at the computer science department at the Otto-von-Guericke-University of Magdeburg, where he leads a research group focused on medical visualization and its application in diagnosis, surgical planning and education. He is also a visiting professor at MeVis Research. He sits on the scientific advisory boards of the International Competence Center on Computer-Assisted Surgery (ICCAS), the German Society for Computer and Robot-assisted Surgery (CURAC) and he is speaker of the working group Medical Visualization in the German Society for Computer Science. He is member of the ACM and the German Chapter of the ACM.

DIRK BARTZ is Professor for Computer-Assisted Surgery at the University of Leipzig. Previously, he was head of the research group on Visual Computing for Medicine of the University of Tübingen. He was member of the executive committee of the IEEE Visualization and Graphics Technical Committee (VGTC), is speaker of the Eurographics Working Group on Parallel Graphics, and founding/steering member of the Gesellschaft für Informatik working groups on Medical Visualization and Data Visualization. His main research interests are in visual medicine and medical imaging, medical mixed reality, visualization of large datasets, man-machine interfaces, parallel/grid computing, and data visualization. He received the NDI Young Investigator Award for his work in virtual endoscopy and intra-operative navigation.

Contents

PART V APPLICATION AREAS AND CASE STUDIES   497

19 IMAGE ANALYSIS AND VISUALIZATION FOR LIVER SURGERY PLANNING   499

Foreword

Visualization in Medicine is an excellent textbook for students, researchers, and practitioners in the field of medical visualization. The field of medical visualization has rapidly evolved in recent years and currently comprises a large and quite heterogeneous body of advanced research work.

This book is concerned with diagnosis, treatment, and therapy planning with a focus on tomographic slice data such as Computed Tomography and Magnetic Resonance Imaging. In detail it covers the elaborate pipeline: from data acquisition, analysis, and interpretation, to advanced volume visualization and exploration techniques. Selected image analysis techniques, which are often used in combination with visualization techniques, are concisely treated. Important application areas and advanced visualization techniques for vascular structures, virtual endoscopy, and liver surgery planning are extensively dealt with.

The acceptance of medical visualization techniques by medical doctors critically depends on issues like performance, robustness, and accuracy. In this respect the book does a very good job in discussing the validation and clinical evaluation of medical-visualization methods. Medical visualization is a highly interdisciplinary research area involving specialists from quite different professional backgrounds. The book will definitely help to bridge the gap between technical individuals who develop visualization methods and the medical doctors who are supposed to apply these methods in their clinical routine.

As the area of medical visualization has blossomed and matured over recent years, a comprehensive overview, as provided by this book, has been urgently needed. The book will be a prime source for students taking courses on medical imaging and visualization, and will be a solid basis for researchers interested in medical visualization. Furthermore, for physicians with research interests in computer-assisted radiology and surgery, the book gives a thorough overview on the state of the art.

The book is well structured. The 21 chapters are classified into five focal themes. Each chapter starts with outlining content to come and concludes with references to further readings. The well-conceived hierarchical composition allows for non-sequential reading and quick focus on specific sub-topics of interest.

The authors have accomplished the laudable feat of nicely structuring a quite diverse research field and delivering a comprehensive piece of work that makes an interesting read for experts from varying areas of expertise. The book will be an authoritative guide to medical visualization for years to come.

DR. EDUARD GRÖLLER
Vienna University of Technology

Preface

The past years have seen tremendous advances in medical technology to acquire data about the human body with ever increasing resolution, quality, and accuracy. At a similar pace, visualization research for medicine has progressed, employing this medical data. Considering this technological revolution, we feel that it is time to write a textbook on this topic to support students, researchers, and practioners in this field, or those who want to become a part of it. This book is based on basic and applied research in computer-assisted radiology and surgery. It combines our knowledge and experiences in research and in computer science education since the year 2000.

In keeping with the character of a textbook, we focus on the visualization and interaction techniques that have a great potential in many areas of diagnosis and treatment planning and skip methods that are strongly bound to a particular application or that rely on rarely available image data. We focus on methods based on tomographic slice data, such as Computed Tomography and Magnetic Resonance Imaging. These are regularly spaced volume data; therefore, the description of volume rendering is focused on such data. We consider single volume data but also dynamic volume data (time-dependent data acquired, for example, to image the blood flow in the human body) and the integration of different volume data from different acquisition devices.

Medical visualization is an advanced topic; we assume that the reader is familiar with computer graphics and possibly with basic visualization methods. Some basic visualization techniques, such as the volume visualization methods, are explained in detail, but others are not. In those cases we recommend the excellent book *The Visualization Toolkit* [SCHROEDER et al. 2001].

Clinical problems cannot be solved by visualization techniques alone. In particular, it is often necessary to analyze the data, to "detect" and delineate important anatomic and pathologic structures. This process, called segmentation, is the basis for many high quality visualization techniques and also a prerequisite for a quantification of spatial relations. Medical image analysis is a closely related area to medical visualization. We describe selected image analysis techniques that are often used in combination with visualization techniques. For readers primarily interested on medical image analysis, we refer to dedicated books, such as [SONKA and FITZPATRICK 2000].

Our book provides a good overview on volume visualization, including specialized algorithms dedicated to clinical applications. Advanced visualization techniques, e.g., for the display of vascular structures and for virtual endoscopy, are another focus of this book. In the application part, we describe several case studies on how medical visualization techniques are combined to solve clinically relevant problems.

Since diagnosis and therapy planning are serious application areas, the validation of visualization methods and the clinical evaluation of the methods is a crucial aspect. We discuss methods to analyze the accuracy of segmentation and visualization methods, and we also describe how the value of medical visualization applications can be assessed.

Intended Audience This book is mainly intended for students taking courses on medical imaging and visualization. As medical visualization is an advanced research–oriented topic, it also serves as a solid base for researchers interested in medical visualization. Furthermore, for physicians who have research interests in computer assisted radiology and surgery, the book provides an overview on the state of the art. Specifically, it introduces into the possibilities and limitations of the field. For computer science researchers and researchers from related technical areas, the book provides a basis, focusing on algorithms and methods with demonstrated clinical use.

Medical visualization is a fascinating and growing research area. For computer scientists and engineers, this fascination may originate in the importance of the application area. Nevertheless, contributing successfully to medical visualization is a challenging task. Among other difficulties one has to face, appropriate interdisciplinary project teams have to be established. It is difficult to achieve a mutual understanding between medical doctors and people from technical backgrounds. It needs patience and a strong desire to understand different positions. For those who develop methods and algorithms and integrate them in software assistants intended for clinical use, it is mandatory to visit physicians in their workplaces (even in the operating room) to gain insight into their work. Reliable information must be extracted as to which information is useful for diagnostic processes, for treatment decisions, and for the strategy of surgeons. The difficulty of understanding each other starts with terminology. Even if the words used are familiar they might have different meanings to different team members. As an example, we cite RON KIKINIS, Director of the Surgical Planning Laboratory of the Department of Radiology, Brigham and Women's Hospital and Harvard Medical School. "If I say 'this is urgent' to a medical doctor, he puts his cup of coffee to the table and answers 'Let's go,' expecting that immediate action is required. If I say 'this is urgent' to a computer scientist, he will start to think about it next week and perhaps come with a solution next month." Cultures, attitudes, and working procedures are very different; maybe this is another reason for the fascination of medical visualization.

ACKNOWLEDGEMENTS

We have to thank many people for their support, for fruitful discussions and for collaboration which was essential to write this book. BERNHARD PREIM wants to thank PROF. KARL J. OLDHAFER (General hospital Celle), DR. GERO STRAUß, DR. ILKA HERTEL, PROF. ANDREAS DIETZ and PROF. JÜRGEN MEIXENSBERGER (University hospital Leipzig), PROF. MICHAEL GALANSKI, DR. HOEN-OH SHIN and DR. GEORG STAMM (Medical School Hannover), PROF. HAUKE LANG and DR. ARNOLD RADKE (University hospital Essen), DR. KAI LEHMANN (University hospital Berlin), PROF. HUBERTUS FEUSSNER (Munich University of Technology, Department of Surgery) for their support in long-lasting cooperations, for discussions on requirements for treatment planning, and for their substantial help concerning the evaluation of medical visualization applications. DR. ALF RITTER of Brainlab provided images and much background information with respect to measurement and navigation. DR. PREIM also wants to thank his former colleagues at the Center of Medical Diagnosis Systems and Visualization (MeVis) for their support, for the implementation of algorithms and applications, for proofreading chapters, and for providing images and substantial background information over and above published work. Many thanks go to PROF. DR. HEINZ-OTTO PEITGEN, DR. MARKUS LANG and DR. GUIDO PRAUSE, SARAH BEHRENS, DR. TOBIAS BOSKAMP, DR. HOLGER BOURQUAIN, STEFAN DACHWITZ, DR. VOLKER DICKEN, ANJA HENNEMUTH, MILO HINDENNACH, DR. HORST HAHN, OLAF KONRAD-VERSE, DR. SVEN KOHLE, DR. FELIX RITTER, DR. MATTHIAS SCHLÜTER, DR. DIRK SELLE, ANDREA SCHENK, and WOLF SPINDLER. We also want to acknowledge the support of the visualization group at the University of Magdeburg (RAGNAR BADE, ALEXANDRA BAER, JEANETTE CORDES, JANA DORNHEIM, ARNO KRÜGER, KONRAD MÜHLER, STEFFEN OELTZE, and CHRISTIAN TIETJEN) as well as the Master students DÖRTE APELT, CHRISTIAN BENDICKS, CHRISTINA DÖRGE, JENS HAASE, BJÖRN MEYER, SEBASTIAN MIRSCHEL, DIANA STÖLZEL and ANDREAS TAPPENBECK. Many thanks go to the secretaries of the Institute for Simulation and Graphics, MRS. PETRA JANKA,

PETRA SPECHT, STEFANIE QUADE and BEATRE TRAORE, for substantial support in proofreading, drawing illustrations, and handling correspondence related to the book.

DIRK BARTZ is in particular thankful to his clinical research partners at the University of Tübingen, namely PROF. DR. JÜRGEN HOFFMANN, DR. DIRK REUDENSTEIN, PROF. DR. FRANK DUFFNER, PROF. DR. MARCOS TATAGIBA, PROF. DR. JOACHIM HONEGGER, PROF. DR. SIEGMAR REINERT, PROF. DR. FLORIAN DAMMANN, PROF. DR. MARCUS MAASSEN, and PROF. DR. HORST BECKER. His appreciations also includes colleagues and friends at other hospitals, DR. ÖZLEM GÜRVIT (University of Frankfurt), PROF. DR. MARTIN SKALEJ (University of Magdeburg), and DIRK MAYER (University of Mainz). He is also grateful for many discussions with other colleagues from the computer science community, such as PROF. DR. EDUARD GRÖLLER (Vienna University of Technology), PROF. DR. JOACHIM HORNEGGER (University of Erlangen-Nürnberg), PROF. DR. ARIE KAUFMAN (Stony Brook University), DR. CRISTIAN LORENZ (Philips Research Hamburg), PROF. DR. HEINRICH MÜLLER (University of Dortmund), PROF. DR. KLAUS MUELLER (Stony Brook University), PROF. DR. AMITABH VARSHNEY (University of Maryland, College Park), DR. RAINER WEGENKITTL (GWI-Tiani), and DR. KAREL ZUIDERVELD (Vital Images)

DR. PREIM is especially grateful to the members of his research group at the University of Tübingen: DR. JAN FISCHER, MARTHA KERSTEN, DR. ÁNGEL DEL RÍO, DR. ZEIN SALAH, and DR. DIRK STANEKER; his colleagues at WSI/GRIS of the University of Tübingen: DR. DOUGLAS CUNNINGHAM, DR. MICHAEL DOGGETT (now at ATI Research), ALEXANDER EHLERT, DR. OLAF ETZMUß, DR. MICHAEL HAUTH, URS KANUS, DR. MICHAEL KECKEISEN, DR. STEFAN KIMMERLE, DR. MICHAEL MEIßNER (now at Vital Images), RALF SONDERSHAUS, RALF SONNTAG, PROF. DR. MARKUS WACKER (now at the University of Applied Science Dresden), DR. GREGOR WETEKAM, and many more.

Most of the research work could not have been done without students, in particular SILVIA BORN, JIRKO CERNIK, LUDWIG GAUCKLER, JASMINA ORMAN, MATTHIAS PFEIFLE, EUGEN RESCH, CHRISTINE SCHALLER, and BENJAMIN SCHNAIDT. Last but not least, he would like to thank PROF. DR. WOLFGANG STRAßER for continuing support.

Both authors would like to express special thanks to DR. STEFAN ZACHOW from the Zuse-Institute Berlin for carefully proofreading the whole book and for many suggestions based on his profound insight in medical visualization. Many other colleagues and researchers in our exciting fields have provided us with advice and images that they have generated, which we have included in our book. We thank you all for your support.

The book proposal and some sample chapters have been carefully reviewed by DR. DREW BERRY, DR. DAVID EBERLY, PROF. DR. THOMAS ERTL, PROF. DR. NIGEL JOHN, and PROF. DR. KLAUS MUELLER, as well as two anonymous reviewers. Many thanks for the constructive and helpful comments on early versions of the book.

We also want to acknowledge the support of the German Research Foundation (DFG), in particular the Focus Program 1124, "Medical Robotics and Navigation." Funding for projects on computer support for liver surgery planning, surgery planning for sinus surgery and neck dissections, navigated virtual endoscopy, and surgery planning of the mastoid was crucial to carrying out the work on which this book is based.

Last but not least, we want to acknowledge the intensive and fruitful cooperation with Morgan Kaufman, in particular with JESSIE EVANS, MICHELLE WARD, DARICE MOORE, ALAN ROSE, and DENISE PENROSE and TIM COX, our publisher and senior editor at Morgan Kaufman, who provided substantial support and encouragement in all stages of book preparation. It was a privilege to work together with you.

MAGDEBURG, LEIPZIG,
February 2007

Chapter 01

Introduction

Visualization in medicine, or, for short, medical visualization, is a special area of scientific visualization that established itself as a research area in the late 1980s. The roots of scientific visualization are manifold; on one hand, the long tradition of scientists who illustrate their work with carefully crafted graphics laid the foundation for scientific visualization. Anatomical illustration, starting with da Vinci's work, is a prominent example. On the other hand, scientific visualization is based on computer graphics, which provide representations to store 3D geometry and efficient algorithms to render such representations. Additional influence comes from image processing, which basically defined the field of medical image analysis (MIA). MIA, however, is was originally the processing of 2D images, while its 3D extension was traditionally usually credited to medical visualization.

1.1 VISUALIZATION IN MEDICINE AS A SPECIALTY OF SCIENTIFIC VISUALIZATION

Scientific visualization deals primarily with the visualization, exploration, and analysis of datasets arising from measurements or simulation of real world phenomena. The investigation of air flow around planes and cars is a well-known application area. The underlying data of scientific visualizations are often very large, which makes it necessary to consider the efficiency and hence the time and space complexity of algorithms.

Important goals and research scenarios of scientific visualization are:

- To explore data (undirected search without a specific hypothesis)
- To test a hypothesis based on measurements or simulations and their visualization
- The presentation of results

Many relevant examples in medical visualization address these general visualization goals. Whether or not a patient is suffering from a certain disease is a hypothesis to be tested through clinical investigations and medical imaging. If a physician cannot sufficiently assess a disease based on the symptoms described by the patient and by clinical examinations, radiological image data might be acquired without a particular hypothesis. Computer support—in particular image processing, quantitative image analysis and visualization—may improve the radiologist's diagnosis.

Finally, if a radiologist has performed a diagnosis specifying the stage and severity of a disease, certain visualizations are generated to present the diagnosis to the referring physician. Such visualizations might include measurements (extent of a pathologic structure) and annotations (encircled regions or arrows) to enhance their interpretation. The ultimate goal of such visualizations and the attached report is to support treatment decisions. The presentation goal is also relevant for medical visualizations; visualizations are generated to be discussed among colleagues, to employ them for educational purposes or as being part of a publication. Figure 1.1 shows images that have been generated for neck dissection planning.

There are several lessons from general scientific visualization literature that are true and inspiring for the design of medical visualization systems. The most important is to consider visualization as a process

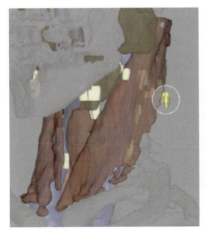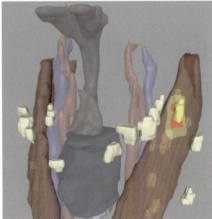

FIGURE 1.1 *Medical visualization for neck dissection planning. Left: Relevant anatomical structures and potentially pathologic lymph nodes are displayed to support neck dissection planning. Right: The distance between an enlarged and potentially malignant lymph node is color-coded to a muscle to support the decision as to whether the muscle should be removed. From: [KRÜGER et al. 2005]*

directed to understand the data. "The purpose of visualization is insight, not pictures," as MCCORMICK et al. [1987] state in their field-defining report on scientific visualization.[1] If "insight" is the goal of visualization, it is essential to understand what kind of "insight" particular users want to achieve.[2] For medical visualization systems, an in-depth understanding of diagnostic processes, therapeutic decisions, and intraoperative information needs is indispensable to providing dedicated computer support. It is also essential to consider organizational and technical constraints.

Another consequence is that interaction methods play a crucial role in the design of adequate medical visualization systems. Interaction facilities should support the user in navigating within the data, in selecting relevant portions of the data during their exploration, in comparing data from different regions or different datasets, and in the adjustment and fine-tuning of visualization parameters that define after all the optical properties observable by a human. The whole exploration process should support the interpretation and classification of the data. Examples for this classification in the medical domain are statements such as "The patient suffers from a certain disease," or "The patient can be treated by a certain intervention. A particular surgical strategy was selected."

Finally, interaction methods should support users in the storage of results (static pictures and image sequences, along with annotations). Medical visualization is primarily based on 3D volume data. Our discussion of interaction facilities therefore has a focus on 3D interaction techniques which allow the immediate exploration of 3D data.

Regarding scientific and medical visualization as an analysis process leads to the consequence that image generation and visual exploration is not the only way to get "insight." Equally important are tools to mathematically analyze the data: for example, to characterize the distribution of numerical values in

---

1   This quote is a reference to the famous quote of RICHARD W. HAMMING, "The purpose of computing is insight, not numbers" [1962]. Less known is his 1997 add-on quote "The purpose of computing is not yet insight" [HAMMING 1997].

2   An in-depth discussion of the scientific data analysis process is given in [SPRINGMEYER et al. 1992].

certain regions of the data. Radiological workstations and therapy planning software systems therefore should integrate functionality to derive quantitative information concerning the underlying data.

We should keep always in mind the limitations of the data, which is in the focus of our work. Its discrete nature defines boundary conditions for interpretation and analysis. Specific structures (i.e., tumors) may not show up at their full size; other structures are so small that their analysis might lead to a high error rate, or is highly subjective. Knowing the limitations of the used methods is therefore an important key to their successful application.

1.2   COMPUTERIZED MEDICAL IMAGING

Medical visualization deals with the analysis, visualization, and exploration of medical image data. Main application areas are:

- **Educational purposes.** Visualization techniques are the core of anatomy and surgery education systems. As an example, the VOXELMAN, an advanced anatomy education system, combines high-quality surface and volume rendering with 3D interaction facilities and a knowledge base to support anatomy education [HÖHNE *et al.* 2001, 2003] (see Fig. 1.2).

  While anatomy education relies on static models, surgery training requires *deformable models* which simulate the behavior of tissue if force is applied. In particular, minimally invasive surgical procedures require extensive training, for which interactive 3D visualization plays an essential role.

  Often, nonclinical data are used for educational purposes. In particular, the Visible Human male and female dataset provided by the National Institutes of Health provides attractive material for educational systems [SPITZER *et al.* 1996]. These datasets contain photographic images as well as CT data. Due to the high dose of radiation that could be applied, a high resolution and a very good signal-to-noise ratio were achieved, which would not have been possible with clinical data of a living patient. Clinical data are often not perfect and suffer from various shortcomings in image

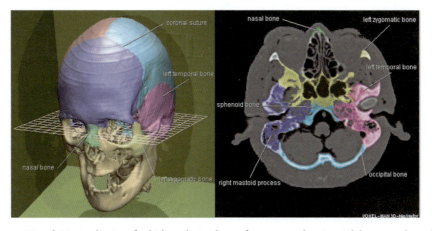

FIGURE 1.2   2D and 3D visualization of a high-resolution dataset for anatomy education. Labels support the student's understanding. Screenshot of the VOXELMAN system. Copyright: Institute for Mathematics and Computer Science, University Hospital Hamburg-Eppendorf.

quality. High quality at one hospital is frequently not matched at other sources of the data that must be processed in medical visualization.

- **Diagnosis.** The diagnosis of radiological data benefits from interactive 2D and 3D visualizations. In particular, if the situation of a particular patient is very unusual (complex fractures, defective positions), 3D visualizations are a very useful way to get an overview of the morphology. More and more, functional and dynamic image data are employed to assess effects such as blood perfusion or contrast agent enhancement and metabolism. Various measures are derived from these image data. Appropriate visualizations depict the spatial correlation between these measurements.
- **Treatment planning.** Interactive 3D visualizations of the relevant anatomical and pathologic structures may enhance the planning of surgical interventions, radiation treatment, and minimally invasive interventions. The spatial relations between pathologic lesions and life-critical structures at risk may be evaluated better with 3D visualizations. Since the early work on craniofacial surgery planning [VANNIER et al. 1983], the visualization of anatomical structures has been steadily improving due to the progress in image acquisition, graphics, and computing hardware, and better rendering. Visualizations may also include information that is not present in radiological data, such as the simulated dose distribution for radiation treatment planning or simulated vascular territories. Treatment planning systems have found their way to many applications in, for example, orthopedic surgery, neurosurgery, abdominal surgery, and craniofacial surgery (see Fig. 1.3) [ZACHOW et al. 2003a, b].
- **Intraoperative support.** Medical visualization based on 3D data is, more and more often, entering the operating room (OR). Preoperatively acquired images and intraoperative images are integrated to provide support during an intervention. Flexible and smart displays are needed for such applications (see Fig. 1.4 and [SCHWALD et al. 2002, FISCHER et al. 2004, DEL RÍO et al. 2005]).

It is essential to note that the computer support described above is not intended to replace medical doctors. Instead, physicians should be supported and assisted to perform their tasks more efficiently and/or in a higher quality.

The data, on which medical visualization methods and applications are based, are acquired with radiological scanning devices such as computed tomography (CT) and magnetic resonance imaging (MRI). These devices have experienced an enormous development in the last 20 years. Although other imaging modalities such as 3D ultrasound, positron emission tomography (PET), and imaging techniques from nuclear medicine are available, CT and MRI dominate due to their high resolution and their good signal-to-noise ratio. Image resolution increased considerably with the introduction of multislice CT devices in

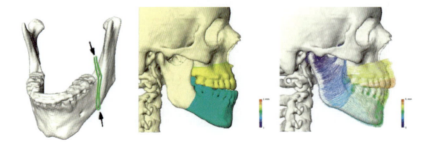

FIGURE 1.3 Left: Intuitive 3D osteotomy planning on polygonal bone models. Middle: Colorcoded distance of the planned osteotomy. Right: direction of the bone movement illustrated by arrows. (Images courtesy STEFAN ZACHOW, Zuse-Institute Berlin)

FIGURE 1.4 *Intraoperative use of medical visualization: Left: Semitransparent screen positioned over the OR-situs. Virtual information is displayed on the screen, and the OR-situs is visible through the screen. (Image courtesy* BERND SCHWALD *of the* MEDARPA *project, ZGDV Darmstadt). Right: A volume-rendered image of an MRI dataset is augmented with a video of the OR-situs. (Image courtesy* ÁNGEL DEL RÍO, *University of Tübingen)*

1998. Also, acquisition times have decreased—this development contributes to the quality of medical volume data, because motion and breathing artifacts are reduced considerably. The acquisition of time-dependent volume data, which depict dynamic processes in the human body, has been improved with respect to spatial and temporal resolution. Today, intraoperative imaging has become a common practice to support difficult interventions, for example, in neurosurgery. With the improved quality and wide availability of medical volume data, new and better methods to extract information from such data are feasible and needed.

More and more, a radiologist uses software instead of conventional lightboxes and films to establish a diagnosis. The development of monitors with sufficient gray value and spatial resolution was an essential prerequisite for the clinical application of image analysis and visualization techniques. Contrast and brightness may be adjusted with digital image data, which often allows the interpretation of images in a convenient manner, even if the data acquisition process was not optimal.

With the increased resolution of the image data, reliable measurements can be derived: for example, cross-sectional areas and volumes of certain structures can be determined with a reasonable amount of certainty. Measurements of cross-sectional areas are valuable in the diagnosis of vascular diseases (detection of stenosis and aneurysms). Volume measurements of pathologic structures are highly relevant to assessing the success of a therapy. However, the quality of these measurements depends heavily on the quality of the image data. Specific artifacts (i.e., flow artifacts in MRI angiography) may reduce the accuracy significantly.

Note that image analysis and visualization may provide comprehensible views of the data, but the results strongly depend on the original data. Physicians tend to overestimate what can be achieved by using sophisticated algorithms; it is important to convey realistic expectations to users. If physicians complain about the results of medical visualization, the problem is often due to deficiencies in the image acquisition process. Structures with a 2 mm diameter cannot be reliably displayed with 2 mm slice thickness, for example. It is essential that the requirements are stated precisely and that the scanning parameters of the image acquisition are adapted to these requirements.

The increased resolution and improved quality of medical image data also has a tremendous effect on therapy planning. With high quality data, smaller structures—for example blood vessels and nerves, whose locations are often crucial in the treatment—can be reliably detected. In some cases, this enables the physician to refine the decision as to whether or not a particular disease can be successfully treated through surgery: for example, whether or not a malignant tumor can be removed entirely. Still, too often such decisions have to be made intraoperatively. In so-called explorative resections, the body is opened and the relevant structure is exposed through surgery to find out whether or not the intervention is feasible. If a resection needs to be canceled, the patient has been subjected to a potentially risky intervention without effect. Visualization and computer support for treatment planning aim at reducing such unfavorable situations.

1.3   2D AND 3D VISUALIZATIONS

Medical imaging started with X-ray imaging at the end of the 19th century. Since that time, diagnosis has been carried out by inspecting X-ray films or, more recently, digital X-ray images. With the advent of computed tomography, many slices showing X-ray absorption in a particular region of the body have to be inspected. Slice-by-slice inspection of medical volume data is still a common practice. Despite all the efforts to accelerate volume rendering, employing high-quality reconstruction filters, and to ease the adjustment of the necessary parameters, the inspection of 2D slices is still dominant. A typical explanation of this phenomenon is the assumed ability of a radiologist to mentally fuse the 2D slices in a 3D representation. This ability, however, is not generally accepted and is disputed even between radiologists.

Another aspect seems to be a tradition in radiology: well-established techniques are preferred despite their obvious disadvantages when compared to more recent techniques. A thorough analysis of the radiologic workflow, however, reveals that there are still real benefits to using slice-by-slice inspection. In 2D views of the slices, each and every voxel can be seen and selected (for example, to inquire the density value). 2D slice views support precise exploration and analysis of the data. This is probably the reason radiologists are legally obliged to inspect every slice. Volume rendering or other 3D visualization, on the other hand, provides an overview. Radiologists use such overviews if for example, very unfamiliar spatial relations occur, such as judging branching patterns of vascular structures or assessing complex fractures. While radiologists rarely rely on 3D visualizations, physicians who carry out interventions (radiation therapy, surgery) strongly benefit from interactive and dynamic 3D visualizations. On the one

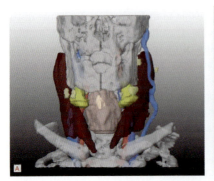 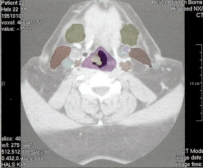

FIGURE 1.5 *Left: A 3D surface visualization of the relevant anatomical structures for surgery planning. Right: The CT slices from which the data have been extracted. The colored objects shown in the left view are represented in the slice view (right) with colored overlays. The relationship between the underlying data and the resulting visualization becomes obvious. (Images courtesy JEANETTE CORDES, University of Magdeburg)*

hand, they do not have the radiological training to mentally imagine complex structures based on a stack of cross-sectional views. On the other hand, they have to understand the 3D spatial relations better than radiologists. While radiologists "only" describe the data; the surgeon actually intervenes in the spatial relations—with all the consequences that might have.

In summary, 2D *and* 3D visualization techniques are needed and should be connected closely. While 3D techniques provide often a more comprehensible overall picture, 2D slice-oriented techniques typically allow a more accurate examination and, hence, processing. An example of a simultaneous employment of 2D and 3D visualizations for surgery planning is shown in Figure 1.5.

1.4   ORGANIZATION

This book is structured in five parts.

The first part provides the fundamentals of medical image data acquisition, perception, interpretation, and computer-supported analysis. These fundamentals are used later in the book to describe visualization techniques related to medical image data and derived information, such as image analysis results.

The first part starts with an introduction into the characteristics of medical volume data (see Chap. 2). This chapter provides an introduction into the characteristics of discrete data organized in (uniform) cartesian grid datasets with scalar values, which is the typical structure of medical image data. In particular, we will shed light on the limitations of the data through artifacts and perception. In Chapter 3 we introduce imaging modalities, with a focus on CT and MRI, and provide an overview of other modalities. Chapter 4 deals with the clinical use of medical image data. It turns out that the software used for the analysis of medical volume data must be carefully integrated in the information-processing environment in hospitals. This chapter is followed by an overview on medical image analysis (see Chap. 5). Image processing and image analysis, in the context of this book, are meant as an introduction to the basics of medical image analysis. The chapter illustrates selected image analysis tasks and results. Image segmentation, the identification and delineation of relevant structures, is the most important aspect of this chapter. Visualization benefits from image segmentation, because it allows the selective emphasis of relevant objects. Moreover, image segmentation is the prerequisite for many interaction techniques to explore data and carry out treatment planning.

The second part of the book is devoted to the visualization of medical volume data. Hardware and software aspects, quality, and speed of algorithms are discussed. Chapter 6 presents the fundamentals of volume visualization, including in particular data analysis tools such as the histogram, transfer functions, and lighting.

Volume data can be visualized by directly projecting the data to the screen (direct volume rendering, DVR) or by generating an intermediate representation, which is subsequently rendered (indirect volume rendering). Chapter 7 is devoted to indirect methods (primarily surface-based visualization). Such techniques are known as isosurface techniques in the visualization community. Isosurfaces are based on an isovalue selected by the user and represent the surface that connects all elements of a volume data set where this isovalue occurs. On medical workstations, the same technique is known as surface shaded display (SSD). Chapter 8 discusses a theoretical model for direct volume rendering, which leads to the volume rendering equation. Different volume rendering pipelines are presented, with strategies of implementing the theoretical model in different ways. Finally, various compositing techniques are described. Chapter 9 is more algorithm-oriented and discusses in detail how the different strategies are realized. Image- and object-based methods are introduced. Hybrid combinations of direct and indirect volume rendering are motivated by frequent requirements in therapy planning and surgery simulation systems.

The realization of such combinations is also discussed. Finally, the comparison of medical visualization algorithms and the validation of visualization techniques is discussed.

While Chapters 7 to 9 consider static volume data, Chapter 10 describes techniques to explore and analyze time-dependent volume data. These data have a great potential for medical diagnosis. An example is the assessment of tumors in the female breast. Whether or not these tumors are malignant is often difficult to decide with static images. With dynamic MRI data, the blood flow around a tumor can be assessed as an important criterion to characterize the tumor. Techniques for the efficient visualization and analysis of such data are important, because the huge amount of dynamic volume data cannot be evaluated without dedicated software support.

Part III discusses techniques for the exploration of medical volume data. The topics covered in this part focus on the user and discuss how certain interactions can be accomplished. Ease of learning and use, as well as accuracy, are important aspects of exploration techniques. The first chapter of this part deals with advanced transfer function design for volume rendering (see Chap. 11). Transfer functions map data to visualization parameters, such as gray values and opacity. Without dedicated support, users have to experiment with many possible transfer function settings before an appropriate specification is found. The focus of this chapter is task analysis (what are the structures the user probably wants to assess?) to support the specification.

In Chapter 12, two related interaction tasks and functions are described: clipping and virtual resection. With clipping and virtual resection, the user can specify subvolumes of the data that will be removed in the subsequent visualization. Clipping, virtual resection, and transfer function design are often combined to specify which parts of the data should be displayed. With transfer function design, parts of the data with values in a certain interval are removed by mapping their visual contribution to zero, whereas with clipping planes or other clipping geometry, parts of the data are removed based on a geometric specification. Finally, 2D and 3D measurement techniques are discussed in Chapter 13. The qualitative analysis of spatial relations is added through measurements by a quantitative assessment. Such measurements may directly support treatment decisions. The size and extent of a tumor strongly influences applicable therapies; the angle between bony structures may influence whether the anatomy is regarded as normal or whether treatment is necessary. Interactive measurements and automatic measurements that employ segmentation information are covered.

Part IV is devoted to advanced medical visualization techniques. It starts with the visualization of anatomic tree structures, such as vascular trees and the bronchial tree (Chap. 14). Due to the complexity of these structures, it is difficult to visualize them in such a way that important information, such as the type of branching pattern, can be easily inferred. We describe different methods that produce comprehensible visualization at different levels of detail and accuracy. The next chapter (see Chap. 15) is dedicated to intraoperative visualization and navigation. Here we will discuss how medical image data are integrated with an intervention itself. This requires several different operators, which enable the mapping of the data directly to the patient. Chapter 16 is devoted to virtual endoscopy. Virtual endoscopy is inspired by real (or optical or video-) endoscopic procedures, which are carried out for diagnosis (e.g., detection of polyps in the colon) or as minimally invasive intervention. In real endoscopy, a small camera is inserted in the human body through small incisions or anatomical openings (e.g., the colon) and it is moved to inspect vascular structures or structures filled with air. In virtual endoscopy, similar images are produced through 3D visualization on the basis of medical volume data. Virtual endoscopy has a great potential for surgery training and treatment planning, as well as for diagnosis and intraoperative navigation, because it has less restrictions than real endoscopy (the virtual camera can go everywhere) and is more comfortable for the patient. Visualization and navigation techniques in the virtual human are the issues discussed in this chapter.

In Chapter 17, illustrative rendering and emphasis techniques are described. These techniques are essential for medical education and for therapy planning. One scenario is that the user selects an object via its name from a list, and this object will be highlighted in the related visualization. In general, emphasis is difficult to carry out because most objects are at least partially occluded.

A special variation of MRI is diffusion tensor imaging (DTI). With this modality, the inhomogeneity of the direction of (water) diffusion can be noninvasively determined. Strongly directed diffusion occurs, for example, in the white matter of the human brain, and thus indicates the direction and location of fiber tracks. This information is highly relevant, in particular in neuroradiology and neurosurgery. The analysis and visualization of DTI data pose many challenges, which are discussed in Chapter 18.

Part V covers specific application areas and a comprehensive case study. In these applications many of the techniques described before are combined, integrated with other software, and fine-tuned to serve a particular purpose. However, special application needs are not fulfilled by only combining existing techniques. New technical problems and appropriate algorithms are also presented, along with the application problems that gave rise to their development. Examples are the problem of labeling 3D models and the design of effective animations—both motivated from challenges in medical education.

The descriptions should clarify how real medical applications can be approached. Important aspects are:

- A brief description of the necessary medical background (anatomy of the particular region, imaging techniques used, and treatment strategies)
- The analysis of tasks and requirements for computer support
- The design, test, and refinement of prototypes

In Chapter 19, we discuss image analysis and visualization for liver surgery planning (tumor surgery and liver transplantations). Validation and evaluation are carefully described to provide orientation for designing such studies. In Chapter 20, the use of medical visualization techniques for educational purposes, in particular for anatomy and surgery education, is discussed. Beside describing application areas, this chapter introduces some new techniques, such as labeling and animation of medical volume data, collision detection, and soft tissue deformation for surgical simulation.

The book will be concluded with an outlook on future developments of medical imaging, computer-assisted surgery, and visualization techniques.

An appendix will provide information on available and sometimes free software systems, libraries, and frameworks used for medical visualization.

PART I

Acquisition, Analysis, and Interpretation of Medical Volume Data

In the first part, we specify the foundation for the discussion of visualization techniques related to medical image data and derived information.

The fundamentals of 3D medical image data are introduced in Chapter 2. The chapter provides a detailed introduction to the characteristics of (uniform) cartesian grid datasets with scalar values, which is the typical structure of medical image data. Since all the data originates from measured data and has a discrete nature, it is subjected to diverse visual artifacts, which we will also examine. This includes a careful discussion of general problems, such as aliasing and interpolation problems. Important parameters for the diagnostic quality are also discussed, as well as the basics of visual perception.

Chapter 3 introduces important image acquisition modalities in radiology, with a focus on computed tomography (CT) and magnetic resonance imaging (MRI), the prevailing modalities for the diagnosis of severe diseases as well as for therapy planning. Other modalities, such as conventional X-ray, ultrasound, and the imaging techniques used in nuclear medicine (positron emission tomography, PET and single-photon emission computed tomography, SPECT) are discussed to provide a broader view on image data acquisition.

A discussion of the image interpretation by radiologists follows in Chapter 4. This discussion is focused on soft-copy reading, where radiological workstations are used and where interaction methods are provided to browse through the data and to perform specific analysis tasks. We consider the integration of soft-copy reading in digital radiology departments as well as the cooperative work of radiologists, referring physicians, and assistant medical technicians.

Chapter 5 is dedicated to image analysis—the computerized assistance for extracting clinically useful information concerning anatomical and pathologic structures. While some of the more straight-forward image analysis techniques can be found in modern radiological workstations, most of them are not widely available. Image analysis is a challenging problem that requires specialized solutions and careful consideration of interaction functionality. Image analysis provides important information that may be incorporated in visualization algorithms and, ultimately, in clinical applications such as therapy planning software assistants.

Chapter 02

Medical Image Data and Visual Perception

In this chapter, we characterize important concepts of medical volume data as discrete regular data. We discuss general data artifacts in medical image data due to noise, limited resolution, and other general problems of the imaging modalities. This discussion is complemented later in Chapter 3, where the different imaging modalities are described in more detail. In this chapter, we also discuss general aspects of diagnostic quality and how it is influenced by artifacts. The interpretation of medical image data requires a basic understanding of the human visual system. Since human perception is an extensive topic, we focus on some aspects that are crucial for the use of medical image data and related information.

Organization In the following sections, we will discuss the structure of volumetric data and introduce the respective terminology (see Sect. 2.1). This section is complemented by a discussion of frequent image data artifacts and their sources (see Sect. 2.2). We discuss the quality of diagnostic procedures with respect to the accuracy and reliability of detecting a pathology (see Sect. 2.3) and finally how aspects of the human visual perception—in particular, the perceived brightness and contrast—influence the interpretation of medical image data (see Sect. 2.4).

2.1 MEDICAL IMAGE DATA

Medical image data are usually represented as a stack of individual images. Each image represents a thin slice of the scanned body part and is composed of individual pixels (picture elements). These pixels are arranged on a two-dimensional grid, where the distance between two pixels is typically constant in each direction. For most medical image modalities,[1] the horizontal (x) and vertical (y) directions have identical distances, which are called the *pixel distance*. A constant pixel distance allows the calculation of the actual position by multiplying the respective distance value with the respective pixel index i. If we assume that i is indexing the horizontal x position and j is indexing the vertical y position, the position of pixel $P_{i,j}$ is determined. Figure 2.1 (left) displays the 2D image grid arrangement.

Volumetric data combine individual images into a 3D representation on a 3D grid (see Fig. 2.1 (right)). The data elements are now called *voxels* (volume elements), and they are located on the grid points. In addition to the horizontal (x) and vertical (y) dimensions, we now also have a dimension representing the depth (z). The distance between two neighboring images (slices) is called *slice distance*. The three distances in every direction are also called *voxel spacing*. Similar to the pixels, the position of a voxel $V_{i,j,k}$ is determined by the distance values and the voxel index (i, j, k) (see Fig. 2.2).

If the pixel distance is identical to the slice distance, we speak of an isotropic grid or dataset. If this is not the case, we speak of an anisotropic grid. Most datasets in medical imaging are anisotropic and in many cases the slice distance is several times larger than the pixel distance (see Fig. 2.2). Eight neighboring voxels form a cuboid (see Fig. 2.1 (right)) called a *volume cell* or short a *cell*.

---

1 A modality in our context is identical to a specific image acquisition technique, such as CT or MRI.

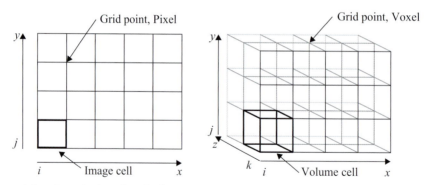

FIGURE 2.1 *Left: A 2D grid, where all pixels of an image are arranged on the grid points of the grid. Right: In volume datasets, the voxels are arranged on a 3D grid.*

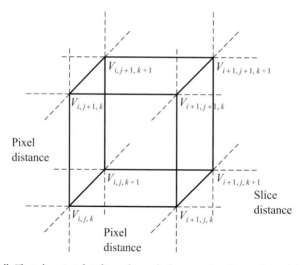

FIGURE 2.2 *Volume Cell: The indices i, j, k indicate the voxels that span the volume cell. Pixel distances are the spaces between the voxels that are indexed via i and j (within one image slice), and slice distance is the space between the voxels indexed via k (between image slices).*

Since the grid points can be seen as being aligned on a cartesian coordinate system, this grid type is also called cartesian or uniform grid. Its special features are:

- Constant or regular spacing in each dimension
- Regular geometry that can be computed by the grid index and the spacing
- Regular topology (it has the same connectivity for all grid points)
- It is only composed of cuboid (volume) cells

While most datasets in medical imaging are defined on such grid types, it is important to be aware that there are other grid types with varying spacing, varying geometry, varying topology, and, lastly, with

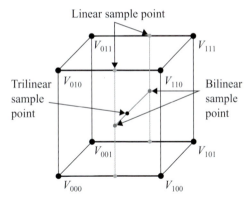

FIGURE 2.3 *Trilinear interpolation: Linear sample points are computed on the frontal and backward edges of the volume cell. Based on these points, bilinear interpolation is computed by linear interpolation. Finally, the trilinear sample point is computed by linear interpolation between the bilinear sample points.*

varying cell types. These grids can be of a non-uniform, curvilinear, or irregular type. More information on these grid types can be found in the literature on scientific visualization [SCHROEDER et al. 2001].

A volume dataset is defined only at the discrete grid positions. In many cases, however, we need to calculate sample points within a volume cell. In the early days of volumetric data processing, this was achieved by nearest-neighbor interpolation, where a sample point within a volume cell was assigned the voxel value of the voxel with the smallest distance from that sample point.[2] While nearest-neighbor interpolation introduced only very modest computational costs, its visual quality became quickly unacceptable. The low visual quality was due to the discontinuous interpolation results between neighboring voxels, resulting in a very blocky appearance of reconstructed surfaces.

Today, more sophisticated interpolation schemes are used. The most popular scheme is trilinear interpolation, which is composed of seven linear interpolations (see Fig. 2.3). In the first composition step, four linear interpolations compute the weighted sample points between two neighboring voxels on an edge of a volume cell along one direction (either x, y, or z). In the second composition step, the result of two such linear interpolations between voxels located on the same face of the volume cell are combined by linear interpolation to compute the result of a bilinear interpolation. Finally, the result of the two bilinear interpolations on opposite faces of the volume cell are combined by a linear interpolation into the final trilinear sample point within the volume cell.

As described above, three levels of linear interpolations are chained into one function. Since each interpolation uses its own variable, it is technically a trivariate linear function. However, if an isosurface[3] with a specific isovalue c is extracted, a root-finding operation is performed. One variable is successively substituted by the remaining ones, and we get a cubic function for the isosurface, or a quadratic function for an isocontour in 2D (see Fig. 2.4.)

For a more simple representation of the interpolations in Equations 2.1–2.3, we will abbreviate terms like $V_{i,j,k}$ with V_{000} and terms like $V_{i+1,j+1,k+1}$ with V_{111}, where the index represents the increment

---

2   The concept of nearest-neighbor interpolation was also the basis of a now-outdated voxel concept, where a voxel was considered the whole space that had a constant voxel value, similar to the volume cell in the modern voxel concept.

3   An isosurface typically represents a boundary surface in a volume dataset that has the same (hence, "iso") intensity values, similar to contour lines in a map, which respresent levels of the same height. (Isosurfaces will be discussed in detail in Section 7.2.)

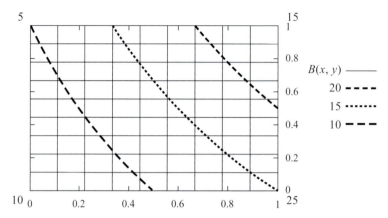

FIGURE 2.4 Bilinear contours in a volume cell. The bilinearly interpolated 2D cell B(x,y) is seen from above. The voxel values on the corners are 5, 15, 25, 10 (clockwise, starting from the upper left corner). Three isocontours with the isovalues 10, 15, and 20 are shown.

of the position indices i, j, k. $V_{i+1,j,k}$, for example, is abbreviated as V_{100}. Equation 2.1 shows a linear interpolation between two voxel values, and Equation 2.2 shows the respective bilinear interpolation between four voxel values. α, α_1, and α_2 represent the respective interpolation weights for linear and bilinear interpolation, and x, y, z for the trilinear interpolation.[4]

$$L(\alpha) = \quad V_0 * (1 - \alpha) + V_1 * \alpha | 0 \leq \alpha \leq 1 \qquad (2.1)$$

$$B(\alpha_1, \alpha_2) = \quad L_0(\alpha_1) * (1 - \alpha_2) + L_1(\alpha_1) * \alpha_2$$

$$= \quad (V_{00} * (1 - \alpha) + V_{10} * \alpha) * (1 - \alpha_2)$$

$$+ (V_{01} * (1 - \alpha) + V_{11} * \alpha) * \alpha_2 \qquad (2.2)$$

$$T(x, y, z) = \quad B_0(x, y) * (1 - z) + B_1(x, y) * z$$

$$= \quad (L_0(x) * (1 - y) + L_1(x) * y)* \qquad (1 - z)$$

$$+ (L_2(x) * (1 - y) + L_3(x) * y)* \qquad z$$

$$= \quad (V_{000} * (1 - x) + V_{100} * x) * (1 - y) +$$

$$((V_{010} * (1 - x) + V_{110} * x) * y)* \qquad (1 - z)$$

$$+ (V_{001} * (1 - x) + V_{101} * x) * (1 - y) +$$

$$((V_{011} * (1 - x) + V_{111} * x) * y)* \qquad z \qquad (2.3)$$

Trilinear interpolation involves only the immediate voxel neighborhood of a sample point, which are the voxels of the enclosing volume cell (see Fig. 2.3). Other schemes involve higher-order interpolation functions, such as triquadratic or tricubic spline functions, which take a larger voxel neighborhood into account. Alternatively, the sample value can be reconstructed by convolving the voxel values with a Gaussian filter kernel.

---

4 Since these interpolations can be computed in all three directions, we use only one voxel index for linear and two voxel indices for bilinear interpolation, and α, α_1, and α_2 as parameters, respectively.

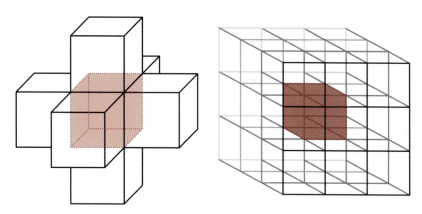

FIGURE 2.5   Left: 6-neighborhood—*every face of the current cuboid (red) has a neighbor. Right: 26-neighborhood—every face, every edge, and every vertex of the current cuboid (red) has a neighbor.*

The final concept we introduce in this section is the concept of *neighborhood*. This concept will be employed throughout the various chapters of this book, since it defines the *support* or area of influence for many operations. In some contexts, it will be also called *connectivity*, e.g., for region growing segmentation (see Sect. 5.3.3). These operations are typically computed not only on one voxel, but also on the voxels in its neighborhood. If, for example, only the voxels on the left/right, top/bottom, front/back of the current voxel are considered, we speak of a *6-neighborhood*, since six neighboring voxels are considered. According to the formalism introduced earlier, we denote the current voxel with V_{000} and the voxels in the 6-neighborhood as V_{-100}, V_{100}, V_{0-10}, V_{010}, V_{00-1}, and V_{001}. In other words, we selected the neighborhood according to regular grid topology (a cartesian grid) of our dataset. Often, the analogon of cuboids for voxels is also used. In this case, the 6-neighborhood represents all neighboring cuboids that share one face with the current cuboid (see Fig. 2.5 (left)). This also motivates the term *6-adjacent*. Sometimes, this neighborhood is also called a *direct neighborhood*.

Next to the 6-neighborhood, the other frequently used neighborhood is the *26-neighborhood*. As the name suggests, it includes a neighborhood of 26 voxels. To the original six neighboring voxels the 26-neighborhood adds the voxels on the major and minor diagonals from the current voxel. In our formalism to enumerate voxels, this includes all index combinations with negative and positive index offsets, except 000 for the current voxel. With the cuboid analogon, we now also include cuboids that connect to the current cuboid through shared edges (12) and shared vertices (8) (see Fig. 2.5 (right)). In other words, we have a *26-adjacent* neighborhood. Sometimes this neighborhood is also called a *complete neighborhood*. Other neighborhood concepts include an 18-neighborhood, which includes the 6-neighborhood and the cuboids that are connected through a shared edge. Note that neighborhood considerations are not limited to the immediate neighborhood. If we also take into account the second-order neighbors, which are connected through one immediate neighbor, or even higher order neighborhoods, more complex schemes are possible.

2.2   DATA ARTIFACTS

Data artifacts are virtually omnipresent in medical imaging. Nevertheless, the source and appearance of these artifacts are often not clear to people in charge of the acquisition and representation of medical image data. Fortunately, medical imaging data have their theoretical roots in digital signal processing, and, therefore, artifacts can be explained by and traced back to the foundations of signal processing. In this section, we provide a brief introduction to the sampling theorem and its influence on medical imaging. Specifically, we describe and explain the major data artifacts in medical volumetric data, based on medical 3D scanners.

Important concepts for the discussion of many data artifacts are the spatial domain and the frequency domain. So far, we have only examined datasets represented in the spatial domain, where the data are arranged as voxels or pixels on a 3D or 2D grid. Since this grid spans into space, depending on the number of voxels in each dimension and the spacing between the voxels, they are a representation in the spatial domain.

The frequency domain is a different representation of spatial data that have been Fourier transformed. Now the data (or signals) are represented by a band of different frequencies, hence the name frequency domain. To transform the signals from the frequency domain to the spatial domain, we need to apply the inverse Fourier transformation.

2.2.1 SAMPLING THEOREM

The main basis in signal theory is the sampling theorem credited to Nyquist [NYQUIST 1924]—who first formulated the theorem in 1928—and to Shannon [SHANNON 1949]—who formally proved it in 1949.

The sampling theorem essentially says that a signal has to be sampled at least with twice the frequency of the original signal. Since signals and their respective speed can be easier expressed by frequencies, most explanations of artifacts are based on their representation in the frequency domain. The sampling frequency demanded by the sampling theorem is also called the Nyquist *frequency*, or the reciprocal term Nyquist *rate*.

The transformation of signals into the frequency domain (see Fig. 2.6) is done by the Fourier transformation, which essentially reformulates the signal into a cosine function space. If, for example, we transform the sine function into the frequency domain, this results in a peak (or Dirac impulse/function) at the frequency of the sine function (see Fig. 2.6 (right)). Due to the symmetry of the Fourier transform for real values, there are two peaks on both sides of the ordinate (y) axis.

However, we present here only a very compact explanation of sampling, which we based—with a bit of hand-waving—in the spatial domain. More details on that transformation and the frequency-domain-based interpretation can be found in the books by LEHMANN et al. [1997a] and GLASSNER [1995].

As all image data can be interpreted as a spatial or Fourier-transformed signal, we base our discussion on a simple example of a one-dimensional signal, the sine function. This function has a straightforward

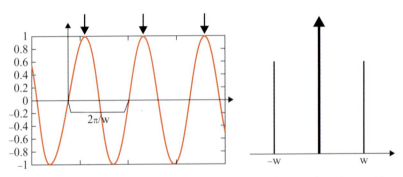

FIGURE 2.6   *Sine-function is sampled (arrows) at same speed as sine periodicity of $T = 2\pi/w$. Left: spatial domain representation, right: frequency domain representation, where the frequency is represented by two symmetric peaks at $-w$ and w.*

representation in the spatial and the frequency domain. Figure 2.6 (left) shows a section of the sine function around the origin. If we transform this continuous representation into a discrete representation, we need to take samples of the continuous sine function to measure its characteristics. Figure 2.6 (left) demonstrates what happens if we take the samples at the same speed (or frequency) as our original function. Since the sine function has the periodicity $T = 2\pi/w$ (or the frequency of $w/2\pi$), this sampling speed would also be T. As Figure 2.6 (left) shows, sampling the sine function at the same speed would always recover the same sine value in different periods, thus pretending that we are recovering a constant function.

If we increase the sampling speed to half of the periodicity of the continuous function (the minimum demand of the sampling theorem), we can now recover the correct characteristic of the sine function, as can be seen in Figure 2.7 (left). However, depending on the exact position of the sample, in the period T of the original function, we recover different amplitudes of the original signal. In an unfortunate case, we always sample the zero crossing of the sine function, as shown in Figure 2.7 (right). In this case, the characteristics could be correctly recovered, but the amplitude of the signal was recovered in an unfortunate way, so we are back with a constant signal. Overall, sampling at a rate that satisfies the sampling theorem does not guarantee that the full signal strength is reconstructed, although higher sampling rates usually approach the original strength.

In the frequency domain, sampling of the original signal is described as the convolution of the original signal with a comb function (with peaks repeating at the sampling frequency). Due to the periodicity of the comb function (taking samples at regular positions), the convolved signal also exposes a replicating pattern. Since exactly one of these signal patterns is used, we need to select one copy of it with a low pass filter, a technique that is explained in the next section. If the sampling rate is not high enough, it will result in an overlap of the replicating patterns and, hence, in the inability to select one copy of the pattern.

Finally, it is important to keep in mind that medical image data do consist of a full spectrum of frequencies, which are revealed once the Fourier transform of the data is calculated. Therefore, the respective limiting cut-off frequency of this spectrum should be taken into account, when estimating the correct sampling frequency.

2.2.2 UNDERSAMPLING AND ALIASING

Aliasing is a phenomenon that is directly related to sampling. Essentially, it is caused by an incorrectly reconstructed signal, due to insufficient sampling. Therefore, the signal is mistaken for another signal, its *alias*. A typical visual result of aliasing is the Moiré artifact pattern, which can also be observed in our daily

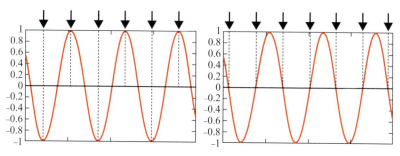

FIGURE 2.7 *Sine-function is sampled (arrows) at Nyquist rate. Left: Sampling at optimal position (detects peaks and valleys); right: Sampling phase shift—only a constant (zero) amplitude is sampled.*

environment, e.g., when looking through two fences while we are moving. The top row of Figure 2.8 shows examples of the Moiré artifact, where the surface of the scanned phantom object is sampled at a speed below the Nyquist rate. This insufficient sampling is also called undersampling. Another undersampling artifact is shown in the middle row of Figure 2.8, where an insufficient slice distance is not able to recover the full geometry of the scanned object.

There are basically two possible solutions to overcome undersampling: first of all, the sampling rate can be increased until we satisfy the Nyquist rate. Figure 2.8 shows in the top row how the Moiré artifacts are reduced by increasing the sampling rate.

The other solution is to band-limit the original signal by performing a low pass filtering step first. As mentioned above, a signal will be represented by a spectrum of frequencies in the frequency domain. If this spectrum extends into a higher frequency range that we cannot correctly reconstruct, we remove those frequencies from the spectrum by convolving the original signal with a low pass filter (removing higher frequencies and keeping lower frequencies; hence, a low pass filter). This means the convolved signal does not contain the offending higher frequencies; the band of frequencies has been limited.

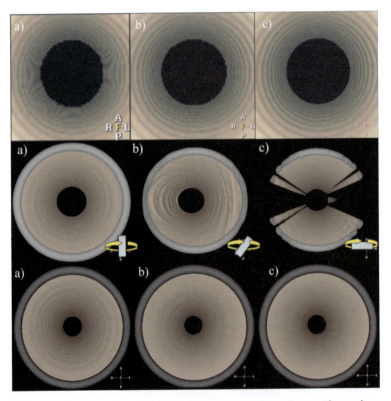

FIGURE 2.8   *Tube phantom with perspective projection from an endoscopic viewpoint. Top row: The sampling rate is increased from the left to right and the Moiré artifacts are reduced. Middle row: Different slice and pixel distance in anisotropic datasets can lead to insufficient sampling, if the object orientation is changed. Bottom row: If too many frequencies are removed by a low pass filter, details will disappear (the number of removed frequencies is increasing from left to right). (Images courtesy FLORIAN DAMMANN and ANDREAS BODE of the University Hospital Tübingen.)*

In the spatial domain, this results in a smoothed or blurred signal (or image). The blurring of the new signal depends on the size and quality of the low pass filter; the more high frequencies are removed, the more blurred the new signal. The bottom row of Figure 2.8 demonstrates what happens when too many high frequencies are removed.

Extensively band-limited signals often lead to excessively blurred data, in which more details than intended are removed. Therefore, the low pass filter has to be carefully designed in terms of its size (or extent). The choice of which low pass filter to use is also important. Typically, three different low pass filters are considered: a box filter, a triangle filter, and a Gaussian filter. The box filter is so called because of its frequency domain representation as a rectangle (see Fig. 2.9 (left)). If it is convolved with the spectrum of the original signal, only the frequencies covered by the box are kept in the convolved signal. The triangle filter works similarly, except that it introduces different weights for frequencies off-center of the triangle filter. Both filters have one common drawback: while they have a simple representation in the frequency domain, their representation in the spatial domain is the sinc function whose oscillating infinite extent must be truncated (see Fig. 2.9 (right)). This truncation however, leads to an imperfect box filter representation in the frequency domain.

This situation is less difficult with the third low pass filter candidate, the Gaussian filter, which essentially is a Gaussian function in the frequency and the spatial domain. Furthermore, it has a better weighting cut-off than the triangle filter. While it still has an infinite extent that needs to be truncated, it lacks the oscillating behavior. Furthermore, it always has positive weighting values.

More information on filtering can be found in Glassner's book [GLASSNER 1995].

2.2.3 PARTIAL VOLUME EFFECT

The partial volume effect is an issue that specifically concerns medical image data. Due to limited resolution at volume reconstruction—when the volume dataset is reconstructed from the measured signals—large intensity differences cannot properly be reconstructed. In order to avoid undersampling artifacts, the signal is band-limited, resulting in a smoothed intensity in the transitional region between the low and high intensity signals. Therefore, this sample represents a local neighborhood of the original signal values.

The practical consequences for medical image data are broad. Large differences in intensities can be caused, if neighboring tissues create significantly varying signal responses. If, for example, a bone is measured with a CT scanner, neighboring tissue with a significantly lower density will create a steep intensity difference that cannot properly be reconstructed. Hence, the voxels on the boundary between the two tissue materials will be low pass filtered. While low pass filtering is a good approach to avoid aliasing

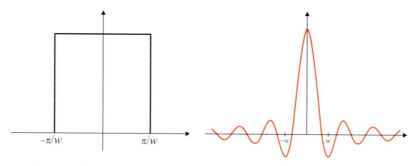

FIGURE 2.9 *The (1D) box filter has the shape of a rectangle in the frequency domain (left) and is a sinc function (right) with infinite support in the spatial domain.*

artifacts, the smoothed intensities create at the same time false connections or holes in the resulting image data. Figure 2.10 (left) demonstrates this effect. A thin membrane located in the area indicated by the yellow oval is affected by the partial volume effect. Since the neighboring cavities, which are separated by this membrane, are represented with high intensities, the low intensity thin membrane could not be fully reconstructed. Figure 2.10 (right) shows a similar situation. The measuring resolution of the MRI scanner is not sufficient to represent the (low intensity) septum between the (high intensity) upper cerebral ventricles, resulting in false connections between the upper ventricles.

Partial volume effects are omnipresent in medical image data and must therefore be taken into account for segmentation, classification, and quantitative image analysis. If a small anatomical structure with a significantly different intensity than the surrounding voxels needs to be scanned, the resolution must be chosen accordingly. HAHN [2005] discussed the impact of the partial volume effect on quantitative image analysis.

2.2.4 INTERPOLATION ARTIFACTS

As mentioned earlier in Section 2.1, many visual representations use interpolation schemes to compute data at positions between defined grid points. One of the most popular schemes is trilinear interpolation (Eq. 2.3), which is used for position and normal computation. Since the normals in volume datasets are usually approximated by gradients, central differences are typically used to estimate the gradients [HÖHNE and BERNSTEIN 1986]. Unfortunately, standard central differences will generate artifacts if the intensity differences are large or the grid spacing is anisotropic.

In the case of binary segmentation, individual voxels are labeled as part of the segment (on) or not part of the segment (off). If the respective isosurface representing the material interface between the segment and its neighborhood is computed, large intensity differences on the material interface (all off-voxels are set to zero, all on-voxels contain the original voxel value) occur. In these situations, the positions of the isosurface and in particular their normals will experience the above mentioned artifacts and result in a blocky appearance (see Fig. 2.11). This blockiness is aggravated if the isosurface is computed on the label

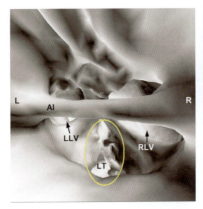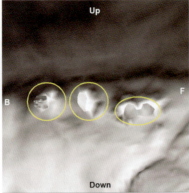

FIGURE 2.10 *Partial volume effect in an MRI scan of the cerebral ventricular system: The thin membrane Lamina Terminalis (LT, yellow marking) at the floor of the third cerebral ventricle could not be fully reconstructed (left). False connections (yellow markings) are due to the incompletely reconstructed septum between the upper lateral cerebral ventricles (right). L and R point to the left and right directions, B points to the back direction (or posterior), and F points to the frontal direction (or anterior). Up and down point to the respective directions. AI depicts the Adhesio Interthalamica, and LLV and RLV the entrance of the left and right cerebral ventricles (Foramen of Monro).*

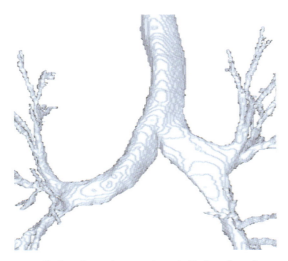

FIGURE 2.11   *Binary segmentation block artifacts. The image shows the block artifacts of an isosurface reconstruction of the label volume of a bronchi dataset. (Data courtesy* DIRK MAYER, *University Hospital Mainz)*

volume itself, where only one (for voxels of the segment) and zero intensities are available. In these cases, all smoothing effects of the partial volume effects are gone.

Fortunately, there are several remedies for these interpolation artifacts if the original data are used for isosurface computation and the label volume is only used as a map to indicate the voxels of the segments. The first remedy adds a layer of off-voxels around the segment voxels. This additional off-layer allows smoother local gradients on the material interface of the segment, since the intensity differences are significantly smaller than to zero intensities, due to the partial volume effect [HÖHNE and BERNSTEIN 1986]. Another possible remedy changes the original data values and might hence be less appropriate for certain situations, particularly in diagnostics. Here, the material interface in the voxel values is smoothed by applying a low pass volume filter, which generates a smooth transition between the segment and the off-voxels. However, this also changes the resulting isosurface and, therefore, must be applied with great care.

A related interpolation issue arises with the normal estimation based on central differences on anisotropic grids. Typically, the normal at a computed sample point within a volume cell is based on the trilinear interpolation of normals approximated by central differences at the surrounding voxels of this volume cell. This gradient estimation scheme, however, assumes an isotropic grid, since all three vector components are computed the same way. Unfortunately, anisotropic datasets have different voxel distances in the three different spatial orientations; usually the slice distance (z) is significantly larger than the pixel distance (x,y). Since these differences are not properly addressed in most rendering approaches, the normals at the computed sample points are distorted in the different spacing direction (typically in slice direction). Figure 2.12 (left) demonstrates this *staircasing artifact*, while the right figure shows the normals in the marked area of the left image in a polygonal isosurface representation.[5] Note that the flipped normal direction causes the staircasing artifact; the vertex positions are already correct.

Fortunately, there are also possible remedies, which address the anisotropic grid spacing. Probably the easiest approach is to correct the sample point normals according to the spacing. Figure 2.13 top row shows a possible solution in which the central differences of the normal estimation scheme are scaled by the voxel spacing, a solution that is similar to curvilinear or structured grid datasets, in which

---

5   Staircasing artifacts can appear in direct as well as indirect volume rendered images.

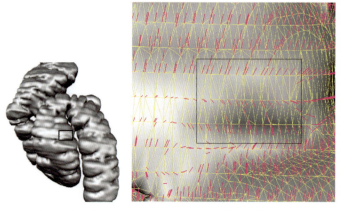

FIGURE 2.12 *Staircasing artifacts in the polygonal reconstruction of the left flexure of a colon dataset. The right image shows a magnification of the marked area in the left overview image. Here, the flipping (red) normal direction (up/down) at the staircase artifact (in the black rectangle) demonstrate the origin of the artifact.*

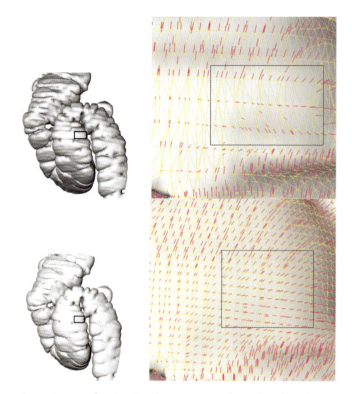

FIGURE 2.13 *Corrected normals to significantly reduce the staircasing artifact in the polygonal reconstruction of the left flexure of a colon dataset. The top row shows the correction based on the scaled gradient components, and the bottom row shows a corrected representation based on a Gaussian resampling of the volume. The left column shows the overall result, and the right column shows a magnification of the marked staircase region in the left image with the now corrected normals, compared to Figure 2.12.*

the normals also need to be corrected to address different cell sizes. As a variation of this approach for a polygonal representation, we can also compute the normals of the polygons (e.g., the cross product for triangles) and distribute a weighted average of these normals to the participating vertices. However, this normal computation scheme produces less smooth normals than the (corrected) gradient based method.

Alternatively, the data volume can be resampled into an isotropic grid dataset using an appropriate reconstruction filter (e.g., a Gauss-filter). The results of this approach can be seen in the bottom row of Figure 2.13. While the quality of the resampling solution is better than that of the rescaled version, a drawback to this solution is the significantly increased volume size, which requires more memory and rendering resources.

There are several other possible solutions that reduce the appearance of staircasing artifacts. An overview of normal estimation schemes was provided by MÖLLER et al. [1997]. More recently, NEUMANN et al. [2000] suggested the use of linear regression to estimate better gradients.

2.2.5 SIGNAL ARTIFACTS

One class of artifacts in medical volume data is caused by the data acquisition techniques themselves. While artifacts due to malfunctions of the measurement units (e.g., the detector array of a CT scanner, see Sect. 3.2) or other parts of the mechanical and electronic components became rather uncommon with the improving technology, other artifacts still persist.

Among the most notorious signal artifacts are *metal artifacts*, which appear if metal (e.g., steel or gold) is present in the body part to be scanned. Unfortunately, metal is used for many implants, such as tooth fillings, which are present in virtually every scanned mandible or maxilla bone; more rarely, one will find a metallic projectile. Similar to the partial volume effect, metal artifacts are partially due to an insufficient sampling of the very high metal/tissue intensity difference [KALENDER 2000]. Furthermore, the X-rays are almost blocked by the metal, what actually contributes most to the signal artifacts and can affect large areas of several image slices in a CT dataset (see Fig. 2.14 (left)).

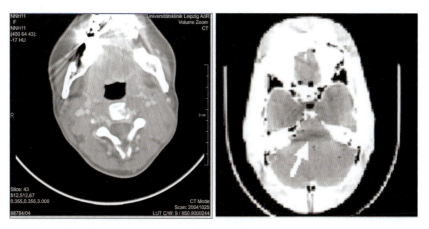

FIGURE 2.14   CT artifacts: Left, metallic implants degrade CT image quality in the maxillary region. (Image courtesy THOMAS SCHULZ, University of Leipzig) Right, beam-hardening artifact (white arrow) near the base of the skull. (Image courtesy WILLI KALENDER, University of Erlangen-Nürnberg)

MRI image data are also degraded in the presence of metal, since it causes inhomogeneities in the magnetic field (see Sect. 3.3). These inhomogeneities can lead to distortions of the image data (suggesting a somewhat different geometry) and to local changes of signal intensity [HOLDEN 2001].

Other artifacts occur due to patient movement (e.g., breathing, voluntary movements, moving body organs, etc.), because even small movements can lead to distortions to the whole image stack. In most cases, this kind of artifact can be significantly reduced with an increased scanning speed.

2.3 SENSITIVITY AND SPECIFICITY

Diagnostic procedures as a whole, as well as imaging procedures, are evaluated with respect to their diagnostic quality. The diagnostic quality is high if every pathologic abnormality is correctly reported and, on the other hand, all reported abnormalities are real abnormalities. The determination as to whether an abnormality was missed or incorrectly reported requires a comparison to a method which is believed to be correct. This method must be established and explored in detail. It is often referred to as the gold standard. The gold standard, however, might be limited in its correctness as well. Even an accepted and established method does not replace a ground truth, which serves as a reliable baseline for comparisons. With this in mind, it is clear that the comparison to a gold standard might be even misleading if a diagnostic procedure were introduced that was actually better than the (existing) gold standard. Partially, artificial phantoms can be used to compare the diagnostic quality of different imaging modalities. Since phantoms are created manually, all properties are exactly known.

Table 2.1 summarizes the different situations [BOWYER 2000].

Sensitivity is the probability of correctly reporting an abnormality; it is defined as:

$$sensitivity = \frac{TP}{TP + FN} \qquad (2.4)$$

Specificity is the probability of correctly reporting that no abnormality exists, and it is defined as:

$$specificity = \frac{TN}{TN + FP} \qquad (2.5)$$

If a diagnostic procedure has a parameter, the choice of this parameter determines sensitivity and specificity. As an example, we briefly look at colonoscopy, a screening procedure to detect colon cancer at an early stage or even before a lesion has converted to a malignant cancer. In this process, based on CT or MRI data and an appropriate contrast agent, polyps are searched for so that polyps that exceed a certain size can be removed. The procedure is laborious and cumbersome for the patient, because the colon lumen must be cleaned beforehand in order to avoid interpreting residual material as a colonic mass, a polyp. Colon cleansing is achieved by drinking a large amount of liquids or by administering medications to induce bowel movements [CHEN et al. 2000]. Colonoscopy is not the only method for colon cancer

	abnormality present	abnormality not present
abnormality present	true positive (TP)	false negative (FN)
abnormality not present	false positive (FP)	true negative (TN)

TABLE 2.1 *Categories for the evaluation of diagnostic procedures.*

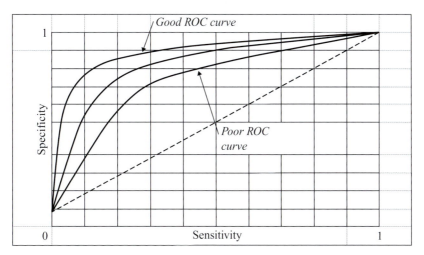

FIGURE 2.15 *Examples of ROC curves. A "good" curve indicates that a diagnostic procedure has a high sensitivity and specificity at the same time. The dotted line represents the worst performance of a diagnostic procedure. (Image courtesy PETRA SPECHT, University of Magdeburg)*

screening: the fecal occult blood test and digital rectal examination are widespread, cheaper alternatives. The sensitivity and specificity of detecting significant polyps allow a comparison of these methods.

The size of the polyps, which is considered *significant*, is the parameter of all screening methods. With a very low threshold for the polyp size, the sensitivity is very high but the specificity is low, since many persons have very small polyps that are not malignant. On the other hand, a higher threshold ensures that specificity is increased, at the expense of sensitivity. This tradeoff is characterized in so-called receiver-operator curves (ROC analysis, see Fig. 2.15). The area under the curve (AUC) is a measure for the quality of a diagnostic procedure. The imaging modalities described in the following chapter differ in sensitivity and specificity for diagnostic questions such as detection of cancer, soft tissue abnormalities, or pathologic variations of vascular structures.

2.4   VISUAL PERCEPTION

In this section, we introduce some fundamental aspects of the human visual perception. We focus on gray values and their perception and discuss color perception more briefly. The attention to gray values is due to the fact that gray value images dominate in conventional diagnosis as well as in volume rendering. Although in the visualization community colors are used intensively also for visualization of medical volume data, this does not reflect the clinical use of medical volume data.

2.4.1 GRAY VALUE PERCEPTION

When we discuss gray value perception, we have to consider the physical parameter luminance (the amount of light intensity per unit area) and the perceived brightness. As one would expect, the relation is monotone: the more light intensity applied to a CRT monitor, the brighter we perceive the image. However, this relation is distinctly non-linear. The human eye is relatively less sensitive in the brightest areas of an image. This variation in sensitivity makes it easier to see small relative changes in luminance in darker areas of an image.

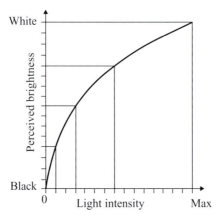

FIGURE 2.16 *When the light intensity (luminance) is increased, the perceived brightness increases quickly in the low intensity areas. Later, larger steps are necessary to achieve the same perceived brightness difference. (Adapted from [WARE 2000].)*

Figure 2.16 shows the relation between image intensity and perceived brightness with a dark background. Note, however, that the measurement of perceived stimuli, in particular of the human visual system, is a complex task that requires a careful design of the experiments. The design of a gray scale such that adjacent perceived differences between similar gray values is called (perceptual) *linearization*.

Just-Noticeable Differences   An important term in the discussion of visual perception is the *just-noticeable difference* (JND). With respect to gray value perception, this term characterizes the smallest luminance difference of a given reference intensity (under given viewing conditions) that the average human observer can still perceive. The JND is not an absolute value, due to the non-linear characteristic of our visual perception. Instead, the JND for darker values is smaller than for brighter values. With this in mind, quantitative data, such as CT data, can be displayed so that humans can discriminate approximately 100 gray levels simultaneously [RHEINGANS 1992].[6] The number of discernible gray values also depends on the type of display. Display systems with a wider luminance range are capable of presenting more just-noticeable luminance differences.

It should be noted, that 100 is a relatively small number: the CT scanner produces 4096 different intensity values, and MRI scanners may produce 256, 4096, or even 65,536 different intensity values. On the other hand, the gray level resolution of current display facilities is below 4096 (12-bit). Usually, 8-bit resolution (256 gray values) is available on standard displays. Only specialized displays are able to reproduce 10-bit resolution (1024 gray values). Therefore, the gray level resolution of medical data must be mapped to intensity values that can be reproduced on the screen. This mapping process should not be linear (cutting the least important bits) but instead should consider the curve presented in Figure 2.16. Our discussion is based on a simplified view of visual perception; we ignore, for example, the influence of the image content and the viewer's visual capabilities.

For experts in perception, non-linear visual perception is a special example of non-linear effects of the human perception in general. Also, our perception of sound and our perception of differences in length are characterized by distinctly non-linear relations to the underlying physical quantity. This is generally

---

6   Note that the JND is always a relative difference; if we select an arbitrary luminance intensity from a range that cannot be differentiated, the JND may point to a different intensity than it would for the intensity at the lower boundary of the range.

expressed in Weber's law, which states that for each stimulus, the JND is a constant proportion of the original stimulus.

Spatial Resolution   So far, we have discussed perceivable gray level differences. Another important aspect for our ability to interpret image data is the spatial resolution of our visual system. To discuss this issue, it is essential to discuss some aspects of our retinal image processing. Incoming light is perceived by the retina, which consists of many light-sensitive cells (except at the blind spot, where the optical nerve starts and no such cells can be found). Humans possess two kinds of light-sensitive cells, namely rods and cones. The cones are the smaller cells (width of 3 mm) and respond to incoming light very fast. Cones are responsible for color perception (three classes of cones allow the perception of colors with different spectra of the visible light). Rods are the second type of light cells, which allow the perception of different gray values.

We will not go into detail here, but it is important to know that the spatial resolution of the retina is strongly different between a small central area, where we can perceive small details, and other regions on the retina, where the spatial resolution is an order of magnitude lower. The *fovea* is the region where we have a high density of light-sensitive cells, primarily cones, that permit detailed perception (*foveatic vision*). The spatial resolution inside the fovea is approximately one arc minute (measured as the visual angle between the borders of an object). It is interesting to note that the cells in the fovea are not aligned along a regular grid, but instead on a jittered grid (see Fig. 2.17). It is assumed that this distribution effectively avoids aliasing problems [WARE 2000].

Outside the fovea, the density of the sensory cells is strongly reduced, which causes peripheral vision (see Fig. 2.18). Whereas the cones are concentrated in the fovea, the rods occur in the periphery. The distribution of the cells is not perfectly symmetric. There are slightly more cells at the half where the blind spot occurs (probably to compensate for the missing cells there). If an image is interpreted, it takes some time to focus on an area that is relevant for diagnosis. For the development of software to support diagnostic processes, it is therefore highly desirable that interaction facilities for adjusting an image, for example, its lightness, do not force the user to lose his or her focus.

Contrast Perception   Another important aspect of visual perception that is relevant for reading medical data is the perceived *contrast*. As one would expect, the perceived contrast at the boundary of objects depends on the difference between gray values. However, the absolute difference of gray values is not

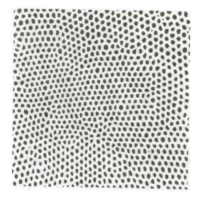

FIGURE 2.17   *Jittered position of cells in the fovea. (From [WARE 2000].)*

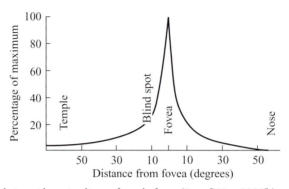

FIGURE 2.18   *Spatial resolution with varying distance from the fovea. (From [WARE 2000].)*

sufficient to characterize contrast. Instead, the image intensities have to be taken into account, according to Equation 2.6.

$$C = \frac{I_{light} - I_{dark}}{I_{light} + I_{dark}} \tag{2.6}$$

It is desirable to generate images with a high contrast between adjacent tissues, because the resolution of the visual system depends on the contrast: we can recognize smaller structures if they exhibit a good contrast to the surrounding. The contrast in an image is affected by a transfer function that maps data to optical properties such as gray values. A simple kind of transfer function specification, called *windowing*, will be discussed in Section 4.3.2.

The human visual system enhances contrasts by sophisticated "image processing." The signals detected at adjacent light sensitive cells are combined, resulting in the perception of a larger brightness difference than would be expected with respect to the actual intensity difference. Therefore, humans are very sensitive to aliasing problems (recall Sect. 2.2).

2.4.2 COLOR SPACES, COLOR SCALES, AND COLOR PERCEPTION

In medical visualizations, color is frequently used to display complex information—for example, in the diagnosis of dynamic image data (see Chap. 10) and diffusion tensor data (see Chap. 18). The use of colors is primarily motivated by its higher dynamic range compared to gray scales. Despite the fact that the number of just-noticeable differences can be considerably increased by means of appropriate color scales, color is not always a better choice than gray scale. This was demonstrated in an experiment in which simple detection tasks in medical image data had to be solved; gray scale lead to better results [LEVKOWITZ and HERMAN 1992].

Color perception is a complex issue, which is worth a book on its own. We will briefly introduce some concepts that are needed later in this book. A detailed discussion of color perception can be found in [LEVKOWITZ 1997].

As described above, humans possess three different kinds of light-sensitive cones that capture color sensations. These three kinds of cones have different absorption maxima in the spectrum of visible wavelength. For the design of color scales, it is essential that the cones with an absorption maximum in the blue area of the spectrum are relatively rare (cones that perceive primarily green and red light occur

10 times more often). This explains why humans are relatively less sensitive to blue light and small changes in bluish colors. Before we discuss color scale, it is necessary to introduce and discuss *color spaces*.

Color Spaces   A *color space*, sometimes also called a color model, is a space spanned by three orthogonal basis vectors, each of them representing one component of a color model [RHEINGANS 1992]. These components may be strongly different: for example, the basis can be formed by three primary colors either added (to black) or subtracted (from white) to describe a particular color. Almost all color spaces are characterized by three components, which corresponds naturally to the three kinds of cones at the retina. The following categories of color spaces can be distinguished (see [RHEINGANS 1992]):

- *Device-oriented color spaces*, where color is defined in a way which corresponds to the physical realization of color output of that device (e.g., a printer or a computer monitor)
- *Intuitive color spaces*, where color is defined in a way that adheres to natural properties of color, such as brightness
- *Perceptually uniform color spaces*, where color is defined such that the Euclidean distance between a pair of colors corresponds to the perceived difference between these colors

All three categories have their place. Device-oriented color spaces are necessary to control output devices. Intuitive color spaces make it easier to specify colors so that the expected result is achieved. Finally, perceptually uniform color spaces are useful if colors are interpolated. Since different color spaces are used, it is often necessary to transform a color specification from one space to another, and vice versa. In the following, we briefly describe each category.

Device-Oriented Color Spaces   The APIs of computer graphics libraries, such as OpenGL, usually require the specification of color as a triple with a red, green, and blue component (RGB). The RGB color space is based on an additive color model and motivated by the working principle of the cathode ray tube, in which a color is composed by adding red, green, and blue components. If the creator of a visualization considers appropriate colors (for example, to highlight values in a critical range) the RGB space is not well suited to this task.

Intuitive Color Spaces   The most widespread intuitive color space is the HSV space, which consists of a triplet of hue, saturation, and value (see Fig. 2.19). Hue interpolates between the six base colors, and it is modified with respect to saturation (0 represents a gray value and 1 a perfectly saturated color). The value component indicates the brightness. Geometrically, the HSV space has the shape of a cone. All saturated colors are represented along the base of the cone. The center line of the cone connects all gray values. Dark colors are therefore close to the apex. The hue is specified as an angle, with 0 degrees representing red. In HSV space, for example, it is straightforward to specify a moderately saturated color. Closely related intuitive color spaces are HLS (hue, lightness, saturation) and HSB (hue, saturation, brightness).

Perceptually Uniform Color Spaces   The design of a perceptually uniform color space is motivated by the goal that the perceived distance of two pairs of colors, $pd(c_1, c_2)$ and $pd(c_3, c_4)$, should be the same exactly when the Euclidean distance between $dist(c_1, c_2)$ and $dist(c_3, c_4)$ in the color space is equal. None of the device-oriented and intuitive color spaces is, in this sense, perceptually uniform. The CIELUV color space, developed by the COMMISSION INTERNATIONALE DE L'ECLAIRAGE (CIE) [1978], is specifically designed for this purpose. The first letters of CIELUV are due to the organization which defined it; LUV stands for the names for the components of the color space. We will not describe it here in detail; however, it should be noted that it is difficult to verify whether the desired property is completely fulfilled. In general, it is agreed that for large distances between colors, perceptual uniformity is not achieved. There is some

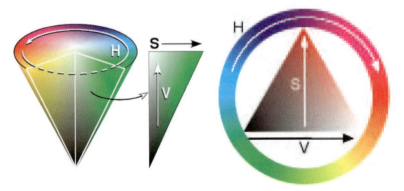

FIGURE 2.19 *The HSV color space has the shape of a cone. The angle between a point's connection to the center with a reference line denotes the hue component (see also the right image), the distance to the centerline denotes saturation (S), and the height of a point in HSV space denotes darkness (V). (Image courtesy* ERIC PIERCE)

debate whether the color space developed by ROBERTSON and O'CALLAGHAN [1986] is more perceptually uniform [LEVKOWITZ and HERMAN 1992].

Color Scales for Encoding Scalar Values Color is often used to encode a single scalar value. As an example, bone thickness has been analyzed in ZUIDERVELD [1995b] and color-coded onto the bone surface. Color coding is controlled by color scales or colormaps. A color scale is a one-dimensional parametric curve in a color space [RHEINGANS 1992]. The concept of linearization is also known for color scales. It denotes that additional colors are inserted in the scale such that the perceived distance between adjacent colors of the extended scale is as uniform as possible [LEVKOWITZ and HERMAN 1992].

In visualization libraries, a variety of color scales are usually provided. The most prominent color scale is the rainbow scale, where the full hue range of the HSV color model is mapped to a selected color range. Unfortunately, hue is not a linearly perceived range, which can lead to interpretation problems of accordingly colored data [ROGOWITZ et al. 1996]. Better are isomorphic colormaps, such as saturation or luminance maps where either saturation or luminance is increased in a monotone manner. Such color scales also have a distinct and obvious start and endpoint, which is an essential aspect of perceptually oriented color scales [LEVKOWITZ 1997]. Color scales that have monotone behavior with respect to brightness and saturation also enable people with deficient color vision to recognize differences. The heated body (often called temperature scale) is an example of a perceptually oriented color scale that uses primarily reddish and orange colors, for which human sensitivity is high (see Fig. 2.20) [LEVKOWITZ and HERMAN 1992]. Another good method is to vary both hue and intensity to get a spiral color in color space.

The design of color scales must also consider predefined meanings of colors. In western countries, red is considered a signal for danger and thus is used for values in a critical range. Green, on the other, hand indicates that values are in a normal range. Yellow and orange are appropriate for values that are neither normal nor highly critical.

The appropriateness of color scales, in particular if new color scales should be used, can only be assessed by means of a systematic user study. A user study should compare familiar images color-coded with different scales. The recognizability of differences needs to be assessed separately in different portions. ROGOWITZ and KALVIN [2001] carried out such a study to compare the most frequently used color scales. Their experiment design may serve as an orientation for similar experiments.

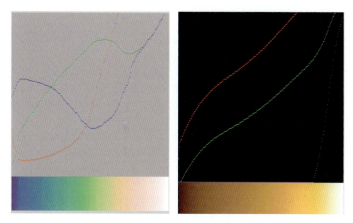

FIGURE 2.20   *The rainbow and the heated body color scale, together with the related RGB values. The heated body scale is perceived better sorted and perceptual differences in the colors are roughly the same in all portions of the scale. (Images courtesy HAIM LEVKOWITZ, University of Massachusetts at Lowell)*

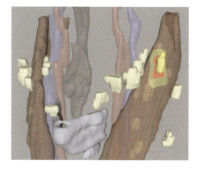

FIGURE 2.21   *Color-coding distances between a malignant tumor and a critical structure. (Image courtesy of ARNO KRÜGER, University of Magdeburg)*

Discrete Color Scales   Continuous color scales map scalar data in high precision. Often color is used instead to convey whether a value is in a certain interval. In such cases, discrete color scales with clearly distinct colors are used. As an example, for surgery planning it is often essential to recognize whether a critical structure is close to a tumor. To convey this information, a discrete scale with red representing distances below 2 mm and orange representing distances between 2 and 5 mm is appropriate (see Fig. 2.21).

Bi- and Trivariate Color Scales   Since color spaces have three components, it is feasible to map two or three scalar values to a single color by using separate components of a color space. This is referred to as bi- and trivariate color mapping. The HSV color space is often used for bivariate color scales. It must be noted that continuous bi- and trivariate color scales often lead to complex visualizations, for example, if they are mapped onto complex anatomic surfaces.

2.5   SUMMARY

CT and MRI data, as well as PET and SPECT data, are volumetric datasets arranged on a cartesian voxel grid. Data values between the grid points are usually computed by trilinear interpolation within the voxel cells. Since this is a discrete representation of the data, all the datasets are subject to the sampling theorem, which specifies the boundary conditions for an alias-free representation. Next to possible sampling artifacts (if the sampling theorem is violated), other causes of artifacts are the partial volume effect, interpolation artifacts, and signal artifacts at data acquisition.

While most direct image representations of medical image data are represented as gray intensities, some representations—in particular visualizations—use colors. Gray intensities are not perceived linearly; the human visual system is less sensitive to brightness changes in dark regions, than in bright regions. This needs to be considered when a black and white (gray) representation is chosen.

The same problem arises in color representations, since not all color scales are perceived linearly. In particular, the often-used rainbow color scale includes catches, where different colors at the same metric distance in the color space suggest different interpretation distances. This is less problematic with luminance color scales.

FURTHER READING

Since data artifacts are largely based on violations of the sampling theorem, the interested reader will find background material in books on signal theory. An excellent introduction into the computer graphics side of signal theory can be found in Glassner's books [GLASSNER 1995]. Signal artifacts are examined in the respective literature. For CT, this information can be found in [KALENDER 2000], and for MRI, advanced information is provided through MRI-TIP [accessed 2005] and GREGORY [accessed 2005].

Theories of visual perception are an important source for designing computer-supported visualizations. We discussed this topic briefly, but want to point to additional information. With respect to perceptually linearized visualizations, we refer to PIZER [1981]. SWETS and PICKET [1982] discuss studies of the performances of users in diagnostic tasks depending on different color-coded visualizations. LEVKOWITZ and HERMAN [1992] proposed an "optimal" color scale that maximizes the number of just-noticeable differences and that is perceived as ordered. The heated body scale and its application to ultrasonography is discussed in [PIZER and ZIMMERMANN 1983]. The appropriateness of color scales depends on specific tasks and users. This relation is investigated in [TREINISH 1999] and [RHEINGANS 1999]. Experiments concerning the appropriateness of color scales are described in [ROGOWITZ and KALVIN 2001]. More information on color can be found in Stone's excellent book [STONE 2003] and in the very useful color FAQ [POYNTON 2006].

For readers who are interested in visual perception and the improvement of computer-generated display and visualization systems based on perceptual considerations, we refer to the excellent book of WARE [2000]. A more psychophysics-oriented book is [GOLDSTEIN 2006].

Chapter 03

Acquisition of Medical Image Data

Medical image data are acquired for different purposes, such as diagnosis, therapy planning, intraoperative navigation, and postoperative monitoring. The most important and widespread use of medical image data is for diagnostics. The acquisition of medical image data is usually not the first step in a diagnostic process; exceptions are urgent cases or severe accidents with unconscious patients. Usually, a patient describes his or herproblem to a medical doctor who interprets these statements, while also considering the patient's previous diseases or accidents and habits as well as diseases which occurred in the family (anamnesis). As a second step, simple diagnostic procedures such as palpation, auscultation with a stethoscope, and blood pressure measurements are carried out. As a further building block of diagnosis, clinical tests are performed in which liquids of the body, such as blood and urine, are analyzed. Many diagnostic procedures can be completed with these examinations.

Medical image data are acquired primarily when the previously described diagnostic steps raised the suspicion for a severe disease, such as a malignancy or heart disease. In the large majority of cases for which image data are acquired, a specific suspicion exists. The image acquisition and interpretation are specifically performed to determine whether the suspicion can be confirmed or excluded. Therefore, it is essential that the relevant information from previous diagnostic steps is available to the radiologist. From a computer science perspective, this situation is the motivation for developing electronic patient records and hospital information systems, which contain this information and share it among all doctors involved in the diagnosis and treatment of the patient. Important issues of hospital information systems, such as security, networking standards, and data protection, are beyond the scope of this book, but it is essential to understand that image data acquisition and interpretation cannot be regarded as an isolated problem. Instead, it is part of a complex process in which information from previous diagnostic steps must be integrated and in which the results produced must be made available for other medical doctors.

Organization We start with an overview on X-ray imaging (see Sect. 3.1). X-ray images were the first medical image data that exposed information about inner structures of the human body, and they are still by far the most used image modality in modern health care. In this section, we will also discuss various flavors of X-ray imaging, such as angiography and rotational X-ray. We continue with a discussion of CT data acquisition, which is based on the same physical principle, but represents a tomographic modality generating volume data (see Sect. 3.2). The second widespread tomographic modality is MRI which is described in Section 3.3. This versatile imaging modality exploits the different characteristics of human tissue in magnetic fields. Although most of the applications and algorithms discussed in this book are based on CT and MRI data, we also discuss other modalities that have a great importance in clinical reality and might be used more intensively in the future in computer-assisted diagnosis and therapy planning systems. In Section 3.4, we describe the principle of ultrasound generation. Finally, positron emission tomography (PET) and single-photon emission computed tomography (SPECT) (see Sects. 3.5 and 3.6) are considered the most widespread modalities in nuclear medicine.

3.1   X-RAY IMAGING

The discovery of X-rays by Wilhelm Konrad RÖNTGEN in 1895 was the birth of medical imaging. For the first time, interior parts of a body could be seen without actually cutting into it. Figure 3.1 shows examples of X-ray imaging. The left image shows one of the first images made by RÖNTGEN; it is said to be the hand of his wife. The right image shows a more recent X-ray image of a left hand. The name X-rays was coined in RÖNTGEN's original paper [RÖNTGEN 1895], where it denoted a new, unknown ("X") kind of radiation. They are also known as RÖNTGEN rays. Note that Figure 3.1 shows two X-ray images that have inverted intensities, due to different recording techniques. In the left image, low densities (e.g., air) are mapped to white, and high densities (e.g., bone) are mapped to dark. In contrast, the right image shows high densities in white, and low densities in black.

X-ray images are based on the attenuation of X-ray quanta travelling through the scanned object. The attenuation is based on two processes: X-ray quanta are *absorbed* by the object that is hit, and X-ray quanta are *scattered* due to the so-called Compton effect. The Compton effect occurs if photons arrive at an atom with high energy and cause electrons from the outer hull of that atom to be detached and moved in a certain angle to the direction of the incoming photon. The Compton effect actually limits the contrast and quality of X-ray images.

The denser the current part of that object is (e.g., bone or metal), the more the X-ray quanta are absorbed. The absorption also depends on the thickness of the object to be passed.

The X-ray quanta are generated by electrons accelerated through an electric field. When these electrons hit the target material (the anode), the kinetic energy is transformed into heat (approximately 99% [LEHMANN et al. 1997a]) and X-ray quanta. The target material is often tungsten, which exhibits characteristic X-ray energies that are appropriate for imaging bones. For other applications such as mammography, where soft tissue is imaged, other target materials are required, for example molybdenum.

The speed (and hence the energy) of the electrons depends on the strength of the electric field that accelerates the electrons. If the generating voltage is larger than 100 kV, we speak of hard beam X-rays; otherwise, we speak of soft beam X-rays. If hard beam X-rays are used to generate X-ray quanta, the scattering effect dominates the interaction with the object. Consequently, the quanta are only absorbed

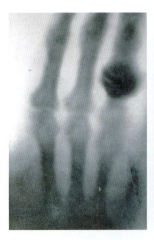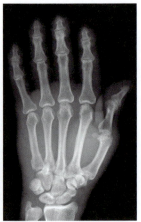

FIGURE 3.1   *X-Ray imaging: Left, an X-ray image of the right hand of the wife of RÖNTGEN; right, a recent X-ray scan of a left hand. (Right image courtesy HARVARD Medical School)*

in very dense material. In medical imaging, this is exploited for the representation of bone structures. In contrast, soft beam X-rays result predominately in absorption; hence, this can be used for the representation of soft tissue. This technique, however, results in more energy intake by the tissue itself, which in turn leads to more tissue damage. Therefore, soft beam X-rays are more harmful than hard beam X-rays.

A film behind the patient records the X-ray attenuation. The varying brightness of the film is a result of the interactions of X-rays with the different tissue types that have been passed. Tissue types that absorb a large fraction of X-ray intensity lead to a low density of radiographs and appear bright.

Skeletal structures exhibit the highest absorption rates and are therefore the brightest structures. Tissues with lower absorption rate lead to a high density of radiograph, resulting in dark or even black areas. In the human body, air has the lowest absorption rate and appears black. The resulting intensity I depends on the thickness of the material that is passed, as well as on a coefficient μ that characterizes the attenuation S. The initial intensity I_o drops exponentially with increasing distance d (see Eq. 3.1).

$$I(d) = I_0 * e^{-\mu * d} \tag{3.1}$$

The product $\mu * d$ characterizes the attenuation S. Usually, different tissue types are involved, which leads to the approximation of the attenuation S as a sum of different materials with individual attenuation coefficients μ_i and a certain distance d_i (see Eq. 3.2).

$$S = \sum \mu_i * d_i \tag{3.2}$$

Note that the elements of an X-ray image characterize the whole pass of the radiation through the body and produce a weighted average value of X-ray attenuation. Primarily, only the silhouettes of objects

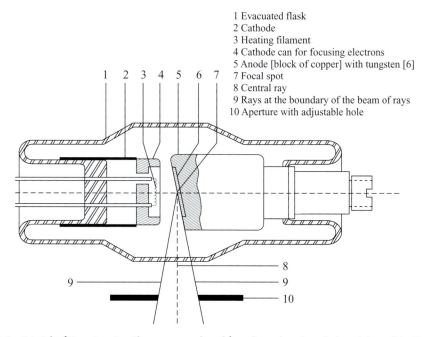

1 Evacuated flask
2 Cathode
3 Heating filament
4 Cathode can for focusing electrons
5 Anode [block of copper] with tungsten [6]
7 Focal spot
8 Central ray
9 Rays at the boundary of the beam of rays
10 Aperture with adjustable hole

FIGURE 3.2 Principle of X-ray imaging. Electrons are accelerated from the anode to the cathode, and the resulting X-ray quanta are deflected towards the patient, where they are focused by means of an appropriate aperture. (Adapted from [LEHMANN et al. 1997b])

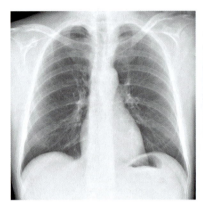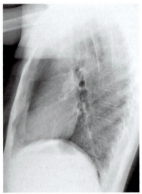

FIGURE 3.3 *A frontal and a lateral view of a thorax (no pathologies were detected). (Images courtesy HANS-HOLGER JEND, Hospital Bremen-Ost)*

and structures are recognizable. Therefore, individual X-ray images cannot be used to accurately localize structures. As a consequence, X-ray images are often generated in two different imaging planes (see Fig. 3.3).

Today, images generated by X-rays are typically provided as digital image data. The necessary digitalization can basically be achieved in two ways. If they are recorded on film material, they need to be scanned afterwards ("computed radiographs"). Alternatively, the X-ray images can be directly recorded digitally by a detector array ("direct radiograph").

Digital Mammography A special variant of digital X-ray images is digital mammography, where digital X-ray images of the female breast are acquired. Because of the epidemiologic importance of breast cancer, digital mammography experienced enormous development, which led to dedicated workstations aiming at an improved diagnosis of mammographic images. While reading mammographies, it is often essential to detect very small features that could be early signs of breast cancer. To enable the detection of these small features, monitors with high spatial and gray value resolution are required. It is often essential to compare the current mammography (from two viewing angles) with previous images to evaluate the progress of suspicious regions over time. Since these mammography images are available in a digital form, they can be processed algorithmically to improve their interpretation. A problem of mammography is that it requires soft beam X-rays, which in turn increase the potential tissue damage of the patient.

Fluoroscopy Fluoroscopy is a special version of direct radiographs, where the result can be immediately represented on a screen. Since the permanent exposure to X-radiation requires a significantly lower intensity, the overall image quality does not equal the quality of regular still X-ray images. However, the focus here is on dynamic processes that are visible over time. Typical examples are angiographies, where an injected contrast agent is tracked while it travels through the respective blood vessels. Typically, fluoroscopy images are acquired intraoperatively by a C-arm[1] scanner (see Fig. 3.4).

---

1 The "C" characterizes the shape of the device.

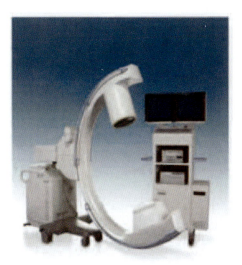

FIGURE 3.4 *C-arm scanning for intraoperative imaging, e.g., of fluoroscopy images. (Image copyright SIEMENS Medical Solutions)*

3.1.1 ANGIOGRAPHY

Angiography is an imaging technique in which an X-ray picture is acquired to display the inner open space (lumen) of blood-filled structures. The resulting X-ray image is called an *angiogram*. Angiography is employed to depict arteries; the most widespread applications are cerebral angiography (depiction of blood vessels inside the brain) [OSBORN 1999] and coronary angiography (depiction of the coronary vessels around the heart). Angiography is an invasive procedure that requires the insertion of a catheter. A catheter is a long, thin, flexible tube employed to administer contrast agent in a target area. Coronary angiography, for example, is performed by inserting a catheter in an artery in the arm and then advancing the catheter into a major coronary artery. The concept of angiography was developed by Egas Moniz, a Portuguese physician, in 1927 (documented in his book [MONIZ 1940]).

Digital Subtraction Angiography Digital subtraction angiography (DSA) tracks the blood flow through contrast agent–enhanced imaging. In order to maximize the representation of the blood vessels, a "mask image" of the object before injecting the contrast agent is taken. During the contrast-enhanced phase, this mask image is subtracted from acquired images, thus leaving only the changing parts of the images, which in case of a DSA is typically a blood vessel tree. Other potential visually obstructing structures are removed with the mask image (see Fig. 3.5). There are many applications of this principle to guide neurosurgical procedures, such as the treatment of significant cerebral aneurysms (sacklike enlargements of vascular structures with a high risk for rupture).

3.1.2 ROTATIONAL X-RAY

Rotational X-ray is a recent scanning technology based on DSA. Hence, most of the associated applications are angiography applications, and this technique is frequently referred to as rotational angiography (see Fig. 3.6) [FAHRIG 1999, GÜRVIT et al. 2000]. Rotational X-ray acquires a series of X-ray images while

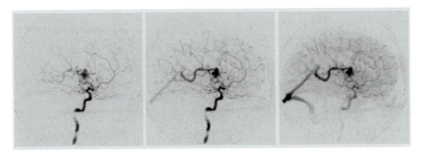

FIGURE 3.5 *Digital subtraction angiography to analyze cerebral blood vessels. (Images courtesy* BERND TOMANDL, *University Hospital Erlangen-Nürnberg)*

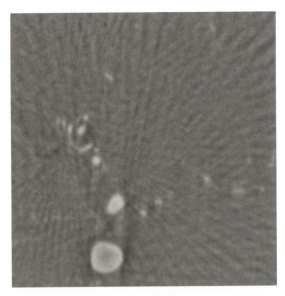

FIGURE 3.6 *Rotational angiography of cerebral arteries. Due to the used reconstruction algorithm, only bones (not visible) and blood vessels enhanced with a contrast agent can be represented well. The image shows a large aneurysm of the anterior cerebral artery in the lower left. (Data courtesy* ÖZLEM GÜRVIT, *University Hospital Tübingen)*

rotating around the subject to be scanned. Since the rotation of the emitter/detector system is performed on a C-shape mounting, it is also called C-arm X-ray. Many systems consist of a pair of emitter/detector systems to acquire two projections at a time. These systems are named rotational biplanar X-ray.

To generate volumetric datasets, a series of up to 132 X-ray projections are taken from a rotation range of 200 degrees around the scanning object. In contrast to CT, rotational X-ray is using a full array of up to 1024^2 detectors, which allow the measurement of a full cone of rays. To account for reconstruction errors, a modified back-projection algorithm is used [FELDKAMP et al. 1984, KALENDER 2000]. Additionally, special filter kernels are used to further reduce potential artifacts. Current rotational angiography systems provide very high resolution, isotropic datasets, good reconstruction quality (for selected organs, such as bones and contrast agent enhanced blood vessels), and a high data acquisition speed of up to 13 seconds for a full scan.

3.1.3 DISCUSSION

Compared to other (especially 3D) image modalities, 2D X-ray imaging provides only a projection image of the scanned object. Hence, the representation of positional relationships is difficult. In most cases (in particular the diagnosis of bones), two X-ray images are acquired from two different viewing directions (biplanar) to provide a better spatial understanding of the different anatomical structures.

Despite the availability of many different 3D modalities and their advantages, 2D X-ray imaging is still the standard image acquisition method in clinical practice.

A general problem of X-rays is that they have the potential to impair the genetic material, which may contribute to the outbreak of cancer. The danger for the patient depends on the dose of radiation (measured in Sievert). In general, there is a trade-off between image quality (high signal-to-noise ratio) and the dose of radiation. Lower doses of radiation tend to compromise image quality. Despite this correlation, image quality has improved considerably over the years while the necessary radiation has been reduced.

3.2   COMPUTED TOMOGRAPHY

The introduction of X-ray computed tomography (CT) in 1968 by GODFREY HOUNSFIELD [HOUNSFIELD 1972][2] provided for the first time a volumetric representation of objects, and not only a 2D projection of a volumetric object. Generally, it is seen as one of the major milestones in medical imaging [CHO et al. 1993].

In essence, CT data represents a series of individual X-ray images that are composed into one volume dataset. These X-ray images are acquired by an emitter/detector system that rotates around the object to be scanned (see Fig. 3.7 (left)). Each X-ray image represents an intensity profile measured by the detectors. From the intensity profiles of a full rotation, the slice image of the scanned object is computed based on the Radon transform [RADON 1917, CHO et al. 1993], which essentially is based on the Fourier theorem. Afterward, the table on which the scanned object is positioned will be moved forward and the next image slice of the object will be acquired.

3.2.1 COMPUTED TOMOGRAPHY COMPARED WITH X-RAY IMAGING

CT has a variety of advantages as an imaging modality compared to the conventional use of X-rays [HOUNSFIELD 1980]. These are:

- **Localization of anatomical structures.** Most notably, CT can provide accurate localization of objects in depth. While X-ray images superimpose the X-ray absorption values of many tissues along a ray, CT records X-ray attenuation for small volume elements independently.
- **Sensitivity.** CT data are two orders of magnitude more sensitive than X-ray images. X-ray images are not able to distinguish different soft tissues such as liver and pancreas, whereas CT image data discriminate these tissues. The contrast between soft tissues, however, is small with CT data. Better soft tissue contrast is achieved with MRI data.
- **Quantitative measurements.** Since the X-ray absorption is computed with high accuracy for individual volume elements, it is possible to analyze CT data quantitatively. For example, the mean X-ray absorption in a selected region can be determined and used as an indicator for the severity of a disease, such as osteoporosis.

---

2 The patent was filed in 1968 and granted in 1972.

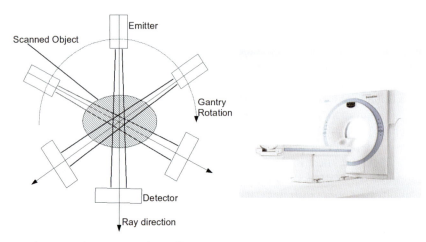

FIGURE 3.7 *Left: A series of measurements from different angles are reconstructed to a 2D cross-sectional image. Right: A photo of a modern CT scanner. (Right image copyright SIEMENS Medical Solutions, Somatom Sensation)*

In general, CT produces detailed anatomic information and allows for many pathologic variations to discriminate pathologic regions from healthy tissue. It was soon recognized that precise anatomic localization is crucial for diagnosis as well as for therapy planning. Craniofacial surgery planning [VANNIER et al. 1983] was the first application area, primarily because for these interventions, bones are crucial and could be discriminated from their surroundings well with CT data. Precise craniofacial surgery planning is important, as functional and aesthetic aspects are involved. Later, many other application areas, such as radiation treatment planning [LEVOY et al. 1990] followed. CT data, therefore, also fostered cooperation between medical doctors from different disciplines.

3.2.2 PRINCIPLE OF CT DATA GENERATION

The major differences between the development stages of CT [KALENDER 2000] are different projection reconstruction algorithms and the emitter and detector architecture (data acquisition). The first generation of CT scanners was basically the experimental setting of Hounsfield's CT scanner. It used a single pencil-like X-ray beam emitter and a single detector on the opposite side of the object. To acquire a data slice, the pencil beam was translated along the object and rotated afterwards for the next series of beams. All together, the costly mechanical movement of emitter and detector caused long scanning times, ranging from several minutes to several hours at a resolution of 80 × 80 pixels per scan/slice. Furthermore, the single emitter/detector architecture enabled only a poor utilization of the emitted radiation.

The next generation and first commercial generation of CT scanners used small angle fan beams (which were computationally transformed into parallel beams) and multiple detectors to scan two neighboring rotational projections at the same time. This technique reduced the number of necessary rotations, and hence the required scanning time (10 to 60 seconds, up to several minutes per slice) needed for a sufficient reconstruction. It also provided a better utilization of the emitted radiation. Both first-and second-generation techniques are parallel beam devices, deploying different reconstruction algorithms than the next fan beam devices.

The next improvement increased the fan beam angle and the number of detectors to cover the whole object, thus the translating movement became unnecessary and reduced the scanning time to five seconds

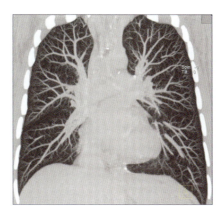

FIGURE 3.8 *Example image of multislice CT data of the most recent generation. With 0.4 mm slice thickness even small blood vessels and bronchial tubes can be depicted clearly. Image acquisition times dropped to less than 10 seconds, which strongly reduces artifacts from patient motion or breathing. (Image copyright* SIEMENS *Medical Solutions)*

per slice. Similar to the previous techniques, the radiation was emitted at fixed time intervals and was measured by the detectors.

In the fourth generation, the rotating detector was replaced by a fixed circular ring detector, which reduced the technical effort of moving the larger mass of emitter and detector. Here, the radiation was permanently emitted and only the detectors were enabled at certain intervals. However, several problems with ring detectors led to further developments in favor of third-generation scanners. Besides the higher costs for the detector ring, specific X-ray scattering problems reduced the image quality of these systems, while collimator technology could reduce the scattering problems with a third-generation rotating emitter/detector system.

Currently, the state-of-the-art systems are spiral or helical CT, where the emitter/detector system rotates permanently around the object, while the object is moving continuously in a perpendicular direction to acquire a full data volume. This technique allows faster scanning, due to the continuous rotating movement of the emitter/detector system, and saves the time previously required to accelerate and slow down these heavy parts of the scanner. Since 1999, multiple layers of emitters and detectors have been combined to create multislice CT scanners (twin or quad slices), realizing fast and near-isotropic scanning of large object areas. Today (2007), the state of the art in multislice CT scanners acquires up to 64 slices (actually spirals) at a time (see Fig. 3.7 (right)). Figure 3.8 shows an example image generated by this scanner.

Besides the architectural development, different volume/slice reconstruction algorithms are used in the various systems and generations. The basic approach is the back transformation of the slice projections into the volume slices by the Radon transform [CHO et al. 1993]. In the early days of computed tomography, algebraic reconstruction techniques (ART) were used to solve this back-projection problem. However, the high computational costs of iteratively solving large matrices[3] meant this approach was not feasible for standard applications [KALENDAR 2000]. The standard method today is filtered back-projection (parallel beam [RAMACHANDRAN and LAKSHMINARAYANAN 1971, SHEPP and LOGAN 1974] and cone-beam [FELDKAMP et al. 1984] reconstruction), in which each projection is composed according to the measured direction. While there are parallel and fan beam methods to perform this back-projection, the

---

3   The size of a reconstruction matrix is equal to the resolution of the slice.

current fan beam methods for CT are more complex and less efficient than state-of-the-art parallel beam reconstruction algorithms. Hence, the projections of today's fan-beam scanners are re-sorted in parallel beams before the actual reconstruction. Another modification is required to address the continuously moving object tray of modern spiral CT scanners, where a z-interpolation corrects the measured projections according to the tray movement [KALENDER 2000]. In the future, cone beam reconstruction algorithms will probably replace the current methods [KALENDER 2000], which are successfully used in rotational X-ray (see Sect. 3.1.2) already.

The intensity profiles of the projection images are subject to a filter process at data reconstruction, which may enhance or soften boundaries (see Fig. 3.9). Figure 3.10 shows the effect of two different

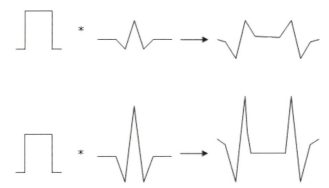

FIGURE 3.9 *Principles of CT reconstruction filters. The original signal (left) is modified according to the filter (middle) to produce the reconstructed signal (right). Reconstruction filters change the amplitude of the signal and the form of edges. In general, the output signal exhibits more contrast than the input image. These filters are applied in all three dimensions in the actual image acquisition process.*

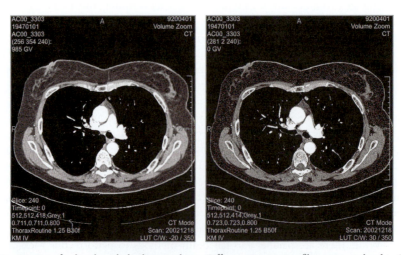

FIGURE 3.10 *A portion of a slice through the thorax is shown. Different reconstruction filters were employed in CT imaging. Left: a soft (smoothing) filter; right: an edge-enhancing filter. (Images courtesy BERTHOLD WEIN, Aachen)*

reconstruction filters of one particular CT dataset. The user of a CT scanner can choose one of these filters (actually, there are more than two).

New CT devices are currently under development and in first clinical trials. With flat panel detector CTs, the whole range of the human body can be imaged with one rotation: the spatial resolution improves with this device to 0.2 × 0.2 mm [KALENDER 2003]. Another line of development is the Dual Source CT, in which two detector units are placed in the scanner [FLOHR et al. 2006]. While the spatial resolution is not changed, the acquisition times are reduced by a factor of two. The increased spatial and temporal resolution of these devices is important for a variety of complex diagnostic and therapeutic processes. The diagnosis of coronary heart disease, in particular the detection and classification of calcifications in coronary arteries, is a major field of application.

3.2.3 PARAMETERS OF CT SCANNING

Datasets acquired by a CT scanner can be described by their spatial resolution, composed of the *number of slices*, the *number of pixels per slice*, and the *voxel distances*[4] (see Sect. 2.1). The number of pixels in one slice is also referred to as *image matrix*; an image matrix of 512 × 512 simply describes an image slice of that resolution. If we have a CT dataset with an image matrix of 512 × 512 and 300 slices, we have a volume dataset with the resolution 512 × 512 × 300. The distances between the voxels are differentiated into the slice (out-of-plane) and pixel distance (in-plane). As already mentioned in Section 2.1, a dataset with a slice distance different than the pixel distance is described as an anisotropic dataset, while equal distances constitute an isotropic dataset.

The resolution of the data has an influence on the noise level: data with higher resolution are more noisy if the radiation dose remains the same (see Fig. 3.11). The dose of radiation also has an influence on the image quality. With a higher dose of radiation, a better signal-to-noise ratio is achieved. Naturally, there is a trade-off between the desired image quality and undesirable amounts of radiation. This conflict has to be resolved such that the image quality is just sufficient to answer the diagnostic question at hand. This trade-off is one of the reasons why visualizations based on clinical data do not achieve the quality that can be achieved with data acquired by a cadaver, such as the Visible Human Dataset [SPITZER et al. 1996].

A slice in a volumetric dataset from a scanned resource does not represent an infinitesimally thin data slice; it represents a specific area of the image matrix times the *slice thickness*. This is essentially based on the fact that a reconstructed image pixel value is a weighted average of the local spatial neighborhood. This neighborhood in z-direction (between slices) can be seen as the slice thickness.

The rotating emitter/detector system of a CT scanner—through which the table with the scanned object is moved—is called the *gantry* (see Fig. 3.7 (left)). The tilt of the gantry defines also the tilt of the image slices. Since most CT datasets are of anisotropic spacing, it can be useful to adapt the gantry tilt to the target organ of an examination, e.g., to ensure optimal sampling of the respective organ structures. Therefore, the *gantry tilt* is an additional parameter of CT scanning. If data are processed with a non-zero gantry tilt, they should be warped to compensate for the gantry tilt in order to generate correct 3D visualizations. Figure 3.12 illustrates this process.

When X-rays are cast from the emitter, they usually diverge like a fan from the emitter. Since these diverging X-rays will influence neighboring signal acquisition, it is useful to focus the rays along the

---

4   Note that the typical definition of resolution only describes how much detail can be represented in an image (or volume). It does not describe how accurately the original objects are represented. Our concept of resolution also includes the voxel distance and therefore also describes (to some extent) the acquisition accuracy.

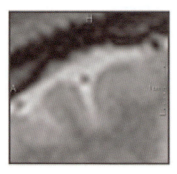 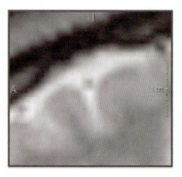

FIGURE 3.11 *Portion of a CT slice. Left: Noisy high resolution image (512×512 matrix); right: low resolution image (256×256 matrix) with better signal-to-noise ratio. For both images, the same reconstruction filter is employed. (Images courtesy* BERTHOLD WEIN, *Aachen)*

FIGURE 3.12 *A tilted CT dataset (left) is warped according to the tilting angle represented in the image data. This warping step is essential for a correct 3D visualization (right). Images are generated by means of volume rendering. (Screenshot of Amira®)*

main direction of the emitter. This is achieved by an aperture that limits the fan-out of the X-rays and is called *collimation*. The related collimation parameter specifies how open the aperture (the collimator) is.

Two more important parameters for CT scanning are *pitch* and *table increment*, also known as *table feed*. The latter parameter (table feed or table increment) specifies how far the table (on which the object to be scanned is positioned) is advanced through the scanner during one rotation of the gantry. The pitch *p* defines the ratio between the table increment *d* and the *total slice collimation*, which is the factor of number of slices per rotation M (one for a regular spiral CT scanner, or four for a four-slice multislice CT scanner) and the slice thickness *S*. Therefore, we can compute the pitch as $p = d/(M \cdot S)$. If, for example, we have a four-slice CT scanner ($M = 4$), a slice thickness of $S = 1$ mm, and a table feed of $d = 6$ mm, we can compute the pitch as $p = 1.5$ [CT, accessed 2005].

Radiation Dose   CT exposes a patient to a moderate or high radiation dose, which may be considered a serious problem in special cases, for example in young children. Radiation efficiency has been considerably improved in the development of CT scanning devices. However, some new and complex scanning techniques, as well as the goal of providing high resolution images, have compensated this effect—leading to an increased radiation dose in some cases.

Contrast-enhancement Many CT examinations concern the blood vessel system. However, blood vessels are difficult to read in standard CT scans. Therefore, a contrast agent (usually iodine) is injected into the venous system to enhance the representation of the arteries (and later, during the venous cycle, the respective veins). Important parameters to consider for a contrast-enhanced CT scan are quantity of contrast agent (typically between 300–400 mgI/ml) and the injection parameters that determine how the contrast agent is administered (as bolus, continuously, or in a varying distribution). Depending how long the scan is performed after the injection and what kind of injection parameter was chosen, the visual representation of the arterial (high iodine flow of 3–4 ml/s) or venous system (low iodine flow of 2 ml/s) will be enhanced (with an increased voxel intensity). Note that the image intensity of adjacent organs can also be slightly increased, due to the contrast agent, which has a positive effect on the segmentation of this organ (see Chap. 5).

3.2.4 STANDARDIZATION WITH HOUNSFIELD UNITS

The computed intensity value represents the densities of the scanned object. In medical imaging, these intensity values are normalized into Hounsfield units (HUs), named after Godfrey Hounsfield (see below). This normalization maps the data range into a 12-bit range, where the intensity of water is mapped to zero and air is mapped to -1000. This normalization is formalized in Equation 3.3, where I_{H_2O} represents the intensity value of water. Note that while only 12 bits are occupied by the dynamic range of the intensity values, they are typically packed into two bytes (16 bits) to provide easy voxel data access.

$$HU = \frac{\mu - \mu_{H_2O}}{\mu_{H_2O}} * 1000 \qquad (3.3)$$

Table 3.1 lists Hounsfield density values for different organs and tissue types. The table indicates that parenchymatous organs, such as the heart and liver, have similar or even overlapping intensity values.

Historic Remarks The CT as imaging modality was developed by Godfrey Hounsfield in 1972 and was first applied to get cross-sectional images of the brain in order to evaluate a lesion which turned out to be a cyst [HOUNSFIELD 1973]. The invention of the CT is the birth of modern tomographic imaging modalities and was recognized with the Nobel prize for Physiology or Medicine in 1979. Soon after the advent of functional MRI in 1992, medical imaging began to play an essential role in the neurosciences.

Tissue type	Hounsfield Value Interval
Air	−1000
Lung tissue	−900...−170
Fat tissue	−220...−30
Water H_2O	0
Pancreas	10...40
Liver	20...60
Heart	20...50
Kidney	30...50
Bones	45...3000

TABLE 3.1 *Hounsfield values for selected tissue types. (From [*LEHMANN *et al. 1997a])*

The notion of a functional segregation and specialization in the brain was established due to advanced neuroimaging.

3.3   MAGNETIC RESONANCE IMAGING

Magnetic resonance imaging (MRI) is based on different properties of human tissue in a (strong) magnetic field. In particular, the occurrence of hydrogen nuclei in human tissue is exploited for image generation. They can be considered as small dipole magnets aligning themselves either parallel or anti-parallel along a strong external magnetic field. While aligned in that field, the hydrogen protons (a hydrogen nucleus consists only of a proton) spin arbitrarily around the axis of the field. There is a slight difference in the number of parallel and antiparallel aligned protons (see Fig. 3.13). This difference results in a net magnetization. To measure this magnetization, a magnetization component perpendicular to the magnetic field must be generated. This is achieved by a radio-frequency pulse signal at the *Larmor* frequency.[5] As a result of the RF pulse, the protons perform a precession movement with the *Larmor* frequency (see Fig. 3.14). The nuclear resonance forces the protons to receive some of the energy from the RF. This pulse also forces all the protons to spin synchronously, or *in phase*, and increasingly to flip into the antiparallel orientation of higher energy, until the number of parallel protons is equal to the number of antiparallel oriented protons.

A 90 degree RF pulse moves the protons perpendicular to the magnetic field, resulting in a zero z-component (along the magnetic field). After the stimulation of the protons, they slowly release the received energy, *dephase*, and realign with the magnetic field. This *relaxation* is described as *free induction decay* (FID) and is divided into the transverse and longitudinal relaxation. The first relaxation of the transverse magnetization, also called spin-spin relaxation, describes the dephasing of the x/y-component of the precession (see Fig. 3.15). The transversal relaxation is an exponential decay. The time required for a 63% decay $(1-1/e)$ relaxation is called T2 and is in the order of a few milliseconds. The longitudinal, or spin-lattice (or spin-grid), relaxation describes the realignment according to the magnetic field, and thus the restoration of the z-component (see Fig. 3.16). This relaxation has a logarithmic increase. The time until 63% of the original magnetization is restored is called T1 and is in the order of a second. T1 largely depends on the material (tissue), its structure, and its surrounding tissue. Since water has a long T1 and T2 relaxation time, tissue that contains a large ratio of water will also have a long T1 and T2 time. The actual measured volumetric information is the proton density σ, which needs to be reconstructed at the specific voxels. In Figure 3.17, the relaxation curve for different brain tissue and the corresponding T1 and T2 times are shown. The different times are due to different densities of hydrogen protons in different tissue types; cerebrospinal fluid has the highest water content, at 97%. Gray matter and white matter have, respectively, an 84% and 71% water content.

To reconstruct the spatial information of the measured signal, two additional gradient magnetic fields are applied [LEHMANN *et al.* 1997a]. The first field selects the slice in z-direction of the volume, since only one layer of protons suffices the *Larmor* frequency for the main and gradient magnetic fields. An additional gradient field in x-direction selects a *y*-slab. By rotating the gradient fields, other projection directions are measured. This feature in particular is very useful, since the slice direction can be adapted to the medical exam. This is not possible with a CT scan (which is always axial).

An alternative approach became available with the 2D Fourier reconstruction, which requires only one gradient field. Here, the x/y-coordinate is encoded into that signal [LEHMANN *et al.* 1997a] by

---

5   The *Larmor* frequency can be described as the resonance frequency of the protons in a magnetic field. It is determined by the *gyromagnetic ratio* of the protons (which is constant for the respective protons, e.g., hydrogen protons) and the strength of the magnetic field.

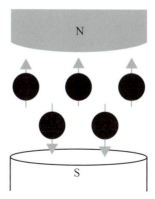

FIGURE 3.13 *The protons are aligned according to the external magnetic field. Some protons are aligned parallel to the magnetic field, while some are aligned antiparallel.*

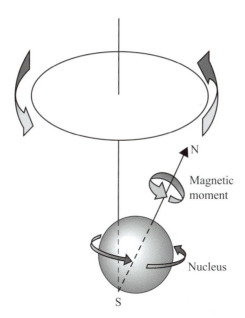

FIGURE 3.14 *Spin and precession of the protons. Next to their self-rotation (spin), they perform an additional precession movement around the direction of the magnetic field. (Image courtesy Ragnar Bade, University of Magdeburg)*

the increasing dephasing signal of the transverse relaxation along the x and y directions, which generates specific frequencies into the signal. Thus, the RF intensity (proton/spin intensity) is encoded into the intensity of the signal, while the position is encoded into the frequencies [Cho et al. 1993, Lehmann et al. 1997a]. Note that the quality of the image data strongly depends on the homogeneity and strength of the magnetic field [Hahn 2005].

MR imaging is performed in a ring magnet that is large enough to enclose the whole patient. Inside this magnet, gradient coils are embedded in such a way that magnetic field gradients in three orthogonal directions (x, y, and z) can be generated. The coils used for the MR image acquisition are very different,

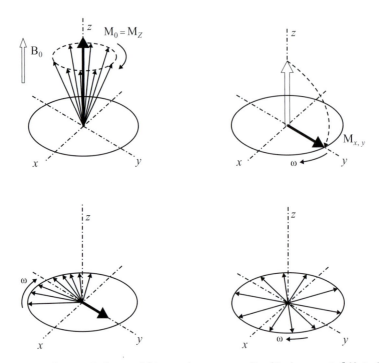

FIGURE 3.15 Spin-spin relaxation. In the upper left image, the protons are aligned in the magnetic field. In the upper right image they are moved due to a 90 degree RF impulse. In the lower left and right image, the protons dephase. (Images courtesy PETRA JANKA, University of Magdeburg)

depending on which body region is to be imaged. In Figure 3.18, some frequently used coils are depicted. The coils are either integrated sender and receiver (such as head coils) or separate sender and receiver coils.

Depending on the strength of the magnetic field, MRI scanners are characterized as "low field" scanners, with a magnetic field strength of up to 0.8 T (Tesla), as "full field" scanners, with a magnetic field strength of 1.5 T, or recently as "high field" scanners, with a typical magnetic field strength of 3 T or more.

3.3.1 PARAMETERS OF MRI SCANNING

MRI acquisition itself is characterized by a huge parameter space. In general, 90-degree pulses as well as additional 180-degree pulses are applied to the magnetic field. The additional pulses compensate for inhomogeneities in the magnetic field and lead to more reliable results than would be achieved by directly measuring the FID. The common MRI sequences, composed of 90-degree and 180-degree impulses, are referred to as *spin echo* sequences. The signal intensity (SI) in these sequences is computed according to the following equation [RUMMENY et al. 2002].

$$SI \sim PDe^{\frac{-TE}{T2}}(1 - e^{\frac{-TR}{T1}}) \qquad (3.4)$$

PD is the proton density and T1 and T2 are the relaxation times of the specific material.

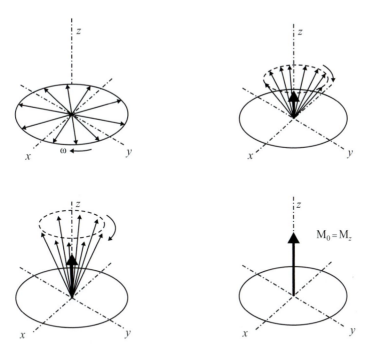

FIGURE 3.16 In the upper left image, the protons move in the transversal plane due to an RF impulse. In the upper right, lower left, and the lower right image the protons are again realigned according to the magnetic field—the transversal magnetization decreases. (Images courtesy PETRA JANKA, University of Magdeburg)

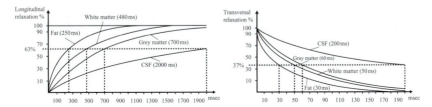

FIGURE 3.17 Longitudinal (left) and transversal (right) relaxation of different brain tissue. The dotted lines indicate the resulting T1 and T2 times. (Images courtesy RAGNAR BADE, University of Magdeburg)

Different protocols describe sequences of various RF pulses and the actual measurement of the signal, where the time between the initial stimulation and the measurement is called *echo time* T_E and the time between two (initial) stimulation cycles is called *repetition time* T_R. By varying T_E and T_R, different weight data can be achieved:

- With short echo (< 25 ms) and short repetition times (< 500 ms), the signal is mostly dominated by the T1 relaxation time (T1 weighted)
- With long T_E (> 1500 ms) and long T_R (>50 ms), the T2 relaxation time dominates the signal (T2 weighted)
- With a long T_R and a short T_E (< 25 ms), the resulting data are neither T1 nor T2 and can be seen as "the pure (proton) density function" (proton-weighted) [CHO et al. 1993].

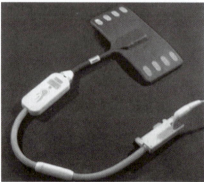

FIGURE 3.18 *Coils used for MRI imaging. Left: a head coil; right: flexible surface coils that may be attached at the stomach and at the back of the patient. (From [RUMMENY et al. 2002].)*

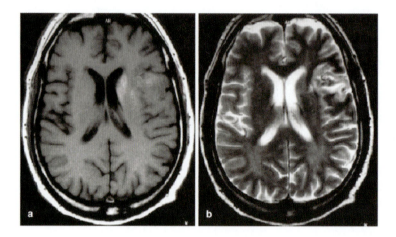

FIGURE 3.19 *Comparison of T1- and T2-weighted cerebral MRI data. In the left T1-weighted image (TR: 4000 ms, TE: 96 ms), the cerebrospinal fluid appears dark, whereas in the right image (TR: 500 ms, TE: 17 ms) the same region appears white. Also gray and white matter exhibit different intensity values in these images. (Data courtesy MARTIN SKALEJ, University of Magdeburg)*

A frequent protocol is echo planar imaging, or EPI, which is a very fast acquisition method. EPI protocols are often used in functional MRI and diffusion tensor MRI, as discussed later. The drawback of EPI protocols is the increased geometric distortion. Recently developed volumetric MRI acquisition methods resample the data in an isotropic resolution.

Figure 3.19 compares T1- and T2-weighted images acquired for neuroradiological diagnosis. While T1-weighted acquisition sequences emphasize tissue signals, it de-emphasizes fluid signals with a very low image intensity. In contrast, T2-weighted acquisition sequences emphasize fluid signals with a high image intensity.

Orthogonal to the T1/T2-weighting, a variety of acquisition sequences are available. Each sequence puts emphasis on different optimization targets. An MRI FLASH (fast low angle shot) sequence, for

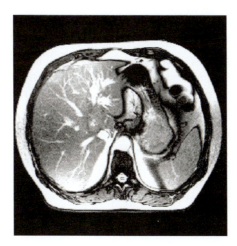

FIGURE 3.20 *Abdominal MRI data. The liver appears light in the peripheral regions and darker in the central regions. (Data courtesy* JÖRG DEBATIN, *University of Essen)*

example, enables a very rapid image acquisition. Combined with a T1-weighted image acquisition, it is often used for the acquisition of dynamic phenomena, e.g., the blood flow. Other pulse sequences, such as 3D CISS (constructive interference steady state) combined with T2-weighting, emphasize high spatial resolution. Further sequences focus on different aspects of the metabolism. MRI angiography (MRA) focuses on vascular imaging with or without a contrast enhancing agent. Typical examples of these (noncontrast agent) imaging protocols are time-of-flight (TOF) and phase-contrast-angiography (PCA). Note that flow artifacts can reduce the quality and, in some cases of turbulent blood flow, lead to pseudostenosis.[6]

The large potential parameter space of MRI leads to a high number of imaging protocols that emphasize different functional or physiological properties of the tissue. Therefore, an MRI examination often contains a variety of five or more different MRI scans. New pulse sequences are also continuously explored and developed by MRI physicists to optimize for special diagnostic procedures.

A typical MRI scan takes between 2 and 25 minutes. This relatively long scanning time is dominated by the relaxation of the spins, not by the time required for the measurements. MRI is also characterized by a certain spatial resolution. In general, MRI data—acquired with a full-field MRI scanner—have a lower resolution compared to CT image data (the in-plane resolution/pixel distance is often between 1 and 2 mm, and the slice distance between 2 to 5 mm). The resolution also depends on the acquisition time (more pulses are required for a higher spatial resolution, which leads to increased acquisition times). However, this can be different with modern high field MRI scanners, which acquire significantly higher (spatial and/or temporal) resolution image data.

Contrast Enhancement The usual T1- and T2-weighted images are often not sufficient to show the target structures adequately. As a consequence, either a sophisticated acquisition technique is used (e.g., to suppress certain structures such as fat) or a contrast agent is employed. Most commonly, contrast agents with special magnetic properties are employed. Gadolinium compounds are frequently used in connection with a T1-weighted image. Structures enhanced by gadolinium appear bright on T1-weighted images. Vascular structures or strongly vascularized tumors become clearly visible with contrast enhancement.

---

6   A stenosis that appears in the image data although it is not actually present.

MRI Image Artifacts While we discussed image artifacts in general in Section 2.2, we will briefly summarize typical MRI artifacts in this paragraph. MRI image artifacts can be sorted into

- Artifacts by physiological causes (e.g., artifacts due to [body] motion or [blood] flow)
- Hardware problems, such as inhomogeneities of the magnetic field
- Problems with the inherent physics (chemical shift, presence of metal, etc.)

Inhomogeneity is probably the most severe of these artifacts. It strongly depends on the geometry of the coils employed in the scanner. Head coils only have one open end (near the shoulder), which leads to an intensity variation from the head towards the neck. Surface coils, which are used in abdominal imaging for example, lead to stronger inhomogeneities. The intensity strongly depends on the distance to coils. In Section 5.2.5, we discuss algorithms to account for these problems. A discussion of MRI artifacts can be found at [MRI-TIP 2005] with images of the respective artifacts at [GREGORY 2005].

3.3.2 INTRAOPERATIVE MRI DATA

MRI data are also an attractive imaging modality for intraoperative use, since no harmful radiation is involved. Special "open" MRI scanners are used, which allow interventions while acquiring intraoperative images. This, however, also requires the use of MRI-compatible instruments that can be used in or near a strong magnetic field. Due to the significantly less powerful magnetic field of an open MRI of 0.5–0.8 T ("low field"), the quality of the images is also significantly lower, caused by limited resolution and a high noise level. Nevertheless, it provides intraoperative imaging, in which the surgeons still can access the patient in the MRI scanner.

Recently, full magnetic field MRI scanners (1.5 T, "full field") have been introduced into the operating room (OR) [NIMSKY et al. 2003]. Since these scanners are not open, the patient has to be moved while lying on the operating table into the scanner for the image acquisition and moved back to the surgeons,who wait outside the area immediately influenced by the magnetic field. Next to the space required for the full-sized MRI, additional space in the OR is needed to operate in a safe distance from the scanner, as well as for the transportation of the anesthetized patient. Because of these challenges, full-field intraoperative MRI is very difficult to install, since regular ORs will not be able to accommodate the required space. In addition to the required additional space, intraoperative full-field MRI scanners are expensive devices that are not affordable for many hospitals.

One of the phenomena targeted by intraoperative MRI is the brain-shift effect in neurosurgery. This effect describes the local changes of location and shape of the brain, after opening of the skull and dura mater [NABAVI et al. 2001]. These changes render the preoperatively acquired image data (at least partially) useless, since they do not represent the current situation with sufficient accuracy.

3.3.3 FUNCTIONAL MRI

Functional MRI, or fMRI, detects changes in cerebral blood flow and oxygen metabolism as a result of neural activation. These changes are recorded in time-intensity curves [FRISTON et al. 1994]. The "blood oxygen level-dependent" (BOLD) effect is employed for image acquisition. Besides neuroanatomical studies, fMRI is clinically used to support access and resection planning in minimally invasive epilepsy and brain tumor surgery [GUMPRECHT et al. 2002].

fMRI data are acquired while the patient performs cognitive or behavioral tasks in an MRI scanner, which leads to measurable changes of local blood flow and oxygenation. Sensorimotor and language regions, such as the Wernicke area and the Broca area, can be identified by tracking these changes. Significant research has been dedicated to identifying simple tasks that reliably indicate the responsible brain region. For the identification of the language region, for example, patients are asked to tell the names of the month, to generate words starting with a given character, or to fit words to a given noun [PROTHMANN et al. 2005]. The measured activation is represented by time-intensity curves.

fMRI data are acquired along with anatomical MRI data. Activation signals are superimposed on MRI data to convey the anatomical location of certain regions (see Fig. 3.21). The correct mapping of functional data to the anatomy requires the *registration* of the two datasets. This challenging task is described in Section 5.9.

Most of the difficulties in analyzing fMRI data are due to long acquisition times and the complex nature of the recorded phenomena, which causes various artifacts. The visualization of activation patterns is guided by thresholds relating to the probability of an activation and to the minimum size of a cluster that is regarded as activated region.

To address inevitable motion artifacts, modern MRI scanners provide motion correction. Various common toolkits analyze fMRI data. The BrainVoyager® (www.brainvoyager.com/) supports retrospective motion correction and noise reduction, volume-based statistical analysis methods, and a variety of visualization techniques. The second widespread software tool for the analysis of fMRI data is Statistical Parametric Mapping (SPM), provided by the Department of Imaging Neuroscience, University College of London. It provides even more advanced methods for the statistical analysis of fMRI data and also supports other functional modalities, such as PET (see Sect. 3.5). The fundamental text on SPM is the *Human Brain Function* book [FRACKOWIAK et al. 1997]. The SPM suite and associated theory were developed by Karl Friston for routine statistical analysis of functional neuroimaging data, primarily PET, and were released in 1991.

Before the advent of fMRI, activation patterns were determined intraoperatively by stimulating the patient (with electro-encephalography [EEG] and magneto-encephalography [MEG]). fMRI, in contrast, allows noninvasive mapping of functional areas to anatomical regions. Comparisons with the previous gold-standard intraoperative activation show a good correlation [LURITO et al. 2000, RUTTEN et al. 2002]; therefore, fMRI is now widely used. A combination of intraoperative and fMRI data to enhance neurosurgical interventions was proposed by ROUX et al. [2001] and TALOS et al. [2003].

3.3.4 DIFFUSION TENSOR IMAGING

As another important MRI variant, MRI diffusion tensor imaging (DTI), has recently become an image modality of high interest. DTI exploits the anisotropic nature of water diffusion to estimate the fiber direction of neural pathways and heart muscles. Water diffusion occurs primarily parallel to the fiber direction, since membranes act as barriers to a diffusion perpendicular to the fiber. At each voxel, diffusion

 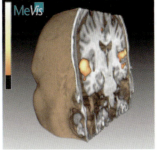

FIGURE 3.21 *Functional MRI data are acquired after auditory stimulation and overlaid with anatomical image data. (Images courtesy of Horst K. HAHN, MeVis Bremen; Data courtesy FREDERIK GIESEL, DKFZ Heidelberg)*

is characterized as a diffusion tensor. An important aspect of the analysis of DTI data is the eigenanalysis of diffusion tensors, which allows the evaluation of the major fiber orientation as well as the amount of anisotropy. This modality and the interpretation of the acquired images will be explained in detail in Chapter 18.

3.3.5 HISTORIC REMARKS

The dependency of the resonance frequency of protons on the magnetic field strength has been well known for a long time. In the 1950s, it was also known that this dependency could be used to distinguish their localization. MRI as an imaging modality in medicine was suggested by LAUTERBUR [1973] and was later refined by a number of people. Most notably, extremely fast echo-planar image acquisition was developed by Sir Peter Mansfield [MANSFIELD 1977]. Lauterbur suggested that magnetic field gradients could be used to determine the spatial distribution of protons in water by different frequencies. Later, he became known for his work on contrast agents for MRI. Finally, John Mallard should be mentioned because he headed the development of the first practical human MRI scanner [HENNIG 2003].

The work of Mansfield was recently characterized in an editorial in the following way: "It took great perseverance and a firm belief in the further technical process for Sir Peter to keep continuously working on echo-planar imaging over nearly two decades until MRI technology was sufficiently advanced to give us today's image quality" [HENNIG 2003].

Lauterbur and Mansfield were awarded the Nobel prize for Physiology or Medicine in 2003 for these inventions.

3.3.6 CT VERSUS MRI DATA

CT and MRI were introduced as imaging modalities used in radiology to overcome the limitations of X-ray imaging. Over and above advanced imaging, these imaging modalities played a significant role in the collaboration between computer scientists and medical doctors: "For the first time, it seemed to scientists, engineers and doctors that computers might have a genuine role in medicine, permitting the introduction of procedures that simply were not possible without them" [YOUNG 2003].

CT and MRI are rather complementary: MRI—since it depends on a sufficient water content—does not produce a good quality signal for skeletal structures, whereas CT is less appropriate (and sometimes completely insufficient) to discriminate soft tissues. The inability of CT to discriminate soft tissue is due to its similarity to X-ray attenuation in soft tissues.

Compared to CT data, MRI is able to provide a high soft tissue contrast. Therefore, MRI is often used in neuroimaging (to discriminate white and gray matter) and for the diagnosis of joints, such as the shoulder and the knee. Magnetic fields, such as those used in MR imaging, do not harm the patient (at least, nothing is known about harmful effects so far). The disadvantages of using MRI data are the relatively high costs and the difficulties of correctly interpreting such data. CT data can often be understood by the referring physician, whereas MRI data are carefully commented upon by radiologists.

For computer-supported analysis and visualization of medical data, the standardized Hounsfield units are an enormous help, as they allow the predefinition of parameter values. With MRI data, one and the same structure can have very different intensity values even within one dataset (see the liver in Fig. 3.20). For the diagnosis by a radiologist, a 10% variation of the gray value is not prohibitive; for the algorithmic selection of a threshold to discriminate a particular tissue, it certainly is. In Section 5.2.5, we discuss algorithmic corrections of inhomogeneities in MRI data.

CT is available in significantly more hospitals, since it is the cheaper imaging modality. However, MRI has the advantage that no ionizing radiation is required.

As a summary, we cite Hounsfield for a comparison of the two kinds of image data: "At the present time, the two techniques should perhaps be seen not as potential competitors but rather as complementary techniques that can exist side by side" [HOUNSFIELD 1980]. Although it is more than 25 years old, this assessment is still valid and probably will continue to be valid for the foreseeable future.

3.4   ULTRASOUND

Ultrasound is a cheap, widespread modality for many diagnostic tasks and for intraoperative target localization. Ultrasound scanning is based on sound waves emitted at very high frequencies (more than 20 kHz, 1 to 15 MHz) from the ultrasound probe ("transducer") into the respective body part. The sound waves penetrate human tissue at a speed of 1450 to 1580 meters per second [SAKAS et al. 1995]. The waves are partially reflected if they hit an interface between two tissue types (see Fig. 3.22). The reflected waves are recorded by sensors located next to the sound sources. Similar to sonar, the reflections of these sound waves are received by the transducer and used to generate the respective images.

The use of ultrasonic images requires knowledge of their typical problems to prevent the drawing of wrong conclusions [SAKAS et al. 1995]. Typical problems are:

- A significant amount of noise and speckle
- A much lower intensity range, resulting in lower contrasts compared to tomographic images
- Unsharp boundary regions
- Partially or completely shadowed surfaces from objects closer to and within the direction of the sound source
- Boundaries with varying gray values due to variations of the surface orientation

In the B-mode or brightness mode, the resulting pixels represent the echoes received by the transducer and show the respective body parts. Images generated by this mode typically show anatomical details. In contrast, the A-mode is only used to measure distances within the body, the M-mode to measure motion (e.g., of the heart), and, finally, the Doppler-mode is used to measure velocities. Combined with the B-mode, the Doppler-mode is typically employed to examine blood vessels, showing their anatomy and the blood flow simultaneously.

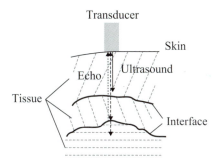

FIGURE 3.22   *Principle of ultrasound imaging. The acoustic waves are partially reflected by interfaces between different tissue types.* (From [SAKAS *and* WALTER 1995].)

In fluids the sound is transmitted without attenuation due to echoes. The fluids are hypoechogenic (black), and since there is no attenuation, increased echoes will occur behind them. Metastases are also hypoechogenic, but do not show an increased signal behind them. Figure 3.23 presents two ultrasound images from the human liver, whereas Figure 3.24 depicts the kidney and the spleen.

The major advantage of ultrasound is the real-time availability of data that can be widely used for, e.g., cardiac diagnosis to evaluate kinetic features, or intraoperative imaging. Ultrasound is used as navigation tool in traditional surgical interventions and in guided biopsies, such as fine-needle aspiration biopsy of breast tumors [FORNAGE et al. 1990]. Another advantage is that no ionizing radiation is employed.

Due to the importance of ultrasound in clinical medicine, dedicated conferences, journals, and books on the subject are available. A very good introduction and at the same time a comprehensive text is provided by MEIRE et al. [1993]. A more recent book with focus on the basics of physics, artifacts, and instrument handling is KREMKAU [2002]. The normal anatomy and physiology from an ultrasound perspective is described in CURRY and TEMPKIN [2004].

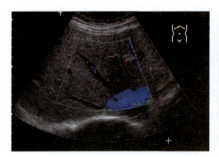
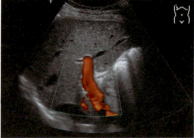

FIGURE 3.23 *Ultrasound images depicting vessels in the human liver. The small pictogram in the upper right indicates the position and orientation of the ultrasound probe. The left image shows the hepatic veins and the inferior vena cava (dark and blue regions), and the right image shows the portal vein. The blue-coded regions depict blood flow away from the ultrasound probe, whereas the red-coded regions (right) represent blood flow towards the probe. Only the main stem of the portal veins are coded, since the flow in the right and left portal veins are perpendicular to the probe in this orientation. (Data courtesy SKADI WILHELMSEN, University Hospital Magdeburg)*

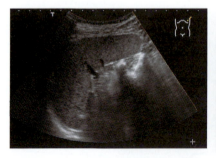
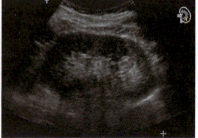

FIGURE 3.24 *Ultrasound images depicting the spleen (left) and the kidney (right). The outer portions of the kidney appear dark (low echo) whereas the fattier inner parts appear brighter. The dark stripes at the spleen represent the vessels in the hilum. The left portion of the left image appears black (acoustic shadow); the signal is strongly attenuated due to the air-filled lungs. (Data courtesy SKADI WILHELMSEN, University Hospital Magdeburg)*

Intravascular Ultrasound (IVUS)   Similar to angiographic imaging, a catheter can be inserted into a vascular system to enable selective ultrasound imaging in a particular region. For this purpose, the catheter is attached with a tiny 1D transducer. With this device, a polar cross-section image of the blood vessel may be generated. IVUS is used, for example, to depict the coronary arteries and has a high sensitivity in detecting plaques. Present day catheters are less than 1 mm in diameter and operate at 30 to 40 MHz frequencies. MINTZ et al. [2001] describe standards for IVUS in cardiac diagnosis.

3D Ultrasound   Some ultrasound scanning devices allow also 3D image acquisition by acquiring and accumulating multiple scans while tracking the movement of the ultrasound probe (performed by the physician). 3D ultrasound is acquired either by a parallel scanner—resulting in axis-aligned images—or by rotation around a swivel. Depending on the chosen acquisition technique, different side effects must be considered; the rotational scan leads to a curvilinear organization of the data, while the parallel scan leads to an average gray value that differs from slice to slice.

Freehand acquisition of 3D ultrasound data is an extension of 2D ultrasound and is hence feasible with most conventional devices [RICHTSCHEID et al.1999]. In contrast, however, it acquires a volumetric dataset that can provide additional views that are not available in 2D. In particular, the latter difference is similar to the difference between CT and X-ray.

Principle of 3D Ultrasound Acquisition and Processing   In a very few cases, 3D ultrasound devices provide a DICOM interface to export the data in a digital format. Unfortunately, digital data acquisition in most cases requires a video framegrabber card in a computer connected with the video output of the ultrasound device [RICHTSCHEID et al. 1999, NELSON and ELVINS 1993] (see Fig. 3.25). During data acquisition, all B-scan images are digitized by the framegrabber. A magnetic receiver is attached to the ultrasound probe to record positional information (six degrees of freedom: x-, y-, and z-coordinates as well as θ_1, θ_2, and θ_3 which specify the orientation).

Discussion   Ultrasound is frequently used for diagnosis and intraoperative navigation. Application areas include abdominal tumor diagnosis, artery plaque measurements, and fetal examinations. Compared to most other modalities, the interpretation of ultrasound images requires considerable experience.

3D ultrasound might also be employed for advanced diagnostic and therapy planning tasks. In partic-ular, for the localization of tumors and vascular structures in soft tissue, 3D ultrasound plays an essential

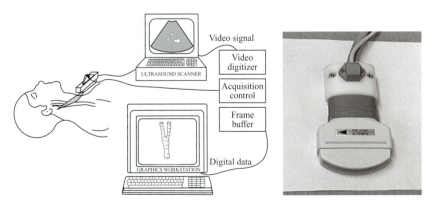

FIGURE 3.25   Left: Block diagram of a 3D ultrasound display. (From [NELSON and ELVINS, 1993]) Right: Mounting the magnetic receiver for tracking on the ultrasound transducer. (From [SAKAS and WALTER, 1995].)

role. However, widespread use of 3D ultrasound for computer-supported planning systems is currently hampered by technical problems. Whereas CT, MRI, and many other devices export their data in the DICOM standard (see Sect. 4.1), the export of 3D ultrasound data remains a serious problem, with a lack of accepted standards. The noisy and blurry nature of ultrasound data makes any kind of 3D visualization challenging. However, as we will see in later chapters, with appropriate filtering and noise removal, expressive 3D visualizations may be generated.

3.5   POSITRON EMISSION TOMOGRAPHY (PET)

Positron emission tomography (PET) is a nuclear medicine imaging technique. PET scans generate 3D images of functional processes, such as metabolistic activity. A short-lived radiopharmaceutical substance ("tracer") is injected and traced throughout the body to its target area. At the target area, the substance is processed by the metabolism and the radioactive isotope decays, which emits positrons. If a positron interacts with an electron, it annihilates, which in turn generates two gamma photons (rays) in opposite directions (180 deg). These photons are then measured by the detector array of the PET scanner (see Fig. 3.26). Since annihilation photons are always emitted in exactly opposite directions, it is possible to localize their source along a straight line. Since the tracers are processed by the metabolism, they are processed primarily in currently active regions. Therefore, the location of a current metabolistic activity— e.g., brain activity while performing a specific task—is revealed.

Due to the short-lived nature of the radionuclides, they must be produced close to the PET scanner. A frequently used radionuclide is (18 F) fluorodeoxyglucose (FDG). The spatial resolution of a PET image dataset is significantly lower than CT and MRI data; the pixel size equals 1–2 mm for neuroimaging and 2–3 mm for other parts of the body. This low resolution can be observed in Figure 3.27, which shows orthogonal slices of PET data.

Due to the low resolution of PET image data, it is often combined with CT or MRI data to enhance the low resolution functional data with high resolution morphological data of the respective body parts. This requires the alignment ("registration") of the generated volumetric datasets. This registration, however, is quite difficult, since the scanned patient has to be moved to another scanner. This movement will change the position and orientation of the body, and hence it will complicate the matching of a set of landmarks. These obstacles are aggravated by the different resolutions of CT/MRI and PET image data, which renders the matching of properties difficult (this matching process is described in Sect. 5.9). One of the proposed

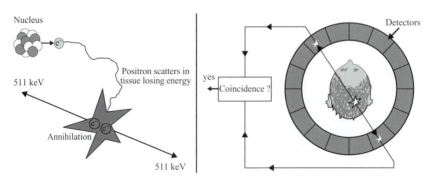

FIGURE 3.26 *Principle of PET data acquisition.*

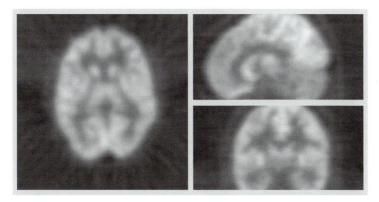

FIGURE 3.27   *Orthogonal slices of PET data. (Images courtesy* PETER HASTREITER, *University of Erlangen-Nürnberg)*

solutions for this situation is the recently introduced combined PET/CT scanner, which basically removes the problem of patient movement and simplifies the registration difficulties tremendously.

Next to the rather low resolution of PET images, the tracer substances have to be produced on site with a cyclotron, right before they are injected. This renders PET scanning a quite expensive image modality.

PET Applications in Oncology   Due to the ability of PET scanners to characterize metabolistic activity, they play a crucial role in the diagnosis of cancer and in the search for metastases. PET is also used to evaluate the success of a cancer therapy, which is often possible earlier with PET than with CT or MRI [YOUNG et al. 1999]. Oncology scans with FDG account for the large majority of all PET scans.

PET and fMRI   PET was developed prior to fMRI (first studies are reported in 1988) and had been the primary choice for neuroanatomical studies. PET data were employed to generate *parametric maps* that convey the amount of brain responses based on a per-voxel statistical analysis. These parametric maps indicate the probability that an activation occurred in a particular region. The methodology and concepts of statistical parametric mapping were developed for PET data first [FRISTON et al. 1990, 1991] and later used and refined for the analysis of fMRI data, in particular with the SPM toolkit. In general, activations are modeled as Gaussian fields, a variant of stochastic processes, that allows characterization of *significance* of an activation. The significance indicates the probability that the detected changes are indeed caused by an activation. The signals of PET data are spatially independent, whereas in fMRI data the signals are spatially dependent. As a consequence, PET data only require simpler models for the stochastic process to determine the significance of activations. The rigorous statistical analysis of activation patterns was necessary to make sure that the hot spots shown in publications are really caused by activation patterns. As a consequence, the sensitivity of PET data analysis was improved.

3.6   SINGLE-PHOTON EMISSION COMPUTED TOMOGRAPHY (SPECT)

Single-photon emission computed tomography (SPECT) scanning is based on gamma cameras that acquire multiple images of the 3D distribution of a radiopharmaceutical. A gamma ray camera reveals the location of the body part where the tracer is processed. Typically, projections are acquired every 3 or

6 degrees, and a full 360-degree rotation is performed. The total scan time is typically between 15 and 20 minutes.

Heavy metals, such as thallium (Tl) and technetium (Tc) are used as tracer elements. Technetium 99-m is by far the most frequently used tracer, since it has a low half-period and only weak radioactivity. For use in medical imaging, the heavy metal must be combined with a biologically neutral substance.

In contrast to PET, SPECT is more limited in terms of spatial and temporal resolution, and more limited with respect to the effects that can be monitored. However, SPECT tracers decay more slowly than PET tracers, thus allowing the examination of longer-lasting metabolistic functions. SPECT is applied for example for diagnosis in oncology, for bone imaging, in neuroimaging, and to investigate myocardial perfusion in the left ventricle (see Fig. 3.28).

With SPECT imaging, only one gamma photon is emitted from the nucleus of the tracer that needs to be detected by the gamma camera. Therefore, collimators at the cameras are needed for path estimation. Due to the collimators, fewer signals are recorded and only lower resolution is acquired. Typically, the voxel spacing is between 4 and 7 mm, and a typical SPECT image slice consists of 64 × 64 or 96 × 96 pixels. Images are provided either as gray scale images or as pseudo-colored images. Like PET, SPECT imaging has been recently integrated with CT imaging in a combined scanner.

Dynamic SPECT Dynamic SPECT, or dSPECT, is employed to observe the motion of a radiotracer through the body by acquiring a series of planar images over time. Each image is a result of summing data over a short time interval, typically between 1−10 seconds [CELLER et al. 2000, FARNCOMBE et al. 2001]. This way, dSPECT allows the evaluation of the temporal and spatial distribution of a radioactive tracer. Nevertheless, the analysis of dSPECT (and of SPECT) signals is difficult, since the data are geometrically distorted and have a low signal-to-noise ratio. Figure 3.29 shows the change of a particular slice in dSPECT data over time.

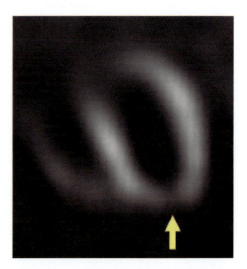

FIGURE 3.28 *Slice view of SPECT data. The arrow points to a gap in the left ventricle of the heart, which is due to an infarct. The remaining parts of the left ventricle are normally perfused. (Data courtesy ANNA CELLER, Medical Imaging Research Group, University Hospital Vancouver)*

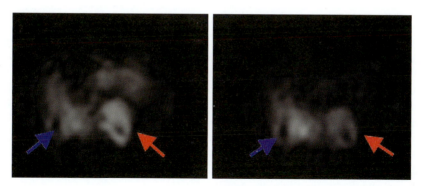

FIGURE 3.29 *Left: slice in the middle of the data set at the beginning of the time sequence. Right: the same slice four minutes later. It is clearly visible that the activity in the liver region (blue arrow) has increased while the activity in the left ventricle has decreased (red arrow). (Data courtesy* ANNA CELLER, *Medical Imaging Research Group, University Hospital Vancouver)*

3.7   SUMMARY

Medical image data can be acquired through several different scanning modalities. The most typical are X-ray, computed tomography (CT), magnetic resonance imaging (MRI), and ultrasound. While X-ray is still the standard modality for diagnosis and intraoperative navigation (through a C-arm X-ray scanner), it provides only a 2D projection image through the body. For additional 3D cues, a second X-ray image is frequently acquired from an orthogonal direction. Typically, X-ray is employed for standard fracture diagnosis, mammography, and lung diagnosis.

CT is based on X-ray, but computes a volumetric image dataset from a series of X-rays acquired from different angles around the scanned body. Recent multislice CT scanners allow fast scanning at a very high resolution. Therefore, they are also used for the scanning of fast-moving organs, like the heart (synchronized with an ECG). CT is the standard modality for all diagnostic purposes that require more information than an X-ray can provide, e.g., more spatial differentiation. Typically, CT is also used for scanning in emergency situations, in particular if the head must be scanned. While CT is well suited for the representation of (contrasted) blood vessels and skeletal structures, its soft tissue differentiation is limited.

MRI is a scanning technology based on the spin of protons in a strong magnetic field. While it is usually slower than CT and often provides only a coarser resolution (except with high-field scanners), it is the standard modality if soft tissue needs to be discriminated. Furthermore, it is well suited for contrast-agent free blood vessel scanning, for scanning functional information (fMRI), and for a representation of fiber structures (DTI), e.g., the communication network of the brain.

Ultrasound is based on the penetration of human tissue with sound waves. The interpretation of ultrasound data with its various sources of artifacts requires considerable experience. On the other hand, ultrasound is a cheap, real-time imaging modality that allows representation of soft tissue and vascular structures in high quality. The reconstruction of 3D volumes from freely acquired ultrasound slices is demanding, but represents a great potential for further developments.

FURTHER READING

There are many books on medical imaging. CHO et al. [1993] present the classical, signal-theory oriented book on data reconstruction. More recently, SUETENS [2002] discussed various aspects of medical imaging and their related artifacts. DHAWAN [2003] is an excellent book on medical imaging modalities. Most books on medical imaging relate to a single modality and its use for specific diagnostic questions, such as pediatric radiology, neuroradiology, or the diagnosis of (some special) vascular structures, for example, OSBORN [1999]. We cannot provide a comprehensive review on radiology teaching material. As an example, in cardiac imaging, a variety of books have been edited in the last few years [DE FEYTER 2004, BUDOFF and SHINBANE 2006, MILLER 2004, BOGAERT et al. 2005]. These books provide an overview on the specific requirements and processes in image acquisition, present many examples of normal and pathological cases, and discuss their interpretation.

Chapter 04

Medical Volume Data in Clinical Practice

Medical volume data are acquired by a variety of imaging devices from different manufacturers and are displayed at very different output devices. It is crucial that these data can be exchanged flexibly and displayed at every appropriate device. It is also essential that the appearance of the image data on the output devices is equivalent. Therefore, image data storage and representation is an important topic (see Sect. 4.1). Image interpretation is, of course, a huge topic. In radiology, dozens of books are available covering special aspects of diagnosis of certain diseases or with special imaging modalities. We discuss general aspects of image interpretation that provide hints on the design of software systems to support this process. We start the discussion with conventional film-based diagnosis (see Sect. 4.2) and continue with the diagnosis using CRT monitors and appropriate software (radiological workstations) (see Sect. 4.3).

4.1   STORAGE OF MEDICAL IMAGE DATA

Medical image data are physically stored together with the information that is essential for the interpretation of the images. This information is highly standardized as a result of dedicated and long-term standardization activities. These led to the DICOM standard (Digital Imaging and Communications in Medicine), which was established by the NEMA (National Electrical Manufacturers Association). The current version, 3.0, was established in 1993. At the same time, publicly available software tools that support the standard were presented—this turned out to be essential for widespread acceptance and support. DICOM is the industry standard for transferral of radiological images and other medical information between computers and medical devices. DICOM enables digital communication between diagnostic and therapeutic equipment and systems from various manufacturers. For example, workstations, CT and MRI scanners, film digitizers, shared archives, laser printers, and host computers and mainframes made by multiple vendors can communicate by means of DICOM. Currently, most manufacturers of CT and MRI scanners are officially accredited as being DICOM conform, which means that their output meets the specification of the DICOM standard.

4.1.1 SCOPE OF DICOM

DICOM is continuously refined by the DICOM committee, which includes 26 leading manufacturers as well as several organizations, such as the American College of Radiology, that represent the users. In addition to the DICOM committee, 22 working groups deal with special topics, such as *Cardiac and Vascular Information*, *Nuclear Medicine*, and *Digital Mammography*.

The standard is rather voluminous, with 18 parts and more than 2000 pages (2007). 26 working groups discuss on enhancements and special solutions. Although they are not a mandatory standard, many of these supplements contain useful recommendations for the design and development of software support. As an example, we discuss digital hanging protocols in Section 4.3.4 based on a corresponding supplement to the DICOM standard.

There are different kinds of DICOM data. In case of computed or direct radiography (CR, DR), individual images are represented as DICOM files (often two images per study). The results of a CT or MRI examination are a series of DICOM files, each of which represents one slice. Usually, it is necessary to analyze such a stack of images to detect which of them belong together (forming a volume dataset). Only those data with identical image acquisition parameters such as unique identifiers (study-id) are regarded as belonging together. Postprocessing refers to the task of generating 3D volumes from contiguous slices.

4.1.2 STRUCTURE OF DICOM DATA

DICOM data contain information concerning a variety of aspects of medical image data. These are organized in a hierarchy, with patients on the top. For each *patient* one or more *studies* are available; each study may contain several *series*, and finally each series consists of *images*. For volume data, an image represents one two-dimensional slice.

In the following, we briefly mention some important parts of DICOM data. The official term of these parts is *group*; each group consists of the elementary specification of DICOM tags.

- **Identification.** This section contains information essential for locating a series of image data in a database. This includes date and time of image acquisition. Some information is essential for the use of the results—for example, the name of the referring physician.
- **Acquisition parameters.** This section contains information concerning the imaging modality (CT, MRI, DR, etc.), the specific scanning parameters (sequence name, sequence variants) and the administration of a contrast agent. Also, the name of the manufacturer and its product are recorded. Finally, the position and orientation of the patient are also stated. Some information is specific for a certain modality (and restricted to that modality), such as magnetic field strength, echo, and repetition time for MRI data.
- **Patient data.** The patient's name, unique patient ID, date of birth, and sex (female, male) are part of this section. The patient's weight and height are optional tags that are useful—for example, to relate certain findings to the patient weight.
- **Image data.** For the localization and evaluation of images, a variety of numbers are essential. The corresponding tags are part of the *image data* section. Examples are a study-id, a series number, an image group, and an acquisition number.
- **Image presentation.** This section contains the slice distance and the *pixel spacing*, which describes the in-plane resolution. The range of values (min, max) and the number of bits allocated are also represented in this section. Finally, a default configuration for the display of the data can be specified (*WindowWidth*, *WindowCenter*). In Section 4.3, we discuss these parameters and their influence on image interpretation.

Some of these data have an immediate influence on image interpretation. It is therefore common practice in radiological workstations to include this information in a legend when the radiological data are viewed (on a CRT monitor or on a screen). In particular, patient data as well as some image interpretation data are usually displayed. Figure 4.1 gives a typical example of the visualization of image data and related information.

For medical visualization, part 14 of the DICOM standard is particularly important. It describes a *Grayscale Standard Display Function*. DICOM contains a model of the image acquisition process, as well as a presentation chain and the *Standardized Display System*. The Grayscale Standard Display Function describes the transformation of measured values to observable luminance values in a device-independent manner. The goal of the function is to transform measured values to be perceptually linear (taking into account

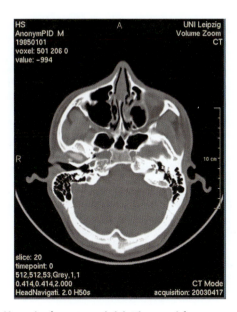

FIGURE 4.1 *A CT slice with additional information included. The upper left corner presents patient-specific information. The name and the ID of the patient were modified in the anonymization process. The third row represents the year of the patient's birth. The "voxel" entry indicates the coordinates of the currently selected voxel (represented by the mouse cursor) and the "value" entry represents the Hounsfield value at this location. The upper right corner refers to the institution where the images were acquired. The lower left corner shows which slice and which point in time is currently visible. The size of the dataset (number of voxels in x-, y-, and z-direction) is also presented. The fourth row indicates the size of one voxel, the first two numbers (0.414, 0.414) represent the in-plane resolution, and the third number (2.0) represents the slice distance (in mm).*

that our visual perception is actually not linear; recall Sect. 2.4). The purpose of defining this Grayscale Standard Display Function is to enable applications to know *a priori* how measured values are transformed to visible luminance values by a Standardized Display System.

4.2   CONVENTIONAL FILM-BASED DIAGNOSIS

The conventional way of reporting is by means of transmissive films which are put on a lightbox (see Fig. 4.2), where the radiologist inspects them. This way of reading images was also employed for the new 3D image data. This was accomplished in the following way: a workstation is attached to the scanning devices (CT, MRI). At this workstation, images are preprocessed and a subset is selected to be printed on film. The resulting films were read at the lightbox and later archived in film folders.

For the design of computer support, it is essential to understand the conventional diagnosis of medical image data by means of a lightbox. On one hand, radiologists are accustomed to this kind of reporting. On the other hand, the lightbox has been very efficiently organized in a way dedicated to specific diagnostic questions. The design of efficient software solutions to replace conventional diagnosis strongly benefits from the lessons of experience.

4.2.1 COOPERATION OF RADIOLOGISTS AND RADIOLOGY TECHNICIAN

Reporting medical image data is a cooperative process involving radiologists (experienced medical doctors with a long-term postgraduate education) and radiology technicians. This cooperation is designed

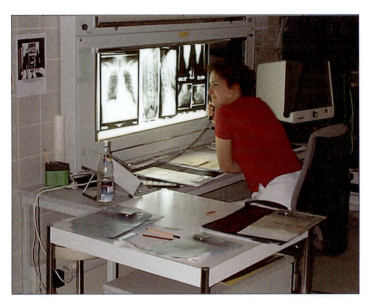

FIGURE 4.2 *The conventional lightbox as traditional workplace of radiologists. (Photo: SEBASTIAN MEYER, MeVis Diagnostics Bremen)*

such that the expert knowledge of the radiologist is used as effectively as possible. All tasks that involve the localization and initial arrangement of the images are carried out by a radiology technician. The preparation includes affixing images to the lightbox in such a way that a certain diagnostic process is supported in an optimal manner. This process is based on *hanging protocols* that define how images are arranged. Hanging protocols are neither formalized nor standardized. They differ from department to department and even from radiologist to radiologist. Hanging protocols are individual agreements between a radiologist and the radiology technician. They allow the radiologist to form a habit of inspecting images. With these hanging protocols, examination reporting is highly reproducible and very effective.

An example for a hanging protocol for X-ray thorax images is to use a lateral and a frontal image (this is actually the image acquisition protocol) and to always place the lateral image on the left and the frontal image on the right. Hanging protocols differ based on the body region being inspected, the diagnostic question, and the modality (e.g., CT, X-ray).

4.2.2 TASKS IN CONVENTIONAL FILM-BASED DIAGNOSIS

There are some general and frequent tasks in film-based diagnosis. Radiologists often compare current images with previous images of the same patient. This comparison is facilitated if the image acquisition parameters are identical or at least very similar. Whether or not a pathologic lesion is regarded as malignant might depend on its difference from previous images. Whether or not a therapy with drugs is considered effective depends on the comparison of pathologic lesions, and in particular on the assessment of their volume. Locating the previous images for a particular patient is often a tedious process if no digital archive is available.

Another typical task, in particular in the reading of X-ray images, is to inspect suspicious regions in detail. Often this is difficult, because it involves small regions that may reveal the characteristics of an early stage of a disease. A magnifying glass is used for this purpose.

Quantitative image analysis is strongly restricted with conventional diagnosis. Radiologists employ rulers to assess distances and protractors to assess angles. Distances are often essential for radiation treatment and surgery planning (distances between pathologic structures and vital structures), whereas angular measures enable assessment of the spatial relation between bones, which is crucial in orthopedics. The accuracy of these measures is limited, because they are carried out based on (axial) 2D slices. Other measures, such as cross-sectional areas, volumes of structures, or mean gray values, cannot be assessed reliably at all.

Finally, diagnostic findings are documented. This documentation is often recorded with a voice-recorder and later transformed to a written report (either manually, by a secretary, or by employing voice-recognition software). The diagnostic findings are often discussed with referring physicians to establish an appropriate treatment. Radiologists explain their findings by means of selected images and answer questions with respect to therapeutic decisions.

4.3   SOFT-COPY READING

Digitalization of radiological departments and soft-copy reading was established in the last years to compensate for some of the obvious drawbacks of conventional film-based diagnosis. Within a completely digital radiology department, image data are stored in a database (a picture archiving and communication system, or PACS). Storage in a database is more reliable and allows faster access to image data. Also, the cost of developing and printing film is saved—on a long-term scale, this is an enormous amount, which justifies the investment in software and infrastructure. Usually, the modalities (CT or MRI scanners) send the image data (via DICOM) immediately to the PACS. From there, the data are distributed to the workplaces of the radiologist. While early PACS-systems were indeed controlled by SQL-like database queries [ASSMANN and HÖHNE 1983], current systems hide query specification behind a graphical user interface.

4.3.1 INTEGRATION OF SOFT-COPY READING IN DIGITAL RADIOLOGY DEPARTMENTS

Before we discuss soft-copy reading, we describe the typical infrastructure and workflow in a digital radiological department, including the reading process. This description is based on BREITENBORN [2004]. The process starts with an order from the referring physician, which is registered in the radiological information system (RIS). The RIS entry is either created manually or generated automatically if the referring physician and the radiology department share a common information system (such as a hospital information system, or HIS).

By means of the RIS, a date and time are scheduled to carry out the examination and the referring physician is notified about this. Also, relevant prior image data are prefetched (from the PACS) and provided. The patient is welcomed by a radiology technician who knows from the RIS which examination should be carried out. The RIS submits relevant information to the imaging modality, such as patient name and patient ID. This automatic process saves time and avoids confusion. These data are later part of the DICOM data, which are transferred from the modality to the radiologist's workplace. After the image data acquisition, the RIS is notified about the completion of the procedure and the images are stored in the PACS. The images are retrieved at a diagnostic workstation, where a report is generated, sent to a *report repository*, and finally returned to the referring physician.

The RIS supports the management of different users based on their permissions to read and write image data and reports. In particular, *task lists* for each individual radiologist and for each modality are created and managed to support the diagnostic processes within a department. The support provided by a RIS is valuable, because there are orthogonal views on the orders and procedures that are accomplished in a radiology department. On the one hand, there are workplaces where images from a certain modality are processed by one radiologist; on the other hand, there are referring physicians—the "customers"—who place orders to different modalities.

The results of the diagnostic process are selected images and a written report, which often follows a special structure. The images contain diagnostically relevant information, often enhanced by annotations such as arrows, encircled regions, or labels. The enhanced images are sent back to the PACS, where again the DICOM format is employed to represent the information.

Finally, radiologists demonstrate diagnostic results to the referring physicians. In university hospitals, for example, there is a regular demonstration for neurosurgeons, general surgeons, neurologists, and most of the other medical specialties (these demonstrations are often scheduled on a daily basis for operating specialties and on a weekly basis for others). These demonstrations start with a presentation of the diagnostic findings and provide room for questions from the referring physicians relating to therapeutic decisions. In a digital radiology department, such demonstrations are carried out by means of a laptop and a projector. Figure 4.3 illustrates this process.

Soft-copy reading became a viable alternative when the quality and speed of diagnostic procedures were similar (or better) than with conventional methods. Several iterations were necessary to achieve these requirements. With respect to speed, the enormous amount of data is a major problem. A digital mammography, for example, is represented as a 4096×4096 matrix. Experienced radiologists are very fast at evaluating a mammography; therefore, a radiological workstation should enable to load and display such images very quickly.

With respect to the quality of the diagnosis, two aspects are crucial: the display device and the interaction facilities for exploration of the data.

Display Devices for Soft-Copy Reading For radiological diagnosis, only CRT monitors that meet high quality standards are permitted. The standards require that distortions in the resulting images are minimal and

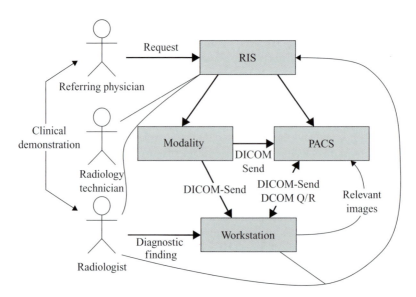

FIGURE 4.3 *Workflow in a digital radiology department. (Adapted from* BREITENBORN *[2004])*

that high spatial resolution is provided (more than 1600×1200 pixels). The requirements are especially high if image data with high spatial resolution are to be handled. One example is digital mammography, where the typical size of the data is 4096×4096. Special monitors with a resolution of 2500×2000 pixels have been developed to support reading these images (see Fig. 4.4). Another important aspect of soft-copy reading is the gray-level resolution of the display device, in particular for screening purposes where early signs of (potential) malignancy must be detected. Conventional display devices support only the display of 256 different gray values (8 bits). Advanced devices, such as those manufactured Barco$^{(TM)}$, are able to display 1024 different gray values (10 bits). It is not quite clear yet whether the enhanced gray level resolution has a significant effect on the radiologist's performance. Therefore, more conventional display devices with 256 gray levels are also used for soft-copy reading.

4.3.2 TASKS IN SOFT-COPY READING

Soft-copy reading starts with a selection of a task from the modality worklist. This task often consists of several series of image data relating to a particular patient. These series are loaded and quickly browsed to assess whether or not they are useful for diagnosis. An interaction facility to step through the slices of 3D data is therefore essential.

Windowing   After images are selected, they are displayed with a certain mapping of data to gray values applied. This process was historically necessary before printing (data were reduced to 256 gray levels). In the context of soft-copy reading, windowing is employed to map the data to the 256 gray levels of a conventional screen.

To restrict the interaction effort, only simple transformations are offered. The simplest mapping is a so-called *windowing*. This mapping is characterized by a *window center* and a *window width*. These two values specify a linear transformation where all intensity values below $center - width/2$ are mapped to black,

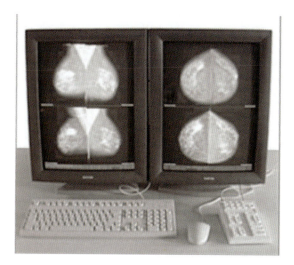

FIGURE 4.4 *Soft-copy reading of digital mammograms. The two vertical monitors support comparisons between the current images and previous images. The keypad on the right provides access to the most important functions, such as changes of the layout. (Image courtesy MeVis BreastCare, Bremen)*

and all values above *center* + *width*/2 are mapped to white. The gray values are employed for all values in this interval (see Eq. 4.1). Figure 4.5 illustrates windowing.

$$G = \begin{cases} 0 & I \le center - \frac{width}{2} \\ \frac{I - center - \frac{width}{2}}{width} & I > center - \frac{width}{2} \text{ and } I \le center + \frac{width}{2} \\ 1 & I > center + \frac{width}{2} \end{cases} \tag{4.1}$$

The width of the window defines the steepness of the function and thus the contrast. The center defines the level of intensity values the user is interested in. Radiological workstations provide so-called presets for typical tasks. Presets are particularly useful for CT data, where the standardized Hounsfield units are employed (recall Table 3.1).

The generalization of windowing is often called *adjusting a lookup table* (LUT). The LUT is in fact a table with two columns: the first contains the intensity values and the second contains the associated gray values defined by a mapping process. "Lookup" implies that the display system looks up the gray value associated with an intensity value.

Lookup tables are not directly edited. Instead, users define the graph of a function with an appropriate editor. This function is called *transfer function*, and the LUT results from the discretization of the transfer function. There is much research on advanced methods to adjust transfer functions and to automate this process. These methods are described in Chapter 11.

Browsing Slices An important interaction facility is to browse through the slices. The layout may consist of one large slice display or several slices shown simultaneously. If one slice is shown, the user should step forward and backward. If several slices are shown, either all slices are replaced when the user moves forward or backward or only one new slice is presented while the other slices move (see Fig. 4.6). The simultaneous view of several images is closer to conventional diagnosis with the lightbox. However, with CRT monitors, four or more images displayed at once are often too small to recognize small features reliably. Therefore, layouts with several images serve primarily as an overview.

A feature that is completely unknown in conventional diagnosis is to provide an animated movement through all slices (referred to as *cine mode*). The cine mode is effective because the continuous movement

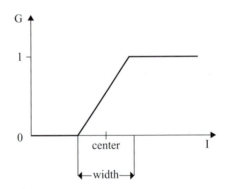

FIGURE 4.5 *Windowing as a simple transform from intensity values* I *to gray values* G. *For CT data, the Hounsfield values would be represented at the abscissa. The gray value "1" represents the brightest value that can be displayed (white), whereas "0" represents black.*

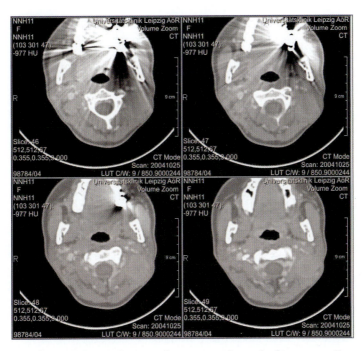

FIGURE 4.6 *Four slices of CT neck data are shown in a slice viewer simultaneously. (Data courtesy* THOMAS SCHULZ, *University of Leipzig)*

smoothly blends one cross-sectional slice with the next, which considerably reduces the cognitive effort required to mentally integrate these images.

Evaluating Image Data in Different Orientations   One of the advantages of soft-copy reading is the ability to reformat the stack of slice data. With this facility, the three orthogonal views (axial, coronal, or sagittal), as well as arbitrary oblique slices, may be created. Radiological workstations often support the simultaneous display of the three orthogonal slicing directions (see Fig. 4.7).

4.3.3 QUANTITATIVE IMAGE ANALYSIS

A variety of features of radiological workstations refer to the quantitative analysis. Distance measurements are accomplished by selecting the corresponding measurement mode and selecting two pixels. The pixels may be located in different slices, which allows the measurement of distances between positions that do not belong to the same (axial) slice. Angular measurements are carried out in a similar way. Here, a third position has to be selected. These measures are more precise than those carried out in conventional diagnosis.

Another kind of quantitative analysis refers to the intensity distribution in a selected region. As a prerequisite for this analysis, the user must be able to define a region of interest (ROI). For this purpose, predefined shapes, such as circles, ellipsoids, or rectangles, are provided; these can be scaled and translated by the user. In addition, it is often possible to create arbitrarily shaped ROIs by manually drawing on the slices. As feedback, the system presents how many pixels have been selected and which area is comprised by the ROI. In addition, the mean intensity value and the standard deviation are calculated. This information may be used to assess the severity of a disease, in particular when CT data are involved where intensity values are standardized. As a first example, the mean intensity value of an ROI in the bones—the vertebral

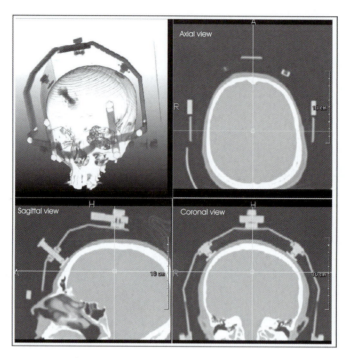

FIGURE 4.7 *Simultaneous display of three orthogonal views and a 3D view (upper left). The crosshair cursor is synchronized between these views. The ruler (on the right) is employed to assess the order of magnitude of distances. (Data courtesy* THOMAS SCHULZ, *University of Leipzig)*

mineral density—is an indicator for the severity of osteoporosis [KALENDER *et al.* 1989]. To further support quantitative image analysis, algorithms that automatically place an appropriate ROI are promising in order to increase the reproducibility. As an example, the determination of vertebral mineral density could be enhanced by automatic ROI definition [LOUIS *et al.* 1988].

Example 1: Regional Lung Function Determination   With respect to CT thorax data, the mean intensity value of an ROI in the thorax is related to functional defects of the lung [HAYHURST *et al.* 1984, SAKAI *et al.* 1987]. In normal conditions, a value between −500 and −900 Hounsfield units is expected [WU *et al.* 2002]. If the mean value is above this range, the patient probably suffers from a fibrosis.[1] On the other hand, if the mean value is less than −900 Hounsfield units, an emphysema[2] is likely where lung tissue is degraded. The severity of the disease is related to the mean value; the more strongly it deviates from the normal interval, the more severe the disease is. Figure 4.8 ROI selection in a suspicious region of CT thorax data to derive the mean gray value. To assess the severity of an emphysema, not only the mean value but also the portion of voxels with HU values below −900 and below −950 are registered [PARK *et al.* 1999].

The lung function may be also assessed with functional tests, which are much faster to accomplish. However, these tests evaluate the global lung function. The quantitative CT analysis supports a regional

---

1   Pulmonary fibrosis involves scarring of the lung. Gradually, the air sacs of the lungs become replaced by fibrotic tissue. When the scar forms, the tissue becomes thicker, causing an irreversible loss of the tissue's ability to transfer oxygen into the bloodstream. (Source: Wikipedia)

2   An emphysema is a chronic lung disease characterized by a loss of elasticity of the lung structures. Emphysema leads to the destruction of some lung structures, causing small airways to collapse during expiration. (Source: Wikipedia)

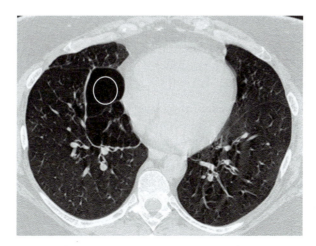

FIGURE 4.8 *Quantitative analysis of CT thorax data to assess the severity of an emphysema. The mean intensity value in the encircled region is defined to evaluate the severity of an emphysema. (Data courtesy* HANS HOLGER JEND, *Zentralkrankenhaus Bremen-Ost)*

analysis of the lung function, which is essential for therapeutic decisions such as surgery planning. For surgery planning, analysis of the lung function in the remaining lung tissue is essential for evaluating the postoperative lung function and, thus, the feasibility of surgical intervention.

Example 2: Response Evaluation in Solid Tumors   The measurement of tumor size is another essential and frequent task in the routine work of radiologists. Tumor size determination is crucial for evaluating the success of a drug therapy and for many treatment decisions. Measurements are based on CT or MRI data; X-ray is also "allowed" [PARK et al. 2003] for lung nodule quantification, but it is less accurate than CT data.

To standardize these measures, the WHO (World Health Organization) established criteria in the early 1980s [MILLER et al. 2000]. According to the WHO standard, tumor size is evaluated by the product of two diameter measurements: the longest diameter in a slice and the orthogonal diameter. Such measures are not reproducible (different users would perhaps select different slices and even in the same slice they would probably not achieve exactly the same result). They are also difficult to accomplish.

The more simplified RECIST criteria (response evaluation criteria in solid tumors) were later introduced [THERASSE et al. 2000] and are based on just one measurement of the (perceived) largest diameter. The RECIST criteria are supported by the National Cancer Institute in the United States are now common practice in many countries.

RECIST criteria offer a simplified, conservative extraction of imaging data for wide application in clinical trials. They presume that linear measures are an adequate substitute for 2D methods and register four response categories:

- CR (complete response) = disappearance of all target lesions
- PR (partial response) = 30% decrease in the sum of the longest diameter of target lesions
- PD (progressive disease) = 20% increase in the sum of the longest diameter of target lesions
- SD (stable disease) = small changes that do not meet above criteria

WORMANNS [2005] discusses the limitations of these criteria and points out possible future developments, such as computerized measurement of tumor volume.

Manual Segmentation For some advanced image analysis facilities, identification and delineation of certain structures (*segmentation*) are a prerequisite. Facilities are provided to manually outline a structure. This is similar to the definition of an arbitrarily shaped ROI. However, the process has to be repeated in several slices. As feedback, it is common to overlay the segmented region onto the slice data as a semitransparent colored region.

Annotation Annotation is the process of enhancing selected images with information to convey the findings of the radiologist. There are different kinds of information that can be added for this purpose. One example is the use of arrows that point to some pathologic variation. The arrow might be placed near textual information that labels this region. Another annotation facility is to encircle a region.

4.3.4 DIGITAL HANGING PROTOCOL

The digital hanging protocol is the further development of hanging protocols for conventional diagnosis.[3] Like the conventional hanging protocols, it is targeted at achieving optimal cooperation between a radiologist and a radiology technician. Digital hanging protocols include more information than conventional hanging protocols, due to the extended capabilities of soft-copy reading.

A digital hanging protocol may contain information with respect to the initial transfer function, the initially selected slice, and the information presented in the legend. Besides the layout of images, a digital hanging protocol may include synchronization specifications that define how one view should be adapted if certain modifications occur in another view. Synchronization may refer to the presentation center/width specification of the presentation LUT and the selected slice. This type of synchronization supports the comparison between different visualizations.

Another crucial aspect of digital hanging protocols is the user's ability to create such protocols or to refine existing protocols, tailoring the diagnostic process to the diagnostic workflow in this particular department or to the personal habits of the radiologist. To further illustrate the spirit behind digital hanging protocols, we introduce a scenario elaborated in the DICOM Digital Hanging Protocol supplement (slightly modified):

"Physician sits at a workstation with two 1280×1024 screens and selects a chest CT case from the worklist. He decides to customize the viewing style and uses the viewing application to define what type of hanging protocol he would like (layout style, interaction style) by pointing and clicking on graphical representations of the choices. He has chosen to define a three columns by four rows tiled presentation. He places the new exam on the left screen and the old exam on the right screen before he saves his preferences in a hanging protocol located at the DICOM server."

If digital hanging protocols are consequently supported, a large variety of such protocols are needed to adapt the diagnostic process to the imaging modality, the characteristics of the display device, the image data characteristics (such as slice distance), and the region of the body that is depicted. It is highly desirable that the most appropriate protocol is chosen automatically. This can be accomplished if image data are represented by means of the DICOM standard, where appropriate tags represent these characteristics.

4.3.5 GUIDELINES FOR SOFTWARE ASSISTANTS TO SUPPORT SOFT-COPY READING

In this subsection we give hints on user interface design for general radiological workstations as well as for dedicated software assistants that support special tasks, such as thorax diagnosis.

---

3   The term digital hanging protocol is not formally defined and (currently) not part of the DICOM standard. There is a supplement to the standard that discusses digital hanging protocols.

The most essential aspect of reading images is that radiologists have to focus on the images. Software assistants have to provide as much space as possible to images rather than to labels, pushbuttons, status bars, and other interaction facilities. User interface facilities should be partitioned so that only a small subset is required in a special situation.

Interaction With Pointing Device and Function Keys   To support the focused observation of images, frequently required interaction tasks should be carried out using a mouse. Mouse buttons, modifier keys, and function keys can be employed to select the appropriate function. For the most important of these functions, there are widespread interaction techniques. As an example, browsing through the slices is accomplished using the middle mouse button or the mouse wheel. Windowing is often accomplished with the right mouse button. Movements from left to right control the width of the window (and thus the contrast), whereas movements in the vertical direction control the brightness. As feedback, the current values for window and center are included in the legend at the margin of the image view.

Radiologists require these functions very often; they will soon learn them. If they were forced to select slices or adjust contrast by means of some sliders, they would be heavily distracted and annoyed. The information in the legend, such as center/window and current slice, is crucial to enable another person to reproduce the images.

Other frequent interaction tasks, such as zooming or rotating, are also provided with mouse-based interaction in many radiological workstations. Shift or Ctrl buttons are often employed to select the appropriate function. We discussed interaction tasks, such as defining an ROI or selecting positions for distance measurements. Whenever objects are created, it should be possible to modify these objects. For this purpose, it is essential that the control points of such objects can be easily selected—so they should be displayed enlarged.

For special purpose workstations, even more functions might be provided by means of a keypad (see Fig. 4.4, in which a special keypad accommodates functions for mammography reading).

4.3.6 DIAGNOSIS WITH 3D VISUALIZATIONS

3D visualization techniques are explained in detail in Part III. In this subsection, we briefly discuss which techniques are widespread and what can be achieved by using them. For a discussion of the use of 3D image data to clinical diagnosis, we refer the reader to MEGIBOW [2002].

Maximum Intensity Projection   A frequently used technique is the maximum intensity projection (MIP). With this technique, images are generated by tracing rays from the viewing plane to the 3D volume data in the direction of the virtual camera. For each pixel of the viewplane, the voxel with maximum intensity is displayed. MIP images do not convey depth-relations reliably, but they allow assessment of contrast-enhanced vascular structures (these are often the voxels with highest intensity; other structures are therefore effectively suppressed). Diagnosis of vascular structures is therefore the most important application of MIP images. An advantage of the MIP display mode is that no user interaction is required.

Surface Shaded Display   Another visualization technique available in many diagnostic workstations is surface shaded display (SSD). Images are generated based on a threshold supplied by the user. 3D surfaces are created by generating polygonal meshes connecting adjacent voxels with the given threshold value (or a value very close to the threshold). Usually, some lighting is applied to produce shaded visualizations, which convey depth relations well.

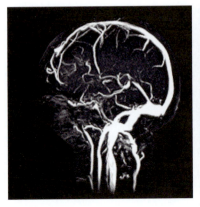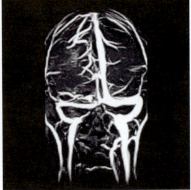

FIGURE 4.9 *Maximum intensity projection of cerebral MRI data. (Data courtesy BURKHARD TERWEY, Institute for Magnetic Resonance Imaging Diagnosis, Bremen)*

Visualization researchers have coined the term isosurface visualization. SSD is a useful visualization option if surfaces of anatomical structures can be created based on an intensity-threshold that holds—for example, for bones in CT data. Surface generation is described in Chapter 7.

Volume Rendering In contrast to SSD, in which a binary decision classifies voxels as belonging to the surface, volume rendering produces semi-transparent renditions based on a transfer function. A transfer function is in principle the same as we have discussed in Section 4.3.2 with respect to windowing. For volume rendering, two transfer functions are defined: one for mapping intensity values to gray values (as in 2D visualization), and one for mapping intensity values to transparency values. According to these transfer functions, voxels are overlaid from front to back. Opaque voxels block all voxels behind. If several semitransparent voxels are encountered that are projected to the same pixel, the gray value is determined as an interpolation of the gray values of these voxels. Figure 4.10 gives two examples of volume renditions created for radiological diagnosis.

Volume rendering does not produce any intermediate representation, such as polygonal meshes. To emphasize this property, volume rendering is often referred to as direct volume rendering (DVR), whereas SSD is an indirect method of rendering volume data.

Multiplanar Reformatting Another 3D visualization technique is multiplanar reformatting (MPR). This technique enables the user to define oblique slices throughthe volume data, which might be useful, for example, to adapt a slice to the orientation of a relevant structure. MPRs might be defined automatically (based on segmentation and image analysis of certain objects) or interactively (as shown in Fig. 4.11). The section of a rectangular plane with a parallelepiped is a plane with three, four, five, or six vertices.

Virtual Endoscopy Virtual endoscopy is a procedure inspired by real endoscopy, in which an endoscope is moved through air-filled or water-filled structures for diagnostic or therapeutic purposes. Virtual endoscopy is based on CT or MRI data and simulates the view through a real endoscope. The virtual camera is moved along a path in the center of the relevant structure. The calculation of this path requires segmentation and center-line extraction of the relevant structure (see Sect. 5.7). The relevant structure may be visualized by means of SSD or volume rendering.

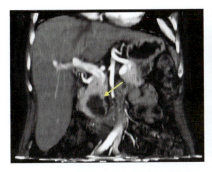
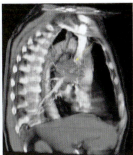

FIGURE 4.10 Clinically relevant examples of direct volume rendering. Left: the location of a tumor in the pancreas (see the arrow) is evaluated. Right: a bronchial carcinoma (see the arrow) is assessed. (Images courtesy HOEN-OH SHIN, Hannover Medical School)

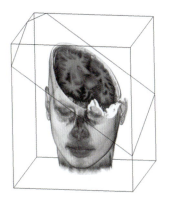
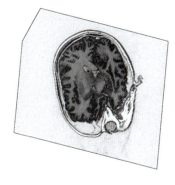

FIGURE 4.11 Interactive definition of a multiplanar reformatting of cerebral MRI data. The 3D visualization on the left is used to define an oblique plane, which is depicted undistorted on the right. (Images courtesy WOLF SPINDLER, MeVis Bremen)

The most important application is virtual colonoscopy, in which the virtual endoscope is moved through the colon to detect polyps (which are often a prestage of colon cancer).[4] Computer support for virtual colonoscopy (path planning and navigation support) is provided by a number of manufacturers and has matured over the last years.

3D Interaction All 3D visualization techniques are combined with interaction techniques that allow the adjustment of arbitrary viewing directions and zooming into relevant regions. To support depth perception, interactive rotation is essential. In particular, the investigation of MIP images benefits from smooth rotations. To convey the current viewing direction, some sort of orientation indication is essential. Often, a so-called orientation cube is included in the 3D visualization and rotated together with the 3D scene. Its faces are labeled "A"nterior, "P"osterior, "L"eft, "R"ight, "H"ead, or "F"oot, which refer to the anatomical names of viewing directions (see Fig. 4.12). It might be surprising that viewing directions are not always obvious for medical doctors. Actually, this kind of support is valuable in particular for organs that have large anatomical variation between different persons and do not exhibit clearly recognizable landmarks.

---

4   A polyp is a smooth-coated abnormal growth (tumor) projecting from a mucous membrane. (Source: Wikipedia)

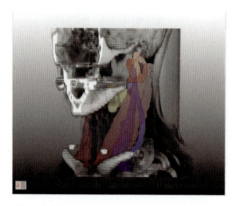

FIGURE 4.12   *The orientation cube (lower left) indicates that the 3D visualization shows the anterior (A) and left (L) view of the data. Volume rendering and surface rendering are combined to show structures relevant for planning neck dissections. (Image courtesy JEANETTE CORDES, University of Magdeburg, data courtesy THOMAS SCHULZ, University Hospital Leipzig)*

4.4   SUMMARY

Medical diagnosis has evolved into a highly efficient routine task, strongly integrated in the treatment planning process. Computer support for diagnosis and clinical demonstration must permit radiologists to retain the efficiency they achieve at the lightbox. In this vein, the collaboration between radiologists and radiology technicians, as well as the communication between radiologists and referring physicians, must be considered. It will be possible to further enhance the quality of medical image data. However, this advance will require additional effort, which is justifiable primarily for enhanced therapy planning and additional monitoring. Imaging methods are being used by surgeons more and more. In addition to preoperative planning, imaging support during interventions has become feasible.

Standardization plays a crucial role in achieving reproducible and efficient diagnosis. Digital hanging protocols that adapt the initial layout, windowing and other parameters to the modality, and other image acquisition parameters are an essential means to achieve the goals of digital radiological departments.

Visualization is the core of medical diagnosis and interactive interdisciplinary discussions of therapeutic decisions. The selection of images, the adjustment of contrast and brightness, the magnification of relevant regions, and some image analysis facilities such as ROI selection are essential interaction facilities. How these interaction facilities should be actually provided is not formally standardized. However, established and widespread solutions exist and should be considered when similar features are developed.

The DICOM standard has experienced widespread acceptance because it supports many of the requirements of modern radiology departments. DICOM will continue to evolve in the future. Topics currently under discussion in the standardization committee are 3D presentation facilities as well as the presentation of colored visualizations. There are publicly available tools for preprocessing and viewing DICOM data, such as ezDICOM and Dicom3tools Software, as well as the DICOM toolkit (DCMTK) provided by the OFFIS institute (Oldenburg, Germany). Software for medical image analysis, such as Amira (www.amiravis.com/), ITK (www.itk.org), and MeVisLab (www.mevislab.de), provide support for handling DICOM data.

2D and 3D Visualization   Currently, the investigation of 2D slice images is still dominant in medical diagnosis. 3D visualization is used to get an overview when rare anatomical variants or complex fractures are involved. For the referring physician, and in particular for surgeons, 3D visualizations are more important. On the one hand, these doctors are less familiar with reading cross-sectional images. On the other hand, their task is not to "describe" a pathology but to destroy or remove it in their 3D surroundings, which leads to additional requirements in the visual representation. Therefore, 3D visualizations play an essential role in clinical demonstrations for surgeons as well as in radiation treatment planning.

FURTHER READING

Concerning DICOM, the Web page medical.nema.org/ is the official portal, with in-depth information and many links. Two books include more information about DICOM [CLUNIE 2001, OOSTERWIJK and GIHRING 2002].

Chapter 05

Image Analysis for Medical Visualization

In this chapter, we discuss image analysis techniques that extract clinically relevant information from radiological data. We focus on extracting information for generating high-quality visualizations and for deriving quantitative information about relevant structures. Image analysis is crucial for many diagnosis and therapy planning tasks. As an example, the identification and delineation of a tumor is often a prerequisite to determining its extent and volume. This information is essential for the selection of viable therapy options. The goal of this chapter is to provide an overview of important image analysis tasks and some established solutions. The overview includes validation of image analysis approaches, because of the particular relevance of accuracy and reproducibility for medical applications.

We shall discuss not only algorithms that detect and analyze features in medical image data, but also interaction techniques that allow the user to guide an algorithm and to modify an existing result. Since medical doctors usually work under severe time pressure, it is preferable that no interaction at all be required—the whole task is initiated with one mouse-click and performed reliably and precisely in a fully automatic manner. However, this scenario is not realistic for typical image analysis tasks, and it will probably be unrealistic for most application areas in the foreseeable future. Medical image data, anatomical relations, pathologic processes, image modalities, and biological variability exhibit such a large variety that automatic solutions for the detection of certain structures cannot cope with all such cases.

Image analysis is often carried out as a pipeline of individual steps. This pipeline starts with preprocessing and filtering, which is designed to support subsequent algorithms. The restriction of the image data to a relevant subset, as well as methods to improve the signal-to-noise ratio, is an example of tasks to be carried out in this stage. Image segmentation usually represents the core of image analysis.

This process assigns labels (unique identifiers) of anatomical or pathologic structures to parts of the image data. Image segmentation is often a sophisticated, time-consuming process that produces geometric descriptions of the relevant structures. There are two basic strategies to address segmentation problems:

- The edge-based approach, which searches for discontinuities in th.e image data that belong to the border of the segmentation target structure.
- The region-based approach, in which the target structure is regarded as a homogeneous region determined by a search process guided by appropriate criteria for homogeneity.

Often, the results of the segmentation algorithm are enhanced by some kind of postprocessing; smoothing the boundary of segmentation results or the removal of small holes are among the tasks in this process. Image segmentation results may be the input for a higher level of analysis. As an example, the shape of objects may be characterized to classify the objects (benign or malignant tumor), or the skeleton of an object might be determined to assess its branching structure. Skeletonization results are also essential for visualization purposes. As an example, skeletons of elongated structures serve as a path for a virtual fly-through (virtual endoscopy, see Chap. 15). Often, skeletons are further processed to assess

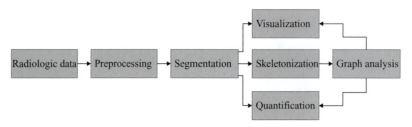

FIGURE 5.1 *Image analysis pipeline for many diagnosis and therapy planning tasks. While segmentation results are often used as input for visualization and quantification, for some structures, such as vascular structures, additional image analysis steps are required.*

the branching pattern of anatomical structures. Figure 5.1 presents a typical image analysis pipeline in which *quantification* and *visualization* are the final goals of image analysis.

The discussion in this chapter is by no means complete; we refer to dedicated textbooks on medical image analysis, such as SONKA and FITZPATRICK [2000], for further information.

Organization This chapter starts with a discussion of general requirements for image analysis (see Sect. 5.1). The core of this chapter is organized according to the pipeline presented in Figure 5.1. In Section 5.2, we shall discuss preprocessing and filtering. The discussion of segmentation methods is subdivided into two parts: more general semi-interactive approaches (see Sect. 5.3) that do not require dedicated assumptions about the shape and appearance of objects, and specialized methods (see Sect. 5.4) for narrow fields of applications that can carry out segmentation tasks (almost) automatically. We deal with interaction techniques to guide segmentation algorithms in Section 5.5. Postprocessing is discussed in Section 5.6. As an example for further analysis, we deal with the skeletonization of anatomical structures (see Sect. 5.7). At the end of this chapter, we describe strategies to validate image analysis methods. From the visualization point of view, it is crucial that the image analysis results on which visualization methods are based are reliable (see Sect. 5.8).

5.1   REQUIREMENTS

Before we describe detailed problems and solutions, it is essential to discuss some general requirements for medical image analysis. The following requirements are essential:

- **Robustness.** To be useful in the clinical routine, image analysis solutions have to be robust; they must work for a large variety of cases. It is acceptable that the interaction effort increases in difficult cases with abnormalities in the anatomy or in pathologic structures, but there should be support even in those cases. Automatic solutions that only work under certain circumstances might be part of a software system but must be complemented by a solution for other cases.
- **Accuracy.** Image segmentation and subsequent operations should provide accurate results. Validation studies are required to determine whether accuracy is achieved with high certainty. Such studies are essential, although they have a limited scope, typically for a specialized imaging protocol.
- **Reproducibility.** This requirement is closely related to the previous one. Reproducibility means that a single user would get a very similar result if an algorithm is applied several times (intra-observer reproducibility) and that different users also would produce very similar results (inter-observer reproducibility). This requirement is a little weaker than accuracy, but it might be sufficient in

some applications to demonstrate a reasonable reproducibility. This requirement is easier to prove because no correlation to some ground truth is necessary. A synonym for reproducibility, *precision*, is often employed. We use the term reproducibility because it is less likely to be confused with accuracy.

- **Speed.** There might be excellent solutions that are computationally extremely demanding. Sophisticated filtering or clustering techniques are among them. If it is not possible to accelerate these methods to a level for which an interactive use is feasible, they should not be used. The growing power of computers alleviates the situation; however, the increasing sizes of image data often compensate for the additional computing power.

While these requirements are general, the importance of each individual requirement differs strongly with respect to the application context. Speed might be the dominant requirement if image analysis is carried out under severe time pressure—for example, in the operating room. Reproducibility is crucial, if radiological data are acquired and analyzed for monitoring the progress of a disease over time. Similar discussions of requirements can be found in [HAHN 2005 and UDUPA and HERMAN 2000].[1]

5.2   PREPROCESSING AND FILTERING

Radiological image data exhibit artifacts such as noise and inhomogeneities. Shading artifacts often occur in MRI data, and metallic implants, for example in the teeth, cause artifacts in CT and MRI data. Additionally, motion of the patients and breathing might locally decrease image quality. For image analysis as well as for direct visualization, it is crucial to improve the quality of images. While some techniques, such as contrast enhancement, improve visual quality only, other techniques also enhance the signal-to-noise ratio and favor subsequent image analysis. Noise reduction leads to more homogeneous regions, which might be delineated with less interaction effort. On the other hand, noise reduction might compromise the detection of small relevant features.

Preprocessing and filtering summarize all aspects that restrict the amount of data and enhance data for further processing.

5.2.1 ROI SELECTION

Often, a first step is the definition of a region of interest (ROI) that comprises all relevant structures. The term ROI is usually applied to a region in 2D image data; in the context of 3D image data, volumes of interest (VOI) is also a common term. We use the term ROI for the selection of subimages in 2D data as well as for the selection of subvolumes in 3D data.

The ROI usually has the shape of a cuboid. Even if the ROI selection reduces the extent in each direction by 10% only, the overall amount of data is reduced by some 27%, which accelerates subsequent computations and enhances visualization because irrelevant information is not included. The interaction to accomplish ROI selection should be a combination of direct manipulation (drag the border lines of the ROI) in an appropriate visualization of the data and the specification of numbers (precise input of ROI position and extent in each direction). The precise numerical specification of an ROI is in particular welcome if several datasets are processed and compared. Often, in such scenarios, the same ROI should be selected, which is difficult to achieve with direct manipulation.

---

1   Hahn's excellent Ph.D. thesis is available online: www.elib.suub.unibremen.de/publications/dissertations/E-Diss1252_Hahn.pdf.

It might be necessary for certain segmentation tasks to define further ROIs as a subset of the first ROI. These additional ROIs may serve as barriers that reduce the search space for segmentation information. In contrast to the primary ROIs, these often have an irregular shape, which might be defined by drawing in a few slices and interpolating between them.

5.2.2 RESAMPLING

As already pointed out in Section 2.2, the anisotropic nature of many datasets can be a severe quality issue for image analysis and visualization techniques. Therefore, a resampling step is often included to transform data to an isotropic grid. In this process, the accuracy of the data should not be degraded. Therefore, resampling is driven by the highest resolution (usually in-plane) and interpolates additional data in the dimension with lower resolution (usually the z-dimension). There are many algorithms available that can accomplish the interpolation; they differ in their quality and computational effort. Fast methods interpolate the value at a particular position by taking into account the neighboring voxels only (trilinear interpolation, Sect. 2.1). Better results are achieved with triquadratic or tricubic interpolation. Based on reconstruction theory, the *Lanczos* filter, based on the sinc-function, has optimal properties, but its infinite extent renders a practical implementation difficult. A detailed overview on image interpolation can be found in THÉVENAZ et al. [2000]. Since resampling increases the amount of data, it is carried out after ROI selection to increase the resolution only in relevant areas.

Resampling is a challenging issue in 3D ultrasound processing (recall Sect. 3.4). The slices acquired in freehand mode are neither parallel nor equidistant. Although available 3D visualization techniques can directly process the data available at irregular grids, the general strategy is to convert the data to a regular grid (see Fig. 5.2). Without special care, gaps would result in the regular volume in places where the original slices were too far. Different interpolation schemes have been suggested to handle the resampling problem with 3D ultrasound: LALOUCHE et al. [1989] employed cubic spline filters, which incorporate many voxels in the neighborhood. OHBUCHI et al. [1992] proposed an adaptive interpolation scheme based on the Gaussian filter. With this filter, smooth transitions of the data and their derivatives are achieved. The standard deviation of the Gaussian is adapted to the resolution of ultrasound data. In principle, the Gaussian has infinite support (all voxels contribute to the resampling at each point). For the computation, the filter is limited to a certain size, which is again adaptive with respect to an error term.

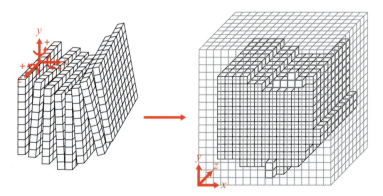

FIGURE 5.2 *Resampling the 3D ultrasound data into a regular three-dimensional grid* [SAKAS and WALTER 1995]. *(Image courtesy* GEORGIOUS SAKAS, *Fraunhofer Institute, Darmstadt)*

However, it must be noted that all resampling schemes lead to problems with respect to the reliability of the results in case of irregularly sampled data. The Gaussian filter, for example, is a low pass filter that effectively blurs the image (see Sect. 5.2.4).

5.2.3 HISTOGRAM AND HISTOGRAM EQUALIZATION

For many operations applied to image data, we employ the *histogram* to select appropriate parameters. The term histogram inherently relates to discrete data (data sampled on a discrete grid and represented in a discrete range). Histograms indicate the frequency distribution of data values and indicate the probability that an image element exhibits a certain value. Therefore, a histogram represents a discrete probability density function.

Usually, histograms are presented as vertical bars, the height of which represents the frequency over a horizontal axis of values (e.g., Hounsfield values in case of CT data). Each bar represents a value or an interval of values. More formally, if we have a total number of N pixels or voxels, and values in the range $[0, \ldots, G-1]$, the probability of the occurrence of a particular value G_i is computed as:

$$p(G_i) = \frac{n_i}{N} \qquad (5.1)$$

Histograms are analyzed, for example, with respect to their significant local maxima (or simply peaks). The definition of a significant local maximum is difficult and application-dependent: in general, a local maximum that strongly exceeds adjacent values and is not too close to another significant local maximum is considered significant. In medical image data, a peak in the histogram is often related to one tissue type. Depending on the tissue types and the imaging modality, the tissue types may overlap each other in the histogram, so that the number of peaks is lower than the number of tissue types. Figure 5.3 presents a slice of an MRI dataset of the shoulder region along with the histogram (of the whole dataset). Besides the global image histogram, the histogram within a local neighborhood is often used to derive parameters for filtering operations.

Some preprocessing operations are directly based on the histogram—for example, the histogram equalization, the most common histogram transformation technique, which enhances the image contrast. With this transformation T, an image is transformed such that a new histogram results, in which

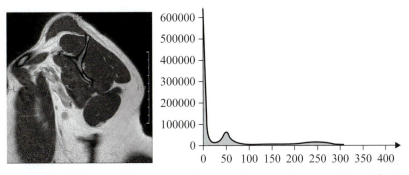

FIGURE 5.3   *A slice of an MRI dataset and the histogram of the whole 3D dataset. The large peak in the left relates to background voxels, the second peak corresponds to muscles, and the smaller third peak to soft tissue structures with higher image intensity. (Image courtesy ARNO KRÜGER, University of Magdeburg)*

all brightness values are approximately constant. The precise computation of the output value G_o from the input value G_i is as follows:

$$G_{out} = T(G_{inp}) = \sum_{j=0}^{k} pG_j = \sum_{j=0}^{k} n_j N \qquad (5.2)$$

Although the result is not a perfectly uniform histogram, the histogram of the output image is spread over a wider range of (gray) values (see Fig. 5.4).

T is a monotonically increasing function in the whole interval of intensity values. This property ensures that pixels that were darker in the original image remain darker in the resulting image. Histogram transformations may strongly enhance the perception and interpretation of images. However, due to their strict monotonic behavior, image segmentation usually does not benefit from prior histogram transformations. For segmentation purposes, noise reduction is essential. GONZALES and WOODS [1998] discuss these and other histogram operations in detail. Histograms, in particular histogram presentations, are described in more detail in Section 6.2.1, since it is relevant to direct volume rendering.

5.2.4 GENERAL NOISE REDUCTION TECHNIQUES

Medical image data exhibit random noise due to stochastic processes in the image acquisition. Noise is characterized by a certain amplitude and distribution. The noise level is often measured as the signal-to-noise ratio in the whole image. In fact, the noise level depends on the imaged tissue and on its mean gray value and is thus locally different. The noise level also depends on the spatial resolution of the data; high resolution data, such as CT data with 0.5 mm slice thickness, exhibit more noise. In X-ray and CT imaging, the noise level depends on the amount of radiation. To minimize the negative effects, the amount of ionizing radiation is kept at a minimum, at the expense of a low signal-to-noise-ratio.

Noise reduction filters are employed to enhance the data. In general, it is assumed that noise occurs in high frequency. Therefore, low pass filters are used for noise reduction. The design of these filters is based on assumptions concerning the amplitude and distribution of noise. A variety of filters have been designed to reduce noise with a Gaussian distribution. The Gaussian filter kernel is represented by Equation 5.3, where μ represents the centroid of the function and σ represents the standard deviation and thus the width of the function.

$$G(x, \sigma, \mu) = \frac{1}{\sigma \cdot \sqrt{2 \cdot \pi}} \cdot e^{\frac{x-\mu}{\sigma^2}} \qquad (5.3)$$

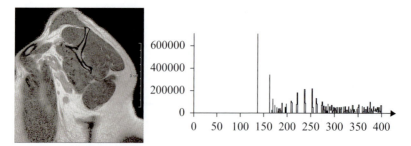

FIGURE 5.4 *Histogram equalization applied to the MRI shoulder dataset shown in Figure 5.3. The large peak in the left is cut again. (Image courtesy ARNO KRÜGER, University of Magdeburg)*

The Gaussian is an example of the general concept of filtering a function g with a filter F, which is often represented as a convolution (see Eq. 5.4).

$$g'(x) = g(x) \otimes F(x) = \int_{-\infty}^{\infty} g(x) \cdot F(x - x_1) \cdot d_x \qquad (5.4)$$

where $\otimes$ denotes the convolution operator.

To apply this concept to discrete image data, the convolution is expressed as a weighted sum of the signal g over the filter kernel F with $2N + 1$ elements (see Eq. 5.5).

$$g'(u) = \sum_{i=-N}^{N} g(u) \cdot F(u - i) \qquad (5.5)$$

Simple filters are *local filters* that modify the image intensity at each voxel by a combination of image intensities at neighboring voxels. Discrete local filters are characterized by a kernel—a matrix of elements with the same size as the neighborhood being considered. Usually the matrix has the size $(2N + 1) \times (2N + 1) \times (2M + 1)$, with N usually being 1, 2, or 3 and M being 0, 1, or 2. In cases of isotropic data, M and N usually have the same value, whereas in (typical) anisotropic data a smaller M is chosen to account for the larger extent in the z-direction. Odd numbers for the matrix size ensure that a central element exists.

With $M = 0$, the filter is applied to each slice separately and has no effect on other slices. This is the typical situation when data have a highly anisotropic voxel spacing with a slice distance s being more than twice as large as the pixel distance r within a slice. In such situations, the differences of the images' intensities between adjacent slices are relatively large, and these voxels should not be considered for filtering.

If the elements of the matrix are constant, the corresponding filter is *static*. Filters that adapt their content to local image characteristics are called *dynamic*. We will briefly discuss examples of both kinds of filters.

Static Noise Reduction Filters   Static noise reduction filters are scaled so that the sum of their elements is 1, with the result that the mean gray value of the image remains the same after the filter was applied. This normalization is important to maintain the overall image intensity.

The filter is applied by iterating over all pixels and replacing the image intensity with a weighted average of neighboring pixels. The weights of the neighboring pixels are characterized by the filter matrix. The simplest filter is the average filter, in which each neighbor voxel has the same influence. Better results are achieved with a filter that takes the distance to the central voxel into account. A frequent example is the binomial filter, a discretized version of the Gaussian function.[2] The elements of the filter are binomial coefficients. Figure 5.5 shows the result of a 2D binomial filter with kernel size 5×5. As a second example, we present the effect of Gaussian filtering on 3D visualizations derived from ultrasound data (see Fig. 5.6). In Section 3.4, ultrasound data were characterized as particularly noisy image data. Gaussian filtering improves the quality of the data; however, it is not sufficient to generate expressive 3D visualizations [SAKAS and WALTER 1995].

The 5×5 filter has the following kernel matrix:

To normalize the kernel elements, we divide them by the sum of all elements (256 for the 5×5 binomial filter). For the efficient application of filters with larger kernels to large volume data, *separability* is an important issue. Separable filters with a two (or three)-dimensional kernel can be replaced by

---

2 This filter is called *Gaussian* in many image processing systems.

1	4	6	4	1
4	16	24	16	4
6	24	36	24	6
4	16	24	16	4
1	4	6	4	1

TABLE 5.1 5×5 binomial filter.

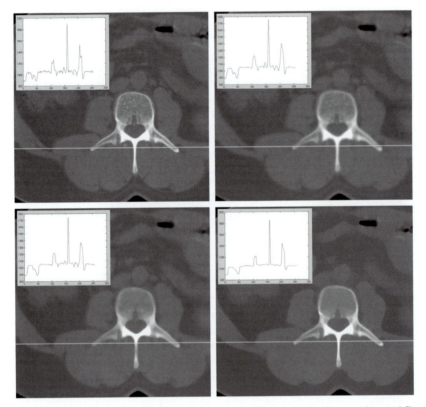

FIGURE 5.5 *Portion of a slice of a CT neck dataset (original data: upper left) processed with a 5×5 binomial filter (upper right), with a 5×5 median filter (lower left), and a diffusion filter (lower right) to reduce image noise. The intensity profile along the horizontal white lines is displayed in the upper left inset. (Image courtesy ARNO KRÜGER, University of Magdeburg)*

combining two (or three) one-dimensional filters. This way, the quadratic (cubic) complexity can be reduced to a linear one. The binomial filter is an example for a separable filter. The drawback of implementing a filter for *n* dimensions as a sequence of separable one-dimensional filters is the additional memory consumption necessary to store intermediate results.

The inherent problem of local filters with a static matrix is that they are not adaptive. Features such as edges are not preserved and appear washed out. Static local filters do not exhibit adaptive behavior; neither the size of the filter nor its elements can be adapted to local image characteristics.

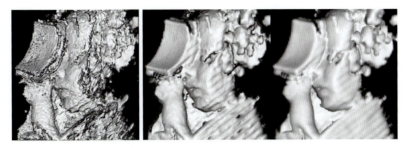

FIGURE 5.6 *3D visualization of ultrasound data of a fetus. Left: original data, middle: after binomial filtering with a $5 \times 5 \times 5$ kernel, and right: after filtering with a $7 \times 7 \times 7$ kernel. Further processing steps are required for the generation of expressive visualizations from 3D ultrasound [SAKAS and WALTER 1995].* (Image courtesy GEORGIOUS SAKAS, Fraunhofer Institute Darmstadt)

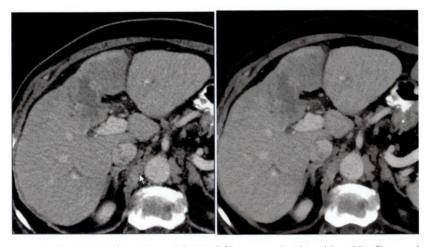

FIGURE 5.7 *Portion of a CT slice of an abdominal dataset (left) is processed with an $11 \times 11\sigma$ filter to reduce image noise (result image right).* (Data courtesy JÖRG DEBATIN, University of Essen)

Dynamic Noise Reduction Filters Better results can be achieved in general with *dynamic* filters, which analyze and consider image intensities in the local neighborhood. An important example is the median filter. With this filter, the voxels in the neighborhood of the current voxel are sorted into bins according to their image intensity, and the median is determined (intensity of the voxel that is in the middle of the sequence). The central voxel is then replaced by the median value. Compared to Gaussian filtering, extremely high and low outlier values do not significantly influence the result. The sorting stage, however, takes considerable time; therefore kernel sizes should not be too large. In general, dynamic filters are computationally more demanding but allow to adapt to features in the data.

Another instance of a dynamic noise reduction filter considers the *histogram* of image intensities in the local neighborhood. If it turns out that the current voxel has a very high or very low value compared to the average in its neighborhood, it remains unchanged. An example of this strategy is σ-filtering, which restricts the filter to voxels with an intensity that does not differ strongly from the local average (see Fig. 5.7).

σ is the parameter of the filter that quantifies how strongly the image intensity may deviate from the average (avg). With $\sigma = 1$, all voxels deviating less than the standard deviation from the average ($avg \pm \sigma$) are considered. If the central voxel has an intensity inside the specified interval, the image intensity is replaced by its local average. A drawback of this method is the computational effort it requires (the computation of the average intensity and the standard deviation in each local neighborhood requires a significant amount of time, particularly for larger kernels and 3D objects).

Another adaptive variation of filtering is to restrict the application of the filter to an intensity interval that has been successfully realized as a first step for the analysis of vascular structures [SELLE et al. 2002].

Diffusion Filtering There are many more advanced filtering techniques that try to preserve features. A family of advanced edge-preserving filter techniques is diffusion filtering, where the physical process of diffusion is simulated. Diffusion occurs between adjacent regions, in which concentrations of a liquid, for example, are different. These differences are adjusted in the diffusion process. As a result of diffusion, a stable balance arises that is characterized by Fick's law (see Eq. 5.6):

$$j = -D\nabla(u) \qquad (5.6)$$

Here $\nabla(u)$ is the gradient of the concentration, D is the diffusion tensor (a symmetric matrix), and j is the energy flow necessary to achieve the balance.

The goal of advanced diffusion filtering techniques is to restrict the diffusion to areas without edges as well as along edges (see Fig. 5.8). To realize this behavior, an edge detector is included in the calculation of the diffusion tensor.

Nonlinear anisotropic diffusion effectively reduces the noise level and leads to clear boundaries of different regions. In particular for the analysis of cerebral MRI data, diffusion filtering is a frequent initial step [GERIG et al. 1992]. An overview on diffusion filtering is given in WEICKERT [1997]. The original ideas that underlie the simulation of diffusion processes in image smoothing go back to MUMFORD and SHAH [1989] and PERONA and MALIK [1990].

Filtering at Boundaries With both static and dynamic filters, problems occur at the boundary of images (where voxels do not have a complete neighborhood). For a matrix sized 5×5, the first and the last two rows and columns of an image are involved. In typical CT and MRI data, the border of the data contains background information that is not relevant. Therefore, virtual rows and columns filled with the background color can be added to the images to provide the necessary neighborhood for filtering.

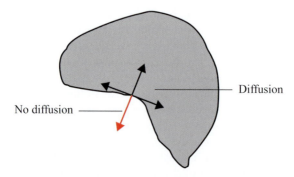

FIGURE 5.8 *Principle of non-linear anisotropic diffusion. Diffusion may occur along borders and inside homogeneous regions. No diffusion is applied perpendicular to edges.*

If 3D kernels are used, at least the first and last slices of the volume do not have the neighborhood information relevant for filtering. In such cases, it is more suitable to leave these slices unfiltered or to apply a reduced filter that only contains the non-zero elements for the available voxels. The implementation of such a filtering scheme is a bit more complex, because special variants of the filter have to be provided for each border and for each corner of the image data.

Multiresolution Filtering   The general problem of noise reduction is to prevent relevant features from being degraded. In particular, if large filter kernels are applied, removing degradation of features is a crucial problem. These problems may be alleviated by means of multiresolution schemes. An image pyramid, for example, contains voxels at different levels, in which each voxel at level n represents a low pass filtered version of eight voxels at the level $n - 1$. Such a data structure might be used to detect important features, such as larger surfaces at a higher level (coarser representation of the data). This information can be used to restrict or modify filtering at lower levels. As an example, SAKAS and WALTER [1995] employed a multiresolution filtering scheme to enhance filtering of 3D ultrasound data.

5.2.5 INHOMOGENEITY CORRECTION

MRI signal intensities are usually not uniform, primarily due to inhomogeneities of the magnetic field induced by the radio-frequency coils. The character and amount of inhomogeneity depend on the geometry of the coil. Surface coils, for example, produce different intensity values depending on the distance to the coil. While intensity variations of 10% to 20% do not affect the visual diagnosis severely, they strongly degrade the performance of intensity-based segmentation algorithms [SLED et al. 1998]. For MRI data, inhomogeneity is a more serious problem than image noise [STYNER et al. 1998]. In those cases, an automatic correction of this inhomogeneity (often referred to as gainfield correction) may be urgently needed. This requires models of the inhomogeneity. In general, radio-frequency (RF) inhomogeneity results in low spectral frequency variations of the signal intensity (see Sect. 3.3).

A wide-spread and generic method for inhomogeneity correction was introduced by SLED et al. [1998]. It is based on the observation that a background distortion blurs the image histogram. Starting from assumptions about the smoothness of the background distortion and the probability distribution of the background values, the image histogram is deconvolved with the (modeled) background distribution. Subsequently, an intensity map is computed from the original and the deconvolved, sharpened histogram. The difference between the mapped and the original image is smoothed according to the above-mentioned assumptions, thus yielding an estimate of the background distortion. This procedure is iterated until convergence is achieved (see Fig. 5.9). This method has also been used as preprocessing step for the segmentation and analysis of vascular structures (see Sect. 5.7 and BOSKAMP et al. [2004]).

Another approach has been presented by STYNER et al. [1998]. In contrast to the method of SLED et al. [1998], which relied on the image histogram only, STYNER'S method is based on known statistics for the intensity distributions of the tissue classes in the image. The method is therefore more specialized, but produces better results if the necessary information can be provided. Application examples are breast MRI data and cerebral MRI data, which employ statistical information concerning the distribution of gray matter, white matter, and cerebrospinal fluid. This method is widely available as part of the OpenSource software ITK (see www.itk.org and the related books [IBANEZ and SCHROEDER 2005, YOO 2004]).

5.2.6 GRADIENT FILTERING

Gradient filtering is a preprocessing operation that is particularly useful for subsequent edge detection and edge-based segmentation methods. The gradient of a function f is the vector consisting of the

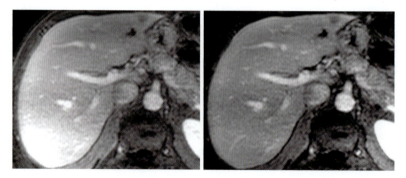

FIGURE 5.9 *Inhomogeneity correction for a slice of an abdominal MRI dataset. (Image courtesy Andrea Schenk, MeVis Bremen; data courtesy* JÖRG DEBATIN, *University of Essen.)*

partial derivatives in each direction. The gradient has a direction (the direction of steepest descent) and a magnitude (*mag*) that is determined as the length of the gradient vector. For a two-dimensional function $f(x, y)$, the gradient magnitude is computed according to Equation 5.7. With respect to discrete image data, gradients have to be approximated by differences between neighboring voxels. Often, the gradient magnitude at each pixel location is essential for subsequent operations, such as segmentation with the watershed transform (see Sect. 5.3.4). To yield an image with gradient magnitude per pixel, a suitable filter must be applied. The simplified denotation of such images is *gradient image*.

$$mag(\nabla f) = \sqrt{\left(\frac{\delta f}{\delta x}\right)^2 + \left(\frac{\delta f}{\delta y}\right)^2} \qquad (5.7)$$

Gradient filters are often 3×3 filters that are applied similarly to noise reduction filters (again the images are convolved with a filter). Widespread gradient filters are the Sobel-operator and the Roberts-Cross-operator. Another variant is to calculate the average intensity in the local neighborhood in a first step and sum the absolute differences of all pixels in the neighborhood. This sum is a good indicator of the gradient magnitude. GONZALES and WOODS [1998] describe gradient filtering in detail.

5.2.7 ENHANCEMENT OF RELEVANT STRUCTURES

Beside correcting inhomogeneities and suppressing noise, the preprocessing stage might also involve the enhancement of relevant structures. The general concept is to incorporate assumptions with regard to the shape and/or intensity variations of the relevant objects to explicitly highlight these structures.

For example, for vascular structures, special filters are used to enhance long tubular structures. FRANGI *et al.* [1999] introduced an approach where the Hessian matrix (approximating second-order derivatives) is computed in different scales for each voxel position. The eigenvalues of the Hessian matrix are analyzed to detect and enhance elongated, vessel-like structures. The underlying model assumption is that the elongated shape of vascular structures results in one large eigenvalue λ_1 and two small eigenvalues λ_2 and λ_3 ($\lambda_1 \gg \lambda_2 \gg \lambda_3$). The enhancement of vascular structures is described in more detail in the context of their visualization (see Sect. 14.1.1). Figure 5.10 gives an example for vessel enhancement. Usually, this technique is applied to angiography data after the selection of an appropriate ROI so that only vascular structures are enhanced.

In a similar way, bony structures might be enhanced [DESCCTEAUX *et al.* 2005]. Again, the eigenanalysis of the Hessian is the basis for characterizing image elements with respect to their probability of belonging

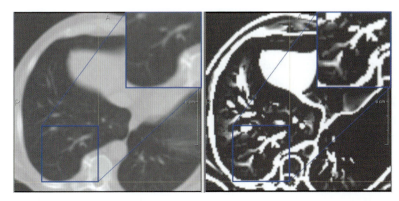

FIGURE 5.10   *Applying the vessel enhancement filter to CT thorax data. Left: original; right: resulting image. The insets in both image clearly reveal the differences. The filter might be applied in different ways. In this case, structures that are not considered tubular are strongly suppressed. Primarily, vascular and bony structures are enhanced. (Image courtesy ARNO KRÜGER, University of Magdeburg)*

to bones. The eigenanalysis of the Hessian is an efficient means to characterize shapes. Nodules, for example, are characterized by three eigenvalues of approximately the same size.

5.3   GENERAL SEGMENTATION APPROACHES

Segmentation is the task of decomposing image data into meaningful structures that are relevant for a specific task. Segmentation has two aspects:

- Relevant objects should be identified, which means they must be recognizable as particular anatomical structures.
- They should be delineated, in the sense that their borders are precisely specified.

In a way, a segmentation imposes a semantic on the image data.

Recognition is a high-level task that humans usually perform better than computers. Delineation, on the other hand, is a task where accuracy is essential. Carefully designed algorithms may lead to excellent solutions for the delineation problem. A challenge for segmentation processes is therefore to combine the strength of the user with the potential of computer support.

Technically, a unique label is assigned to each voxel representing the membership to a particular structure. In medical applications, it is usually sufficient to segment the relevant structures only, and not all anatomical structures—the segmentation is incomplete. We shall refer to the structures that should be delineated as *target structures*.

Significance of Segmentation   In the context of this book, we are primarily interested in segmentation as prerequisite for visualization. Segmentation information is required to selectively show certain (segmented) objects. On the other hand, segmentation is sometimes applied to suppress a structure that hampers the visualization. As an example, bones in CT angiography data are often segmented to be removed from a visualization of contrast-enhanced vascular structures (FIEBICH et al. [1999]).

Another application of segmentation is quantitative image analysis—for example, with respect to gray values, volumes, sizes, or shape parameters of relevant structures. In general, the required accuracy is larger for any kind of quantitative analysis. For visualization it is more important to support a comprehensible display of anatomical or pathologic structures. A segmentation result that leads to smooth (surface) visualization is essential for this process. Accuracy is, of course, also an issue in this application scenario to prevent misleading visualizations, but a submillimeter accuracy is often not necessary (and not supported by the dataset resolution).

Computer Support for Image Segmentation   Much effort has been spent on the development of segmentation approaches. These rely on some homogeneity criteria that are fulfilled for all voxels belonging to a certain structure. This criterion might be a certain range of intensity values—for example, with respect to the Hounsfield scale if CT data are involved. Another example for such a criterion is the existence of a border line characterized by large gradient magnitude. We discuss first segmentation approaches that rely on image features to delineate structures. It turns out that such approaches require substantial interaction effort. More advanced model-based approaches make use of assumptions concerning the shape, size, location, or gray-level distribution of objects to identify a certain structure.

We begin the discussion of general segmentation techniques with a brief discussion of manual segmentation and provide a more detailed description of threshold- and region-based methods. Another important class of segmentation techniques that we will describe are edge-based methods, in which the boundary of an object is detected. Finally, we discuss model-based segmentation approaches, in which available knowledge on the target structure is exploited.

Segmentation methods usually compute a map that identifies which voxels belong to a target structure. Since this map may contain several segmented target structure it is also called a *label volume*, where each voxel in this auxiliary volume is considered a label of one (or more) segment.

5.3.1 MANUAL SEGMENTATION

The most general and easy-to-accomplish method for image segmentation is manual drawing on slices of radiological data: the user outlines the relevant structures with a pointing device. To modify the contour, it is often possible to redraw a particular portion, which replaces the previously drawn portion of the contour.

This approach is robust (always applicable); however, it is time-consuming, not reproducible, and not precise, because the user often deviates slightly from the desired contour. Despite these problems, manual segmentation is widespread, particularly if objects are very difficult to delineate due to low contrasts and an unexpected shape. As an example, tumor segmentation is often performed manually.

5.3.2 THRESHOLD-BASED SEGMENTATION

With a global threshold or an interval of a lower and upper threshold applied to the image intensity, a binary image is generated. Equation 5.8 specifies the typical situation, in which a threshold interval is defined by an average value a and a tolerance ϵ. All voxel values $I(v)$ that lie within the resulting interval ($[a - \epsilon, a + \epsilon]$) are selected.

$$\epsilon = |I(v) - a| \tag{5.8}$$

Threshold-based segmentation can be extended to using multiple intensity intervals $D_1, D_2, \ldots D_n$. Any kind of threshold-based segmentation may be supported by the presentation and analysis of the image histogram, which may support the selection of thresholds.

Usually, this will not produce a segmentation of the target structure immediately, but it may serve as a usable starting point. In the next step, a connected component analysis may be carried out to detect connecting regions.

The most typical application of threshold-based segmentation is the identification of bones in CT data, as bones can be characterized by large Hounsfield values. However, even in this application, the accuracy of threshold-based segmentation is limited, since thin bones usually are not correctly identified. This is due to the partial volume effect, which averages image intensities and leads to lower intensity values for voxels that only partially represent bony structures.

Threshold Selection   Threshold-based segmentation can be made faster and more reproducible if the threshold-selection process is supported. There are a variety of methods to "suggest" meaningful threshold values. Most of these methods rely on the histogram of image intensities.

A local minimum in the histogram often represents the threshold, which is optimal to distinguish two tissue types. The local minimum is a reasonable suggestion if the frequency at this position is low. If the image intensities of two tissue types strongly overlap, there might be no image intensity for which the histogram entry is small. A useful suggestion for a threshold might be derived by analyzing the approximated curvature of the image histogram. A popular threshold selection method, introduced in OTSU [1979], maximizes the separability between different threshold classes in the data based on an initial guess of the thresholds (e.g., $t_1 = max(V)/3, t_2 = 2max(V)/3$, where $max(V)$ is the maximal voxel value in data volume V).

If knowledge about the tissue types in the data and their distribution of gray values is available, threshold selection may be even further supported. In cerebral T2-weighted MRI data, for example, three tissue types, corresponding to white matter, gray matter and cerebrospinal fluid, are available after segmenting the brain. The intensity distribution of these tissue types can be modeled as normal distribution with two parameters μ and σ. Meaningful thresholds can be suggested by fitting the parameters (μ and σ for each of the three tissue types) of the normal distribution to the image histogram (see Fig. 5.11).

Since boundaries between different tissue types are typically represented by rising and falling edges of peaks in the histogram, the distinctness of these peaks is important for threshold-based

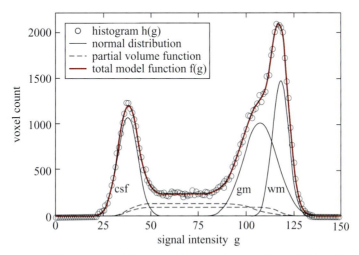

FIGURE 5.11   Fitting normal distributions to the histogram of brain voxels extracted from MRI data. The parameters are optimized by a least square fit. The analysis is employed for brain segmentation by means of thresholding and morphologic operators. "csf" refers to cerebrospinal fluid (the liquid in the cerebral ventricles), "gm" refers to gray matter, and "wm" to white matter [HAHN and PEITGEN 2003]. (Image courtesy HORST HAHN, MeVis Bremen)

segmentation. However, this distinctness is reduced by the partial volume effect and thus by the lack of sufficient spatial resolution. Small structures with a large portion of boundary voxels tend to be blurred and lose this distinctness. With high spatial resolution and low noise level, the histogram contains more clearly discernible peaks. The histogram analysis shown in Figure 5.11 is carried out to support brain segmentation (or skull stripping, as it is often called) [HAHN and PEITGEN 2000]. Brain segmentation is accomplished by thresholding and subsequent morphological operations that will be discussed in Section 5.6. The idea of threshold-based selection can be extended to derived information such as gradient magnitude, where two intervals for intensity and gradient magnitude are specified. Such multidimensional thresholding can also be supported by presenting an appropriate histogram (a 2D histogram in this example). Instead of selecting rectangular regions in a 2D histogram, the user may also specify arbitrary polygons. With such a facility, threshold-based segmentation can be applied to more complex segmentation problems [BOTHA 2005].

Connected Component Analysis   A connected component analysis (CCA) considers the binary image and initializes a first component with the first pixel. The algorithm recursively looks for adjacent pixels in the binary image and adds them to this component. If no more connected pixels are found, and there are still pixels that have not been visited, a new component is initialized. This process terminates when all pixels are processed and assigned to one region. These should be conveyed to the user—for example, by assigning individual colors. For some segmentation tasks, the result corresponds basically to one of the regions. Minor corrections can be carried out in the postprocessing stage (see Sect. 5.6). The CCA is often employed in combination with thresholding—the user selects one component from a previous thresholding operation to segment a particular object (see Fig. 5.12 for bone segmentation by means of a CCA). The combination of threshold-based segmentation, connected component analysis, and morphologic postprocessing (see Sect. 5.6) is a powerful concept for segmentation tasks in which the target objects are represented by homogeneous gray levels. Combined with immediate visual feedback, this concept was introduced and extensively used in the preparation of the VOXELMAN [HÖHNE et al. 1992].

5.3.3 REGION GROWING

A family of segmentation algorithms is based on the concept of growing a connected volumetric region. The standard approach of region growing is similar to threshold-based segmentation (again, a threshold determines which voxels belong to the segmentation result). The major difference to intensity-based thresholding is that *one* connected component is considered (which corresponds to the combination of thresholding and the selection of one connected component by means of a CCA). We start the description with the simple region growing approach and later discuss refined homogeneity criteria.

The growing process is initiated by one or more user-selected seed points and aggregates successively neighboring voxels until a user-selected inclusion criterion is no longer fulfilled (see Fig. 5.13). This inclusion criterion is usually a threshold for the intensity values (collect all voxels with an intensity lower than or equal to the seed point's intensity and above the threshold). With this approach, the user simply specifies seed points that certainly belong to the target structure. Additionally, the user has to provide the threshold as additional parameter. The threshold selection is often a trial-and-error process; the segmentation is started with a certain threshold and then modified until a desired result is achieved. The problem with threshold selection is that the user cannot employ his or her expert knowledge on anatomy and radiology.

Basic region growing is based on a fixed condition, usually one or two thresholds. For the interactive adjustment of these parameters, the basic strategy is too slow. SELLE et al. [2002] introduced a progressive

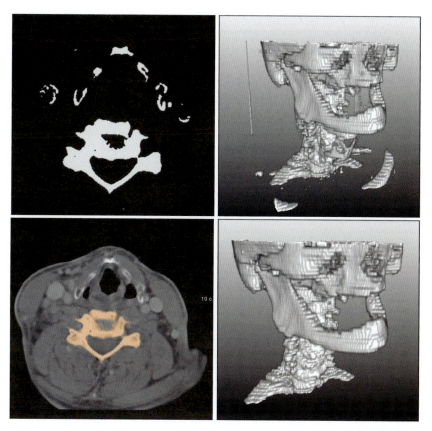

FIGURE 5.12   *Thresholding (above, left and right) as input for a connected component analysis. The largest component represents major parts of the skeletal structure (below, left and right). (Image courtesy JEANETTE CORDES, University of Magdeburg; data courtesy THOMAS SCHULZ, University of Leipzig)*

FIGURE 5.13   *Different stages of a region growing algorithm. Starting from one user-defined seed point (left), successively more voxels are aggregated that fulfill an inclusion criterion. X marks the voxels of the current active wavefront [SELLE et al. 2002]. (Image courtesy DIRK SELLE, MeVis Bremen)*

region growing in which the segmentation is performed for a whole range of thresholds in parallel. This can be effectively accomplished using the fact that the segmented voxel set for a higher (lower) threshold is completely included in the voxel set for a lower threshold. Region growing is often used for the segmentation of contrast-enhanced vascular structures (see [SELLE et al. 2002 and BOSKAMP et al. 2004]). Ideally, one seed point placed in the root of the vascular tree is sufficient to delineate the target structure. In practice, often several seed points have to be chosen and the segmentation results relating to each seed point are combined. The results are often acceptable; however, some kind of preprocessing, such as noise reduction, is often employed to yield good results.

If the goal is to trace vascular structures as far as possible into the periphery, there are better approaches available. Conventional region growing terminates if at one voxel no neighboring voxel is found that satisfies the homogeneity criterion. Due to partial volume effects, there might be regions where voxels of vascular structures are missing because they are surrounded by voxels that do not satisfy the criterion.

As a strategy to improve region growing for vessel segmentation, an initial segmentation result with an appropriate global threshold may be frozen and incrementally expanded, guided by seed points specified by the user. Based on an analysis of the neighborhood of these additional seed points, local thresholds are estimated. With this strategy, the periphery of vascular structures is segmented with other (lower) thresholds than the central parts. Another strategy for handling vessel segmentation is to look for voxels not only in the immediate neighborhood (either with a sophisticated region growing variant or with a completely different segmentation approach).

Advanced Region Growing Methods Region growing might be improved by combining different inclusion criteria. As an example, a lower and an upper threshold define an intensity interval, representing two boundaries, as a criterion. This approach is used in the vessel analysis pipeline introduced by BOSKAMP et al. [2004] to delineate contrast-enhanced vascular structures. The second (upper) threshold prevents leaking into bones, which appear even brighter in CT data. They also incorporate a second criterion: a limit to the gradient magnitude. For a discussion of applications and advanced variants of region growing, please consider SALAH [2006].

Adaptive Threshold Intervals Small inhomogeneities in image data can sometimes lead to situations in which a specified threshold or threshold interval does not fully select a target structure. In those cases, the threshold (interval) needs to adapt to the data. If we extend Equation 5.8 with Equation 5.9 and use the adaptive average threshold a_i instead of a, the threshold interval $[a_i - \epsilon, a_i + \epsilon]$ is adapted after each added voxel $I(v)$. n_{i-1} is here the number of voxels in the current segmentation before adding this voxel (step $i-1$), and a_{i-1} is the respective average threshold before adding [ADAMS and BISCHOF 1994].

$$a_i = \frac{a_{i-1}n_{i-1} + I(v)}{n_{i-1} + 1} \tag{5.9}$$

There are situations where sophisticated criteria do not help to discriminate adjacent structures reliably. In such cases, it is necessary to provide additional interaction facilities. As an example, the user may specify a direction of the growing process or specify barriers that should stop growing.

5.3.4 WATERSHED SEGMENTATION

Watershed segmentation is another region-based method that has its origins in mathematical morphology [SERRA 1982]. The general concept was introduced by DIGABEL and LANTUEJOUL [1978]. A breakthrough in applicability was achieved by VINCENT and SOILLE [1991], who presented an algorithm that is orders of magnitudes faster and more accurate than previous ones (see also HAHN [2005] for a discussion of the "watershed segmentation history"). Since then, it has been widely applied to a variety of medical image segmentation tasks and can now be regarded as a general and important segmentation method.

Watershed segmentation is based on the idea of regarding an image as a topographic landscape with ridges and valleys. The elevation values of the landscape are typically defined by the gray values of the respective pixels or their gradient magnitude. Based on such a 3D representation, the watershed transform decomposes an image into regions called *catchment basins*. For each local minimum, a catchment basin comprises all points whose path of steepest descent terminates at this minimum (see Fig. 5.14). Watersheds are the border lines that separate basins from each other. The watershed transform decomposes an image completely and thus assigns each pixel either to a region or a watershed. With noisy medical image data, typically a large number of small regions arise. This is known as the "oversegmentation" problem, since these regions are generally much smaller than the anatomical target structures (see Fig. 5.15).

The most widespread variant employs the gradient images (recall Sect. 5.2.6) as the basis for the watershed transform. Gradient magnitude, however, is strongly sensitive to image noise. Therefore, appropriate filtering is essential. There are many variants in how the watershed transform may be used as a basis for a general segmentation approach. The "oversegmentation" problem must be solved by using some criteria for merging regions, and the user must be provided with facilities to influence the segmentation result. We describe the approach introduced by HAHN and PEITGEN [2000] and later refined in [HAHN and PEITGEN 2003].

Merging Basins   The decomposition of the image into regions is the basis for merging them. In the metaphorical sense of a landscape, catchment basins are merged at their watershed locations by flooding them. While some regions merge early (with low flooding level), other regions are merged later (with higher flooding levels) (see Fig. 5.16). To support interactive merging, HAHN and PEITGEN [2003] introduced a *merge tree*. This tree consists of the original catchment basins as leaves and of intermediate nodes that represent *merging events*. A merging event is characterized by the nodes merged and by the flood level necessary for merging. As the first step of segmenting an image with the watershed transform, a certain amount of flooding may be applied ("preflooding", see [HAHN and PEITGEN 2000]). The watershed transform can be also applied to 3D images. In this case, 4D height images arise by regarding intensity values of 3D data as height values. If the segmentation target structure corresponds to one region achieved after some preflooding, the segmentation is completed.

Marker-based Watershed   Often, however, no examined flooding level is sufficient to segment target structures precisely. Therefore, the user may specify image locations that belong to the target structure (include

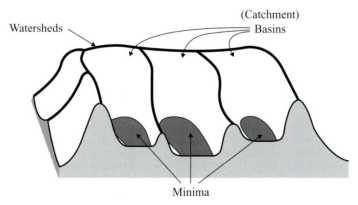

FIGURE 5.14   *Principle of the watershed transform, in which the intensity values define hills and basins. For segmentation purposes, basins may be flooded in order to combine corresponding regions* [HAHN 2005]. *(Image courtesy HORST HAHN, MeVis Bremen)*

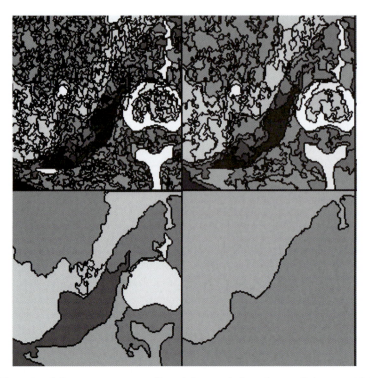

FIGURE 5.15 *Illustration of the oversegmentation problem of the watershed transform applied to an axial slice of a CT image. Individual basins are merged to form successively larger regions. (Image courtesy* THOMAS SCHINDEWOLF, *MeVis Bremen)*

points), or that do not belong the target structure (exclude points). If the user specifies an include point and an exclude point, an additional watershed is constructed at the maximum level between them. The watershed prevents the regions represented by the include and exclude points from being merged (see Fig. 5.17). The merge tree is traversed so that each region contains either include points or exclude points, but not both. This interaction style is called *marker-based watershed segmentation*.

Applications   The watershed transform has been successfully applied to a variety of segmentation tasks. HAHN and PEITGEN [2000] demonstrated that the brain could be extracted with a single watershed transform from MRI data. Also, the cerebral ventricles were reliably segmented with minimal interaction (see Fig. 5.18). HAHN and PEITGEN [2003] show, among other applications, the solution to the challenging problem of delineating individual bones in the human wrist (see Fig. 5.19). KUHNIGK et al. [2003] employ the above-described variant of the watershed segmentation to the delineation of lung lobes in CT data.

Other Variants of the Watershed Transform   There are many variants of the watershed transform, making it possible to adapt the method to a variety of applications. For example, merging may consider also gradient information or other criteria for homogeneity. A frequently used variant is to merge regions where the difference of the mean gray value is below a threshold. This process can be carried out iteratively and results in a hierarchical merging tree.

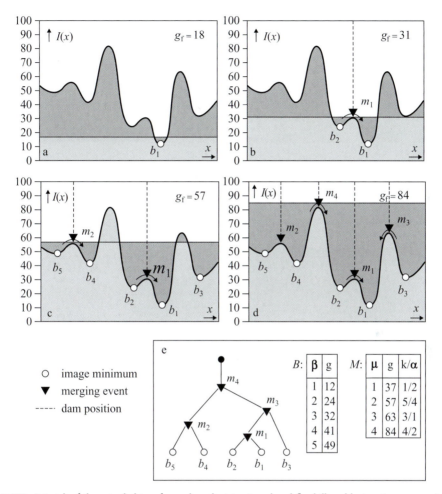

FIGURE 5.16 Principle of the watershed transform where the intensity values define hills and basins. For segmentation purposes, basins may be flooded in order to combine corresponding regions. As result, a merge tree arises [HAHN and PEITGEN 2003]. (Images courtesy HORST HAHN, MeVis Bremen)

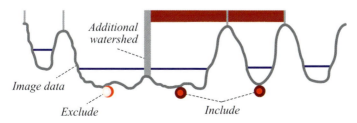

FIGURE 5.17 The image data are considered as a landscape and flooded to merge small basins. To prevent merging, an additional watershed is erected between an include and an exclude point specified by the user. (Image courtesy HORST HAHN, MeVis Bremen)

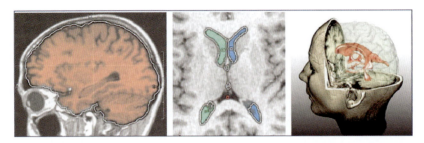

FIGURE 5.18 *Watershed segmentation of the brain (left) and the cerebral ventricles (middle) from T1-weighted MRI data. The segmentation result is shown as enhanced contour. The right image shows the segmentation result as semitransparent 3D isosurface rendering* [HAHN and PEITGEN 2003]. *(Image courtesy HORST HAHN, MeVis Bremen)*

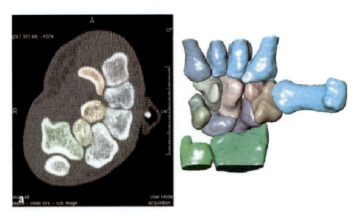

FIGURE 5.19 *Watershed segmentation was successfully applied to the segmentation of individual bones from CT data. While bones are relatively easy to distinguish from other structures, the challenge is to delineate individual bones* [HAHN and PEITGEN 2003]. *(Images courtesy HORST HAHN, MeVis Bremen)*

5.3.5 LIVEWIRE SEGMENTATION

While region growing directly generates the region that belongs to the target structure, livewire and its variant, live-lane, are edge-based segmentation methods [FALCAO et al. 1998]. Livewire was introduced by MORTENSEN et al. [1992] and UDUPA et al. [1992]. It is also known under the name "Intelligent Scissors." As a result of livewire segmentation, the contours of the target structure in each slice of a 3D dataset are available.

Livewire is based on the definition of a cost function, and it selects paths with minimal costs (movements along boundaries with strong gradients in general have low costs). Minimal cost paths are computed by Dijkstra's graph search algorithm [DIJKSTRA 1959]. For this purpose, an image is represented as a graph, with vertices representing image pixels and edges representing costs of connections between neighboring pixels. The edges are directed and the orientation is opposite to each other. The "inside" of a directed edge is considered to be the left of this edge. Costs are assigned to every directed edge [KIM and HORLI 2000]. Intensity to the left and to the right, gradient magnitude and direction, and the

Laplacian zero crossing (the approximated second-order derivative of the image data) may be part of the cost function computation. Equation 5.10 is a general cost function for the computation of the local cost of an edge connecting the pixels p and q. It is a weighted sum of different components: the Laplacian zero crossing $f_z(q)$, which indicates proximity of the pixel q to an edge; $f_g(q)$, which represents the gradient magnitude at pixel q; and $f_D(p, q)$, which represents the gradient direction. The latter term is employed as a smoothness constraint: high costs are associated with sharp changes in the boundary direction. The weights w_z, w_g, and w_d can be adapted to the properties of the segmentation target object.

$$l(p, q) = w_z \cdot f_z(q) + w_g \cdot f_g(q) + w_d \cdot f_D(p, q) \qquad (5.10)$$

Figure 5.20 illustrates the traversal of the graph using the Dijkstra algorithm. Starting from seedpoint s, minimal cost paths are searched. After four iterations, during which the costs to all local neighbors are considered, minimal cost paths to eight neighbors are computed. This process can be repeated until all pixels have been processed; it results in a *cost image*.

Since the computed connections in the graph are directed, it is essential that the user draws the contour in the same way that the cost function computation assumes (usually counterclockwise).

Costs are computed from a user-selected control point to the current mouse position. The contour associated with the lowest accumulated cost is highlighted. Ideally, the resulting path wraps around the target object. If the path deviates from the target object's boundary, the mouse is moved back until the suggested contour and the desired contour coincide and an additional control point is marked interactively. Thus, a first path segment is specified. The second control point becomes the new seed point and is used to define the next path segment. This process is repeated until the boundary is

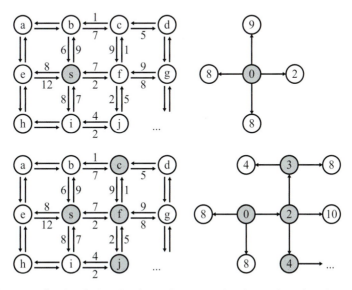

FIGURE 5.20 *Illustration of Dijkstra's algorithm for searching minimal paths in a directed graph. In each iteration, the local neighbors of all nodes which have been processed are considered with respect to their costs. After three iterations, it turns out that the path from s to b via f and c is associated with lower costs than the direct edge between s and b. Therefore, the edge from s to b was removed. (Image courtesy ANDREA SCHENK, MeVis Bremen)*

closed. The name "livewire" describes the appearance of a wire that trembles between a few possible paths, if the mouse is moved.

The success of this segmentation method critically depends on the suitability of the cost function. In general, the cost function considers gray values of the relevant object (mean value and standard deviation), gray values of surrounding objects, strength of image gradients, and second-order derivatives in the gradient direction. Each factor might be assigned a certain weight that determines its influence. If the cost function perfectly fits to the target structure, the contour of an object might be defined with two mouse-clicks (see Fig. 5.21). If the cost function is less suitable, the contour typically deviates from the target structure and the user must specify a larger number of control points. In worst-case situations, livewire is not better than manual drawing. The choice of a good cost function can be supported by appropriate default values for certain structures. In particular, the standardized Hounsfield values of CT data are useful for the generation of cost functions.

It is a good strategy to compute the costs of all possible paths and to generate a *cost image* based on that information. An appropriate cost function would generate a cost image in which the target structure's boundary had a strong contrast to its surroundings, ideally in the whole image. If the user has to specify many control points, he or she should attempt to change the cost function and verify whether the cost image more clearly delineates the target object. In Figure 5.22 (left), the cost function is not suitable to efficiently segment the liver from CT data. The right cost image certainly allows a faster segmentation, since the target object exhibits a clear boundary.

Livewire and Shape-based Interpolation   Livewire is a segmentation approach operated in a slice-oriented way. Since radiologists and their technical assistants are used to analyze and explore medical image data in a slice-oriented way, this approach is well accepted.

However, the original livewire approach is still rather laborious for the segmentation of larger 3D objects. Depending on the image resolution and the object size, an object might well be part of 100 or more slices. Therefore, the overall effort to segment an object with livewire may take 20 minutes, even if a suitable cost function is chosen. Another problem is the 3D slice consistency, since the defined contours of neighboring slices may deviate significantly.

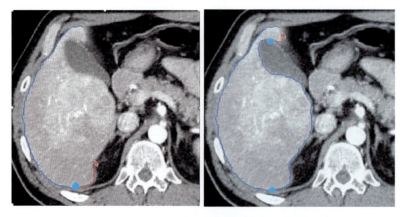

FIGURE 5.21 *Two stages in the segmentation of an organ with livewire. Two control points are necessary to precisely define the liver outline based on a suitable cost function. (Image courtesy ANDREA SCHENK, MeVis Bremen)*

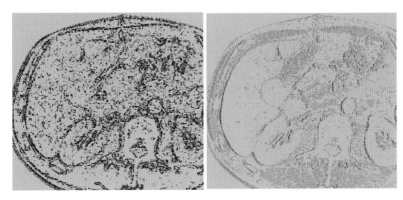

FIGURE 5.22   *Cost images related to livewire segmentation. The target object is the liver, which is not clearly visible in the left cost image; in the right image, the liver is clearly delineated. (Image courtesy* ANDREA SCHENK, *MeVis Bremen)*

To reduce the interaction effort and potential slice inconsistencies, livewire has been combined with interpolation methods [SCHENK et al. 2000]. Interpolation is employed to skip *intermediate slices* and reduce the specification of control points to a subset of *key slices*. If the interpolation is carried out for intermediate slices S_1 and S_2, a binary image of the two slices is generated, with "1" representing the pixels on the contour and "0" representing all other pixels. Based on these binary images, a distance transformed image is computed (entries represent the Euclidean distance to the object contour with positive values for inside pixels and negative values for outside pixels). The interpolation is performed as a gray value interpolation of the distance values (recall SCHENK et al. [2000]). In intermediate slices, the pixels with an assigned "0" are regarded as interpolated contours.

The interpolation of contours, however, does not produce ideal results; better correspondence to the target structure is achieved if the cost function is also employed for interpolated slices, to pull the contour to the target structure. Figure 5.23 shows how an interpolated contour of the liver in CT data is improved (automatically) by means of the cost function.

For the segmentation of the liver in CT data, SCHENK et al. [2000] were able to demonstrate that the number of slices and the overall segmentation effort could be considerably decreased while only minimally reducing accuracy. The number of slices that can be skipped depends on the image resolution: for CT liver data, it turned out that it was sufficient to manually segment slices in a distance of 12 mm (for 4 mm slice distance, two slices are skipped; for 2 mm slice distance, five slices are skipped).

However, the selection of slices for which the contour is specified manually should be carried out carefully. If the topology changes, for example, it is advisable to specify more contours. Topology changes typically occur if, for example, the target structure consists of a closed contour in one slice and two contours in other slices, e.g., in case of branching structures. This situation can be handled by shape-based interpolation; however, deviations from the desired result are more likely to occur.

Livewire and Adaptive Propagation   Another alternative to the specification of intermediate slices is the adaptive propagation of livewire control points into the next slice with an as-yet unspecified contour [SALAH et al. 2005b]. Similar to shape-based interpolation, the control points are pulled toward the contour of the local target, based on the cost function. In contrast to shape-based interpolation, the contour of adaptive propagation depends only on the control points of the previous slice, and thus may adapt better to

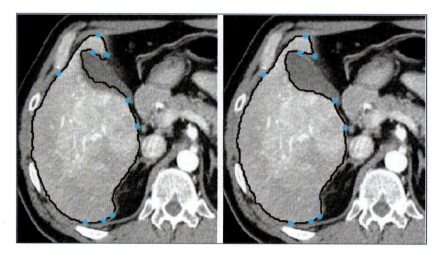

FIGURE 5.23 *Abdominal CT data with segmented liver parenchyma: Left: Image with shape-based interpolated contour and approximated control points from the two adjacent userdefined slices; larger deviations occur at the gallbladder (dark gray). Right: contour after automated optimization with livewire* [SCHENK *et al.* 2000]. *(Images courtesy* ANDREA SCHENK, *MeVis Bremen)*

local changes of the anatomy. However, topological changes may not be handled and may require the interactive specification of the control points.

As another potential feature, adaptive propagation does not rely on closed contours. In particular, livewires that perform a clipping operation to remove an oversegmented region ("separation wires") or that correct already established contours can be propagated through several slices.

Overall, adaptive propagation enabled the automatic contour specification of intermediate slices. In the context of the highly variable contour of the petrous portion of the temporal bone ("mastoid"), up to 46% of the slices were successfully generated by adaptive propagation, while only up to 27% could be computed by shape-based interpolation. However, these results may vary significantly with different organs, depending on their variability.

Discussion The result of livewire segmentation (and other edge-based methods) is a stack of contours represented as polygons or parametric curves. To use these results for a quantitative analysis as well as for visualization, it is necessary to convert the contours to regions (sets of voxels that represent the inner part of the target structure). The transformation of a (closed) contour to a region is carried out by a filling algorithm—a basic algorithm in computer graphics [FOLEY *et al.* 1995]. Since a livewire contour is a (possibly partial) directed line loop, the inside can be determined easily.

Livewire is a general segmentation method. It works best for compact and large objects that do not have many indentations. Brain segmentation, for example, would be a task for which livewire is not appropriate—the user would have to set at least one seed point in every sulcus. In addition to using livewire for the primary segmentation, it may also be used to correct segmentation results, even if they were generated using other methods. The slice-oriented process is again attractive for physicians [SALAH 2006]. Livewire is also less suited if the data are rather inhomogeneous, such as MRI data. In such data, a completely different cost function might be required in different regions of an image [SCHENK *et al.* 2001]. MRI-inhomogeneity correction would be required to apply livewire successfully to MRI data. Similar to other segmentation methods, livewire benefits from filtering; simple noise reduction filters are often sufficient (recall Sect. 5.2.4).

5.4   MODEL-BASED SEGMENTATION METHODS

In this section, we give an overview of strategies that better support specialized segmentation tasks. These strategies all employ knowledge of the size and shape of objects or of gray level distributions for the segmentation. Characteristic landmarks, symmetry considerations, or typical orientations of the target structure may also be employed. In therapy planning applications, there is often a variety of segmentation target objects. Some of these objects have a rather fixed location in relation to other's. With an appropriate sequence of the segmentation steps the relative location might be employed for the segmentation.

Segmentation methods which rely on such kind of knowledge are referred to as *model-based segmentation*. Strictly speaking, livewire is also a model-based approach. Assumptions concerning gray value distributions and gradient characteristics are part of the cost function. We discussed it as a general method, since the knowledge incorporated in the livewire cost function is rather low level and can be easily adapted to other structures.

We start the discussion of model-based segmentation approaches with *active contour models*, a widespread variant of the general approach of fitting *deformable models* to the segmentation target structure. Deformable models are based on a flexible geometric representation, such as b-splines, that provides the degree of freedom necessary to adapt the model to a large variety of shapes. The process of fitting the model to the target structure is guided by physical principles and constraints, which restrict, for example, the curvature along the boundary. The application of *deformable models* is guided by principles of elasticity theory, which describe how a deformable body responds to the forces exerted on it. The resulting shape variations depend on some assumed stiffness properties of that body. The use of deformable models for image segmentation was suggested by TERZOPOULOS et al. [1988] and has been used intensively since.

5.4.1 ACTIVE CONTOUR MODELS

Active contour models or *snakes*, as they are often called, are a variant of deformable models, in which initial contours are algorithmically deformed towards edges in the image [KASS et al. 1988]. They are primarily used to approximate the shape of object boundaries under the assumption that the boundaries are smooth. The name *snake* is motivated by the behavior of such models, which adapt a contour between two control points like a snake.

Active contour models rely on an initial contour, which is either supplied by the user or derived from *a priori* knowledge (concerning geometric constraints, data constraints such as range of expected gray level, and knowledge concerning object shapes). Starting from the initial contour, an energy functional is minimized based on contour deformation and external image forces. This optimization process cannot guarantee that a global minimum is actually found. Instead, a local minimum based on the initial contour is accepted.

The energy function with a parametric description of the curve $v(s) = (x(s), y(s))^T$, where $x(s)$ and $y(s)$ represent the coordinates along the curve $s \in [0, 1]$ is described by Equation 5.11.

$$E_{contour} = \int_0^1 [E_{int}(v(s)) + E_{ext}(v(s))]ds \qquad (5.11)$$

The inner energy E_{int} (see Eq. 5.12) represents the smoothness of the curve and can be flexibly parameterized by α and β to encode expectations concerning the smoothness and elasticity of the target structure's contour. High α values, for example, contract the curve. Usually, α and β are constant [LEHMANN et al. 2003].

$$E_{int} = \alpha(s) \left| \frac{dv}{ds} \right|^2 + \beta(s) \left| \frac{d^2v}{ds^2} \right|^2 \qquad (5.12)$$

The external energy E_{ext} counteracts the inner energy and is derived by the gray values and the gradient of the image according to Equation 5.13.

$$E_{ext} = w_1 f(x, y) - w_2 |\nabla(G_\sigma(x, y) * f(x, y))|^2 \qquad (5.13)$$

w_1 and w_2 are weights that represent the influence of the gray value ($f(x, y)$) and the gradient $\nabla(G)$. The gray values are assumed to be normally distributed. The σ value characterizes the standard deviation of this distribution. The suitability of the parameter values strongly depends on the initialization; if it can be assumed that they are close to the final results, for example, lower σ values are suitable.

The curves are usually represented as (cubic) b-splines, which has the advantage that the resulting segmentation is smooth (continuous first-order derivatives). The actual realization of the functional is very application specific—similar to the cost function on which livewire is based (recall Sect. 5.3.5).

3D Extension For 3D segmentation, active contour models are applied slice by slice, which is not only laborious but also poses problems in the composition of a continuous surface based on a stack of contours. To better support 3D segmentation, the fitted contour in one slice may be used as the initial contour in neighboring slices [LIN and CHEN 1989]. This process of contour propagation can be applied in a similar way to livewire segmentation. Also, a combination with shape-based interpolation is feasible.

Active contour models have been extended to 3D, which is known as balloon segmentation [TERZOPOULOS et al. 1988]. Balloon segmentation is based on deforming surfaces instead of contours. This variant of deformable models is accomplished by interactively fitting a polygonal representation of the initial shape to the target structure. There are two approaches to initiating the segmentation process: either the user selects small volumes that are iteratively inflated until the forces converge, or the user specifies enclosing volumes that are iteratively deflated. Figure 5.24 illustrates the inflation approach with an application to tumor segmentation.

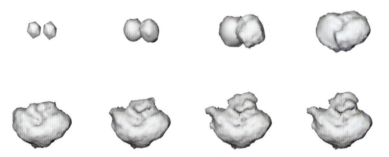

FIGURE 5.24 *Infiltrating balloon segmentation starting from the two small volumes in the upper left. After 40 iterations the final result is achieved (lower right image). (Image courtesy OLAF KONRAD-VERSE, MeVis Bremen.)*

These 3D extensions bear great potential; however, they pose some challenging user-interface problems (e.g., 3D interaction with 2D input and output devices).

Discussion   The internal energy constraints of active contour models restrict their flexibility and prevent the formation of tube-like shapes, branching structures, or objects with strong protrusions [MCINERNEY and TERZOPOULOS 1996]. Therefore, they are generally not applied for the segmentation of vascular or bronchial trees.

A problem of active contours (and their 3D extension) is the strong dependence on a proper initialization; the contour might otherwise be attracted by a "wrong" edge in an image. Although nice results can be presented in many publications, active contour models are (still) not widespread in clinical applications due to their difficult parameterization. This may change in the near future, provided that solutions are carefully fine-tuned and evaluated for special segmentation tasks.

5.4.2 LEVEL SETS AND FAST MARCHING METHODS

If region growing is considered as a dynamic process, the progressing boundary can be regarded as wave front propagating through the target object. This interpretation is the basis for level sets and fast marching methods [SETHIAN 1999]. The wave propagation is guided by image features such as image intensity and gradient. Level sets are considered an implicit formulation of deformable models. However, the contour is not manipulated directly. Instead, the contour is embedded as the *zero level set* in a higher dimensional function, the level set function $\psi(X, t)$. The parameters are specified in such a way that progression toward the target object's boundaries slows. More precisely, the level set function is evolved under control of a partial differential equation. The evolving contour can be determined by extracting the zero-level set.

$$\Gamma((X), t) = \psi(X, t) = 0 \tag{5.14}$$

Applying Equation 5.14 determines all points at height 0 of the embedding function. Level set segmentation is able to handle complex anatomical shapes with arbitrary topology. Fast marching methods are closely related. They are used for segmentation tasks where the wave front always moves either forward or backward. In comparison, level set segmentation is slower but more general than fast marching methods.

There are many applications of level set methods for image segmentation. As an example, AVANTS and WILLIAMS [2000] and VAN BEMMEL et al. [2002] segment vascular structures with level sets. The segmentation of layered anatomical structures, such as the cortex (the outermost layer of gray matter in the brain), can be performed well with level sets [ZENG et al. 1999].

5.4.3 ACTIVE SHAPE MODELS

Active shape models (ASMs) are parameterizable descriptions of the shape of anatomical structures. In contrast to deformable models, ASM are based on a statistical analysis of a representative sample of training data. Due to their origin in statistical analysis, ASMs are also referred to as *statistical models*.

The parameterization allows to adapt the default model to different shape variants. For segmentation, parameters are searched that optimally adapt the shape model to the target structure in a particular dataset. The model is derived from appropriate training data with a set of shapes $S_i (i = 1, ..., N)$, each of which is represented by the same set of M points (this set is referred to as *point distribution model*). These points should be roughly equally spaced along the surface. Note that it is essential to be able to find a corresponding landmark point for each landmark in the other dataset.

After all the landmarks for the individual shapes are determined, they are aligned with each other. In this process, the shapes are translated, rotated, and scaled to minimize the differences between corresponding landmarks. An important tool for analyzing the variability of the landmarks' positions is the principal component analysis (PCA). This statistical method delivers a set of ordered orthogonal basis vectors that represent the directions of progressively smaller variance. The dimensionality of the correlated datasets can be reduced with the PCA results by retaining the first principle vectors [MORRISON 2005, JOLLIFFE 1986]. The use of PCA for statistical models is described in detail in the following.

The mean shape vector $\bar{v}$ represents the average of each point M_i. The variability of the points can be expressed by means of the covariance matrix C (see Eq. 5.15). The PCA of the point distribution model is a high-dimensional problem (the number of dimensions corresponds to the number of landmarks and is thus often greater than 50).

$$C = \frac{1}{N-1} \sum_{1=1}^{N} (S_i - \bar{S})(S_i - \bar{S}^T)) \qquad (5.15)$$

With a PCA, the eigenvectors e_i and eigenvalues λ_i of C are determined, fulfilling Equation 5.16.

$$C \cdot e_i = \lambda_i \cdot e_i \qquad (5.16)$$

They are determined by calculating the roots of the characteristic polynomial of C of degree n. Each shape vector can be expressed as a linear model of the form:

$$S_i = \bar{S} + Cb_i = S + \sum_{k=1}^{n} E^k b_i^k \qquad (5.17)$$

where $E = e^k$ is the matrix of eigenvectors of the covariance matrix.

The eigenvalues are sorted ($\lambda_i \geq \lambda_{i+1}$) and the eigenvectors are labeled so that e_i corresponds to λ_i. The order of the λ_i characterizes the influence of points on the object shape. Usually, a small number of points account for most of the variation. This gives rise to an approximation with the largest t eigenvalues, which explain, for example, 95% of the object shape's variability. A shape is then approximated by finding optimal weights b_s for the significant modes of variations ($e_1, e_2, \ldots, e_t$). These eigenvectors are concatenated to a matrix P_s. Equation 5.17 can now be replaced by an approximation (see Eq. 5.18).

$$S_i \approx \bar{S} + P_s b_s \qquad (5.18)$$

If too many parameters are necessary to characterize individual shapes precisely enough, very large training data sets would be required and the search process would be too laborious.

The shape parameters b represent weights that control the modes of variation and thus the variability of the shape. The variability of a particular landmark is suitably restricted. A common restriction is to permit a variance related to the statistical variance of this landmark. If the shapes are assumed to represent a Gaussian distribution, 99% of all shapes in the training data are within the bounds $\pm 3\sqrt{\lambda_i}$. With such restrictions, the ASM represents an *allowable shape domain* [COOTES et al. 1994]. In other words, with an ASM it is feasible to segment shapes correctly, provided that each landmark does not deviate more from its mean value than all shapes in the training set. As an example, an ASM for an organ derived from adult data will most likely not successfully segment the same organ in a small child, where not just the size but also the shape might differ significantly.

For 3D segmentation, finding the correspondence of landmarks between surfaces is the most challenging problem. Mathematically, an optimal match between anatomically equivalent features is determined.

Model Fitting   The fitting of the model must be properly initiated—for example, by a user-selected central point or roughly defined shape. Starting from the mean shape, all landmarks (starting with the most significant mode of variation) are translated perpendicular to the contour and evaluated until the contour remains stable.

Requirements   Although the basic idea of segmenting objects by means of ASMs is easily explained, it is demanding and time-consuming to realize it. The quality of the segmentation strongly depends on the quality of the acquired model. The model is derived by segmentations from a training data set and has to fulfill several requirements:

- The training data set should be large enough to statistically characterize shape parameters. It is not reasonable to present a minimum number of test cases covering all applications, but as a rule of thumb, there should be more than 20 training cases.
- The training set of datasets should comprise a representative selection of the anatomical variants. If certain variants occur, they must be part of the training set. Otherwise, the model cannot be used to fit to such parameters. If it turns out that an initial ASM of the target structure has many variables that characterize its shape, a larger training set will be needed compared to shapes with little variability.
- The quality of the segmentations must be very high, which means that the segmentation result is either produced manually, as accurately as possible, or—if generated with a semi-interactive approach—carefully verified and modified, if necessary.
- A prerequisite for the comparison of training data sets is that all coordinates refer to a common reference frame. Therefore, the surfaces have to be aligned (translated, scaled, and rotated) so that the correspondence between the shapes is optimal (the distances between corresponding points are minimal).
- The model generation process relies on the definition of corresponding landmark points, which allow comparison of the shapes. It is necessary to determine enough points that actually have a correspondence with all other segmentation results.

The list of requirements makes it clear that the effort to create an appropriate model is significant. Therefore, this effort is only justified if it addresses a frequent segmentation task.

Applications   The first application of ASM was the segmentation of the left heart ventricle in echocardiograms and MRI data [COOTES et al. 1994]. Successful applications have been realized for liver segmentation (see Fig. 5.25) [LAMECKER et al. 2002] and pelvic bone segmentation (see Fig. 5.26) [LAMECKER et al. 2004].

For both applications, it turned out to be difficult to realize correspondence for the whole anatomical structure. Instead, the structures are subdivided into substructures; the liver, for example, in four substructures, three of which represent liver lobes. The pelvic bone was subdivided into 11 substructures. This process has to be carried out for each dataset; therefore, automatic support is a very important goal. LAMECKER et al. [2002] suggest that substructures are chosen that can be identified automatically by locating and connecting features with high curvature.

The model generation for the pelvic bone was more challenging because of the complex topology (genus three; that means that the pelvic bone has three holes). On the other hand, the shape of the pelvic bone is less variable; three main modes of variation were considered. The liver model, in comparison, considers 21 modes of variation resulting from 43 datasets. Probably a larger training set would still increase the number of significant modes.

Both models have been carefully validated. The statistical liver model was validated using 30 datasets that were not part of the training set.

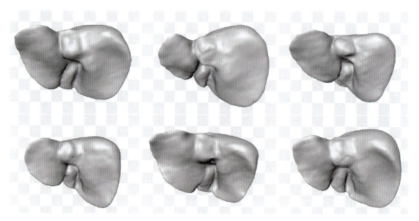

FIGURE 5.25   *Variability of the ASM of the liver. In each column, one eigenmode is varied. The left column presents the variability of the largest eigenvalue, the middle and the right columns the 2nd- and 3rd-largest eigenvalues, respectively [LAMECKER et al. 2004]. (Image courtesy HANS LAMECKER, Zuse-Institute Berlin)*

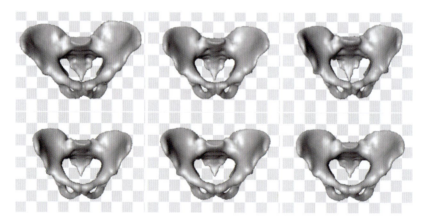

FIGURE 5.26   *Variability of the ASM of the pelvic bone. Similar to Figure 5.25 the variation with respect to three largest eigenvalues is shown in each column LAMECKER et al. [2004]. (Image courtesy HANS LAMECKER, Zuse-Institute Berlin)*

There are many more applications of ASMs for medical image segmentation, including tubular structures and structures with different topologies. For 3D segmentation, establishing correspondences between landmarks is the most challenging problem. Different problem-specific strategies to the correspondence problem have been described [BRECHBUEHLER et al. 1995, BRETT et al. 1997, LORENZ and KRAHNSTÖVER 1999, DE BRUIJNE et al. 2002].

5.4.4 ACTIVE APPEARANCE MODELS

ASMs capture assumptions on the variability of the target structure's shape, but they ignore gray value distributions. In contrast, active appearance models (AAM) are based on active shape models and take the gray value distributions into account. An AAM is constructed by adjusting differences between the shapes using the point distribution model and the PCA. With this strategy, each shape is transformed to the mean shape $\bar{S}$. As the shapes are sized and oriented in a different way, the transformation requires a resampling of the gray values (new pixel values in the normalized dataset are determined as weighted average of pixels in the original dataset).

In these normalized shapes, the gray value distribution is analyzed, and again a PCA is employed to find out which modes of variation are significant. The most advanced variant also considers the correlation between the variability of gray values and object shapes [COOTES et al. 1998b]. It is performed by another PCA applied to a matrix that contains information from the shape model analysis and from the appearance model analysis.

For the segmentation with AAM, the model must be fitted to the (new) dataset. This fitting process can be guided by intensity profiles along the surface normal, which represent expectations concerning gray values and gradients. To enhance the correspondence between these profiles in the training data and the real data, diffusion filtering might be very useful (recall Sect. 5.2).

Summary   ASMs were introduced by COOTES et al. [1998a]; the extension to active appearance models has also been suggested by COOTES et al. [2001]. AAMs are more specialized; for example, they cannot be applied to CT and MRI data simultaneously.

A comparison of AAMs and ASMs carried out for MRI data of the knee and brain documented the benefit of including assumptions concerning gray level distributions [COOTES et al. 1998b, COTIN et al. 1999]. Segmentation with active shape models is feasible, if the variability of the shapes of an anatomical structure is not too large. The required effort to build such a model is considerable; STEGMANN et al. [2000] contributed a flexible and publicly available implementation of AAMs [STEGMANN et al. 2003].

Discussion   AAMs were introduced more recently than active contour models. They are also more specialized and require a very time-consuming model-building process. In principle, they may reduce the interaction effort considerably, compared to active contour models or livewire. However, despite some successful segmentation applications, AAMs and ASMs are considerably restricted in their applicability. For anatomical structures that exhibit a strong variability or complex folding patterns, such as the brain, they are not appropriate.

5.4.5 INCORPORATING MODEL ASSUMPTIONS IN REGION-GROWING SEGMENTATION

In this section, we discuss how a general segmentation method, namely region growing, can be refined and adapted by incorporating some model assumptions. If region growing is employed for the segmentation of vascular structures in contrast-enhanced data, it is a reasonable assumption that the cross-section of these structures is roughly elliptical. It is also reasonable to assume that these structures are at similar locations in adjacent slices. With these assumptions, region growing may be initiated by a seed point specified by the user. The interval for the growing process may be estimated by analyzing the 3D surroundings, and evaluating how many voxels would be segmented with a particular threshold (a sudden increase in this number indicates a crossing of the border of contrast-enhanced structures). The assumption of an elliptical cross-section is employed by fitting an ellipse to the detected cross-section (see Fig. 5.27) and to restrict the segmentation result to this ellipse. The segmentation result in one slice is propagated to the next slice and refined with respect to the thresholds. HENNEMUTH et al. [2005] designed this approach and refined it even further with assumptions suitable to delineate coronary vessels. They showed that even in the presence of noise and plaque, reasonable segmentation results were achieved based on only one seed point specified by the user (see Fig. 5.28).

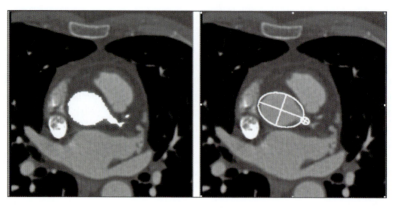

FIGURE 5.27 *An ellipse fit is applied to restrict a segmentation result (cross-section of the coronary artery [HENNEMUTH et al. 2005]. (Image courtesy ANJA HENNEMUTH, MeVis Bremen, data courtesy University of Münster, Institute of Clinical Radiology)*

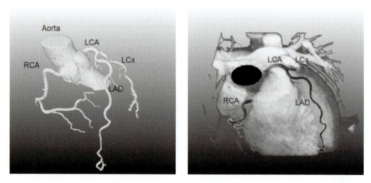

FIGURE 5.28 *Coronary tree automatically segmented with an advanced region-growing. LCA and RCA denote the left and right coronary artery, LCx denotes the circumflex artery, and LAD the left anterior descending artery [HENNEMUTH et al. 2005]. (Image courtesy ANJA HENNEMUTH, MeVis Bremen, data courtesy University of Erlangen Department of Radiology)*

5.5   INTERACTION TECHNIQUES

The feasibility and acceptance of image analysis methods strongly depend on the required amount and style of user interaction. Some methods may produce excellent results with almost no interaction in many cases, but lack appropriate interaction facilities in other cases. Often, segmentation is an iterative process where intermediate results are fine-tuned. While some methods support a directed improvement of intermediate results, others are based on trial and error. The topic of interaction issues in image segmentation is widely ignored; research and development are strongly focused on algorithms. A dedicated effort to understand interaction issues in image segmentation has been attempted by OLABARRIAGA and SMEULDERS [2001]. They emphasize that medical doctors have no difficulties in specifying points inside or outside the target structure or roughly encircling it for the initialization. However, they found that difficulties arise when users have to specify numerical input, such as the average gradient magnitude of the target structure. The following considerations are based on their work.

The discussion of user interface issues for image segmentation is guided by some general considerations regarding human computer collaboration based on SHNEIDERMAN [1997]. He emphasizes that computers are generally better at:

- Counting or measuring physical quantities
- Processing quantitative data in prespecified ways
- Maintaining performance over extended periods of time

Humans, on the other hand, are better at:

- Detecting stimuli on noisy background
- Adapting decisions to specific situations
- Selecting alternatives if an original approach fails

The design of interaction techniques for image segmentation should take into account the strength and weaknesses of human beings.

5.5.1 INTERACTION TECHNIQUES FOR REGION GROWING

An efficient support for region-growing methods is a diagram that indicates the size of the segmentation result for a range of thresholds (see Fig. 5.29). The creation of this diagram requires initiation of the algorithm for all integer values in a certain interval (recall Sect. 5.3.3). We refer to this diagram as the threshold-volume diagram. With this feature, users can deliberately specify a threshold that prevents

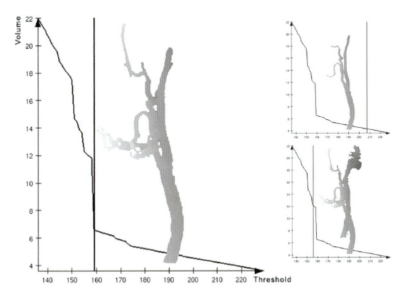

FIGURE 5.29 *The volume of the segmented structure is shown for a range of intensity values. With the vertical bar the user can specify a threshold. The visualization result is shown as a point cloud* [SELLE et al. 2002]. *(Image courtesy* DIRK SELLE, *MeVies Bremen)*

segmentation leaks into surrounding structures. Reasonable candidates can be identified as locations of large steps in the threshold curve.

Similarly, these thresholds can also be estimated directly from the histogram value distribution near the seed point [SALAH et al. 2003] or by further analysis of the region around the seed point to estimate parameters for the growing process. Mean gray value and standard deviation might be used to suggest a threshold for the user. Adaptive region-growing variants are discussed in [POHLE and TOENNIES 2001, 2002].

5.5.2 INTERACTION TECHNIQUES FOR WATERSHED SEGMENTATION

The basic interaction of image segmentation with the watershed transform is to specify include and exclude points or regions, referred to as markers. On one hand, it is easy for users to specify which point belongs to the target structure and which does not. On the other hand, it is often difficult to estimate how many include and exclude markers have to be specified until a reasonable result is achieved. Similar to region growing, the user cannot force the boundary to be at a particular location where he or she expects the boundary to be.

Another issue of watershed segmentation is the difficulty of predicting the effects of the specification of include and exclude points. Under unfavorable conditions, the following sequence of interactions arises: the user specifies (several) markers in slice S_1 until a desired segmentation in this slice is achieved. He moves to another slice S_2 and recognizes that the target structure is not well segmented. Again, include and exclude markers are specified until the result is satisfying in S_2. The user goes back to slice S_1 to assess the effect of the new include and exclude markers on the segmentation result there (which was satisfying before) and detects that the recent markers resulted in a now poor segmentation result of S_1. If the user—without actually understanding the underlying algorithm—has this experience, he or she might have no idea how to proceed to achieve a satisfying result in all slices.

Although this described scenario is not common—often a single include and a single exclude point are sufficient for segmentation—it might happen. In such cases, a completely different segmentation method might be better suited. In other words, the watershed transform often fails, if large parts of the object boundaries cannot be discerned in the images.

5.5.3 INTERACTION TECHNIQUES FOR LIVEWIRE

Livewire is a segmentation method that is very well accepted by medical users because they have a good understanding what contour it selects (which is not necessarily true for the region-oriented approaches). In general, livewire has nice characteristics concerning the interactive control. The modification of an intermediate result may be laborious, but it is easy to understand. If a contour turns out to be wrong, a control (or seed) point c_i can be interactively translated. This modification influences the path between the previous and the next control point (c_{i-1} and c_{i+1}). If the translation of a seed point does not lead to the desired result, additional seed points may be introduced. An essential interaction technique for new applications of livewire is a learning function that estimates the parameters of the cost function based on a manually selected contour. This estimation process considers the mean gray value, the standard deviation of the gray value, and the other factors that are part of the cost function. Similar to the threshold in region growing without dedicated support, the choice for a suitable value might be a tedious trial and error process.

5.6   POSTPROCESSING OF SEGMENTATION RESULTS

Threshold-based and region-oriented segmentation methods in particular often produce results that need some postprocessing to be accurate. Examples are holes within a segmentation result that should be filled (if a tumor with a central necrosis occurs, region-growing typically would not include the central necrosis, although it should be part of the tumor segmentation result[3]).

There are typically two tasks in the postprocessing stage. The first task is to correct minor errors in the segmentation result by adding and removing voxels. The second task is relevant to achieve high-quality visualizations of the segmentation result: the segmentation result should be enhanced to support smooth visualizations. The goal here is not to add or remove voxels completely but to transform the binary segmentation result to a multivalued segmentation result, so that smooth boundaries arise.

5.6.1 MORPHOLOGICAL IMAGE ANALYSIS

Segmentation results can often be enhanced by morphological operators SOILLE and TALBOT [2001]. Morphological operators add or remove voxels inside or from the border of the segmentation. Such filters operate on binary image data (1 represents a voxel that is part of the segmentation result and 0 represents other voxels). Similar to noise reduction filters, morphological filters are described by a kernel matrix with a certain size. The elements, however, are restricted to 1 or 0 to produce binary results. The simplest morphological operators are *erosion* and *dilation*. Erosion with a 3×3 kernel, with all elements set to 1, removes all pixels with a neighbor pixel outside the segmentation result and, hence, shrinks the segmentation. Typically, erosion is used to remove erroneous ("false") connections between regions. In contrast, dilation grows the segmentation (thus closes holes and bumps in the boundary) if at least one voxel below the kernel is set.

Since erosion and dilation reduce or increase the segmentation, *opening* and *closing* operators are introduced that maintain the overall size. Opening consists of an erosion and a subsequent dilation. Note that the image really changes via these two operations; dilation is not exactly the inverse transformation of erosion. For example, a 2×2 square would be completely removed in the erosion process, and does not reappear in the dilation. Also, small connections between parts of a segmentation result are removed. In general, opening is employed to remove small objects and to reduce convex bulges.

Closing, on the other hand, dilates the segmentation result first and erodes it subsequently. Closing fills concave notches and closes (small) holes. Other parts of the segmentation result remain unchanged. This is useful in, for example, tumor segmentation, where a central necrosis may be added by a closing operation with an appropriate scale. Note that the morphological filter kernels ("structure elements") may not be a fully set $N \times N$ matrix to achieve specific result shapes. In these cases, we speak of *active* and *inactive* kernel entries. The application of morphologic operations may depend on certain conditions (referred to as, e.g., conditional dilation, conditional erosion, etc.). For complex segmentation tasks, (conditional) morphologic operators are essential. BOTHA [2005] describes a comprehensive system for planning implants at the shoulder and using morphologic operators in a pipeline for segmenting skeletal structures in the shoulder.

Noise Reduction with Morphologic Operators   Although morphologic operators are often used in a later stage of an image analysis pipeline (e.g., after segmentation) they are sometimes useful in earlier stages—for example, as part of the noise reduction process. In particular, morphologic operators are useful if the data

---

3   A necrosis describes the death of cells in an organ or tissue from disease or injury.

contain not only stochastic noise but also speckles of a certain size that need to be removed for further analysis and visualization. Ultrasound data are an example of this situation. Iterative erosion may be used to separate regions that contain the relevant information from a noisy environment (see Fig. 5.30). In the ultrasound processing pipeline described by SAKAS and WALTER [1995], erosion and opening were applied before general noise reduction filters (Gaussian and median) were applied to the relevant portions of the data.

Postprocessing methods of segmentation results are also used for volumetry (see Sect. 13.5).

5.6.2 SMOOTHING SEGMENTATION RESULTS FOR VISUALIZATION

Postprocessing, as discussed above, is essential to achieve more accurate segmentation results, for example, for quantitative analysis. Smoothing, which is discussed here, attempts to improve the appearance of visualizations based on the segmentation results.

Usually, 3D binary segmentation results are used as input for an isosurface visualization (see Chap. 7). The segmentation result is characterized by a data structure called a *segmentation* or *label volume*. One value represents voxels belonging to the segmentation mask and a second value represents background voxels. The intermediate value is used as isovalue for the surface generation. As an example, 100 may denote voxels belonging to an object, 0 represents background voxels, and 50 is used as isovalue. The simple isosurface generation suffers from strong aliasing artifacts (see Sec. 2.2.4), which become obvious as discontinuities in the surface normals. These artifacts are due to the discontinuity of the inside-outside function. Therefore, it is useful to "smooth" the boundary in the segmentation result at the voxel level, or to smooth the resulting visualization (which will be discussed in Sect. 7.3.3). In the following, we describe a viable and efficient approach to smooth the segmentation result, which was introduced by [NEUBAUER et al. 2004].

We denote with v_1 the value of the segmentation result and with v_2 the value of the background voxels. t_{iso} represents the isovalue computed as $(v_1 + v_2)/2$. The method is based on morphologic operations performed in a defined distance of the original object boundary, and it is constrained in a way that maintains the original in-out classification of the segmentation step.

Each voxel near the object boundary is assigned a new value v, with $v_1 \leq v \leq v_2$ using the following algorithm: a reference mask V_{ref} is created by eroding the segmentation result. After the erosion, all

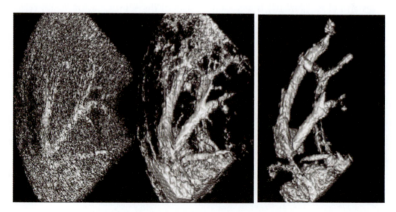

FIGURE 5.30   *3D visualization of ultrasound data from vascular structures in the liver. Left: without morphologic suppression of irrelevant regions, middle: after 20 iterations of an erosion with a 3D structure element, right: after 30 iterations with the same structure element* [SAKAS and WALTER 1995]. *(Image courtesy* GEORGIOS SAKAS, *Fraunhofer Institute Darmstadt)*

voxels of V_{ref} are assigned the value v according to Equation 5.19, which in essence moves the isosurface closer to the background value and thus farther away from the original segmented object.

$$v = v_2 - (v_2 - v_1) * \frac{1}{3} \qquad (5.19)$$

During erosion, the algorithm checks whether the shape has significantly changed, in the sense that small features on the boundary of the segmented object would be lost [NEUBAUER 2005]. Significant changes are defined as removed voxels that are not adjacent (or not at the boundary) to the original segmentation. In such case, these voxels are not removed (see Fig. 5.31 for an example).

After the modified erosion, two dilation operations are performed. The boundary voxels of the reference mask are tracked as reference voxels with the dilation front. Each voxel V that is added through dilation is therefore associated with a reference voxel from V_{ref} and acquires the value

$$v = v_{ref} - (v_2 - v_1) * \frac{d}{3} \qquad (5.20)$$

with d being the Euclidean distance from V to V_{ref} and v_{ref} the value of the associated voxel from V_{ref}. The method can be generalized to a wider filter region (with more erosion and dilatation steps). To optimally preserve the original segmentation result, it is desirable that all voxels belonging to the segmentation result yield a value above t_{iso}. This is achieved by a correction with a small positive δ in a final step.

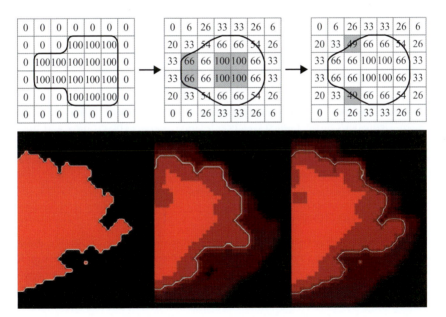

FIGURE 5.31 *Top row: Smoothing binary segmentation results (left) through morphologic operators and with $v_1 = 0, v_2 = 100$, and $t_{iso} = 50$. The dark gray voxels in the left part (middle) would be removed by an erosion. This is avoided to preserve the object shape. In a last step, voxels that belong to the segmentation result and have a value below 50 are corrected (right). Bottom row: A real world example. Bright red represents the original label value v_2 of the segmentation, dark red the smoothed voxel value. White indicates the the isosurface. Left: Binary input segmentation, middle: smoothing after erosion, right: smoothing after erosion with correction. (Images courtesy ANDRE NEUBAUER, VRVis Wien)*

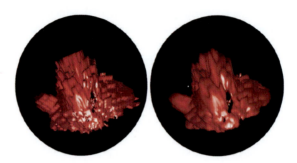

FIGURE 5.32 *3D visualization based on the raw segmentation result and on two smoothed segmentation volumes (middle, right). The distracting interpolation artifacts on the left are effectively reduced, in particular on the right, where a larger filter region is applied. (Image courtesy ANDRÉ NEUBAUER, VRVis Wien)*

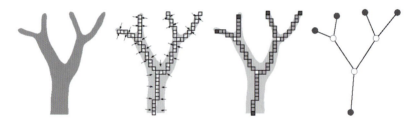

FIGURE 5.33 *A vessel analysis pipeline with vessel segmentation, skeletonization, analysis of branching points, and transformation to a branching graph branching [SELLE et al. 2002]. (Image courtesy DIRK SELLE MeVis Bremen)*

This algorithm yields a near-linear value degradation from the reference mask outwards (see Fig. 5.31). The algorithm by Neubauer can be applied to smooth larger regions (by eroding and dilating several times); see Fig. 5.32, in which the results of different sizes of the smoothing filter are compared. Here, we described a restricted and simplified variant. As demonstrated in NEUBAUER et al. [2004], the algorithm retains the basic object shape and volume.

5.7   SKELETONIZATION

A reliable segmentation result may be useful as input for subsequent analysis tasks. For example, tumor segmentation is often followed by a decision concerning the dignity (malignant or benign lesion). The roundness of the lesion (relation between longest and smallest diameter or relation between volume and surface area) and the relation between the circumference and the cross-sectional area are some of the parameters that might support this decision. For anatomical tree structures, such as vasculature, the vessel skeleton and the local vessel diameter are often required. As an example, we discuss dedicated visualization techniques that require this kind of input in Chapter 14. The skeleton representation makes it easy to assess the branching structure (skeleton voxels with more than two neighbors represent a branch). The branching graph is a useful data structure for surgery planning software. It can be used to answer questions such as "What happens if I have to cut a vascular tree at a particular position?" Figure 5.33 shows a typical vessel analysis pipeline.

In a continuous space, the skeleton is a set of (infinitely thin) space curves. In a discrete space, the skeleton is a one-voxel wide line representation that proceeds in the center of a volumetric object. A definition in 2D is that each point on the skeleton is the center of an enclosing circle with maximum diameter. The differences between this definition for continuous objects and skeletons of discrete representations are shown in Figure 5.34. The deviation between the continuous skeleton and an ideal discrete skeleton is less than one voxel.

Algorithms that compute skeletons may successively erode the segmentation result until a one-voxel wide line remains. Skeletonization based on erosion is called *thinning*.

Actually, skeletonization of discrete 3D objects with anisotropic voxels (slice distance is different from pixel distance) is more difficult. The anisotropic character must be explicitly considered to compensate for the fact that an erosion in the z-direction may be considerably larger than for the x- and y-directions. Some problems occur with small branches of the skeleton (see Fig. 5.35). Small side branches may correctly

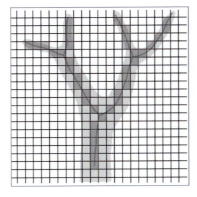

FIGURE 5.34   *The dark line represents the skeleton of the gray shape. The dark gray pixels represent the discrete skeleton [SELLE et al. 2002]. (Image courtesy TOBIAS BOSKAMP, MeVis Bremen)*

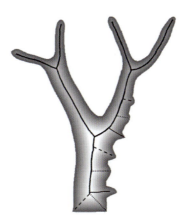

FIGURE 5.35   *Irrelevant side branches are suppressed by a threshold applied to distance transform gradient. All lines represent the skeleton with a threshold of 0.8 (only a few branches are filtered out). With the threshold reduced to 0.6 the dotted branches are removed. Further reduction to 0.4 removes the dashed branches also. The solid lines, which probably represent the interesting shape information here, are obtained with a threshold of 0.0 [SELLE et al. 2002]. (Image courtesy TOBIAS BOSKAMP, MeVis Bremen)*

reflect the anatomical situation but may also be the consequence of the discrete representation. A filter that controls these side branches may consider the length of a side branch in relation to the length of an adjacent branch, as well as the gradient along the branch. A sensitivity parameter is used to control how much information is filtered out. Examples for such filter functions are described in SELLE et al. [2002] and BOSKAMP et al. [2004]. Figure 5.35 gives an example for the results produced with the filter described in BOSKAMP et al. [2004].

For the diagnosis of vascular diseases, even the skeleton is only an intermediate result. It might be used for the visualization of cross-sectional areas orthogonal to the local vessel centerline. A stenosis can be detected much better with such images compared to axial slices. As an example for further analysis, cross-sectional areas, minimal, average, and maximum diameters are determined. These measures support the diagnosis of a vessel stenosis and allow assessment of its severity.

Direct Skeletonization   So far, we described skeletonization as an image analysis step carried out after segmentation using the segmentation result as input. There are also algorithm that compute the vessel skeleton immediately (without prior segmentation). Similar to the livewire segmentation they are based on a minimal path computation that considers gray values and local contrasts, as well as the length and curvature of the resulting path. Usually, the user has to specify an initial point (on the centerline) and an initial direction, and the algorithm extrapolates in the given direction with a small increment and searches for a new centerline point [WINK et al. 2000].

Direct skeletonization is fast; however, the resulting paths may strongly deviate from the true centerlines, in particular at branchings. Direct skeletonization methods are discussed in FRANGI et al. [1999] and HERNANDEZ-HOYOS et al. [2002].

Comparison Between Direct and Indirect Skeletonization   The direct skeletonization approach is usually faster, since the segmentation step, which is tedious and error-prone, is completely avoided. However, direct skeletonization is often less accurate, particularly in strongly bended parts of a vessel and near branchings. If noticeable deviations occur, the user has to fine-tune the parameters of the underlying optimal path calculation, which is probably difficult, and it is not clear that this process converges against the true centerline. Accuracy is critical for centerline determination, both for visualization as well as for the diagnosis of vascular diseases. With respect to the requirements discussed in Section 5.1, in particular *robustness* and *reliability*, there is an advantage for indirect methods. The segmentation result is a verifiable intermediate result which may be fine-tuned by specifying seed points for example. Consequently, indirect skeletonization currently dominates in clinical applications.

5.8   VALIDATION OF SEGMENTATION METHODS

Validation indicates the accuracy of a given method, which can be achieved with a particular segmentation method. The design of a study to assess accuracy is difficult, in particular, if the result strongly depends on user interactions or careful choices with respect to many parameters of an automatic algorithm. Validation is carried out primarily for automatic segmentation or for automatic support in semi-interactive segmentation methods (such as the influence of shape-based interpolation on the accuracy of livewire; recall SCHENK et al. [2000]).

If segmentation results primarily depend on a user-selected threshold (flooding level, intensity, or gradient threshold) validation studies are carried out to evaluate the sensitivity of the parameter. If very similar results would have been obtained with slightly different parameter values, it is likely that different users would gain similar results.

5.8.1 PHANTOM STUDIES VERSUS CLINICAL DATA

In general, it is necessary to have a representative sample of segmentation results available. The size of the required sample depends on the variability of the target structure and the variability of the image acquisition parameters. Validation studies include clinical data and phantoms. The use of clinical data has the advantage that the results of a validation study can be reliably transferred to the real clinical use. Phantoms, on the other hand, are artificial data that exhibit characteristics similar to real data. Phantom data may be flexibly parameterized with respect to noise levels and noise distribution, inhomogeneity artifacts, and image resolution. Thus, they allow simulation of many aspects of the variability of the images. Modified clinical data are often a viable trade-off that combines the flexibility of phantom data and the authenticity of clinical data. Based on real clinical data, a modification of the noise level for example is carried out by adding different types and different levels of noise. With these modifications, different acquisition parameters can be simulated. Such modifications are useful to draw conclusions on the noise level for which (still) acceptable results may be expected. A reasonable strategy is to use a very high-quality dataset with a high resolution, and degrade the image quality by adding noise or transforming it to lower resolution.

Validation studies are targeted at quantitative expressions concerning the accuracy. For this purpose, validation metrics are required to compare the results achieved with different segmentation methods. It is desirable to use several metrics and thus to study different aspects of accuracy. Which aspect is particularly important and which level of accuracy is acceptable depends strongly on the specific application. As mentioned before, accuracy is more important, if segmentation is the basis for quantitative analysis. It is difficult to make a general statement concerning the accuracy requirements for visualization purposes. If the local neighborhood of a tumor is evaluated, the visible border surfaces should correctly reflect the spatial relations. If on the other hand, should the location of a tumor inside a larger organ should be evaluated, the requirements for the accuracy of the segmentation of the organ would be reduced.

5.8.2 VALIDATION METRICS

Validation metrics refer to distances between segmentation results or to volume overlaps between the *gold standard* and the (new) segmentation method. The *gold standard* typically is a high-quality reference segmentation carried out by an expert. Note however, that this reference is not perfectly accurate or reliable; however, the use of such gold standards is often the most feasible approach. An alternative is the use of *phantoms*. In phantom studies, the *ground truth* is generally available. The challenge is to develop phantoms realistic enough to permit conclusions about segmentation accuracy for real data.

Distances between contours or boundary surfaces allow the assessment of worst case scenarios (maximum distance between surfaces), whereas the metrics based on the volume overlap represent average values. In the following, R denotes our reference segmentation and S our segmentation with a new method.

The following distance metrics are widespread:

- Mean symmetric distance (*avg*). For the contour or surface of S, the distances between each vertex and the closest vertex of R is calculated. Subsequently, for each vertex of R, the distance to the closest vertex of S is computed. *avg* represents the mean value of these distances (see Eq. 5.21).

$$d_{avg}(S, R) = \frac{\sum_{S_i} min_{R_k} d(S_i, R_k) + \sum_{R_k} min_{S_i} d(R_k, S_i)}{|S_i| + |R_k|}$$

(5.21)

- Hausdorff distance $d_{Hausdorff}$ (see Eq. 5.22) represents the maximum deviation between two contours or surfaces.

$$d_{Hausdorff}(S, R) = max(min\{d(S_i, R)\}, min\{d(S, R_k)\})$$ (5.22)

- Euclidean distance between the centers of gravity of S and R.

The above described distance measures do not differentiate between over-segmentation, where S is constantly larger than R and under-segmentation, where S is smaller than R.

To evaluate the volume overlap, the dice coefficient is a widespread measure. It computes the union of the volumes of R and S and relates it to the sum of the volumes of R and S (see Eq. 5.23).

$$d_{Dice}(S, R) = \frac{2 * |S| \cap |R|}{|S| + |R|}$$ (5.23)

The dice coefficient has values in the range 0 to 1, with 1 representing perfect overlap.

5.8.3 DISCUSSION

Validation is a crucial issue in medical image analysis. Usually, scientists perform "their" validation, by analyzing and interpreting some data. For other scientists, the image data and the reference are usually not available, and it is impossible to reconstruct the conclusions. Also, it is almost impossible to reliably compare the quality achieved by different research groups with different methods. Fortunately, databases that provide access to medical datasets and segmentation results are emerging.

The correlation between the results achieved with the above-mentioned metrics is rather low. In general, metrics that characterize the volume overlap lead to different assessments of the segmentation than surface distance measures. The two surface distance measures may also lead to different assessments. In general, several metrics should be employed in a validation. ZHANG [1996] gives an overview and discusses also other validation metrics.

A promising validation strategy is to employ a collection of expert segmentations to account for the inter-observer variability. However, there is no standardized approach to how these different segmentation results are processed. WARFIELD et al. [2002] and MADDAH et al. [2004] described an approach where a probabilistic estimate of the "ground truth" is attempted with an expectation-maximization algorithm.

5.9   REGISTRATION AND FUSION OF MEDICAL IMAGE DATA

Image registration is the process of aligning images so that corresponding features can easily be related [HAJNAL et al. 2001]. In many clinical scenarios, it is crucial to mentally combine information extracted from different sources to draw conclusions. Registration is essential to compare image data and to analyze different image data in a common frame. The image data to be analyzed and compared often relate to the same patient but are acquired at different points in time, or they are acquired with different imaging modalities. To name a few examples, where registration is required:

1   *Registration of image data acquired at different points in time.* In dynamic imaging, image data are acquired at different time points. A robust mathematic analysis of these data requires the correction for motion artifacts. Follow-up studies after initial treatment involve the acquisition of images at various stages, such as three, six, and twelve months after a therapy. The evaluation of these images involves a comparison, for example, with respect to tumor growth.

2   *Registration of pre- and intraoperative data.* Therapy monitoring is based on intraoperative imaging. It is desirable to relate intraoperative data to analysis results derived from preoperative data. Together with navigation systems, a correct transformation of intraoperative data to preoperative data might be used to support the localization of a pathology.

3   *Multimodal registration.* A wide area of application is multimodal image registration, in which different acquisition techniques, such as CT and MRI, are used complementarily.

4   *Atlas-based matching.* Finally, image registration is often employed to compare the data of a particular patient with an *atlas* that represents normal anatomical variations.

The first three categories relate to data of the same patient, whereas the last category relates to the registration of data from either different patients or a particular patient with an "average" patient.

The commonality of these different application areas is the need to geometrically adapt several images to each other or to some kind of model. The goal of image registration is to deform or transform one dataset to optimally match another dataset that provides different information as well as similar information. The dataset to which a new dataset is adapted is referred to as *reference data*. According to the applications named before, the reference data may be data from the same patient but in another modality, e.g., data acquired at a different time.

There is a huge amount of scientific literature on image registration, including whole books on subclasses of registration problems. Usually, single components of the registration process (transformations, similarity measures, optimization, interpolation, image representation) are considered in research publications. As in segmentation, there is no standard approach.

The registration problem can be formulated as follows: "Transform a floating image dataset geometrically so that it fits optimally to a given reference image under a given aspect." This problem statement contains several components:

-   Transformation: geometric transformation of voxel coordinates
-   Fitting: requires a quantification by means of a similarity measure
-   Optimally: The transformation should be accomplished in such a way that the similarity measure is maximized.
-   A given aspect: The criteria for optimal matching are chosen such that particular structures are matched as good as possible. As an example, the goal might be to match vascular structures, or skeletal structures, or organs. It is essential to note that optimal correspondence with respect to a given aspect is often achieved at the expense of other aspects.

Transformation   "Global" and "local" transformations are discriminated.

Global Transformations   Translation and rotation of (all) coordinates are examples for global transformations. These transformations are described by a small set of parameters that is applied to all coordinates. With global transformations, simple movements may be corrected. The modification of one parameter has an influence on all voxels, which is not desirable if more complex transformations have to be represented. With increasing complexity, we can discriminate *rigid, homomorph, affine,* and *polynomial transformations.*

Local Transformations   These transformations are described by a *large* set of parameters that correspond to a mesh of control points. Modifications of a single parameter (control point) affect only a local neighborhood. Examples for local transformations are cubic b-spline transformations [RUECKERT *et al.* 1999] and Bézier transformations [OTTE 2001]. For each voxel coordinate, a new set of parameters is employed. Local transformations enable the accounting of more complex movements. Other local approaches utilize elastic models [CHRISTENSEN 1994, 1999, 2001] or fluid models to characterize movements

[BRO-NIELSEN and GRAMKOW 1996, BRO-NIELSEN 1996]. The numeric solution of these models is accomplished by means of partial differential equations, which is computationally extremely expensive.

Comparison: Global and Local Transformations   While a global transformation can be used to compensate for simple movements, local movements can in principle account for any complex movement. The computational effort for a global transformation is low: a matrix-vector operation is carried out for each coordinate. In contrast, elastic transformations are computationally highly demanding. In general, a global transformation is used as a preprocesssing step for a local transformation.

Fitting   Similarity measures characterize how similar two images are. Basically, similarity measures based on intensities of voxels and on geometric measures are discriminated:

- *Intensity-based similarity.* Gray values of voxels in the floating image are compared with voxels in the reference image.
- *Geometry-based similarity.* Positions of voxels in the floating image are compared to those in the reference image [ROHR 2001].

There are three categories of intensity-based similarity measures [ROCHE *et al.* 1999]:

- *Voxel-based.* The intensities of the two images are compared for each voxel in a 1:1 relation. This measure is only applicable if the two images have the same resolution and if both images contain the same content with similar intensities. This assumption is not fulfilled in multimodal registration where different modalities are involved. An application example is time-dependent data with limited motion artifacts, such as cerebral perfusion.
- *Statistic.* The normalized correlation of intensities in both images is computed. The application of this measure also requires that the same content be represented in both images. Linear transformations of intensity values can be compensated.
- *Entropy-based.* These methods are based on information theory. The mutual information [VIOLA 1995, MAES *et al.* 1997a] of the common 2D histogram of both images is computed. Normalized mutual information is a similarity metric, which may be used even if the content of the images is slightly different [STUDHOLME 1997]. The relationship between the intensity values may be statistical. Registration based on normalized mutual information is able to match multimodal image data, such as CT and MRI.

All these similarity measures might be computed automatically (without any interaction). The determination of landmarks in the floating image, as well as in the reference image in general, requires user input. The automatic localization of corresponding landmarks is difficult. In many cases, branching points of vascular trees are appropriate [AYLWARD and BULLITT 2002, TSCHIRREN *et al.* 2002]. Intensity-based and similarity-based registration are also combined [JOHNSON and CHRISTENSEN 2002]. Normalized-mutual information is the most frequently used similarity measure in particular for multimodal registration. However, the use of this measure also has considerable drawbacks [HABER and MODERSITZKI 2005]. Typically, it has many local minima, which make the optimization process difficult.

Optimization Process   For the maximization of the selected similarity measure, a numerical optimizer is used to approximate "optimal" transformation parameters. Numerical optimization is either applied to the similarity values (for example, simplex, Powell, or Hooke approach) or considers derived information [MAES *et al.* 1997b]. The registration with landmarks is often based on the Levenberg-Marquardt algorithm [DENNIS and SCHNABEL 1983].

Discussion   Local registration processes are often guided by some constraints. For example, the volume of certain tissue, in particular a tumor, should be preserved. Without constraints, arbitrary deformations may arise, resulting in misleading visualizations. For example, with contrast-enhanced perfusion data, some bright spots become larger over time as a consequence of the wash-in behavior. Unconstrained registration would try to match smaller and larger spots by scaling the region correspondingly. Volume preserving registration is often desirable [HABER and MODERSITZKI 2004, ROHLFING et al. 2003].

Local registration is a time-consuming process; therefore, it is usually employed as a batch process. Recent advances allow the transformation of the necessary operations to the graphics hardware, which accelerates the computation considerably [SOZA et al. 2002, HASTREITER et al. 2004].

For interactive registration, primarily global transformations are employed. Several attempts have been made to accelerate local registration by employing either graphics hardware [SOZA et al. 2002] or parallel computer [FERRANT et al. 2001, RUIZ-ALZOLA et al. 2002]. Another alternative is to employ a priori knowledge relating to the specific question. As an example, AZAR et al. [2002] employ a model for breast deformations to accelerate local registration.

In the clinical routine, landmark-based registration is primarily used. This is probably due to the fact that with this kind of registration it is relatively easy to control which regions of the target image are mapped to certain portions of the reference image. In general, it is difficult to understand and verify the registration process. KÖNIG and PEITGEN [2005] discussed visualization techniques to convey the locally different amount and direction of transformation in a nonrigid local registration. Such techniques need to be refined and employed to increase acceptance of advanced registration techniques.

Integrated Visualization of Registered Image Data   Once the target image is transformed to the reference image, both image data can be explored in an integrated visualization. The integrated visualization also serves as a visual control of the registration quality. Integrated visualizations may be explored in slice-based views (see Fig. 5.36) or in 3D visualizations (see Fig. 5.37) where clipping planes might be used to restrict which portions are visible from the reference image and from the target image. In both 2D and 3D visualization, movable and scalable lenses are frequently used to control which portions of the data are visible. In particular, for quality control, checkerboard visualizations are frequently used to evaluate the registration accuracy in different portions of the data. Neurosurgical interventions are an example, where multimodal information, in particular CT and MRI data are frequently acquired. The registration and integrated visualization of both image data provide an overview on soft tissue structures within

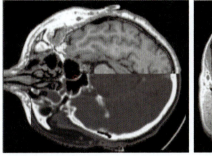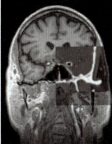

FIGURE 5.36   *Fusion of T1-weighted MRI and CT angiography data. Integrated and synchronized slice views are displayed and explored with a "fusion" lens [*HASTREITER *and* ERTL *1998]. (Images courtesy* PETER HASTREITER, *University of Erlangen-Nuremberg)*

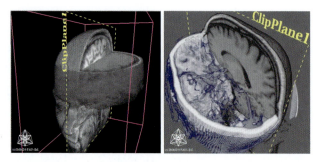

FIGURE 5.37 Fusion of T1-weighted MRI and MRI angiography data (left). Fusion of T1-weighted MRI with CT angiography data. 3D visualizations are explored by means of clipping planes [HASTREITER and ERTL 1998]. (Images courtesy PETER HASTREITER, University of Erlangen-Nuremberg)

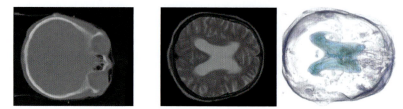

FIGURE 5.38 The fusion of skeletal structures from CT (left) and cerebral soft tissue from MRI data (right) allows to generate integrated 3D visualizations highlighting the cerebrospinal fluid inside the skull. (Images courtesy MATTHIAS KEIL, Fraunhofer Institute Darmstadt)

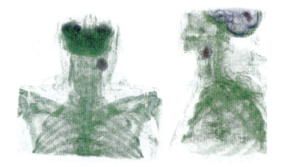

FIGURE 5.39 Fusion of PET and CT data to convey the location of a neck tumor. The tumor is visualized based on its characteristic signal in PET data, while the skeletal structures are extracted from CT data. (Images courtesy MATTHIAS KEIL, Fraunhofer Institute Darmstadt)

the context of skeletal data (see Fig. 5.38). As a final example, we present two integrated visualizations of PET and CT data. Due to its increased metabolism, a tumor in the neck region is detected with PET data and integrated in a volume visualization of the skeletal structures based on CT data. The integrated visualization supports the localization of the tumor (see Fig. 5.39).

Discussion   HAJNAL 2001 provides the first comprehensive coverage of this emerging field. This monograph details the theory, technology, and practical implementations in a variety of medical settings. International experts thoroughly explain why image registration is important, describe its applications in a nonmathematical way, and include rigorous analysis for those who plan to implement algorithms themselves.

5.10   SUMMARY

In this chapter, we discussed a typical image analysis pipeline that processes medical volume data, such as CT and MRI data, and produces segmentation information concerning the object shape. For clinically useful applications, it is a good strategy to attempt automatic solutions that produce acceptable results in the majority of the cases. These solutions should be complemented by more general semiautomatic solutions for the remaining cases. Image analysis and visualization are closely connected parts of computer support. Fast 3D visualization techniques are very useful for evaluating segmentation results. These visualizations might also be used to fine-tune the segmentation. On the other hand, segmentation is the prerequisite for high-quality visualizations of the relevant structures. While visualization techniques in general have a broad applicability, image analysis is necessarily more dependent on the specific data to which it is applied. As an example of a complex image analysis task, we discussed vessel analysis. We will revisit that topic in Chapter 14 on the visualization of vascular structures.

FURTHER READING

Many aspects and techniques of image analysis could only be touched in this chapter. Readers with interest in image analysis are referred to respective textbooks (SONKA and FITZPATRICK 2000, GONZALES and WOODS 1998, UDUPA and HERMAN 2000). LOHMANN [1998] focuses on 3D image analysis and efficient methods for computing distance maps.

Skeletonization was briefly discussed. Recent and advanced algorithms are available, for example TELEA and VAN WIJK [2002] and STRZODKA and TELEA [2004]. The latter provides a solution which is directly supported by the graphics hardware. TER HAAR ROMENEY [1994] discusses the application of diffusion processes to image analysis problems.

Many algorithms briefly discussed in this chapter are available in dedicated software libraries. The platform-independent OpenSource project Insight Toolkit (ITK), for example, contains algorithms and annotated examples for a variety of segmentation tasks (www.itk.org). YOO [2004] describes the concepts for the algorithms contained in the toolkit. IBANEZ and SCHROEDER [2005] explain how to assemble the algorithms and adjust the parameters appropriately. The ITK also contains source code, which allows the user to understand and explore algorithms in detail. Another software library that is (in a basic version) freely available is MeVisLab (www.mevislab.de). Most of the images in this chapter were generated using this platform.

Mathematical models of (pixel) noise in medical image data are discussed in HAHN [2005]. MACOVSKI [1996] and MCVEIGH and BRONSKILL [1985] characterize noise in MRI data depending on acquisition parameters, such as volume size and acquisition time. The most substantial work on noise characteristics in MRI data is SIJBERS Ph.D. thesis [SIJBERS, 1998]. Jan SIJBERS maintains a thorough passing reference list on this topic (www.ruca.ua.ac.be/visielab/sijbers/snr_ref.html).

Concerning livewire segmentation, several modifications of the basic approach, including quality studies, have been published (BARRETT and MORTENSEN 1997, FALCAO et al. 1998, FALCAO et al. 1999). These publications discuss the accuracy, efficiency, interaction issues, and reproducibility of the segmentation results. FALCAO and UDUPA [1997] extend livewire segmentation to 3D. With this extension, users select a few orthogonal slices and segment the target structure with livewire. Based on these contours on the surface boundary, the complete boundary is extracted automatically. Interactive segmentation with special input devices is discussed in HARDERS and SZEKELY [2003].

The analysis of vascular structures exhibits some peculiarities due to their complex topology. Alternative and evaluated algorithms for vessel segmentation were also presented by AYLWARD and BULLITT [2002] and YIM et al. [2000].

A whole branch of image analysis methods attempts to overcome binary decisions (does a pixel belong to an object? (yes/no)). They rely on principles of fuzzy logic; one example is region-growing methods, which rely on a fuzzy definition of connectedness. General concepts are described in UDUPA and SAMARASEKERA [1996]. A specific application of fuzzy connectedness, the quantification of multiple sclerosis lesions, is described in UDUPA et al. [1997]. Fuzzy segmentation relates to statistical probability of connected components. This concept is a special aspect of statistical pattern recognition [DUDA et al. 2001].

While some of the algorithms described here were attempted for the identification of homogeneous regions (region-growing, watershed), others were aimed at the delineation of discontinuities that are supposed to be the boundaries of the target structure (livewire, active contour models). A variety of research papers deals with the combination of region-based and edge-based methods. FREIXENET et al. [2002] give an overview of these attempts, based on an appropriate classification.

We omitted several segmentation strategies completely. For example, graph-cut methods [WU and LEAHY 1993, BOYKOV and JOLLY 2001, BOYKOV and VEKSLER 2006] have been successfully employed for a variety of clinically relevant problems, such as heart segmentation in CT data [FUNKA-LEA et al. 2006]. We discussed selected categories of advanced segmentation methods. Active shape and appearance models are an area of active research. The most relevant goal of this research is the identification of more reliable methods for determining shape correspondence. FRANGI et al. [2002] give an overview and present a new method with an application to cardiac imaging. A detailed description of active contours is given in BLAKE and ISARD [1998]. A collection of research papers on active contours and other variants of deformable models has been edited as a book [SINGH et al. 1999]. MCINERNEY and TERZOPOULOS [1996] is an excellent and detailed survey on deformable models.

A flexible class of model-based segmentation techniques is based on M-reps [JOSHI et al. 2002, PIZER et al. 2003]. M-reps are based on *medial atoms*, parts of medial axes and surfaces. They are particularly well suited to the modeling of anatomical objects, producing models that can be used to capture prior geometric information effectively in deformable model segmentation approaches.

Mass-spring models are another class of deformable models that have been refined recently for applications in image segmentation (segmentation of the left ventricle from dSPECT data and segmentation of neck lymph nodes from CT data) [DORNHEIM et al. 2005a,b; 2006]. This model-based technique allows the incorporation of a variety of information with respect to gray values and object shapes and generates good results even in portions of the target object where no image information is available (for example, in case of pathologic changes of the anatomy).

The segmentation of 4D (time-varying) data is currently not the focus of much research. It might be inspiring to look at a few examples, such as POHLE et al. [2004] (segmentation of the left ventricle in dSPECT data) and QIAN et al. [2005] (segmentation of 4D cardiac MRI data). Of all application areas in medical imaging, the analysis of cardiac image data of different modalities is particularly advanced. In particular, sophisticated model-based techniques are used in this area (see FRANGI et al. [2001], LELIEVELDT et al. [2006] for survey articles and MITCHELL et al. [2002] for the application of active shape and active appearance models for MRI and ultrasound data).

The appropriate solution to real world segmentation problems depends not only on the use of the most sophisticated algorithms. Often, a careful combination of preprocessing, segmentation, and postprocessing techniques provides an acceptable or even appreciated support. While we focused on individual methods in this chapter, a few validated examples of complex segmentation applications are documented: SELLE et al. [2002], and BOURQUAIN et al. [2002] describe *HepaVision* (planning of liver surgery), SALAH [2006] discusses segmentation for planning mastoidectomy, and CORDES et al. [2006] describe *NeckVision*—a system for neck dissection planning.

As a general and comprehensive overview on medical image registration, we recommend HAJNAL et al. [2001]. Fast numeric solutions to registration problems are described in MODERSITZKI [2004]. Recent overviews on registration methods can be found in FITZPATRICK et al. [2000], HALLPIKE and HAWKES [2002], BARBARA ZITOVÁ [2003]. MAINTZ and VIERGEVER [1998] provide a good survey on medical image registration, although it is several years old.

In the validation section, we discussed the problems associated with the gold standard used as reference. Specialized databases with validated segmentation results improve the situation. An excellent example is the simulated brain database (www.bic.mni.mcgill.ca/brainweb/, [COLLINS et al. 1998]). Another dedicated effort is the development of the lung image database consortium, which aims to stimulate the development of computer-aided detection algorithms for lung nodules in CT data [ARMATO et al. 2004]. The lung image database was initiated by the National Cancer Institute in the United States (imaging.cancer.gov/programsandresources/InformationSystems/LIDC).

PART II

Volume Visualization

In the previous part, we introduced the structure (see Chap. 2) and the analysis (see Chap. 5) of medical volume datasets. In this part, we will focus on the rendering of medical volume datasets through the means of volume visualization, namely volume rendering.

Before we actually start with the different volume rendering methods, we look into the fundamentals of volume rendering (see Chap. 6). Specifically, we will discuss the volume rendering pipeline, the classification and the basic design of transfer functions, and how voxel contributions are illuminated.

After the introduction of the fundamentals of volume visualization, we will look into the two main avenues for the visualization of medical volume data: indirect volume rendering (see Chap. 7) and direct volume rendering (see Chaps. 8 and 9). While we have already discussed the basics of direct volume rendering in Chapters 6 and 8, more advanced methods of transfer function specification will be discussed in Chapter 11 of the following part of the book. In Chapter 9, we describe advanced methods and algorithms for the visualization of medical volume data, e.g., the hybrid visualization of surface and volume data as well as the validation of visualization algorithms. In the last chapter in this part, we deal with dynamic medical volume data, in particular with perfusion data (see Chap. 10). We describe methods for processing, analyzing, visualizing, and interactively exploring such data, with applications in stroke and tumor diagnosis. It turns out that methods described earlier in this part can be extended to dynamic medical volume data.

Finally, note that direct or indirect volume rendering are not the only options for the rendering of scalar volumetric datasets. However, they are the most important in the context of medical volumetric data.

Chapter 06

Fundamentals of Volume Visualization

Volume visualization is concerned with the generation of a visual representation of volumetric data. As described in Chapter 2, medical volumetric data can be considered as a stack of aligned images or slices of the same resolution and adjacent position in z. This motivates the standard examination mode in radiology departments, where the individual images are examined.

Volume visualization aims at a visual representation of the full dataset, hence of all images at the same time. Therefore, the individual voxels of the dataset must be selected, weighted, combined, and projected onto the image plane. The image plane itself acts literally as a window to the data, representing the position and viewing direction of the observer who examines the dataset.

Organization The individual steps in that process are discussed in this and the following chapters. In particular, we will examine how these steps are organized (see Sect. 6.1) and how the contributing voxels are weighted (see Sect. 6.2). The voxel selection process was already discussed in the chapter on Image Analysis (see Chap. 5). In Section 6.2, we will focus on the classification of volume datasets based on histograms and discuss the ways classification is different from segmentation. An important part of the projection step is the illumination model. In Section 6.3, we will briefly introduce the standard illumination model in computer graphics, the Phong illumination model, which is also widely used in visualization.

6.1 THE VOLUME VISUALIZATION PIPELINE

The volume visualization pipeline shown in Figure 6.1 describes how the different steps and avenues of volume visualization fit together. After data acquisition, the dataset may be filtered (e.g., to enhance the data quality) and objects are segmented. After the possible selection of a subrange of the voxels (e.g., due to clipping or cropping of the dataset) the normals of the voxels are computed. As the last step before the actual rendering, the voxels are classified. Finally, the voxels are projected onto or rendered into an image by either indirect or direct volume rendering.

Please note that normals are typically computed after classification (which is discussed in the next section). The rationale behind this order lies in the fact that voxels with zero contribution (as determined by the classification) do not require the costly computation of their normal.

The related term volume rendering pipeline describes the order of operations for direct volume rendering. More details on the volume rendering pipeline and its implications for the volume rendering process will be discussed in Chapter 8.

6.2 HISTOGRAMS AND VOLUME CLASSIFICATION

An important question in the context of volume visualization is how the individual voxels contribute to the final image. This question is addressed by the classification step of the volume visualization pipeline. Here, the voxel values of a volume dataset are mapped to optical properties by one or several *transfer functions*. Transfer functions (TF) are functions in a mathematical sense that specify the mapping from

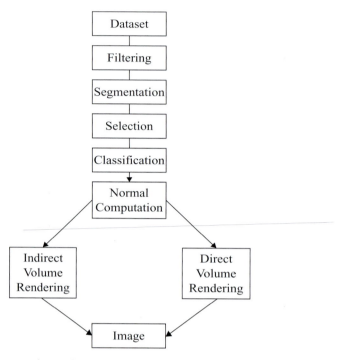

FIGURE 6.1 *Volume visualization pipeline.*

the voxel values—V_i, as different data properties at each voxels—to a set of optical properties O_i (see Eq. 6.1). The cartesian product of the voxel values V_i specifies the domain of the function, while the product of the optical properties O_i specifies the range of the transfer function. In the context of medical volume datasets, we typically have only one data value V per voxel, which is usually also called voxel intensity (see Chap. 3 for a discussion of these voxel values). The resulting transfer functions are hence called one-dimensional transfer functions (with a 1D domain) or transfer functions of a scalar volume dataset (one scalar value field). In the following, we limit ourselves to that case. A discussion of more complex transfer function design (including higher dimensional domains) is provided in Chapter 11.

$$tf : V_0 \times V_1 \times \ldots \times V_{n-1} \longrightarrow O_0 \times O_1 \times \ldots \times O_{n-1}$$ (6.1)

Depending on the used formalism, the voxel values V are either mapped by one transfer function to a tuple of optical properties O_i (see Eq. 6.2), or the voxel values are mapped to each optical property by an individual transfer function (see Eq. 6.3). In the following sections, we will adopt the second formalism.

$$tf : V \longrightarrow O_0 \times O_1 \times \ldots \times O_{n-1}$$ (6.2)

$$tf_0 : V \longrightarrow O_0$$
$$tf_1 : V \longrightarrow O_1$$
$$\ldots$$
$$tf_{n-1} : V \longrightarrow O_{n-1}$$ (6.3)

FIGURE 6.2   Left: linear histogram. Right: vertical zoom into the bottom end (frequencies 0–10) of the linear histogram. The linear horizontal scale is inappropriate for the histogram of this CT dataset of a human thorax, since the large majority of voxel values is concentrated on the left side. A vertical zoom can provide more information on the upper voxel values. The colored rectangle on the bottom marks the different materials in the intensity value spectrum. The respective classification can be found in Figure 6.4 (right).

Many different options for optical properties can be specified by transfer functions. These options depend on the used color and lighting model.[1] Typically, the adopted model is the RGB color model, although alternative color models like HSV are also frequently used. In addition to the base color parameters, the transfer function specifies the opacity α, which is the complement of transparency, thus specifying how "solid" the respective voxel value should appear. Putting the RGB-model and the opacity together, we get four transfer functions that map each voxel value to (R, G, B, α) values:

$$
\begin{aligned}
tf_R &: V \longrightarrow R \\
tf_G &: V \longrightarrow G \\
tf_B &: V \longrightarrow B \\
tf_\alpha &: V \longrightarrow \alpha
\end{aligned}
\tag{6.4}
$$

Ideally, every voxel could be classified individually. Since this mapping would result in a function range of many millions or billions of voxels, the specification of that classification is clearly infeasible. Therefore, the standard classification considers only their voxel values. In case of 12-bit deep voxels, the transfer function specifies the mapping of 4096 values to $RGB\alpha$ tuples. This in turn results in a one-dimensional classification that does not depend on the individual voxel position.

The distribution of voxel values or voxel intensities is typically represented in a histogram, where the x-axis or abscissa represents all possible voxel values, and the y-axis or ordinate represents the number of voxels of that value. In the following two sections, we will discuss histograms (see Sect. 6.2.1) and how they are used to specify transfer functions (see Sect. 6.2.2).

6.2.1   HISTOGRAMS

Histograms are discrete distribution functions that represent the frequency of their domain values. In the context of scalar volumetric data, the histogram represents the frequencies of the different voxel values. Figure 6.2 (left) shows a histogram of a CT dataset of a human thorax. The figure shows a variety of peaks where the frequency of the respective voxel values are particularly high. Considering that different tissue types normally map to different intensity values (e.g., different densities in a CT dataset[2]), we can

---

1   Here we use the Phong illumination model, which is discussed in Section 6.3.

2   As discussed in Section 3.2, CT voxel intensities are measured in Hounsfield units (HUs), that range from −1024 to 3071. Here, we consider only positive voxel intensities, which can be achieved by translating the HUs range into a positive range starting at zero.

differentiate these materials by different intensity ranges in the histogram. Peaks in a histogram indicate a large number of voxels in the dataset that have the same intensity value. If we assume that our dataset contains meaningful information with a reasonably low noise level, the large number of voxels with the same intensity value suggests a homogenous region with the same material.[3] Figure 6.2 shows an example of these ranges below the histograms, and the respective result of the classification in Figure 6.4 (right). Blue specifies the background intensity range and magenta the low intensity range air-filled space of the lungs. The gray part classifies the tissue between some organs that is mostly subject to the partial volume effect. The low intensity organ tissues are classified in cyan, while the higher intensity organs are classified in yellow. The green area marks higher intensity tissue, such as bones. Finally, the red area marks the very high intensity tissues, also typically bone tissue. Note that while the number of voxels with very high intensity values is small, their contribution is often important and cannot simply be ignored.

Unfortunately, different organ tissues often do not map to different intensity ranges. Furthermore, the histogram does not provide any information where voxels of the same intensity range are located within the dataset; they might not be located in the same area. Hence, we cannot always differentiate organs by classification alone. In those cases, we require an explicit segmentation step, as described in the volume visualization pipeline in Section 6.1.

Note that the histogram does not need to be computed on the whole volume dataset. Instead, only a subset of volume slices (e.g., one slice) or even a local region of interest can be selected for the computation of the histogram.

The vertical appearance of linear histograms is set by its y-scaling, which is dominated by the highest peak. This peak is commonly created by background voxels, which have a zero or near-zero intensity value (cf. the example in Fig. 6.2). Since the frequency of these background voxels is typically several orders of magnitude higher than the smallest peaks, the latter ones will essentially be unnoticeable in the histogram (right end of Fig. 6.2 (left)). This is, for example, the case for the very bright spot near the lung on the left side of Figure 6.4 (marked in yellow or classified into red in the right image). This situation can become even more extreme after a windowing operation, where basically all background voxels are mapped to zero, increasing the background peak several orders of magnitude higher.[4]

Zoomed Histograms   As one remedy to that situation, we can zoom into the histogram area of interest. Figure 6.2 (right) shows such an example, where the low frequency part of the upper intensities becomes visible due to a vertical zoom. However, this solution does not allow the simultaneous analysis of the high frequency part on the left.

Figure 6.2 (right) also exposes another problem that affects virtually all histogram representations—aliasing. Since the drawing of the histogram does not provide enough pixels for all histogram buckets (4096 buckets for a 12-bit dataset), thin peaks are subject to undersampling. Some of these thin peaks will be visible, some will be not visible. This issue is clearly visible on the right half of Figure 6.2 (right). Note that this aliasing artifact, visible or invisible, affects all histograms presented here.

Logarithmic Histograms   A better solution for dealing with very high and low peaks is the application of logarithmic scaling to the voxel values, as demonstrated in Figure 6.3. Now all peaks are roughly scaled to a comparable height and the upper voxel intensities become visible. Note that there will be situations in which logarithmic scaling is not appropriate. In particular, in cases where we have a similar voxel

---

3   As we will point out later, histograms do not provide any spatial information. Here, we simply exploit knowledge about the scanned objects.

4   Note that due to noise in scanned datasets, background voxels can have intensities higher than zero. After windowing, these background voxels are mapped to zero.

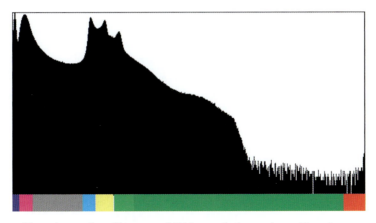

FIGURE 6.3 *Vertical logarithmic scaling of histogram of CT dataset of a human thorax. The peaks are now of comparable height and the upper intensity voxel values become visible on the right side. The color code marks the same intensity ranges as in the linear histograms in Figure 6.2.*

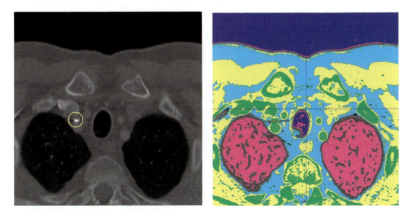

FIGURE 6.4 *Original (left) and classified (right) slice of CT thorax dataset used in Figure 6.2. The circle marks an area with very high intensity values. The slice image on the right is classified according to the colors in the bottom end of the linear histogram.*

distribution, a linear scaling (linear histogram) provides easier interpretation than a logarithmic scaling. Furthermore, a logarithmic histogram can overemphasize value variations due to noise, as can be seen in the right area of Figure 6.3. Another example of linear/logarithmic histograms is shown in Figure 6.5. In contrast to the CT thorax dataset shown in Figure 6.2, the background voxel peak is even more dominating than higher intensity value peaks.

Finally, please note that one-dimensional histograms can only differentiate different materials; they cannot differentiate material boundaries and the resulting interface between three or more materials (*material interfaces* or *material boundaries*). Achieving this differentiation requires multidimensional histograms that at least employ gradient information between the voxels. A detailed discussion on that topic can be found in Section 11.1.1 in the chapter on transfer function specification.

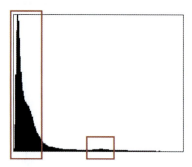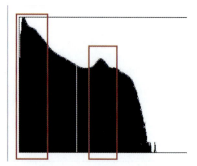

FIGURE 6.5   *The linear TF horizontal scale is inappropriate for the histogram of a particular MRI dataset, since the large majority of the values is concentrated on the very left. The logarithmic scale is better suited and allows a fine-grained specification with respect to significant peaks in the histogram. The rectangles indicate the same peaks in both histograms.*

6.2.2 TRANSFER FUNCTION SPECIFICATION

As described earlier in this chapter, transfer functions (TFs) assign optical properties to voxel values. Specifically, the case we examined here is a standard one, in which the voxel values are mapped to RGBα colors and opacities.

Typically, the voxel values are not individually mapped to a quadruple of RGBα values. Instead, piecewise functions are used to specify a whole intensity range at once. Depending on the application, these piecewise functions can be very flexible or quite restricted. Figure 6.6 shows typical examples of transfer functions, which consist of piecewise linear functions. These piecewise linear functions are manipulated by changing the position of the control points at the end of each line segment. If additional control points are added (or removed), the line segments can be refined (or coarsened). Once a whole section of a transfer function is specfied, it is useful to group the respective control points to allow simultaneous modifications of that section. Rapid changes of a transfer function may not always introduce an improvement of the transfer function. In those cases, an undo function helps to remove the recent changes.

While linear line segments are a frequent choice for piecewise transfer functions, higher order functions are also often used to achieve a smoother transition. Furthermore, the piecewise functions can be voxel value specific, if the transfer function editor allows pencil-like drawing operations (see Fig. 6.7 (right)). In medical applications, transfer function editors provide only limited flexibility. Similar to the transfer function editor in Figure 6.6, they provide only trapezoids and ramps as specification primitives. These primitives can be translated on the abscissa, and scaled horizontally and vertically. Furthermore, the slope of the rising and falling edges of the trapezoids can be manipulated.

In the process of specifying a transfer function, intensity ranges of materials need to be identified. Colors and opacities are then assigned to the intensity ranges of these materials in the histogram. Important structures are typically assigned a high opacity (to increase their visibility), while surrounding context information (e.g., skin) is assigned a significantly lower opacity. Colors are used to differentiate the different material types. Figure 6.4 (right) shows the result of such a color classification, whereas the opacity is set to maximum. The bottom part of Figure 6.3 shows the intensity ranges of the different colors. In contrast, different opacities are assigned in Figure 6.6; the upper row shows a low opacity ramp for the low intensity voxel values of soft tissue, and a high opacity assignment for the bone and contrast enhanced structures. The lower row shows no low opacity ramp, but a steep opacity ramp for the soft tissue, hence more soft tissue becomes visible.

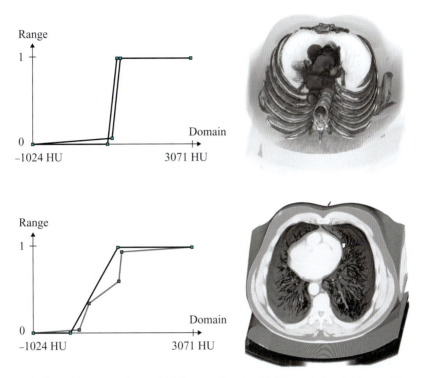

FIGURE 6.6   Left column: adjustment of a gray-level (gray) and opacity (black) transfer function in a graphical transfer function editor. Control points (small quadrilaterals) define the shape of the function. Right column: resulting rendition of a CT thorax data. Top row: only structures with high X-ray attenuation are visible according to the transfer function. Bottom row: the different transfer function specification (left) leads to a different result (right). Lung tissue and abdominal fatty tissue are now visible, due to the shifted opacity curve. The units shown in the histograms are Hounsfield units (HUs).

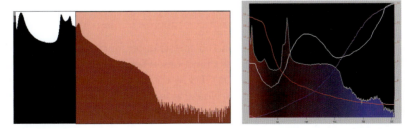

FIGURE 6.7   Left: binary opacity transfer function. All voxel values below the specified rising edge of the red area are assigned a zero opacity, and all voxel values above and equal (below the red area) are fully opaque. Right: transfer function editor with pencil function to draw color (red and green) and opacity transfer function. The background shows the histogram with the resulting colors.

A special case of TFs are *binary TFs*. In contrast to the flexible specification of TFs as described above, they typically consist of one (or two) very steep rising (see Fig. 6.7 (left)) or falling edges. These edges indicate a *threshold* or an *isovalue*, since they essentially classify all voxels with an intensity below the threshold as invisible (zero opacity) and all voxels with an intensity value above or equal as opaque (maximum opacity). Typically, binary transfer functions are used if an isosurface is specified (see Chaps. 7 and 8).

Transfer functions can have an additional impact on a visual representation based on them; depending on the function, they increase the frequency spectrum of the classified dataset. In Section 2.2, we described how important it is to provide a sufficient sampling, in order to avoid artifacts. If we assume that the cut-off frequency of the dataset is f_{ds} and the cut-off frequency of the transfer function is f_{tf}, then the resulting cut-off frequency of the classified dataset is $f_{all} = f_{ds} \times f_{tf}$. Obviously, a binary TF will introduce significantly higher frequencies than a smooth higher order function.

Note that the specification of the opacity allows also a decision on the visibility of the respective voxels; an opacity of zero (e.g., below the threshold of a binary TF) results in a zero contribution of those voxels. However, this allows only a very limited selection of semantic structures in the datasets, like specific organs, since no spatial or organ-specific information is considered. Since organs do not just differ by intensity values, classification is typically not suited for the selection or identification of objects in a dataset. This task requires specific segmentation methods. Nevertheless, the classification as described in this section is equivalent to threshold-based segmentation (see Sect. 5.3.2).

Presets for TF Specification   On radiological workstations in a clinical setting, the complex manual specification of transfer functions for every patient dataset would be too time consuming. Consequently, the specification is usually supported by a variety of predefined TFs ("preset") for certain types of data and diagnostics questions. This concept is particularly useful for CT datasets, since CT maps tissue consistently to the same intensity values. This ensures a very similar classification, even for different scanning subjects.

Presets are chosen based on the DICOM tags that describe the datasets. The Vitrea® Workstation, provided by VitalImages, has pioneered such presets and presents for each kind of image data a so-called *gallery* with up to six volume renderings, each of which emphasizes the different structures of this dataset. As we have discussed in Section 4.3.4, presets for transfer functions may be part of digital hanging protocols. As such, they may be distributed to other users or stored as personal preference.

Interactivity and Preview   The process of manually specifying a transfer function can be very complex and cumbersome. Numerous techniques have been proposed to provide more intuitive or even automatic schemes for their specification. Chapter 11 presents a detailed discussion of the various approaches. In many cases, however, we end up with a manual specification. To facilitate the process of specification, rapid feedback on how the classification will change the volume rendering results is necessary. Therefore, an interactive preview on the results of this trial-and-error approach is important.

Color Versus Gray-Level Transfer Functions   As mentioned before, transfer functions specify color and opacity. Figure 6.7 (left) shows an example of RGBα transfer functions, whereas the transfer function of the green color channel maps only to zero (no contribution). Below the histogram, we see the color map of the intensity values specified by the red and blue TFs. Note that in areas of a low opacity, the resulting color contribution is smaller than in areas with a higher opacity. This effect, however, is not visible in Figure 6.7 (right).

A special category of color transfer functions is gray-level transfer functions, where R, G, and B are manipulated simultaneously. Hence, the resulting colors vary between black and white only. Figure 6.6 shows such gray-level (and opacity) transfer functions. Again, the gray values of voxels with a low specified opacity also have a low contribution.

One of the motivations for using either color or gray-level transfer functions lies in the target community; if the resulting visualizations are meant for radiologists, very often a gray-level representation is preferred. In contrast, surgeons typically prefer color representations of the dataset.

6.2.3 SELECTION OF ISOVALUES

One of the specific tasks of specifying a transfer function is the determination of organ structures. In most practical cases, this is achieved by selecting isovalues that represent the boundaries of these organ structures. These isovalues are used to specify an isosurface for indirect volume rendering (see Chap. 7), or direct volume rendering (see Chap. 8). In both cases, the isosurface will be specified through TFs, where binary TFs are typically used for indirect representations. For direct representations, these TFs are specified through ramps and trapezoids centered at the isovalue. This way, a smoother transition is ensured.

Since isovalues are obviously relevant for the TF specification, we will briefly look into their selection process. As we have pointed out in Section 6.2.1, regions of homogeneous materials tend to create peaks in the histogram. Consequently, these peaks may also indicate the transition area between materials—the material boundaries. However, it is not the peak itself that may represent those boundaries, but their flanks. Figure 6.3 and 6.4 show this relationship: the dark blue area indicates the background, and the purple area indicates the non-background voxels of the lower airways in the lungs. The purple area at the bottom of Figure 6.3 covers not only the peak, but the whole area between the rising and falling flank of that peak.

As we have seen above, the process of isovalue determination is basically driven by the identification of peaks and the following selection of the area between the flanks of the peak. Note, however, that this is not always sufficient. We can also see in Figure 6.3 that the dark green area of high density bone material is not exposed by a peak, but by something like a plateau or a slowly falling line, and the high intensity red spot (marked by the circle) does not show up at all in the histogram. In those cases, we need to carefully analyze the voxel data to identify relevant structures. The application of a colormap (a color transition or color band assigned to a range of voxel values) may be applied to expose interesting material transitions.

Figure 6.3 shows the classification for a CT dataset. As we have pointed out in Section 3.2, certain tissue types (Table 3.1) can be identified by specific Hounsfield values, which are also exploited for the TF presets described in the previous section. This, however, does not work for MRI data, since no stable intensity values can be determined for specific tissue types. In those cases, a dataset-specific analysis must be performed, possibly taking into account more advanced data analysis methods (see Further Reading in Sect. 6.4).

6.3   ILLUMINATION IN SCALAR VOLUME DATASETS

Similar to standard computer graphics, volume visualization uses illumination information to provide more visual structure to the represented information. This section provides a brief summary of the local illumination model that is typically used, the Phong illumination model [PHONG 1975]. Note that while this is the standard model for many computer graphics application and also of the OpenGL Application Programming Interface (API), it is by no means the sole or most accurate model. In particular, global illumination and, more recently, direct illumination models [KAUTZ 2003] are used to achieve a higher level of photorealistic rendering. However, the goal of visualization, and of medical visualization in particular, is the comprehensive and visual representation of information. The sources of this information typically do not represent our world as perceived by our visual system. Hence, photorealism usually does not increase the understanding of the data; in the best case, it is only an expensive add-on method, but in the worst case, it can actually make interpretation more difficult. For this reason, we limit our presentation here to the Phong illumination model.[5] For a more detailed discussion of illumination models in general, and global illumination in particular, we refer to FOLEY et al. [1995], and GLASSNER [1989].

6.3.1 PHONG'S ILLUMINATION MODEL

The illumination model of PHONG [1975] combines three components in its formula; ambient light, diffuse reflection, and specular reflection (see Eq. 6.5).

$$I_{total} = I_{amb} + c_{att} \sum_{i=0}^{n-1}(I_{diff,i} + I_{spec,i}) \qquad (6.5)$$

Ambient light can be seen as a general and uniform background light, while diffuse and specular reflections describe specific properties of the objects. In the case of volume rendering, these objects are sampling points in the volume datasets. Diffuse and specular reflections depend on the light sources, hence their contribution iterates over all n specified light sources. Furthermore, c_{att} models light attenuation to enable the differentiation between different objects with the same orientation.[6] A standard interpretation of c_{att} introduces a term that models the distance between sampling points and viewpoint.

Ambient Light Ambient light models the background illumination with no specific light source. Often, ambient light is described as a self-luminous phenomenon, where the constant k_{amb} specifies the material properties. If we add a specific color C_{amb} of the background light and a diffuse object or sampling point color O_{diff}, we yield Equation 6.6:

$$I_{amb} = k_{amb}C_{amb}O_{diff} \qquad (6.6)$$

Diffuse Reflection Ambient light alone does not allow for good discrimination of object features, since the illumination will be constant from all viewing directions and positions. Diffuse reflection, also known as Lambertian reflection, adds dependencies of the light direction and the surface structure to our illumination model. Specifically, we add a normal $\vec{N}$ of the sampling point and the light direction $\vec{L}$ as a scalar product, describing the angle θ between both vectors (see Eq. 6.7, Fig. 6.8):

$$I_{diff} = k_{diff}C_{light}O_{diff}(\vec{N} \cdot \vec{L}) \qquad (6.7)$$

where C_{light} describes the color of the light source, O_{diff} is again the diffuse color of the sampling point, and $(\vec{N} \cdot \vec{L}) = cos(\theta)$. k_{diff} models the overall intensity of the diffuse reflection.

Specular Reflection Diffuse reflection provides a reflection that resamples matte surfaces without any highlights. In contrast, the third component of the Phong illumination model introduces specular reflection, which can be usually observed on shiny surfaces. Since this term models the specular reflection, it needs to consider the direction of the reflection $\vec{R}$—which is the light vector $\vec{L}$ mirrored at the normal $\vec{N}$—and

---

5   Some visualization systems even use only a simplified Phong illumination model.

6   Objects at different locations but same orientation are not differentiated by the reflection terms, since those only consider directional information.

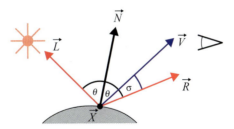

FIGURE 6.8 Phong Illumination Model: The normal $\vec{N}$ is located at sampling point $\vec{X}$ of an object. $\vec{V}$ points to the viewing point, and $\vec{L}$ indicates the light direction. θ describes the angle between $\vec{N}$ and $\vec{L}$, while $\vec{R}$ describes the reflection of $\vec{L}$ at the normal $\vec{N}$. σ describes the angle between $\vec{R}$ and $\vec{V}$.

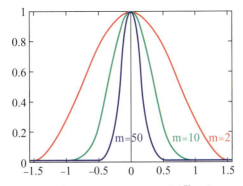

FIGURE 6.9 Drop-off of specular highlights of view-dependent part $cos(\sigma)^m$ with increasing exponent m.

the direction to the viewing position $\vec{V}$. If $\vec{R}$ and $\vec{V}$ are normalized, we can transform the viewpoint dependent part: $(\vec{R} \cdot \vec{V})^m = cos(\sigma)^m$.

$$I_{spec} = k_{spec} C_{light} O_{spec} (\vec{R} \cdot \vec{V})^m \qquad (6.8)$$

Equation 6.8 for the specular reflection looks now very similar to Equation 6.7 for diffuse reflection, except for the viewpoint depending part $(\vec{R} \cdot \vec{V})^m = cos(\sigma)^m$, which takes into account the angle σ between the reflection and viewing vector. k_{spec} describes again the overall intensity of specular reflection and O_{spec} describes the specular color of the object at the sampling point. C_{light} is the same as in Equation 6.7.

The exponent m in $cos(\sigma)^m$ determines the sharpness of the specular highlights. The larger m is, the stronger the drop-off of the highlights. Figure 6.9 illustrates how the term $cos(\sigma)^m$ changes with different exponents. Figure 6.10 shows an example for the Phong illumination model. All three components are displayed separately (leftmost three images) and combined in a weighted sum (right image). The example shows an aneurysm at the cerebral t-junction of one of the carotid arteries and one of the frontal and middle cerebral arteries.

In summary, several parameters have to be specified for the Phong illumination model. Material properties (O_{diff} and O_{spec}) and the weighting coefficients (k_{amb}, k_{diff}, and k_{spec})[7] are typically specified

7   The sum of the coefficients must be normalized to one.

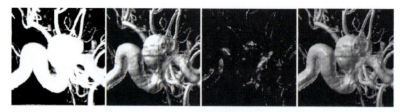

FIGURE 6.10 *The images show the different components of the Phong illumination model. From right to left: Ambient light, diffuse reflection, specular reflection, and combined result with weight factors $k_{amb} = 0.1$, $k_{diff} = 0.5$, $k_{spec} = 0.4$. The dataset itself was generated by a rotational angiography of one of the cerebral t-junctions of carotid and frontal and middle cerebral arteries. (Images courtesy MICHAEL MEIßNER, University of Tübingen)*

by transfer functions. While the viewing positions and direction $\vec{V}$ depend on the current viewing transformation, we usually have constant light parameters (direction $\vec{L}$ and light colors C_{amb} and C_{light}).[8] All that remains is the normal vector $\vec{N}$, which we will discuss in the next section.

6.3.2 APPROXIMATION OF NORMAL VECTORS

Normals are typically defined as normalized vectors on surfaces, and they are computed as vectors orthogonal to the tangent plane at that position. In polygonal computer graphics, this means that they are either provided through a generating function (e.g., for splines) or they are computed for a polygon (e.g., a triangle) through a cross product. Vertex normals are then computed by a weighted average of the normals of the polygons of which that vertex is part.

Volumetric data, however, do not contain surfaces, and hence no surface normals. Therefore, we need to construct a meaningful normal for our sampling points. The de facto standard approach in volume graphics is the use of gradients of the voxel values as normals [HÖHNE and BERNSTEIN 1986], even if no surface is present. Gradients are motivated essentially by the partial volume effect, which is due to low-pass filtering of insufficiently sampled large intensity differences (see Sect. 2.2.3). Since the partial volume effect ensures smooth voxel intensities in that area, it also ensures that no large intensity differences are present. Hence, the gradients in the affected areas will also be smooth, which renders them as excellent candidates for normals.

In the following, we will explore the various options for the approximation of the gradient vector in sampled datasets. Specifically, we will look into intermediate and central differences [HÖHNE and BERNSTEIN 1986] and the Sobel operator [PINGLE 1969].

Central Difference The approximation of the local gradient with the central difference operator and its use as normal was independently proposed by HÖHNE and BERNSTEIN [1986]. It is also known as gray-level gradient shading. The operator itself approximates the gradient at a voxel V_{000} by calculating the intensity difference in its close neighborhood. It considers all voxels in the 6-neighborhood of V_{000} except those of V_{000} itself, as shown in Figure 6.11 (left).

$$D_{000} = \begin{pmatrix} D_{000,x} \\ D_{000,y} \\ D_{000,z} \end{pmatrix} = \begin{pmatrix} V_{100} - V_{-100} \\ V_{010} - V_{0-10} \\ V_{001} - V_{00-1} \end{pmatrix} \tag{6.9}$$

---

8 Note that all the material and light parameters are wavelength-dependent, which we ignored here for simplicity.

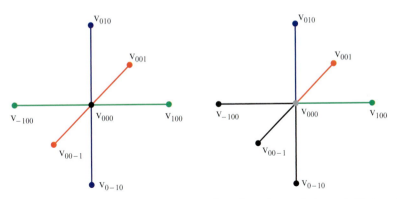

FIGURE 6.11 Left: central differences—the red, blue, and green colors indicate the contributing voxels. The intensity value of V_{000} itself does not contribute to the computation of the gradient. Right: intermediate difference considers the intensity value of V_{000} in contrast to the central difference operator.

Equation 6.9 formalizes this relationship. For use as normals, the computed difference vectors must be normalized $\vec{N} = \nabla V_{ijk} = \|D_{000}\|$. In the case of anisotropic voxel spacing, we need to scale the gradient vector with the respective voxel spacing (x_s, y_s, z_s), before we normalize the gradient vector. The need for this scaling was already discussed in Section 2.2.4. Equation 6.10 expresses this scaled gradient vector. Note that this scaling is required for all anisotropic datasets to avoid interpolation artifacts. In the following, however, we will continue with the simpler isotropic situation.

$$D_{000}^{sc} = \begin{pmatrix} x_s\, D_{000,x} \\ y_s\, D_{000,y} \\ z_s\, D_{000,z} \end{pmatrix} = \begin{pmatrix} x_s(V_{100} - V_{-100}) \\ y_s(V_{010} - V_{0-10}) \\ z_s(V_{001} - V_{00-1}) \end{pmatrix} \tag{6.10}$$

The operator to compute the central difference of a voxel is essentially a highpass filter, which can also be expressed as a filter kernel: $[-1, 0, 1]$. Note that this filter needs to be applied for every gradient vector component and the respective directions within the volume. Figure 6.12 (left) shows the results of central difference–based normal approximation. In comparison, the result of intermediate difference–based normal approximation is shown on the right side.

Intermediate Difference The intermediate difference operator considers only a limited neighborhood of the current voxel, which consists of the intensities of the "next" voxels (with an incremented index) and the current voxel V_{000} itself (see Fig. 6.11 (right)):

$$D_{000} = \begin{pmatrix} D_{000,x} \\ D_{000,y} \\ D_{000,z} \end{pmatrix} = \begin{pmatrix} V_{100} - V_{000} \\ V_{010} - V_{000} \\ V_{001} - V_{000} \end{pmatrix} \tag{6.11}$$

As an alternative to the "next" voxels, a variation of intermediate difference uses the "previous" voxels with a decremented index. Due to the different possible directions of the intermediate difference operator, they are sometimes also called *forward* (with incremented indices) and *backward* (with decremented indices) differences. Both variations are highpass filters, which also can be expressed as a filter kernel with $[-1, 1]$ (for the forward difference) for each direction within the volume. Figure 6.12 (right) shows the

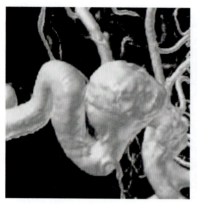 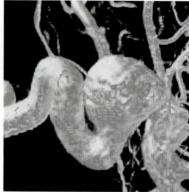

FIGURE 6.12 *Visualization of the aneurysm dataset from rotation angiography. Left: central differences are used to approximate the normal. Right: intermediate differences are used to approximate the normal. (Images courtesy* MICHAEL MEIßNER, *University of Tübingen)*

results of intermediate difference–based normal approximation for the aneurysm dataset from rotational angiography.

Sobel Operator Of all gradient estimators discussed here, the one with the highest complexity, but also the smoothest visual quality, is the Sobel operator. The Sobel operator is another highpass filter that was apparently first credited to Sobel by PINGLE [1969]. It considers the intensity value of V_{000} itself, and of the full 26-neighborhood of V_{000}. Since the equation for the computation of the gradient for each voxel is quite complex, we show in Equations 6.12 through 6.14 only the filter kernel for the x (see Eq. 6.12), y (see Eq. 6.13), and z components (see Eq. 6.14). The respective kernels are obtained by rotation of the filter kernels. The first matrix is for the previous slice, the second matrix for the current slice, and the third matrix for the next slice.

$$\begin{bmatrix} -1 & -3 & -1 \\ -3 & -6 & -3 \\ -1 & -3 & -1 \end{bmatrix}, \quad \begin{bmatrix} 0 & 0 & 0 \\ 0 & 0 & 0 \\ 0 & 0 & 0 \end{bmatrix}, \quad \begin{bmatrix} 1 & 3 & 1 \\ 3 & 6 & 3 \\ 1 & 3 & 1 \end{bmatrix}, \qquad [6.12]$$

$$\begin{bmatrix} 1 & 3 & 1 \\ 0 & 0 & 0 \\ -1 & -3 & -1 \end{bmatrix}, \quad \begin{bmatrix} 3 & 6 & 3 \\ 0 & 0 & 0 \\ -3 & -6 & -3 \end{bmatrix}, \quad \begin{bmatrix} 1 & 3 & 1 \\ 0 & 0 & 0 \\ -1 & -3 & -1 \end{bmatrix}, \qquad [6.13]$$

$$\begin{bmatrix} -1 & 0 & 1 \\ -3 & 0 & 3 \\ -1 & 0 & 1 \end{bmatrix}, \quad \begin{bmatrix} -3 & 0 & 3 \\ -6 & 0 & 6 \\ -3 & 0 & 3 \end{bmatrix}, \quad \begin{bmatrix} -1 & 0 & 1 \\ -3 & 0 & 3 \\ -1 & 0 & 1 \end{bmatrix}, \qquad [6.14]$$

Other Approaches Although gradient estimation-based shading methods are doubtless the standard approaches, there are several others. In particular, depth shading uses the depth value (after its recovery from the z-buffer) or the distance from the viewpoint to estimate a normal. This method was particularly used in combination with the cuberille method [CHEN et al. 1985]. However, with the increase of computing power, more expensive methods with a significantly better quality—such as the central difference operator—replaced depth shading. A further discussion of gradient-based and depth-based normal estimators is provided by TIEDE *et al.* [1990].

Another shading technique was recently published by DESGRANGES *et al.* [2005]. Somewhat similar to depth shading, they use the accumulated opacity through an outer shell object to attenuate the intensity. They furthermore introduced a shading technique using shadows and approximated the specular term of the Phong lighting model with the computed diffuse intensity. The advantage of this technique is that a gradient as a normal approximation is not required. This is in particular helpful for datasets inflicted by noise, or if the gradient magnitudes are very small, thus being very sensitive to small inhomogeneities.

The methods of gradient-based normal approximation consider the immediate voxel neighborhood of the current voxel. BENTUM *et al.* [1996] and later MÖLLER *et al.* [1997] also discussed higher order interpolation methods that take into account a larger neighborhood. Until now, however, these methods have not widely been adopted, due to the significantly increased computation time.

Quality of Normal Estimators

The choice of a normal estimator is a trade-off question between quality and resource consumption. Figure 6.13 shows the results for the normal estimators we have discussed, namely intermediate difference, central difference, and the Sobel operator. Clearly, the Sobel operator results in the best visual quality with very smooth normals. In contrast, the intermediate difference operator exposes significantly more normal interpolation artifacts and is more sensitive to noise.

The Sobel operator takes into account a larger neighborhood than the difference operators and it performs well if a surface-like structure is to be reconstructed. However, it might at the same time remove fine and small structures. In particular, structures perpendicular to the main gradient direction can be

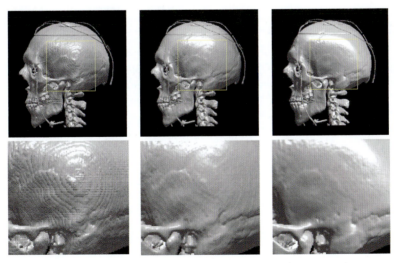

FIGURE 6.13 *Comparison of the three main candidates for gradient computation. The upper row shows a view of the full dataset, the lower row shows a close-up of the area within the yellow rectangle. From left to right: results for the intermediate difference operator, the central difference operator, and the Sobel operator.*

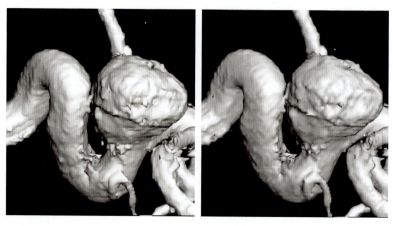

FIGURE 6.14 *Left: vertex normals are computed based on the triangle normals. Right: voxel normals are computed based on central difference.*

affected by it. In these cases, the central difference and in particular the intermediate difference operator are more appropriate for the normal approximation.

Overall, the Sobel operator provides superior visual quality (for surface-like structures), while consuming by far the most computational resources. The central difference operator offers somewhat reduced visual quality at modest costs. In contrast, the intermediate difference operator has the poorest visual quality at the same costs as the central difference operator, but it is more faithful to the original local data. All things considered, this leads to the very high acceptance of the central difference operator as the today's standard method of computing voxel-based normals for indirect and direct volume rendering.

Voxel Normals versus Vertex Normals

In the case of indirect volume rendering, or polygonal isosurface rendering, we can choose between two alternatives for the approximation of normals. We can compute the vertex normals directly from the corresponding cross product (of the triangles and the following averaging of all triangle normals contributing to that vertex) or we can use gradient-based voxel normals.

Figure 6.14 compares both approaches in a close-up of the aneurysm dataset. The vertex normals computed by the cross product clearly expose a patch structure (left), while the gradient-based method (right) shows a much more coherent and smooth surface, due to the partial volume effect [HÖHNE and BERNSTEIN 1986].

6.4   SUMMARY

In this chapter, we laid out the foundations for volume visualization, which are used for both indirect and direct volume rendering. In particular, we briefly discussed the individual steps of the volume visualization pipeline that lead from a volumetric dataset to the rendered visual representation in an image (see Sect. 6.1).

Section 6.2 was concerned with the analysis of the datasets based on their histogram. This analysis was then used for the specification of transfer functions that determine the visual appearance of the data values of the dataset in the final image. Furthermore, this section discussed how meaningful isovalues may be extracted from the volume dataset.

Finally, Section 6.3 explained how illumination and shading effects are computed for volume visualization using the Phong illumination model. An important part of the illumination is the computation of the normal at the contributing samples. Since a mathematical description of a surface may not be available (in particular for direct volume rendering), this normal is approximated by the local gradient. This gradient in turn can be estimated by different gradient operators with different impacts on quality and performance.

FURTHER READING

Among the first researchers, DREBIN et al. [1988] showed how a classification of tissue types can be conducted based on a histogram in the context of direct volume rendering. Unfortunately, most useful classifications cannot be achieved that easily. Advanced transfer function design will be discussed in more detail in Chapter 11. For the identification of meaningful isovalues, BAJAJ et al. [1997] proposed the *Contour Spectrum*. Alternatively, KINDLMANN and DURKIN [1998] suggested the use of the first (gradient) and second partial derivative to derive useful isovalues. Local higher order moments (LHOMs) were used by TENGINAKAI et al. [2001] and TENGINAKAI and MACHIRAJU [2002] for isovalue identification, and PEKAR et al. [2001] used a special Laplace-weighted histogram.

While the illumination model we discussed is pretty straightforward, plenty of research has been devoted to the computation of good normals. Today's standard approach of using central differences as normal approximation has been introduced independently by HÖHNE and BERNSTEIN [1986] and BARILLOT et al. [1985]. Using higher order gradient operators such as the Sobel operator is discussed in PINGLE [1969] or more recent image processing books. BENTUM et al. [1996] and later MÖLLER et al. [1997] also discussed other higher order interpolation methods. An alternative illumination technique was recently proposed by DESGRANGES et al. [2005].

Chapter 07

Indirect Volume Visualization

Volumetric data are composed of a very large number of individual voxels. One approach to extract information from this large set of information attempts to do so by focusing on a subset of that information. In this chapter, we will concentrate on two different avenues for indirect volume rendering: plane-oriented visualization (see Sect. 7.1) and surface-oriented visualization (see Sect. 7.2), which we will discuss in the following sections. In the last section of this chapter, we will also examine postprocessing methods to reduce the amount of generated rendering data and ways to smooth this data (see Sect. 7.3).

7.1 PLANE-BASED VOLUME RENDERING

A widely used technique in medical routine is the *cine mode*, in which the individual slices of a volumetric dataset are examined subsequently. Due to the frequently anisotropic nature of volumetric datasets, the cine mode examination mode is mostly used along the DICOM slice orientation, which is specified by the acquisition protocol (e.g., axial for CT), since slice resolution and voxel spacing are then identical.[1] If another slice orientation is chosen, the resolution and voxel spacing will be different in most cases,[2] as the slice is now spanned by one image dimension and the number of slices of the volume dataset. If we examine the data with more than one slice orientation, we speak of a multi-planar reconstruction (MPR).

So far, all our slice reconstructions are aligned with the cuboid that is spanned by the slice images and that encompasses our volume dataset (see Fig. 7.1). Each of the different slice orientations is orthogonal to the other ones. Unfortunately, most anatomical structures are aligned neither to the dataset nor to any regular geometric structure. Consequently, a standard slice orientation will usually provide only an insufficient representation of the target structure.

For these situations, *oblique* volume slices provide a better representation, since they can be arbitrarily oriented within the dataset. Like all planes, oblique slices are defined by a position vector inside the volume dataset and the normal vector of the plane. The voxels on the intersection of the volume dataset and that slice are the visual representation of the oblique slice (see Fig. 7.2).

Technically, the computation of oblique slices is a 3D scan-conversion problem, in which we need to compute the voxels intersected by the plane. This is traditionally achieved with a three-dimensional version of BRESENHAM's classic 2D scan conversion algorithm [BRESENHAM 1965], e.g., KAUFMAN's approach [KAUFMAN 1987b]. The today's standard approach, however, employs 3D texture-mapping, which is also called 3D texture slicing [CULLIP and NEUMANN 1993]. In this approach, the volumetric dataset is interpreted as a 3D texture, which is mapped as a texture on a polygon [WESTERMANN and ERTL 1998]. If that polygon represents an oblique slice through the volume dataset, the texture-mapping functionality of the graphics hardware will fill it with the respective voxels (see also Sect. 9.4). Since texture mapping is

---

1   e.g., 512 × 512 and 0.3 mm × 0.3 mm.

2   e.g., a slice resolution of 512 × 220 with a voxel spacing of 0.3 mm × 1 mm.

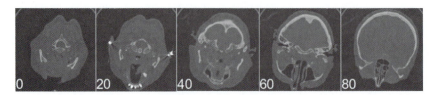

FIGURE 7.1   *Cine mode examination of a CT angiography dataset. Every 20th slice image is displayed.*

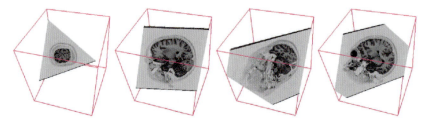

FIGURE 7.2   *Oblique slice mode examination of a MRI dataset. The oblique slice is clipped to the boundaries of the volume dataset. (Images courtesy* PETER HASTREITER, *University of Erlangen-Nürnberg)*

performed on modern graphics cards in hardware, it is fast. Furthermore, it uses trilinear or quadlinear[3] interpolation (see Sect. 2.1) to provide a high quality reconstruction. For more information on texture-mapping for volume rendering, please refer to Chapter 8.

Yet another plane-based representation is *curved planar reformation* (CPR). This technique addresses the problem that most organs are not aligned with the volume dataset, and hence are not well represented in either plane. As an example, blood vessels cannot be represented well in one plane, since their location typically changes quite rapidly. Instead, CPR computes a curve along a selected blood vessel and a respective curved slice, using the vessel curve as profile and the largest vessel diameter as spanning vector [KANITSAR *et al.* 2001] (see Fig. 7.3). Technically, the CPR image is computed similar as the oblique slice with a 3D rasterization approach. Note that several issues are associated with a CPR representation. First, the chosen method for the computation of the vessel curve (and the largest diameter) influences the quality of the CPR. Second, the varying vessel diameter may be not well represented within the reformatted plane. Further discussion on CPR can be found in the work of KANITSAR *et al.* [2001, 2002a, 2003].

7.2   SURFACE-BASED VOLUME RENDERING

Structures of interest in volumetric data are typically differentiated from the surrounding image data by a boundary or a material interface. The surface-based variation of indirect volume rendering aims at a visual representation of that boundary, which needs to be specified. Typically, this boundary is on voxels that have the same or a similar intensity value. Hence, the resulting surface on these voxels is called an *isosurface*. This concept is analogous to *contour lines* on a map, which mark lines of the same altitude. Isosurfaces are also known as the 3D extension of contour lines, and they are also called 3D *contours* or sometimes *contour surfaces*.

---

3   Quadlinear interpolation combines two trilinear interpolation results in different resolution levels (mipmaps) with a linear interpolation.

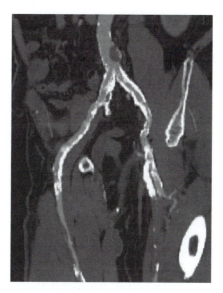

FIGURE 7.3   *Curved planar reformation of the femoral arteries from a patient CT dataset* [KANITSAR *et al.* 2002a]. *(Image courtesy* ARMIN KANITSAR, *Vienna University of Technology)*

An isosurface can be specified as an implicit surface, where the implicit function equals the isovalue (also called threshold)[4] or where the difference of the implicit function and the isovalue is zero. Equation 7.1 describes this relationship; x is the voxel position and τ is the isovalue or threshold.

$$i(x) = V(x) - \tau = 0 \tag{7.1}$$

Effectively, an isosurface separates a volume dataset into an *outside* and an *inside*. This can be specified by adapting Equation 7.1; the outside is described by all voxels with an intensity value smaller than the isovalue τ: $i(x) < 0$. In contrast, all voxels with an intensity value larger than the isovalue τ are part of the inside $(i(x) > 0)$, and all voxels with an intensity value equal to the isovalue τ are part of the isosurface $(i(x) = 0)$. Note that the specification of an isosurface is equivalent to a binary transfer function (see Sect. 6.2.2), and hence is equivalent with threshold-based segmentation. This is a special case, in which classification and segmentation cannot be separated. However, isosurfaces can also be directly computed on segmented data (see Sect. 7.2.3).

If the implicit function itself is known as a polynomial, its gradient can be computed analytically by taking the partial derivatives in all three directions. While this is not uncommon in scientific visualization, where many datasets are generated by computed simulations, this is rarely the case in medical visualization, where most datasets are acquired by 3D scanners like CT or MRI. In those cases, normals are approximated. In Section 6.3.2, we provided a discussion on different gradient operators that are commonly used for normal approximation.

---

4   The process of identifying meaningful isovalues is discussed in Section 6.2.3.

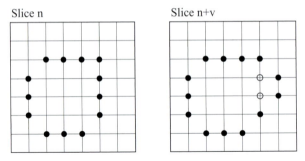

FIGURE 7.4 *A contour in slice n is changing its shape to slice n+1. The outlined positions are the changed previous positions of the contour vertices. Note that contour vertices do not need to be located right on the voxel positions.*

7.2.1 CONTOUR TRACING

Contour tracing is a classic method from image processing to extract boundaries in a digital image. Contour tracing can also be used to extract a 3D contour or isosurface from a volume dataset by applying a standard 2D contour tracing algorithm [GHUNEIM, accessed 2005] to each image slice of the volume dataset individually. Typical examples of such 2D contour tracing algorithms are the approaches by KLEIN et al. [2000] or by VAN WIJK and TELEA [2001]. Once the 2D contours are extracted, they need to be connected with each other. The major issue here is the *correspondence problem*, where we must decide which contour vertex $v_{i,n}$ of slice n corresponds to vertex $w_{j,n+1}$ of the contour in slice $n + 1$. While this task sounds trivial on first sight, it can be very complex. First of all, an object typically changes its shape from slice to slice. Consequently, the corresponding vertex $w_{j,n+1}$ probably has different x, y coordinates (see Fig. 7.4). Fortunately, the shape of the contour generally does not change dramatically, so most vertices of the next slice will have similar coordinates, which can be found by simple local search algorithms, e.g., along the local gradient. However, if the slice distance of the dataset is too large, the contours in the different slices might not overlap any more, which might lead to disconnected parts of one object.

The more difficult issues are topology changes within the contour ("branching problem"). If, for example, the anatomical structure bifurcates into two or more substructures—as it frequently happens with blood vessels or the bronchi—the respective vertex correspondence must be split and merged, as shown in Figure 7.5. Once this problem is solved and the correspondence between neighboring slices is established, the resulting contour surface can be triangulated.

7.2.2 CUBERILLE VOXEL REPRESENTATION

In 1979, HERMAN and LIU introduced the *Cuberille* approach, in which an object boundary is approximated by a large number of polygonal cubes. Each cube represents one voxel and its neighborhood halfway to the next voxel, implementing a nearest-neighbor interpolation scheme (recall Sect. 2.1). Since the polygonal faces of the voxel cubes are always axis-aligned, their normals too are aligned to the axes of the coordinate system, exposing a very blocky surface representation (see Fig. 7.6). Essentially, the cuberille approach generates a binary voxelization[5] of the displayed object (see Fig. 7.6 (left)).

---

5 A voxelization is the 3D scan conversion of a geometric—and hence continuous—object into a discrete voxel description. Here, we refer only to binary voxelization, in which a binary decision determines whether a voxel is set or reset. Voxelization itself is introduced in Section 7.3.4.

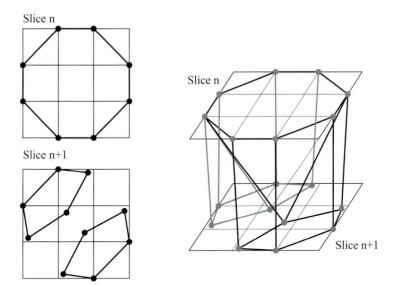

FIGURE 7.5   *The shape and the topology of the contour in slice n are changing at a bifurcation. Left: Consecutive slices with an object bifurcation. Right: One solution to the correspondence problem, where some vertices of slice n are split into several vertices in slice n+1.*

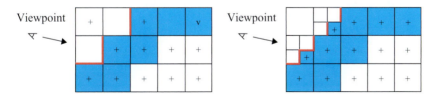

FIGURE 7.6   *Cuberille voxel representation. Left: Boundary voxels (cyan) are selected in a 26-neighborhood if the voxel value is greater equal threshold: $V(x) \geq \tau$ (+). Only faces visible from the viewpoint are rendered (red). Right: Adaptive refinement of the boundary voxels.*

To overcome the problem of the low visual quality, essentially two methods were proposed. CHEN et al. [1985] refined the the normal approximation scheme to improve the visual quality. In particular, they introduced *normal-based contextual shading*, in which the orientation of the neighboring cubes is taken into account. These neighbor orientations index a lookup table of different normal vector orientations that are finally used as normals.

As an alternative to the refined normal computation, the voxel grid can be adaptively voxelized. In areas, where the cuberille surface is particularly inaccurate, a voxel can be subdivided in subvoxels until the cuberille primitives approximate the surface of the object sufficiently accurately (see Fig. 7.6 (right)). An example of a cuberille representation is shown in Figure 7.7.

7.2.3 POLYGONAL ISOSURFACE EXTRACTION

Among the many available approaches and algorithms for the extraction of isosurfaces from volumetric image data [HANSEN and JOHNSON 2004], there is one classic algorithm that has motivated many other

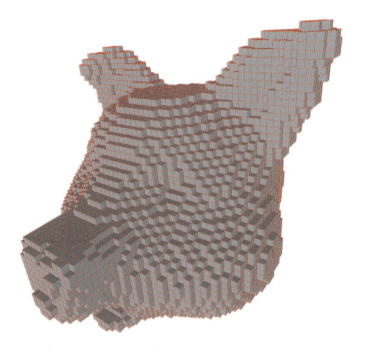

FIGURE 7.7 *One example of a cuberille representation. (Image courtesy* ANDREAS BÆRENTZEN, *Technical University of Denmark)*

approaches, and its publication is one of the most cited scientific papers in computer graphics: the Marching Cubes algorithm [LORENSEN and CLINE 1987].[6] Essentially, the Marching Cubes algorithm examines each individual volume cell and generates a triangulation in it, in case the isosurface is crossing through it. The major innovation of Marching Cubes was the use of a lookup table—the case table—for every possible triangulation. This enabled a significantly faster triangulation of the specified isosurface.

Since Marching Cubes has only a local focus—one cell at a time—and since it has no high-level control, the coherence of the generated isosurface must be maintained inherently. This, however, is a problem of the original version of Marching Cubes, as presented in LORENSEN and CLINE [1987], and it resulted in holes in the triangulation, due to inconsistencies of the triangulation in neighboring cells.

In the following, we will first briefly discuss the 2D version of Marching Cubes, the Marching Squares algorithm. Marching Squares demonstrates all the advantages and drawbacks of Marching Cubes, but at a much more illustrative level. Afterward, we continue with Marching Cubes itself.

Marching Squares

If we limit Marching Cubes to two-dimensional images, we get a variation of it called Marching Squares [SCHROEDER *et al.* 2001]. In essence, Marching Squares examines all image cells of four pixels if the contour passes through it. For each cell, the pixels (or corners) are examined if they are greater than or equal to the isovalue or threshold. If that is the case, the respective pixel states are set, or reset otherwise. In total,

---

6   Interestingly, the Marching Cubes patent, held by General Electric Corporation, expired in June 2005.

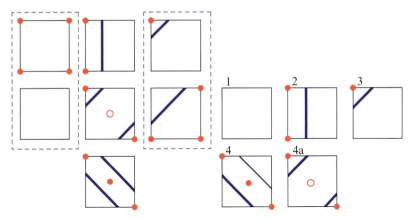

FIGURE 7.8 *Marching Squares case table after reduction through rotation (left) and after further complementing (right).*

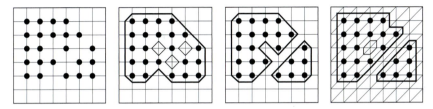

FIGURE 7.9 *Possible contours for Marching Squares. From left to right: Discrete set of pixels; contouring with case 4; contouring with case 4a; contouring after triangulation of cell domain.*

this generates 2^4 (=16) possible combinations of set or reset pixels.[7] In the following, we will call the grid connections between pixels (and voxels in 3D) *cell borders* or *cell edges*. Marching Squares assumes that a contour is passing through a cell border between two neighboring pixels with different states exactly one time. Based on that assumption it generates a contour crossing through the respective cell borders.

If we interpret the different pixel states as digits of a number (similar to Fig. 2.3), we can use this number as index to a table that enumerates all 16 possible cases (of the lookup table) for a contour and the respective contour lines. Most of these 16 cases are very similar. With rotations of the set/reset pixel states, we can reduce the number of cases to seven (see Fig. 7.8 (left)), and with inversion of the pixel states to five possible configurations (see Fig. 7.8 (right)).

Unfortunately, Marching Squares has one serious drawback, which is also visible in Figure 7.8 (right); case 4 has an ambiguous solution that cannot be decided without further information. Both set pixels can either be connected or separated. Depending on that (unavailable) information, Marching Squares should either choose case 4 or case 4a. Figure 7.9 shows the impact of the chosen case on the resulting contour. One standard remedy to avoid the case ambiguity is to use a different cell type, e.g., a triangulation, which in turn would generate a unique contour (with an even simpler case table). The resulting contour is also shown in Figure 7.9.

---

7   This process is sometimes also called classification, not to be confused with the classification of the voxels themselves.

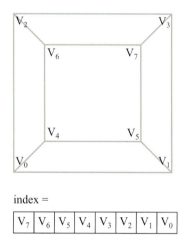

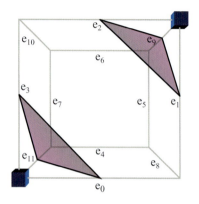

index =

V_7	V_6	V_5	V_4	V_3	V_2	V_1	V_0

Intersected edges:
e_0, e_3, e_{11}; e_1, $e_2$ve$_9$

FIGURE 7.10 *Voxel and edge indexing of the Marching Cubes algorithm. Left: To compute the case table index, the voxel indices compose an 8-bit binary number* **index**, *depending on whether they are set or reset. (Note that the voxel indexing is similar to the one in Figure 2.3, except that the binary string is reversed:* $001 \rightarrow 100$.) *Right: The case table contains a list of the intersected edges. In this example of case 9, edges* e_0, e_3, e_{11} *and edges* e_1, e_2, e_9 *are intersected. The blue cubes at the voxel positions indicate a set voxel state (all other voxels have a reset state).*

Marching Cubes

After discussing Marching Squares, the 2D version of Marching Cubes, we will now look in detail into the Marching Cubes algorithm [LORENSEN and CLINE 1987], and describe how the case index is computed and how the respective triangulation of the volume cell is generated. Subsequently, we will also look into different solutions for the above-mentioned ambiguity.

Indicated by its name, Marching Cubes processes each volume cell individually. However, unlike its name, it typically processes only one cell at a time. As mentioned above, the basic assumption of the Marching Cubes algorithm is that each edge of a volume cell is intersected at most only once. Hence, the algorithm needs only to compute up to one intersection point per cell edge. Very similar to the 2D case, the eight voxels of the volume cell have an assigned state indicating whether their respective voxel value is greater, equal to, or smaller than the specified isovalue τ. The state of each voxel is interpreted as a binary digit (1 for inside, or 0 for outside) and composed into an 8-bit number index. Figure 7.10 (left) shows which voxel state goes to which position.

Figure 7.11 (left) shows an example of case 9 ($9 = 1*2^0+1*2^3$), in which the states of voxels V_0 and V_3 are set. Equivalent to the 2D case, we have 256 possible configurations of voxel states, and hence we have 256 possible triangulations of a volume cell. However, not all of these 256 configurations generate different triangulations. Most cases can be sorted into 15 equivalence classes,[8] taking into account rotation or mirroring (on a plane) and the complement of the configuration. Figure 7.11 (right), for example, shows case 130, which is a simple rotation of case 9. Figure 7.12 shows a rendering of all 15 classes, as listed in the original paper by LORENSEN and CLINE [1987].

---

8 Some papers or lecture notes mention only 14 equivalence classes, but there really are 15 classes. Since only 14 classes actually contain a part of the isosurface, this might be the cause of the confusion.

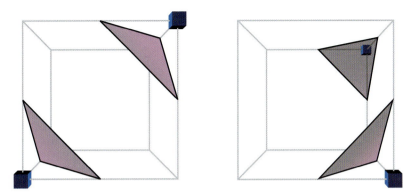

FIGURE 7.11 *Marching Cubes Cases 9 and 130 are in the same equivalence class, since case 9 can be mapped to case 130 by a simple rotation. The blue cubes at the voxel positions indicate a set voxel state (all other voxels have a reset state).*

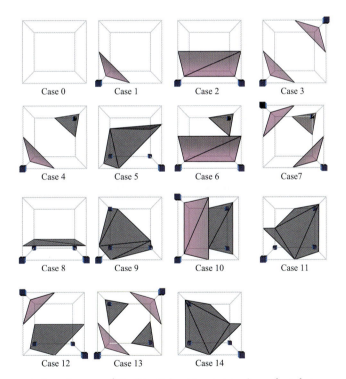

FIGURE 7.12 *Fifteen equivalence class cases of Marching Cubes. Magenta triangles are front-facing, gray triangles are backfacing. The blue cubes at the voxel positions indicate a set voxel state (all other voxels have a reset state).*

After the case for the cell is determined, the cell edges that are intersected by the isosurface can be looked up in the case table. Figure 7.10 (right) shows an example of case 9, where six cell edges are intersected by the isosurface. Once the intersected edges are determined, the intersection itself is calculated by linear interpolation. Equation 7.2 shows how the interpolation parameter t is calculated based on the isovalue τ, and the voxel values V_j and V_{j+1} on both sides of the edge. If we assume that X_j and X_{j+1} describe the coordinates of the respective voxels, we can compute the respective edge position X_e with Equation 7.3.

$$t = \frac{\tau - V_j}{V_{j+1} - V_j} \qquad (7.2)$$

$$X_e = X_j + t \cdot (X_{j+1} - X_j) \qquad (7.3)$$

Figure 7.13 shows an example, where the edge vertex of edge e_0 is changing depending on the isovalue τ. If the isovalue τ is closer to the voxel value V_1, the respective edge vertex moves closer to that voxel (see Fig. 7.13 (left)). Respectively, the edge vertex moves closer to the left voxel if τ is closer to the voxel value V_0 (see Fig. 7.13 (right)).

If we combine the interpolated edge vertices with the information on how the edge intersections are composed into triangles—which is also stored in the case table—we can now compute the vertices of the triangulation of the cell. The final components that need to be computed are the edge vertex normals. The Marching Cubes algorithm approximates these normals based on the voxel normals of the edge, weighted with the same parameter t as in Equation 7.3. In the example in Figure 7.13, it would be the normals of the voxels V_0 and V_1, which we denote with N_0 and N_1 in Equation 7.4. Note that the new edge normal needs to be renormalized:

$$N_e = \| N_j + t \cdot (N_{j+1} - N_j) \| \qquad (7.4)$$

After the computation of the triangulation within one volume cell, the algorithm *marches* to the next unprocessed volume cell. Since voxels are typically indexed first in x, then in y and z, the next cell has an incremented x-position. However, this is often not the optimal addressing scheme. As in most algorithms for large volumetric datasets, only a part of the dataset can be stored in first (L1) and second (L2) level caches of the CPU. Hence, the memory access speed for the voxel values will greatly vary depending if the voxels of the next volume cell are already stored in the CPU cache. Every voxel that generates a page miss and needs to be loaded into the cache will slow down the isosurface extraction significantly. Therefore, an implementation of the Marching Cubes algorithm will benefit enormously if it adopts *cache-sensitive* processing that takes into account how the voxels are organized in memory, in particular in the caches.

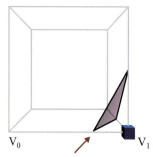 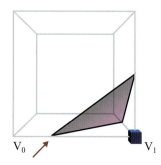

FIGURE 7.13 *The position of the edge vertex (indicated by the red arrow) changes depending on the chosen isovalue. Left: The isovalue is closer to the voxel value V_1. Right: The isovalue is closer to the voxel value V_0.*

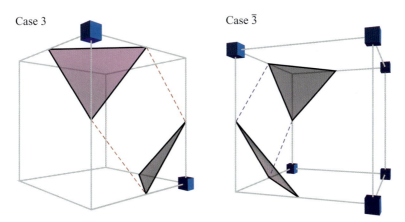

FIGURE 7.14   *Possible Marching Cubes triangulations for two neighboring volume cells. The left cell is triangulated to separate set voxels (case 3), the right neighboring cell is triangulated to connect set voxels (case $\bar{3}$). Both are valid triangulations, but they generate an inconsistent triangle interface with holes. The dashed lines indicate the triangle edges of the respective other cell.*

Ambiguities in 3D

Similar to the above-discussed 2D case, Marching Cubes suffers from ambiguities. Depending on how set voxels (the voxel state is set) are triangulated connected or separated, and due to the lack of a higher level control, inconsistencies may arise. Figure 7.14 shows such an inconsistency in the triangulation, where a connecting and separating triangulation causes holes. This problem (and others) with the Marching Cubes algorithm was detected quite rapidly after its publication [DÜRST 1988], and a number of remedies have been suggested.

Asymptotic Decider   NIELSON and HAMANN [1991] suggested the interpolation of a point on the face that is shared by both cells to provide information if the set voxels should be connected or separated. They assume that the contours on that face are hyperbolic and reconstruct the face interpolation point (or bilinear saddle point) with the asymptotes of the hyperbolas. A somewhat related approach was proposed by NATARAJAN [1994] to fix a similar problem in 3D, where inconsistencies may be generated not on the face of a volume cell, but in its interior.

Case Table Refinement   An alternative solution to the computation of additional interpolation points is the refinement of the original Marching Cubes case table. CHERNYAEV [1995] modified the case table to 33 cases to address the above-mentioned face and cell ambiguities. In a similar approach proposed by CIGNONI et al. [2000], the triangulation is progressively refined to address ambiguities. Possibly the most widely used solution is implemented in VTK [SCHROEDER et al. 2001], where the full 255-case table[9] is used to avoid inconsistencies.

Marching Tetrahedron   In the section on Marching Squares, we already discussed the use of alternative cell types to avoid inconsistencies. Similar to the 2D case, in which triangles were used as cells, SHIRLEY and TUCHMAN [1990] proposed the use of tedrahedrons as cell types. To generate the respective tessellation of the cartesian grid dataset, every cuboid cell is decomposed in five tedrahedrons with a consistent choice of

---

9   Only case 0 (no set voxel) and case 255 (eight set voxels) are combined into one case that does not contain an isosurface.

primary and secondary diagonals. The new tetrahedron-based case table contains only four cases without any ambiguities. On the downside, however, the number of generated triangles is approximately twice as large as for the Marching Cubes algorithm.

Artifacts

One other problem of the Marching Cubes algorithm is its interpolation, which is composed of a linear interpolation for the edge vertices and a Gouraud interpolation of the color values inside the triangles (or the normal vectors for Phong shading). This, however, is not equivalent to cubic trilinear interpolation and results in visual artifacts if the individual triangles become visible. FRÜHAUF [1995] pointed out this difference by comparing the results with a ray casting direct volume rendering approach that uses trilinear interpolation (see Chap. 8). ALLAMANDRI et al. [1998] proposed a solution to this problem, in which the volume cells were subdivided with a trilinear filter to improve the approximation quality. Figure 7.15 shows an example of the so-called *diamond artifacts* that occur if the volume cells are not further subdivided.

A different kind of artifact can appear if Marching Cubes is applied to segmented volume datasets. In cases where the segmentation is more complex than simple thresholding and region-growing, the decision criterion is different from that of the Marching Cubes algorithm. This usually leads to abrupt material interfaces, in which the intensity values vary from high values inside the segmentation to zero outside of the segmentation. The resulting normals will be distorted by this intensity difference, exhibiting staircasing artifacts (see Sect. 2.2). In some cases, it helps to add an additional voxel layer around the segmentation to smooth the intensity difference. In other cases, however, we need to explicitly smooth

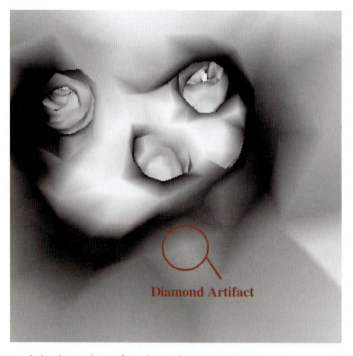

FIGURE 7.15   *The triangle-based interpolation of Marching Cubes generates the typical diamond artifact if the individual triangles become visible. The image shows a close-up of a virtual bronchoscopy (see Chap. 16).*

this material interface with methods discussed in Section 7.3.3. Note that this smoothing must be applied with great care, as it changes the original information, which in turn might have serious consequences on the interpretation of the data.

Another possible artifact due to segmentation is noise on the normal vectors. If the segmentation limits the voxel selection through an area of relative homogeneity, the gradient magnitude of the normals is very small. This situation is very sensitive to noise. Even small intensity changes in that relatively homogeneous region can lead to drastic changes in the normal direction and hence in the shading. In Section 6.3.2, we discussed a remedy to that problem, based on gradient-free shading [DESGRANGES et al. 2005].

Finally, note that in particular the latter segmentation-caused artifacts do not affect only the Marching Cubes algorithm, but all indirect and direct volume rendering approaches.

Segmented, Multiple Objects, and Transparency

Isosurface extraction approaches are often used to extract one surface. This, however, is not the limit of isosurface extraction. In particular for the visualization of multiple segmented anatomical structures, different objects need to be distinguished and rendered accordingly. A basic distinction can be achieved by using different material parameters, e.g., different colors, for different objects. Unfortunately, some objects contain other objects, and they will hence occlude them.

The most frequently used solution for this problem is the use of transparency. A containing object, specifying the context, is rendered semi-transparently with an α value between $(0; 1)$. Examples of this kind of solutions can be found in BARTZ and MEISSNER [1999], where each object is assigned a specific α value. Note that for the correct rendering, all geometry primitives must be depth-sorted from back to front to allow the correct alpha-blending in OpenGL or other graphics APIs (application programming interfaces). Figure 7.16 shows two examples of such segmented isosurface models using different colors. Some advanced examples of this constant transparency modulating for anatomical models have been presented by SALAH et al. [2005a].

While this approach allows viewing of virtually all objects (except those behind too many semi-transparent objects), it does not enable a good perception of how deep inside the context object a

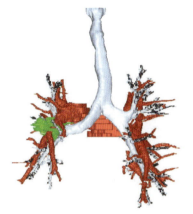
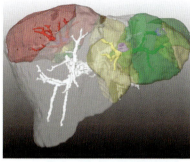

FIGURE 7.16 *Segmented Marching Cubes models. Left: Model of the lung with airways (gray), pulmonary arteries (red), and a lung tumor (green). Right: Model of the liver where the colored regions indicate risk areas with respect to the portal vein (see Chap. 19). (Right image courtesy MILO HINDENNACH, MeVis Bremen)*

focus object is. To address this, the transparency can be modeled for each individual triangle. STALLING *et al.* [1999] discussed such an approach, where the transparency of a triangle is modeled based on its orientation towards the viewer. If it is parallel to the user, a small α-value is chosen, and a larger α-value is chosen if the triangles are oriented more orthogonally to the user. This is a variation of a much older idea presented by KAY and GREENBERG [1979], which basically assumes that a light ray will be more attenuated if it traverses a medium with a more acute angle. Figure 7.17 (left) shows an example of this technique, while Figure 7.17 (right) shows an example of constant transparency modulating. Overall, transparency modulating results in an emphasis on the boundary of the semi-transparent objects.

The idea of modeled transparency has also been used by VIOLA *et al.* [2004a] for importance-driven volume rendering. Here, a template slightly larger than the focus object is rendered with high transparency to improve the visibility of the focus object.

7.2.4 OTHER ISOSURFACE EXTRACTION ALGORITHMS

While Marching Cubes is certainly the most popular isosurface extraction algorithm, it is not the only one. Here, we discuss only a small subset of such algorithms. The first approach—quite similar to Marching Cubes, but older—was presented by WYVILL *et al.* [1986], and it polygonized each volume cell through which the isosurfaces pass. In contrast to Marching Cubes, however, it did not use a case table, but polygonized the isosurface of every cell individually. On the positive side, the *soft objects* approach did not suffer from ambiguity problems, as the Marching Cubes algorithm did.

A variation of Marching Cubes, *Dividing Cubes*, was introduced by the Marching Cubes inventors [CLINE *et al.* 1988]. It specifically addressed situations in which Marching Cubes generated too many triangles. Instead, Dividing Cubes used attributed points (points with a normal) as basic primitive and is thus one of the earliest point-based rendering approaches in raster-display-based graphics, almost 20 years before they resurfaced in computer graphics. Depending on the screen resolution and the respective volume cell size, the cell was subdivided until it fitted the screen resolution, thus generating an output-sensitive point-based rendering.

MÜLLER and STARK [1993] proposed a different approach, the *splitting box* algorithm. In contrast to Marching Cubes, its cell selection is based on a top-down subdivision of the volume dataset. In essence,

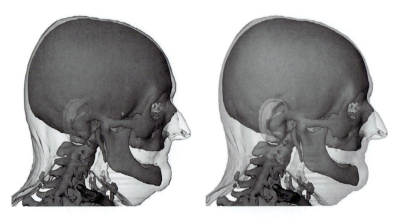

FIGURE 7.17 *Transparency modelled Marching Cubes models [STALLING et al. 1999]. Left: oriented transparency modulating; right: constant transparency modulating. (Images courtesy DETLEV STALLING, Zuse Institute Berlin)*

the bounding box of the grid of the whole dataset is successively subdivided until the edges of the respective boxes only contain one intersection with the isosurface. In contrast to Marching Cubes, this might already happen at higher resolution levels, and not only at the volume cell level. Next to the one-intersection-only criterion, an approximation quality metric controls this subdivision process.

7.2.5 DATA STRUCTURES FOR ACCELERATING ISOSURFACE EXTRACTION

The most costly part of extracting an isosurface is the detection of the cells that intersect with the isosurface.[10] Frequently, the number of these cells is orders of magnitude smaller than the total number of cells in a volumetric dataset. Hence, most acceleration methods aim at improving that search process by applying hierarchical or special data structures. An overview of some of the approaches can be found in the *Visualization Handbook* [Hansen and Johnson 2004].

Data Structures

Before we discuss the different methods, we give a very brief introduction on the used hierarchical data structures. A more detailed discussion can be found in Samet [1994]. An *octree* is a hierarchical data structure that subdivides a volume dataset in all three dimensions in half, resulting in eight child blocks, the octants. This process is continued until one octant represents one volume cell of eight voxels. This of course also implies that the volume dataset has a resolution of a power of two in each dimension, e.g., 512 × 512 × 256. In case the resolution in one or more dimensions is not a power of two, a NULL pointer must be provided instead of the respective child blocks. In this case, the subdivision plane of the respective dimension will be positioned at the nearest power-of-two position. The two dimensional version of an octree—decomposing a single image—is called a *quadtree*, where only four child blocks of a block (or node) are generated at every subdivision step.

A *kd-tree* is a slightly different data structure. Instead of subdividing the volume (or image) dataset in all three (or two) dimensions at the same time, only one dimension is chosen, generating a binary partition at every subdivision step. Note, that the orientation of subdivision plane can be changed step by step. A very similar data structure is the *BSP-tree* (Binary Space Partitioning Tree), which uses arbitrary oblique subdivision planes [Fuchs et al. 1980].

Octrees, quadtrees, kd-trees, and BSP-trees are hierarchical and recursive tree structures, where the root node represents the whole dataset. The depth of the tree is determined by the maximum subdivision level, usually the cell level where a block (or node) is represented by a volume cell of eight voxels.

The final data structure is the *lattice*, which subdivides a 2D space (e.g., the 2D space of the span space) in uniform (or non-uniform) intervals. Similar to the uniform (or non-uniform) grids of a volume dataset (see Sect. 2.1), the lattice elements can be addressed rapidly by an index and the voxel spacing information, similar to the bucket-sorting algorithms. In contrast to the previous tree structures, the lattice is neither recursive nor hierarchical.

Branch-On-Need-Octrees

Among the first effective approaches was the *branch-on-need-octree* (BONO) of Wilhelms and van Gelder [1992]. The key innovations of this approach are that the generated octree was not a full octree with eight child blocks at every inner node, hence saving a significant amount of memory. Furthermore, it stored the isovalue interval (minimum and maximum isovalues) of every octree block. Consequently, the isosurface extraction could be limited to octree blocks with an isosurface interval containing the isovalues.

---

10   These cells are sometimes also called *relevant cells*.

All other octree blocks can be skipped, since they do not contain blocks (or volume cells on the highest resolution level) that intersect with the isosurface. While the BONO approach could significantly reduce the isosurface extraction time, the construction of the octree for large volumetric datasets can be still quite time consuming. BARTZ et al. [1998] suggested constructing the octree (and the subsequent extraction) in parallel by a thread-based processing model.

Span Space

LIVNAT et al. [1996] proposed the *span space*, a data structure that represents every volume cell in a 2D coordinate system by using its minimum voxel value as x-coordinate and its maximum voxel value as y-coordinate, similar to the isovalue interval of the BONO. This has the advantage that cells with a similar minimum/maximum interval are located close to each other in the 2D coordinate system (see Fig. 7.18). The difference between several of the isosurface extraction methods is in the way the span space is organized for searching the cells that are intersected by the isosurface. LIVNAT et al. [1996] proposed the use of a kd-tree, which in turn allows rapid search for cells intersecting with the isosurface. An optimization for this cell searching was proposed by SHEN et al. [1996], who replaced the kd-tree with a lattice of $L \times L$ non-uniformly spaced rectangles, the lattice elements. The non-uniform spacing is due to a better adaption to the data samples in the span space. At isosurface extraction, the lattice elements are searched by a simple binary search either along the rows or the columns, once it is established that the cells are located in a specific column or row.

Yet another variation was proposed by CIGNONI et al. [1997], who generated a balanced binary tree (the *interval tree*) as access function to the span space. The root node of the interval tree contains a sorted list of intervals that contain the median of extremal interval values. The child nodes contain the intervals that are larger (left) and smaller (right) than the median. The respective child interval trees are constructed accordingly with an adapted right (left tree) and left (right tree) boundary of extremal interval values. Due to the fact that the access is organized as a balanced binary tree, the theoretical complexity of the worst case is lowest with the interval tree [CIGNONI et al. 1997].

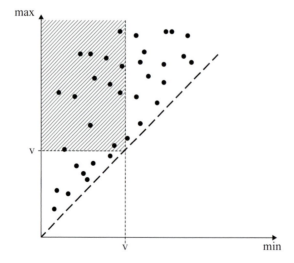

FIGURE 7.18 *Every volume cell of a dataset is a sample in the span space. The x and y coordinates are the minimum and maximum voxel values in that cell. The hatched area marks all the cells that intersect with the isosurface with threshold v.*

Extrema Graph

The *extrema graph* is a data structure that searches for seed cells of isosurfaces and propagates from these seed cells throughout the isosurface [ITOH and KOYAMADA 1995]. It is thus an isosurface propagation method. The important question that remained was how to find these seed points rapidly. ITOH and KOYAMADA [1995] achieved this by classifying all grid points as maximum points, minimum points, or neither. A maximum point here is a grid point with a voxel value larger than all adjacent grid points, while a minimum point has a voxel value smaller than all adjacent grid points. Thus, maximum and minimum points are local extremum points. These extremum points are connected through sorted lists of cells, the *arcs*. Together with the extremum points, the arcs form the *extrema graph*.

Every (closed) isosurface will intersect the connections between the respective extremum points; thus, searching the extrema graph will generate appropriate seed cells for the isosurface propagation. In addition to the extrema graph, two lists of cells on the boundary of the volume—the *boundary cell lists*—are maintained to allow the detection of open isosurfaces that do not necessarily intersect with the arcs of the extrema graph. The boundary cell lists are sorted according to their minimum and maximum voxel values to allow faster detection of a cell that intersects with the isosurface.

Isosurface extraction with the extrema graphs works well if the number of extremum points and boundary cells is reasonably small. If a dataset is inflicted by noise, however, its number of extremum points can be very large, which in turn increases the overall number of arcs in the extrema graph. In this case, volume filtering by a low pass filter might be a solution to reduce the number of extremum points. In the case of a large number of boundary cells (e.g., for unstructured grids), ITOH et al. [2001] suggested the volume thinning method, which eliminates the need to check the boundary cells separately.

Bounding Volumes

Many algorithms do not process the actual geometric data, but only a representation of it. Typically, this representation completely encloses the geometry; it is frequently a convex closure of it and is generally denoted as a bounding volume. In particular, the inner nodes of a tree representation of a scene (e.g., an octree) are represented not by the actual geometry of all leaf nodes but only by such a bounding volume of all leaf nodes. In those cases, we also speak of a bounding volume hierarchy.

Depending on the specific application of the bounding volume, different types of bounding volumes are used. Important aspects to be considered for the selection of the right bounding volumes are the costs associated with its computation, costs associated with its representation, costs of the interference test (e.g., intersections or visibility), and its approximation quality. Particularly in the context of visibility computation, BARTZ et al. [2001b, 2005b] provide a discussion and evaluation of various bounding volumes.

Axis-Aligned Bounding Box   One of the most frequently used bounding volume types is the axis-aligned bounding box (AABB) (see Fig. 7.19(a)). It is a cuboid composed of six faces (twelve triangles) that is computed based on the minimum/maximum x, y, z positions of the vertices of an object. Its faces are parallel to the major planes in a cartesian coordinate system, hence the name axis-aligned. In terms of costs, it can be computed very rapidly as it consists of only six polygons. Furthermore, it usually allows very simple interference tests; intersections can be computed based on the six planes and their orientations, visibility tests are typically conducted based on its rasterized framebuffer representation. The only drawback of an AABB is its poor approximation quality in cases of elongated and non-axis-aligned objects, such as a long rod with a 45 degree rotation on all three axes (thus being positioned on a major diagonal).

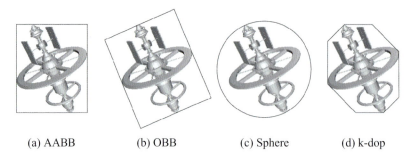

    (a) AABB   (b) OBB   (c) Sphere   (d) k-dop

FIGURE 7.19 *Approximations of an object using bounding volumes: (a) an axis-aligned bounding box (AABB), (b) an oriented bounding box (OBB), (c) a bounding sphere, and (d) a k-dop (where $k = 8$). (Images courtesy JAMES T. KLOSOWSKI, IBM TJ WATSON Reasearch Center, Hawthorne, USA)*

Oriented Bounding Box   Very similar to the AABB is the oriented bounding box (OBB) (see Fig. 7.19(b)). It also consists of six faces (twelve triangles) and enables a simple interference test. However, its approximation quality is theoretically better than the AABB, since it is not axis-aligned and adapts its three spanning axes according to the vertex data. In case of our rotated rod, the OBB will align itself along the rod. In other words, the OBB is rotational invariant in contrast to the AABB. However, for the computation of the orientation, we need to compute a principal component analysis (PCA) of the vertices (recall Sect. 5.4.3), which is quite an expensive operation with a complexity of $O(nlogn)$. One issue with the OBB is the numerical accuracy of the eigenanalysis required for the PCA. In cases of three very similar eigenvalues, the resulting orientation may suffer from rounding errors.

Bounding Sphere   A bounding sphere (BS) (see Fig. 7.19(c)) is another simple bounding volume that can be computed very cheaply. Furthermore, its representation can be straightforward (center and radius) if only the mathematical description is used for the interference test, e.g., an intersection test. However, if we need to rasterize the BS for a visibility test, we need several hundred triangles for a decent tessellation. Furthermore, our rotated rod is approximated very poorly with a BS.

Bounding Cylinders   A mixture of a BS and an OBB is the bounding cylinder (BC). Like the OBB, its major axes are also oriented according to a PCA of the object's vertices, while the radius of the cylinder is chosen so that the cylinder contains all vertices. The main application of the BC, however, is not to simplify any interference tests but to create a visual representation of tubular objects like blood vessels. More details on this specific use can be found in Chapter 14.

Convex Hull   The bounding volume with the tightest (convex) approximation of the original geometry is the convex hull (CHULL). However, its computation is complex ($O(nlogn)$) [O'ROURKE 1993] and its representation may consist of several hundred polygons. Furthermore, the complex geometrical structure may lead to an expensive interference test. All things considered, we must carefully determine whether the better approximation quality warrants the higher representation and computational complexity.

k-Dimensional Orientation Polytopes   Our final discussed bounding volume is the k-dimensional orientation polytope (k-DOP) (see Fig. 7.19(d)), which approximates the object with k halfplanes chosen from the major and minor diagonals and axes. In case of $k = 6$, the 6-DOP is identical to the AABB (six axis orientations). For $k = 14$, in addition to the six AABB planes, the 14-DOP uses eight halfplanes based on the eight major diagonals, thus they approximate the object by cutting from the vertices. For

$k = 26$, the 26-DOP additionally approximates the object from the 12 AABB edges. The 26-DOP can be computed by a simplified convex hull algorithm that mimics the minimum/maximum calculation process of the AABB and is thus very fast. It consists of up to 26 polygons (92 triangles) and enables relatively cheap interference tests [KLOSOWSKI et al. 1998, BARTZ et al. 2001b]. It provides a significantly better approximation quality than the AABB, but does not introduce significant computational or interference test costs. It thus strikes a good compromise between an AABB and a CHULL.

7.3   SURFACE POSTPROCESSING

So far, we have discussed various methods for the extraction of a polygonal isosurface, focusing on the Marching Cubes algorithm [LORENSEN and CLINE 1987] and several of its variations. Furthermore, we presented several approaches to accelerate the extraction of the volume cells that intersect with the isosurface. The result of all these discussed variations and combinations of extraction methods is a polygonal mesh, which is typically composed of triangles. In this section, we discuss how to accelerate the rendering of these meshes and how we can improve their visual quality.

7.3.1   GEOMETRY CULLING

When isosurfaces are extracted from large medical image datasets with the Marching Cubes algorithms, the resulting polygonal models consist often of many million triangles. If an interactive rendering performance of 20 frames per second (fps) or more is required, the graphics subsystem must have a sustained rendering performance of significantly more than hundreds of millions of triangles per second. While modern graphics cards already reach this performance, the growing dataset size will create even larger models.

There are basically two approaches to deal with the rendering complexity of large polygonal models. Mesh reduction (see Sect. 7.3.2) reduces the number of polygons that represent the isosurface, and geometry culling reduces the number of pixels that are drawn in the framebuffer before they are rasterized and tested by the z-buffer [FOLEY et al. 1995].

Geometry culling essentially removes from the rendering pipeline groups of polygons (objects) that are not visible. To maintain efficiency, several heuristics are employed. Hence, not all not visible polygons (or polygon groups) are culled, but only those detected by the heuristics. At the same time, a culling approach must maintain conservatism to ensure that only polygons are culled that are not visible. This is in particular important for visualization in medicine, since an incompletely rendered isosurface might lead to a wrong medical therapy decision. If a very limited potential reduction of quality is acceptable, quantitative or adaptive culling can be used. Here, the number of not-occluded pixels of the object representation can be used to select a specific fidelity level of the object geometry ([BARTZ et al. 1999a], see also Sect. 7.3.2).

Essentially, three different classes of culling can be employed. *Backface culling* is the simplest approach and removes all triangles that face away from the viewpoint and are, hence, showing their backface to the current viewpoint. Since the back- and frontfaces of a triangle are decided through the direction of its normal, this test essentially only checks if the normals are pointing away from the viewpoint [WOO et al. 1997]. Note that backface culling requires a correct and consistent orientation of the tested triangles. This essentially means that the vertices of all triangles are enumerated in either anticlockwise or clockwise fashion, which already includes a decision on what is the frontface of a triangle.

The second geometry culling approach is *view-frustum culling*. It tests to determine whether the object is at least partially located within the view-frustum. If not, the whole object cannot be visible from the current

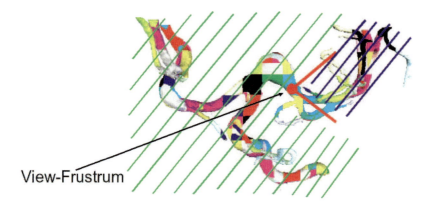

FIGURE 7.20 *An arterial cerebral blood vessel tree is culled. The different colored blocks are an octree decomposition of the geometry of the model. The red lines show the view-frustum, whereas the red circle indicates the view-position. The green hatched area shows the geometry culled by view-frustum culling, the blue hatched area shows the geometry culled by occlusion culling.*

viewpoint. In a typical setting, view-frustum culling will not check the whole object, but only the vertices of its bounding volume (BV), which consists of n vertices. These vertices are transformed according to the viewing transformation and then tested if they are within the view-frustum [GARLICK *et al.* 1990]. Unfortunately, this approach has one major drawback: if the BV contains the whole view-frustum—a rare but possible configuration—none of the BV vertices will be within the view-frustum, and the test will incorrectly return that the object is not visible. While this problem could be solved by adding interior vertices, BARTZ *et al.* [1999a] solved the problem differently. By employing the OpenGL selection buffer, they rendered the whole object and specified the whole screen an active area for the selection process. If the hit buffer of the selection mode contains any contribution of the object—a polygon, a vertex, or a line—the object is at least partially located within the view-frustum.

While the previous culling techniques are fairly standard, the actual used *occlusion culling* approach can be very diverse. COHEN-OR *et al.* [2003] presented a survey of a variety of culling and visibility approaches. Here, we only present one standard approach that utilizes occlusion queries in hardware, which are present on the recent graphics subsystems of the major vendors. The functionality of this *occlusion culling* flag was first presented by SCOTT *et al.* [1998], and the first use was reported by BARTZ *et al.* [1999b], BARTZ and SKALEJ 1999. After view-frustum culling, the remaining objects intersecting the view-frustum are processed from front to back (view-frustum culling implicitly depth-sorts the objects).[11] First, the BV of the frontmost object is tested for occlusion using the occlusion culling flag. If the BV of this object is not occluded (which does not mean that it is visible, since we are conservative), it is rendered. Otherwise, it is culled and the algorithm tests the next object. There are numerous improvements of the basic algorithm, such as using a test hierarchy [STANEKER *et al.* 2004], using tighter bounding volumes [BARTZ *et al.* 2001b], using an occupancy map to avoid redundant occlusion queries [STANEKER *et al.* 2003] and grouping individual queries [STANEKER *et al.* 2006, BITTNER *et al.* 2004] to reduce the query overhead. Furthermore, recent graphics hardware also provides functionality to compute the degree of occlusion

---

11   The actual occlusion status of the tested objects depends on the traversal order. Since frontmost objects typically occlude objects in the back, they should also be tested and rendered first.

by counting the number of pixels that would alter the depth-buffer. This information can be used to specifically decide what to do with a partially occluded object, e.g., selecting a specific level-of-detail. All these approaches test for occlusion in the framebuffer; therefore, they belong to the class of image-space occlusion culling approaches.

Note that transparency modulation and occlusion culling do not fit well together. First of all, a translucent representation allows the viewing of objects behind the translucent object, a concept that violates the very idea of occlusion. Second, occlusion culling queries are best processed in a front to back manner, while transparency requires a back to front sorting for correct blending. However, if the respective scene elements are carefully sorted and tested, they can be still used together, as demonstrated in BARTZ *et al.* [2001c, 2003a].

Overall, the effectiveness of occlusion culling varies depending on the application. For virtual endoscopy, it has been reported that more than 90% of the geometry can be always culled by a combination of view-frustum and occlusion culling [BARTZ and SKALEJ 1999].

7.3.2 MESH REDUCTION

While occlusion culling aims at the reduction of the depth complexity of a rendered model—e.g., reducing the number of times a pixel is painted over in a scene—mesh reduction aims at the different goal of reducing the overall number of polygons of a model. Note that this does not necessarily reduce the depth complexity, since the number of times a pixel is painted over is typically not significantly different.

Simplification may be performed by a global simplification algorithm, which considers the whole polygonal object, or by local operations, which consider only the local neighborhood. The decision whether to accept a proposed simplification depends on a decision function driven by accuracy (fidelity-based) or by time constraints (budget-based). In a medical visualization scenario, fidelity is usually the criterion of choice, since accuracy is highly important.

Another differentiation evolves along the question if the simplification is performed progressively [HOPPE 1996] or if discrete levels-of-details are computed. The first option enables a smoother or continuous transition between different levels-of-detail, while the latter one produces large visual differences between the different levels. Another variation of continuous levels-of-detail are view-dependent simplifications, which refine the polygonal mesh based on the current viewpoint [XIA and VARSHNEY 1996]. In practice, however, most rendering frameworks provide only discrete levels-of-detail. As indicated in the section on geometry culling, these discrete levels-of-detail can also be used in connection with quantitative occlusion queries, where the number of visible pixels of the bounding volumes (e.g., a AABB) of the objects are used to select the specific fidelity level of those objects [BARTZ *et al.* 1999a].

Local simplification operators enable only local changes in the geometry. This can be an *edge collapse* [HOPPE *et al.* 1993]—an edge is replaced by a vertex and the resulting degenerated triangles within the local neighborhood are removed. Alternatively, the *vertex pair collapse* combines two previously unconnected vertices into one vertex. The resulting triangulation also contains degenerated triangles with no area, which are hence removed. Typical examples are the algorithm by SCHROEDER [1997] and by GARLAND and HECKBERT [1997]. Other approaches remove vertices [SCHROEDER *et al.* 1992], triangles, or cells and might require a local retriangulation.

The question which difference metric should be used is one of the most important in the context of mesh simplification. In theory, it depends on how much a model is visually changing. In practice, however, this is difficult to specify. Hence, a number of specific difference metrics are used, such as the geometric distance in object-space (e.g., the Hausdorff distance), the pixel distance in screen space, or the differences in the attribute space (e.g., normals, colors, or textures).

Overall, the chosen simplification approach depends largely on the required accuracy for the simplified model. In particular, the requirements for the boundary between the different objects are important. If adjacent objects are simplified separately, cracks between the polygonal surfaces may appear and will need to be retriangulated.

There are a number of surveys available that provide an overview over the variety of mesh reduction algorithms. GARLAND [1999] provided such a survey on multiresolution modeling. More recently, LUEBCKE et al. [2004] discussed a large variety of simplification approaches, error metrics, and applications.

7.3.3 MESH SMOOTHING

Medical image data are usually based on a measuring process inflicted with measuring errors. Furthermore, the measurements are filtered, weighted, and rearranged to reconstruct a volume dataset, which also involves several possibilities for rounding errors, incomplete reconstruction, and many more sources of errors. Finally, the image data are processed by a variety of algorithms, such as segmentation, filtering, cutting, etc. Each of these operations can lead to an abrupt change of intensity values, resulting in holes, connections, incomplete objects, or severe staircasing artifacts. To provide a satisfying visualization, the respective data must be smoothed to fill holes and reduce artifacts. Note that the required degree of smoothing (how much smoothing is needed) depends on the previous data acquisition and preprocessing. In particular, it depends on the specific segmentation and cutting operations. While some segmentation methods inherently ensure a smooth boundary (e.g., snakes in see Sect. 5.4.1), others perform simple binary transitions (e.g., manual cutting/editing operations), which in turn generate abrupt intensity changes.

One of the major issues that need to be addressed sufficiently is volume conservation. Generally, most smoothing operators reduce (or sometimes enlarge) the object. For many medical applications, this is not acceptable. Hence, an adequate smoothing approach must maintain the overall volume of an object within tight bounds.

One well-known standard approach to smoothing is to apply a 3D low pass filter ($n \times n \times n$) to the volume area of interest, e.g., the segmented volume dataset. To maintain the overall volume of the segmented object, the 3D low pass filter should be normalized. Afterwards, a polygonal isosurface is extracted from this smoothed volume. However, this filtering approach is not very sensitive to small object details, which will be smoothed away.

LAKARE and KAUFMAN [2003] presented a related approach, where a (near) binary intensity transition is smoothed by reconstructing a fuzzy boundary. A similar approach was proposed by NEUBAUER et al. [2004] for isosurfaces, employing morphological operations to maintain the overall shape of the segmented object (see also Sect. 5.6.2). STALLING et al. [1998] suggested an approach to extract smooth surfaces from label volumes. Since label volumes contain only identification tags for the different objects after a segmentation, they are exposed to severe staircasing artifacts. This situation is similar to binary segmentations, where objects are identified by 1, and the background by 0. These staircasing artifacts are substantially reduced by weighting the labels on the boundary appropriately, which in essence enables subvoxel accuracy.

A different class of smoothing approaches addresses the fairing of meshes. Since traditional surface fairing methods from geometric modelling are computationally too expensive to be considered, a variety of local fairing methods are frequently used. Most local fairing operators take into account the weighted average of the direct neighbors of the current vertex (the *umbrella* region) to reposition the current vertex (see Fig. 7.21). However, it is not trivial for an application to select from the class of umbrella operators appropriate smoothing algorithms and parameters (neighborhood, number of iterations, weighting factor). Different choices are needed for different categories of anatomical objects, such as compact organs or elongated tubular structures. BADE et al. [2006a] compared several variations of umbrella operators for the applicability for segmented medical datasets.

The simplest approach is to apply the well-known Laplacian filter, which smooths every vertex in the mesh. Unfortunately, this filter tends to shrink the smoothed object. Hence, it is usually considered unsuitable for the smoothing of medical segmentations [BADE et al. 2006a]. An extension of Laplacian fairing was proposed by VOLLMER et al. [1999]. In this approach, the smoothed umbrella regions are corrected in a second stage by moving the current vertex back towards its original position, thus maintaining the overall volume of the object. Another approach to surface smoothing based on signal theory was presented by TAUBIN [1995]. Here, the discrete Fourier theory is used to provide low pass filtering to (two-dimensional discrete) surface signals by interpreting the eigenvalues of the Laplacian matrix as frequencies. Model shrinking is controlled by alternating low pass filtering with different filter sizes. Yet another technique was presented by DESBRUN et al. [1999], who introduced mesh fairing based on geometric diffusion and curvature flow. Volume preservation is achieved by computing a scale factor from the measured volume before and after smoothing.

Bilateral mesh denoising is based on methods from image filtering [FLEISHMAN et al. 2003], in which a bilateral filter is applied to remove noise from a polygonal mesh. Bilateral image filtering combines closeness metrics in the spatial and the frequency domain to obtain smoothing and edge preserving at the same time [TOMASI and MANDUCHI 1998]. For this reason, FLEISHMAN et al. [2003] introduced bilateral mesh filtering to remove noise for meshes while preserving edges. However, this may mean that staircasing artifacts are considered as edges that need to be preserved, which in turn reduces the effectiveness of the smoothing operation.

The final smoothing approach that we discuss here, is a variation of Marching Cubes itself, the Dual Marching Cubes algorithm [NIELSON 2004]. After computing a quadrilateral patch structure from an original Marching Cubes–generated mesh, the dual mesh of the patch mesh is generated. A dual of a mesh replaces a patch surface cell with a vertex and connects every neighboring dual vertex with an edge. Thus,

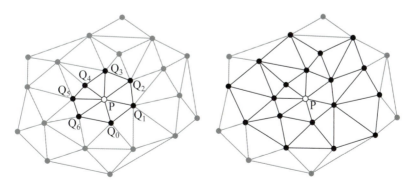

FIGURE 7.21 *The umbrella operator takes the local neighborhood into account. Left: First-order umbrella operator, taking into account the immediate neighbors. Right: Second-order umbrella operator, taking into account immediate neighbors and their neighbors. (Images courtesy JENS HAASE, University of Magdeburg)*

every dual edge crosses an edge of the patch mesh, and every dual mesh cell contains a patch vertex. This also means that in contrast to the original triangular mesh, the dual mesh is composed of quadrilaterals. By iteratively applying this dualing operator, the original Marching Cubes mesh is successively smoothed. Figure 7.22 shows an example of the smoothing of a staircase artifact–inflicted model of the cerebral ventricular system (left), and the Dual Marching Cubes generated smoothed version of it (right).

All local mesh smoothing algorithms have the serious problem of terracing artifacts, where the steps represent the slices of the original data. To successfully remove these artifacts, a local filter with the same size as the terrace width is needed. Such large filters would result in serious loss of imaging detail.

In summary, numerous approaches exist to smooth a polygonal isosurface. For medical applications, it is important to maintain the overall volume of the objects represented by the isosurface. Unfortunately, many smoothing approaches do not address volume preservation sufficiently, in particular for differently shaped objects. Recently, BADE et al. [2006a] discussed some of the smoothing approaches in that context for compact, flat, or long objects. The results showed that smoothing by signal processing by TAUBIN [1995] and the Laplace + HC approach by VOLLMER et al. [1999] preserved the object volume best (see also Fig. 7.23). For elongated, branching objects, e.g., vascular trees, no parameterization of the discussed smoothing algorithms achieved satisfying results. This leads directly towards model-based techniques for the visualization of anatomical tree structures (see Chap. 14).

Constrained Elastic Surface Nets Due to the problems of general mesh smoothing algorithms, dedicated attempts have been made to wrap binary volume data with smooth surfaces. This principle is closely related to the segmentation with snakes (recall Sect. 5.4.1), in which energy-minimizing surfaces are fitted to the image data and attracted to features such as edges. In fact, the same principles for energy-minimization are applied.

GIBSON [1998] developed a special algorithm dedicated to binary medical volume data. In particular, the terraces in binary segmented data can be handled appropriately by the method of fitting a surface around the binary segmentation result. The iterative relaxation process is constrained by a voxel

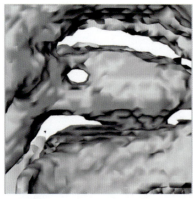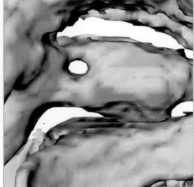

FIGURE 7.22 *A Marching Cubes generated isosurface is smoothed by the dual Marching Cubes algorithm. The mesh shows a close-up of a segmented isosurface of the third cerebral ventricle. The hole in the third ventricle is the adhesio interthalamica, which connects the two parts of the thalamus of the central nervous system through the third ventricle. Left: original Marching Cubes mesh of the cerebral ventricles. The segmentation of the ventricular system exposes staircasing artifacts. Right: smoothed Dual Marching Cubes surface of the ventricular system.*

FIGURE 7.23 *Smoothed models of a segmented sternocleidomastoid muscle of the neck. From left to right: Model of the original segmented data (0%), Laplacian smoothing (13.5%), Laplace + HC [V*OLLMER *et al. 1999] (0%), Signal Processing [T*AUBIN 1995] (0.7%), 2nd-order Laplace + HC (5.5%), 2nd-order Signal Processing (2.9%). The numbers in brackets measure the volume loss compared to the original segmented data after 10 iterations. Implementations are based on VTK [S*CHROEDER *et al. 2001]. (Images courtesy J*ENS *H*AASE, University of Magdeburg)*

environment. This environment is created by volume cells that contain at least one boundary voxel of the binary segmentation and and at least one background voxel, thus creating a 26-neighborhood voxel layer as limit for the relaxation. The constrained elastic surface nets improve earlier work on fitting parametric (spline) surfaces to binary volume data [MCINERNEY and TERZOPOULOS 1996, TAKANAHI et al. 1998]. The major problems of the earlier approaches are the strategy for adjusting the control point density and a variety of other parameters.

7.3.4 VOXELIZATION

The result generated by an indirect volume rendering algorithm is typically a polygonal mesh, which is rendered by standard computer graphics hardware. In some cases, however, it is necessary to convert this continuous presentation back to a discrete volume representation of voxels to enable a crossover from indirect to direct volume visualization. This process is called *voxelization* or *3D scan conversion*. In this section, we will discuss some of the approaches to the voxelization of general polygonal meshes. This process in a way is similar to the scanning of an object and requires advanced filter operations to generate a smooth voxelized representation.

As one of its names suggests, voxelization can be considered as the 3D extension of 2D scan conversion, a technique that has been developed to represent lines and polygons on raster displays [FOLEY et al. 1995]. KAUFMAN [1987a] extended the standard 2D scan conversion techniques to 3D, which is essentially a 3D extension of the 2D scan conversion algorithm of BRESENHAM [1965]. The result of this scan conversion process is a binary voxelization of the mesh, where each new voxel can be considered as a point sample of the mesh.

One of the special concerns at the time was how to avoid holes in the voxelized mesh, while later on the quality issues of the binary and block-like nature of the voxelized object arose, which is also known as object-space aliasing [BLINN 1989]. To address this problem, WANG and KAUFMAN [1993] proposed a weighted sampling to address object and image-space aliasing. Several samples in a spherical neighborhood of the voxels are sampled and weighted with a Bartlett function, which linearly decreases the influence of more distanced samples. For fast computation of the filtered volume, precomputed lookup tables were used, addressed by the distance from the voxel to the voxelized mesh element. Later, SRAMEK and KAUFMAN [1998] showed that a smooth voxelization filter must also consider interpolation

FIGURE 7.24 *A voxelized geometric model of a teapot and of a cogwheel* [SRAMEK *and* KAUFMAN *1999b*]. *(Image courtesy* MILOS SRAMEK, *Austrian Academy of Sciences)*

and normal estimation techniques to provide a correct surface orientation through the normals. This method was later extended [SRAMEK and KAUFMAN 1999a] and the respective VXT voxelization library was described [SRAMEK and KAUFMAN 1999b]. Figure 7.24 shows an example of this voxelization approach.

Next to the filtered voxelization, signed distance fields are used for voxelization. Here, a distance larger than zero usually indicates the outside, while a distance below zero indicates the inside of an object. A zero distance indicates the object boundary. JONES [1996] presented such an approach for the voxelization of polygonal meshes.[12] An improved version of signed distance field computation was recently presented by BRENTZEN [2005].

7.4 SUMMARY

In this chapter, we explored the various options of indirect volume rendering. Next to the various plane-oriented displays, such as orthogonal, oblique, and curved reformatted slice displays, we focused on a surface-based display of the structures of interest. Specifically, we looked into contour tracing and the classic cuberille method [HERMAN and LIU 1979]. The major focus of this chapter, however, was on the de facto standard of indirect volume rendering, the Marching Cubes algorithm [LORENSEN and CLINE 1987]. After introducing Marching Squares as 2D isoline extraction algorithm, we explored its 3D extension.

---

12 In contrast to the mentioned convention, Jones interprets negative distances as outside and positive distances as inside the object.

Among the major issues of Marching Cubes is that surface artifacts are caused by triangulation ambiguities. We discussed several solutions to this artifacts, among them the asymptotic decider, various case table refinements, and Marching Tetrahedron. Next to triangulation artifacts, visual artifacts appear due to the limited quality of the vertex interpolation of Marching Cubes. Finally, we discussed the proper use of colors and transparency to visualize multiple segmented objects computed by an isosurface extraction algorithm.

Although Marching Cubes is probably the most popular indirect volume rendering algorithm, it is by no means the only one. We discusses a few other methods, some of which are related to Marching Cubes, and some that were proposed even earlier [WYVILL et al. 1986].

The major performance consuming part of isosurface extraction is the detection of relevant volume cells. Relevant cells are the volume cells through which the isosurface(s) passes. We discuss several classes of methods that aim at the rapid detection of these cells. Furthermore, we briefly described some of the relevant basic data structures used by these methods, such as octrees or kd-trees.

In the final section of this chapter, we focused on various postprocessing operations that accelerate visualization by limiting the rendering to not-occluded geometry, or by reducing the number of polygons that approximate our isosurface(s) (mesh reduction). Since segmented objects from volumetric image data often contain jaggy edges and corners, mesh smoothing is necessary to remove or at least reduce those features. Various approaches for mesh smoothing were discussed. The last postprocessing operation discussed in this chapter is voxelization. Voxelization converts a continuous polygonal model into a discrete volume dataset. To generate a satisfying visual quality, filtering and specific processing techniques must be employed.

FURTHER READING

Numerous sources provide additional information on the topics covered in this chapter. The book by SCHROEDER et al. [2001] on VTK covers many different aspects of indirect volume rendering. Also, the *Visualization Handbook* [HANSEN and JOHNSON 2004] discusses fast isosurface extraction algorithms and extensions to 4D isosurface extraction, which also incorporates time as a dimension of time-varying phenomena, similar to those we will describe in Chapter 10. SAMET [1994] provides an in-depth discussion of hierarchical data structures, which are intensively used for efficient indirect volume rendering.

Approaches for solutions to the correspondence and branching problems of contour tracing were proposed originally by KEPPEL [1975] and FUCHS et al. [1977], based on contour stitching. Recently, a level set-based morphing mechanism was proposed by NILSSON et al. [2005].

Non-manifold surfaces may appear if more than two materials (resulting in three material interfaces) are present in one volume cell. Since the Marching Cubes algorithm provides only a binary classification, it cannot deal with such situations. HEGE et al. [1997] presented a solution to this limitation with the generalized Marching Cubes algorithm, which allows an arbitrary number of materials in a volume cell. The theoretical foundations of this approach were discussed in HEGE [1998]. This idea was later rediscovered by BANKS and LINTON [2003]. A different approach for non-manifold surfaces was presented by BLOOMENTHAL and FERGUSON [1995], who propagated a volume cell along the surface. According to the classification of that cell, it was tessellated into tetrahedrons to construct an appropriate surface.

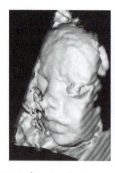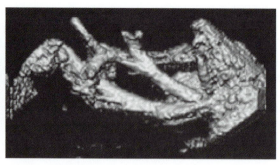

FIGURE 7.25 *Surface visualizations generated from 3D ultrasound data. After applying different noise reduction and speckle removing techniques, expressive 3D visualizations may be generated. Left: rendering of the face of a fetus, right: rendering surface inside the liver. (Images courtesy GEORGIOS SAKAS, FRAUNHOFER-Institute Darmstadt)*

The methods presented in this chapter are devoted to the visualization of surface data from regularly sampled medical volume data such as CT and MRI. With appropriate preprocessing, surface extraction is also feasible for irregularly sampled 3D ultrasound data [SAKAS and WALTER 1995]. Resampling to a regular grid, speckle removal, and noise reduction, as well as surface normal smoothing, belong to the surface extraction pipeline for 3D ultrasound data (see Figure 7.25). Advanced and more recent techniques for surface extraction from 3D ultrasound data are described in FATTAL and LISCHINSKI [2001] and ZHANG et al. [2002].

Chapter 08

Direct Volume Visualization

In the previous chapter, we introduced indirect volume visualization as a popular way of visualizing volumetric image data. Indirect volume visualization generated an intermediate representation of the dataset that is rendered afterwards. In case of the Marching Cubes algorithm, this is a polygonal representation of an isosurface. Since this is not the original dataset itself, it is called indirect. Direct volume visualization provides a different strategy; here, the volumetric dataset is directly represented visually without generating a meta representation. Furthermore, the complexity of direct volume visualization algorithms is driven by the number of voxels of the dataset and by the number of pixels of the viewing plane. In contrast, the complexity of a polygonal meta representation of an isosurface is driven by the number of polygons, and not by the viewing plane resolution. Consequently, many polygons will have only a small or even evanescent contribution, in particular if they have a projected size of one pixel or less.

Organization   Direct volume visualization is frequently depicted as direct volume rendering, or, in short, volume rendering (in contrast to indirect volume rendering and surface rendering). In this chapter, we will focus on the theoretical aspects of direct volume visualization, in particular the employed physical model (see Sect. 8.1) and the mathematical foundation of the resulting *volume rendering equation*. Section 8.2 addresses the processing order of the volume rendering pipeline that evaluated the volume rendering equation and its components, such as sampling and compositing (see Sect. 8.3).

In Chapter 9, we will look into the practical aspects of direct volume rendering; in particular, we will discuss major volume rendering algorithms. Since this book's focus is on visualization in medicine in general, our discussion of direct volume rendering is by definition limited to a few chapters. A more in-depth discussion can be found in the recent book by ENGEL *et al.* [2006].

8.1   THEORETICAL MODELS FOR DIRECT VOLUME RENDERING

Rendering in general is the interaction of light, objects, and the medium in between, which in practice breaks down into the interaction of particles and media. It is typically described with absorption, emission, and scattering and has its physical foundation in the *transport theory of light* [KRÜGER 1990a]. This theory is evaluated in its steady state (or stationary) version by the linear Boltzmann equation, which describes increase or decrease of the intensity of particles in space [KRÜGER 1990c]. Since this is a quite complex model, we will reduce the complexity by simplifying our model.

We will ignore the influence of a changing medium (participating media) and we will not consider different wavelengths or diffraction. If we also skip scattering, we are down to the traditional rendering equation as introduced by KAJIYA [1986].[1] If we further remove refraction and reflection[2] from the

---

1   Note that scattering found its way into the global illumination research area with the introduction of bidirectional reflectance distribution functions (BRDFs) and subsurface scattering (SSS).

2   There is still a diffuse specular lighting component as part of the Phong lighting model.

model—a *low albedo* scenario [BLINN 1982a]—we have reached the standard physical model of volume rendering, the *density emitter model* introduced by SABELLA [1988]. This model only considers *emission* and *absorption* and essentially models every contributing particle in our volume as a tiny light source attenuated by absorption while traveling through the volume dataset. Note that the density-emitter model has only a macroscopic view on the physical model and models the medium as one homogenous density cloud. All the variations of physical models are also referred to as "optical models" for direct volume rendering.

8.1.1 EMISSION

The general assumption of the emission part of the physical model is that each contributing particle in a volume dataset is a tiny light source that emits its light throughout the volume. In the emission-only physical model, this light is not attenuated and not scattered; hence, it is without any interaction with the volume [HEGE et al. 1993, MAX 1995]. An example of this situation is a glowing but mostly transparent (no absorption and no scattering) gas. This light source is modeled by the *source term* $Q_\lambda(s)$, where λ specifies the wavelength of the emitted light and s specifies the direction of the light. Later, we will model s as a ray that travels from the view point eye through the volume and that accumulates the light (see Fig. 8.1).[3] From now on, we will further simplify the source term by computing it for one fixed wavelength, thus using only $Q(s)$ as source term. Equation 8.1 implements the computation of the intensity $I(s)$ at position s along a ray S, based on the source term $Q(s)$, by the following differential equation:

$$\frac{dI}{ds} = Q(s) \tag{8.1}$$

We yield the solution of this differential equation by computing the integral

$$I(s) = I_{s_0} + \int_{s_0}^{s} Q(t)dt \tag{8.2}$$

where s_0 is the entry point into the volume. Here, I_{s_0} is the initial value of light intensity when the ray enters the volume. In a way, it can be considered as some kind of ambient background light. The source term $Q(s)$ represents the actual contribution of the volume dataset to the final image and can be specified by $Q(s) = c \cdot v(s)$, where c is a constant and $v(s)$ is the sample value in the volume dataset at position s. If we also consider the transfer functions defined in Section 6.2.2, we can specify the source term as $Q(s) = T_F(v(s))$, with $T_F(.)$ as transfer functions. Note that the source term at position s will also be illuminated, typically by the Phong lighting model [FOLEY et al. 1995] (see Sect. 6.3.1). This, however, extends the basic density-emitter model of SABELLA [1988], which assumes just a (homogenous) participating media cloud. Instead, the Phong illumination model interprets each sample as an object illuminated by external light sources.

8.1.2 ABSORPTION

Since our physical model interprets the volume dataset as a cloud of a homogenous medium, we also need to specify how this medium attenuates light. Our absorption-only physical model assumes any light

---

3   Different publications present these models with varying conventions. Either the ray moves towards the view point (eye), or away from the view point. Our convention is the same as in HEGE et al. [1993], MAX [1995], while SABELLA [1988] casts the ray away from the view point.

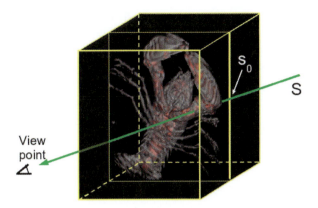

FIGURE 8.1 *A ray S traverses a volume dataset and accumulates contributions starting from the entry point s_0 towards the view point.*

intensity will absorb all the particles [MAX 1995]. Equation 8.3 defines this absorption at position s along ray S within the volume with the following differential equation:

$$\frac{dI}{ds} = -\tau(s) \cdot I(s) \tag{8.3}$$

MAX [1995] calls $\tau(s)$ the extinction coefficient that attenuates the intensity along the ray within the volume dataset. It also corresponds to the transparency of the sampling value at s specified by the opacity transfer function[4] (see Sect. 6.2.2). If we integrate the differential Equation 8.3, we yield

$$I(s) = I_{s_0} \cdot e^{\left(-\int_{s_0}^{s} \tau(t)dt\right)} \tag{8.4}$$

in which $T_{s_0}(s) = e^{\left(-\int_{s_0}^{s} \tau(t)dt\right)}$ attenuates the initial intensity I_{s_0} at position s along ray S.

8.1.3 VOLUME RENDERING EQUATION

The standard physical model for direct volume rendering employs emission and absorption [MAX 1995]. Hence, we combine both terms:

$$dI/ds = Q(s) - \tau(s) \cdot I(s) \tag{8.5}$$

and yield as a solution for that differential equation the *volume rendering equation 8.6*:

$$I(s) = I_{s_0} \cdot e^{\left(-\int_{s_0}^{s} \tau(t)dt\right)} + \int_{s_0}^{s} Q(p) \cdot e^{\left(-\int_{p}^{s} \tau(t)dt\right)} dp$$

$$= I_{s_0} \cdot T_{s_0}(s) + \int_{s_0}^{s} Q(p) \cdot T_p(p)dp \tag{8.6}$$

with $T_x(.)$ as attenuation function.[5]

---

4   Transparency and opacity are complementary values. If we assume a transparency range of $\tau \in [0..1]$, we can compute the opacity by $\alpha(s) = 1 - \tau(s)$.

5   Note that the previously mentioned different conventions of the direction of the ray use different integration ranges of the attenuation function, reflecting the accumulation ranges. With our convention, the attenuation accumulates from the current sampling point p (see Eq. 8.6) to the volume exit point s towards the view point. The other convention would use switched integration bounds.

Unfortunately, this equation cannot be solved analytically for all transfer functions and interpolation functions. Hence, we must solve it numerically, which is typically done with a Riemann sum and a fixed step size Δs that scales the current sampling position k along ray S with $k \cdot \Delta s$ (see Fig. 8.2). Before we discretize the volume rendering equation, we first discretize and simplify the attenuation term T_{s_0} into T_0, where we assume that the entry point of the ray S into the volume is now at location 0 instead of s_0:

$$T_0(s) = e^{-\int_0^s \tau(t)dt} = e^{\left(-\sum_{k=0}^{n-1} \tau(k \cdot \Delta t)\Delta t\right)}$$

$$= \prod_{k=0}^{n-1} e^{-\tau(k\Delta t)\cdot \Delta t} = \prod_{k=0}^{n-1} t_k \tag{8.7}$$

with $n-1$ as the final position $(n-1) \cdot \Delta s$ along the ray S, and with t_k as the transparency at the discrete sample point k. If we now discretize the volume rendering equation (see Eq. 8.6) with $s_k = k \cdot \Delta s$, $Q_k = Q(s_k)$, and the discretization of the attenuation term in Equation 8.7, we get

$$I(s) = I_0 \prod_{k=0}^{n-1} t_k + \sum_{k=0}^{n-1} Q(k \cdot \Delta s) \cdot \Delta s \prod_{j=k+1}^{n-1} t_j \tag{8.8}$$

This equation describes how a ray S with the initial value of the first summand in Equation 8.8 traverses the volume dataset and accumulates at discrete locations k contributions. These contributions are based on the local source term Q_k that is attenuated by the transparency (or opacity) that has been accumulated from t_j at the sample locations j along that ray. While this equation provides the theoretical basis for direct volume rendering, it also governs how the voxels of the volume datasets contribute to the final rendered image. The specifics of how the volume rendering equation is evaluated are determined by the volume rendering pipeline.

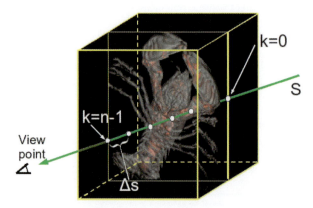

FIGURE 8.2 *A discretized ray S traverses a volume dataset and accumulates contributions at sampling points s_k starting from the entry point $k = 0$ through $k = n - 1$. Note that appropriate sampling would require many more samples as illustrated in this figure.*

8.2   THE VOLUME RENDERING PIPELINE

The volume rendering pipeline specifies the order of the individual operations used to evaluate the discrete volume rendering equation (see Eq. 8.8). An overview of these operations is given in Figure 8.3. Note that the difference between the direct volume rendering algorithms is based essentially on variations of the order of operations or on the individual operations, such as interpolation.

Sampling   The volume rendering equation describes a ray that traverses a volume dataset. Along this ray, contributions are accumulated at discrete locations. The process of selecting these specific locations is called *sampling*. As indicated by its name and by the nature of discrete data, the sampling process is subjected to the *sampling theorem* that we discussed already in Section 2.2.1. Its influence on the sampling is basically twofold: first, the sampling locations along the ray have to be picked depending on the grid resolution of the dataset, which essentially leads to a sampling rate twice as high as the respective grid spacing to avoid major artifacts.[6]

Second, the interpolation method should be picked accordingly. As we discussed in Section 2.1, the actual dataset values are only defined on the grid locations, and the values between these grid values must be interpolated. The choice of an interpolation method also influences sampling, since the order of the interpolation methods specifies the support on which that interpolation is defined. A first-order trilinear interpolation function, for example, takes into account the immediate voxel neighborhood of the sample value. In contrast, a third-order tricubic interpolation function considers a significantly larger voxel neighborhood and hence provides a lowpass filtering of that sampled region. This becomes even more clear if we consider that interpolation functions are volumetric data filtered with the respective filter kernel.

Classification and Illumination   Once the location and the value of the sampling point is determined, its contribution Q_k must be computed. The sample value is first classified according to the transfer functions (see Sect. 6.2). The result of this classification is a color value[7] that is then used in the lighting model to compute the illuminated contribution (shading). Typically, the Phong illumination model is used for that purpose (see Sect. 6.3). As we mentioned in Section 8.1, all volume samples act as a light source that emits light throughout the volume dataset. The contribution of this volume sample, however, is computed based on specified external directional light sources that provide an orientation to these volume samples.

Also part of the classification is the determination of the attenuation factor t_j, which is also based on the sampling value, using the *opacity transfer function* (OTF). This OTF in particular removes non-contributing sampling values, such as background samples, by setting the attenuation factor to fully transparent.

Compositing   Once the sample values are computed, classified, and illuminated, they must be accumulated along the ray according to the physical model. This accumulation is called compositing; it is the numerical approximation of the volume rendering integral and will be discussed in more detail in Section 8.3.

FIGURE 8.3   *Post-classified volume rendering pipeline.*

---

6   Note that depending on viewing parameters, these artifacts may not show up if the sampling rate is insufficient.

7   In case of gray-level visualization, all three color channels are set accordingly. For the RGB color model, R, G, B are set to the same value.

Preclassified Volume Rendering Pipeline

The previous paragraphs (Figure 8.3) described the post-classified[8] volume rendering pipeline, where the sampling is performed before the classification and illumination. Figure 8.4 describes a different order of operation, where the volume dataset is first classified (and possibly illuminated) and the resulting color volume dataset is then sampled. Since classification (and illumination) is now performed before sampling, it is called *preclassified volume rendering*.

The big advantage of preclassified volume rendering is that classification and illumination are computed for every voxel, hence we can tell in advance which voxel will contribute and which voxel will not based on the classification. Furthermore, we can perform most of the expensive illumination calculations, such as the approximation of the normal, in a preprocess, albeit increasing the memory footprint by the need to store the normals for every voxel. Finally, the preclassified color volume can be used in cases where no on-the-fly illumination can be performed, as it was the case for the original volume rendering approaches based on 3D-texture-mapping [CULLIP and NEUMANN 1993, VAN GELDER and KIM 1996]. For more details, please refer to Section 9.4.

In addition to the advantages, there are several disadvantages associated with preclassified volume rendering. First, changing the sampling value domain—from data values to color values—introduces several problems. Interpolation in color space is not as straightforward as in the original data space. Depending on the color model, a sampling value between two different colors, e.g., on the boundary of an object, can result in a third color, as can be seen in Figure 8.5. This artifact is known as *color bleeding*,

FIGURE 8.4   *The preclassified volume rendering pipeline changes the order of classification and sampling.*

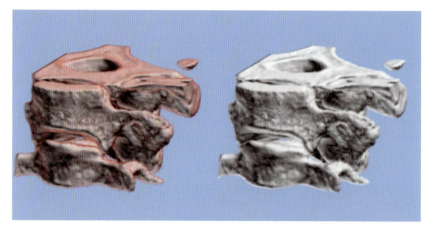

FIGURE 8.5   *Color bleeding artifact on a reconstructed vertebra dataset [WITTENBRINK et al. 1998]. (Images courtesy CRAIG WITTENBRINK, NVIDIA Corporation, and Tom Malzbender, Hewlett-Packard Corporation)*

---

8   Also known as post-shaded or post-illuminated.

due to the red color shift, and it is similar to the interpolation artifacts known as staircasing. WITTENBRINK et al. [1998] analyzed this issue and provided a solution to it: the *opacity-weighted interpolation*. This variation of the interpolation rescales the color value of the voxels by dividing them by their respective transparency values before interpolating the contribution of the sample point. Second, high-frequency details in the transfer functions cannot be presented properly by preclassification [MUELLER et al. 1999a].

8.3   COMPOSITING

As we briefly discussed in the previous section on the volume rendering pipeline, *compositing* describes the way that the individual contributions from the sample points are accumulated. *Compositing* is the discrete, numerical approximation of the volume rendering equation (Eq. 8.8). Since the contribution per sampling point may be small and is further affected by the accumulated attenuation factors, datatypes for compositing are required to provide high accuracy and fidelity. These requirements are increased by opacity-weighted interpolation, since it requires an additional division for every computed color at the samples. These requirements, however, are not always met. Several direct volume rendering systems provide only limited accuracy, which in turn leads to color staircasing, a variation of the color bleeding and interpolation artifacts. An example of this is shown Figure 8.6.

The basic compositing operator is the *over-operator* introduced by PORTER and DUFF [1984] for the compositing of images. Equation 8.9 shows how the over-operators works for a ray with three sampling points ($n = 3$) and $C_k = Q_k \cdot \Delta s$:

$$
\begin{aligned}
I(s) &= I_0 \prod_{k=0}^{2} t_k + \sum_{k=0}^{2} C_k \prod_{j=k+1}^{2} t_j \\
&= I_0(t_0 \cdot t_1 \cdot t_2) + (C_0 \cdot t_1 \cdot t_2 + C_1 \cdot t_2 + C_2) \\
&= C_2 + t_2(C_1 + t_1(C_0 + t_0 \cdot I_0)) \\
&= C_2 \text{ over } (C_1 \text{ over } (C_0 \text{ over } I_0))
\end{aligned}
\tag{8.9}
$$

 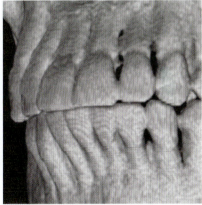

FIGURE 8.6 *Compositing accuracy issues. Left: probability cloud of electrons in a protein molecule. The fidelity of compositing data type does not allow for a sufficiently accurate accumulation of highly transparent samples. Right: skull from 3D X-ray. Insufficient compositing fidelity is causing color staircasing [MEISSNER et al. 2000]. (Images courtesy MICHAEL MEIßNER, University Tübingen)*

The over-operator is associative, but not commutative. This means that the order of composited samples cannot be changed, but the order of evaluation can. This gives rise to two directions of composition, *back to front* and *front to back*. The former composes samples on the ray from the back end of the volume dataset to the front (towards the view point) [LEVOY 1988a]. Back to front compositing is described in Equation 8.10, in which the contribution at sample position k is computed by the previous contribution weighted by the transparency t_k at the current sample, plus the color C_k at the current sample. The initial value I_0 is given by boundary condition or the ambient background light. The final result is given by I_{n-1}, the accumulated intensity at the final sample position.

$$I_k = I_{k-1} \cdot t_k + C_k, \forall k = 1, ..., n-1 \qquad (8.10)$$

In contrast, the latter *front to back* composes samples from the front (entry point into the volume from the view point) of the volume dataset along the ray to the back end of the dataset [DREBIN et al. 1988, UPSON and KEELER 1988] (see Fig. 8.2). This is described by Equation 8.11, where we start at the volume exit point $n-1$ of the ray and accumulate color I_{k-1} at the next sampling position, based on the accumulated color I_k at the current sampling position plus the color at the current sample position C_k weighted by the accumulated transparency $\hat{t}_k$. In contrast to back-to-front compositing, we now must also explicitly compute the accumulated transparency $\hat{t}_{k-1}$ at the next sampling position, based on the transparency t_k at the current sampling point and the already accumulated transparency $\hat{t}_k$. In contrast to back to front compositing in Equation 8.10, the final result is stored in I_0 and $\hat{t}_0$.

$$
\begin{aligned}
I_{n-1} &= C_{n-1} \\
\hat{t}_{n-1} &= t_{n-1} \\
I_{k-1} &= I_k + C_k \cdot \hat{t}_k, \forall k = n-2, ..., 0 \\
\hat{t}_{k-1} &= t_k \cdot \hat{t}_k, \forall k = n-2, ..., 0
\end{aligned}
\qquad (8.11)
$$

In the case of front to back compositing, we can exploit *early ray termination* [LEVOY 1990b], in which we stop compositing once the accumulated transparency $\hat{t}_k$ is too large (or the accumulated opacity too small), and more sampling points have virtually no contribution. The precise termination is specified with a transparency (opacity) threshold, which, once reached, terminates the ray sampling process. Typically, this threshold is set to 95% accumulated transparency (5% opacity). If we do not stop for early ray termination, we can still terminate compositing, once zero transparency (or full opacity) is reached, since nothing will be visible behind this point. Both compositing directions have their advantages and disadvantages, while in most cases the chosen volume rendering algorithm picks one compositing direction.

8.3.1 COMPOSITING VARIATIONS: PSEUDO X-RAY, MIP, AND CVP

Now that we have specified the basic compositing operator, we can employ it in different ways of compositing (see Figs. 8.7 and 8.8). If we sample the casted rays until we find two sample points below and above a certain intensity threshold, we reconstruct the isosurface of that threshold. This compositing mode is called *First Hit*, since it terminates once the sample points hit the isosurface with the specified threshold. This compositing mode is essentially similar to polygonal isosurface extraction. However, we only sample the isosurface. If our sampling rate is too low, we experience aliasing and visual artifacts. Furthermore, first hit compositing does not compute the exact intersection of the ray with the isosurface; it only computes the nearest sample points. Hence, small details of the isosurface may be missed if

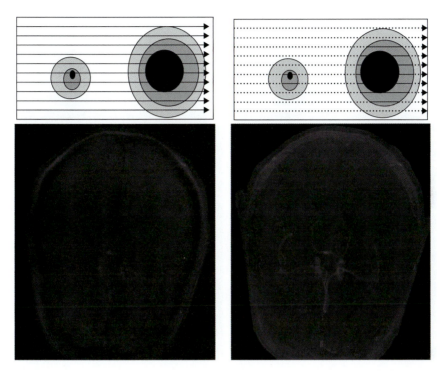

FIGURE 8.7   *Compositing variations. Top row: the arrows point to the structure along the ray that will be shown by the specific method. In all examples, the threshold (if used) is set to middle gray, not to bright gray. The dotted lines show the ray traversal through the volume, and the full lines shows which parts of that ray contribute to the final value. In some cases (pseudo X-ray), the dotted lines are covered by the full line. Bottom row: examples of the pseudo X-ray compositing based on an MRI angiography dataset. Left: pseudo X-ray accumulates all samples (full line) along the ray through the volume. Right: threshold-sensitive compositing accumulates all samples along the ray (dotted line) that are above the threshold (full line). The threshold for the bottom row image was set to 10% of the maximum intensity.*

they are too small for our sampling rate. Some compositing algorithms therefore explicitly calculate the intersection point and its contribution to the compositing.

Similar to the standard compositing as described above, *pseudo X-ray* or *averaging* is traversing and accumulating sample values along the rays throughout the whole volume (see Fig. 8.7 (left)). In contrast, however, it uses an attenuation factor that shrinks reciprocally to the voxel value; the higher the value, the smaller the factor. In other words, the opacity grows proportionally to the voxel value. Furthermore, color and lighting information are typically not considered. Overall, this leads to a representation that has a similar appearance as X-ray images (Röntgen images), hence its name. Unfortunately, this method also takes into account dark background voxels that may darken the composed image. This can be prevented by considering only sample values above a certain intensity threshold. This variation is called *threshold sensitive compositing* and is demonstrated in Figure 8.7 (right).

A popular compositing mode is *maximum intensity projection (MIP)*, which searches for the sample point with the highest intensity value. MIP therefore uses the MAX-operator along the compositing ray (see Fig. 8.8 (left)). With MIP compositing, anatomical structures with highest intensities can be visualized

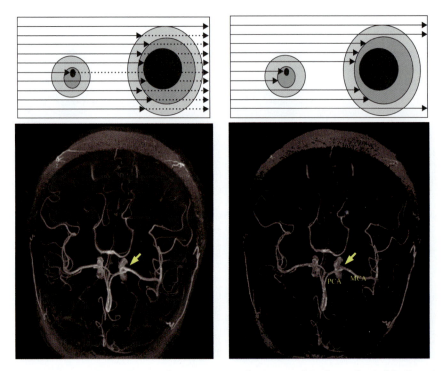

FIGURE 8.8 *Compositing variations. Top row: the arrows point to the structure along the ray that will be shown by the specific method. In all examples, the threshold (if used) is set to middle gray, not to bright gray. The dotted lines show the ray traversal through the volume, and the full lines shows which parts of that ray contribute to the final value. In some cases (CVP), the dotted lines are covered by the full line. Bottom row: examples of the respective composition variation based on an MRI angiography. Left: maximum intensity projection (MIP) picks the sample value with the highest intensity value (end of full line) along the ray through the volume (dotted line). Right: closest vessel projection (CVP) picks the sample value with the first local maximum above the threshold (end of full line). The difference in depth perception is visible at the left carotid siphon (yellow arrow) of the left internal carotid artery (ICA), where the MIP suggests that the left middle cerebral artery (MCA) and left posterior communicating artery (PCA) are located in front of the siphon.*

efficiently. This is in particular useful for bone structures (CT) and contrast-enhanced vascular structures, where the measured intensity is significantly above the regular tissue signal (see Chap. 3). Since MIP is searching for the maximum sample value along the ray, it must traverse the whole volume dataset to locate it, which can involve significant time consumption.

Another drawback of MIP, however, is that it does not provide information on how deep the shown structure is located in the volume, since no attenuation information is used. This leads to the peculiar effect that two MIP projections from opposite directions (e.g., the front and back of the volume) will be identical for the same orientation. Furthermore, small and usually darker vessels are outshone by the larger and brighter vessels. For such cases SIEBERT et al. [1991] proposed the *closest vessel projection* (CVP), which takes the first sample with a local maximum that surpasses a specified threshold (see Fig. 8.8 (right)). As we have discussed earlier, scanned datasets always experience some sort of noise, which will create very small local maxima along the ray. Therefore, the sensitivity of detecting the local maximum must be carefully tuned. In some cases, it might be necessary to traverse the ray a few samples further to ensure that we found a true local maximum. CVP is closely related to the first hit method, but differs in the choice of the sample point. The difference can be seen in Figure 8.8 (right), where the sixth ray from the top finds the local maximum of the black ellipsoid. First hit stops already at the larger middle gray ellipsoid (similar to the seventh ray), which already satisfies the threshold.

8.3.2 THIN SLAB VOLUME RENDERING

All of the above-mentioned compositing variations consider the full volume. While this is a useful setting for many applications, it is difficult to use if only the local neighborhood of a specific location is examined. NAPEL et al. [1993] proposed the use of *thin slabs* in the context of a MIP, to focus only on pulmonary (see Fig. 8.9) and cerebral blood vessels (see Fig. 8.10). Thin slab volume rendering considers only a small number of slices from the full volume dataset, specified by two synchronized clipping planes, and thus allows to inspect the local image data. This allows a better representation of the spatial coherence between individual slices (see Fig. 8.10 (left)). One of the major motivations for thin slab MIP was better depth perception of local blood vessels. While this goal is better achieved with CVP, thin slab rendering became a popular technique for more general thin slab volume rendering. In that context it is also known as *thick slice volume rendering* or simply as *slab volume rendering*.

Slab rendering is an accepted variant for certain diagnostic tasks, particularly if a large amount of slices is involved, such as in CT thorax examinations [NAPEL et al. 1993]. In particular maximum-intensity projections (MIPs) are frequently slab volume rendered (see Fig. 8.10 (right)). The user may change the displayed portion of the data by moving the mouse over an image (typically using the mouse wheel) thus sliding through the data. The acronym STS for *sliding thin slab* is often used for this type of exploration

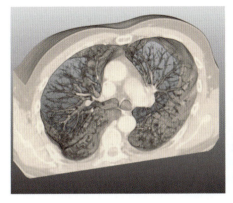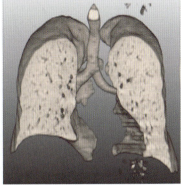

FIGURE 8.9 *Slab volume rendering of about 10 cm of CT thorax data. The left image shows the arterial and venous part of the blood vessel tree of the lungs. Right below the heart, we can also see the beginning of the left and right bronchi (empty tube-like structure with staircases). In the right image, another transfer function was specified to analyze the lung. Left: a sagittal view, right: an axial view. (Images courtesy VOLKER DICKEN, MeVis Bremen; Data courtesy BERTHOLD WEIN, Aachen)*

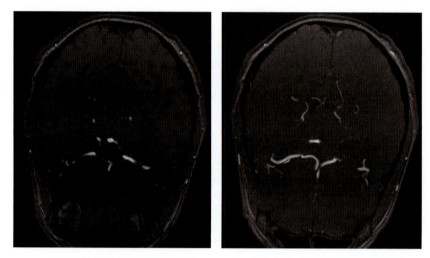

FIGURE 8.10 *Representations of an MRI angiography dataset. Left: single slice representation; right: thin slab maximum intensity projection.*

(recall NAPEL et al. [1993]). Slab rendering and other visualization techniques to explore CT thorax data are discussed in DICKEN et al. [2003].

8.3.3 PRE-INTEGRATED VOLUME RENDERING

As we mentioned earlier, the frequency range of a volume dataset can be increased depending on the used transfer function. In particular a binary transfer function that specifies a threshold for an isosurface will increase the frequency spectrum tremendously. This effect can be demonstrated if we consider that a sampling ray has a sample point before and after the isosurface. Therefore, the actual intensity transition will be missed. The obvious solution for this situation is to increase the sampling rate of the ray. This, however, will also increase the computational costs of sampling significantly. An alternative was proposed as *pre-integrated volume rendering* by ENGEL et al. [2001]. Instead of composing the contributions at sample points, they propose to compose ray segments between the sample points. This assumes that there is only a linear variation of the intensity between the sample points. While this is not totally true for all scanned datasets,[9] it is a reasonable approximation of the situation.

The ray segments represented a pre-integrated contribution along the rays. Their values depend on the local transparencies τ_k, τ_{k+1} and the source terms C_k, C_{k+1}. Furthermore, the contribution depends on the distance Δs_k between the two sampling points. In our current discrete volume rendering model, we use a constant sampling distance Δs. Hence, the ray segment contributions depend only on the sampling values at position k and $k+1$. If we precompute all possible combinations of current (k) and next ($k+1$) sampling values, we get a 2D lookup table of values, in which each dimension has as many entries as we have possible voxel values. For an 8-bit voxel depth, the 2D table has 256×256 entries. Since we

---

9   Voxels in measured volume datasets are computed by a complex set of filter operations based on the measured raw data. Most of these
    filter operations are not linear.

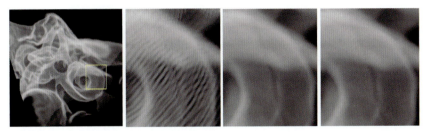

FIGURE 8.11 *Volume rendering of a CT dataset of the inner ear with vestibule and cochlea (leftmost image), with a close up of a part of the vestibule. Middle left: Post-classified volume rendering with 128 slices; the interpolation artifacts are clearly visible. Middle right: Pre-integrated volume rendering with 128 slices; no artifacts are visible. Right: Post-classified sampled volume rendering with 284 slices, with the same quality as the middle right image* [ENGEL et al. 2001]. *(Images courtesy* KLAUS ENGEL, *Siemens Corporate Research)*

precompute the transparencies and the source terms, we need two such lookup tables. Note that we need to recompute the lookup tables for every change in the transfer functions.

8.4   SUMMARY

In this chapter, we provided a brief presentation of the theoretical foundations of direct volume rendering. Specifically, we described a physical model that consists of emission and absorption in a low albedo situation with the volume rendering equation. SABELLA [1988] named this model the *density emitter model*, and it omits the influence of scattering, diffraction, refraction, reflection, participating (inhomogeneous) media, and wavelength. Also, relativistic effects are completely ignored.

Direct volume rendering is organized by the volume rendering pipeline, which allows for pre- and post-classified volume rendering with different consequences for the quality and the accuracy of the direct volume rendering algorithms. The final step of compositing the various contributing samples enables different modes, which in turn generate different visual representations of the data. In the next chapter, we will discuss the various direct volume rendering algorithms that evaluate the volume rendering equation and process the volume rendering pipeline.

FURTHER READING

There are many articles that describe the foundations of direct volume rendering. A comprehensive presentation of the physical models typically used for volume rendering was prepared by MAX [1995]. HEGE et al. [1993] provide also an excellent overview of the theoretical foundations.

The basis of the physical model is the transport theory of light and was described by KRÜEGER [1990b, c]. It is the more general version of the rendering equation presented by KAJIYA [1986], which omits the participating media and assumes a vacuum and that light is emitted, scattered, and absorbed on surfaces only. The rendering equation also ignores any kind of wavelength dependencies. BLINN [1982a] described the physical model of single scattering events or low albedo situations with an example of the dust particle rings of Saturn. In that paper, he first introduced the notion of a density cloud with certain optical properties. KAJIYA and HERZEN [1984] extended the model to multiple scattering events, or high albedo situations.

Four important articles on direct volume rendering were published in 1988. SABELLA [1988] specified the optical basis of direct volume rendering with the density emitter model. The use of the Phong lighting model was proposed by DREBIN et al. [1988], UPSON and KEELER [1988], and LEVOY [1988a], and the specification of opacity transfer functions was proposed in all four papers. Although the opacity transfer function already implied the classification of different materials, this was only discussed by DREBIN et al. [1988]. Furthermore, they introduced color transfer functions in addition to the opacity transfer function. LEVOY, however, also proposed the use of gradient magnitudes to emphasize boundaries [LEVOY 1988a].

While most direct volume rendering applications work sufficiently well with the discussed models, RAU et al. [1998] and WEISKOPF et al. [1999] also modeled relativistic effects for ray tracing, where in particular the geometric distortion [RAU et al. 1998] and the Doppler and searchlight effects [WEISKOPF et al. 1999] were examined.

Chapter 09

Algorithms for Direct Volume Visualization

In the past chapter, we discussed the theoretical foundations of direct volume rendering. This chapter focuses on how these foundations are used in practice, through implementation in the various direct volume rendering algorithms. Note, however, that there are many variations of the basic algorithms and we cannot cover all of them in this book. For a more in-depth discussion of algorithms, please refer to ENGEL *et al.* [2006].

All direct volume rendering algorithms can be classified into two groups; *image-space* approaches, sometimes also called *backward-mapping* approaches, and *object-space* approaches, also called *forward-mapping* approaches. However, many advanced variations cannot be strictly classified as one or the other, but fuse aspects from both groups into one algorithm.

Organization In the following sections, we will discuss the most important (i.e., the most frequently used) direct volume rendering approaches. We start with the two major image-space approaches: *ray casting* in Section 9.1 and *shear warp* in Section 9.2. Afterwards, we will examine the two dominating object-space approaches, *splatting* (see Sect. 9.3) and *texture-mapping* (see Sect. 9.4). Other approaches will be summarized in Section 9.5. Section 9.6 discusses one approach to rendering segmented volume data with high visual quality. The question of hybrid volume rendering, in which we combine direct and indirect volume rendered objects, is the focus of Section 9.7. Next to the discussion of algorithmic aspects of volume rendering, we also have to look into the validity of volume rendering algorithms (see Sect. 9.8).

Finally, we will briefly discuss questions of which direct volume rendering approach to use and the maybe more important question of when to use direct and indirect volume rendering (see Sect. 9.9).

9.1 RAY CASTING

The classic direct volume rendering algorithm is the image-space oriented *ray casting*, which is a variation of *ray tracing*. In both cases, rays are cast from the eye or viewpoint through the image-plane and through the dataset. In the case of ray tracing, contributions are typically computed at the intersections of the rays with the objects of the scene. Depending on the material properties of the objects, the rays are refracted or reflected. If both effects take place, secondary rays are cast from the intersection point, while the primary rays proceed in the current or new directions.

In contrast, standard ray casting does not traverse a scene containing various objects, but a volumetric dataset. Consequently, it does not compute intersections with objects, since all voxels of the dataset may be contributing. Instead, the ray samples the volumetric dataset along its path. Depending on the specified properties (specified by the transfer functions), the samples may be contributing (having opacity values larger than zero) or not contributing (having opacity values of zero). The positions of the samples on the ray within the data volume depend on the direction of the ray and the sampling rate, which governs the distance between neighboring samples on that ray. Since in most cases these positions will not be located

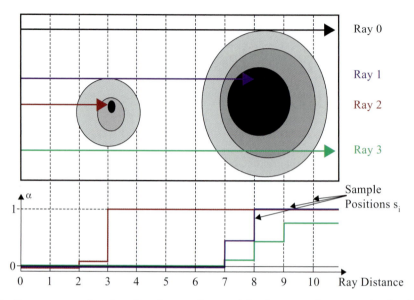

FIGURE 9.1 *Four rays are cast through a volume dataset and are sampled at discrete sampling points. Note that the sampling rate is only chosen for illustration purposes. The diagram in the lower part shows the accumulated opacity α of the rays at the sampling positions, with 0 as totally transparent (no contribution) and 1 as fully opaque. Ray 0 samples through fully transparent empty space, hence its opacity α_0 remains zero. Ray 1 samples first through empty space and detects a contributing sample at s_7, and a full opaque sample at s_8, which triggers early ray termination. Ray 2 finds its first contributing, semi-transparent sample at s_2, and a fully opaque sample at s_3. Finally, ray 3 finds the first contributing sample at s_7 and accumulates the opacity through samples s_7-s_9.*

directly at voxel positions, we need to compute the sample values by an interpolation method. The typical used method is trilinear interpolation, which we discussed in Section 2.1.

Next to the difference between computing intersections and sampling, the other big difference between ray casting and ray tracing is the lack of secondary rays, since here the rays are neither refracted nor reflected at the sampling points. Nevertheless, some visualization approaches do use sampled ray tracing with secondary rays on volume datasets, such as SOBIERAJSKI and KAUFMAN [1994].

Similar to ray tracing, ray casting expects at least one ray to be cast per pixel of the image-plane (hence it is classified as an image-space approach). However, the sampling theorem tells us that this is not enough to avoid sampling artifacts. Therefore, 2×2 or more rays per pixel should be cast. Since this increases the computational load fourfold, this is rarely done. Fortunately, only very few features are small enough to witness the sampling artifacts. In Figure 9.2 (left), we see a two-times oversampling.

Alternatively, a coarse sampling rate is used for a rapid exploration mode, while the full quality rate is used to refine the current image into the final image, once the viewing parameters are set by the rapid exploration mode.

Note that also the distance of the sampling positions on the cast rays are subject to sampling issues, as the name already suggests. Hence the selected sampling rate should reflect the smallest voxel spacing with at least two samples per volume cell. Figure 9.2 shows that even twofold oversampling is sometimes not enough. In particular the middle image shows twofold oversampling of a close-up in comparison to fivefold oversampling in the right image.

Ray casting is the direct algorithmic implementation of the discrete volume rendering equation (see Eq. 8.8) introduced in Section 8.1.3. The sampling distance translates directly to the step size Δs.

FIGURE 9.2 *Ray cast image of an electron distribution in a protein molecule. Left: An overview of the three classified distribution areas with twofold oversampling in x, y, and depth (z). Middle: Undersampled close-up with twofold oversampling. Right: Sufficiently sampled close-up with fivefold oversampling.*

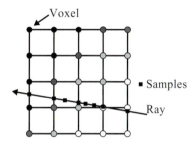

FIGURE 9.3 *Adaptive ray sampling in the gray area of the material boundary.*

9.1.1 QUALITY

In contrast to the extraction of isosurfaces using Marching Cubes [LORENSEN and CLINE 1987], discrete ray casting typically does not compute the exact intersection. Consequently, isosurfaces rendered with ray casting will appear somewhat smaller, and small features might be missed if the number of samples is insufficient or no samples represent them. Typical solutions include ray tracing (compute the exact intersection of the ray with the isosurface) [SOBIERAJSKI and KAUFMAN 1994, TIEDE et al. 1998, PARKER et al. 1998] and the adaptive subsampling of the ray, once a material boundary has been detected (see Fig. 9.3) [LEVOY 1990b, DANSKIN and HANRAHAN 1992]. However, this detection is tricky without any data representation of the respective volume region.

Most medical applications use a parallel or orthographic projection, in which all rays remain parallel along their way through the volume dataset. Hence, the density of sampling points remains constant, if the sampling rate is not changed. This, however, is different with perspective projections, where the rays diverge from each other on their way through the volume dataset. This ray divergence reduces the sampling rate along the rays and causes aliasing. In particular, voxels in the rear part of the volume dataset might be missed completely (see Fig. 9.4 (left)). Several remedies are possible for this issue; the most simple remedy is to increase the number of rays cast through the volume. However, this solution will significantly increase the rendering costs, which might be disproportionate to the gained visual quality. Alternatively, a multiresolution representation of the volume dataset can provide an appropriately low pass filtered subvolume, similar to a mipmap, that is sampled by the rays that are further advanced through the volume [LEVOY and WHITAKER 1990]. Finally, NOVINS et al. [1990] suggested an adaptive sampling technique in which each ray is split into four subrays once undersampling is detected. Their respective contribution must be composited into the original ray at the split location (see Fig. 9.4 (right)).

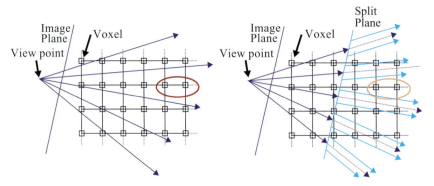

FIGURE 9.4 *Ray divergence in perspective ray casting. Left: the red ellipse indicates two voxels on the grid that are completely missed by the diverging rays. Right: rays are split if voxel sampling becomes too low. Their contribution must be composed with the respective original ray on the split plane.*

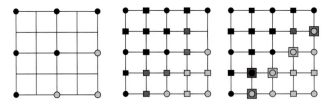

● Image plane pixels that is set by a ray
■ Image plane pixels that is set by interpolation
◎ Image plane pixels that is set by a refinement ray

FIGURE 9.5 *Adaptive image sampling. In areas of a large gradient or color differences, the interpolated pixel values are replaced with the result of refinement rays.*

Other quality issues may arise from other sources of undersampling, i.e., due to high frequencies introduced by transfer functions. In this case, higher sampling rates are required. Alternatively, pre-integrated volume rendering can be used to avoid aliasing artifacts (see Sect. 8.3.3).

9.1.2 ACCELERATION METHODS

Historically, most acceleration methods tried to reduce computational time by reducing the number of samples. More recently, approaches focus on the memory access, which proved to be a major bottleneck.

For ray casting, the reduction of samples means that either less rays are cast through the volume, or less samples are taken along the rays. The first avenue is adopted by LEVOY [1990c], where one ray is cast for every four pixels (2 × 2). For the remaining pixels, the color is bilinearly interpolated. Subsequently, the rendered image is successively refined to provide the full image-space resolution. This concept of image coherence was further exploited in [LEVOY 1990a], where more rays are cast if the color values of neighboring rays vary too much (see Fig. 9.5). In contrast, DANSKIN and HANRAHAN [1992] suggested that a user-specified hierarchy level be used throughout the image generation.

The alternative way of reducing samples along the rays aims at subsampling regions of little or no contribution (*empty space*). LEVOY [1990b] suggested a hierarchy of binary volumes, similar to LEVOY and

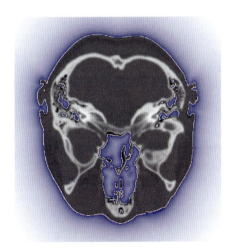
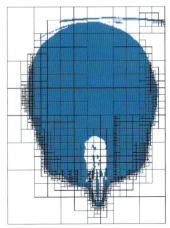

FIGURE 9.6   *Ray casting acceleration techniques. Left: distance transform of the empty (not relevant, hence not contributing) space. The high saturation indicates a very short distance to the CT data of a head. Right: adaptive octree decomposition of a slice from a CT scan of a (different) head. The decomposition level depends on the view direction and the respective occlusion [MORA et al. 2002]. (Right image courtesy BEN MORA, Swansea University)*

WHITAKER [1990], to identify empty regions as regions with a low opacity value in coarse resolution hierarchy levels. The respective regions can then be represented by a smaller number of samples and a respectively larger sampling distance. Furthermore, *early ray termination* (also called α-*termination* or *adaptive termination*) was proposed to stop compositing once a certain level of opacity has been reached [LEVOY 1990b] (see Sect. 8.3).[1]

Other methods accelerate empty space traversal by calculating distance fields that encode the distance of the current position to the next relevant[2] (non-empty) object [ZUIDERVELD et al. 1992, COHEN-OR and SHEFFER 1994]. Figure 9.6 (left) shows an example of a distance field that encodes the distance to the object (the darker the pixel color gets, the closer the current location is). AVILA et al. [1992] introduced PARC (polygon assisted ray casting), which uses the depth buffer and a polygonal approximation of the objects to be rendered to compute the positions of the first contributing samples of an isosurface; they extended their approach to accumulative volume ray tracing, which sums up the weighted (classified) samples along the ray, including the contributions from secondary rays [SOBIERAJSKI and AVILA 1995]. A quite similar method was proposed by WESTERMANN and SEVENICH [2001], who use texture-mapping (see Sect. 9.4) and the alpha test to provide empty-space skipping. Specifically, the alpha test discards all as transparent classified voxels, when the dataset is rasterized by the texture-mapping hardware. This leaves only the nontransparent (contributing) voxels, which represent the entry points for the subsequent ray casting process.

A different approach to reducing the number of not contributing samples is a hierarchical subdivision of the volume dataset (see Sect. 7.2.5 for a discussion in the context of isosurfaces). Octrees are frequently used to store minimum and maximum voxel values (see branch-on-need-octrees in Sect. 7.2.5), which can guide the determination of relevant volume cells [WILHELMS and VAN GELDER 1992, NEUBAUER et al.

---

1   Originally, early ray termination depicted a reached 100% opacity, while α-termination depicted termination at a lower opacity threshold.

2   In this context, relevant means that the respective voxels may have a contribution, depending on the classification and the view position.

2002, MORA et al. 2002, GRIMM et al. 2004] (see Fig. 9.6 (right)). Most intermediate data structures store the complete volume dataset and select the relevant parts when necessary. This way, the data structures do not need to be recomputed if the transfer functions are changed. This, however, is somewhat different for empty space skipping, where empty dataset regions are often completely removed from the data structure, and hence must be recomputed completely if the definition of empty changes.

Quite a large share of computations for ray casting is spent on the calculations of the next sampling positions. YAGEL and KAUFMAN [1992] tried to reduce these costs by using ray templates for parallel projections to simplify ray traversal. Once a sample is found relevant, the calculation of the respective gradient is consuming significant resources. If, instead, precomputed per-voxel gradients are used, it is only a trilinear interpolation of the gradient vector, but it may require up to six times more space to store the gradients [ZUIDERVELD 1995a]. In contrast, VAN GELDER and KIM [1996] suggest storing quantized gradient value in a lookup table to reduce the space requirements with modest quality degradation (see Fig. 9.7). MORA et al. [2002] also precompute gradients.

More recently, researchers have focused on efficient memory architectures. Furthermore, they exploited concurrent (parallel) computing, either using threads on one computer, message-passing processes on clusters, or SIMD (single instruction stream, multiple data stream) on the CPUs and GPUs, a technique that has been adopted from the vector processors of supercomputers. By far, most efficiency gains have been achieved by arranging memory management in a cache-sensitive way. Here, data are arranged so that the access to data in the significantly slower main memory is avoided.

While memory-sensitive processing is not new,[3] it was first proposed for interactive ray casting/tracing by PARKER et al. [1998], who reorganized the data volume into smaller blocks (bricks). Furthermore, they arranged the data in a volume hierarchy that provided meta information on the data (i.e., maximum and minimum voxel values [WILHELMS and VAN GELDER 1992]) to quickly determine the relevant volume cells, and used thread-based multi-processing on a large SGI Origin 2000 system. In addition to a brick-oriented memory-sensitive processing with an octree hierarchy, MORA et al. [2002] reorganized the ray casting pipeline into an object-space approach. Ray casting is applied to each brick, and the results are projected onto the image-plane. Furthermore, they provide a technique for removing not-visible parts of the volume to reduce the number of samples, using an occlusion culling approach. The used hierarchical occlusion map (HOM) [ZHANG et al. 1997] is in essence an image pyramid of the framebuffer that contains occlusion information. The higher the pyramid level, the faster the occlusion query can be made, at the expense of a higher number of false positives (that are found to be not occluded, but that are in fact occluded). The lowest pyramid level represents the full framebuffer content.

Unfortunately, this approach is inflicted with a large memory overhead, largely due to the precomputed voxel gradients. Although precomputed gradients can reduce the computational load significantly, they render this approach impractical for the dataset sizes acquired in currently used clinical scanners. Hence, GRIMM et al. [2004] provided another variation that does not pre-compute gradients, but stores already-computed gradients of the local data brick in a cache-like structure. Brick-local octrees provide spatial information to rapidly skip transparent regions with one data brick, thus enabling a rapid ray casting approach. Due to lean data structures, the memory overhead sums up to only 10%, allowing the representation of larger (clinically relevant) dataset sizes.

A general approach to adapt voxel organization to a provided memory hierarchy is the *voxel cache* of KANUS et al. [2003]. The brick organization of a volume dataset is mapped to a customizable memory

---

3   Memory-sensitive processing is a common and well-known technique for distributed memory or non-uniform memory access architectures (NUMA). It is also common for out-of-core processing, when the data does not fit into main memory and the currently needed data must be swapped from mass storage. This was for the example used by COX and ELLSWORTH [1997].

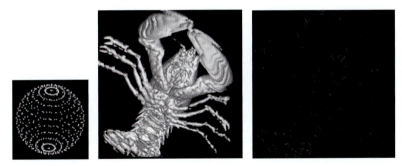

FIGURE 9.7 *Ray casted images with quantized gradients. Left: quantized gradients stored in the lookup table. Middle: famous ray cast lobster dataset using quantized gradients. Right: difference image for ray cast lobster with computed gradients* [MEIßNER *et al.* 1998]. *(Images courtesy* MICHAEL MEIßNER, *University Hospital Eppendorf)*

system that can consist of local memory cache, slower main memory, or even external diskspace. Each memory brick is organized in a two-level hierarchy of voxel blocks aligned in cache memory, enabling a sustained hit ratio of more than 98%. Although this approach was originally designed for a hardware volume rendering architecture, its concept can be mapped to software- or hardware-supported rendering approaches.

Finally, note that cache-sensitive memory management also benefits all other processing stages, not just ray casting or other direct volume rendering methods.

9.2   SHEAR WARP

The *shear warp* volume rendering approach is a highly optimized version of the basic ray casting algorithm. However, it is no longer a pure image-based approach, since it also incorporates object-space aspects. The basic idea of shear warp is to simplify the volume sampling to reduce memory access costs. Ray casting samples the volume in arbitrary directions, depending on the position and orientation of the image-plane (which intrinsically defines the view transformation).

Shear warp instead casts the rays from a base-plane, which is always parallel to the side of the data volume that faces the viewpoint most. The resulting ray direction is now perpendicular to the respective volume face, which enables a very regular data access pattern. However, we need to *shear* the volume slices to get the same sampling pattern as for the original image-plane (see Fig. 9.8 (middle)). Furthermore, the resulting base-plane image (or intermediate image, see Fig. 9.9 (middle)) is *warped* to the original image-plane to correct for the different viewing position and direction (see Fig. 9.9 (right)). In total, we factorize the viewing transformation V into the principal axis transformation P (to rotate (permute) the volume towards the face that is most parallel to the image-plane), the volume shear transformation S, and the final warping W. For a perspective projection, there is also a scaling transformation included in the shear transformation S_{persp} (see Fig. 9.8 (right)). This scaling, however, causes approximately 50% additional time costs, as SCHULZE *et al.* [2001] have shown. Since the view transformation, the permutation, and the shear transformation are known or can be constructed, we can compute the warping matrix W through matrix Equation 9.1:

$$V = P \cdot S \cdot W \tag{9.1}$$

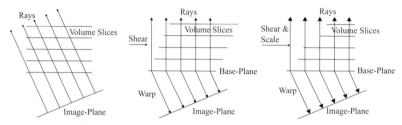

FIGURE 9.8 *Shear warp transformation. Left: rays are cast from the image-plane. Middle: parallel projection—rays are cast from the base-plane. To correct the sampling positions, the slices are sheared and the base-plane image is warped to the image-plane. Right: perspective transformation—the shear transformation now also contains scaling to adapt to a perspective transformation.*

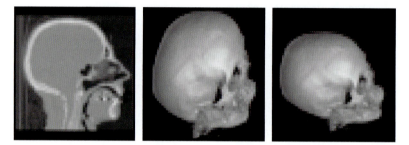

FIGURE 9.9 *Shear warp planes. From left to right: Volume slice, base-plane image; final (image-plane) image* [LACROUTE 1995]. *(Images courtesy* PHILIPP LACROUTE)

Shear warp factorizations to simplify voxel access patterns were originally proposed by CAMERON and UNDRILL [1992], YAGEL and KAUFMAN [1992], and SCHRÖDER and STOLL [1992] and later extended by LACROUTE and LEVOY [1994]. However, they are based on even earlier work on the decomposition of rotations into scale-shear [CATMULL and SMITH 1980, DREBIN et al. 1988] and shear-only transformations [PAETH 1986, TANAKA et al. 1986]. Today's shear warp volume rendering is essentially based on Lacroute's approach. The data access is organized by pre-computing three rotated versions of the volume to provide better caching for accessing the voxels after the principal axis transformation. To further simplify the voxel access, Lacroute's version of shear warp sampled the rays cast from the base-plane only within the volume slices. This way, only a bilinear interpolation between four voxels on the sheared slices is necessary. However, this operation also introduced significant aliasing effects, since the sampling distance is as large as the distance between the slices.[4] Even worse, the more the view transformation approximates a 45° angle, the larger the sampling distances get. Figure 9.10 shows such aliasing artifacts.

In addition, Lacroute proposed several other optimizations, such as a run-length encoded (RLE) representation of the volume dataset and of the image compositing. For the former, the volume dataset is preclassified to identify empty regions that do not contribute to the final image and regions of identical properties, such as homogenous regions. This RLE representation allows faster loading of the (now smaller) volume and faster processing, since we already know how many voxels have the same property. The preclassification may lead to a reduced quality, as discussed in Section 8.2.

---

4   Depending on the currently used volume permutation, this distance can be as large as the *slice distance* of an anisotropic volume dataset.

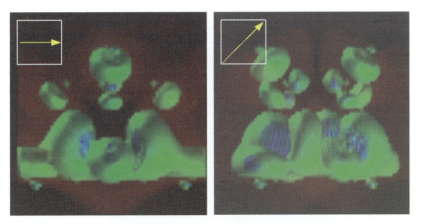

FIGURE 9.10 *Shear warp varying sampling distances. The small squares represent the respective sampling distance. Left: 1:1 sampling when view-plane is parallel to volume. Right: 1:1.41 sampling when viewed at* 45°.

Shear warp enables the simultaneous traversal of all rays at the same time, hence the compositing is organized slice-by-slice, and not ray-by-ray, as for the standard ray casting approach. This compositing style represents the hybrid image-space and object-space orientation of Shear warp. The slice-by-slice orientation enables an RLE representation of each scanline of the base-plane image if the pixels have already accumulated enough opacity for early ray termination. All other pixel runs are composited with the next voxel scanline of the next volume slice but can also be run-length encoded, if parts of the next voxel scanline are fully transparent (no contribution) and can thus be skipped.

9.2.1 QUALITY

Overall, the regular voxel access patterns and the other acceleration techniques render Shear warp one of the fastest software direct volume rendering techniques. However, the fast rendering is obtained with several quality penalties. Next to the already mentioned preclassified volume rendering pipeline and the insufficient sampling along the rays, the standard Shear warp algorithm of LACROUTE and LEVOY [1994] casts only one ray per base-plane pixel. Since the base-plane resolution is typically identical to the resolution of the respective volume face, it quickly becomes obviously insufficient for large view-plane images. In this case, the base-plane image is bilinearly enlarged in the warping step, which in turn introduces heavy blurring.[5] Finally, as we have already indicated earlier, Shear warp uses only bilinear interpolation within one slice to compute the ray samples, which is a reconstruction filter with a much lower quality than trilinear interpolation, in particular for highly anisotropic datasets.

All these drawbacks led to strong visual artifacts, which become particularly obvious if zoom factors larger than one are used. To compensate for these problems, several variations of Lacroute's algorithm were proposed. PFISTER et al. [1999] described a hardware implementation that provided already trilinear interslice interpolation and a higher base-plane resolution. The higher base-plane resolution was also later briefly described for a software approach by SCHULZE et al. [2001], who required zoomed and perspective views, for their virtual environment application. More details on how to achieve this higher resolution were discussed by SWEENEY and MUELLER [2002]. Furthermore, SCHULZE et al. [2001] discussed the use of

---

5   In cases where a higher resolution is needed, VOLPACK, Lacroute's publicly available implementation of Shear warp, provides a tool that computes a resampled higher resolution volume. This way, however, the computational costs are increased significantly.

FIGURE 9.11 *The engine dataset has been rendered with the modernized shear warp algorithm with post-classification, high-resolution base-plane image, and higher depth sampling [SWEENEY and MUELLER 2002]. (Image courtesy KLAUS MUELLER, Stony Brook University)*

texture-mapping functionality to implement the final warping step, a technique that was also proposed by PFISTER et al. [1999] for the VolumePro volume rendering board.

Additional improvements were suggested by SWEENEY and MUELLER [2002]. Next to a quantized normal map (see also VAN GELDER and KIM [1996], and Fig. 9.7), they provided a post-classified volume rendering pipeline with small modifications. Furthermore, higher depth sampling is provided through interpolated intermediate slices that are located between the sheared volume slices. Extra care has to be invested to compute the correct interpolation weights for the trilinear interpolation in the now sheared volume cell. Also, compositing of the intermediate slices with the current scanline of the base-plane image requires extra effort to decode the scanline voxel runs properly. An example of a dataset transparently rendered with these techniques can be seen in Figure 9.11.

9.3   SPLATTING

The previous two approaches gather contributions along a ray that is cast through the data volume. *Splatting*, in contrast, projects the voxels onto the image-plane [WESTOVER 1989, 1990, 1991]. It is therefore an object-space approach. Voxels itself are infinitesimal small points in 3D with a scalar value.[6] Therefore, we need to convolve the voxels with a volume filter to provide them with a geometric extent. This volume filter is typically a Gaussian function. Being a spherical kernel, it has the advantage of being invariant to rotations, hence we can use this filter kernel without considering the view direction. This, however, works only for isotropic grids, where all voxel distances are identical and the screen projection, the footprint, is a circle. For anisotropic grids, we need to scale the filter with the voxel distances, resulting in an ellipsoid kernel, which has an ellipsoid screen projection. This projection is no longer invariant to the view-direction.[7]

---

6   In many scientific volume rendering applications, voxels can consist of several scalars, vectors, or even tensors (e.g., DTI). Here, however, we examine only single scalar values, which is the typical case for medical image datasets.

7   Alternatively, the volume can be resampled into an isotropic volume grid.

Once the voxels are convolved with the filter kernel, they are projected onto the image-plane. Since the projected contribution, the footprint, for an orthogonal projection will always be the same scaled with the voxel value, it can be precomputed and stored in a table, the footprint table. In the case of anisotropic grids, this footprint table must be adapted for every new view-direction. Details on that adaption are provided in WESTOVER [1990]. If a perspective projection is used, the screen extent of the footprint and its position must be corrected for each sample. Furthermore, the perspective screen projection of an ellipsoid may be no longer an ellipse. However, the actual size of the footprints may be only a few pixels, hence this error is ignored in WESTOVER'S published work.

As we have learned in Section 8.3, the compositing of samples is not commutative, hence we must ensure that the voxels are convolved in the correct order. WESTOVER [1990] used an axis-aligned *sheet-plane* (or *sheet-buffer*) that is most parallel to the image-plane (see Fig. 9.12 (right)).[8] This way, splatting selects the relevant voxels from the respective slices of the dataset—an approach similar to the previously described shear warp volume rendering approach. This sheet-plane traverses the volume dataset back-to-front to select the voxels, compute their contributions, and accumulate them in the final image.

For classification, WESTOVER'S original splatting approach used preclassification, where every voxel is classified. If the classified voxels are contributing (the transparency value is larger than zero), they are afterwards convolved and projected. Otherwise, they are simply ignored.

One of the advantages of splatting is the voxel orientation of the approach. This way, it is less sensitive to changes of the image-plane size, which are typical factors for increased costs in the ray casting approach. Instead, the filter kernel—and hence the footprint—size is adapted to the higher (or lower) image-plane resolution. Larger filter sizes can also be used to provide a lower fidelity representation of volume regions with high data coherence. This advantage, however, comes with several drawbacks, such as preclassification volume rendering, illumination artifacts due to axis-aligned sampling, and potentially excessive blurring.

In general, the size of the filter kernels (splats) should be chosen so that they slightly overlap to include all voxels and their respective volume cells. CRAWFIS and MAX [1993] suggested a splat size of 1.6

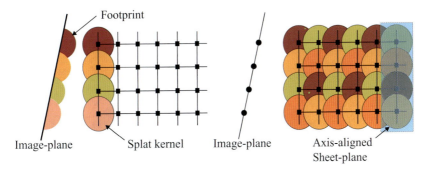

FIGURE 9.12 *Splatting after* WESTOVER [1989, 1990]: *Left: Voxels are convolved with a splatting kernel and projected to the image-plane. Right: Axis-aligned splatting; all voxels are splat to the image-plane in an axis-aligned order, either front-to-back, or back-to-front, to ensure a correct compositing order.*

8   The first splatting approach presented in WESTOVER [1989] did not make any specific assumptions on the splat projection order. This in turn led to bleeding artifacts, since some of the local splat contributions may have been composited in the wrong order, thus violating the noncommutative nature of compositing.

to ensure a sufficient overlap of the splats while at the same time limiting the overlap, thus allowing accurate splatting. Note that in general, too-small splat sizes will result in aliasing, and too-large splats will result in excessive blurring.

9.3.1 QUALITY

WESTOVER's original splatting approach suffered from several quality problems. First of all, the outlined approach for perspective projections introduced aliasing, due to insufficient sampling of the back parts of the volume dataset—the same perspective undersampling problem that was described as *ray divergence* for ray casting in Section 9.1.1. MUELLER and YAGEL [1996] approached this undersampling problem with cone-beam ray casting, which accumulates the local splats table. Later, this hybrid ray casting/splatting approach was complemented by a pure splatting approach that used appropriately scaled splats (filter kernels) to cover the otherwise-not-included areas of perspective undersampling in uniform grids [SWAN et al. 1997]. One of the drawbacks of this approach was discussed by ZWICKER et al. [2001], who pointed out that the uniform scaling of the spherical splats does not translate well to non-uniform grids; spherical splats do not provide a good approximation of non-spherical kernels like elliptical filter, resulting in unnecessary blurring, a well-known issue in texture-mapping (see Fig. 9.13) [SCHILLING et al. 1996]. Instead, they suggest the use of elliptically weighted average filters, introduced by HECKBERT [1989], which combine elliptical Gaussian splats and low pass filtering.

Although bleeding artifacts due to the locally incorrect composition of splats were addressed by the axis-aligned sheet-plane [WESTOVER 1990], this method still generates popping artifacts. These artifacts occur when the slice orientation of the most-parallel slice changes at 45° rotation angles. Figure 9.14 (left/middle) demonstrates this artifact, where the two sides of the binary cube dataset are illuminated differently, although they should be identical [MUELLER and CRAWFIS 1998]. Figure 9.14 (right) explains the reason for this artifact: most samples of the left face of the cube are simply added, since most samples are on the same sheet-plane. In contrast, most samples of the darker right face are located in different sheet-planes, hence there are not simply added, but composited, which yields a smaller intensity than a sum. In fact, both illumination results are incorrect, since both faces should not only have a similar illumination, but the bright face should be darker, and the dark face should be brighter. MUELLER and CRAWFIS [1998] suggest a solution of this problem, where the axis-aligned sheet-plane is replaced by an *image-aligned sheet-buffer*. This sheet-buffer[9] is now parallel to the image-plane that accumulates the final image (see Fig. 9.15 (left)).

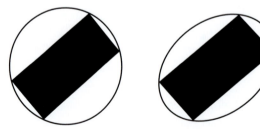

FIGURE 9.13 *Filter kernels are approximated through spherical splats (left) and through elliptical splats (right).*

---

9   With the introduction of the image-aligned sheet-buffer by MUELLER and CRAWFIS [1998], the terminology changed from WESTOVER's sheet-plane to MUELLER's sheet-buffer.

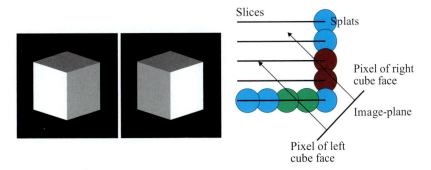

FIGURE 9.14 *Illumination artifacts with axis-aligned sheet-plane splatting. Once the orientation of the most parallel slice orientation changes from 45° (left) to 45.2° (middle) it exposes the illumination artifact. The reason for these artifacts lies in the different accumulation of the splats. In the right image, the red splats are combined by attenuated compositing into the respective pixel of the image-plane (dark face), and the green splats are combined by summation into the respective pixel of the image-plane by summation (bright face) [MUELLER and CRAWFIS 1998]. (Left images courtesy KLAUS MUELLER, Stony Brook University)*

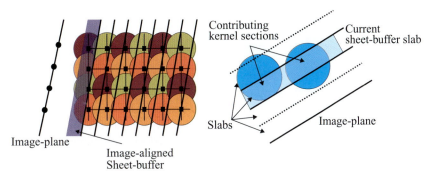

FIGURE 9.15 *Image-aligned sheet-buffer. Left: the sample-selecting sheet-buffer is now parallel to the image-plane. Right: sections of the splat kernels (blue) of one slab (turquoise) are composed into one sheet-buffer [MUELLER and CRAWFIS 1998].*

Since now the splat samples are taken consistently with the same plane orientation, the compositing is consistent as well and can accumulate its contribution into the image-plane. However, while every voxel—and hence its splat—was represented by exactly one sheet-plane in axis-aligned sheet-planes composition, this is no longer the case for image-aligned sheet-buffers. Instead, parts of the splats extend into neighboring sheet-buffers and need to be considered for correct compositing with that sheet-buffer. To enable the composition of splat sections, MUELLER and CRAWFIS [1998] propose the organization of the splat into many small overlapping pre-integrated splat kernel sections (slabs) that can also be reused due to the spherical nature of the splats (see Fig. 9.15 (right)). Here, the number of slabs and their respective size is a tradeoff between quality (small size) and efficiency (large size). MUELLER et al. [1998] found that a slab size of 1.0 yields a good compromise.

As we mentioned above, splatting uses a preclassification volume rendering scheme, where the voxels are first classified and then resampled by the splatting filter kernel and the sheet-buffer. This, however, leads to blurred object edges, an issue that is even stressed in splatting due to its implicit low pass filtering by the Gaussian filter kernels. MUELLER et al. [1999] suggested a reformulation of the splatting algorithms into a post-classification scheme to reduce the edge blurring. The gradient estimation in particular is different from the previous preclassification scheme and is now based on the central difference within one sheet-buffer and the central difference between the preceding and following sheet-buffer. Since now the smoothed edge transition shown in Figure 9.16 (left/middle) is combined with a classification afterwards, it creates a crisp edge transition (see Fig. 9.16 (left/bottom)).

9.3.2 ACCELERATION METHODS

One standard approach in volume rendering to accelerate the visual representation is the exploitation of data coherence. Typically, a hierarchical representation is generated, where the different hierarchy levels represent different fidelity levels of the data. Thus, a higher level with lower fidelity can be chosen if the respective data region has a high data coherence. For splatting, this approach was first suggested by LAUR and HANRAHAN [1991]. Depending on an error metric based on the standard deviation of the (preclassified) color values, large splats representing the lower fidelity regions are used instead of the smaller leaf block splats. However, replacing small splats with larger splats typically leads to reconstruction artifacts; if not, a costly global re-parameterization step is performed [JANG et al. 2004]. These artifacts are in particular located in the areas where the large splats overlap with the small splats. While these artifacts are less noticeable with preclassified splatting, they become very annoying with post-classified splatting [NEOPHYTOU et al. 2006a].

One advantage of splatting lies in the use of precomputed footprints through a lookup table. However, these footprints must still be rasterized into the framebuffer to generate their visual contribution. This rasterization represents one of the most costly steps of the splatting approach. Consequently, many researchers attempted to reduce the costs of the splat rasterization. Among the first approaches was the use of texture-mapping support in the graphics hardware by CRAWFIS and MAX [1993]. Here the footprint of a high-resolution template splat is rasterized into a texture-map, which in turn is then scaled and rasterized through one polygon by the graphics hardware into the framebuffer for each splat.

In contrast to ray casting, splatting has to project every relevant (nontransparent) voxel on the image-plane, even if it would have no contribution because the respective image-plane area has already reached full opacity. This means that every relevant voxel has to be convolved with the splat kernel, and

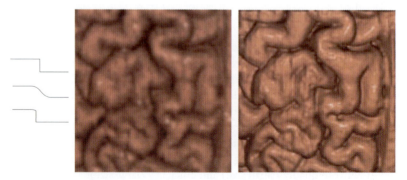

FIGURE 9.16 *Pre- and post-classification splatting. Left: Edge filtering after classification; top-original edge, middle-blurred edge after low pass filtering due to splatting (preclassification); bottom-crisp edge after thresholding (classification) of the filtered (interpolated) signal (post-classification). Middle: preclassified magnified view onto a brain. Right: post-classified magnified view onto a brain [MUELLER et al. 1999a]. (Images courtesy KLAUS MUELLER, Stony Brook University)*

its projection has to be rasterized in the framebuffer. While the number of relevant but not contributing voxels may be relatively small for sparse datasets like blood vessel trees, it can be significant for compact datasets like a human head [MEISSNER et al. 2000]. For this reason, MUELLER et al. [1999b] devised a scheme for early detection of splats that will not make a contribution to the framebuffer, which they called *early splat elimination*. MUELLER et al. use an occlusion buffer similar to the hierarchical occlusion map (see Sect. 9.1.2) to determine whether the respective area of that splat is already fully opaque. This occlusion buffer is in fact the opacity channel of the image-buffer that accumulates the contribution of the sheet-buffers. Since testing every pixel of the screen-projected splat (footprint) with the content of the underlying opacity buffer would be too expensive to be worthwhile, a simpler test must be found. Figure 9.17 (left) illustrates the use of only the center of the footprint for the test. Unfortunately, this test can result in inaccuracies, since the extent of the footprint of the splat might not be covered by the fully opaque region of the opacity buffer. Instead, MUELLER et al. exploit the fact that if all pixels of the opacity buffer below the splat are fully opaque, this is also true for their average opacity. Hence, it would be enough to test the average opacity at the splat center to determine the visibility status (see Fig. 9.17 (right)). Fortunately, this average operation can be implemented efficiently using a convolution of the opacity buffer with a box filter the size of the footprint's bounding box [MUELLER et al. 1999b]. For conservative early splat elimination, an opacity threshold of 100% must be used. Smaller thresholds implement a somewhat relaxed conservative splat elimination akin to the α-acceleration of ray casting [LEVOY, 1990b]. Note, however, that recovering the result of a hardware-supported convolution from the graphics pipeline may be an expensive operation. To circumvent this costly framebuffer readback, HUANG et al. [2000a] replaced the convolution-based solution with summed-area tables (SAT) [CROW, 1984]. These SATs represent specific parts of the region, thus allowing quick pixel area operations (see Fig. 9.18 (left)). If a splat is finally rasterized, the involved SATs are simply incrementally updated by adding the additional opacities. Note that effective early splat elimination requires a front-to-back compositing of the sheet-buffers to access potentially occluded voxels **after** the occluding voxels have already been splatted.

Early splat elimination and required flexibility triggered the need for a fast software-based rasterization of splats, since framebuffer readbacks are too costly to be done in large numbers. An early approach by MACHIRAJU and YAGEL [1993] suggested fast DDA (digital differential analyzer) rasterization approaches to map splats to a software framebuffer. HUANG et al. [2000a] propose *1D Squared FastSplats* that incrementally compute the footprint contribution with subpixel accuracy based on a large 1D footprint function, akin to BRESENHAM'S [1997] rasterization algorithm for circles. For isotropic datasets, this 1D footprint function is sufficient, since the used splat kernels and the respective footprints are spherical. For anisotropic grids and

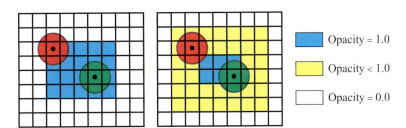

FIGURE 9.17   *Early splat elimination. Left: the opacity buffer yields inaccurate results if only the voxel center is tested for occlusion. Right: the opacity value below the voxel center in the averaged opacity buffer represents the results of the respective neighborhood. If its average opacity is below 100%, at least some pixels are not fully opaque [MUELLER et al. 1999b].*

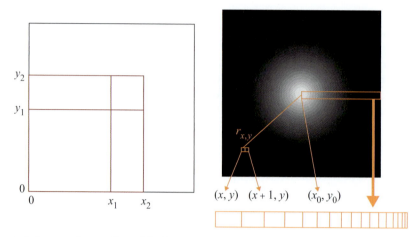

FIGURE 9.18 *Left: summed-area table used for fast region average computation. An SAT entry s_{ij} contains the sum of pixel intensities in the pixel interval $0, .., i - 1 \times 0, .., j - 1$. The average of a screen area $(x_1, .., x_2] \times (y_1, .., y_2]$ can be computed by the sum $(s_{x_2,y_2} - s_{x_1,y_2} - s_{x_2,y_1} + s_{x_1,y_1})/A$, where A is the screen area. Right: radial line of 1D Squared FastSplats, indexing with $r_{x,y}^2$. (x_0, y_0) indicates the center of the splat, and (x, y) an arbitrary location within that splat. (Right image courtesy JIANG HUANG, University of Tennessee, Knoxville)*

perspective projections, the 1D footprint function evaluation can be adapted. Alternatively, a 2D footprint can be composited with the underlying pixels with a bit block transfer operation (bitBLT). To avoid aliasing artifacts, the blocks are snapped to a subpixel grid instead of to the pixel centers [HUANG et al. 2000a]. Although this alternative achieves a high rasterization speed, its image quality requires a reasonably large subpixel resolution, which may increase the memory requirements too much. Figure 9.18 (right) shows an illustration of these FastSplats.

Finally, splatting has also been adapted to exploit modern GPUs. CHEN et al. [2004] map the EWA volume splatting approach of ZWICKER et al. [2001] to the GPU, while uploading the whole dataset onto the GPU. While they achieve a significant speedup, this method only implements axis-aligned sheet-buffers to avoid the sorting costs of the voxel splatting. Unfortunately, axis-aligned splatting is prone to popping artifacts. In contrast, NEOPHYTOU and MUELLER [2005] describe a mapping of an image-aligned sheet-buffer splatting approach described in MUELLER et al. [1999b]. After establishing the correct visibility order on the CPU, the voxels are transferred to the GPU. Previous texture splats (each requiring one quadrilateral with four vertices to be mapped to the framebuffer) are replaced by single vertex point sprites. To reduce the costs of transferring these point sprites to the graphics pipeline, vertex arrays are used. Furthermore, the RGBα buffer is used to process four slices of splat kernels with the extent of two at the same time, thus saving rasterization bandwidth. Recently, this approach was extended for more general radial base functions as filter kernels [NEOPHYTOU et al. 2006b].

9.4   TEXTURE-MAPPING

One of the most recent direct volume rendering approaches is based on the *texture-mapping* support of computer graphics hardware. Although CABRAL et al. [1994] are usually credited for this approach, it was originally described in CULLIP and NEUMANN [1993] and later in WILSON et al. [1994]. In essence, a volume dataset is loaded into texture memory and is subsequently resampled by the texture-mapping functions of the graphics hardware and mapped to a rasterized polygon (the *proxy geometry*) on the screen. Since it collects the relevant samples directly in object-space, it is considered an object-space approach.

This resampling through the texture-mapping capabilites is (re-)slicing the volume dataset and combines the contribution of the newly resampled slices through OpenGL's alpha-blending functions in the framebuffer. Figure 9.19 demonstrates this volume slicing process. A slice, parallel to the view-plane and perpendicular to the view vector, is computed through resampling of the volume dataset. It is mapped (rendered) back-to-front (mapping the farthest slices first) to the framebuffer through a rectangle rasterized to the framebuffer (left). Note how the front-most polygon is clipped to the clip-volume, resulting in a triangle. The middle image shows how the clipped polygons are now texture-mapped with the slice information. Since only a small number of slices are used for illustration purposes, we can see strong staircase artifacts. If we increase the number of computed slices, thus reducing the distance between the slices, we significantly reduce the staircase artifacts (right).

Figure 9.19 illustrates direct volume rendering that employs 3D texture-mapping to resample the volume dataset. This technique enables arbitrary slice orientations, particularly slice orientations that are parallel to the image-plane. Furthermore, high quality interpolation functions can be used to compute the individual texels. However, 3D texture-mapping capabilities were, until a few years ago, only available on high-end graphics systems, such as the RealityEngine® graphics of SGI [AKELEY 1993]. Specifically, this graphics subsystem enabled quadlinear interpolation of the samples, where two resolution levels of the textures (through a mipmap) were combined with trilinear interpolation.

Some graphics accelerators provide only 2D textures. Therefore, volume resampling has to be organized differently (see Fig. 9.20). Two Dimensional textures cannot be resampled arbitrarily in the volume dataset using the hardware acceleration, as with 3D textures; they have to be treated like single images. Consequently, we exploit the cartesian grid organization of the volume dataset to arrange the 2D textures as slices of the dataset. This, however, implies that the textures are not oriented parallel to the image-plane, which would be the proper orientation. Instead, we follow the same approach as for the Shear warp algorithm, where we choose an orientation that is most-parallel to the image-plane. Hence, we need to store the data volume with the three orthogonal orientations of the cartesian grid, which unfortunately increases the basic texture memory requirements threefold.[10] This leads to one of the major challenges of texture-based volume rendering approaches: for optimal performance, the volume dataset has to be fitted into the texture memory, or at least to the graphics memory onboard the graphics accelerator. Unfortunately, this is only the case for relatively small datasets, which do not

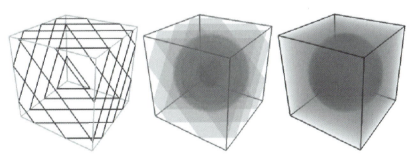

FIGURE 9.19 *Volume rendering with 3D texture-mapping* [WESTERMANN *and* ERTL *1998*]. (*Images courtesy* PETER HASTREITER, *University of Erlangen-Nürnberg*).

---

10   Some graphics accelerators provide texture compression for a more compact data representation. However, the employed compression schemes might be using a lossy representation, which in turn can lead to visual artifacts or an otherwise imperfect data representation.

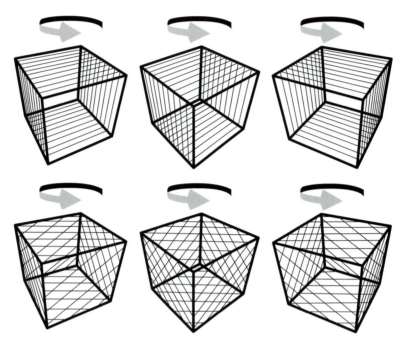

FIGURE 9.20 *The slice-orientation changes during rotations. Top row: slice-orientation switches from one slice stack to the next slice stack, which is now most parallel to the image-plane. Bottom row: 3D textures enable an always parallel-to-the-view-plane slice-orientation* [REZK-SALAMA *et al. 2000a*]. *(Images courtesy* CHRISTOF REZK-SALAMA, *University of Siegen)*

reflect the dataset sizes in today's clinical practice. Therefore, it is necessary to swap parts of the data from main memory, or even from disk space, if the dataset does not fit into main memory. Loading data from the main memory into the texture memory—and even worse from disk—is associated with a significant penalty that may slow an application severely.[11] Therefore, many approaches reorganize the volume dataset into data bricks (small parts of the volume dataset, see Fig. 9.21) that are exchanged, depending on which part of the dataset will be rendered next. In Section 9.4.2, we will examine these techniques further.

In general, and for preclassification pipelines in particular, classification of volume datasets is done through lookup tables, which store the transfer functions. Here, the scalar value of the volume dataset is interpreted as an index to a color lookup table (or transfer function) that returns an RGBα color tuple, which is interpreted as a texel and then rasterized and composited in the framebuffer. Note that, in particular, previous graphics accelerators performed the lookup in the colortables before the texture interpolation, thus implementing a preclassification pipeline that requires opacity-weighted interpolation. More recent accelerators provide also a lookup after the texture interpolation through a second 1D texture. If this texture encodes the transfer functions, it also enables post-classification.

Another shortcoming of early texture-mapping-based volume rendering was the lack of shading, which limited the spatial perception significantly. This was caused by the lack of flexibility in early

---

11   Interestingly, a 3D texture requires significantly more time to be downloaded into the texture-memory than a 2D texture of the same size, as pointed out by VOLZ [2000]. Hence, texture swaps of 3D texture bricks are more expensive than texture swaps of 2D textures.

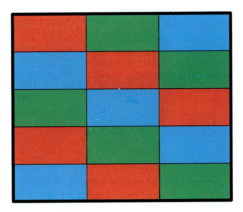

FIGURE 9.21 *A volume dataset is split into small subvolumes—bricks—that fit into the target memory, e.g., a memory cache. This way, the processing (and rendering) can be optimized for speed.*

programmability of the texture-mapping functionality, which did not allow for flexible per-voxel normal handling. The first solution to this problem was proposed by VAN GELDER and KIM [1996], who suggested the use of preilluminated or preshading (colored) volume datasets, which do not require extra space if only gray-level illumination is used. Since early texture-mapping capabilites allowed only for preclassification anyway, it did not add significantly more constraints to the volume rendering approach. Only the predefined positions of light sources are fixed in the necessary preprocessing (to compute the preshaded volume dataset). WESTERMANN and ERTL [1998] developed a two-pass method that provided shaded isosurfaces through texture-mapping volume rendering by exploiting new graphics extensions that became available. Specifically, they loaded the voxel gradients into the RGBα components of the volume texture and the intensity value into the α-channel. Depth testing through the Z-buffer and the OpenGL alpha-test ensured that not-visible voxels and voxels with an intensity (in the α channel) below the specified value of the alpha-test were removed from the pipeline, thus selecting the voxels that represent the currently visible isosurface. In the second pass, the gradient vectors in the RGBα channels were processed again—by re-applying the texture volume—and were transformed (dot product) by the color matrix, which encodes the light direction (allowing only one light directional light source), resulting in a shaded (gray-level) isosurface. Shortly afterwards, this approach was modified by MEISSNER et al. [1999] to compute shading of the whole texture volume, thus allowing classification of the volume dataset. This was achieved through several advanced (at the time) image and pixel extensions, which are now available through pixel shaders. Later, shaded isosurfaces and shading of semitransparent samples was adapted into a single-pass implementation on PC graphics accelerators by REZK-SALAMA et al. [2000a]. So far, ambient and diffuse lighting components were addressed and accompanied by the specular component in [ENGEL et al. 2001] (see Fig. 9.22). By now, advanced illumination models can be implemented through the use of vertex and pixel shaders, such as reflection and environment maps [REZK-SALAMA 2002].

9.4.1 QUALITY

To increase sampling for 3D textures, more slices are resampled from the volume dataset, as we discussed above and (recall Figure 9.19 (right)). Similarly, higher image-plane sampling is achieved when the textures of the volume dataset are mapped to a larger image-plane. This way, the 3D texture-mapping hardware provides filtered (interpolated) samples that represent the respective higher sampling rate.

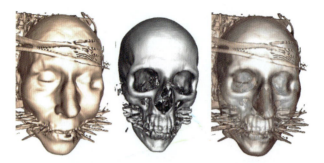

FIGURE 9.22 *Illuminated CT dataset of a head rendered with texture-mapping using programmable shaders. Left: skin isosurface; middle: skull isosurface; right: semitransparent skin and skull [ENGEL et al. 2001]. (Images courtesy KLAUS ENGEL, Siemens Medical Solutions)*

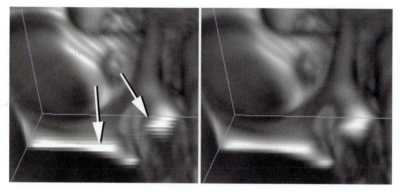

FIGURE 9.23 *Artifacts due to bilinear slice interpolation. Left: bilinear interpolation and insufficient depth sampling generate staircase artifacts. Right: these artifacts can be avoided with intermediate slices, realizing trilinear interpolation and sufficient depth sampling [REZK-SALAMA et al. 2000a]. (Images courtesy CHRISTOF REZK-SALAMA, University of Siegen)*

Note, however, that this works sufficiently well for parallel projections, which employs a cuboid proxy geometry to map the textures to the screen. Perspective projections may need extra care to adapt for the perspective distortion. This is typically done through a different proxy geometry, e.g., spherical shells as suggested by LaMAR et al. [1999].

One of the major drawbacks of 2D texture-based volume rendering is the fixed slice organization, once one of the three base orientations has been chosen. This leads to similar artifacts as the Shear warp approach, since the contributing samples are always located within the textures. Hence, that approach experiences insufficient sampling between the slices along the depth orientation and provides only bilinear interpolation (see Fig. 9.23 (left)). Another source of artifacts is the situation when the chosen base slice orientation changes during rotations. Here, the sampling points of the new volume slices are typically not identical to the previous sampling points, thus generating visual artifacts, similar to popping artifacts. Furthermore, and also similar to Shear warp, 2D texture-mapping introduces a varying sampling distance, when the volume is not viewed from an angle perpendicular to the textures. Beside the potential violation of the sampling theorem, this also introduces inaccuracies in the accumulated opacities in the framebuffer. REZK-SALAMA et al. [2000a] suggested a remedy for this situation, using multitexturing extensions of OpenGL to compute intermediate textures. These textures are linear combinations of two (neighboring) stored textures, thus allowing sufficient depth sampling with one or more intermediate textures. Furthermore, the linear combination of bilinearly interpolated textures yields trilinearly interpolated samples, thus improving the quality even further (see Fig. 9.23 (right)). The opacity is corrected by taking into account the original and the current sampling rates [ENGEL et al. 2004]. Note that intermediate texture coordinates are typically mapped to the same proxy polygon. With perspective projections, this requires a correction of the texture coordinates to avoid intermediate slice artifacts [REZK-SALAMA et al. 2000a].

One of the major quality drawbacks of early texture-based volume rendering approaches was the limited accuracy of the framebuffer. Since sample compositing is realized through OpenGL blending, small contributions are accumulated in the alpha (and color) buffer of the framebuffer. Until a few years ago, this alpha-buffer provided only 8–12 bit accuracy that is insufficient for small contributions and leads to quantization artifacts, which can be seen in Figure 9.24. This situation deteriorates if we use opacity-weighted interpolation (see Sect. 8.2) for preclassified volume rendering, since the individual contributions become even smaller. Fortunately, the major manufacturers of graphics accelerators introduced floating-point accuracy pipelines in 2002, which enabled sufficient composition accuracy.

Another cause of aliasing in direct volume rendering is transfer functions, as discussed in Section 6.2.2. Specifically in the context of texture-based volume rendering, ENGEL et al. [2001] introduced pre-integrated volume rendering, where precomputed slabs—which already incorporate the higher frequency through the classification—are composed. More details on pre-integrated sample composition are discussed in Section 8.3.3.

Finally, bricking causes an artifact that requires special attention. Since textures cannot be interpolated and treated across individual bricks, incorrect texture samples are computed on the boundary between the bricks, due to the lack of information. This situation is illustrated in Figure 9.25 (left), where the bricked texture now has a visible seam (see Fig. 9.25 (left/middle)). The typical solution for this situation is to provide a voxel boundary that overlaps with the neighboring bricks (see Fig. 9.25 (left/bottom)). At render time, these overlaps are blended with each other, resulting in a seamless brick transition

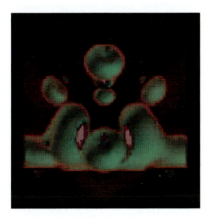 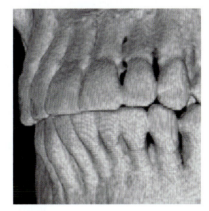

FIGURE 9.24 *Accuracy artifacts at compositing are caused by a limited precision of the alpha-channel. Left: electron density distribution of a protein molecule. The low density areas (red) are insufficiently represented due to limited precision (compare with Fig. 9.2 (left)). Color-bleeding (opacity-weighted interpolation of the preclassification rendering algorithm is not used due to the limited available compositing precision) is also visible. Right: enlargement of the jaw of a skull scanned by 3D X-ray. The lack of compositing precision is causing the dark quantization artifacts [MEIßNER et al. 2000]. (Images courtesy MICHAEL MEIßNER, University of Tübingen)*

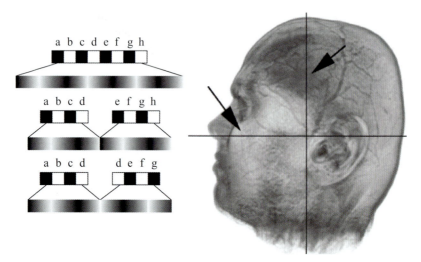

FIGURE 9.25 *Bricking artifacts are caused by incorrect interpolation on the brick boundaries due to the lack of neighborhood information. Left: Top—a texture of eight texels is split into two bricks (middle). However, due to the lack of a common boundary, a seam will be created at rendering (see right image in this figure). To eliminate that seam, the texture bricks must overlap by one texel (for a central difference gradient interpolation). Note that the full texture is no longer represented in this four-texel brick (bottom) [GRZESZCZUK et al. 1998]. Right: four seams are visible at the boundaries of four texture bricks (arrows). (Images courtesy PETER HASTREITER, University of Erlangen-Nürnberg)*

[GRZESZCZUK et al. 1998]. The size of the overlapping boundary depends on the used interpolation method. If only one neighborhood layer is needed, one voxel layer is a sufficient overlap.

The current trend of texture-mapping-based volume rendering is directed towards hybrid rendering algorithms that employ object-space techniques of texture-mapping and high-quality ray casting [WESTERMANN and SEVENICH 2001, RÖTTGER et al. 2003].

9.4.2 DATASET MANAGEMENT

One of the major issues of texture-mapping-based volume rendering is the availability of the respective voxels in the texture or graphics memory. Since the size of volume datasets is typically growing faster than the size of texture (or graphics) memory, specific memory management techniques have to be applied to allow a mostly seamless exchange of data between the main memory and the texture memory. While early approaches tried to fit the full volume into the texture memory, it became quickly clear that this would too often require a downsampling of the dataset [CULLIP and NEUMANN 1993]. Hence, the volume was partitioned into smaller texture volumes, which are subsequently downloaded into texture-memory and rendered into the framebuffer [VAN GELDER and KIM 1996]. More details on this bricking technique were presented by GRZESZCZUK et al. [1998]. In contrast, TONG et al. [1999] proposed a volume hierarchy in main memory that is preclassified in a volume buffer. After removing the nonrelevant (transparent) parts, the remaining volume leaf blocks are merged into larger chunks in the texture buffer. The choice of the block size depends on the boundary conditions of the texture-mapping hardware, which at the time required a certain size of a power of two for all texture dimensions, and on the transparent block culling efficiency. Clearly, small blocks increase the culling performance while at the same time reduce the texture-mapping effectiveness. This, however, was in part compensated by merging several relevant leaf block into larger chunks in the texture buffer.

Instead of selecting blocks at the same resolution level, LAMAR et al. [1999] suggested a multiresolution approach that enables full resolution in parts close to the viewer, and coarser resolutions in volume parts farther away. This approach is quite similar to the mipmap approach for ray casting [LEVOY and WHITAKER 1990], but requires more care for a texture-based approach to avoid aliasing artifacts. LAMAR et al. organize the data volume into different resolution levels based on an octree. Each resolution level is then organized in tiles to allow a flexible texture block selection. At render time, the texture slices are computed based on the respective hierarchy level and the proxy geometry. Figure 9.26 shows a rectangular proxy geometry which is aligned to the view-plane. One difference between the mipmap approach of LEVOY and WHITAKER [1990] and the hierarchy level generation of LAMAR et al. [1999] relates to the computation of the lower resolution levels. While the former used a low pass filter, LAMAR et al. claimed that undersampling (selecting every other voxel) produced better results, a claim that is at odds with the sampling theorem.

A different approach to managing large volume datasets is data (de-)compression interweaved with rendering, which was proposed by GUTHE and STRASSER [2001]. Here, the volume is encoded by wavelets, where the wavelets' coefficients are quantized and arranged in an octree hierarchy. This scheme was later extended to a full hierarchic volume compression and decompression scheme for large volume datasets [GUTHE et al. 2002]. In particular, it enabled fast on-the-fly decompression and interactive level-of-detail rendering of large volume datasets by employing a cache filled with decompressed volume blocks.

9.5   OTHER DIRECT VOLUME RENDERING APPROACHES

So far, we have discussed four direct volume rendering approaches, which are the most popular or the ones that are used most of the time. However, they are by no means the only ones. There are other approaches that are well suited for specific circumstances. In this section, we briefly describe some of them.

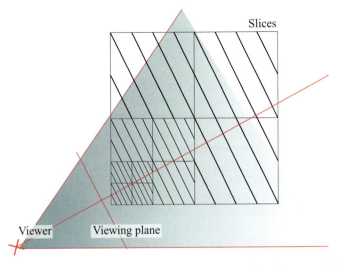

FIGURE 9.26 *Multiresolution slicing. All texture slices are parallel to the view-plane* [GUTHE et al. 2002]. *(Image courtesy* STEFAN GUTHE, *University of Tübingen)*

Cell Projection

This class of algorithms is based on methods that project object-space primitives, e.g., voxels, to the screen in a specific depth order. Early methods projected a cube for every voxel of interest to the screen, for example in a back-to-front manner [FRIEDER et al. 1985], while later these voxels were splatted to the screen (see Sect. 9.3). Here, we briefly discuss a related method that projects volume cells to the image-plane.

SHIRLEY and TUCHMAN [1990] suggested *cell projection*, which projects whole volume cells to the screen. Since the volume cells have typically a simple screen projection (footprint), this projection can be represented by few polygons. Each polygon then represents the color and opacity contribution of the respective part of the projected cell and is rasterized by computer graphics hardware into the framebuffer. SHIRLEY and TUCHMAN provided a solution for various grid types by tessellating the cells into tetrahedrons. These tetrahedrons are then transformed into view-space, and their projection footprint is tessellated into up to four triangles.

Computer graphics hardware typically rasterizes triangles using Gouraud shading, in which the color and opacity are computed at the vertices and interpolated on the face. This image-space interpolation does not usually reflect the physical properties of the respective data volumes, but is only a simple approximation. While this is hardly noticeable if the volume cells, and hence the triangles, are very small, it quickly becomes obvious with high zoom factors, where the individual cells are projected to larger screen areas. Consequently, WILHELMS and VAN GELDERN [1991] suggested improved compositing and interpolation methods, which are limited to cartesian (rectilinear) grids.

9.5.1 SHELL RENDERING

Shell rendering, by UDUPA and ODHNER [1993], aims at the extraction of fuzzy boundaries. These fuzzy boundaries are essentially voxels, each representing a cuboid. These cuboids are within an intensity value interval of an isosurface, with at least one neighboring voxel in the 6-neighborhood (see Sect. 2.1) not larger than the upper bound. The major difference from an isosurface is the fuzzier definition of the boundary, which is here called a shell. All selected voxels (cuboids) of the shell are stored in a linked list data structure that allows fast addressing and view-dependant sorting of the voxels to facilitate back-to-front or front-to-back traversal. This way, early ray termination (similar to ray casting) is possible. Every voxel is thereafter projected on the image-plane, an approach similar to splatting. Recently, the voxel rendering has been improved by BOTHA and POST [2003] through a better splatting method.

Note that the major benefit of shell rendering comes through the selection of the voxels on a fuzzy boundary, the shell voxels, which are of a significantly smaller number than the total number of voxels in the volume dataset. This allows rapid rendering after the boundary is selected in a much slower process. This selection process is similar to the isosurface extraction methods of the Marching Cubes algorithm (see Sect. 7.2.3), except that a fuzzy boundary is selected, and not an accurate one.

Fourier Domain Volume Rendering

In Section 3.2, we briefly discussed how a volume dataset can be reconstructed from a series of projection images generated by X-ray scans of an object taken from different angels. *Fourier domain volume rendering* exploits similar techniques to go the reverse way: from volume dataset to a projection image from a specific angle. This relationship is defined by the *central or Fourier projection slice theorem*, which states that the Fourier transform (2D) of such a (parallel) projection is equal to the slice at the perpendicular angle of the Fourier transform (3D) of the dataset. In practice, this means that once the volume has been Fourier transformed in a preprocess, we can use the inverse fast Fourier transform of the slice perpendicular to the viewing angle to compute the view projection. The advantage of this projection (volume rendering) process is that the complexity can be reduced from $O(N^3)$ to $O(N^2 * log(N))$, where N is the resolution of the volume dataset in every dimension [MALZBENDER 1993]. Unfortunately, this method does not account for any depth representation, such as occlusion or attenuation. This has been partially addressed by TOTSUKA and LEVOY [1993], who include some attenuation and a modified shading model. Nevertheless, Fourier domain volume rendering is limited to X-ray-like images.

Dedicated Hardware

The computational complexity of direct volume rendering led early to the idea of using special purpose hardware. While many ideas were proposed in the past, only a few of them have been implemented in real hardware, and only one can be purchased and used in a standard PC. The following paragraphs will briefly describe some of the realized special purpose hardware solutions for direct volume rendering.

One of the first real implementations of direct volume rendering hardware is the VIRIM system of the University of Mannheim [GÜNTHER et al. 1994]. This system used an array of signal processors (DSPs) and dedicated logic combined with memory (DRAM) to implement volume rotations and a ray tracing algorithm.

Shortly after the VIRIM system, the first version of the VIZARD system of the University of Tübingen had been presented. Here, a PCI-interfaced FPGA-board implemented a simplified ray casting scheme. A special voxel compression scheme was used, which enabled fast voxel access [KNITTEL and STRASSER 1997]. Later in 1998, the VIZARD II board, using a FPGA-chip and a signal processor, was proposed [MEISSNER et al. 1998] and later demonstrated [MEISSNER et al. 2002]. VIZARD II provided a fully functional ray casting pipeline implemented on the FPGA-board combined with special memory management that enabled fast and full accuracy voxel access.

The only commercially available system is the VolumePro-board by TeraRecon, originally built at Mitsubishi Electric Research Labs (MERL), based on the Cube4 architecture of Stony Brook University [PFISTER et al. 1999]. This board implements an improved version of the shear warp algorithm. In particular it enables a high resolution base-plane that provides a much higher visual quality than the original shear warp algorithm (see Sect. 9.2). While the VolumePro-board provides superior rendering speed even for large datasets, it unfortunately does not support high-quality perspective projection in the current VP1000 version, in contrast to other hardware systems.

The latest implemented hardware system is the SaarCOR system from the University of Saarbrücken. It implements a fully functional version of the ray tracing algorithm on a FPGA-chip [SCHMITTLER et al. 2002] and provides flexible shading programming [WOOP et al. 2005]. Note that ray casting is a specialized version of ray tracing in which sampling is used instead of intersection computations (see Sect. 9.1).

9.6   DIRECT VOLUME RENDERING OF SEGMENTED VOLUME DATA

In Section 7.2.3, we discussed ways that segmented datasets could be rendered using indirect volume rendering. Here, we focus on the same issue for direct volume rendering.

An early approach for the rendering of multiple segmented objects is based on preclassified datasets. The voxels of different objects can be assigned specific classification parameters that are encoded directly into the color volume used by the preclassified volume rendering pipeline (see Sect. 8.2). Note that this approach is not the same as classifying a volume dataset, since every voxel in the color volume is classified individually and segmentation information can be taken into account. However, preclassified volume rendering is afflicted by a reduced visual quality. This situation is aggravated with segmented color volumes, since the color values are chosen based on the segmentation information, which may exhibit significantly larger color differences than a voxel value-based classification. Furthermore, the assignment of one voxel to exactly one object is not always correct in areas inflicted by partial volume effects, which blurs the boundaries between neighboring anatomical objects.

TIEDE et al. [1998] suggested a solution to many of these issues in a ray casting environment that provides several additional features for segmented datasets. In particular in cases where the segmentation is generated with methods that are not threshold-based, e.g., manual segmentations, their scheme provides techniques to approximate the object's surface.

Manual segmentation has the advantage of exploiting user knowledge for the labeling of objects in a volume dataset. This, however, comes with several side effects that may reduce the visual quality of standard volume rendering. One of these side effects is staircase artifacts on the object's surface due to the non-threshold nature of the boundary specification. In such a case, the object's surface must be reconstructed based on the label volume that stores the segmentation information. Unfortunately, this is not a straightforward process since a labeled object does not contain smooth boundaries; a voxel is either part of one object (possibly of many), or part of the background. For this case, TIEDE et al. suggest reconstructing a smoothly sampled surface based on trilinear interpolation of the sample in the label volume, considering only one object label at a time. This means that all voxels of the volume cell that contains the sample are set to 1 if these voxel belongs to the respective object, and to 0 otherwise. Since trilinear interpolation of a specific isosurface (0.5 is this case) yields a cubic interpolation (see Fig. 2.4), the overall surface is smooth.

Another issue that has been addressed by TIEDE et al. [1998] is the computation of an accurate surface from the original volume dataset (see Fig. 9.27). In contrast to earlier discussed approaches that actually compute the intersection of a cast ray with the object's surface (see Sect. 9.1.1), they approximate the surface with a bisection approach. This approach successively bisects the ray segment between the last non-object sample and the first object sample until the difference between trilinearly interpolated intensity value at the bisection point and the threshold is below a specified bound ϵ. Note that in case of multiple objects, several surfaces may occur. TIEDE et al. only render the surface that has a normal vector towards the sample point, thus showing the frontface. If the surfaces cannot be distinguished (because they overlap), the above described method for manual segmentations is used. Furthermore, this interpolation in the label volume has potentially similar problems to interpolation in color volumes. Nevertheless, this scheme is only used to reconstruct the surface, not to compute the color values, which are set in a binary fashion according to whether the sample is considered part of the object or not. One convenient feature of the more accurate surface computation is that the calculated surface samples vary significantly less if the view direction is changing. Hence, it reduces animation artifacts, which are caused by slightly changing sampled surface points of the traditional ray casting approach.

For thin objects, TIEDE et al. use oversampling in ray direction with a sample distance similar to the size of the pixels of the image-plane. This distance value has been picked heuristically by experience of the authors, but is also reflected by the sampling theorem.

An alternative method of rendering segmented volume datasets is *two-level volume rendering*, proposed by HAUSER et al. [2001]. Two-level volume rendering decomposes the combined rendering in a *global* and *local* rendering step. Local rendering is responsible for rendering individual objects, while global rendering composes the contributions from the local rendering into the final image. An efficient GPU-based implementation was later introduced by HADWIGER et al. [2003a]. More details on two-level volume rendering will be discussed in the next section.

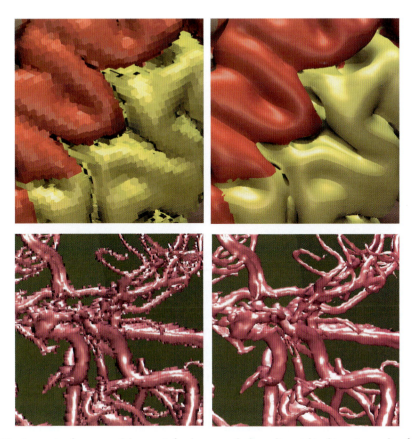

FIGURE 9.27   *Ray casting for segmented datasets. Left column: standard sampling; right column: improved surface computation and label interpolation. Top row: rendered brain surface—the rendered boundaries on the right have been significantly improved. Bottom row: reconstructed blood vessel from an MRI angiography. The representation of small blood vessels on the right has been significantly improved [TIEDE et al. 1998]. (Images courtesy ULFTIEDE, University of Hamburg)*

9.7   HYBRID VOLUME RENDERING

In many application scenarios discussed in this book, it is essential to combine geometrically defined objects such as protheses with medical volume data. Surgery simulation, in which geometric models of surgical devices are employed to manipulate volume data, is another example. The integrated visualization of surface and volume data is challenging, since occlusions within the surface and the volume representation (as well as between both representations) must be considered. After classification, volume data contains opaque, semitransparent, and fully transparent voxels. Surface representations may also include semi-transparent portions. The correct representation of depth relations in semi-transparent surface and volume representations is the most demanding aspect of hybrid volume rendering.

Another motivation for hybrid volume rendering is to adapt the rendering process to specific diagnostic questions as well as to the peculiarities of medical image data. While in some scenarios the interior of anatomic structures is not relevant, it is essential for other structures or regions in the data. The use of surface visualization in cases where sharp boundaries exist and only these boundaries matter is appropriate. Since sharp boundaries in the data often cannot be visualized by means of transfer-function based volume rendering, segmentation and surface visualization restricted to the segmented portion of the data is a useful option.

Basically, there are two different approaches to integrating geometric surface models and volume data into one visualization.

- One representation is converted in the other and fused with it.
- Both representations are rendered separately and the rendered results are finally combined.

With respect to the first choice, either volume data are transformed to a polygonal representation, for example with a Marching Cubes variant, or the surface representation is converted to a voxel representation (this process—*voxelization*—was discussed in Section 7.3.4). The transformation of volume data to polygonal data may be very inefficient, since many isosurfaces are necessary to roughly achieve the effect of a semitransparent volume rendering. The opposite transformation, the voxelization, can be performed efficiently. This volumetric representation is merged directly with the sampled voxel data, resulting in a new grid that is refined in regions where voxels originating from the surface representation have been inserted. Since the integrated representation of voxelized surfaces and voxel data in general leads to an irregular grid, some volume rendering methods are not directly applicable. The basic image- and object-space techniques, however, might be easily modified in such a way that they can process these multigrids. It should be noted that voxelization means to sample a continuous representation and thus may lead to aliasing problems, in particular at sharp edges or in regions with high curvature.

Consequently, the better choice in general is to preserve the original representations, render them separately, and combine the results in a final 2D pixel image. There are different strategies about which stage of the pipeline the results should be combined. GOODSELL et al. [1989] and KAUFMAN et al. [1990] describe hybrid rendering algorithms where both rendering modes generate a shaded image and a Z-buffer that are combined afterwards according to the depth values. The limitation of these algorithms is that they are not able to represent multiple layers of semitransparent surfaces within the volume data.

The first detailed description of a rendering algorithm without this limitation was provided by LEVOY [1990a], partly based on earlier work [JOHNSON and MOSHER 1989]. LEVOY's *ray merging* method, which has been used widely, extends a volume ray casting algorithm. In the following, we shall briefly describe his hybrid ray tracer. Parallel rays are traced from the observer to both polygonal and volumetric data. Polygonal and volume data are treated separately (see Fig. 9.28). Colors and opacities for points at surfaces and in the volume are determined and collected in two vectors of samples. The final image value is determined in a compositing step that considers these two vectors.

The current transfer function and the lighting specification are applied to generate a classified and shaded volume, which contains opacities $\alpha_v(i)$ and colors $c_v(i)$ for each voxel (i is the index to the volume data). The rays are sampled at evenly spaced locations, resulting in a vector of colors and opacity values. The samples are indexed by a vector $U = (u, v, w)$ where u, v represent the image-plane index and w the position along the ray. The sample opacities $\alpha_v(U)$ and colors $c_v(U)$ are used in the compositing step.

Polygonal data are also ray traced, resulting in point intersections with the polygonal surface. At these intersections, shading with the Phong illumination model is performed, resulting in opacities and point colors at the intersection points. This intermediate result is used in a compositing step. The number of contributions affecting a ray equals the sum of all volume samples plus the number of polygons intersected by the ray.

Computing Visibility at Polygon-Volume Intersections

Compositing at evenly spaced sample locations along a viewing ray approximates the visibility of a volume composed of equally sized rectangular slabs [LEVOY 1990a]. When a polygon is embedded in the volume

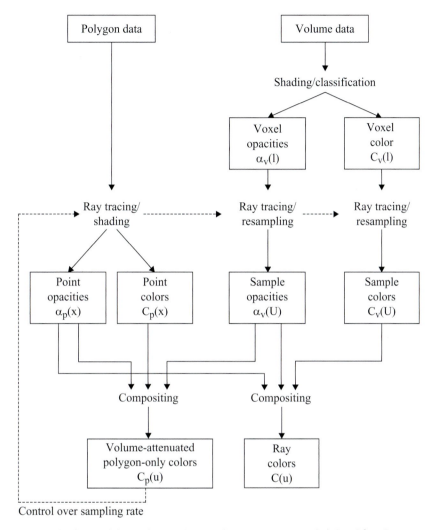

FIGURE 9.28   *Hybrid indirect and direct volume rendering with a ray casting approach (Adapted from [LEVOY 1990a].)*

data, some of these slabs are intersected. As a consequence, some portions of these slabs are obscured by the polygon and some portions obscure the polygon. Two different types of polygon-volume intersections have to be discriminated for proper supersampling:

- *The polygon intersects only the side faces of the slab.* In this case, the exact solution can be produced without supersampling. The contributions made to the trapezoidal volumes lying in front of and behind the polygon are equal to those made by rectangular volumes separated by a plane perpendicular to the ray and placed at the intersection of the ray with the oblique plane forming the trapezoidal volume (see Fig. 9.29 (top row)).
- *The polygon intersects the frontface of the slab, the rear face, or both.* In this case, the polygon intersects more than one slab along a ray. To achieve an exact solution, more rays have to be traced as discussed in the

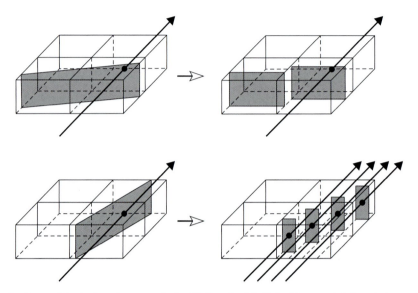

FIGURE 9.29 *Top row, left: A polygon intersects only the side faces of a slab. Right: The exact visibility solution can be be computed without supersampling. Bottom row, left: A polygon intersects front and rear faces of a slab. Right: The exact solution of the visibility requires supersampling* [LEVOY 1990a]. (Images courtesy MARC LEVOY, Standford University)

previous paragraph. For each ray, the trapezoidal hidden volume corresponds again to a rectangular volume as discussed for the first case (see Fig. 9.29 (bottom row)).

Adaptive Supersampling

Ray tracing is a sampling process that is subject to aliasing problems. LEVOY [1990a] suggested applying an adaptive supersampling in regions where the range of colors in a pixel-sized region in the image-plane exceeds a threshold.[12]

Supersampling is primarily required in case of sharp polygon edges and polygon-polygon intersections. If a large color difference occurs in a region where only volume data are sampled, no supersampling is necessary, provided that the data are properly filtered (e.g., trilinear interpolation). To accomplish the desired behavior, two sets of colors are computed for each region (see the two boxes in the lower part of Fig. 9.28). The ray color is computed by solving Equation 9.2, which evaluates N depth-sorted contributions of either a volume sample or a ray-polygon intersection point.

$$C = \sum_{n=1}^{N}[C(n)\alpha(n)\prod_{n'=1}^{n}(1 - \alpha(n'))]$$
(9.2)

If the color $C(n)$ is set to 0 for all volume samples, a color C_p is computed that evaluates only the contributions of polygonal data but is attenuated by passing the volume data (*volume-attenuated polygon-only colors*). If the range of the C colors exceeds the threshold and the range of the C_p colors does not, the difference is due to the volume data, and no supersampling is required. Only if the range of the C_p colors exceeds a threshold is the sampling rate in this region increased.

---

12   The maximum distance between pairs of red-, green-, and blue-triples is computed to assess the homogeneity.

The major ingredients for hybrid volume rendering were described above. Since hybrid volume renderings are computationally demanding, various optimizations, such as early ray termination and hierarchical data structures to identify non-empty voxels quickly, are essential [LEVOY 1990a].

Figure 9.30 presents some examples of hybrid volume renderings. While the left image just illustrates the expressiveness that can be achieved by combining direct volume rendering with isosurface rendering, the right image is a typical example used for neck dissection planning [KRÜGER et al. 2005]. In Chapter 17, we will elaborate the discussion of hybrid rendering styles and discuss how volume-, surface-, and line-based renderings can be combined.

Hybrid Renditions with Two-Level Volume Rendering

A more recent and appreciated method of hybrid rendering is two-level volume rendering. It is based on a tagged volume, in which segmentation results are represented on a per voxel basis, and enables the rendering method to change for each object. Two-level volume rendering aims at a flexible assignment of rendering styles to individual objects of a volume dataset. If additional instruments (e.g., surgical instruments) must be integrated, these need to be voxelized first. Moreover, some priority assignments are required to specify which object is actually visible in regions where the surgical instrument is located in the data. In principle, two-level rendering is also applicable for these situations.

The first version was employed to combine MIP rendering and DVR in one image [HAUSER et al. 2000]. More recent versions allow the combination of DVR, MIP, surface rendering, and even more different rendering styles [HAUSER et al. 2001, HADWIGER et al. 2003a]. The basic idea of two-level volume rendering is to consider the rendering process as composed of a *global* and a *local* rendering step (see Fig. 9.31). Conceptually, both the local and the global step can be thought of as ray casting, which is in particular true for the global rendering method. Whenever the rays meet an object boundary, a different local rendering style might be applied. If the ray leaves the object again, the rendering mode is switched back to the global method. The contributions of different rendering styles along a ray are combined according to the global rendering style. Figure 9.32 shows rendition of two-level volume rendering, integrating DVR, MIP, and surface rendering. As another example in Figure 9.33 the benefit of two-level volume rendering compared to conventional volume rendering is shown.

One advantage of two-level volume rendering is the flexible treatment of assigning transparency values. One object might have an opacity valid for all of its voxels, a situation typical for indirect volume

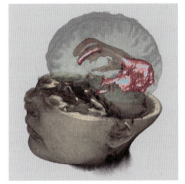
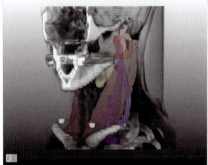

FIGURE 9.30 *Hybrid combinations of indirect (IVR) and direct volume rendering (DVR). Left: the ventricles and the brain are rendered as surfaces from segmented data, whereas the skull is created with DVR (Image courtesy HORST HAHN, MEVIS). Right: for neck dissection planning, hybrid renditions of segmented anatomical structures combined with DVR are clinically used. Bone structures are included through DVR as anatomical context. (Image courtesy JEANNETTE CORDES, University of Magdeburg)*

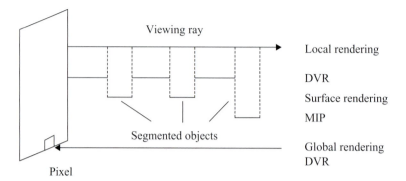

FIGURE 9.31 *Object segmentation partitions viewing rays into segments. Local rendering styles may be applied on a per object basis. By choosing DVR, MIP, and surface rendering, hybrid combinations of the most common rendering styles are achieved. (Image courtesy* PETRA SPECHT, *University of Magdeburg)*

FIGURE 9.32 *Combining DVR, surface rendering, and MIP. Bones are rendered with DVR using a sharp transfer function, vessels are rendered as surfaces, and the skin is rendered as MIP [*HAUSER *et al. 2001]. (Image courtesy* HELWIG HAUSER, *VRVis Wien)*

rendering. Other objects may use transfer functions to map opacity values to individual voxels. Both specification methods can be combined in the sense that the object-specific transparency is modulated on a per-voxel basis by a transfer function using appropriate weighting factors.

The actual implementation by HAUSER et al. [2001] is not ray casting, due to performance considerations. Instead, they employed a fast object-order implementation based on the shear warp transformation using several acceleration techniques such as empty space skipping.

9.8   VALIDATION OF VOLUME VISUALIZATION ALGORITHMS

Validation is crucial for all aspects of the analysis and visualization of medical image data. We already discussed validation of image analysis techniques in Section 5.8. Although validation is urgently needed for visualization[13] it is rarely considered.

---

13   POMMERT and HÖHNE [2003] state: "For clinical applications, it is of course important to ensure that the 3D images really show the true anatomic situation or at least to know about their limitations."

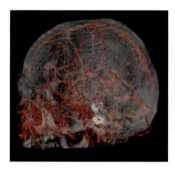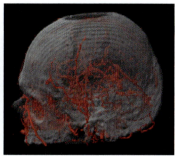

FIGURE 9.33 *With conventional volume rendering, parts of the cerebral blood vessels are barely recognizable in the brain. Two-level volume rendering using MIP for the bony structures and the skin enables recognition of the vascular structures much better [HAUSER et al. 2001]. (Image courtesy HELWING HAUSER, VRVis Wien)*

Visualization algorithms usually incorporate a variety of parameters that influence the accuracy of the results. Images rendered by ray casting, for example, depend on the spacing between rays and along ray samples, as well as on parameters such as the accumulated opacity threshold for early ray termination and on the filter kernel applied at each sampling point. The sequence of classification and interpolation also has an influence on the image quality (see Sect. 8.2). Moreover, rendered images depend on acquisition parameters of the volume data, such as slice thickness, reconstruction filter, and noise level.

After a variety of isolated investigations, primarily with respect to normal estimation (recall Sect. 6.3.2) and interpolation filters, the first encompassing effort to characterize the accuracy of volume visualization algorithms was accomplished by POMMERT [POMMERT and HÖHNE, 2003, POMMERT, 2004]. The discussion in this section is inspired and based primarily on this work.

A general issue of validation is the determination of a ground truth that serves as a *standard* or *reference*. The validation task can be characterized as a systematic comparison between the results achieved by the investigated algorithm and the reference.

9.8.1 VALIDATION CRITERIA

A straightforward definition of image quality is based on the question? "How well does an image communicate information?" in other words, what is the *intelligibility* of the image [PRATT, 1991]. For example, an image used in diagnostic imaging is good if it enables a radiologist to establish the right diagnosis (*diagnostic image quality*). Diagnostic imaging quality relates to the influence of a visualization technique on sensitivity and specificity (recall Sect. 2.3). An important criterion for the acceptance of new visualization techniques relates to the trust of a physician in his or her diagnosis based on different visualization techniques [VANNIER 2000]. There are a number of studies that compare 2D and 3D visualization techniques with respect to their image quality [ALDER et al. 1995, KAUCZOR et al. 1996]. These studies give hints on the appropriateness of certain visualization options for answering diagnostic yes/no-questions, such as "Is there a relevant stenosis?" However, these studies do not allow characterization of the influence of visualization options on more complex therapy planning decisions. Moreover, the accuracy of visualizations is not quantitatively characterized. Therefore, a technical definition of image quality is still required. This definition relates to the question "How much does an image deviate from an ideal image of the scene?" This is called the *fidelity* of the image. The evaluation of both aspects requires the comparison of quality to a ground truth.

In Section 5.8, several measures were introduced to assess the accuracy of segmentation methods. A group of these measures are distance-based, such as the Hausdorff and mean Euclidean distance, between a reference segmentation and the segmentation with a new method under investigation. Distance-based measures are also relevant for the validation of surface visualization algorithms. They allow quantitative characterization of the deviation between the surface of an object that is regarded as "perfect" (the reference) and the computed surface. For validating visualization algorithms, it is also essential to analyze the local distribution of distance errors—and not only to derive global distance measures. Local distributions may directly reveal which kinds of anatomical shapes are not correctly depicted.

Besides distance measurements, it is also essential to analyze whether the surface orientation is correct. The surface orientation is characterized by the surface normal, hence the orientation accuracy—or the *normal error* (the angle between two surface normals)—is an obvious choice as a metric [POMMERT 2004]. The normal error is computed according to Equation 9.3 [TIEDE et al. 1990]. The computation of the distance and normal error is illustrated in Figure 9.34.

$$error_{normal}(s) = \arccos(\vec{N}_{computed}(s) \times \vec{N}_{true}(s)) \qquad [9.3]$$

9.8.2 GEOMETRIC MODELS FOR VALIDATION

A crucial question relates to the geometric models employed for the comparison between a new visualization method and a reference. Basically, the same aspects are considered here that we have discussed for validating segmentation algorithms (recall Sect. 5.8.1). Either phantoms, a set of "real" datasets, or a combination of both are employed for a validation study. The Visible Human dataset and the CT Head dataset (provided by the University of North Carolina, Chapel Hill) are examples of real datasets that are publicly available, and therefore are frequently used to compare visualization algorithms and parameters. However, it is difficult to precisely analyze the differences in case of such a complex anatomy. Furthermore, the rapid progress in medical image acquisition devices quickly renders small datasets (as the CT Head) outdated for clinical standard dataset sizes.

Phantoms The selection of test data or phantoms should attempt to provide simple and general shapes that highlight rendering differences. The flexible parameterization is the most salient advantage of phantoms. Simple geometric shapes, such as a sphere, have the advantage that their surface can be computed accurately. The use of analytically representable shapes has another advantage; the shapes can be sampled in different resolutions and the influence of the sampling density on the visualization result can be assessed.

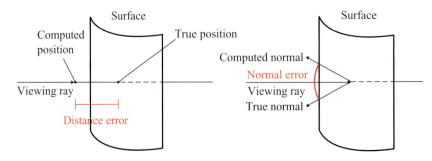

FIGURE 9.34 *Computation of the distance and the normal error. (Adapted from [POMMERT 2004])*

A validation—similar to the validation of a segmentation method—should encompass several geometric models so that different kinds of possible problems can be detected. A sphere allows easy detection of any deviations from the smooth shape; however, it does not contain any thin structures where specific undersampling problems may occur. Another special situation relates to objects that are in close neighborhood to each other (the validation in this case characterizes the ability of a visualization technique to distinguish the objects).

POMMERT [2004] described a validation based on three geometric shapes:

- A sphere
- A star-shaped object
- A spiral

The star-shaped object is also called the SIEMENS star, since it is just the 3D extension of a phantom for evaluating imaging devices and protocols by SIEMENS Medical Solutions. This phantom with its 12 cones enables the evaluation of how accurate structures with different thicknesses are visualized. The cylinder with its gaps is similar to a thin bone with fractures.

Other shapes that have been used for elucidating differences in volume rendering approaches are points, lines, cones, pyramids with slots, and tori (see [KIM et al. 2001] for a survey). In contrast to these general geometric shapes, special analytic functions are used to analyze the fidelity of visualization algorithms. One of the most widespread analytic functions is the Marschner-Lobb dataset [MARSCHNER and LOBB 1994] (see Fig. 9.35). The Marschner-Lobb dataset incorporates very high spatial frequencies, where inaccuracies show up quickly.

The selection of a geometric representation of the phantom and a rendering approach, which is regarded as the reference, is crucial. POMMERT [2004] discusses typical choices such as polygonal representation and concludes that these are too crude approximations for this purpose. Instead, he suggests directly applying ray casting to the analytic description of the phantom (see Eq. 9.4).

$$\rho(x, y, z) = \frac{1 - \sin(\frac{\pi z}{2}) + \alpha(1 + \rho_r(\sqrt{x^2 + y^2}))}{2(1 + \alpha)} \tag{9.4}$$

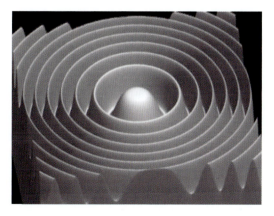

FIGURE 9.35 *The unsampled Marschner-Lobb test data* [MARSCHNER and LOBB 1994]. *(Image courtesy STEVE MARSCHNER, Cornell University)*

FIGURE 9.36 *Different renditions of the Marschner-Lobb phantom. The three leftmost images and the rightmost image are created with standard ray casting, whereas the next image (second from the right) was generated with a coherent projection approach. The rightmost image is created with ray casting using a preclassified volume rendering pipeline. All images are generated with trilinear interpolation, except the middle image, which employed a cubic interpolation filter [KIM et al. 2001]. (Images courtesy KWANSIK KIM, University of California, Santa Cruz)*

$$\rho_r(r) = \cos(2\pi f_M \cos(\frac{\pi r}{2}))$$ (9.5)

In Figure 9.35, α is set to 0.25 and f_M is set to 6; the signal is sampled on a $40 \times 40 \times 40$ lattice with $-1 < x,y,z < 1$. The function has a slow sinusoidal variation in the z-direction. Other phantoms are provided by the Montreal Neurological Institute, which provides a simulator that allows the creation of a large variety of cerebral MRI data by adjusting the relevant parameters [COLLINS et al. 1998].

9.8.3 IMAGE- AND DATA-LEVEL COMPARISONS

In contrast to the validation of segmentation approaches, validation of visualization algorithms may be accomplished at two principally different levels:

- *Image-level*, where image statistics are used to characterize differences in the final output
- *Data-level*, where intermediate rendering results are compared

Image-level comparisons are easier to accomplish. Statistics such as the root mean-square measure (see Eq. 9.6 [KIM et al. 2001]) or more perceptually based wavelet-metrics are employed to quantitatively characterize the comparison [GADDIPATTI et al. 1997]. While these comparisons are enlightening for studying the effects of different algorithms, they do not directly characterize their accuracy.

$$RSME = \sqrt{\sum_{i,j}[A(i,j) - B(i,j)]^2/N^2}$$ (9.6)

A and *B* are images of size $N \times N$. A general problem of image-level comparisons is that the analysis is performed at the level of quantized data. In general, image-based comparisons are preferred to describe differences between different parameters of *one* algorithm.

Data-level comparisons [KIM et al. 2001] allow a more precise description of differences between different volume rendering approaches. Metrics of the surface curvature are analyzed as part of data level comparisons.

9.8.4 PRESENTATION OF RESULTS

Finally, the question arises as to how the results of a validation are presented and communicated. The calculation of representative numbers, such as the Hausdorff distance, should be added by presenting appropriate visualizations that indicate the local distribution of inaccuracy. There are different methods to accomplish this task. An expressive and intuitive way is to render the reference object and color-code the distances.

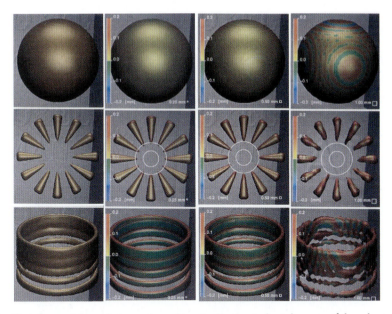

FIGURE 9.37   *The influence of the resolution on the resulting visualizations is shown by means of three phantoms. The left image is a surface rendering based on the analytic description. The following images result from rendering discretized variants, where a cubic voxel spacing of 0.25 mm, 0.5 mm, and 1 mm is employed. The color scale clearly indicates the sign of the surface distances related to the original surface [POMMERT 2004]. (Images courtesy ANDREAS POMMERT, University Hospital Eppendorf)*

Figure 9.37 shows the influence of different resolutions on the visualization result, whereas the influence of the noise level on the distance error is indicated in Figure 9.38.

In a similar way, the local distribution of the normal error can be illustrated. The images presented thus far relate to the influence of imaging parameters. POMMERT [2004] investigated many more aspects, such as direct volume renderings with different transfer functions, different normal estimation schemes, as well as different thresholds for isosurface renderings.

Discussion   The retrospective evaluation of existing visualization algorithms and specific configurations may be regarded as a diligent but unnecessary undertaking. On one hand, only a small subset of possible anatomical shapes, imaging parameters, and visualization options can be investigated. On the other hand, it seems more elegant to design algorithms and parameters that adhere to certain error bounds or can be operated with an adjustable trade-off between (guaranteed) accuracy and speed. There have been several attempts to realize strict error control, e.g., MACHIRAJU and YAGEL [1996], where interpolation filters are adaptive to the position of the sampling point and the values in its neighborhood. However, these methods are not only prohibitively slow, but they are based on a variety of assumptions with respect to the image acquisition that are not always fulfilled. Therefore, a combination of an analysis of algorithmic details and simulation studies, such as the studies conducted by POMMERT et al. are necessary. In summary, POMMERT [2004] recommends considering the following observations:

- The in-plane resolution should be carefully adapted to the finest structure that should be visualized.
- Smoothing reconstruction kernels compromise the discrimination of small objects. Neutral or edge-enhancing reconstruction filters lead to better results. (Reconstruction filters are discussed in Sect. 11.3.2 with respect to their influence on gradient-based transfer functions.)

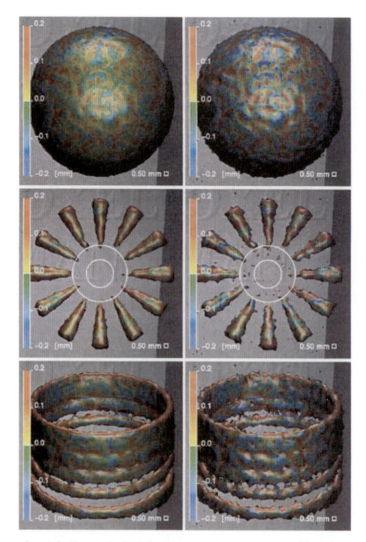

FIGURE 9.38 *The influence of different levels of additive Gaussian noise on the resulting visualizations is shown for three phantoms. The right image is based on a higher level of noise. The visualization of the star-phantom on the right includes many small and disconnected regions* [POMMERT 2004]. *(Images courtesy ANDREAS POMMERT, University Hospital Eppendorf)*

- Relevant but thin structures should be oriented perpendicular to the image-plane, since the in-plane resolution is usually the highest.
- Normal estimation schemes that consider 26 neighbors lead to significantly lower errors.
- Trilinear interpolation is, in general, sufficiently accurate. Only the visualization of very small structures benefits from cubic interpolation. Among different variants of cubic interpolation, Catmull-Rom splines lead to the best results.

While the research discussed in this section covered many aspects of CT data acquisition and the visualization of the corresponding data, considerably more aspects have to be investigated to derive recommendations for 3D visualizations of MRI data.

9.9   SUMMARY

In this chapter, we have described several popular direct volume rendering algorithms that are used in various systems for medical visualization. Specifically, we described in detail the ray casting algorithm, the shear warp algorithm as a special case of ray casting, splatting, and texture-based direct volume rendering. We have pointed out shortcomings in terms of visual quality and rendering performance, as well as optimizations to provide faster or better quality images. Furthermore, we have briefly described other approaches, such as cell projection methods, shell rendering, Fourier domain rendering, and dedicated hardware approaches.

All these algorithms have their advantages and disadvantages with respect to their applicability, their visual quality, and their rendering performance. Some of these aspects are examined in [MEIßNER et al. 2000] on the comparison of the "FabFour" of direct volume rendering that we described in the first four sections. In essence, it shows that ray casting and splatting should be selected for the best visual quality. However, recent development on using programmable standard graphics hardware (GPUs) exhibits the confluence of hardware-based methods (AKA texture-based volume rendering) and ray casting, thus providing excellent visual quality with high speed.

The other major question is when to use indirect volume rendering (see Chap. 7) and direct volume rendering (this chapter). Basically, there is no simple answer to that question. Both methods have their own advantages and disadvantages that make them preferable (or less preferable) in specific situations. BARTZ and MEISSNER [1999] provided an early comparison in terms of computational complexity and visual quality. By now, one of the major advantages of direct volume rendering lies in the seamless integration in a volume visualization pipeline (see Sect. 6.1). No isosurface has to be extracted before we can see the feature of our interest. This led to the situation that most viewing workstations in radiology provide direct volume rendering as major 3D visualization option, while indirect volume rendering (SSD, shaded surface display) plays only a minor role. This, however, is completely different for surgery planning, where more time is typically invested in carefully arranging the visualization parameters of the anatomical structures. Furthermore, the resulting polygonal meshes can be flexibly handled and rendered by any graphics board available on the planning system. The specification of the rendering parameters (color, opacity) of the structures is typically easier than with direct volume rendering. Furthermore, the integration of the patient datasets with polygonal models of additional information (e.g., surgical instruments) is easy with indirect volume rendering, but complex with direct volume rendering.

The last section of this chapter (see Sect. 9.8) focused on the important topic of the validity of visualization algorithms. The question here was, "how truthful are the various visualization algorithms? Do they represent the data properly, or does optimization for faster rendering comprise the data quality too much?"

FURTHER READING

More information on optimized ray casting can be found in [KNITTEL 2000], in which a combination of cache-sensitive memory management, multi-threading (and later cluster-based parallelization), and SIMD optimization provided near interactive framerates on a PC. Similar techniques that also exploited image and object-space coherence were proposed by WALD et al. [2001], MORA et al. [2002], GRIMM et al. [2004], and HADWIGER et al. [2005]. A detailed discussion of these techniques—in particular of cache-sensitive memory management—can be found in [BRUCKNER 2004, GRIMM 2005].

With the advances in programmable Geometry Processing Units (GPU), ray casting has been implemented on graphics hardware, which led to high quality and high speed [PURCELL et al. 2002, NEUBAUER et al. 2004, KRÜGER and WESTERMANN 2003]. In particular the work of HADWIGER et al. [2005] showed how high-quality shading, filtering, and adaptive sampling (also discussed for pre-integrated volume rendering by RÖTTGER et al. [2003]) can be employed on a GPU.

While splatting has originally been proposed for cartesian grids, several contributions describe its adaptation to other grid types. Specifically, MAO et al. [1995] describe splatting on curvilinear grids, while the EWA splatting approach of ZWICKER et al. [2001] can also be used on different grid types. An adaption of splatting for (four-dimensional) body-centered grids has been proposed by NEOPHYTOU and MUELLER [2002]. Finally, HUANG et al. [2000b] proposed a parallelized version of splatting.

An excellent reference to graphics hardware-based volume rendering and texture-based volume rendering in particular are the course notes by ENGEL et al. [2004]. Here a variety of different aspects are discussed and put into perspective. More recently, they published a book on real-time volume rendering [ENGEL et al. 2006]. VOLZ [2000] discussed a variety of techniques to overcome the limits of a small texture-memory. This includes a BSP-tree hierarchy and level-of-detail rendering for large seismic datasets. Also recently, exceedingly large volume datasets are rendered by a cluster of workstations. While software-volume-rendering on clusters has been done for quite some time, the parallel exploitation of multiple graphics subsystems is challenging. KNISS et al. [2001] showed an early example of now-outdated large SGI computer systems with multiple pipes. More recently, the compression-based approach of GUTHE et al. [2002] has been adapted to GPU clusters [STRENGERT et al. 2004].

More information on how to combine polygon-based and voxel-based graphics can be found in [WU et al. 2003], who descibe a multipass approach for the VolumePro 1000 board. In this paper, they also sketch a method on how perspective volume rendering is achived. A similar approach was presented earlier by VILANOVA et al. [2001].

The question of what direct volume rendering algorithm to use has been addressed in the above mentioned paper on the comparison of four different algorithms [MEISSNER et al. 2000]. The more general question on direct or indirect volume rendering has been discussed in the context of computational complexity and visual quality by BARTZ and MEISSNER [1999].

While all direct volume rendering algorithms address general rendering situations, some specific situations may introduce very specific issues and challenges. An example of such a situation is the rendering of 3D ultrasound data, which is difficult due to the special noise artifacts introduced by ultrasound. In many cases, specific compositing methods such as mIP and MIP in connection with ray casting have been successfully applied. For a discussion of these techniques in the context of ultrasound data, see [THUNE and OLSTAD 1991, NELSON and ELVINS 1993, SAKAS et al. 1995, FATTAL and LISCHINSKI 2001].

Chapter 10

Exploration of Dynamic Medical Volume Data

10.1   INTRODUCTION

Static image data allow the assessment of the morphology of anatomical and pathologic structures. With modern devices, high resolution image data are acquired that allow the detection of even small lesions or evaluate spatial relations around a pathology. However, static image data only provide a snapshot; many aspects relevant for diagnostic decisions and treatment planning cannot be judged by means of a single snapshot. This chapter addresses dynamic data, which might change over time. Specifically, we focus here on techniques to acquire and analyze different snapshots in time.

Dynamic image data are acquired to assess blood flow (perfusion) and tissue kinetics by tracing the distribution of contrast agents (CA) or other data changes. A special variant of dynamic data is functional MRI (recall Sect. 3.3.3) where activation patterns after stimulation are recorded. Diagnosis with dynamic data is often based on contrast enhancement. Signal intensities before, during and after the administration of a CA are recorded. Whether or not a contrast agent is delivered and subsequently absorbed within a particular region, how long it takes until the maximum amount of CA is delivered or absorbed, and other parameters are needed for medical diagnosis.

Physiological parameters, such as tumor perfusion and vessel permeability, are reflected by CT or MRI perfusion data [CHOYKE et al. 2003]. Other physiological parameters, such as oxygen metabolism, are reflected by PET data (recall Sect. 3.5). Such parameters support the diagnostic assessment of the malignancy of tumors, the damaged area of an ischemic stroke, or cardiac infarction. These diagnostic questions are examples of highly relevant indications for the acquisition of dynamic data.

Imaging modalities such as CT and MRI now provide markedly improved spatial and temporal resolution. With modern devices, the effects of blood perfusion can be measured in scales of millimeters and seconds and cover complete organs. However, spatial and temporal resolution cannot be increased at the same time. This is due to the limited time available for image acquisition, if a high temporal resolution is needed. Examples include MRI brain perfusion examinations with as many as 20 slices and 40 points in time and MRI mammography with 3D data sets of 80 slices and six points in time. MRI brain perfusion examinations have a low spatial resolution (128×128 matrix), but high temporal resolution (two seconds), whereas MRI mammography has a high spatial resolution (matrix: 512×512) at the expense of a lower temporal resolution (one minute).

Concerning visualization techniques and computer support in general, dynamic image data are extraordinarily interesting and challenging. On the one hand, a diagnosis without computer support is hardly feasible due to the amount and complex structure of the data. On the other hand, efficient computer support is difficult to achieve. Motion correction is typically an important and pressing issue. Visualization options are huge; however, few guidelines exist for meaningful parameterizations and combinations, which hampers a fast and reproducible diagnosis.

Organization   We start this chapter with a discussion of parameters that characterize the dynamic behavior and its use for diagnosis in Section 10.2. We continue with a discussion of basic techniques to visualize and explore dynamic image data (see Sect. 10.3).

The computation of parametric images relies on the correct correspondence of image information in the slices. We therefore discuss processing dynamic data in Section 10.4. Advanced visualization techniques are discussed in Section 10.5. These include combinations of two or more parameters in a single image and 3D visualizations which reflect the dynamic behavior.

At the end of this chapter, we return to medical diagnosis and discuss two case studies as examples for the role of perfusion imaging and the processing of dynamic data. The first case study discusses tumor perfusion (see Sect. 10.6), and the second study focuses on brain perfusion images acquired for stroke diagnosis (see Sect. 10.7).

10.2   MEDICAL BACKGROUND

Radiological diagnosis benefits from a large variety of dynamic data. In Chapter 3, we briefly discussed functional MRI, in which activations of brain areas are imaged, and dynamic SPECT, in which the temporal distribution of a radioactive tracer is registered. In the following, we discuss perfusion data in more detail, since these data have a broad clinical relevance. The measurement of blood perfusion is essential in a variety of medical disciplines, e.g., perfusion of the brain for stroke diagnosis. Other examples are the assessment of vitality of different types and stages of tumors and the detection and diagnosis of ischemia and cardiac infarction. Dynamic contrast enhanced (DCE) images are acquired to study these phenomena. In these examinations, a certain amount of a CA is injected very quickly,[1] and its distribution is measured by a repeated acquisition of subsequent images covering the volume of interest. The CA provides signal changes either in CT or MRI and works as a tracer of the blood. DCE imaging, however, differs strongly from conventional imaging, since much greater care must be exercised in injection rate and dose, image timing, and image analysis. Currently, such imaging techniques are performed mainly at university hospitals and other research institutions [CHOYKE et al. 2003]. Different protocols are used for DCE imaging; T1-weighted MRI images are typically used for breast cancer diagnosis (see Sect. 10.6), whereas T2-weighted MRI images are employed for the diagnosis of ischemic strokes (see Sect. 10.7).

Depending on the physiological process, either the short-term (< 1 min) blood flow or the long-term (> 1 min) diffusion process of the tracer particles through the membranes of the micro-vessels are encoded in the varying signal of the image voxels. The extracted time-intensity curves for each voxel are typically converted into relative concentration-time curves. These are called *enhancement curves*. The conversion is based on the assumption of a linear correspondence between CA concentration and signal intensity. While gradient-echo MRI sequences exhibit a close-to-linear correspondence [CHOYKE et al. 2003], this assumption is not perfectly fulfilled.

The examples discussed here cover short-term distribution as well as long-term diffusion. Figure 10.1 and Figure 10.2 show typical enhancement curves for the assessment of tumor and brain perfusion. T1-weighted images lead to brighter signals for contrast enhancement, the signal increases above the original intensity (see Fig. 10.1). On the other hand, T2-weighted images lead to a decrease of signal intensity where the CA accumulates (see Fig. 10.2).

Tumor Perfusion   The process of CA enhancement in a tumor can be described by the diffusion of tracer particles from inside blood cells into the extracellular space and vice versa before it is excreted in the

---

1   The fast injection is referred to as contrast bolus.

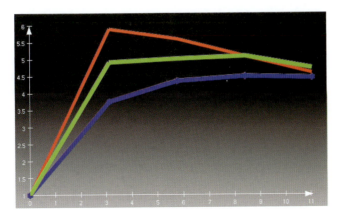

FIGURE 10.1 Enhancement curves of different regions in an MRI mammography. The enhancement relative to the signal intensity at the first points in time is shown. The points in time are connected by straight lines. The red curve is especially suspicious because of its strong wash-out, which is typical for malignant tumors. (Image courtesy SVEN KOHLE, MeVis Bremen)

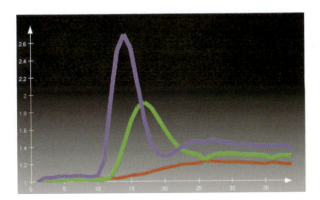

FIGURE 10.2 Enhancement curves of gray matter in the brain. In contrast with the data presented in Figure 10.1, some 40 measurements have been taken in a shorter period of time. The blue curve shows normal brain perfusion, whereas the green and red curves show decreased and delayed perfusion around an infarction. (Image courtesy SVEN KOHLE, MeVis Bremen)

kidneys [FURMAN-HARAN et al. 1997]. The permeability of the vessel walls and the extracellular volume fraction determine the amplitude and the shape of the CA enhancement curve. Enhancement curves—which show a large early enhancement followed by a rapid wash-out, i.e., a significant decrease of signal intensity at later points in time—are especially suspicious (see Fig. 10.1, red curve), because they indicate strong perfusion and high permeability of vessels. Malignant tumors need to form new vessels to grow further (neoangiogenesis), which explains the strong enhancement. The high permeability (wash-out) indicates leaky vessels in which neoangiogenesis can proceed further [KNOPP et al. 1999].

Less suspicious of being malignant are those curves showing a plateau later on, or those that continue to enhance. This is typically observed in benign tumors such as fibroadenoma. More detail on tumor perfusion studies is given in Section 10.6. DCE MRI mammography has been introduced for tumor diagnostics by KAISER and ZEITLER [1989]. However, only recently has the imaging modality gained widespread acceptance, which is partially due to effective computer support.

Brain Perfusion In contrast to leaky vessels in malignant tumors, micro-vessels in normal brain tissue do not leak as a result of the blood-brain barrier. Consequently, there is no enhancement in the extracellular volume over a longer time-period. Instead, we observe the first pass of the CA through the vessel components. About 10 seconds after the first pass of blood circulation, a broadened second pass can be seen (see Fig. 10.2). The volume of blood available in each voxel is diagnostically relevant. It is measured by the *integral* of the enhancement curve and the *mean transit time* of the blood as measured by the first moment of the curve. Brain perfusion studies are discussed in detail in Section 10.7.

The analysis of dSPECT data is also based on the selection of regions and the investigation of curves depicting changes over time in these regions. Since activity of a radioactive tracer is imaged, these curves are referred to as *time activity curves* [POHLE et al. 2004]. The analysis of fMRI data also involves the analysis of time-series [FRISTON et al. 1994]. The basic principles of deriving, filtering, and analyzing time-intensity curves were originally developed for the analysis of scintigrams in the 1970s and refined for the analysis of X-ray image sequences [HÖHNE et al. 1981]; see also the historic review in HÖHNE [2002]. The parameters described in the following are very similar to those used by HÖHNE et al. [1981] for the analysis of angiographic image sequences.

Parameters Concerning the dynamic behavior, some parameters are of general interest for almost all application areas:

- *Peak enhancement* (PE). The maximum value (over all points in time).
- *Time To Peak* (TTP). The point of time where peak enhancement occurs. This parameter allows assessment as to whether blood supply is delayed in a particular region.
- *Integral*. For a certain time interval (often representing one cycle of blood flow), the area below the curve, the approximated integral, is computed. Together, the parameters *peak enhancement* and *integral* give a hint on reduced blood flow. Reduced and delayed blood flow is a strong indicator for a damaged region—for example, in stroke diagnosis. CT perfusion software for stroke diagnosis often referred to this parameter as CBV (cerebral blood volume). The CBV represents for each voxel the portion occupied by micro-vessels (small arterioles and venules).
- *Mean Transit Time* (MTT). In the time interval used for the integral calculation, MTT specifies the time t where the area below the curve is the same on the left and on the right, or, in other words, the center of gravity of the curve.

If the data are appropriately processed (see Sect. 10.4), PE and TTP are easy to determine because the user does not need to specify any parameter. MTT and CBV, on the other hand, are determined for a certain interval representing a pass of blood circulation. Therefore, the user has to specify two points in time. It might be difficult to select the "right" points in time, which hampers the reproducibility of such examinations.

TTP is an essential perfusion parameter. However, it might be misleading to evaluate the TTP parameter exclusively. Even if TTP is significantly increased, the blood flow might be normal. This behavior is caused by strong collateral flow, which takes longer but results in a normal blood flow.

Additional parameters are employed for DCE MRI mammography and other specific applications. The wash-in and wash-out parameter reflect an early increase in signal intensity (wash-in) and the decrease (wash-out) at a later stage. The user, however, has to specify the right points in time to which these measurements refer. Maximum slope is an essential parameter in heart diagnosis and refers to the largest positive change from one point of time t_i to the subsequent point in time t_{i+1}.

10.3   BASIC VISUALIZATION TECHNIQUES

Some straightforward techniques to visualize and analyze such data are:

- Cine-movies, which step through all points in time for a selected slice.
- Subtraction images, which depict the intensity difference between two selected points in time.
- The generation of color-coded *parameter maps* for a selected slice. A parameter map is a 2D display of a selected slice, in which each pixel encodes the value of a selected parameter, such as MTT or TTP. The term parameter map was originally developed for the analysis of activation patterns in PET data and has the same meaning there (recall Sect. 3.5).

The cinematic depiction of gray scale images in a movie loop is helpful to assess image noise and artifacts [CHOYKE et al. 2003]. It is more a vehicle of quality control than an evaluation method itself.

Digital subtraction images may also be used for quality control; the injection of a CA leads to an increase of signal intensity, at least in the early points in time. If the digital subtraction for two early points in time, t_2 and t_1 with $t_2 > t_1$, leads to a negative value, then it is very likely that the pixels do not correspond well to each other, due to motion artifacts. If this occurs often, motion correction is indispensable for a meaningful analysis. (For T2-weighted MRI images with decreasing signal intensity after CA arrival, the quality control would check whether signal intensities do not rise).

Figure 10.3 shows two subtraction images used for diagnosis of an ischemic stroke. Both reveal a dark area in the right image (left part of images). This is suspicious, since it does not occur in the corresponding region of the left image. The area that is dark in both hemispheres depicts the core of an ischemic stroke. Around this region, a larger area appears dark in the early subtraction image (left), but bright in the subtraction image that refers to a later time. This region shows a late contrast enhancement, typical for the penumbra—the tissue at risk around a stroke core.

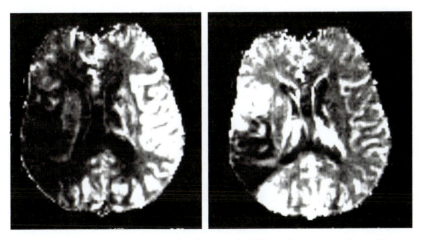

FIGURE 10.3   *Subtraction images to analyze cerebral perfusion. Left: difference between t_6 and t_2; right: t_{17} and t_2. Slice 4 (from 12 total) is selected. The low perfusion in a larger portion of the right image (the left part in the image) becomes obvious. In the right image, the late enhancement in a part of the right image is characterized by a high signal intensity. A brain segmentation algorithm has been applied to restrict the visualization to brain tissue. (Data courtesy JONATHAN WIENER, Boca Raton Community Hospital)*

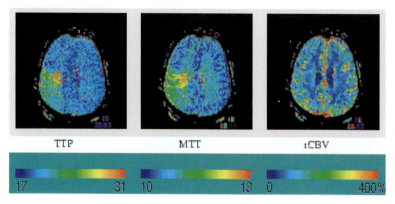

FIGURE 10.4 *Parametric images for slice 4 of a dynamic MRI sequence. TTP, MTT, and the integral (here called cerebral blood volume, CBV) are depicted as color-coded images. The delayed blood flow in the right hemisphere (left part of the images) becomes obvious. (Images courtesy* JONATHAN WIENER, *Boca Raton Community Hospital)*

In principle, subtraction images provide valuable information for the diagnosis. However, there is no assistance in choosing the "right" points in time for subtraction images. Moreover, the 2D data are only used to visually detect abnormalities. Quantitative temporal and spatial information, which could make the diagnostic results more reproducible, is not available.

Parameter maps are derived for a user-selected slice, and they are displayed primarily as color-coded images (see Fig. 10.4). Besides parameter images, it is common to compute enhancement curves for user-selected regions of interest. Often a parameter map is used first to detect interesting or suspicious regions, whereas enhancement curves in selected regions are analyzed later.

10.4 DATA PROCESSING

The analysis of DCE data relies on *comparable* image data. Comparability means that a pixel with coordinates (x, y, z) at time t_1 corresponds to a pixel with the same coordinates at time t_2. Cerebral MRI data are therefore easier to analyze, since the temporal resolution is high and brain structures are little affected by breathing or heartbeat. For other applications, such as MRI mammography, motion correction is required. Depending on the application area, image-processing techniques must be carried out before an appropriate visualization of dynamic information can be achieved.

Image Registration Motion correction is essential when breathing, heartbeat, or muscle relaxation occurs. Figure 10.5 shows the benefit of image registration for a DCE MRI mammography. Without motion correction, the difference volume is filled with bright artifacts. Motion artifacts might hide relevant signal changes, as well as displaying false signal changes that are not actually present.

For DCE MRI mammography, rigid registration approaches that (only) transform the whole static dataset are not appropriate. MRI mammography has a low temporal resolution and relates to a part of the human body where breathing and other motion effects cause considerable soft tissue deformations, which are typically nonlinear. Elastic registration approaches that consider local transformations perform better in terms of registration quality.

The registration algorithm described in [RUECKERT *et al.* 1999] is a good basis, which employs normalized mutual information [WELLS III *et al.* 1996] as a similarity measure. The process is computationally expensive and may take up to several hours on a state-of-the-art PC, depending on the size of the dataset.

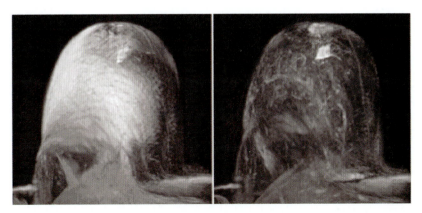

FIGURE 10.5 *Subtraction images of a DCE MRI mammography rendered as MIP. Due to breast motion, the data (left) exhibit bright artifacts in regions that are not aligned. After aligning the data (right) the volume becomes more transparent and reveals an enhancing tumor. (Images courtesy SVEN KOHLE, MeVis Bremen)*

Although faster calculation is desirable, the algorithm is suitable, since no user interaction is required and the quality of the alignment is very high in the majority of the cases.

Calibration of Signal Intensities   While CT imaging provides calibrated signal intensities in Hounsfield units, MRI signals are dependent on the scanning sequence used. Therefore, the raw signals are converted into relative concentration of the CA. The calibration relies on a linear correlation of signal intensity changes and contrast enhancement (recall Sect. 10.2, see also [PRICE 1995]).

Segmentation   Projection methods such as MIP are established for visualization of small, enhanced regions embedded in a relatively transparent data volume, e.g., the distribution of filamentary vessels. Regions of interest can be obscured by adjacent tissues. To remove occluding structures, it is necessary to segment them. For other applications, such as stroke or infarct diagnosis, it is useful to restrict the visualization to relevant structures (ventricles of the heart or brain tissue). Segmentation methods for dynamic data must be carefully evaluated and optimized with respect to their performance. As an example, the fast watershed algorithm described by HAHN and PEITGEN [2000] turned out to be useful for tumor segmentation in DCE MRI data (recall Fig. 10.3).

Temporal Denoising and Model Fitting   Noise reduction strongly improves the interpretation of concentration enhancement curves, which typically exhibit high-frequency noise. To achieve enhancement curves that can be reliably analyzed, smoothing in the temporal dimension is essential. Features such as tissue boundaries represented by edges, however, should be preserved. LYSAKER et al. [2003] developed an appropriate filter based on partial differential equations, which simulate a diffusion process, and applied it to DCE MRI data. Figure 10.6 compares the curve relating to the original cerebral MRI data and the curve after applying smoothing. For the generation of parameter maps, such as MTT and CBV, the "right" points in time must be chosen (recall Sect. 10.2). The smoothed visualization supports this selection. Temporal smoothing is not only defined for perfusion data but is also a standard approach in the analysis of time-intensity curves resulting from functional MRI [FRISTON et al. 1995].

Fitting Pharmacokinetic Models   A more advanced support for interpreting contrast-enhanced data is to employ a physiologic model of perfusion. These models relate physiologic parameters such as permeability of vasculature that depend less on the particular scanner and the imaging sequence. Often, these

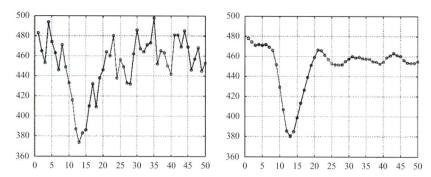

FIGURE 10.6 *Smoothing the temporal dimension of 4D data for an improved interpretation of enhancement curves. The start and endpoint of the V-shaped signal drop becomes obvious in the denoised version. Due to the underlying T2 data, the enhancement leads to negative slopes* [LYSAKER et al. 2003]. *(Image courtesy MARIUS LYSAKER)*

model parameters are more specific for a particular diagnosis. To employ the model, the enhancement curves are fitted to the parameters of pharmacokinetic models.

As an example, we briefly discuss the model developed by TOFTS and KERMODE [1991] which is widely used and carefully validated for tumor perfusion. Similar to other pharmacokinetic models, this model assesses the contrast agent residing in and exchanging between two compartments in the tumor: the vascular space and the extracellular space (ECS) [CHOYKE et al. 2003]. The contrast agent enters the tumor through the vascular space and diffuses into the ECS. The rates of diffusion depend on the interface between capillaries and the ECS, as well as on the concentration of the contrast agent in the ECS and in the vascular space.

The basic parameters are the vascular permeability $K[1/min]$ and the extracellular volume fraction v. The K parameter determines the amplitude of the enhancement curve, and the quotient of K/v determines the shape of the curve.

A least-squares fit to the enhancement curves allows the estimation of the parameters of the Tofts model. The fit is not precise in all regions of the data; in some regions the correlation between the fitted curve and the data might even be poor. Therefore, it is essential that the correlation is also calculated and visualized. Figure 10.7 shows an example where a good fit was produced. A good fit can be expected in active tumor regions, whereas necrotic regions with no capillaries will expose a rather poor fit [FURMAN-HARAN et al. 1997].

The model parameters may also be used for deriving model parameter maps. Instead of showing color-coded distributions of TTP, MTT, and other parameters, K and v values of the Tofts model are visualized to give an overview on regions with suspicious values with respect to the used fitting model.

Usually, time-intensity curves are presented in one view and parameter maps or other visualizations in separate views. This separation makes it difficult to integrate the information from these views. Recently, MLEJNEK et al. [2006] proposed to integrate the time-intensity curves directly in the visualizations similar to a flag "mounted" on top of a surface. This technique can also be used to mount several flags or to integrate the curves of several positions in one view.

10.5   ADVANCED VISUALIZATION TECHNIQUES

In this section, we describe advanced visualization techniques for dynamic data that are currently investigated and neither clinically evaluated nor commercially available. These advanced techniques are

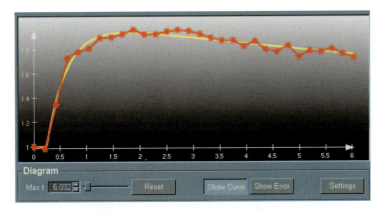

FIGURE 10.7 *Fitting parameters of the Tofts model to enhancement curves. The Tofts model parameters for the fit are* $K = 0.5$
and $v = 50\%$ *which indicates a malignant disease. (Image courtesy* SARAH BEHRENS, *MeVis Bremen)*

motivated by two essential drawbacks of basic visualization techniques (see Sect. 10.3). On the one hand,
basic techniques do not permit the integration of several parameter maps in one image. On the other hand,
dynamic information cannot be integrated with morphologic information that may be based on another
dataset with higher spatial resolution. In particular, the integration of parameter maps with morphologic
information is desirable for the localization of pathologies.

10.5.1 MULTIPARAMETER VISUALIZATION

The integrated visualization of several parameters in a suspicious region is desirable for various diagnostic
tasks. The diagnosis of ischemic stroke, for example, requires an evaluation of MTT, TTP, and CBV (recall
Fig. 10.4). If it turns out that in a particular region the blood flow is delayed (high TTP values), it is
crucial to evaluate whether the overall blood flow is also reduced (small cerebral blood volume).

In principle, color may be employed for two or three parameters as well. However, the widespread
RGBα color specification (red, green, blue) is not appropriate here, because this color space is not perceptually uniform (recall Sect. 2.4). The HSV color space (describing a color by its hue, saturation, and
value component) is better suited (see [LEFKOVITZ and HERMAN 1992] for a discussion of color spaces). To
be compatible with expectations of users, the most suspicious parameter combinations may be mapped
to a red color (hue) with high color saturation and high intensity (value), whereas normal parameter
values are mapped to lower saturation and intensity values and a bluish hue component (see Fig. 10.14).
With this approach, the viewer's attention might be directed to suspicious regions.

Combining Isolines and Color-coding Although commercial software for perfusion analysis relies exclusively
on color to depict dynamic information, more visualization techniques are applicable and useful for this
purpose.

Isolines, height fields, or orientations of textures might be employed to combine several parameters
within a single image [TYLER 2002]. The combination of isolines and colors is particularly effective and
can be easily interpreted.[2] Isolines connect regions where the investigated dynamic parameter has a certain
value. Figure 10.9 gives an example of an isoline visualization of dynamic MRI mammography. The user

---

2 Displays used in weather forecast rely on this combination.

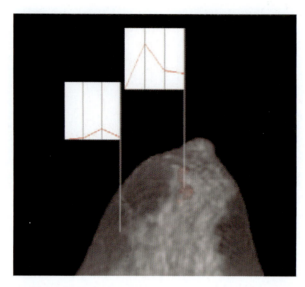

FIGURE 10.8 *Application profile flags for integrating time-intensity curves at selected positions in visualizations of time-varying data (DCE-MRI data)* [MLEJNEK et al. 2006]. *(Image courtesy* MATEJ MLENIK, *University of Technology, Vienna)*

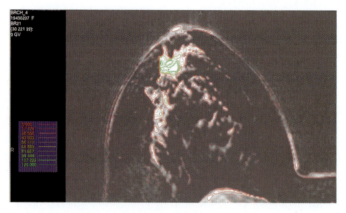

FIGURE 10.9 *Ten isolines depict a dynamic parameter derived from MRI mammography. The data and the resulting isolines are smoothed. (Image courtesy* OLAF KONRAD-VERSE, *MeVis Bremen)*

specifies how many isolines are to be depicted and, as a result, the isovalues are evenly distributed through the whole range of values for this parameter.

Isolines are easily computed by the widely used Marching Squares algorithm [SCHROEDER et al. 2001]. It considers each quadrilateral cell and detects through which cell the isoline proceeds (at least one vertex above or equal to the threshold and one below the threshold). In a next step, edges of the underlying grid that are intersected by the isoline are detected (edges with one vertex above or equal to and one below the isovalue). The precise intersection is determined with linear interpolation (see Fig. 10.10 for a sketch of the approach).

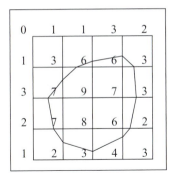

FIGURE 10.10   *Principle of isoline generation with the Marching Squares approach. Isolines for isovalue 5 are computed by linear interpolation along the grid cells.*

There are several issues in isoline generation with respect to noisy image data, where small and jaggy lines may result (many small isolines for a single isovalue). Smoothing the data allows to remove small (and probably) irrelevant isolines. Two strategies are possible:

- Smooth the underlying data (in the spatial domain)
- Smooth the isolines

The choice whether to use the first or the second strategy is not an obvious one. The advantage of the first strategy is that irrelevant noise, which would lead to many distracting isolines, is removed. However, this process involves the loss of some detail that could be relevant, particularly if large filter kernels or very simple filters are used. The second strategy conserves all details of the data. Distracting edges in the isolines are smoothed; however, the number of isolines is not affected with the second strategy.

Often, both techniques are combined, as in Figure 10.9. The data are smoothed with a Gaussian filter and the vertices of the isoline are exposed to Laplacian smoothing. In contrast with color-coding, which supports a fast qualitative interpretation, isolines are not interpreted at a glance but allow a more quantitative interpretation.

Exploration of Multiple Parameter Images with Lenses   Lenses are used to explore conventional images. Digital lenses—working as pixel magnifiers—are also highly welcome in digital image reading to analyze small scale phenomena within enlarged visualizations. In contrast to their conventional use, lenses might also be employed to show different information in the lens region. For parameter maps, lenses are useful for showing information relating to one parameter in the context of a map of another parameter. With this interaction style, the user starts by selecting a foreground and a background parameter (for example, TTP and MTT) and then moves a lens (a rectangle or an ellipse) to select either parameter set.

The interaction with movable viewing lenses is generally useful for the exploration of multidimensional data and was introduced by BIER et al. [1993]. The interaction style is called *see through interfaces* and the lenses are referred to as *Magic Lenses* to emphasize their semantics, which differ from conventional lenses. The motivation here is to analyze the correlation between two parameters.

Instead of completely replacing the foreground display in the lens region, it might be shown as a semitransparent combination of information of the foreground and background parameter (see Fig. 10.11). This is very similar to the semitransparent overlay of segmentation information to original image data. As a second example, we present the exploration of mammography data by means of lenses (see Fig. 10.13).

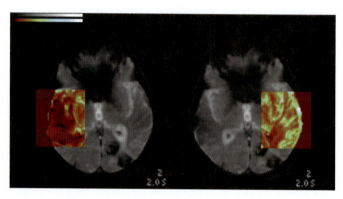

FIGURE 10.11 *Magic Lenses for the exploration of multiparameter maps. The focus region inside the lens shows the parameter cerebral blood volume whereas the gray values show the original MRI data. An optimized color scale is used inside the focus region. The core of an ischemic stroke in the left hemisphere appears dark red or black. (Image courtesy* CHRISTIAN BENDICKS, *University of Magdeburg)*

10.5.2 INTEGRATING DYNAMIC INFORMATION AND MORPHOLOGY

Meaningful dynamic parameters can often be extracted for a restricted region only—e.g., where perfusion takes place. However, other constituents, such as the bony structures, might provide substantial information for displaying the diagnostically relevant regions in their anatomical environment. Therefore, it is useful to add spatial reference information in the regions not containing dynamic information. While the dynamic information is encoded in a color scale, the reference data are displayed in the background using a gray scale. Depending on the resolution of the image data, the integration of dynamic and morphologic information should be carried out in 2D slice visualizations or 3D renderings. For dynamic MRI mammography with more than 50 slices, 3D renderings are appropriate, whereas stroke diagnosis often provides a too-small number of slices.

The assessment of dynamic data might benefit from segmentation information—for example, a suspicious breast lesion. In this case, the visualization of dynamic information might be restricted to the segmented region (see Fig. 10.12 for an example in breast imaging).

10.6   CASE STUDY: TUMOR PERFUSION

The first case study relates to the evaluation of breast tumors. Perfusion imaging is carried out to evaluate whether lesions regarded as suspicious in static images are likely to represent a cancer.

There is strong evidence that both morphologic and enhancement characteristics of DCE MRI examinations must be considered for diagnosing suspicious lesions [KINKEL and HYLTON 2001, KUHL and SCHILD 2000, SCHNALL et al. 2001]. Morphologic changes in static images are often nonspecific (e.g., an enlarged but hyperplastic lymph node [CHOYKE et al. 2003]). Physiologic alterations occur before changes in morphology and thus represent an early indication of tumor growth. These early markers are recorded by means of DCE MRI data.

Perfusion imaging allows the direct assessment of angiogenesis. Angiogenesis—the creation of many new vessels around a tumor—is considered a major event that has to occur if a malignant tumor grows

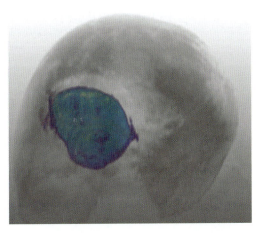

FIGURE 10.12 *The visualization of dynamic information is restricted to the segmented tumor. The surrounding tissue is displayed as conventional volume rendering. (Image courtesy* CHRISTIAN BENDICKS, *University of Magdeburg)*

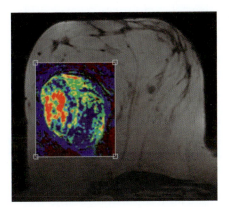

FIGURE 10.13 *Exploration of MRI-mammography data with a lens. Parameter wash-out projected through the lens: a blue color indicates a continuous enhancement for a later period in time (benign); a green color indicates a plateau (suspicious) in the enhancement curve; a yellow and in particular a red color indicate a strong wash-out behavior. This behavior is often observed in malignant tumors. (Data courtesy* JONATHAN WIENER, *Boca Raton Community Hospital)*

beyond a certain size [DOR et al. 2001]. These new vessels are immature and leaky. The high permeability leads to the wash-out effect of a contrast agent.

Angiogenesis is thus a major factor in confirming the diagnosis of a malignant tumor. Therapies, such as vaccines, directly attempt to stop or roll back angiogenesis. The success of such a therapy is reflected in perfusion maps in that region. In summary, perfusion images support diagnosis of tumor diseases and therapy monitoring. It must be admitted, however, that DCE MRI mammography is not able to assess malignancy in all cases reliably. Some malignant tumors may exhibit enhancement curves that appear not to be suspicious (false negatives), and some strongly suspicious curves may actually represent a benign tumor (false positive). Therefore, other clinical examinations—e.g., a biopsy—might be necessary.

Robustness against flow and breathing artifacts as well as the transformation of signal intensities in the local contrast medium concentration are major challenges in the development of an appropriate computer support.

10.6.1 IMAGING

DCE MRI mammography employs T1-weighted images. Contrast enhancement lasts considerably longer than in cerebral blood vessels, because diffusion from inside the vessels to the extracellular space takes places. Therefore, longer acquisition times, such as one to one and a half minutes, are acceptable. The reduced temporal resolution allows a significant increase in spatial resolution. FURMAN-HARAN et al. [1997] emphasize that spatial resolution is more important for tumor perfusion studies than for brain perfusion studies. Typical parameters for DCE MRI mammography are:

- Matrix: 512 × 512
- Slice distance: 2 mm
- Number of slices: 60–80
- Temporal resolution: 1–1.5 min (5–10 measurements)

DEGANI et al. [1997] suggest using only three points in time (3 TP), which should be chosen so that wash-in can be assessed by subtracting image intensities at t_2 and t_1 and (potential) wash-out by considering t_3 and t_2. The 3 TP-method represents the minimum temporal resolution to evaluate dynamics and requires that these points be selected very well to represent the enhancement appropriately. With this scheme, spatial resolution can be enhanced. Malignant tumors with very active and necrotic[3] regions are very heterogenous with respect to their dynamic characteristics. Therefore, (spatial) averaging of those different regions may mislead the interpretation.

Considerable experience is required for the evaluation of DCE MRI mammography. The amplitude and shape of enhancement curves depend, for example, on the patient's age and the time of the examination with respect to menstruation. Pregnant and nursing women also show different enhancement curves. In general, significant enhancements of more than factor two within the first minute after CA-injection are suspicious for malignant lesions.

Imaging strategies for dynamic MRI mammography are described in [HEYWANG-KÖBRUNNER et al. 1997 and HEYWANG-KÖBRUNNER 1994].

10.6.2 COMPUTER SUPPORT

Software solutions are challenging, due to the dynamic nature of DCE MRI mammography. Data processing, in particular motion correction, is more challenging than brain perfusion imaging.

Substantial research to support diagnosis of DCE MRI mammography has been carried out at the Center for Medical Diagnostic Systems and Visualization (MeVis, Bremen). A first software assistant was presented in [BEHRENS et al. 1996]. The display of parameter maps, the selection of ROIs, the calculation of enhancement curves, and the quantitative analysis of these curves was possible. Furthermore, a first version of a search for suspicious regions was realized. Regions with a time-intensity curve similar to a given curve were looked for. MEYER et al. [1999] later presented an improved version, which was carefully adapted

---

3   Active cells split frequently, whereas necrotic tissue consists of dead cells. In case of a fast growing tumor, cells often die because they are not sufficiently supplied with blood.

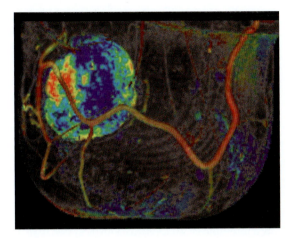

FIGURE 10.14 *A gray scale MIP of the subtraction volume of two early points in time is combined with a color-coded CVP. A color is only assigned to pixels that exceed a threshold. The color encodes the dynamical behavior: bright voxels show a strong enhancement for an early period, less intense voxels show less enhancement. A blue color indicates a continuous enhancement for a later period in time, and a green color indicates a plateau in the enhancement curve. A yellow and in particular a red color indicate a strong "wash-out" behavior. Although this behavior is often observed in malignant tumors, this particular tumor turned out to be benign* [KOHLE et al. 2002]. *(Image courtesy Sven Kohle, MeVis Bremen)*

to the needs of the clinical routine. This software assistant, called MT-Dyna, was evaluated in several hospitals and turned out to be a valuable support for breast cancer diagnosis. With more advanced visualization options, a fast motion correction, and the incorporation of model parameters (recall Sect. 10.4), a new research prototype was presented [KOHLE et al. 2002]. In the following, some visualization aspects of this software are described.

10.6.3 VISUALIZATION TECHNIQUES

Two parameters describing the diagnostically significant shape and amplitude of each pixel's enhancement curve are mapped to color: (1) the slope of the early CA enhancement to brightness and (2) the slope of the late wash-out to the color value, encoding suspicious wash-out in red. Using continuous color values creates a smooth transition between slowly enhancing and depleting regions.

For the integration of morphologic information and dynamic information in DCE MRI mammography, projection methods are very useful.[4] Projection techniques are required that provide a direct link between pixels and the corresponding voxels with its enhancement curve. An interactive tool with point and click functionality in the projected image allows the assessment of the related original image data. Together, the colorized projection image provides morphologic information aligned with its physiological parameters. This visualization technique has been introduced in [KOHLE et al. 2002].

Maximum Intensity Projection The maximum intensity projection (MIP) is conventionally used for gray scale volume data in which the interesting structures have a small volume-filling factor, such as vascular structures. For every pixel of the resulting image, the voxel with highest intensity along the projection

---

4   Every voxel with its corresponding color contains diagnostically relevant information. The use of volume rendering that blends those colors into new colors is problematic, since those mixed colors are difficult to interpret for diagnosis.

ray is determined. The MIP is also applicable with colored volume data when using the HSV color space. Searching for the maximum based on each voxel's intensity value and representing its color in the projection image can display the same regions as in the gray scale MIP but includes the temporal dynamic information in its color encoding.

In general, MIP images are more difficult to assess than volume rendered images, because MIP images typically do not incorporate an illumination model and do not account for occlusion. Direct volume rendering supports the mental understanding. On the other hand, there is the explicit correspondence to the dynamics of every pixel, and there are no more visualization parameters to be adjusted by the physician. The method is therefore easy to use and understand.

Closest Vessel Projection   The closest vessel projection (CVP), also known as local MIP, was developed to add depth information to MIP images (recall Sect. 8.3.1 and NAPEL et al. [1993]). The most intense voxel along the projection ray is no longer selected; rather, the voxel which represents the first local maximum above a certain threshold is selected. The threshold has to be adjusted to segment only the interesting structures. As a rule of thumb, a threshold of 20% relative enhancement is an appropriate suggestion for breast tumors. Similar heuristics may apply to other application areas.

As the name implies, CVP is dedicated to the visualization of vascular structures. Again, because there is a direct link to a single corresponding voxel in the dataset, the projected voxel can be displayed in its inherent color. The local maximum is determined based on its intensity value. Figure 10.15 compares a MIP and a CVP of DCE mammography data. When rotating the dataset or when producing stereoscopic images, the spatial relations are even more evident. Both MIP and CVP are offered as whole-volume visualization techniques and as slab rendering—restricted to a portion of the data characterized by two parallel clipping planes.

Discussion and Clinical Evaluation   The use of DCE MRI mammography and its evaluation with MT-Dyna with the functionality described above was carried out at the Boca Raton Community Hospital [WIENER et al. 2005]. In a prospective study with 65 patients, not only were all (44) breast malignancies reliably detected, but an additional 37 lesions were detected beyond those suspected on mammography or sonography. Twentythree of these lesions turned out to be malignant. The specificity in the detection of malignant breast lesions was 74%.

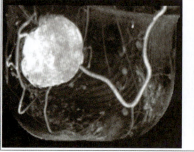 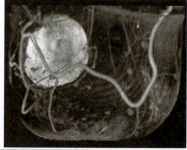

FIGURE 10.15   *Left: a malignant breast tumor visualized using a MIP of the subtraction data derived by subtracting the intensities of the first two points in time of an MRI series. Right: the same data visualized using a CVP. The spatial course of blood vessels becomes much better conceivable [KOHLE et al. 2002]. (Image courtesy SVEN KOHLE, MeVis Bremen)*

Morphologic data (acquired with conventional MRI) and kinetic data were combined for a reliable diagnosis. A modified 3 TP scheme (recall DEGANI et al. [1997]) was employed by WIENER et al. [2005] to optimize spatial resolution.

As criteria for malignancy, relative enhancement of more than 200% between the first and second point of time, combined with a significant drop in signal on subsequent time points (20%), was selected (see Fig. 10.16). In the evaluation, a standardized procedure was developed that includes standardized color scales (e.g., wash-in is color-coded by assigning yellow to > 200%, red to 100%, blue to 50%). Colors that extended over an area of at least four pixels were regarded as reliable. In each lesion, the most malignant region was determined. This region determined the category of the lesion.

In addition to the distinction between malignant and benign lesions, DCE MRI allows the reliable subclassification of malignant lesions [KNOPP et al. 1999] which is essential for therapy decisions. DCE MRI is also crucial for therapy monitoring—particularly for monitoring a chemotherapy, because the success of the therapy can be evaluated earlier compared to static imaging.

10.7   CASE STUDY: BRAIN PERFUSION

Similar to breast cancer, ischemic stroke is among the leading causes of death in all western countries. In the last few decades, a variety of therapeutic options for patients with ischemic stroke were developed and established. Surgical and chemical interventions may salvage at least part of the "tissue at risk" [DEN BOER and FOLKERS 1997].

Once the physiologic mechanisms of a stroke were better understood, it became clear that there is a "window" of three to six hours during which therapeutic options must be initiated to reduce the consequences of an ischemic stroke. As consequence of deeper understanding and improved treatment options, the need for a precise diagnosis increased.

Beside the location and size of an infarction core (in which the function of the brain is already permanently lost), the identification of "tissue at risk" (ischemic penumbra) is crucial before considering any patient treatment. This area is characterized by decreased and delayed perfusion. In this section, we focus on ischemic cerebral strokes. Very similar analysis techniques apply to myocardial infarction. Similar to a

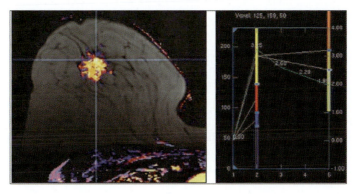

FIGURE 10.16 *Left: a lesion is represented as an area of bright yellow, which indicates a relative enhancement of more than 200%. Right: the graph of the selected voxel is shown and reveals that the rapid increase of signal intensity is followed by a significant signal loss. Screenshot of MT-Dyna. (Image courtesy MeVis Diagnostics, Bremen)*

cerebral stroke, a delay between the onset of clinical symptoms and the development of permanent tissue damage occurs. Within this time, diagnosis of perfusion and initiation of treatment should occur.

10.7.1 IMAGING

A cerebral hemorrhage[5] and an ischemic stroke exhibit similar symptoms. As a first step of imaging, a CT study is carried out, because a cerebral hemorrhage is identified quickly and reliably using this modality. If a hemorrhage can be excluded, diffusion-weighted MRI images are often acquired. While this modality allows establishment of the diagnosis of an ischemic stroke, it does not show hypoperfused tissue around the core of the stroke. Perfusion images are acquired to assess the existence and extent of hypoperfused tissue (the so-called penumbra). Perfusion images also allow assessment of the severity of a stroke and characterization of the subtype of a stroke. This information is highly relevant and urgent for therapeutic decisions. As an imaging modality for perfusion analysis, either CT or MRI might be employed.[6]

MRI Imaging   MRI studies suffer from lower spatial resolution compared to CT, but allow scanning of the entire brain, and are thus better suited to detect an infarction, if its location is not a priori known.

Typical parameters for contrast-enhanced MRI perfusion are:

- Matrix: 128 × 128
- Slice distance: 7 mm
- Number of slices: 10–15
- Temporal resolution: 1–2 seconds (40–80 measurements)

Cerebral blood flow cannot be directly measured. However, as KÖNIG et al. [2001] showed, a good correspondence between mean transit time, cerebral blood volume and time to peak to cerebral blood flow can be established. MTT and TTP maps often present similar information. The "tissue at risk" tends to be overestimated with these maps as compared to CBV maps.

CT Imaging   CT perfusion studies only acquire one slice. To reduce image noise, a large slice thickness (10 mm) is employed. The slice thickness, however, leads to strong partial volume effects. Noise reduction is necessary, as the increase in signal intensity after CA injection is rather small (15 Hounsfield units (HUs) for normally perfused brain tissue and less for tissue with reduced perfusion). If image noise is not reduced carefully, the difference between tissue with reduced perfusion and nonperfused tissue is in the same order of magnitude as the noise level [KÖNIG et al. 2001].

Perfusion Maps   Brain perfusion maps can be quantified in terms of absolute blood flow and blood volume [BARBIER et al. 2001], and they are derived from CT and MRI data. The calibration of these parameters requires the exact measurement of the arterial input function, which is currently not possible with MRI. However, semiquantitative parameters as well as relative perfusion maps have been obtained with MRI and have been shown to allow prediction of infarct growth [GRANDIN et al. 2002]. They evaluated the initial infarct with diffusion-weighted MRI data and the final infarct (six hours later) with a special inversion recovery MRI sequence. Perfusion data were acquired to predict infarct size. A function of peak enhancement, time to peak (TTP), and cerebral blood flow showed good correspondence to the final infarct size.

---

5   Bleeding that may be caused by the rupture of a vascular structure.

6   Before the advent of CT and MRI, perfusion was investigated with imaging modalities from nuclear medicine, such as PET and SPECT. However, the spatial and temporal resolution of these modalities is limited and the noise level is high.

10.7.2 COMPUTER SUPPORT

The principles of CT perfusion imaging and evaluation were developed early [AXEL 1980]. The integration of parameter maps, ROI selection, and analysis of enhancement curves was developed later by KLOTZ and KÖNIG [1999] and KÖNIG et al. [2001]. Software for the evaluation of brain perfusion images has been commercially available for some years. Companies such as SIEMENS and General Electric provide dedicated tools for CT brain perfusion. MRI brain perfusion software is also available; however, it is rarely used.

10.7.3 VISUALIZATION TECHNIQUES

The symmetry of the brain is the basis for diagnostic evaluation of static and dynamic images. Whether or not a part of the brain appears to be pathologic is judged by comparing it with the corresponding part of the other hemisphere. Such symmetry considerations are also highly relevant for CT and MRI perfusion images and might be supported by software assistants. As an example, it is possible to define an ROI in one hemisphere and have the system define the corresponding ROI in the other hemisphere (see Fig. 10.17). For both regions, the enhancement curves are shown to support the evaluation of a correlation between them.

In Section 10.5, we discussed the use of Magic Lenses to explore parameter maps. In Figure 10.17, the symmetric ROIs are used to compute the quotient of CBF. In this particular example, a value of 0.55 was derived. According to this measure, the blood flow in one probably healthy region is almost twice as large as the blood flow in the reference region, which is suspected to be damaged. For brain images, it is useful to provide two synchronized Magic Lenses (see Fig. 10.18).

Both techniques, the synchronization of ROIs and lenses, require that the regions correspond to each other precisely. This assumes that the system "knows" the precise line of symmetry. Initially, the median plane of the axial image data may be used. However, in clinical image data, the symmetry line might be translated by some pixels or even rotated by a small angle. Therefore, it is desirable that robust algorithms for detecting the precise symmetry line are incorporated. If this is not the case, the user should be allowed to fine-tune (translate, rotate) the line of symmetry. Besides the in-plane alignment, the body might also be tilted, resulting in a vertical rotation of the body. This body vertical rotation requires the specification of a symmetry plane in 3D and possibly the re-sampling of the image slices according to that symmetry plane.

Hanging Protocols for Exploring Dynamic Data In Section 4.3.4, we discussed hanging protocols and their extension to soft-copy reading. Digital hanging protocols are essential for the routine diagnosis of dynamic data. They may include the use of certain parameter maps, color maps, time-intensity diagrams, and the layout of several images that should be viewed simultaneously.

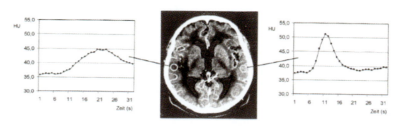

FIGURE 10.17 Enhancement curves are simultaneously derived for the symmetric regions in both hemispheres. Screenshot of the Siemens CT-perfusion software [KÖNIG et al. 2001]. (Image courtesy SIEMENS FORCHHEIM)

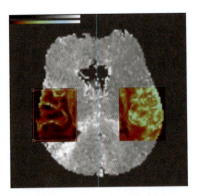

FIGURE 10.18 *Synchronized lenses in both hemispheres of the brain support the comparison between the symmetric regions. The small vertical line represents the line of symmetry. The peak enhancement is the foreground parameter mapped to an optimized color scale and the time to peak parameter is the background parameter. The core of the stroke in the right hemisphere becomes obvious by comparing the regions inside the synchronized lenses. (Image courtesy* CHRISTIAN BENDICKS, *University of Magdeburg)*

10.8   SUMMARY

Dynamic image data have a great potential for enhancing diagnosis and therapy monitoring for important diseases such as stroke and cancer as well as for basic research attempting an understanding of basic principles of metabolism. Although our discussion was focused on perfusion data, many aspects are also essential for other kinds of dynamic image data, such as functional MRI. Appropriate trade-offs between spatial and temporal resolution, the integration and fusion of high resolution anatomical data with lower resolution dynamic data, the correction of motions and breathing artifacts, temporal denoising, and visualization techniques that reveal the spatial distribution of characteristic parameters are among the commonalities between different kinds of dynamic data and application areas.

The acquisition of appropriate data and their interpretation require long term experience. In this chapter, we focused on the role of visualization to support a fast and unambiguous interpretation of such data. The display of parameter maps, the integration of several parameter maps in single images, the exploration of parameter maps with lenses, and the integration of parameter maps with 3D visualizations are crucial visualization techniques. In addition to general visualization and analysis methods, dedicated support for the specific application area is required. As an example, brain perfusion analysis benefits from symmetry considerations, whereas tumor perfusion studies benefit from fitting model parameters to enhancement curves. It should be noted that contrast-enhanced perfusion studies are used in combination with other imaging methods and that clinical diagnosis incorporates findings from these other modalities.

FURTHER READING

We did not discuss performance issues that become relevant if large amounts of data are involved. The visualization of dynamic volume data may be considerably increased by exploiting temporal coherence [SHEN and JOHNSON 1994, LIAO et al. 2003]. A special variant, visualization within a given time budget, is described by LIAO et al. [2004]. In traditional 3D graphics, a binary space partitioning (BSP) scheme is often employed for efficient visualization. A related technique for dynamic volume data is a time partitioning tree [SHEN et al. 1999]. This paper also gives a nice overview on acceleration strategies. Another technique applicable to dynamic volume data is isosurface extraction. Efficient isosurface extraction in dynamic volume data is described in [SUTTON and HANSEN 1999].

The exploration of dynamic medical volume data can benefit from research in other application areas, such as simulations of complex technical processes. In recent years, volume rendering of such data, and in particular transfer function design, has been discussed. Time histograms that show how the frequency of value changes over time are essential in this process [KOSARA et al. 2004, DOLEISCH et al. 2004]. Time histograms are presented either as 2D gray scale images or height fields. The choice of parameters for time histogram presentation is discussed in [AKIBA et al. 2006] with applications in the exploration of turbulent flow.

There are other application areas, such as brain and tumor perfusion. In particular, cardiac perfusion studies by means of CT or MRI gain importance in order to assess coronary artery diseases [OLAFSDOTTIR et al. 2004]. In a research project carried out at the GSF-National Research Center for Environment and Health, Germany, advanced techniques for the exploration of DCE MRI mammography were explored. With virtual reality input and output devices, many depth-cues are provided to support the localization and characterization of lesions in volume renderings [ENGLMEIER et al. 2000]. More details on the first case study are given in [WASSER et al. 2003, KNOPP et al. 1999, KNOPP et al. 2001]. In particular, physiologic characteristics of different benign and malignant breast tumors are discussed as a basis for tumor detection and characterization based on DCE MRI data.

We briefly mentioned the use of cardiovascular perfusion data for the evaluation of the myocardial perfusion reserve. A recent survey on this topic is given in [EDELMAN 2004]. More information on this essential topic can be found in [AL-SAADI et al. 2000, AL-SAADI et al. 2001, NAGEL et al. 2000, NAGEL et al. 2003]. OELTZE et al. [2006] describe a research prototype dedicated to the analysis of cardiac perfusion data in combination with anatomical image data.

Outlook So far, this chapter has illustrated the potential of dynamic image data. However, considerable effort and experience are still necessary to exploit this potential for diagnostic decisions. Therefore, the application of these techniques is limited to the most severe cases (infarct and tumor diagnosis) and to highly specialized hospitals.

Diagnosis with dynamic data can and will be improved in the future. Besides image acquisition, computer support plays an essential role in this improvement. Further research should be directed toward faster and more reproducible diagnostic results. The integration of several parameter maps by using techniques of multifield visualization [TYLER 2002] will support a fast overview on several parameters. For many potential applications, such as liver perfusion, motion correction remains the most challenging task. Feature extraction techniques are needed to direct the radiologist to suspicious regions or to other regions of interest. Dedicated segmentation approaches for series of image data are needed to enhance the ROI selection process. Finally, standardization is necessary to make the diagnosis more reliable.

PART III

Exploration of Medical Volume Data

In this part, we discuss essential interaction techniques for the exploration of 3D medical data. In practical applications, medical visualizations are used interactively to understand and quantify spatial relations and to simulate resection strategies. The three chapters in this part discuss the design of transfer functions for direct volume rendering (see Chap. 11), clipping and cutting techniques for surgery planning and simulation (see Chap. 12), and measurement funtionality to quantify spatial relations (see Chap. 13).

Transfer function design considers interaction facilities to effectively guide the user, as well as semi-automatic methods that analyze the data to suggest transfer functions. Transfer function design is accomplished to adjust the visibility of portions of the data independent of their position. Clipping and cutting techniques, on the other hand, adjust visibility with respect to the position of the data in relation to a clip geometry. The combination of clipping with arbitrary geometry and appropriate transfer functions allows the creation of expressive visualizations that support advanced diagnosis and therapy planning tasks. The description of measurement facilities includes interaction techniques as well as automatic support for frequent measurement tasks. A basis for all these interaction tasks is the theory of 3D interaction. Therefore, we briefly describe crucial terms and concepts of this area.

3D Interaction Interactive manipulations of 3D visualizations require users to select 3D positions or 3D objects and to translate and rotate selected objects. Such interaction techniques are discussed in the field of 3D interaction (see [HAND 1997] for an overview). An intuitive way to accomplish selection and transformation tasks is by means of direct manipulation [SHNEIDERMAN 1983]. With this interaction style, objects are selected via picking and operations are invoked, for example, by dragging the selected object. In combination with 3D visualizations, direct manipulation requires *3D widgets*. This term has been introduced in [CONNOR et al. 1992] and is now widely used to describe interaction facilities comprising a 3D geometry and a behavior to manipulate 3D objects. A crucial aspect is that 3D widgets are clearly recognizable 3D objects, so that their position and orientation in a 3D model can be evaluated by the user. Depth-cues like perspective distortion and shadow projection are thus essential in the use of 3D widgets. Two terms are required for the discussion of 3D widgets:

- The number of *degrees of freedom* (DOF) refers to the number of different interaction facilities available with a 3D widget.
- A *handle* is a single part of a 3D widget that is used to perform a subset of the possible interaction techniques.

Often, there is a 1:1 relationship between handles and degrees of freedom in order to support precise user interaction. For example, for 3D translation, it is common practice to provide one handle for translation in the positive and negative x-, y-, and z-axes.

Two-Handed Interaction   3D interaction might benefit from two-handed interaction. Humans have strong bimanual motor skills. In their daily life, humans perform many tasks, such as composing objects, with a synchronized action of both hands [GUIARD 1987]. The simultaneous use of two input devices is also useful for many 3D interaction tasks, particularly where geometric objects are involved.

In interactive 3D visualization, for example, the selection of objects and the rotation of a virtual camera can be realized simultaneously with two input devices. A sophisticated and carefully refined application is described by HINCKLEY *et al.* [1998], in which two-handed interaction is used for neurosurgery planning.

Chapter 11

Transfer Function Specification

We have already discussed the concept of transfer functions and histograms in Section 6.2. In this chapter, we expand upon these concepts. In particular, we will discuss how transfer functions can be used to flexibly specify rendering parameters (e.g., color and opacity) to generate meaningful visualizations (see Fig. 11.1). However, unconstrained flexibility makes it difficult to define appropriate or even optimal transfer functions for a particular visualization goal. In medical visualization, we can assume that users are familiar with the data and understand the significance of the represented structures. Similar to our discussion of segmentation methods, a high-level support with immediate visual feedback is desirable, because it enables medical doctors to employ their domain-specific knowledge appropriately.

The voxel values of a dataset represent the domain, whereas color and opacity represent the range. In principle, the range may comprise any visual property, such as shininess. In practice, opacity, gray values, and colors are of primary concern. However, the kind of representation chosen—color or gray levels—depends largely on the target audience; while radiologists often prefer gray level renderings, surgeons benefit from colored visualizations with a natural appearance.

TFs determine which structures are visible and how they are displayed. Among the different functions, the opacity transfer function is the most important, since it determines which portions of the data are visible (recall Fig. 11.1). Usually, high opacities are assigned to important features of the data to ensure that they are not obscured by uninteresting regions. TFs are designed to isolate relevant structures and to suppress or hide other structures. Without dedicated support, TF specification is tedious, because the parameter space is huge, and the relation between the modification of a parameter of the TF and the resulting change in the visualization is indirect and hard to predict. Therefore, the focus of this chapter is on functionalities that support the TF specification.

With 1D TFs, the ability to emphasize structures is limited to those that can be distinguished based on their data values. To enhance the ability to discriminate features, multidimensional TFs have been developed that use additionally derived data, such as gradient magnitude or curvature metrics.

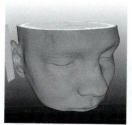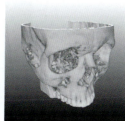

FIGURE 11.1 *Three volume renderings of the same CT dataset produced with different opacity transfer functions. From left to right: the skin, the bones, and the teeth are visible. (Images courtesy* ARNO KRÜGER, *University of Magdeburg)*

In general, 1D TFs allow the separation of *materials*, whereas 2D TFs, particularly with gradient magnitude as the second dimension, also allow an emphasis on *material interfaces* or *material boundaries*. However, the increased flexibility of multidimensional TFs is achieved at the expense of an enlarged parameter space. Therefore, we have to reconsider facilities to guide the parameter specification process.

In a strict sense, TFs relate to features that are independent of the position of data values. They consider locally measured properties or derived quantities, such as the gradient magnitude. Distance-based transfer functions refer to a more general understanding and include positional information, such as distance to a certain point or to a surface, in the transfer function domain.

Organization We start with a discussion of strategies for the specification of 1D TFs and discuss two approaches to support the user in the TF specification (see Sect. 11.1). Interaction techniques for the specification of multidimensional TFs are described in Section 11.2. In the following sections, we discuss special variants of multidimensional transfer functions: gradient-based TFs (see Sect. 11.3) and distance-based TFs (see Sect. 11.4). We describe these TFs and their application to diagnosis and therapy planning tasks. Finally, in Section 11.5, we discuss the use of local TFs that assign different optical properties to different regions of the data.

11.1   STRATEGIES FOR ONE-DIMENSIONAL TRANSFER FUNCTIONS

We discussed the basics of 1D TFs in Section 6.2. In particular, we examined strategies for the specification of binary transfer functions based on single isovalues (see Sect. 6.2.3), which are used in the context of surface-oriented visualization (see Chap. 7). Here, we are focusing on more general methods for arbitrary 1D TFs.

A reasonable basic strategy for TF specification is to increase opacity from one peak in the histogram to the next in order to emphasize this boundary. In Figure 11.2 this strategy is employed to emphasize the white matter in cerebral MRI data. This kind of emphasis is often called *implicit segmentation* (see [REZK-SALAMA et al. 2000b]), because an anatomic structure appears as being (explicitly) segmented. Of course, implicit segmentation is restricted to tissue types with distinct values which do not overlap with other tissue types.

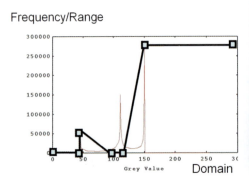
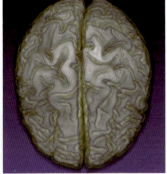

FIGURE 11.2   *The histogram is presented as context for the opacity TF specification of a cerebral MRI dataset (left). The largest change of opacity is assigned to the transition between gray matter and white matter (the right peak) as a linear ramp. The right image shows the resulting volume rendering. (Images courtesy HORST HAHN, MeVis Bremen)*

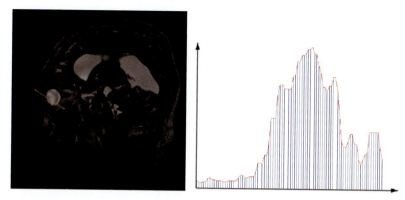

FIGURE 11.3 *Local information in a slice from a volume dataset. Left: slice from an MRI dataset. The orange line indicates the line from where the intensity profile is taken. Right: intensity profile of the orange line (left image). The high-intensity area indicates the eyeball, and the lower intensity area on the right represents the eye muscle tissue on the right end of the orange line.*

Since TF design is largely based on the histogram, it also makes sense to refine the visual representation of the histogram. In Section 6.2.1, we already mentioned methods such as zoomed histograms—limiting the histogram to a specific range of voxel values and value frequencies—and logarithmic scaling of the axes. Furthermore, more meaningful information can be employed by adding basic statistical values such as the standard deviation, average, minimum, and maximum values. The latter two in particular are frequently used to indicate peaks.

Local Histograms   A general limitation of the methods discussed so far is that peaks in the histogram only reveal tissue types that represent a large portion of the data. Minor features that might be essential are not visible in the global histogram. The computation of the histogram in a specific region-of-interest within the dataset or along a line defined in the dataset provides local information. The last-mentioned line histograms are called intensity profiles and may exhibit intensity transitions between different materials. The general concept underlying these facilities is called *probing*, in which the user "inquires" data values that guide the TF specification. The simplest probing functionality, however, is to select a particular position and "read" the value at this position. LINDSTROEM et al. [2005] developed an algorithm that decomposes the volume data into local neighborhoods and computes histograms for these subvolumina, which they call *partial range histograms*. Trapezoid functions are fitted to the local histograms to support the transfer function specification. It is too early to evaluate this method and state its limitations, but it is a promising direction of research.

11.1.1 DATA-DRIVEN TF SPECIFICATION

In this section, we extend the idea of employing the histogram for TF specification. In contrast with the previous section, we do not only present the histogram. Instead, we discuss how the TF design might be restricted and thus become more reproducible. While TF specification discussed so far is a purely interactive process, we regard it now as a semiautomatic process with high-level support to enhance the process.

As mentioned before, TF specification is a more general problem than isovalue or threshold specification for surface rendering. Therefore, all methods that derive salient and potentially appropriate isovalues (recall, for example, [BAJAJ et al. 1997]) are relevant for TF specification where higher opacity is assigned for an interval around critical isovalues.

TF SPECIFICATION FOR BOUNDARY EMPHASIS

In the following, we discuss a boundary model and its application for opacity TF specification. This model is designed to support the user in adjusting opacity TFs that emphasize boundaries at the expense of homogeneous regions.

Boundary Model   The most common and essential visualization goal is to emphasize boundaries in the data. While ideal boundaries are represented by sudden changes in the value, boundaries in medical image data are smoothed due to the image acquisition process. Data-driven specification methods therefore require a model of a boundary. KINDLMANN and DURKIN [1998] argue that boundaries in medical volume data can be modeled by a step function filtered with a Gaussian (see Fig. 11.4). The extent to which boundaries are smoothed depends on the employed reconstruction filter, but the general appearance of boundaries is the same for a wide variety of CT and MRI scanning devices (recall Sect. 3.2).

This model assumption leads to the following considerations: a boundary can be identified by looking for voxels with a local maximum slope (local maximum in the first-order derivative and zero-crossing in the second-order derivative). Actually, this assumption has been used in computer vision for a long time to develop edge-detection filters in image analysis. Figure 11.5 shows the relation between data

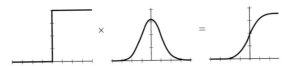

FIGURE 11.4   Boundary model according to KINDLMANN and DURKIN [1998]. The real steep edge is blurred with a (Gaussian) low pass filter, resulting in a gradual change in image intensity. The largest gradient in the resulting image occurs at the position of the original edge. The width of the Gaussian depends on the particular acquisition device. (Image courtesy GORDON KINDLMANN, Brigham and Women's Hospital Boston)

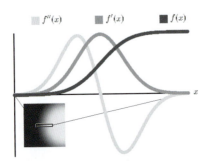

FIGURE 11.5   Relation between image intensity, and first-, and second-order derivative in a neighborhood of a blurred edge, which is spread over a range of positions [KINDLMANN and DURKIN 1998]. (Images courtesy GORDON KINDLMANN, Brigham and Women's Hospital Boston)

values, first-, and second-order derivatives in the vicinity of an edge that corresponds to the model assumptions.

KINDLMANN and DURKIN [1998] presented a method that locates boundaries based on this model. For this purpose they created a histogram volume H in which each entry represents $f(x)$, $f'(x)$, and $f''(x)$ for a particular value x. An essential issue is the resolution of the histogram. For the data value axis ($f(x)$), it should reflect the full resolution of the data. For the other dimensions, a lower resolution is appropriate, as the approximation of first- and second-order derivatives are more sensitive to noise.

In the histogram volume, boundaries are located by searching for curves such as those presented in Figure 11.6. These curves are characterized by adjacent voxels with high first-order and low second-order derivatives. These considerations lead to the definition of a position function p [KINDLMANN and DURKIN 1998] (see Eq. 11.1):

$$p(v) = \frac{-h(v)}{g(v)}$$ (11.1)

where v is a value, $g(v)$ represents the average gradient magnitude for all voxels with value v, and $h(v)$ is the average second-order derivative in gradient direction. $p(v)$ describes the average distance of a data point with value v from a boundary according to the boundary model depicted in Figure 11.5. Together with an algorithm that detects boundaries in the histogram volume, we now have all ingredients to design opacity transfer functions that emphasize boundaries.

Generating Opacity TFs The methods discussed so far detect a boundary and are able to estimate its width. According to the boundary model, a Gaussian is fitted to the data surrounding a boundary. The σ-parameter of the Gaussian characterizes the steepness of the function. Based on this information, the user can select a *boundary emphasis function* that finally determines how the respective boundary is visualized. The predefined functions have different width, height, and shape (see Fig. 11.7).

The opacity TF results from multiplying p with a certain boundary emphasis function. Defining opacity as a function of distance to a boundary is more intuitive and predictable than defining opacity as a function of data value. Figure 11.8 shows some results achieved by the opacity TF specification using the above boundary model. The images in Figure 11.8 consider data and gradient. We discuss gradient-based

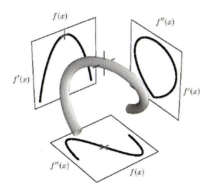

FIGURE 11.6 *Three-dimensional histogram with image intensity, first-, and second-order derivatives as dimensions* [KINDLMANN *and* DURKIN 1998]. *(Images courtesy* GORDON KINDLMANN, *Brigham and Women's Hospital Boston)*

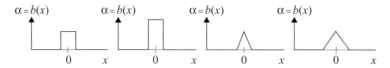

FIGURE 11.7 *Different types of boundary emphasis functions* [KINDLMANN and DURKIN 1998]. *(Images courtesy* GORDON KINDLMANN, *Brigham and Women's Hospital Boston)*

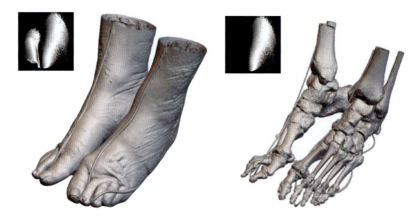

FIGURE 11.8 *Volume rendering results of the feet in the female Visible Human dataset. Left: low data values and low gradient magnitude were removed by means of the 2D opacity TF shown in the inset. Right: the bones are visualized by means of the rightmost portion of the opacity TF (compare the insets)* [KINDLMANN and DURKIN 1998]. *(Images courtesy* GORDON KINDLMANN, *Brigham and Women's Hospital Boston)*

TF specification in Section 11.3. Although the method proposed by KINDLMANN and DURKIN [1998] is based on strong assumptions with respect to the appearance of boundaries, it is a crucial contribution to support TF specification.

In cases, where the assumptions are not valid, such as strongly inhomogeneous MRI data, preprocessing might transform the data so that the boundary model becomes applicable.

11.1.2 EMPLOYING REFERENCE TRANSFER FUNCTIONS

Static presets with a fixed lookup table are an efficient support for direct volume rendering. They are, however, strongly limited in their applicability to structures with standardized and reliable data values. This requirement is not fulfilled, for example, for MRI data. In such cases, only manual editing of the TF is feasible so far.

Therefore, it is highly desirable to develop data-driven support that adapts a preset carefully specified for one dataset to other datasets that have similar pathology, modality, and imaging parameters. This idea has been explored by REZK-SALAMA et al. [2000b]. According to them, we refer to this flexible preset as a reference transfer function (TF_{ref}). If we have defined this function for a dataset D_{ref} and analyze now a similar dataset D_{new}, we are looking for a transformation $t(TF_{ref})$ adapted to the characteristics of D_{new}.

TF Transform According to the Histogram   The first strategy discussed by REZK-SALAMA et al. [2000b] to adapt TF_{ref} is to analyze the histogram H_{ref} and to define how the histogram of a new dataset (H_{new}) has to be transformed to match the histogram of D_{ref} in an optimal way. This can be formalized as follows:

$$H_{new}(v) \approx H_{ref}(t(v)) \tag{11.2}$$

where H_{ref} is the histogram of the reference dataset. The matching process is guided by a similarity metric D_t, which evaluates the differences between the frequencies of all values v in H_{ref} and H_{new} (Eq. 11.3). This metric sums up over all n bins in the histogram.

This matching process has to consider not only that the position and shape of the peaks along the domain are modified, but also that the frequency values might differ strongly. Therefore, the histograms are normalized first.

$$D_t(H_{ref}, H_{new}) = \sum_{i=1}^{n} |H_{ref}(v_i) - H_{new}(v_i)| \tag{11.3}$$

Figure 11.9 illustrates the non-linear transformation of the histogram and its effect on the transformation. The results of this adaption are good but not regarded as precise enough. Better results were achieved by using the *position function p* (recall Eq. 11.1 and [KINDLMANN and DURKIN 1998]) instead of transforming the histogram. In Figure 11.10, we compare the adjustment by means of the histogram and by means of the position function.

11.1.3 IMAGE-DRIVEN TF SPECIFICATION

In contrast to data-driven methods, rendered images instead of the data are analyzed to provide support for TF specification.

The idea of image-driven methods for TF specification is to provide a set of volume rendered images from which the user selects one or a few favorites that guide further image selection. Instead of manipulating TF parameters directly, the user chooses among images which ideally represent a wide scope of

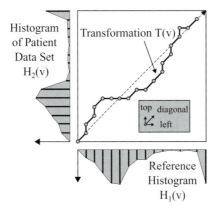

FIGURE 11.9   *A non-linear one-dimensional transformation of the data value range is carried out to adapt a new dataset to the histogram of a reference dataset [REZK-SALAMA et al. 2000b]. (Image courtesy CHRISTOF REZK-SALAMA, University of Siegen)*

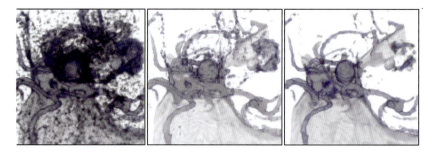

FIGURE 11.10 *TF specification for an MRI dataset to evaluate cerebral aneurysms. Left: default values without adjustment. Middle: the adjustment of a reference TF, accomplished by means of the histogram. Right: adjustment with the position function* [REZK-SALAMA *et al.* 2000b]. *(Images courtesy* CHRISTOF REZK-SALAMA, *University of Siegen)*

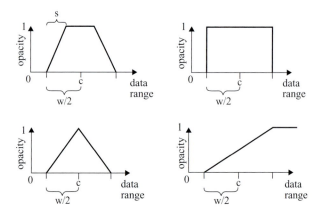

FIGURE 11.11 *Component functions for 1D TF design. All components are characterized by width w and center c. The trapezoid (left) has an additional parameter, which refers to the slope s. From left to right: trapezoid, box, tent, and ramp* [CASTRO *et al.* 1998]. *(Images courtesy* SILVIA CASTRO, *Vienna University of Technology)*

possible TFs. Compared to trial-and-error specification, image-driven specification is more goal-oriented and requires less user knowledge. A technical challenge is to render a sufficient number of preview images fast enough.

The first image-driven method was presented by HE *et al.* [1996]. Their system randomly selects TF parameters and renders corresponding images. The user selects a few of these images and the system generates new images with TF parameters between the selected images. A genetic algorithm is employed to "breed" a TF from the initial "population" that is optimal for the user's needs. This approach is promising; however, it strongly depends on the fitness function underlying the genetic algorithm. This raises the question of how the user can influence the fitness function, which poses a challenging user interface problem because the user cannot be assumed to be familiar with fitness functions and their effect on transfer functions and volume renderings. Therefore, in practice the user relies on the built-in fitness function.

The ideas of HE *et al.* were generalized and enhanced by MARKS *et al.* [1997]. Their "Design galleries" represent a general approach for selecting parameters in a multidimensional space. MARKS *et al.* [1997]

mention camera and light specification as possible applications of their approach. TF specification with this approach is accomplished by selecting previews to guide the search process. The parameter space is more regularly sampled. In contrast with HE et al. [1996], very large sets of preview images are generated and arranged in a "Design Gallery" from which the most appealing image might be selected.

TF Specification by Means of Component Functions   Piecewise linear functions may be defined based on component functions (hereafter CF) [CASTRO et al. 1998]. With the usage of CFs, complex 1D TFs may be composed of simple basis functions such as ramps, boxes, and tents (see Fig. 11.11). To specify a CF, the user has to set a small number of parameters. Often, setting a center, a width, and a maximum opacity is sufficient. The required flexibility to specify 1D TFs is achieved by combining CFs.

In Figure 11.12, we show how a component function is parameterized by means of a histogram that refers to a region selected in a slice. Figure 11.13 shows the definition of two different component functions in which the intensity profile along a ray is used to guide the TF specification. This combination

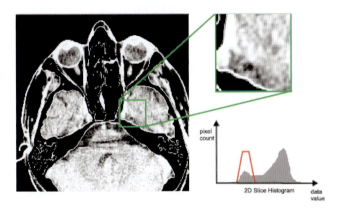

FIGURE 11.12   *The histogram of a rectangular region is derived to guide the placement of a trapezoid component. The selected region is shown enlarged as an inset* [CASTRO et al. 1998]. *(Images courtesy* SILVIA CASTRO, *Vienna University of Technology)*

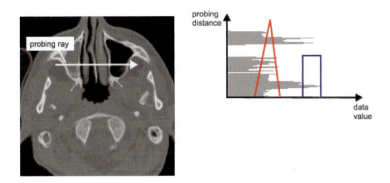

FIGURE 11.13   *An intensity profile along a ray (see the arrow) guides the TF specification by means of two component functions* [CASTRO et al. 1998]. *(Images courtesy* SILVIA CASTRO, *Vienna University of Technology)*

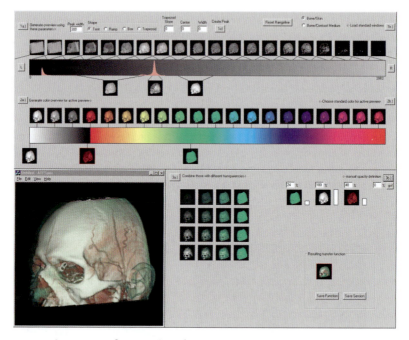

FIGURE 11.14 *Image-driven TF specification with carefully arranged thumbnail images* [KÖNIG *and* GRÖLLER 2001]. *(Images courtesy* ANDREAS KÖNIG, *Vienna University of Technology)*

is a powerful support for TF specification. While the authors relied on special-purpose rendering hardware to achieve the required performance, general GPUs are fast enough for this purpose.

Combining Component Functions With Fast Previews KÖNIG and GRÖLLER [2001] suggest combining fast previews of selected thumbnails with a facility to compose transfer functions by means of component functions (see Fig. 11.14).

11.2 MULTIDIMENSIONAL TRANSFER FUNCTIONS

Multidimensional TFs are employed to improve the discriminative power of TFs. In Chapter 2, we discussed CT data and presented Hounsfield units (HVs) for some structures, such as pancreas (10–40), heart (20–50), liver (50–60), and kidney (50–70). Obviously, transfer functions that only evaluate these values are not able to visually discriminate structures such as the liver and the kidney.

Multidimensional TF is a term that encompasses all TFs with a higher dimensional domain. In addition to data values, gradient magnitude, approximated second-order derivatives, curvature measures, and distance to reference objects have been employed successfully. In principal, multidimensional TFs allow the user to produce excellent visualizations, particularly of CT data. However, much effort is required to specify TFs, and different users (medical doctors) would probably get quite different results.

Similar to 1D TF specification, sufficient flexibility on the one hand and reduced interaction effort on the other hand are desired. The design of appropriate user interfaces is more difficult, since more data dimensions are involved. We elaborate the idea of extending component-based 1D TF specification (recall Sect. 11.1.3) to 2D TFs. The composition of a TF based on predefined but adjustable component functions is a promising idea in general and especially useful for the larger parameter space of 2D TFs. If the components are restricted to linear shapes, the necessary transformation to a lookup table can be accomplished easily by bilinear interpolation. To support interactive exploration, lookup tables must be computed quickly enough.

In the following, we discuss some general concepts of 2D TF specification before we discuss the special cases of gradient-based and distance-based TFs. The dimensions of the TF domain are denoted by V_0 and V_1 (recall Eq. 6.1), in which V_0 represented the voxel values and V_1 represented the gradient magnitude.

Although in principle the TF domain might have even more dimensions, there are no successful applications in routine medical visualization. This is probably due to the fact that the complex specification of such transfer functions is not well suited for the clinical routine.

11.2.1 HISTOGRAMS FOR 2D TF SPECIFICATION

As we have discussed for 1D TF design, the histogram presentation aids the TF specification. Each item in the histogram represents a small range of values in both dimensions. Therefore, we have to consider 2D histograms, which raise the question of how frequency along the two dimensions might be displayed effectively.

Visualization of 2D Histograms   The frequency of each item may be encoded in different ways, for example as height in the third dimension. Due to occlusions, however, this is not an effective technique. A more effective technique is to map frequency to gray values. Often, a frequency of 0 is mapped to white and the maximum frequency is mapped to black. We will see a variety of examples of such 2D histograms in Sections 11.3 and 11.4.

For 2D transfer functions, all considerations related to 1D TFs are also valid: the histogram should be scaled appropriately, taking into account which data actually occur; logarithmic scales might be a useful option; and histogram analysis may facilitate TF specification. The idea of probing is even more valuable for designing 2D TFs. Users select individual voxels or small regions (in 2D slice visualizations) and "inquire" their values in both dimensions indicated in the 2D histogram. This feature is essential, because users are not aware of such values.

Conversion of 2D Transfer Functions to Lookup Tables   The issue of transforming the 2D TF to lookup tables is essential, because lookup tables' sizes should take into account the available hardware support (to facilitate interactive exploration). This may reduce the accuracy of TF specification in both dimensions (for example, to 256 data values instead of 4096). The calculation and presentation of the histogram should reflect the sizes of the lookup tables to which the transfer functions are transformed. Therefore, frequencies are not calculated for each pair of possible values along the two dimensions. Instead, frequency reflects a small interval along the V_0 and the V_1 direction, called a bin. Bin size is chosen to decompose the range in both dimensions into a certain number of equal intervals. A typical number of bins is 256×256, which represents a typical size of hardware-supported lookup tables in modern graphic processing units [VEGA et al. 2004]. It is not necessary that the number of bins be equal in both dimensions. Often, more bins are used to sample the intensity dimension compared to a second dimension, such as distance or gradient-magnitude.

Within the 2D histogram, the user might select regions by means of graphics primitives. Rectangles, trapezoids, and triangles are typical shapes of such primitives. Primitives are modified with respect to position and size either by means of direct manipulation or by means of numeric input (see Fig. 11.15). The selection of regions is the first step in deriving a subset of the TF domain. In a second step, the

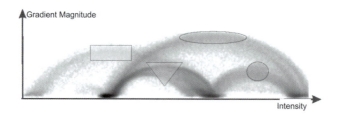

FIGURE 11.15 *Two-dimensional histograms with graphics primitives to select subdomains as basis for 2D TF specification.*

behavior of the TF within that subset has to be specified. A promising approach is the use of component functions.

11.2.2 2D COMPONENT FUNCTIONS

In this subsection, we assume a rectangular region in the 2D TF domain and discuss TF specification based on templates (component functions) for these 2D domains. The following sequence of interactions is carried out to set the parameter of a 2D CF:

- Selection of *intervals* in both dimensions V_0 and V_1
- Selection of a *template* that describes the adjustment of color and opacity values inside the selected ranges
- Selection of an *opacity* and a *color value*

Interval Selection The intervals in the V_0 and V_1 dimension define which tissues are visualized. To specify the intervals, four values have to be defined that represent the borders of ranges (V_{0min}, V_{0max}, V_{1min}, V_{1max}). The adjustment of these values can be supported in different ways.

A valuable support is to convey to the user the relation of the current settings to slice-based visualizations. For this purpose, 2D views of the original radiological data may be combined with colored overlays indicating which pixels are affected by the current interval specification.

Templates The template of a CF defines the optical properties. It is adaptable by the selected intervals of $[V_{0min}, V_{0max}] \times [V_{1min}, V_{1max}]$. For the description of these templates, we need two additional variables: We denote

$V_{0center}$, the center of the line from V_{0min} to V_{0max},
which equals $V_{0min} + (V_{0max} - V_{0min})/2$.
Similarly, $V_{1center}$ equals $V_{1min} + (V_{1max} - V_{1min})/2$.

The following list contains a selection of useful 2D templates (see Fig. 11.16).

1 *Constant values in the selected intervals (2D extension of a 1D box).* The template is assigned a constant level in $[V_{0min}, V_{0max}] \times [V_{1min}, V_{1max}]$. Outside the selected intervals, the template decreases to 0 with high slope or suddenly, without a smooth transition.

2 *Constant values in the selected intervals (2D extension of a trapezoid).* The template is assigned a constant level in $[V_{0min}, V_{0max}] \times [V_{1min}, V_{1max}]$. Outside these intervals, the template decreases slowly towards zero. Zero is reached at the borders of a larger interval $[V_{2min}, V_{2max}]$, $[V_{3min}, V_{3max}]$.

3 *Increasing/decreasing values in the V_0 and in the V_1 dimension.* The template linearly increases from 0 to a maximum between V_{0min} and $V_{0center}$ and linearly decreases above. The CF exhibits the same

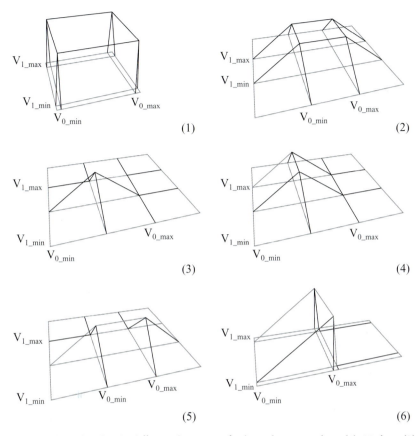

FIGURE 11.16 *Templates that describe different adjustments of color and opacity values: (1) 2D box, (2) 2D trapezoid, (3) pyramid, (4) elongated tent in V_1 direction, (5) elongated tent in V_0 direction, (6) 2D ramp.*

behavior in the V_0 direction, which leads to a pyramidal shape of CF where the maximum is reached at $(V_{0center}, V_{1center})$—the center of the rectangular subdomain selected by the user.

4 Increasing values in the V_0 dimension and constant values in the V_1 dimension. The template is similar to the third. However, the maximum occurs not only at a point but along the line between $(V_{0center}, V_{1min})$ and $(V_{0center}, V_{0max})$.

5 Increasing values in the V_1 dimension and constant values in the V_0 dimension. Similar to template 4, a template with increasing values in the F_2 dimension and constant values in the V_0 dimension. The maximum occurs at the line between $(V_{0min}, V_{1center})$ and $(V_{0max}, V_{1center})$.

6 Increasing values in the V_0 dimension and constant values in the V_1 dimension (2D extension of a 1D ramp). The template linearly increases from 0 to a maximum between V_{0min} and V_{0max} and is constant in the V_1 dimension within $[V_{1min}, V_{1max}]$. Similarly, a template with increasing values in the V_1 dimension and constant values in the V_0 dimension is useful (a ramp in the V_1 dimension).

It is possible to combine CFs so that their intervals overlap. In this case, some rule is necessary to combine several non-zero values from different CFs in the overlapping regions. A simple and general applicable strategy would be to assign the maximum value to the corresponding visualization parameter.

Discussion   The choice of a template is determined by the desired opacity and color function. For example, templates one and two exhibit a constant behavior in the defined intervals. Templates three to six exhibit a linear behavior, which allows the realization of a linearly increasing or decreasing opacity/color TF. In most cases, it is appropriate to use the same template for opacity and color. In addition, the application of different templates can be useful to realize a linear color and a constant opacity at the same time. In these cases, the user has to choose the templates separately.

Color and Opacity Specification   Colors can be selected comfortably from color palettes. If a linear template is selected, a linear interpolation from black to the chosen color is applied. A constant template dyes the tissue with one color. Opacity is defined as numerical input by a scalar value between 0 and 1, which refers to the maximum or constant opacity.

After the selection of intervals, template(s), color, and opacity, the definition of a CF is complete. To create a TF, several CFs can be used.

11.2.3 REPRESENTATION OF 2D TRANSFER FUNCTIONS

The internal representation of 2D transfer functions is essential for their efficient application. One-dimensional transfer functions are usually represented as a linear list of control points with an associated height. The transfer function is an interpolation along the 1D TF domain. Transfer functions for a 2D domain require a 2D grid to represent control points and values.

Regular and Irregular Grids   There is a wide variety of grid types, ranging from *irregular grids*, in which control points may be arbitrarily spread, to *regular grids*, in which the domain is decomposed into equally-sized cells aligned with the coordinate axis. With irregular grids, a sparse distribution of control points in some region may be combined with densely-spaced control points in other regions. This is an important advantage. On the other hand, interpolation schemes along irregular grids are more complex. Another problem is that each and every coordinate has to be explicitly stored.

Regular grids have opposite benefits and drawbacks. Due to their regularity, bilinear interpolation at a particular point P is easy to accomplish by considering the four control points immediately surrounding P. The coordinates of the control points need not be stored. Instead, they are derived by the coordinates of adjacent control points to which only an increment, the constant size of a cell, has to be added. The essential disadvantage of regular grids is their inability to provide more detail locally. Therefore, if high detail is required in a certain region, the whole domain needs to be decomposed into many small cells. Taking into account that transfer functions should be transformed to lookup tables with a limited size, the number of cells may exceed this limit.

Rectilinear Grids   Therefore, neither completely irregular grids nor regular grids are optimal representations for 2D transfer functions. A viable compromise is a rectilinear grid (see Fig. 11.17). This grid type is characterized by rectangular cells aligned with the coordinate axis. The size of cells, however, may be different (which permits a denser representation when required). Rectilinear grids can be stored as 2D arrays with a certain number of control points in V_0, V_1 direction. Within a certain row i, all cells C_{iy} have the same extent in both directions. The same is true for all cells C_{xj} in a column j. We assume that we start with an initial (coarse) resolution of a rectilinear grid. If the user specified control points, either explicitly or by inserting component functions, additional cells in the underlying grid structure are required to reflect the user input. With rectilinear grids, the insertion of a control point p in the 2D array with indices (i, j) requires the insertion of additional control points in the i-th row and j-th column (recall Fig. 11.17, right). These additional control points are necessary to maintain the regularity of the grid.

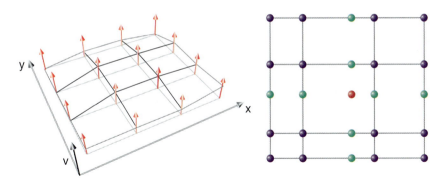

FIGURE 11.17 *Control points are defined over a rectilinear grid to support the transformation to 2D lookup tables. The grid has a coarse initial resolution and is refined if additional control points are necessary. To maintain the rectilinear organization, the insertion of a control point (red point in the right figure) requires the insertion of another row and column of control points (green)* [TAPPENBECK et al. 2006]. *(Image courtesy* ANDREAS TAPPENBECK, *University of Magdeburg)*

With regular Cartesian grids, it would be necessary to insert many control points to achieve higher density in the whole domain. With irregular grids, the insertion of a control point does not require the insertion of any additional point; however, these grids do not have any of the advantages of regular grids.

11.3   GRADIENT-BASED TRANSFER FUNCTIONS

The idea of using gradient magnitude as a second parameter for the TF specification is due to LEVOY [1988b] and was intended to emphasize material boundaries characterized by large gradient magnitudes. In principle, gradient direction could also be used as transfer function domain and could lead to expressive visualizations. However, there are no clinically relevant examples of such visualizations. Basically, gradient magnitude makes it possible to differentiate between homogeneous regions and transition regions. This differentiation is very effective for emphasizing material boundaries in medical visualizations. Gradient magnitude is usually exploited to guide the opacity TF. This is often referred to as opacity-weighted gradient magnitude. Figure 11.18 gives two examples of such visualizations.

11.3.1 GRADIENT ESTIMATION AND STORAGE

Employment of gradient magnitude in the TF domain requires an estimate of gradients. Gradients represent first-order derivatives estimated in discretely sampled data based on some difference (recall Sect. 6.3.2). It is recommended that a low pass filter be applied before the gradient calculation is actually carried out, as gradients are very sensitive to noise.

For high-quality shading, the gradient direction is essential and the accuracy of the approximation strongly determines the visualization result. Here, we are interested in the gradient magnitude, and the accuracy demands are less. Therefore, simple approximations such as central differences are common. Gradient magnitudes may be determined on the fly or precomputed and stored in a separate *gradient volume*. The computation of a gradient can be efficiently accomplished by means of a gradient filter, usually a $3 \times 3 \times 3$ filter that is iteratively applied to the volume and applies the selected differentiation scheme. A scheme of volume rendering by means of gradient-based TFs is shown in Figure 11.19.

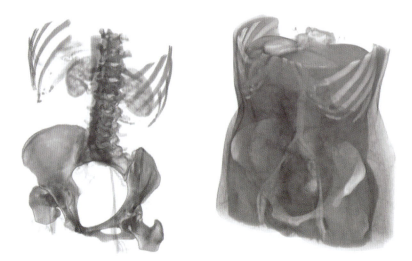

FIGURE 11.18 *Two volume renderings of CT abdominal datasets. Opacity-weighted gradient magnitude specification is applied to highlight transitions. Left: bony structures are visualized; right: the air-skin boundary is accentuated. (Images courtesy HOEN-OH SHIN and BENJAMIN KING, Hannover Medical School)*

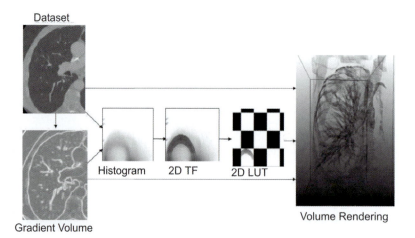

FIGURE 11.19 *Direct volume rendering by means of precomputed gradient magnitude information. (Adapted from STOELZEL [2004])*

11.3.2 USER INTERFACES FOR GRADIENT-BASED TRANSFER FUNCTIONS

User interface design for adjusting gradient-based visualizations is challenging. Again, this process may be supported substantially by presenting a 2D histogram. Gradient magnitude is less standardized than intensity values. The values depend on the reconstruction filter as well as on the voxel spacing. Therefore, fixed presets with respect to the gradient magnitude direction are only applicable if exactly the same image acquisition parameters are used.

In the 2D histogram, gradient magnitude strongly differs, with some very high values and a lot of smaller values. A linear scale would not allow the detection of weaker boundaries in the histogram. Therefore, it is recommended to employ a logarithmic gray level scale for gradient magnitude. The TF specification may be accomplished by means of the interaction facilities discussed in Section 11.2. The specification of rectangular subdomains combined with 2D component functions is a powerful interaction facility. Together with the 2D histogram presentation and slice-based visualizations of the affected regions, TF specification may be carried out effectively. In Figure 11.20, we present an example where a volume rendered image is shown along with its TF specification, carried out by means of 2D histograms.

Arcs in Gradient Magnitude/Intensity Histograms   To provide dedicated support for gradient-based TF specification, it is necessary to investigate the characteristics of the gradient magnitude/intensity histogram. The 2D histograms of gradient magnitude and data values are characterized by *arcs* that represent the transition between two tissue types (see Fig. 11.15). These arcs can be explained by means of the boundary model illustrated in Figure 11.4. Due to the smoothed appearance of a boundary, there is not a single peak in gradient magnitude for a particular value. User interfaces for gradient-based TF should employ the characteristic arcs. In principle, two different ways are possible to support the user.

- Arcs may be automatically detected and parameterized to derive transfer functions, which are subsequently fine-tuned by the user.
- The user may be provided with graphics primitives that are appropriate to select arcs.

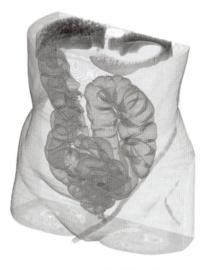
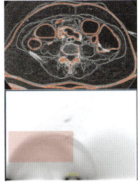

FIGURE 11.20   *The volume rendering (on the left) emphasizes the boundary of the colon, as well as the air-skin boundary. The opacity TF is combined by two rectangular regions in the 2D histogram (lower right), each corresponding to one transition. The rectangles impose a condition to the gradient magnitude as well as to data values. All voxels that fulfill these conditions (those included within the rectangles) are highlighted in the 2D slice visualization (upper right)* [SHIN et al. 2003]. *(Images courtesy HOEN-OH SHIN, Hannover Medical School)*

Automatic Determination of Arcs If the 2D histogram exhibits distinct and clear elliptical arcs, such as the histogram analysis of the tooth dataset (see Fig. 11.21), the determination of these arcs is feasible by means of special algorithms that detect ellipses or parts thereof, e.g., [XIE and JI 2002]. In Figure 11.22, a parabola and an ellipse are fitted to an arc in the histogram. In general, a better fit is obtained with ellipses.

However, if data from the clinical routine are involved, these 2D histograms exhibit a noise level too high for automatic detection of arcs. At least currently, no algorithm is able to reliably identify such arcs. With the interactive specification of arcs, expressive visualizations can be achieved. It should be noted that the gradient magnitude/intensity histogram strongly depends on the particular acquisition parameters, such as the reconstruction filter in CT scanning. In particular, hard reconstruction filters lead to noisy histograms (see Fig. 11.23). The renderings by means of gradient-based TFs may be considerably improved by means of noise reduction filters (see Fig. 11.24).

Interaction Techniques to Specify Half-Elliptical Arcs As support, interaction facilities might be provided which allow the easy parameterization of elliptical arcs [VEGA et al. 2003, STOELZEL 2004]. An additional aid for the user is showing which parts of the data are mapped to non-zero opacity with a particular TF specification (see Fig. 11.25).

Reference TFs for Gradient-Based Visualizations The concept presented in [REZK-SALAMA et al. 2000b] may be extended to gradient-based TFs. This was accomplished in [VEGA et al. 2003] in order to effectively

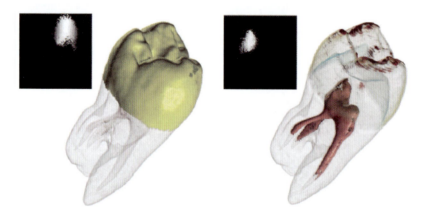

FIGURE 11.21 *Volume renderings of the wide-spread and easy to visualize tooth dataset, which is characterized by the histogram of Figure 11.15. TF specification by data centric analysis [KINDLMANN and DURKIN 1998]. The 2D TF is presented in the inset [PFISTER et al. 2001]. (Image courtesy HANSPETER PFISTER, MERL)*

FIGURE 11.22 *Different geometric shapes (left: an ellipse, right: a parabola) are fitted to the 2D histogram of intensity and gradient magnitude. The ellipse fits better in general. The histograms refer to the tooth dataset (recall Fig. 11.21) where the arcs are clearly represented. (Images courtesy DIANA STÖLZEL, University of Magdeburg)*

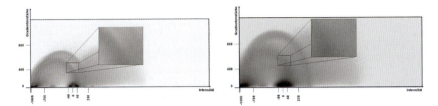

FIGURE 11.23   The gradient magnitude/intensity histogram for a CT dataset. The left dataset was acquired with a soft reconstruction filter, whereas the right image was acquired with a hard reconstruction filter. The adjustment of gradient magnitude–based TFs is easier to accomplish with soft reconstruction filters resulting in a less blurred histogram. (Images courtesy DIANA STÖLZEL, University of Magdeburg)

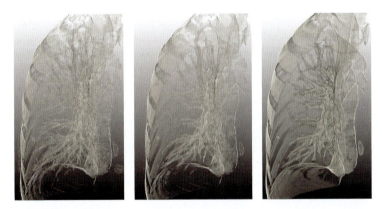

FIGURE 11.24   Gradient magnitude–based visualization of lung vasculature. Left: application to CT data with a hard reconstruction filter. Middle: the CT data were exposed to median filtering. Right: with median and Gaussian filtering, the data were preprocessed to provide improved conditions for gradient magnitude–based transfer functions. (Images courtesy DIANA STÖLZEL, University of Magdeburg)

FIGURE 11.25   TF specification by means of a 2D histogram and slice-based visualizations [STÖLZEL 2004]. (Images courtesy DIANA STÖLZEL, University of Magdeburg)

generate high-quality renderings of cerebral MRI data. They designed a reference function for a particular dataset and transformed the histogram of new datasets to the reference dataset to adjust the transfer function correspondingly. The technique was employed for diagnosis of cerebral aneurysms. For highly standardized image acquisition, the automatic adjustment turned out to be feasible and reliable.

11.4   DISTANCE-BASED TRANSFER FUNCTIONS

In this section, we discuss a special class of multidimensional TFs, where *distance* is employed as a second parameter (in addition to the image intensity). With the use of distance in the TF domain, the local control of the mapping process may be facilitated. Distance refers to reference surfaces of anatomical structures, such as organs. Distance-based TFs require that the reference structures be segmented in advance.

Distance-based TFs are motivated by the fact that the interest of the user is often determined by the distance to reference surfaces, such as margins around a tumor or regions close to an organ's boundary. With distance-based TFs, it is possible to deliberately show voxels that have a certain distance to the (curved) organ surface. If this distance is continuously changed, the user may inspect an organ by slicing orthogonal to the organ surface, which may be very effective, for example, in the search for lung nodules in CT thorax data [DICKEN 2003]. The general concept for distance-based volume rendering is shown in Figure 11.26.

The definition of distance-based 2D TFs is initiated by selecting an object to which the distance specification refers. Subsequently, the distance of all voxels to the boundaries of the selected object will be computed and stored in a separate *distance volume*. Based on this information, the user may start to create a distance-based TF by selecting and composing 2D component functions (recall Fig. 11.16). The intervals in the distance and intensity dimension are chosen by means of the 2D histogram (see Fig. 11.27). Similar to other kinds of TF specification, a valuable support is to convey which voxels are actually affected by the current settings. This can be accomplished by means of 2D slice visualizations (see Fig. 11.28). All tissue which is light-blue colored (intensity interval) and located between the two red lines (distance interval) is visualized with the related CF.

The brightness of a point in the histogram represents the quantum of tissue that features the related values in the two dimensions. Figure 11.27 gives an example for a 2D histogram based on intensity and distance information and a visualization of selected intervals. The intensity interval is displayed as two vertical bars, the distance interval as two horizontal bars. These bars can be modified interactively using the mouse. The structures in the histogram guide this modification. Each structure represents tissue in a limited distance and intensity interval.

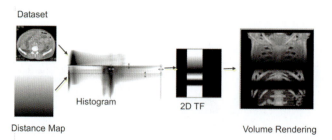

FIGURE 11.26   *Rendering pipeline for distance-based TFs. The distance in this example refers to the top position of the volume instead of a reference shape. (Adapted from [TAPPENBECK et al. 2006])*

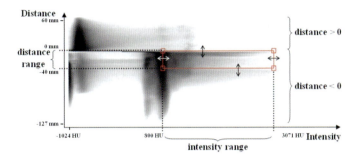

FIGURE 11.27 *2D histogram of distance and intensity information. This view is based on the same dataset as visualized in Figure 11.29. The selected intervals are those that are used to visualize bone [TAPPENBECK et al. 2006]. (Image courtesy ANDREAS TAPPENBECK, University of Magdeburg)*

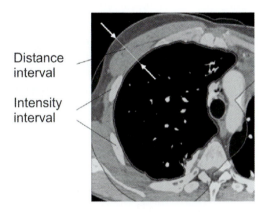

FIGURE 11.28 *The 2D view provides feedback for the selection of an intensity and distance range. Figure 11.28 is based on the same dataset as visualized in Figure 11.29. The distance and intensity interval shown here was used in Figure 11.29 to visualize bones inside a distance interval of [−40 mm, 0 mm] [TAPPENBECK et al. 2006]. (Image courtesy ANDREAS TAPPENBECK, University of Magdeburg)*

11.4.1 DISTANCE CALCULATION AND STORAGE

A crucial issue in the application of distance-based TFs is the representation of distances to the segmented target structure T. For this purpose, an additional volume V_{dist} is required and contains the Euclidean distances to T.

Different metrics might be employed for the calculation of V_{dist}. As an example, the Euclidean distance metric may be employed where the distance D of a voxel p to the reference shape T is calculated as:

$$D(p) = min||p - t||$$

(11.4)

The computational effort of Euclidean distance transform computation is considerable. If a small error can be accepted, there are alternative methods available that approximate the distance calculation. An example is the Chamfer metric, which computes distances with an uncertainty between 2% and 5% with considerably reduced computational effort. The amount of data involved can be strongly reduced by restricting the computation to integer values. Efficient approximate approaches for the distance computation are described in [LOHMANN 1998]. It is important to represent signed distances in order to differentiate between structures inside the target structure and outside. The signs are integrated by a multiplication of the Euclidean distance with 1 for all voxels that are part of T and with -1 for other voxels.

11.4.2 APPLICATIONS

The application of distance-based TFs requires that relevant objects are segmented in advance. In therapy planning scenarios, this assumption is reasonable, since segmentation information is required for different reasons, such as quantitative analysis.

Distance-Based TFs for CT Thorax Diagnostics As a first example, we present the visualization of CT thorax data for diagnostic purposes. In Figure 11.29, where tissue in different distance intervals with respect to the lung surface is visualized, TFs have to be specified in the 2D domain consisting of intensity and distance to the lung surface.

Figure 11.30 shows the color and opacity channels of the TF employed to render Figure 11.29. There are four distance-intensity intervals defined to assign color and opacity values that are unequal.

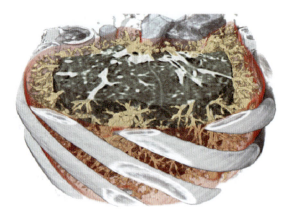

FIGURE 11.29 *Visualization of a lung lobe. Four distance intervals are used according to Table 11.1: bones, lung surface, lung vessels, lung opaque* [TAPPENBECK *et al.* 2006]. (*Image courtesy* ANDREAS TAPPENBECK, *University of Magdeburg*)

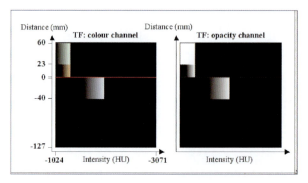

FIGURE 11.30 *Color (left) and opacity channel (right) of TF which is used for visualization in Figure 11.29* [TAPPENBECK *et al.* 2006]. (*Image courtesy* ANDREAS TAPPENBECK, *University of Magdeburg*)

To visualize bones, a distance interval of [−40 mm, 0 mm] and an intensity interval of [100 HU, 1450 HU] is employed. In these intervals, a linear interpolation between black and white in the intensity dimension and a linearly increasing opacity from 0 to 1 in the distance dimension are applied (distance values outside of target structures are negative). For the visualization of the lung surface, lung vessels, and opaque lung tissue, three additional distance-intensity intervals are defined. Table 11.1 and Table 11.2 display the parameters of the used TFs.

In this way, it is possible to visualize opaque tissue in one distance interval and lung surface, lung vessels, or transparent lung tissue in another. In this example, mapping properties are used, which have a constant behavior in the distance dimension. It is also possible to define distance-dependent color and opacity mappings.

In Figure 11.31, we show another example of the way the inner structures of an organ might be visualized by means of distance-based TFs. One lobe of the lung and the internal vessels are visualized. The TF for the lung lobe is specified such that two distance intervals are rendered, the surface [0 mm, 2 mm] and the inner vessels [2 mm, 160 mm]. For both intervals, different opacity and color properties are used. Thus, a special tissue can be visualized in a different manner by exploiting distance, which would not be possible with a conventional 1D TF. In principle, a similar effect could be achieved with gradient magnitude–weighted opacity specification. The interaction, however, would be more tedious.

A second example also refers to the diagnosis of CT thorax data. Here, the idea of anatomic reformatting [DICKEN et al. 2003] is extended: the visualization of slices where each pixel is equidistant to an organ surface. A clinically relevant example for such visualizations is the directed search for lung nodules in the vicinity of the organ surface. With distance-based TFs, different distances can be evaluated within one view, by interactively modifying the shown distance.

	Distance (mm)	Intensity (HU)
Bones	[−40, 0]	[100, 1450]
Lung surface	[0, 1]	[−1024, 3071]
Lung vessels	[1, 23]	[−824, −424]
Lung opaque	[23, 60]	[−1024, −424]

TABLE 11.1   *TF parameters (distance and intensity intervals) of the visualization in Figure 11.29.*

	Opacity	Color
Bones	[0, ..., 1], LI	black—white, LI
Lung surface	0.1, C	red, C
Lung vessels	[0, ..., 1], LI	black—yellow, LI
Lung opaque	1, C	black—light green, LI

TABLE 11.2   *TF parameters (behavior of opacity and color) of the visualization in Figure 11.29. (C—constant values in the intensity and distance dimension, LI—linearly increasing values in the intensity dimension and constant values in the distance dimension)*

FIGURE 11.31 *Three-dimensional visualization of a lung lobe and the vessels inside the lung. The distance-based TF was adjusted so that the surface of the lung lobe and the vascular structures inside are visualized* [TAPPENBECK *et al.* 2006]. *(Image courtesy* ANDREAS TAPPENBECK, *University of Magdeburg)*

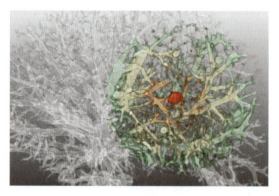

FIGURE 11.32 *Distance-dependent coloring of vessels in the neighborhood of a tumor inside the liver. Four distance intervals are used: tumor red* [0 mm, 3 mm], *vessels red* [−15 mm, 0 mm], *vessels yellow* [−30 mm, −15 mm], *vessels green* [−45 mm, −30 mm] [TAPPENBECK *et al.* 2006]. *(Image courtesy* ANDREAS TAPPENBECK, *University of Magdeburg)*

Tumor Surgery Planning Another application for distance-based TFs is surgery planning, in which the distance from (malignant) tumors to vascular structures is often crucial. A valuable support in such situations can be provided with distance-based TFs with the tumor as reference shape and with colors employed to convey the distance of vascular branches. Such visualizations provide an overview to vascular branches in certain security margins around a tumor (see Fig. 11.32 and Fig. 11.33). It is also possible to completely suppress structures beyond a certain distance of a tumor. These visualizations convey more information than a single distance measure. Figure 11.33 is inspired by liver

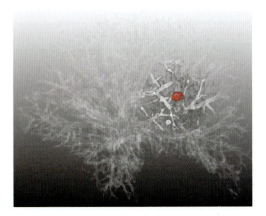

FIGURE 11.33 *Distance-dependent emphasis of vessels (distance to tumor < 30 mm)* [TAPPENBECK et al. 2006]. *(Image courtesy* ANDREAS TAPPENBECK, *University of Magdeburg)*

FIGURE 11.34 *Using distance-based specification for focus and context rendering. The intrahepatic vasculature (left) is the focus object and the liver represents the context. With conventional tagged volume rendering, the visualization of the vasculature is hampered by many occluding liver voxels (middle). In the right image, only the [0–1 mm] distance range of the liver surface is rendered* [TAPPENBECK et al. 2006]. *(Image courtesy* ANDREAS TAPPENBECK, *University of Magdeburg)*

surgery planning and indicates the importance of safety margins. Liver surgery planning is discussed in Chapter 19.

Besides the applications described here, distance-based TFs are probably useful in other medical applications. Thus a distance-dependent removal of undesired tissues can be employed.

11.4.3 DISCUSSION

Distance-based volume rendering is closely related to focus and context rendering [BRUCKNER et al. 2005]. Indeed, distance-based TF specification provides additional facilities for focus and context rendering, as shown in Figure 11.34. The major difference is that the visualization properties are adapted to specific distances. This is crucial for clinically relevant tasks such as tumor surgery planning, where acceptable safety margins are based on established guidelines.

For clinical applications, an efficient interaction is crucial. For 1D TFs, presets are widespread in radiological workstations for all common tasks. Presets are also essential for the distance component of the

TF specification. We discussed such presets for CT thorax diagnostics. As usual, presets are not applicable for all cases. Presets defined for adults are certainly not applicable to children. A facility to adjust and store arbitrary TFs (as new presets) is necessary.

11.5   LOCAL AND SPATIALIZED TRANSFER FUNCTIONS

The expression of volume rendered images is limited by the difficulty to locally control the mapping process. Visual parameters are usually defined globally for the whole dataset. In medical applications, however, selected anatomic structures are relevant, whereas surrounding tissues serve as anatomic context only. In such situations, local TFs [TIEDE et al. 1998] are appropriate because they permit the application of different visual parameters to different subvolumes. Relevant structures may be enhanced by rendering them with higher opacity.

Local TFs are defined for different regions in the dataset. They introduce another feature that increases flexibility and potentially the expressiveness of volume renderings at the expense of an enlarged parameter space. If we want to assign n TFs, we have to define n regions and one TF for each. The use of local TFs is viable if regions are already defined, either as regions-of-interest or as segmentation results.

Local TFs for Detail-and-Context Views   The presentation of an overview combined with the presentation of details on demand is one of the very general principles for effective interactive visualization [SHNEIDERMAN and BEDERSON 2003]. This principle also applies to the exploration of medical volume data. A powerful exploration facility is to let the user navigate through the volume to define a region to be displayed enlarged in a separate detail view. Such views can be enhanced by local TFs, which are fine-tuned to the anatomic structures investigated in them. The use of a local TF for an interesting region was suggested by MEISSNER et al. [1999]. REZK-SALAMA et al. [2000c] defined reference TFs for both an overview as well as a detail view (see Fig. 11.35). Local TFs are designed such that an overview of vascular structures and a detailed analysis of potential intracranial aneurysms is facilitated (see Fig. 11.36). The adjustment of reference TFs (recall Sect. 11.1.2) is very efficient for this kind of exploration.

Local TFs for Segmented Structures   In Figure 11.37, we show an example in which different lung lobes have been segmented. Distance-based TFs are employed, using color to discriminate different lobes. Also, for this kind of analysis it is valuable to carefully define reference TFs as templates.

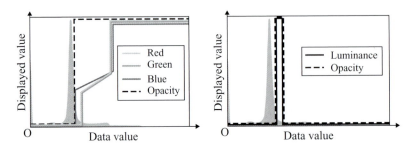

FIGURE 11.35 *Different templates of TFs are used for an overview (left) and detailed analysis (right) of vascular structures* [REZK-SALAMA et al. 2000c]. *(Images courtesy* CHRISTOPH REZK-SALAMA, *University of Siegen)*

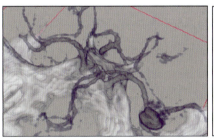 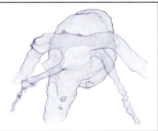

FIGURE 11.36 *Transfer function templates have been manually adapted for the delineation (left) and detailed analysis (right) of vascular structures-[REZK-SALAMA et al. 2000c]. (Images courtesy CHRISTOPH REZK-SALAMA, University of Siegen)*

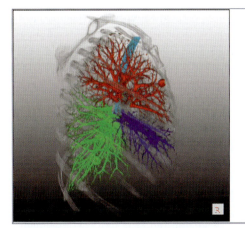 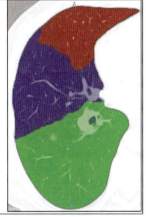

FIGURE 11.37 *Visualization of vessels in different lung lobes. The distance-based TF was adjusted so that only the surface of the lung lobe is visualized to reveal the vascular structures inside [TAPPENBECK et al. 2006]. (Images courtesy ANDREAS TAPPENBECK, University of Magdeburg)*

Compared to a surface visualization of the vessel visualization, direct volume rendering restricted to a lung lobe contains more information, particularly with respect to smaller vessels, which are usually segmented incompletely.

Realization of Local Transfer Functions   Efficient direct volume rendering by means of local TFs is demanding. High performance requires hardware-supported lookup tables that restrict either the number of local TFs or the size of an individual local TF.

With local TFs, the rendering process also has to be modified. A conceptually simple yet inefficient variant is to apply a multipass rendering, in which one region is rendered by means of a different lookup table in each rendering pass. As long as two TFs are employed, for example a focal region and a peripheral region, the stencil buffer of the graphics hardware may be employed. Implementation aspects of local TFs are discussed in detail in [MEISSNER et al. 1999].

Spatialized Transfer Functions   The term *spatialized transfer function* was recently introduced by RÖTTGER et al. [2005]. Spatialized transfer functions are a special variants of local transfer functions in which the positional information is mapped to color. This allows the differentiation of, for example, different objects of the same tissue type, such as different bones. With spatialized transfer functions, expressive images of CTA and MRI head data could be generated.

11.6   SUMMARY

In this chapter, we presented interaction techniques and high-level support for TF design. Transfer functions can be adjusted to emphasize various features in the data. In particular, multidimensional TFs may be employed to create expressive volume renderings. In routine diagnosis and therapy planning, the potential of such visualization facilities, however, can only be realized if the interaction effort can be restricted and the underlying mathematical concepts are effectively hidden.

The most promising approach is a combination of predefined functions, suggestions that are adapted to the histogram of the TF domain, and fine-tuning of facilities to refine presets and suggestions. Except for special applications, fully automatic solutions will not be able to cope with the variety of medical image data. The design of TFs poses some fundamental questions that are typical for providing access to advanced visualization features [GERIG et al. 2002]:

- How much knowledge on the part of the user can be assumed?
- Is it more appropriate to provide guidance in the exploration process without limiting flexibility, or is it more appropriate to restrict parameter settings to some predefined subsets?
- Which context information should be presented to support parameter settings?
- Is it more appropriate to rely on subjective evaluations (selection of thumbnail images) or to guide the process by objective measures, such as those resulting from histogram analysis?

There is a considerable similarity between segmentation and TF design. With segmentation, a binary decision is made as to whether a voxel or a part of it belongs to a certain structure. TF specification is used to visualize and highlight structures. However, visibility is not a binary, but a fuzzy decision based on assigning different opacity values. It is therefore justified to call opacity TF specification a kind of *fuzzy segmentation* [UDUPA 2000]. There is a close relation between segmentation and TF specification with respect to local TFs based on segmentation results. Direct volume rendering that takes segmentation information into account may produce expressive visualizations.

Future Work   A variety of methods is available to support TF specification. For the clinical routine, the idea of a reference TF that is automatically adapted to similar datasets seems to be most promising [REZK-SALAMA et al. 2000b]. In the clinical routine, it is acceptable to limit the flexibility of their specification to explore the data—they need efficient methods to attain sufficiently good visualizations. This approach should be applied to other application areas, carefully evaluated with respect to their limitations, and correspondingly refined. It is also worthwhile to extend this idea to more advanced TFs, such as distance-based TFs. An interesting area for future work is the integrated visualization of several volume datasets after image registration—for example, CT and PET data. Transfer function specification for fused volume data is challenging. Promising first results are presented in [KNISS et al. 2003].

FURTHER READING

PFISTER *et al.* [2001] give an enlightening overview of several approaches presented in this chapter. These approaches are applied to carefully selected CT and MRI datasets, and they discuss how expressive visualizations are attained by means of purely interactive, data-driven, and image-driven specifications.

FANG *et al.* [1998] suggested the analysis of image-properties to combine TF specification with image processing operators, such as edge enhancement, to yield images with some designed properties. Combining image analysis and TF specification is motivated by visualization goals, such as boundary emphasis, with which appropriate image processing *and* TFs yield optimal results even in noisy data, such as those of confocal microscopy. Support for TF design by hierarchical clusterings of material boundaries is described by SEREDA *et al.* [2006]. The idea of local histograms (recall [LINDSTROEM *et al.* 2005]) has been extended and successfully applied to Magnetic Resonance Angiography data [LINDSTROEM *et al.* 2006].

KNISS *et al.* [2002] suggest a local probing of the underlying data using the 2D histograms introduced by KINDLMANN and DURKIN [1998] to detect boundary regions. The user interface to assign color and opacity is advanced and inspiring for those dealing with similar problems. However, it is unfamiliar for many users, and its usability needs to be investigated. An interesting idea is to combine TF design with an analysis of critical isovalues (those that characterize a change in topology) to automatically derive TFs guided by these critical values [FUJISHIRO *et al.* 1999]. BOTHA and POST [2002] argue that fast slice-based previews are essential for TF specification. For this purpose, renditions corresponding to the current TF specification are superimposed on the original slice data. A variety of overlay techniques are introduced. BOTHA and POST [2002] address the problem of providing realistic feedback with respect to the current opacity transfer specification in slices taking into account that opacities accumulate (see also [BOTHA 2005]).

TZENG *et al.* [2003] combine machine learning techniques, such as support vector machines, with a painting metaphor to allow more sophisticated classification. Similar to the reference TF, the TF derived for one dataset can be adapted to another (similar) dataset. For colored volume renderings, color maps have to be defined. This process may also be guided by high-level support regarding human color perception [BERGMANN *et al.* 1995].

The idea of employing distances in the volume rendering pipeline has been presented by KANDA *et al.* [2002] and ZHOU *et al.* [2004] to focus visualizations on a particular region (characterized by the distance to a seed voxel). This idea has been combined with non-linear magnification in the focal region [WANG *et al.* 2005]. An essential aspect of the paper is the realization of smooth transitions between enlarged and "normally" scaled regions of the volume.

A recent idea is to change transfer functions over time along a path [CORREA and SILVER 2005]. An application in medical visualization is to use the centerline of a vascular structure as a path and to parameterize the temporal changes so that the bloodflow can be visually represented.

Three-dimensional ultrasound data is an attractive imaging technique due to the low costs associated with it. However, the data exhibit a low signal-to-noise ratio, and TF design for these data is tedious. A dedicated effort to model tissue boundaries in ultrasound data is described in [HÖNIGMANN *et al.* 2003]. Based on these considerations, boundaries are detected and opacity TF design is directed at illustrating boundaries.

TF design has developed into a large field. We have chosen not to discuss curvature-based TFs in detail, although they considerably enrich the effects achievable by means of volume visualization. The idea of using *curvature* in the TF domain was introduced in [HLADUVKA *et al.* 2000] and enhanced in

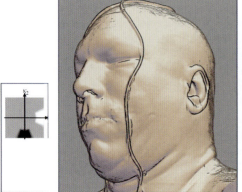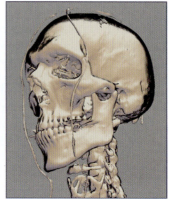

FIGURE 11.38 *Visualizations of the Visible Human dataset by means of curvature information. Left: The transfer function assigns white to ridges and black to valleys. Middle: emphasis on the skin. Right: emphasis on the bones [KINDLMANN et al. 2003]. (Images courtesy GORDON KINDLMANN, Brigham and Women's Hospital Boston)*

[KINDLMANN et al. 2003]. In particular, the principal curvatures κ_1 and κ_2 were employed to emphasize ridges and valleys in volume data and to achieve some effects from non-photorealistic rendering (see Fig. 11.38).

Another interesting field is the design of color-based transfer functions. MORRIS and EBERT [2002] and EBERT et al. [2002] discuss the design of multidimensional color-based transfer functions for photographic volume data using the Visible Human dataset as an example.

Chapter 12

Clipping, Cutting, and Virtual Resection

In this chapter, we describe interaction techniques to explore medical volume data. These techniques have in common that parts of the data are excluded or removed from the visualization. Whereas transfer functions restrict the visualization to those parts with certain properties (intensity values, gradients) in common, clipping excludes certain geometric shapes from the visualization. For many clinically relevant tasks, transfer functions and clip geometries have to be adjusted appropriately. The focus of this chapter is the description of 3D interaction techniques to specify and to modify the clip geometry with medical doctors as intended users. The interaction techniques described in the first part of the chapter are intended for diagnosis. Resection techniques relate to the task of specifying an arbitrarily shaped region that should be removed during surgery. Resection techniques are used to evaluate the basic shape of resections, to determine the resection volume, and, eventually, to explore alternative resection strategies. Cutting techniques relate to the simulation of cutting devices and to the high-quality visualization of cut areas. The largest portion of this chapter is on resection techniques for therapy planning. In the last part, cutting techniques are introduced. These are essential components of surgery simulators, with prospective surgeons as intended users.

Organization We start this chapter with a discussion of the usual clipping procedure with planar faces (see Sect. 12.1. Variants, such as selective clipping (restricting the effect of a clipping plane to certain objects), are discussed with respect to their applications. We continue discussing virtual resection techniques intended for surgery planning. Such areas are usually not bounded by planar faces, because resection areas should be as small as possible to minimize the trauma. The interaction task is thus to specify an arbitrary clip geometry. The intended users for these techniques are experienced surgeons with the goal of investigating the resectability of a particular patient's target organs. After a discussion of general requirements and a description of two simple methods (see Sect. 12.2), we describe a sophisticated approach to virtual resection in Section 12.3. This method is inspired by real surgical procedures, during which the border of the intended resection is marked on the organ's surface.

The most ambitious techniques are those that try to mimic real cut procedures. Such techniques are incorporated in surgery simulators intended for educational purposes. Interest in such systems has grown steadily due to the widespread introduction of minimally invasive surgical procedures with limited visual access and an urgent need for appropriate training (see Sect. 20.6.2). In Section 12.4, we touch upon this area and give a brief overview of the problems to be solved.

12.1 CLIPPING

Clipping is a fundamental interaction technique for exploring medical volume data [HÖHNE et al. 1987]. It is used to restrict the visualization to subvolumes. Clipping planes are translated by the user, and the visualization is continuously updated. Usually, clipping planes can be tilted to optimally represent the target structures. Together with the adjustment of an appropriate transfer function, clipping planes allow the user to effectively specify which portions of the data are visible (see Fig. 12.1 for a diagnostically useful image with a tilted clipping plane).

Rapid feedback is essential for the exploration of the data. In principle, the translation can be accomplished by specifying numbers that represent the coordinates of a clipping plane's center and its orientation. With this indirect method, however, it is very difficult to achieve the desired effect. Clipping is initiated to suppress certain structures. Therefore, it is more intuitive to directly translate and rotate a clipping plane by means of direct manipulation within the 3D visualization. With this interaction style, the clipping plane itself is interactive—representing a 3D widget. The user should be able to recognize whether a clipping plane is currently selected and active. Handles (small iconic arrows) might be displayed to control the translation.

Because clipping planes are widely used, graphics libraries and graphics hardware support their efficient use. In combination with volume rendering, clipping is conceptually easy to accomplish. In the final stage of volume rendering, a voxel is tested as to its spatial relation to the clipping planes. Voxels affected by the clipping plane are discarded completely. Unless the resolution of the underlying volume data is very coarse, or the visualization is strongly enlarged, there is no need to calculate subvoxel representations of the clipping plane. Subvoxel accuracy, however, is desirable in case of illuminated volume rendering to faithfully represent the gradient information. If the clipping plane is moved along the viewing direction, the 3D visualization is similar to conventional slice-based 2D viewing (the difference is that volume rendering is usually semitransparent).

For surface representations—as they are often used for segmented objects—each triangle is tested to determine whether it should be drawn or not. If triangles are larger (covering several pixels in the rendered image), they must be cut, resulting in new vertices. As surface visualizations result in sharp

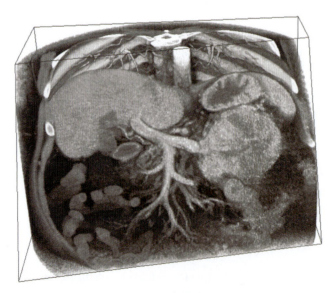

FIGURE 12.1 *By tilting the clip plane vertically, the relationship between the confluence of the superior mesenteric, splenic, and portal veins with the tumor is demonstrated* [JOHN and McCLOY 2004]. *(From the Op3D Project, NIGEL W. JOHN, University of Wales, Bangor, and RORY F. McCLOY, Manchester Royal Infirmary, UK)*

boundaries, the effect of not calculating precise boundaries with cut triangles is more obvious than in volume rendering. In Figure 12.2, a clipping plane is applied to a hybrid rendering of surface and volume representations. By moving the clipping plane, the spatial relations between a mucosal swelling, the optical nerve, and the surrounding bones becomes obvious.

If other than planar clipping is desired, the complexity increases considerably [LORENSON 1993]. A variety of methods for non-linear clip geometries employs the z-buffer of the graphics hardware. As an example, LUCAS et al. [1992] enable arbitrary convex clip geometries by means of rendering into two z-buffers, where the additional z-buffer contains the boundaries of the clip volume.

12.1.1 SELECTIVE CLIPPING

A special variant of clipping, primarily used if segmented structures are available, is *selective clipping*. Selective clipping was introduced almost simultaneously in [LORENSON 1993] and in [TIEDE et al. 1993] and is now widely used to emphasize structures (those not affected by clipping) while presenting contextual information (structures which are partially visible due to clipping, see also [HAUSER et al. 2001]). The original application of selective clipping was anatomy education with the VOXELMAN. Selective clipping is also useful for surgery planning (see Fig. 12.3). second example refers to planning endonasal surgery. Particularly for visualizations of the head region, symmetry might be employed by placing a selective clipping plane as a (vertical) symmetry axis. The concept of selective clipping is not bound to planar faces; it may be applied in combination with arbitrary clip geometries (see Sect. 12.2).

Selective clipping is also feasible without segmentation information. Here, different transfer functions might be applied for regions affected by the clipping plane and the remaining volume. Another common application of selective clipping is *thin-slab volume rendering*, where two synchronized parallel clipping planes specify a set of volume slices that are rendered (see Sect. 8.3.2).

Selective Clipping with Boolean Textures   An elegant and efficient way to accomplish selective clipping is the use of Boolean textures (textures in which each element is in one of two possible states) [LORENSON 1993]. For clipping purposes, the two states relate to being inside or outside of a surface, and this state is mapped to opacity (either zero and full opacity or, more generally, high and low opacity).

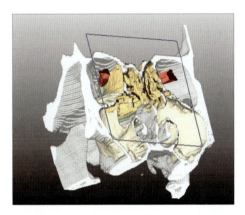

FIGURE 12.2   *Volume and surface rendering with a clipping plane for exploring spatial relations in a CT head dataset. The image was created for sinus surgery planning. (Image courtesy DÖRTE APELT, MeVis Bremen; CT data courtesy THOMAS SCHULZ, University of Leipzig)*

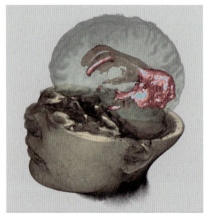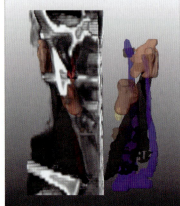

FIGURE 12.3 *Selective clipping. Left: the brain and the ventricles are rendered completely, while the surrounding tissue is clipped. (Courtesy* HORST HAHN, *MeVis Bremen; MRI data provided by* BURKHARD TERWEY, *Institute for Magnetic Resonance Imaging Diagnosis, Bremen) Right: the vertical symmetry is used for selective clipping of a CT head dataset. The image was created for planning neck dissections (view from dorsal). (Images courtesy* JEANETTE CORDES, *University of Magdeburg, CT data courtesy by* THOMAS SCHULZ, *University of Leipzig)*

Boolean textures are constructed by implicit function, such as quadrics. The clip geometry is specified by using a distance metric that is applied to the implicit function (the state of the elements represents whether they are closer than a threshold-distance to the implicitly defined surface). In the general terms of texture-mapping, this means that the Boolean texture is indexed by using the current distance value.

Planes, spheres, cylinders, and cones are examples of objects that can be easily defined with implicit quadrics to be used as clip geometry. This concept is not bounded to a single implicitly defined surface (recall [LORENSON 1993]). With Boolean textures, clipping is activated in the scan conversion step of rendering.

12.1.2 BOX CLIPPING

The combination of six clipping planes might be used to define a subvolume. This variant is often referred to as box clipping. Box clipping is useful for exploring a region in detail, for example, an aneurysm (see Fig. 12.4) or the region around a tumor (see Fig. 12.5). Three Dimensional widgets, such as a handlebox manipulator, might be used to define and modify the clip box. The subvolume might be presented as a single isolated view (see Fig. 12.5) or combined with an overview. The latter variant allows the user to locate the subvolume.

12.2   VIRTUAL RESECTION

Resection refers to the removal of tissue during a surgical intervention. The planning process of such an intervention using medical volume data and derived 3D models is referred to as *virtual resection*. Virtual resection is a core function of many intervention planning systems. In difficult cases, the exploration of resection strategies directly answers the questions of whether or not the resection is feasible at all and how it can be optimally performed. The specification of a virtual resection can be used for a quantitative analysis with respect to the volume of the intended resection or the percentage of an organ to be removed.

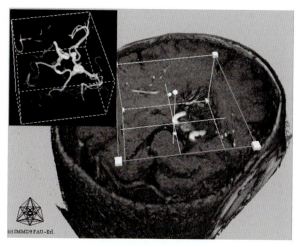

FIGURE 12.4   Box clipping for the analysis of an intracranial aneurysm. A detailed view of the region of interest is combined with an overview rendering. Within the detailed view, a finer resolution of the data is employed. A handlebox manipulator is employed to specify the clipping box [HASTREITER et al. 1998]. (Image courtesy PETER HASTREITER, University Erlangen-Nuremberg)

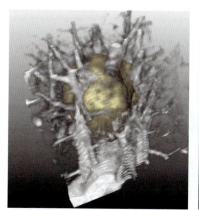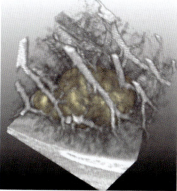

FIGURE 12.5   Local volume rendering for the evaluation of the surrounding of a tumor in CT thorax data. The tumor is visualized as an isosurface whereas the vascular structures around it are rendered as direct volume rendering. (Images courtesy VOLKER DICKEN, MeVis Bremen)

Technically, a user must be able to specify an arbitrarily-shaped 3D clip geometry as resection volume, and the clip geometry should be rendered quickly and accurately. Modern APIs such as OpenGL, however, only support clip geometries composed of clipping planes.

Virtual resection functions have to fulfill several requirements:

1 The user must be able to specify a virtual resection intuitively and precisely.
2 The Modification must be supported to change virtual resections—either to correct them or to explore other variations.
3 Virtual resections should be visualized immediately, with high quality.

The first requirement means that medical doctors should be able to decide in detail which anatomic structures will be removed. For example, the question of whether or not a certain vascular structure will be cut is often essential, because it may have a strong effect on the whole procedure, particularly if a blood vessel needs to be reconstructed. The modification of a virtual resection is crucial to support a flexible exploration of resection strategies and also to correct undesired effects, which occur rather often. It is essential that virtual resections be modified on different scales. The last requirement refers to the update and rendering mechanism, which is used to show the effect of a virtual resection. This aspect has to be considered, since medical volume data is typically large and the update should take place with interactive frame rates.

There are several possible methods to specify a virtual resection. Some methods are restricted by the shape of the resections that can be produced. For example, the extrusion of shapes, such as prisms, along a path cannot serve as a general approach to define arbitrarily shaped resection volumes. On radiological workstations, such techniques are primarily provided to explore data and to enable an unoccluded view to relevant anatomical structures.

In the following, we focus on real-time interaction techniques that can produce any desired shape of the clip geometry. We briefly describe two straightforward approaches to virtual resection in the following subsections. In Section 12.3, we introduce an approach inspired by real surgical procedures.

12.2.1 SPECIFICATION OF VIRTUAL RESECTIONS BY ERASING

A straightforward method to virtual resection is to use scalable 3D shapes as *erasers* that remove the touched tissue [PREIM et al. 2001]. The interaction is similar to *volume sculpting*, a modeling technique in which voxel-based tools are used to iteratively add or remove material [GALYEAN and HUGHES 1991]. The internal representation is inspired by constructive solid geometry (CSG), which has been extended to constructive volume geometry [FANG and SRINIVASAN 1998, CHEN and TUCKER 2000]. Boolean operations on voxel values are used to decide which subset of voxels should be drawn. Virtual resection by means of Boolean operations on voxels are fast, however the visual quality is limited by the resolution of the underlying voxel grid. Aliasing effects are obvious, particularly if strongly enlarged visualizations are generated, in which individual pixels are visible.

The system presented in [PREIM et al. 2001] employed the strategy described above and was used with two-handed input, one hand to rotate the visualization and one to specify the resection. A multilevel undo mechanism and special 3D image processing operations to postprocess the resection volume were included, for example, to remove holes. As a major difference from volume sculpting, a link to the original radiological data must be established. The 2D visualization is used to present the result of the virtual resection in each slice (see Fig. 12.6). However, the evaluation with physicians clearly showed that it was too difficult to specify resections precisely enough. This was particularly the case for fine-grained resection planning with respect to the vascular tree.

12.2.2 SPECIFICATION OF VIRTUAL RESECTIONS BY DRAWING
ON SLICES

Another approach to virtual resection is inspired by the communication between surgeons and radiologists discussing a resection; some slices of the CT or MRI data are copied to paper, and the resection is marked by drawing on the slices with a pen or mouse. Clearly, by drawing on slices a resection can be specified as precisely as desired. However, this process is time-consuming if the entire resection volume should be specified, since often some 50−100 slices are involved. This kind of virtual resection

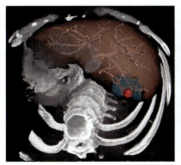
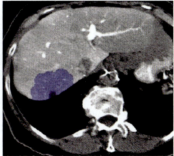

FIGURE 12.6   *A resection area specified by "erasing" liver tissue with a sphere (left). Selective clipping is used to show the branches of a vascular tree that would be affected by the real resection. The result of the virtual resection is also displayed in a 2D view (right)* [PREIM et al. 2001].

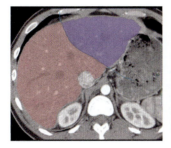

FIGURE 12.7   *Virtual liver resection by drawing on the slices. Using the liver segmentation mask, only one line per slice has to be drawn across the organ. In the 2D view (left image) the contour has been specified on selected slices. After the interpolation, the result is displayed in the 3D view. The virtually resected and the remaining portion of the liver are separated to support the evaluation of the shape of virtual resections.*

is very similar to segmentation with edge-based methods and can therefore be strongly enhanced with interpolation methods. Instead of drawing on all slices, the user might skip many slices on which the contour is computed by shape-based interpolation. While the interaction with this approach is restricted to 2D, the 3D visualization is used to evaluate the result and to discuss the shape of resections (complex shapes are difficult to realize surgically and would lead to long resections with more loss of blood). Figure 12.7 illustrates this approach to virtual resection.

12.3   VIRTUAL RESECTION WITH A DEFORMABLE CUTTING PLANE

In the following, we describe a more sophisticated approach to virtual resection based on a surface representation of an organ, usually achieved with explicit segmentation of that organ. This approach has some similarities with the virtual resection based on erasing in the data (it includes 3D interaction) and some similarities with the virtual resections by drawing on the slices. The user draws lines on the (3D) surface of an organ to initialize the virtual resection. From these lines, which characterize the boundary of the cutting plane, a mesh is generated that represents the initial cutting plane. The plane is deformed locally to fit the lines drawn by the user.[1] This cutting plane can be interactively modified to refine the virtual resection. The virtual resection method described in the following is based on [KONRAD-VERSE et al. 2004].

12.3.1 DEFINING CUTTING PLANE BOUNDARIES

The idea of specifying a cutting plane based on drawing actions dates back to [YASUDA et al. 1990] and was refined by DELINGETTE et al. [1994]. With this approach, the user employs a 2D pointing device and controls the movement of a cursor on a 3D surface. This control is accomplished by casting a ray from the viewpoint through the 2D point (marked by a pointing device) to the 3D position on the surface. The mapping considers the current projection parameters and the z-buffer to select the first visible surface along the projection ray [ZACHOW et al. 2003a]. The mouse motion is tracked, sampled, and represented as a sequence of 3D coordinates. Note that the coordinates are not restricted to coincide with the vertices of the mesh.

The most urgent requirement concerning the usability of this approach is to provide the user with immediate feedback. If this is not sufficiently achieved, he or she will be interrupted from the drawing process, resulting in a serious distraction from the task. This requirement might be difficult to fulfill if the geometric model is very large, due to the effort needed for the ray traversal. ZACHOW et al. [2003a] suggest in such cases to buffer the coordinates of the mouse and to start the ray traversal for all registered mouse coordinates after the mouse button is released. As immediate feedback, only the 2D screen positions are connected with straight lines and displayed during the mouse movement. This is a reasonable trade-off between the desired speed of the interaction and the accuracy of the feedback.

Definition of the Cut Path   If the sampled points of the mouse movement are sufficiently close to each other, the cut path is well defined and the individual connections between points do not matter. Otherwise, different strategies of connecting points on the surface are possible. The Euclidean distance represents the shortest distance between successive points. However, the straight line between these points may intersect the organ's surface. A better choice is to employ the geodesic shortest path which connects points on the 3D surface with a path on that surface (see Fig. 12.8 left).[2] These and other issues of mesh cutting are discussed in [BRUYNS et al. 2002].

The drawing process can be carried out using a mouse as input device or using a pen directly pointed on the screen or a digitizing tablet. The latter is more intuitive (see Fig. 12.9). More advanced interaction hardware, such as tactile input devices, have also been explored for defining borders of cutting planes (see Fig. 12.10). However, their use is only reasonable if tactile feedback is combined with (real-time) collision detection, which represents a challenge due to the high frame rate required for tactile feedback. Currently, the use of such devices is not familiar for the majority of prospective users, and it is questionable whether the effort to use them is justified.

12.3.2 GENERATION OF THE INITIAL CUTTING PLANE

Before we describe the algorithm, the term *covariance matrix* needs clarification. The covariance matrix of a set of 3D coordinates $P(x_i, y_i, z_i)$ is computed according to Equation 12.1.

---

1   In contrast to clipping planes, which are actually flat, cutting planes after deformation are two manifolds but not planar.

2   A geodesic is a generalization of the notion of a "straight line" to "curved spaces." The definition of geodesic depends on the type of "curved space." If the space carries a natural metric, then geodesics are defined to be (locally) the shortest path between points on the space. The term "geodesic" comes from geodesy, the science of measuring the size and shape of the earth. In the original sense, a geodesic was the shortest route between two points on the surface of the earth. (Source: Wikipedia)

FIGURE 12.8 *Euclidean (left) versus geodesic distance (right) between surface points.*

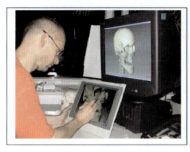

FIGURE 12.9 *Cut boundary specification specified with a pen on a digitizer tablet, which is shown enlarged in the right image. (Image courtesy STEFAN ZACHOW, Zuse-Institute Berlin)*

$$\mathrm{COV}(P,P) = \begin{pmatrix} \sum_{i=0}^{n}(x_i \cdot x_i) & \sum_{i=0}^{n}(x_i \cdot y_i) & \sum_{i=0}^{n}(x_i \cdot z_i) \\ \sum_{i=0}^{n}(y_i \cdot x_i) & \sum_{i=0}^{n}(y_i \cdot y_i) & \sum_{i=0}^{n}(y_i \cdot z_i) \\ \sum_{i=0}^{n}(z_i \cdot x_i) & \sum_{i=0}^{n}(z_i \cdot y_i) & \sum_{i=0}^{n}(z_i \cdot z_i) \end{pmatrix} \qquad (12.1)$$

The following algorithm describes how lines drawn by the user on a surface are converted into an initial cutting plane. The lines are transformed into a pointset (representing each pixel of the digitized mouse movement).

1   **Determine the oriented bounding box of the lines drawn by the user.** The oriented bounding box is computed by a principal component analysis (PCA) of the pointset P forming the lines. Let P be the pointset and v the center of gravity (see Eq. 12.2):

$$P = \{p_0, p_1, ..., p_n\} \subseteq R^3$$

$$v = \frac{1}{n+1} \sum_{i=0}^{n} p_i \qquad (12.2)$$

FIGURE 12.10 *Cut boundary specification with a tactile input device (Phantom, SensAble Technologies).* (Image courtesy STEFAN ZACHOW, *Zuse-Institute Berlin*)

The center of gravity is subtracted from all points p_i resulting in a new pointset P^{norm}. Based on this pointset, the covariance matrix A is determined (see Eq. 12.3).

$$A = \mathrm{COV}(P^{norm}, P^{norm}) \tag{12.3}$$

As can be seen in Equation 12.1, A is a symmetric 3×3 matrix and therefore has three real-valued eigenvectors e_i and three eigenvalues $0 \leq \lambda_0 \leq \lambda_1 \leq \lambda_2$. The eigenvectors define a local right-angled coordinate system of the pointset. Based on the normalized eigenvectors, a transformation matrix M_{rot} can be specified; this matrix describes the mapping from P into the local coordinate system (see Eq. 12.4). With this rotation, a point $p \in P$ is transformed to local coordinates with respect to the cutting plane (see Eq. 12.5).

$$M_{rot} = (|e_0|, |e_1|, |e_2|) \tag{12.4}$$

$$y = M_{rot} \cdot p - v \tag{12.5}$$

2   **Determine the orientation and extent of the cutting plane.** The vectors (e_1, e_2) corresponding to the two largest eigenvalues (λ_1, λ_2) resulting from the PCA of A define the cutting plane's orientation. The plane is determined by the following equation, where x represents any vector that satisfies Equation 12.6.

$$E : (x - v) \cdot e_0 = 0 \tag{12.6}$$

where $\cdot$ denotes the dot product (see Fig. 12.11 for a sketch). This strategy is useful for organs for which the extent is clearly different in the three directions. In case of an almost spherical object, the eigenvalues are very similar and the orientation of the initial plane might be unexpected.

3   The center of the cutting plane (E) is chosen to be v, the center of gravity of P. This plane is then divided into a regular grid with quadrilateral cells. The resolution of the mesh is essential for

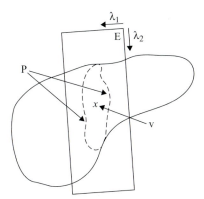

FIGURE 12.11 *Definition of the plane E based on the (dashed) lines P drawn by the user. v represents the center of gravity of P, and λ_1 and λ_2 point in the directions of the two largest eigenvectors of E. (Image courtesy ARNE LITTMANN and OLAF KONRAD VERSE, MeVis Bremen)*

the modification. It is chosen so that it will satisfy the requirements of surgeons to specify typical resection shapes. The default size of the mesh is determined by (λ_1, λ_2); the extent of the mesh is twice as long in the direction of the corresponding eigenvectors. Formally, we can specify the cells of the mesh as follows (see Eq. 12.7), where m and n represent integer values addressing the cells at the mesh and k is a real-valued constant that determines the resolution of the mesh.

$$y_{m,n} = m \cdot k \cdot e_1 + n \cdot k \cdot e_2 \tag{12.7}$$

4   **Project Y into E.**

$$y_i^P = (110) \cdot y_i \tag{12.8}$$

5   **Calculate displacements**. The mesh is displaced in the e_0 direction to fit the original pointset. This is accomplished by scanning all grid cells $y_{m,n}$ and testing whether any of the transformed points y_i are projected in this cell. Figure 12.12 shows that only a small subset of the cells are affected by the y_i. The displacement $d_{m,n}$ is computed as the maximum z-component of all y_i that are projected into $d_{m,n}$ (see Fig. 12.13).

$$d_{m,n} = \|z_i\|_{\max} * \mathrm{sgn}(z_i) \tag{12.9}$$

where the z_i represent the z-component of the y_i and "sgn" represents the signum-function.

$$z_{m,n}^0 = y_{m,n} + d_{m,n} \cdot e_0 \tag{12.10}$$

As an alternative, $d_{m,n}$ could be set to the average distance of the relevant points. The maximum, however, seems better suited, because strong bulges specified by the user are better represented.

6   **Smoothing**. After these distances have been calculated for the whole mesh, they are processed by Laplacian smoothing (recall Sect. 7.3.3). By default, 100 iterations are carried out, and the 3×3 neighborhood is considered ($s = 1$ in Eq. 12.11). However, the smoothing is only applied to the grid cells that have not been displaced in step 5. This prevents the points specified by the user from being translated.

$$z_{m,n}^r = \alpha \cdot \frac{1}{(n+1)^2} \cdot \sum_{i=-s}^{s} \sum_{j=-s}^{s} z_{m+i,n+j}^{r-1} + (1-\alpha) \cdot z_{m,n}^{r-1} \tag{12.11}$$

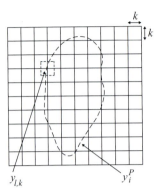

FIGURE 12.12 *Grid and spacing on the plane after projection. (Image courtesy* ARNE LITTMANN *and* OLAF KONRAD VERSE, *MeVis Bremen)*

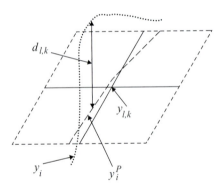

FIGURE 12.13 *The points are displaced orthogonal to* E *to reflect the position of the lines drawn by the user. (Image courtesy* ARNE LITTMANN *and* OLAF KONRAD VERSE, *MeVis Bremen)*

The resulting mesh is rendered as a polygonal surface, which appears smooth due to Gouraud shading. The user can switch between two 3D visualization modes; one shows the complete scene while the other is focused on the structures of interest—namely the tumor, the vessels, and the deformable cutting plane. Higher order interpolations, such as cubic B-splines, can alternatively be used to display the grid smoothly. However, in our experience, this additional computational effort does not pay off.

The initial mesh for the virtual resection is based on a PCA of the points drawn by the user. An alternative would be to use linear regression to fit a plane to the points (for example by minimizing the least square error). The advantage of the PCA method is that not only is the plane defined, but also the extent of the face can be derived with respect to the eigenvalues. The PCA also results in a local coordinate system for the plane, which is employed to determine a grid.

12.3.3 MODIFICATION OF VIRTUAL RESECTIONS

The resection can be refined by translating grid points. The user can define the sphere of influence as well as the amplitude of the deformation. Both functions are controlled with a direct manipulative style (mouse movements at the point that is modified). Usually, the deformation direction is orthogonal to the plane. Within the sphere of influence, the cosine is employed to determine the extent of the displacement (the extent of the displacement decreases from a maximum at the selected point to zero at the border of the sphere of influence). Besides the local modification of the grid, there is also a facility to translate the whole mesh.

Application in Liver Surgery Planning   As only the tumor and the vascular systems are essential for the decision where to cut, the organ surface can be hidden at this stage. Figure 12.14 illustrates the situation when the user starts to modify the plane. In the right image of Figure 12.14, the deformable plane is modified (the modification is slightly exaggerated to show the principle). Figure 12.15 presents an example of an initial plane defined for liver surgery planning.

Of course, the surgeon can visually check the resection in 2D as well. Despite the intuitive clearness of 3D visualization, this ability is indispensable, because sometimes not all important structures can be segmented with reasonable effort. The planning process may be enhanced by a volume calculation of both the resection and of the remaining part (see Fig. 12.16). Such figures are an important criterion for estimating the operation risk—for example, in liver surgery.

12.3.4 DISCUSSION

Some general facilities are required to modify virtual resections. An undo facility is essential, because inadvertent changes occur rather often. The second general strategy is to make use of both the 2D and the 3D visualization for the modification of a virtual resection. Modifying the contour of the resection volume in a 2D slice view requires converting the sequence of pixels into a parametric curve that can be manipulated by translating control points. Interpolation should also be used for the modification (recall Sect. 12.2.2). The virtual resection is typically carried out after several image analysis steps (segmentation of pathologic structures, vascular systems, and organs). The segmentation for the respective organ is required for the virtual resection with the deformable cutting plane.

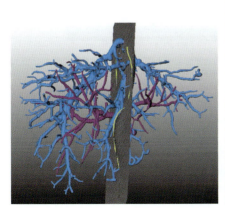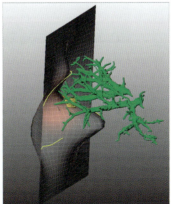

FIGURE 12.14   *Left: as soon as the cutting plane is initialized, the surrounding organ is removed to support fine-tuning of the plane with respect to blood vessels. Right: the initial cutting plane is translated with an adjustable sphere of influence. (Images courtesy* MILO HINDENNACH, *MeVis Bremen)*

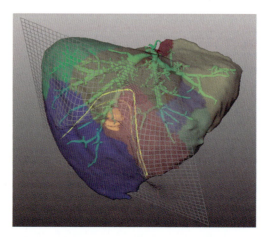

FIGURE 12.15   *Based on the two lines drawn on the object surface, an initial resection has been specified that might be refined by the user. (Image courtesy* ARNE LITTMANN, *MeVis Bremen)*

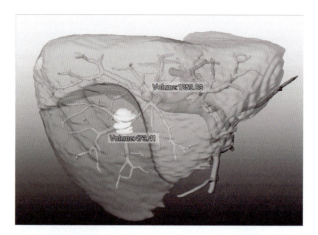

FIGURE 12.16   *The result of a virtual resection by means of a deformable mesh, including information about the volume of the virtually resected and of the remaining tissue. (Image courtesy* ARNE LITTMANN, *MeVis Bremen)*

Transformation of the Resection Boundary to a Resection Plane   There are viable alternatives to the transformation described above, in which a planar projection of the boundary is deformed to represent the points specified by a user. *Minimal surfaces* are another well-defined representation of a surface specified by a given boundary. Minimal surfaces are constructed so that they exactly match the given boundary. The vertices of the inner parts of the surface are determined in an optimization process that generates a surface with the minimum surface area. Minimal surfaces are also characterized by a very low mean curvature, which is a nice property since surgeons also prefer (near) planar surfaces. Figure 12.17 compares minimal surfaces and a flat projection plane as it was computed from a given 3D contour as the initial

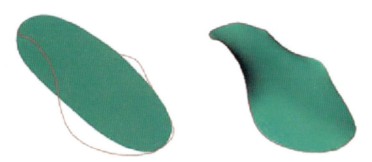

FIGURE 12.17 *A flat surface (left) as approximation of the given boundary compared to a minimal surface (right) of the same boundary. (Image courtesy* STEFAN ZACHOW, *Zuse-Institute Berlin)*

step. Computational methods to generate minimal surfaces are described in [PINKALL and POLTHIER 1993].

Visualization of the Virtual Resection Once the resection plane is specified, the organ should be visualized with the defined cutting region removed. There are many ways to accomplish this. At the surface level, the mesh may be adapted. A coarse approximation is to (completely) remove all primitives (e.g., triangles) influenced by the cut. Depending on the resolution of the grid, this may be regarded as a crude approximation. Remeshing intersected primitives allows the generation of accurate representations of the cut surface. BRUYNS et al. [2002] give a survey on remeshing strategies after mesh cutting. An essential goal of these algorithms is to limit the introduction of new primitives. To generate a closed surface model of an organ after virtual resection, the resection plane and the remaining surface model of an organ must be combined.

In connection with surgical planning, volume models are available and may be employed for a voxel-based visualization. For this purpose, the clipped portion as well as the remaining portion of the organ's volume must be converted into a voxel representation. This representation may be used for either direct or indirect volume rendering. The latter has been performed to generate Figure 12.15.

Application Areas of Virtual Resection Techniques The virtual resection methods described above are illustrated by means of examples from liver surgery, as well as osteotomy planning. A variety of other application areas exist. For example, in craniofacial surgery, conventional planning is based on drawing lines on a stereolithographic model of the patient's bones. Using the techniques described above, the same kind of specification may be applied to plan surgical interventions with 3D models (see Fig. 12.18). Compared to conventional planning methods, there is considerably more flexibility, and it is possible to evaluate the effects of different strategies [ZACHOW et al. 2003a].

12.3.5 EFFICIENT VISUALIZATION OF VIRTUAL RESECTIONS

Efficiency is an important aspect for virtual resection and clipping with arbitrary geometries. For convenient use, the visualization must be immediately updated. It is desirable that a high update-rate be achieved without compromising accuracy (e.g., calculations based on a lower resolution).

The resection volume has to be explicitly represented in a similar way, as segmentation results are stored in binary tagged volumes in which 0-valued voxels represent the clipped geometry. This process can be realized with hardware support or solely in software that is less dependent on particular graphics hardware.

FIGURE 12.18 *Conventional osteotomy planning based on a stereolithographic model (left). Virtual resection based on a 3D model of the patient's bones (middle, right). (Image courtesy* STEFAN ZACHOW, *Zuse-Institute Berlin)*

A very fast hardware-based approach has been described by WESTERMANN and ERTL [1998]. It relies on the stencil buffer to decide which voxels should be included in the visualization. WEISKOPF et al. [2003] described the representation and visualization of complex clip geometries exploiting modern PC graphics hardware. The multitexturing capabilities can be used to combine volume rendering with arbitrary clip regions represented as 3D texture. With this strategy, the corresponding intensity values per voxel are multiplied, resulting in a value of 0 for voxels that are clipped.

In [PREIM et al. 2001], a software-based solution based on hierarchical brick data structures was presented. With this method, it can be decided very quickly which portions of the visualization need to be updated. In general, only subvolumes affected by the local modification of the resection plane are redrawn. For this purpose, the intersection between all modified triangles of the deformable cutting plane with brick boundaries are computed. The resection plane itself is also voxelized and internally represented in the same way as any other segmented object.

Concerning the quality and comprehensibility of the visualization, shading is very effective. In particular, if the boundary of the clip geometry is represented as a (smoothed) surface, it is feasible to achieve high-quality, very efficient shading by employing the usual graphics hardware support.

12.3.6 VISUALIZATION PARAMETERS

Once a virtual resection is specified, it can be displayed in different ways. The realistic approach—to remove the resection volume entirely—is only one of several possibilities. The resection volume can be regarded as a new visualization object that can be flexibly parameterized. In Figure 12.16, for example, it is rendered semitransparently. Other objects within the resection area, such as vascular structures, are not affected. More generally, it might be specified whether objects are clipped against resection volumes or not (recall *selective clipping* in Sect. 12.1.1). Also, it is often useful to display tumors and vascular structures in resection volumes. Again, such adjustments can be specified as default values to enhance the reproducibility and effectiveness of intervention planning.

12.3.7 EVALUATION

As an initial attempt to understand how surgeons use deformable cutting planes, an informal evaluation has been carried out at the Center of Medical Diagnosis Systems and Visualization (MeVis Bremen) with four surgeons. The use of the deformable cutting plane was regarded as promising, which is probably due to the fact that an aspect of real surgical procedures (marking resection lines on organ surfaces) is simulated with this approach.

Some of the surgeons' comments reveal desirable refinements. For example, the distance from the resection plane to a tumor should be continuously displayed to indicate the security margin associated with the virtual resection. In this vein, a useful option would be to prevent the plane from moving too tightly to the tumor (defining a "no go" zone around the tumor). Another desirable function is to render the deformable cutting plane semitransparently.

Usually, the initial viewing direction when the user starts drawing on the organ's surface is not appropriate for drawing the line on the entire organ. Currently, this process must be interrupted to rotate the virtual camera. This process (sequences of drawing, rotating, drawing, . . .) can be improved using two-handed input, where one hand (using one input device) is used to control the virtual camera, and the other hand is used for the specification of the virtual resection. People are very effective in coordinated movements with both hands (see [HINCKLEY *et al.* 1998] for the use of two-handed input in neurosurgery planning).

12.3.8 COMBINATION OF RESECTION PROPOSALS AND VIRTUAL RESECTION

A completely different approach to resection specification is to propose to the surgeon which part of an organ has to be resected. Such a proposal has to consider the position and size of a pathology and the position and structure of important adjacent structures. In tumor surgery, for example, surgeons attempt to completely remove a 10-mm security margin around a tumor. On the other hand, the remaining tissue should be supplied and drained by blood vessels. Such resection proposals have been introduced for liver surgery [PREIM *et al.* 2002a]. The territories that have been presented as resection proposals turned out to be a good orientation for surgeons (see Chap. 19 for a detailed discussion). However, the shape of the resection volumes was often too complex to be realized precisely. While the purely interactive specification of a virtual resection, for example with the deformable cutting plane, does not consider security margins and blood supply, a combination of both is desirable. As a first step, the resection proposal might be presented as additional information when the deformable cutting plane is specified (see Fig. 12.19). A closer integration of both methods could convert the resection proposal in an initial cutting plane that is subsequently modified.

Another way to combine "intelligent" resection proposals and interactive resection specification is to initiate an analysis of vascular structures when the cutting plane is modified. As a result, all branches of vascular structures that are either in the resection volume or are dependent from those branches are highlighted to indicate the consequences of the intended resection. This analysis can be accomplished with precisely the same methods employed for the generation of resection proposals.

12.4   CUTTING MEDICAL VOLUME DATA

Cutting facilities are important for surgery simulation. With such functions, users move a cutting device—often a *virtual scalpel*—through medical volume data and simulate cutting procedures. Collision detection (determining which parts of the geometric model are touched by the cutting device) and tactile feedback are essential for educational purposes when prospective surgeons are trained. The development of surgery simulators is driven by similar reasons to the development of flight simulators used to train pilots. A visually realistic environment and handling should be used to avoid the risks of real-world training with living patients and to reduce the cost involved with training by an expert. In contrast to flight simulators, where the user moves primarily in a static scenery, surgery simulators have to consider many interactions

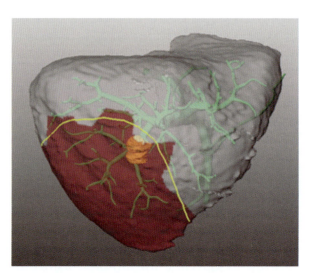

FIGURE 12.19 *Combining resection proposals and interactive resection for liver surgery planning. The resection proposal (dark red) is presented while the user interactively specifies the resection region (with the yellow line). In general, the interactively specified resection line is close to the proposal but smoother and easier to realize in actual surgery. Due to the perspective, it seems erroneously that the tumor is outside the resection proposal. (Image courtesy* ARNE LITTMANN, *MeVis Bremen)*

between cutting devices and human tissue, such as elastic deformations and bleedings. We restrict the discussion here to the cutting procedures in surgical simulators in which the geometry affected by the cutting is regarded as static (and not as deformable soft tissue). In Section 20.6, we give a brief overview of the effects that have to be simulated and also consider soft tissue deformation.

12.4.1 HIGH-QUALITY REPRESENTATION OF CUT SURFACES

As a first step, surgical tools, such as knives, scissors, and drilling devices, are to be included in the 3D scenario. Also, a behavior is associated with the models and facilities to parameterize the geometry. As the tools are moved and operated in the virtual environment, collision detection algorithms are employed to determine whether a cut is performed and which part of the overall model is affected. Surgical cutting is a challenging application for collision detection, because the requirements for accuracy and speed are high, and arbitrary (not necessarily convex) shapes are involved.

If virtual resection is accomplished by means of a volume representation, the resolution of the cut surface is limited to the resolution of the underlying data. For the visualization of irregular cut surfaces that arise after cutting or drilling, this is not appropriate because sharp edges lead to severe "staircase" artifacts. PFLESSER et al. [2002] developed a visualization technique that considers the cut surface at subvoxel resolution and estimates surface normals based on gradients. With their method, tools such as a drilling device can be moved arbitrarily in 3D space. Once shape, position, and orientation are specified, the cutting is voxelized with a weighted filtering technique (see Fig. 12.20). PFLESSER et al. [2002] emphasize that existing cut surfaces should be preserved (the term progressive cutting is used for this feature). Therefore, the portion of an existing cut region that is unaffected by the new cut is determined, resampled, and combined at subvoxel resolution with the new cut (see Fig. 12.21).

The method has been applied in a simulator for petrous bone surgery (surgery in the ear region). A virtual scalpel and adjustable drilling devices might be employed to practice surgery (see Fig. 12.22).

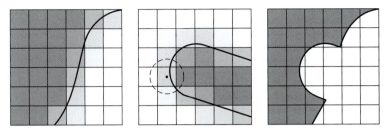

FIGURE 12.20 *Volume cutting. Left: two-dimensional representation of an object surface. Note the different shades of gray representing the partial volume effect. Middle: voxelization of the cutting tool, in which the shades of gray simulate the partial volume effect. Right: the resulting cut surface* [PFLESSER et al. 2002]. *(Images courtesy* BERNHARD PFLESSER, *University Hospital Hamburg-Eppendorf)*

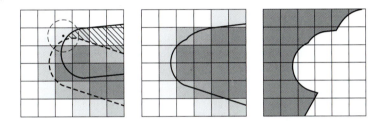

FIGURE 12.21 *Progressive cutting. Left: only the left area has to be considered. Thus, the existing cut (dashed contour) has to be resampled. The support of the filter kernel is indicated by the gray pixels. Middle: representation of the new cut surface. Right: the resulting cut surface (compare with Fig. 12.20)* [PFLESSER et al. 2002]. *(Images courtesy* BERNHARD PFLESSER, *University Hospital Hamburg-Eppendorf)*

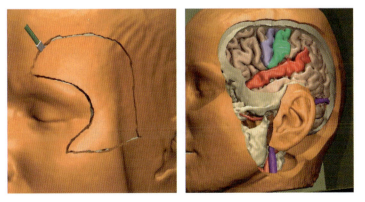

FIGURE 12.22 *Cutting with a virtual scalpel (left). The result is shown in high quality (right)* [PFLESSER et al. 2002]. *(Image courtesy* BERNHARD PFLESSER, *University Hospital Hamburg-Eppendorf)*

The precise simulation of drilling procedures is motivated by the delicate structures in this area (e.g., the facial nerve).

A six DOF-haptic input device, a Phantom® from SensAble Technologies, is used to provide the tactile feedback necessary for surgery training. Appropriate tactile or haptic feedback is difficult to achieve, because a high frame rate is required (1000 updates per second [AVILA and SOBIERAJSKI 1996]).

12.4.2 VIRTUAL RESECTION AND SURGERY SIMULATION

There are some differences and some similarities between surgery simulation and virtual resection. Virtual resection techniques are intended for experienced surgeons who are actually planning a surgical procedure. Specialized hardware, such as those for tactile feedback, should not be assumed for virtual resection. In general, virtual resection is not focused on the realistic simulation of a procedure but on decision support based on the interaction with the data of a particular patient. A brief overview of surgery simulation is given in Section 20.6.

12.5   SUMMARY

After a brief discussion of clipping techniques for diagnostic viewing and exploration of spatial relations, we focused on virtual resection for experienced surgeons as target users. These users need decision support concerning the resectability of a patient. Such decisions depend, among other things, on the anatomical variants of a particular patient.

Virtual resection is an essential feature for surgery planning, particularly for internal organs, such as the kidney, liver, and pancreas. We described two straightforward methods and one more advanced method. With the advanced method (based on a deformable cutting plane), the user can precisely control the orientation of the plane and the displacements orthogonal to the plane by drawing lines on an organ's surface. Fine-tuning methods on different scales are provided to support precise interaction. Both techniques—virtual resections based on drawing in the slices—are clinically used, and the deformable cutting plane has been successfully used in clinical settings for liver surgery planning (see Chap. 19) and planning craniofacial interventions (recall [ZACHOW et al. 2003a]). Careful evaluation is needed to compare the usability and utility of these methods.

Despite many differences, there are some similarities between virtual resection and surgery simulation concerning the representation and the visualization of the data. An additional volume dataset is needed to represent what has been virtually resected. This is necessary to reverse cutting actions and to virtually operate without changing the underlying medical volume data. Hardware support for 3D texture-mapping combined with multitexturing (using both volumes simultaneously for rendering) is essential for a good performance. Virtual resections and cutting actions only affect a small amount of the overall data. To achieve a fast update of the visualization, the rendering should be restricted to the involved region.

While this work is inspired by and targeted at clinical applications, it might be relevant to other areas of interactive 3D visualization as well. We agree with WEISKOPF et al. [2003] who claim that volume clipping has an importance for the exploration and analysis of volume data similar to that of transfer function design. While transfer function design is based on data (intensity values, gradient magnitude, etc.), volume clipping is more intuitive, because the interaction is related to the geometry.

FURTHER READING

Many aspects of surgery simulation, realistic cutting, and particularly soft tissue deformation could only be touched in this chapter. A long-term effort at endoscopic surgery simulation has been carried out at the Research Center of Karlsruhe. Many aspects of real interventions have been carefully modeled in their KISMET (Kinematic Simulation, Monitoring, and Off-Line Programming Environment for Telerobotics) system [KÜHNAPFEL et al. 2000]. An advanced system for craniofacial surgery simulation is described in [KEEVE et al. 1999].

Concerning soft tissue deformation, there are different methods established so far. Accurate physically based representations of manipulations, such as poking, tearing, pulling, and cutting, might be achieved with Finite Element Methods (FEM) (first used by [BRO-NIELSEN and GRAMKOW 1996] for surgery simulation). These solutions, however, are computationally very expensive. A simplified version of FEM solutions (considering only linear elasticity) is presented by [NIENHUYS and VAN DER STAPPEN 2001]. Mass-spring models are generally faster at the expense of accuracy. The majority of surgery simulators are based on these models (see, for example, [DE CASSON and LAUGIER 1999]).

An important aspect of surgery simulation is the representation and subdivision of a grid used for the elasticity simulation. Primarily, tetrahedral grids are used for this purpose. For cutting, it is common to subdivide the affected tetrahedra [BIELSEN et al. 1999]. As an alternative, the nodes are repositioned in [NIENHUYS and VAN DER STAPPEN 2001] to prevent the complexity of the grid from increasing considerably.

Chapter 13

Measurements in Medical Visualization

The quantitative analysis of spatial relations in medical visualizations is crucial for many tasks in diagnosis and treatment planning. The extent of pathological structures is often relevant to discussion of therapeutic options (e.g., tumor staging). Another frequently required measurement concerns the distance between pathological structures and structures at risk (e.g., major blood vessels). This distance often determines whether a surgical intervention or another local therapy is feasible. Quantitative analysis is a useful addition to the qualitative visual assessment. Furthermore, measurements are crucial for quality assurance and for documenting diagnostic or therapeutic decisions.

Currently, it is common practice in radiology to use 2D measurement tools to define measures such as distances, diameters, areas, or angles by means of planar slices of radiological data. This, however, gives only a rough estimation for spatial measurements, such as the extent of a 3D object.

To overcome the limitations of 2D measurements, 3D measurement tools are required to integrate measurements in 3D visualizations. Advanced radiological workstations provide such functions. However, their use can be difficult, because existing line-based 2D measurement tools have been simply transformed to 3D.

The development of usable 3D measurement tools to be applied in the context of a complex 3D visualization is not straightforward, since enough depth cues must be provided to assess the position and orientation of such a measurement tool. Otherwise, the precision suggested by numbers is misleading (recall the discussion of 3D widgets in the introduction of this part). An important aspect of medical 3D visualizations is that they are derived by the analysis of slices of radiological data. Therefore, it is desirable to combine 3D views with 2D views of the original slices where measurement points should be visible and modifiable within the slice data. The interactive use of measurement tools is the most flexible approach. However, it requires a certain effort on the user's part and can introduce inaccuracies. Therefore, we shall analyze which interaction tasks are of primary importance to support these tasks by an automatic approach.

Introductory examples As a first example for measurements in a specific therapy planning task, we briefly discuss Live Donor Liver Transplants (LDLT), a kind of transplantation where a healthy volunteer donates a part of his or her liver to a recipient. The feasibility of such a transplantation depends strongly on the vascular architecture of the potential donor's liver. Among others, the hepatic vein is assessed based on CT angiography. If there is an accessory hepatic vein, its diameter is determined. If it is above 5 mm, the vein needs to be reconstructed. To decide whether there is enough space to perform the vessel reconstruction, the distance between this portion of the accessory vein to the confluence of the left, right, and middle hepatic vein is determined. These measurements are taken with radiological workstations based on the 2D axial display (see Fig. 13.1). For documentation, the measure is annotated (see the emphasized elliptical region in the lower part of Fig. 13.1).

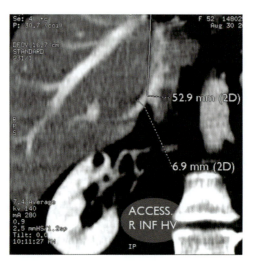

FIGURE 13.1 *Two-dimensional measurements for LDLT-donor evaluation with a radiological workstation. The diameter of an accessory vein (≈ 7 mm) and the distance to the confluence of the left, right, and middle hepatic veins was determined. (Image courtesy* CHRISTOPH WALD, *Lahey Clinic, Boston)*

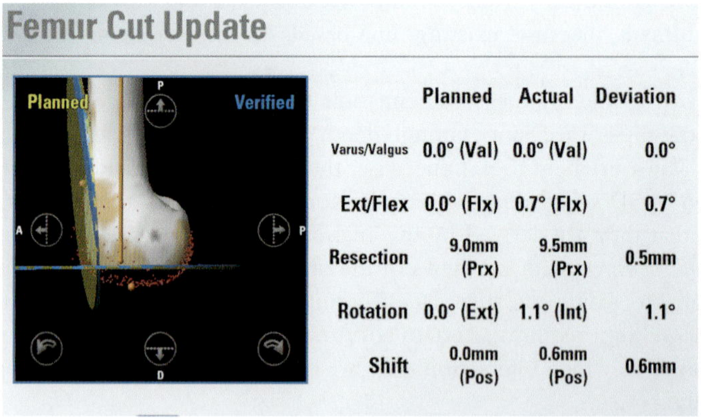

Femur Cut Update

	Planned	Actual	Deviation
Varus/Valgus	0.0° (Val)	0.0° (Val)	0.0°
Ext/Flex	0.0° (Flx)	0.7° (Flx)	0.7°
Resection	9.0mm (Prx)	9.5mm (Prx)	0.5mm
Rotation	0.0° (Ext)	1.1° (Int)	1.1°
Shift	0.0mm (Pos)	0.6mm (Pos)	0.6mm

FIGURE 13.2 *Verification of femoral cut with respect to the planned cut during navigated total knee replacement in* VectorVision® *knee. The orientation of the image is conveyed by "A" and "P" (anterior and posterior) as well as "P" and "D" (proximal and distal).* © *BrainLAB AG 2005. All rights reserved.*

As a second example, we briefly look at a special kind of orthopedic surgery, namely total knee replacement, in which an implant is chosen and its placement has to be carefully planned. A variety of measures are defined in a planning process and stored. During surgery, these measures are used to compare the current position and orientation of the implant with the preoperatively planned values (see Fig. 13.2). Finally, a therapy report—including actual measures of the implant position and orientation—is automatically generated (see Fig. 13.3).

Organization We discuss general design issues for interactive measurement functions in Section 13.1. We continue by introducing the design and implementation of a measurement library, including tools for

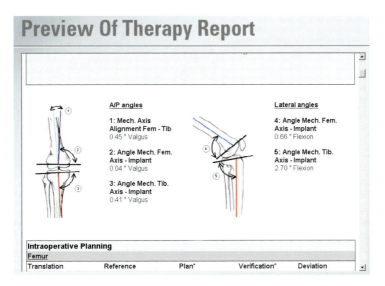

FIGURE 13.3   *Illustration of treatment results with angles, gaps, and alignments in a report.* © *BrainLAB AG 2005. All rights reserved.*

defining distances, angles, areas, and volumes in 3D and 2D visualizations (see Sect. 13.2 through see Sect. 13.5).

Finally, we explain how important distance measurement tasks may be solved automatically and efficiently. In particular, we discuss an algorithm for minimal distance calculation that has its origin in robotics (see Sect. 13.6). Furthermore, the extent of objects as well as the angle between the orientation of elongated objects can be derived automatically. Angular measurements are essential in orthopedic and facial surgery—for example, to assess the major orientation of elongated bones or teeth (see Sect. 13.7).

13.1   GENERAL DESIGN ISSUES

In the introduction of this part, we introduced the term 3D widget, which lays the foundation for the discussion of general design issues. An example of a 3D widget for measurement is presented in Figure 13.4. This 3D widget allows the approximation of the extent of anatomic structures by a box. Eight handles are used to scale the 3D widget, and six handles allow the translation of the widget in 3D.

For the color of measurement widgets, a suggestion should be generated that takes into account which colors can be discriminated preattentively and are recognizable on typical backgrounds in gray level visualizations. The choice of such colors may be guided by [SCHUMANN and MÜLLER 2000], Section 5.4, who propose eight colors that can be easily discriminated.

13.1.1   USABILITY

The usability of measurement tools depends on a number of presentation parameters. Among them are font parameters (size, color) and line style parameters (line width). The selection of presentation parameters is guided by the following requirements:

- *Clear relation between measurements and objects.* It should be clearly recognizable which object or region a measurement refers to.

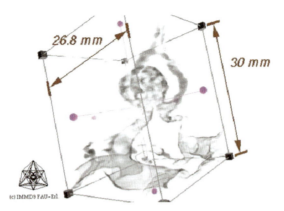

FIGURE 13.4 *Based on the graphics library OpenInventor, a 3D widget was developed to provide a measure corresponding to the current extent of the 3D widget (in x-, y- and z-directions). Each of the small cubes at the corners can be selected and translated separately to scale the widget. The spheres represent the handles for translating the 3D widget. In this example, the approximate size of an aneurysm is determined* [HASTREITER et al. 1998]. *(Image courtesy* PETER HASTREITER, *University of Erlangen-Nürnberg)*

- *Distinct assignment of measurement numbers to measurement tools.* If several measurements are included in a visualization, it is necessary that the affiliation of a measurement number to a measurement tool be shown unambiguously. The placement of numbers relative to a measurement tool and the choice of presentation parameters, such as color, are important for this goal.
- *Flexibility.* Due to the large variety of the spatial relations to be analyzed and due to personal preferences, it is important that the default values concerning font and line parameters as well as units of measurement tools are adjustable.
- *Precision.* Direct manipulation exhibits a lack of precision, which is an essential drawback for measurement tasks. To enable increased precision, it should be easy to zoom in on the visualization. For the specification of measurements, a reduced scale compared to the normal radiological viewing is appropriate. Incremental transformations with cursor keys should be provided to support the fine-grained modifications. In addition to the normal cursor keys, two additional keys (e.g., PageUp and PageDown), may be employed for six DOF (degrees of freedom) interaction. Furthermore, transformations of measurement tools may be specified by numbers, because this interaction style allows arbitrary precision.

All measurement numbers should be presented using two-dimensional text displayed parallel to the viewport. Thus, numbers remain legible after rotations. For optimal readability, the font size used for the numbers must be adapted when the camera is zoomed. Otherwise, measurement numbers appear excessively large or small. To prevent too many changes, the font size might be adapted in discrete steps. A sans serif font is advisable for optimal legibility.

3D Translate Widget For direct-manipulative 3D measurements, all vertices of measurement tools should be translated by means of a six DOF widget. The geometry of such a widget may be composed of three orthogonal 3D arrows. The vertices must be large enough to be easily selected. Spheres and cones are employed to make vertices selectable, independent of the viewing direction. A 3D translate widget is required for the modification of all measurement widgets.

13.1.2 ACCURACY AND UNCERTAINTY

For the interpretation of measurements, the accuracy and the measurement unit itself are crucial. The actual measurement number representing, for example, the distance between two selected voxels is determined using the *voxel spacing-specification* in the radiological data. Such specifications are part of the metainformation added to the image data, for example, in the DICOM-standard.

The voxel spacing-specification provides a lower bound for the accuracy. The selection of a position has an uncertainty of half of the voxel spacing (the uncertainty of the measure is the Euclidean distance between a vertex of a voxel and the center of this voxel). As an example, for a voxel spacing of $0.7 \times 0.7 \times 4.0$ mm, the uncertainty due to the resolution is about 2 mm. A distance measurement is based on the selection of two positions and therefore has twice the uncertainty of an individual selection (in our example about 4 mm).

Presenting this information along with the measurement (+/− uncertainty) is a useful option [HASTREITER *et al.* 1998]. However, such an indication can be misunderstood as a guarantee that the uncertainty is not larger than indicated. This guarantee is obviously not possible. The uncertainty discussed above does not consider whether the user has selected the "right" voxels. Moreover, it is uncertain whether the structures involved are completely visible in the data. As an example, malignant lesions in contrast-enhanced images are often considerably larger than the dark spot representing them in the CT data. In general, a reliable confidence interval cannot be specified.

13.2   3D DISTANCE MEASUREMENTS

Distance measurements are probably the most frequent measurements carried out in medical diagnosis. Two 3D widgets, *distance lines* and *rulers*, are essential to estimate distances in medical visualizations. Distance lines are employed to define distances between objects or diameters of objects as precisely as possible. Rulers, on the other hand, are used to roughly approximate the magnitude of structures, similar to the way a scale is used in maps. Both measurement tools are described in the following subsections (based on [PREIM *et al.* 2002b]).

13.2.1 DISTANCE LINES

Distance lines are employed to precisely determine Euclidean distances. Distance measures are crucial for surgery planning—for example, to evaluate whether there is enough space to separate certain structures or whether vessel reconstruction is required. Similar tasks may be the estimation of the size of the neck of an aneurysm (see Fig. 13.5 left) or the resection planning for lung tumors (see Fig. 13.5 right) [BARTZ *et al.* 2003a].

Geometry   A distance line widget consists of two small cones (3D representation of arrowheads) and a thin cylinder (3D representation of the line). With this design, the distance line is a recognizable 3D object. As an additional orientation aid, distance lines may cast a shadow. To ensure legibility of the measurement number against backgrounds with varying colors, the number might be embedded in a rectangle (see Fig. 13.6). It is reasonable to render the rectangle semitransparently to avoid occlusion of the medical data.

Behavior   The distance line is created with rubberbanding—a direct-manipulative interaction technique for the creation of graphics primitives in which the shape is updated continuously until the mouse is released (see FOLEY *et al.* [1995]).[1] The distance number is also updated continuously (see Fig. 13.7).

---

1   Rubberbanding is widely used in drawing programs to create lines, rectangles, and ellipses.

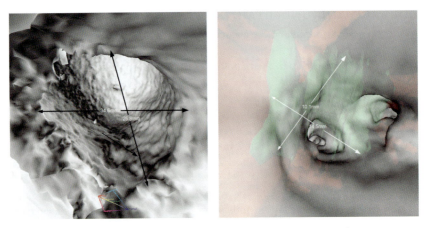

FIGURE 13.5 *Distance measurements in virtual endoscopy (see Chap. 16). Left: the neck of a large aneurysm of an anterior cerebral artery. Right: a tumor in the left lung. The pulmonary arteries are shown in red.*

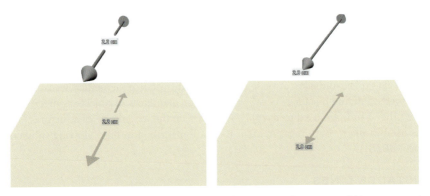

FIGURE 13.6 *Distance lines and their shadow projection. In the left image, enough space is available to accommodate the number inside the distance line, while on the right, it is located near an endpoint. The accuracy is adapted to the voxel spacing [PREIM et al. 2002b].*

FIGURE 13.7 *Rubberbanding for the initialization of a distance line. (Image courtesy HENRY SONNET, University of Magdeburg)*

The placement of the number is adapted to the line length; if the line is long enough, the cylinder is interrupted in the center for the placement of the number. Otherwise, the number is placed near one of the endpoints of the distance line. The distance line is calibrated by exploiting the voxel spacing attribute in the header information of radiological data.

The vertices can be translated by means of the 3D translate widget described above. To simplify adjustments of translated vertices and thus to support measurements of distances between object surfaces, snapping should be provided (as an optional feature). With this feature, the endpoint translated by the user is attracted by the surface of an object as soon as the distance to the surface drops below a threshold. A surface can be detected either as a border of a segmented object or as a voxel with a local maximum of the gradient magnitude. It is important that the user is able to easily recognize to which position his or her input was transformed.

For validating the measured distance, it is crucial to identify the measurement points in the 2D visualization as well. Small quadrilateral marks or circles may be employed for this purpose. However, as often some 100 slices are involved, it is tedious to look for slice n where a measurement point is located. Therefore the mark should also be displayed in a few neighboring slices. In [Preim et al. 2002b], the measurement point in slice n is marked by an opaque quadrilateral and has a close line border. In the vicinity (slices between $n-3$ and $n+3$), a dotted quadrilateral is used to indicate that the measurement point is at that position, although in a nearby slice. The position that corresponds to the measurement point is marked with a semitransparent quadrilateral and a border of dotted lines (see Fig. 13.8, right). Both views should be synchronized (the selection of a vertex in one view also generates feedback in the other view). For example, if a vertex is selected in the 3D view, the 2D view should be adapted to show the 2D representation of this vertex.

13.2.2 INTERACTIVE RULERS

Rulers are well-known measurement facilities from daily life. A simple variant of a ruler can be found in radiological displays; usually, a vertical scale is attached to the right border of a viewer. Interactive rulers are useful for approximating the magnitude of structures and for estimating several distances along a straight line simultaneously.

Geometry   An example of a 3D ruler-widget is composed of a thin cylinder and strokes representing the scaling of a ruler as well as labels which are attached to some of these strokes. An important design consideration refers to the recognizability of the strokes. If rulers are freely rotated to adapt to the target structure, strokes may be perpendicular to the viewing direction and thus are invisible. To prevent this, two

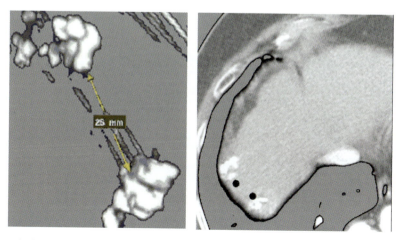

FIGURE 13.8   *The distance between two liver tumors is determined with a 3D distance line (left). Slight rotations of the 3D view allow assessment of the depth relations more clearly. The two endpoints are also visible in the 2D view (right)* [Preim et al. 2002b].

solutions have been investigated in [PREIM et al. 2002b]: the first is to use crosses (two small perpendicular lines) instead of just one line, the second approach is to use circles and thus a two-dimensional mark. The first approach has the advantage that the visualization is less cluttered.

Behavior A crucial design consideration is the behavior of a ruler when it is scaled. In principle, there are two strategies applicable:

- *Constant distance of labels and strokes.* If a constant distance is kept, the number of strokes and labels is enlarged to fill the increasing empty space between the strokes, or it is reduced in the same ratio that the ruler is scaled. This is probably a behavior that meets the user's expectation. However, it may lead to a visualization cluttered by a ruler with many strokes.
- *Adaptable distance of labels and ticks.* The distance between strokes and labels might be adapted to the length of the ruler, for example, in such a way that the overall number remains constant. While this approach may prevent too many strokes and labels from appearing, it may be irritating if the distance between strokes changes frequently while the ruler is scaled.

A trade-off seems to be the superior solution: as long as the user is either scaling the ruler or translating one of its vertices (which also affects its length), the distance between strokes remains constant. If the user no longer controls the ruler, the distance is adapted. The adaption of strokes and numbers, however, is realized at discrete levels. An application of the ruler is shown in Figure 13.9.

13.2.3 PATH MEASUREMENT

As a final measurement task with respect to distances, we briefly discuss path measurement—the task of determining the overall length of a line defined by an arbitrary number of points. A clinical example for this task is to determine the required size of a catheter for reaching a particular position inside the patient's body. Obviously, the path length consisting of different segments of an air-filled organ typically differs considerably from the Euclidean distance between the entry point and the target point.

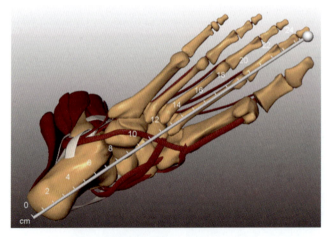

FIGURE 13.9 *The ruler is placed inside a surface visualization of the human foot Several distances can be approximated simultaneously. A small cross indicates each stroke of the ruler to ensure that the strokes are recognizable from all viewing directions* [PREIM et al. 2002b].

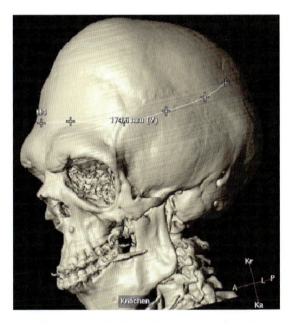

FIGURE 13.10 *A path on the skull's surface is defined by multiple points specified with a cross-hair cursor. The overall length (174.6 mm) is shown. (Screenshot of the Philips Easy Vision workstation)*

It is essential that the user can precisely locate any point to be included in the path in 2D and 3D representations. The minimal feedback after including, deleting, or moving points would be to present the overall path length. It might be useful to display partial distances as well. In Figure 13.10, an example from a radiological workstation is presented. A problem of path definition and the display of the path length is that often there is no appropriate viewing direction to show the whole path at once. As long as the path stays on top of the surface, rotations can be performed to complete a path. This problem is exactly the same one that we discussed in the section on virtual resection, in which a path on an organ's surface is used as input (recall Sect. 12.3).

13.3   ANGULAR MEASUREMENTS

Angular measurements are defined between vectors or lines. In diagnosis and treatment planning, angular measurements are often used to evaluate the orientation of elongated structures with regard to some vector or midline. In these cases, the vectors that define an angle are the directions of the longest extent. These directions are either estimated by the user or determined by means of a principal component analysis, which we will discuss later (see Sect. 13.7.2).

In general, angular measurements are carried out to define angles between anatomical or pathologic structures. The angles at branchings of vascular structures might be essential for vascular analysis; angles that describe different orientations of objects are often important for the assessment of the severity of complex bone fractures (e.g., whether a surgical intervention after fractures of the arm is required depends on the angle between the bones).

Geometry For angular measurements, three coordinates are required, representing the apex of the angle and the termination of the legs. To provide consistency across the measurement tools, properties of the distance line widget may be reused. The angular measurement tool thus consists of two distance lines (which are based on cones and cylinders, recall Sect. 13.2). The apex of the leg is emphasized with a sphere that can be easily selected. It turns out that without orientation aids, it is often very difficult to assess the size of an angle. Therefore, additional planes are displayed when the angle is transformed. Two semitransparent planes perpendicular to each of the legs of the angle are constructed. The use of semitransparent planes as orientation aids is an established concept in the design of 3D widgets. It is used, for example, for some manipulators of the OpenInventor library.

As a first idea, the triangle formed by the three vertices of the angular measurement tool may also be shown semitransparently (see Fig. 13.11, left). The use of a triangle as an orientation aid is restricted, however, to angles of less than 180 degrees (or would be ambiguous for angles larger than 180 degrees). The second idea attempts to avoid this restriction by using a portion of a circle bounded by the legs of the angle. The portion of the circle is smaller than the triangle composed of the legs, which is an advantage because fewer portions of the 3D model are occluded. In Figure 13.11 (right) the circle segment is scaled such that the radius corresponds to half the length of the smaller leg. A typical application of the angular measurement tool is shown in Figure 13.12. In general, the planes should only temporarily be included to prevent the visualization from becoming too cluttered.

Concerning the placement of the measurement number, two strategies were explored and described in [PREIM et al. 2002b]. First, the number has been integrated into one of the two distance lines which represent the legs. The second strategy is closer to the way angles are annotated in conventional technical drawings—the number is placed near the apex of the angle, which also has the advantage that for larger angles, the orientation is unambiguous. However, both strategies differ from conventions of labeling angles in technical drawings, as these conventions are not appropriate for 3D visualizations.

Behavior Each of the three vertices might be selected and transformed with a 3D translate widget. Like the ruler, the angular measurement tool may also be translated as a whole to move the angle's center. In exactly the same way as for distance lines, the placement of the number is adapted. If there is enough space to accommodate the number inside a distance line, the line is interrupted to place the number. Otherwise, the number is placed at the apex. The three vertices are also displayed in the 2D slice view of the original data in exactly the same way that we discussed for the distance line widget.

For angular measurements, a tighter coupling of 2D and 3D views is recommended. When the three not-colinear vertices are defined, a plane can be computed that passes exactly through the three vertices of an angle (see Fig. 13.13). This plane defines an oblique slice through the volume data.

FIGURE 13.11   *Three-dimensional widgets for the measurement of angles. Left: a triangle shows the extent of the angle. Right: a segment of a circle between the legs is used instead. A 3D translate widget is active to translate the right leg [PREIM et al. 2002b].*

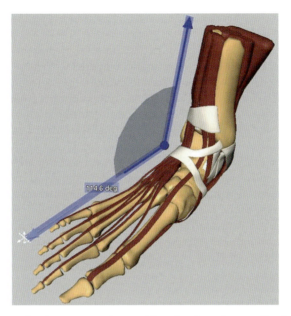

FIGURE 13.12   *Measurement of angles in an example inspired by orthopedic applications. The planes which are displayed during interaction serve as orientation aids [PREIM et al. 2002b].*

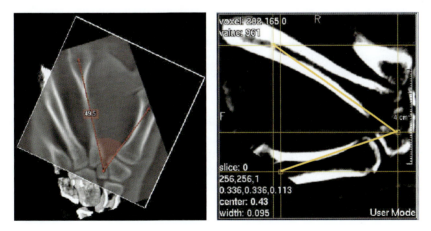

FIGURE 13.13   *Measurement of an angle in CT data of the human hand. Left: a 3D volume rendering with a clipping plane, right: the corresponding oblique display with the three vertices characterizing the angle [PREIM et al. 2002b].*

13.4   INTERACTIVE AREA MEASUREMENTS

Area measurements are more vulnerable to errors, since the second dimension may induce a quadratic error; hence, area measurements are not very reliable. Consequently, computer support can provide a good foundation for these kind of measurements, which may be used to measure the cross section at different parts of a blood vessel. These measurements can be used to assess the state of this blood vessel (Is there a stenosis? How severe is it?).

The definition of an area in an axial slice can be accomplished by drawing a graphics primitive that encloses the target structure. As an approximation, an enclosing circle (or ellipse) can be used as primitive. A better result can be achieved by drawing a polygon around the target structure. Both methods, however, are strongly dependent on the interaction of a specific user. To improve reproducibility, the polygon can be transformed slightly to snap to locations with large image gradients. If the same structure is analyzed frequently, assumptions about the gray value distribution (mean, standard value) can be included in the area approximation.

For an accurate assessment of a vessel cross section, an axial slice (or any other orientation) is not appropriate, as it does not sufficiently reflect the orientation of the vessel. In the worst case, the vessel runs parallel to the selected slice, resulting in a largely overestimated cross section. Instead, a plane perpendicular to the centerline of the vessel provides superior accuracy. Once the areas of oblique cross sections are computed, they can be used to assess the severity of a vessel stenosis. For that purpose, the ratio of the areas before (or behind) and at the stenosis is evaluated; this ratio represents a very significant measure. Often, however, the vessel diameter is used instead of an area measurement because it can be determined faster.

13.5   INTERACTIVE VOLUME MEASUREMENTS

Volumetric measurements are essential to evaluate the success of a therapy. As an example, the change of a malignant tumor's volume in the course of chemotherapy determines the success of the treatment. However, the 3D nature decreases the reliability of traditional ruler-based in-slice measurements to an extreme level. Hence, volumetric measurements can benefit tremendously from computer-based methods.

In general, and particularly for volumetric measurements, the process of measurements can be organized into two stages: first, we need to select the relevant structure (*volume selection*), and second, we need to compute the respective volume of that structure (*volume approximation*). In the following sections, we examine these stages in detail.

13.5.1 VOLUME SELECTION

The identification of a structure to be measured (*target structure*) can be a tedious process and largely depends on how well this structure is represented in the dataset. In particular, the contrast between the voxel intensities of the structure itself and those of the neighboring voxels is important. The larger the contrast, the easier the structure can be segmented. Ideally, it can be identified with a simple thresholding-based method, which would also enable classification-based identification. If the target structure cannot be segmented with (semi)automatic methods, it must be segmented by manually drawing its contour. This, however, is a quite expensive operation and does not always provide the same level of quality. Due to these constraints, a combination of a simple segmentation and optimized interaction through a 3D widget is typically used to select the target structure.

The basic idea for interactive volume selection is that a simple geometric shape is moved inside a 3D representation with the goal of completely enclosing the target structure [HASTREITER et al. 1998]. The visual representation is achieved through a direct volume visualization guided by a transfer function (classification) that suppresses structures that are not relevant for the measurement task. The system displays the volume of this simple shape as feedback. This idea, however, has two drawbacks:

- It is often difficult to locate the target structure in a volume visualization. The specification of an appropriate transfer function requires that intensity values of this structure are already known.

Nevertheless, it is often difficult to suppress irrelevant structures with similar intensity values. Instead, the careful placement of clipping planes is often required.

- Once the target structure is selected, its volume must be computed (see Sect. 13.5.2). This computation, however, is very sensitive to small changes of the boundary definition. For example, if the diameter of a sphere is only increased by 10%, the volume increases by 33%. If the uncertainty of volume selection is below 10%, the uncertainty of the diameter must be below 3%.

In the following, we elaborate the idea of volume selection based on [PREIM et al. 2002b].

Interval-based Volume Selection   To address the first problem, it is crucial that a 3D shape is displayed in the 2D as well as the 3D view, with functionality to modify it in both views synchronously. The lack of precision can be diminished considerably by restricting the volume computation to voxels that are inside the bounding object and that satisfy a condition concerning their intensity values. It is in particular useful and easy for the user to restrict the volume calculation to voxels with intensity values v in an interval $[v_{low}, ..., v_{high}]$. As feedback, the voxels that satisfy the condition are highlighted in both views so that it becomes obvious whether the correct voxels are selected. However, the result may depend strongly on the interval chosen. Therefore, the user may specify an inner and an outer interval, as follows:

- The *inner interval* is intended to cover all voxels that belong with highest probability to the structure.
- The *outer interval* encompasses a wider volume range that will also cover voxels for which there is some degree of uncertainty as to whether or not they belong to the structure.

The volume is later simultaneously calculated for both the inner and the outer interval. The difference between the two values indicates the reliability of the selection.

Enhancing the Volume Selection   Scanned objects are frequently subject to inhomogeneities and attenuation artifacts. While these inhomogeneities are often due to the natural variation of the tissue signal, attenuation artifacts are often caused by inaccuracies of reconstruction algorithms of the scanners. These inaccuracies become particularly noticeable with large-contrast agent-filled cavities, such as large blood vessels [BARTZ et al. 2004].

Due to these inhomogeneities inside the target structures (for example, tumors or blood vessel cavities), some gray values of inner parts may not be within the specified intervals. There are several possible options to address this problem. First, the user can specify that holes and concave notches of a certain size are closed (and added to the volume). This may be accomplished with a morphological image processing filter (recall Sect. 5.6.1). The user can select between some predefined kernel sizes to control the amount of closing (see Fig. 13.14). Second, it should be possible to invert the interval that restricts the volume selection. The invert option means that values within the chosen interval are excluded from the computation, rather than included. In some cases, such a specification is better suited to separate foreground from background voxels. Third, totally encased holes can be closed by inverted flood-filling, where flood-filling is applied to the area *outside* of the currently selected volume.

In cases where these techniques do not lead to a successful volume selection, individual parts of the target structure represented by different gray level intervals can be selected in different steps. These partial selections can subsequently be merged into one selection [BARTZ et al. 2004]. Note that this merging operation can be an arbitrary operation of any logical combination, thus enabling complex merging behavior.

Using Interval-Based Volume Selection

Interval-based volume selection is typically carried out in two steps. In the first step, a shape is chosen and placed so that it encloses the target structure completely (see Fig. 13.15). In the second step, intervals are

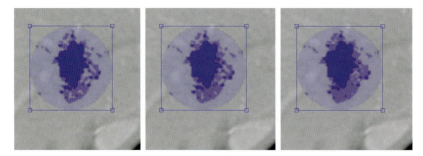

FIGURE 13.14 *Effect of a close gap filter on the volume selection: in the left image, no filter is applied. In the middle and right images, a filter with size 7 × 7 × 3 and 11 × 11 × 3 is applied. The volume changed from 3.5 to 3.6 and 3.8 ml for the inner interval and from 7.6 to 7.7 and 8.0 ml by applying the close gap filter [PREIM et al. 2002b].*

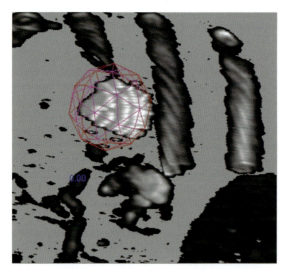

FIGURE 13.15 *An ellipsoid approximated by a polyeder and rendered as wireframe is used to translate the bounding volume inside a 3D visualization (right). The result is also visible in the 2D view (see Fig. 13.14), where it can be explored slice by slice [PREIM et al. 2002b].*

adjusted to restrict the selection. For the interval specification, it is useful to select a probe (either some individual voxels or a small circular region) inside the target structure. As feedback, the *min*, *max*, and *mean* intensity values are displayed. These values may be used to adjust the interval quickly. The interval specification may take some time for the user if an entirely new structure is analyzed. With CT data, the intensity values for certain structures are similar across different cases, which gives rise to standard values that might be stored for later use. For liver tumors in CT data, for example, an interval center of 40 Hounsfield units and widths of 60 and 80 for the inner and outer intervals are often appropriate.[2]

---

2 There are no substantial experiences with this kind of volume selection in MRI data. For smaller structures, where the inhomogeneity has little influence, satisfying results may be possible.

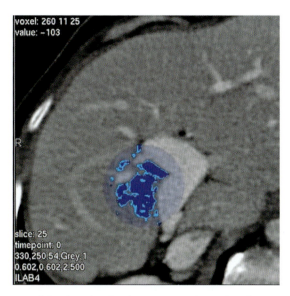

FIGURE 13.16   *The computation of the volume for a liver lesion is restricted to voxels with certain intensity values in the underlying CT data (dark blue voxels). The 2D representation of the shape is transparently overlaid to the original data to verify whether the structure (a liver tumor) is completely enclosed* [PREIM *et al.* 2002b].

Volume selection within the 3D view requires that the target structure is displayed unoccluded (an appropriate transfer function and/or carefully placed clipping planes are therefore needed). To evaluate whether the relevant structure is completely inside the 3D shape, several rotations and transformations of the volume selection tool are necessary. In this case, not only translations, but also scalings and rotations of the measurement tool are required.

Using the 2D view, it is preferable to look first for a slice where the target structure appears largest (hence represented best) and to adjust the scale of the shape in this slice. The use of ellipsoids has the drawback that it is difficult to predict to which extent the 2D cross section is in other slices. This results in frequent modifications of its scaling. Thus, a cylinder is often better suited as the enclosing shape. Whether the target structure is fully enclosed can be evaluated if voxels on the boundary of the structure exhibit intensity values that do not belong to the outer and inner intervals (see Fig. 13.16).

13.5.2   VOLUME APPROXIMATION

Once we have selected all voxels of a target structure, the volume represented by these voxels can be approximated for volumetry. A straightforward approach is to weight every voxel belonging to that selection with the size of a respective volume cell.[3] This method achieves a reasonable approximation for interior *core voxels*. However, it does not reflect the boundary voxels properly, where the separating isosurface may be closer or farther away from the voxels depending on the voxel values and the threshold. While this difference is almost negligible for compact selections—which have a relatively small boundary—it can be significant for small or elongated structures. LUFT *et al.* [1998] showed, for example, that up to

---

3   This size can be computed by multiplying all three voxel spacing values.

50% of all volume cells of the cerebral ventricular system contain a boundary. In [BARTZ et al. 2004], it was shown that 40% of all volume cells of such a ventricular system of a typical patient dataset contained a boundary representing more than 20% of the total volume (see Fig. 13.17). These facts clearly show that the straightforward weighted counting of all voxels will in too many cases compute a very inaccurate volume.

BARTZ et al. [2004] describe a subdivision approach for these boundary voxels. First, the boundary voxels are examined in their volume cell context (see Sect. 2.1), where a boundary cell contains between one and seven selected voxels (see Fig. 13.18). Similar to the case table of the Marching Cubes approach, the boundary cells are classified into simple (one or seven voxels are selected) and complex cases (between two and six voxels are selected). Simple cases can be resolved immediately by weighting the respective volume with the interpolated isovalue parameter. The complex cases are recursively subdivided into eight subcells using trilinear interpolation until either only simple cases remain or the respective full voxel volume is below an error threshold. This way, the difference between phantom measurements and scanned datasets is evaluated.

An alternative method using histogram analysis and weighting of boundary voxels affected by the partial volume effect has been described in [SCHINDEWOLF et al. 1999, HAHN et al. 2001a, HAHN 2005].

13.5.3 VALIDATION

In general, the accuracy of volumetric measurements depends on the segmentation and on the treatment of the boundary, which also includes cavities encased in the target structure. While the latter one can be solved sufficiently (see above), the quality of the volume measurements depends largely on how the segmentation has been achieved. In the case of a threshold-based boundary definition, a variation of 5–10% of the threshold can result in a significant change in the volume of the selection. BARTZ et al. [2004] examined the accuracy of volume measurements based on the physical measurements of contrast agent-filled phantom cavities and of the respective 3D scans, where it could be shown that the difference is less than 5%.

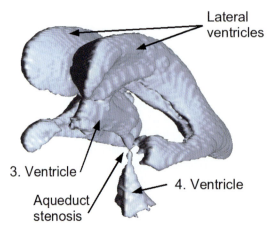

FIGURE 13.17   *Cerebral ventricular system: 40% of all volume cells are boundary cells.*

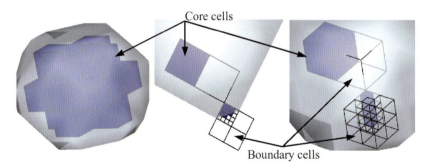

FIGURE 13.18 *Volume approximation on cell level. Left: core cells (blue) that are completely located within the target structure. Middle: core cells (blue) and boundary cells (wireframe). The boundary cells are subdivided three times. Right: same as middle image from a different viewpoint. (Images courtesy* JASMINA ORMAN, *University of Tübingen)*

In this section, however, we examine the results of a volumetry study to analyze liver tumors in CT data [PREIM et al. 2002b]. The analysis of the tumor volume is important, since it is essential for tumor staging as well as for the evaluation of therapies. Due to large variance of the intensity values inside liver tumors, this study faces the above-mentioned issues. Furthermore, this study is too small to draw any reliable conclusions. Despite these limitations, we briefly describe this study as an example for the validation methodology.

Four liver tumors have been manually segmented by an experienced radiologist. The resulting volume is regarded as the correct volume (as different radiologists would probably have slightly different results, this assumption is a simplification). It was hypothesized that:

1 The approximation has the same order of magnitude as the correct result (the mean of the two estimated volumes should be at least 50% and less than 200% of the correct result)
2 The correct result was in between the two volumes calculated with the inner and outer intervals

While the first hypothesis was fulfilled in all four cases, the second hypothesis was only fulfilled in three of four cases. Without the image processing step to close gaps, the results would be less reliable, with a systematic underestimation of the volume. The strong influence of the chosen interval—and hence of the boundary definition—could also be demonstrated; the volumes changed up to 30% if the interval center was moderately shifted by 10 Hounsfield units. Although these results have no statistical significance and are bound to a specific application, they give a hint on the usefulness of such a measurement tool.

Discussion Volume measurement tools are currently not more than prototypes with a preliminary assessment of their reliability. To transfer these and other similar measurement functions into clinical practice, considerably more effort is needed in the validation. For clinicians, it is also essential to compare the results with their current evaluation techniques. With respect to tumor progress, the RECIST criteria (Response Evaluation Criteria in Solid Tumors) are used in current practice (recall Sect. 4.3.3).

13.6   MINIMAL DISTANCE COMPUTATION

Automatic measurements relating to anatomic structures or relations between them require explicit segmentations, which we assume in the remainder of this chapter. As a first example for the automatic support of an important measurement task, we describe the way the minimal distance between two objects, for example a pathologic structure and a vital structure at risk, can be defined. Automatic support for this interaction task is relevant, as it is tedious and error-prone to interactively determine minimal distances.

An algorithm that computes minimal distances between anatomic structures must be very efficient due to the amount of the data (number of vertices of a surface representation) and must be able to handle objects of arbitrary shape. In particular, algorithms that are restricted to convex objects or that require that one object lies outside the convex hull of the other are not applicable for medical visualization. As an example, lesions are mostly located inside a vascular tree's convex hull.[4]

In principle, minimal distances can be computed between object surfaces or in voxel space (taking into account the two sets of voxels that represent both anatomic structures). We focus on minimal distance computation between surfaces.

Accurate minimal distance computations consider edges, faces, and vertices to compute the exact location on the object's surfaces where the distance is minimal. If the surface of the involved objects is represented with a high-resolution polygonal mesh, the computation may be simplified by considering only vertices and determining the pair of vertices with minimal distance. Because the Marching Cubes algorithm, which is usually employed to transform a segmentation result to a surface representation, produces the high-resolution meshes, we consider only algorithms which consider vertices only. The error that arises due to this simplification is lower than the resolution of the radiological data, and thus this simplification is justified.

In the following, we describe a validated algorithm for minimal distance computation in medical visualizations derived from robotics. The key idea is to construct and employ a hierarchy of bounding volumes (bounding spheres) to restrict the computation of distances to subsets of the geometry. Bounding spheres are superior compared to bounding boxes, as the minimal distance between spheres can be computed very quickly.

13.6.1 DISTANCE CALCULATION IN ROBOTICS AND MEDICAL VISUALIZATION

Collision detection between 3D objects in dynamic scenes is a central problem in robotics. A widespread software library for this purpose is V-Collide [HUDSON et al.1997, LIN and GOTTSCHALK 1998a]. The software computes axis-aligned as well as oriented bounding boxes (AABB and OBB) for each object and finally constructs a hierarchy of these bounding volumes. With a bounding volume hierarchy, it is possible to decide quickly which parts of the geometry are close to each other and must be evaluated in detail with respect to possible collisions. Time-consuming computations of intersections between complex geometries are thus avoided in many cases. The problem to be solved here is closely related but differs in some aspects:

1   Objects do not change their positions, because the data of interest is static.
2   The computation involves exactly two objects, instead of a whole scene.
3   The objects might have a complex geometry description of some 100 K vertices. By contrast, in robotics, more objects with a less complex geometry are involved.

Due to these differences, the effort to build similar data structures than in V-Collide and similar systems is not justified. In dynamic scenes, these data structures are reused very often, whereas in a static scene they are employed exactly once. On the other hand, some kind of bounding volumes are required to restrict the computation.

---

4   The convex hull of a vascular tree corresponds well to the whole organ, which is due to the purpose of a vascular system, namely, to provide the blood supply to the whole organ.

While the majority of algorithms for minimal distance computation is restricted to convex shapes, [KAWACHI and SUZUKI 2000, QUINLAN 1994], consider arbitrary shapes. The latter approach is better suited for use in static scenes, because there is less effort to construct hierarchical datastructures. Bounding spheres are used in this approach.

13.6.2 MINIMAL DISTANCE COMPUTATION BASED ON BOUNDING SPHERES

In the following, we describe how the method introduced in [QUINLAN 1994] might be used for minimal distance computation. The two objects are characterized only by their sets of vertices $V_1 = v_{1i}, i = 1, ..., m$ and $V_2 = v_{2j}, j = 1, ..., n$.

A hierarchical data structure is constructed to represent the vertices of both objects. Subobjects and the vertices that belong to them are summarized in nodes n_{1i} and n_{2j}. For each node, a minimal enclosing bounding sphere is determined on the corresponding level g in the hierarchy (for vertices from V_1) and h (for vertices from V_2) in the hierarchy. The algorithm consists of the following steps:

1   Construction of a hierarchical data structure for the representation of V_1 and V_2.

   Initially, the axis-aligned bounding boxes (AABB) for V_1 and V_2 are determined as initial buckets. Vertices v_{1i} are sorted in a bucket until the number (*count*) in the bucket exceeds a parameter *maxEntries*. If *count* equals *maxEntries*, $AABB(V_1)$ is decomposed equally in x-, y-, and z-directions. A parameter *partition* defines the number of subboxes in which $AABB(V_1)$ is decomposed (suitable values are 2^3, 3^3, 4^3, and 5^3). After decomposition, each vertex is assigned to the subbox that contains it. The process of sorting v_{1i} into buckets (with recursive decomposition of the associated space) is terminated when all vertices are part of a bucket containing at most *maxEntries*. The vertices v_{2j} are sorted into buckets in the same way that resulted from the decomposition of $AABB(V_2)$. The buckets correspond to nodes of the hierarchical structure. The first step is illustrated in Figure 13.19.

2   Determination of a bounding spheres hierarchy.

   For all nodes n_{1r} and n_{2s}, the smallest enclosing sphere is determined. It is centered at the center of the AABB of the corresponding node. Thus, a hierarchy of bounding spheres arises for both objects. The spheres encompassing the whole sets V_1 and V_2 (S_{root}^1 and S_{root}^2) represent the roots of both hierarchy trees.

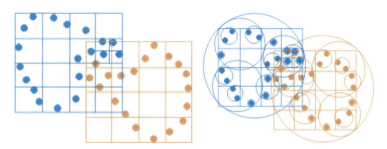

FIGURE 13.19 *Left: hierarchic space decomposition for two pointsets, starting with the axis-aligned bounding box of the whole set. Buckets are decomposed in all dimensions as soon as their capacity (maxEntries) is exceeded (here, 3). Right: for each bucket, a bounding sphere is constructed and a bounding sphere hierarchy is generated, in which each sphere at a higher level completely encloses its "children." Spheres containing only one item are slightly enlarged to discriminate them from the vertex. (Images courtesy CHRISTIAN TIETJEN, University of Magdeburg)*

3 Determination of $d_{current}$ as an upper bound for the minimal distance.

We consider S_{root}^1 and S_{root}^2 and choose the root with the larger diameter. For the larger sphere, we consider the subspheres and compute the distance from the surface to the other (root) sphere. The minimum of these distances is recorded. We assume the minimum occurs for the sphere S_{root}^1 and S_g^2. Again, we select the larger of the two spheres and iterate over subspheres. For all subspheres of the larger sphere, we determine the distances to the larger sphere again and record the minimum. The process is continued until the leaves S_h^1 and S_g^2 of the sphere hierarchy are attained.

For this pair, we iterate over all pairs of vertices (v_{1i}, v_{2j}) represented by these spheres and determine the distances between them. Note that this is the first time that actual vertices (and not bounding volumes) are considered. The minimum distance between these pairs of vertices is our intermediate result $d_{current}$, a first guess of the minimal distance. Actually, $d_{current}$ represents the upper bound of the minimal distance (see Fig. 13.20 for an illustration of this step).

4 Recursive determination of the minimal distance d_{min}.

Our intermediate result $d_{current}$ is employed to exclude all pairs of spheres for which the distance between the spheres' surfaces is larger than $d_{current}$. This is possible because all vertices represented by the spheres S_i^1 and S_j^2 have a distance that is at least the closest distance of spheres' surfaces. With this strategy, the large majority of pairs of spheres can be excluded without analyzing the vertices they represent.

Because the distance of the vertices found in the bounding spheres may be larger than the distance of the bounding spheres, we have to check whether another pair of spheres is also a candidate for the minimal distance. We employ the hierarchical structure of the bounding tree to restrict the test of leaf spheres. We go one step backwards in the recursion (S_{h-1}^1) and look at the other spheres at this level for a distance below $d_{current}$ to S_g^2. If there is a pair of spheres

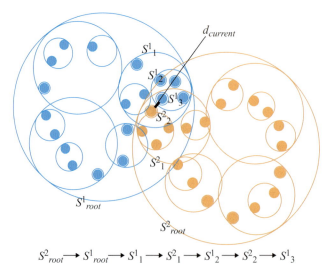

FIGURE 13.20 *Computation of an upper bound, d-current, for the minimal distance. The sequence of the spheres is indicated and all visited spheres are drawn with a thicker line. After step 3, the minimal distance occurs between vertices in the spheres S_3^1 and S_2^2. (Image courtesy* CHRISTIAN TIETJEN, *University of Magdeburg)*

with a shorter distance, we go back to step 3, starting with this pair as root spheres. To prevent an infinite loop, all pairs of spheres that have been checked have to be marked. Using a hashtable is recommended in [QUINLAN 1994]. The stop criterion is true if the roots S^1_{root} and S^2_{root} are reached. After this stage, the minimum distance is determined. A series of 2D examples illustrates the final step of the algorithm (see Fig. 13.21 and 13.22).

The naïve implementation of the above algorithm involves the frequent determination of square roots as part of the Euclidean distance computation. The time-consuming step is required only once, when the vertices between which the minimum actually occurs are identified. For all intermediate results, absolute distances are irrelevant. Because of the monotony of the root operator ($d_1 < d_2$ always implies $\sqrt{d_1} < \sqrt{d_2}$), the square root is neglected for comparisons. As an example of the use of the algorithm, Figure 13.23 shows its application for planning neck surgery.

Choice of Parameters

Parameters are relevant to fine-tune the result. However, it is time-consuming to select parameters; therefore, default values that lead to reasonable results in the majority of the cases are desirable.

A large series of runs of the algorithms were carried out to determine the parameters *partition* and *maxEntries* for typical objects extracted from clinical CT data, such as organs, vascular trees, and lesions with up to 100 K polygons [PREIM et al. 2003]. Both parameters are adapted to the size of the two pointsets (*partition* is assigned $2^3, 3^3, 4^3$, or 5^3). The cube numbers allow partitioning in the space equally in x-, y-, and z-directions.

The choice of *maxEntries* is guided by two conflicting requirements. On one hand, it should be small enough to prevent the comparisons between too many vertices when a pair of spheres is evaluated. On the other hand, the number of spheres and the overhead to traverse the spheres' hierarchy increase if *maxEntries* is a small number. Values between 200 and 1000 turned out to be appropriate. Within this

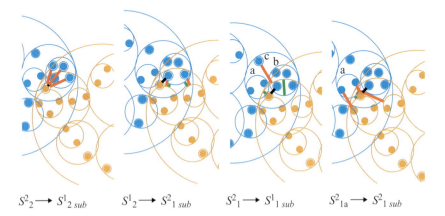

$S^2_2 \longrightarrow S^1_{2\,sub}$ $S^1_2 \longrightarrow S^2_{1\,sub}$ $S^2_1 \longrightarrow S^1_{1\,sub}$ $S^2_{1a} \longrightarrow S^2_{1\,sub}$

FIGURE 13.21   *Recursive determination of the minimal distance (continuation of the example of Fig. 13.20). Four consecutive steps are shown; only relevant portions of the two original pointsets are shown. The red lines indicate distances longer than the current minimum; green lines (may represent negative distances) are smaller than the current minimum, which is rendered in black. S^1_{2sub} relates to all subspheres of S^1_2. The distances between S^1_2 and three subspheres (labeled "a," "b," and "c") are evaluated, and the distances to the spheres "a" and "b" are further explored. (Image courtesy CHRISTIAN TIETJEN, University of Magdeburg)*

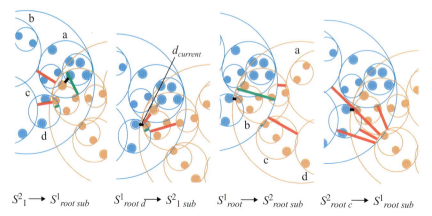

FIGURE 13.22 *Finals steps of the recursive determination of the minimal distance (continuation of the example of Fig. 13.20). In the left image, the distances between S_1^2 and the four subspheres of S_{root}^1 are assessed. The distances to the sphere labeled "a" and "d" are below the current minimum and are further explored by computing distances to the items in the subspheres of S_1^2. In the sphere "d," a new minimum is found. Further tests at the higher levels are performed until the termination criteria is satisfied. (Image courtesy* CHRISTIAN TIETJEN, *University of Magdeburg)*

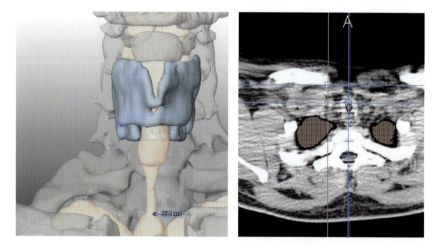

FIGURE 13.23 *A patient with a severe stenosis of the trachea is visualized for surgical planning. To localize the stenosis, the minimal distance between the trachea and the clavicula is determined in 2D and 3D. (Images courtesy* JEANETTE CORDES, *University of Magdeburg, data courtesy* THOMAS SCHULZ, *University of Leipzig)*

interval, maxEntries is adapted to the size of V_1 and V_2. The average number of vertices represented by one sphere is usually far below maxEntries. The upper bound for the number of distance computations that have to be carried out for one pair of spheres is $\textbf{\textit{maxEntries}}^2$. The actual number of comparisons, however, is up to two orders of magnitude below this maximum value.

Discussion and Validation

The brute-force method for minimal distance computation is to iterate over all vertices of both objects, compute all distances, and compute the minimum of these distances. The correctness of the algorithm presented above can be shown by comparing it with the results of the brute-force algorithm. Because the naïve method is very simple to implement, it is very likely that the results produced by this method are correct. This kind of validation, however, is time-consuming, because hours are required to determine the minimal distance between complex anatomical objects with the naïve method.

The minimal distance computation has been extensively used in intervention planning (liver surgery, endoscopic endonasal surgery, and neck dissection planning). As the algorithm operates on point sets, it could also be employed to define the minimal distance between one object and the surface of an enclosing object. As a clinically relevant example, consider tumor ablation inside the liver (more detail on tumor ablation is presented in Sect. 19.5). One criterion for the applicability of this therapy is the distance between a lesion and the organ's surface, which should be at least 1 cm.

Restriction of Minimal Distance Computation for Vascular Trees   A frequent variant of minimal distance calculation refers to pathologic lesions and vascular trees. The relevant question for surgical users is the minimal distance between a lesion and a significant part of a vascular tree. The most important criterion for "significance" is the vessel diameter. To directly address this question, the minimal distance computation should be restricted to the parts of the vascular tree that fulfill a threshold criterion for the vessel diameter (see Fig. 13.24 and [PREIM et al. 2003]).

Distance Transformation   In this book, we encountered other algorithms for distance computations. We mentioned *distance transformation* where the (Euclidean) distance of all voxels to a target structure is represented in a volume dataset—often called a distance map. Distance transformation is part of the concept of distance-based transfer functions (recall [TAPPENBECK et al. 2006, LOHMANN 1998] and see Sect. 11.4). Distance transformation effectively computes many distances between one target object and all other objects. It is essentially an algorithm operating on voxel data. Minimal distance computation, on the other hand, is accomplished between two selected objects only. It returns only the minimum distance and not the distribution of distances.

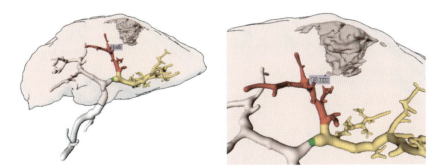

FIGURE 13.24   *Minimal distance between a lesion and a vascular system inside the liver. Only branches of the vascular system with a diameter above 2 mm are considered. Left, an overview; right, a close-up. (Images courtesy CHRISTIAN TIETJEN, University of Magdeburg)*

13.7 FURTHER AUTOMATIC MEASUREMENTS

After discussing minimal distance computation, we describe how the extent of objects, for example of pathologic structures, can be defined. As it turns out, a similar method can be used to determine angles between elongated objects. Both measures are derived using a principal component analysis.

13.7.1 MEASURING THE EXTENTS OF OBJECTS

The extent of an object o can be roughly characterized by its axis-aligned bounding box (AABB), which can be easily computed. This, however, is not a precise measure, since the size of the AABB depends on the orientation of an object. After rotation, a different measure is obtained, although the object itself remains the same size. The oriented bounding box (OBB) avoids this and provides a box with an orientation adapted to the shape of the object. In particular, the longest side of the OBB represents the longest diameter of an object. Guidelines for tumor diagnostics and staging require that the longest diameter be determined. The conventional manual approach of selecting the slice in which the tumor appears to be largest is tedious and unreliable: A conventional ruler is attached to this slice image and diameters in several slices are approximated until the user decides that the maximum was found. However, severe quality issues inflict this approach, even if the slice with the largest (2D) diameter is found, as the largest diameter might be in 3D and does not necessarily show up in any orthogonal slice.

The OBB determination, which can be carried out automatically after image segmentation, produces a reliable result. It is based on principal component analysis, or PCA [SONKA et al. 1999]. The PCA was formally defined in Section 12.3 in the context of a method for virtual resection. We briefly repeat a sketch of this approach. First, the center of gravity (COG) of object o is calculated. The covariance matrix A (a symmetric 3×3-matrix) is computed taking into account all vertices of o. The normalized eigenvectors e_i of A form a local right-angled coordinate system with its origin at the COG of o. The eigenvectors e_i specify a rotation matrix C from the regular Cartesian space into the object coordinate system. To get the exact extent in each of the three directions, o is transformed to o' by rotating o according to the rotation C. As object o' is axis-aligned, the axis-aligned bounding box ($AABB$) of object o' can be easily determined. The length of the axes of the $AABB$ represent the length of the main axis (see Fig. 13.25).

The extent is visualized by either the longest distance line or by three orthogonal distance lines intersecting at the COG (see Fig. 13.26). Numbers are placed at the endpoints to reduce the problem of overlapping information. As the distance lines proceed inside, the object for which these measurements have been carried out is rendered semitransparently.

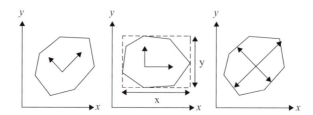

FIGURE 13.25 *Eigenvectors of an object are defined using the covariance matrix (left). Object o is rotated according to the Jacobian matrix to define the oriented bounding box (middle). Object o is rotated back and the main axis is visualized with distance lines (right).*

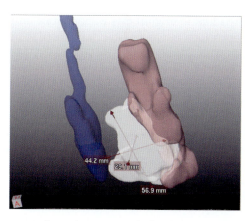

FIGURE 13.26   *The extent of a tumor in the nasal region is visualized with three orthogonal distance lines derived from a principal component analysis. (Image courtesy* JEANETTE CORDES, *University of Magdeburg)*

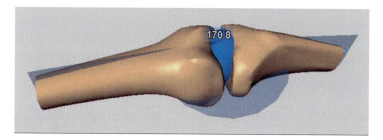

FIGURE 13.27   *Automatic measurement of angles based on a principal component analysis of the two elongated bones [*PREIM *et al. 2002b].*

13.7.2 MEASUREMENT OF ANGLES BETWEEN ELONGATED OBJECTS

Another example of automatic support for a frequent measurement task refers to the angle between two elongated objects. A clinically relevant example can be found in knee surgery planning. Automatic support can be provided again by utilizing segmentation information and performing a principal component analysis for two objects selected by the user. For automatic angular measurements, it is sufficient to know the eigenvector corresponding to the largest eigenvalue for both objects.[5] The angle between these directions is automatically calculated, and an angle measurement tool (recall Sect. 13.3) that conveys this angle is placed. The legs of the angle are parallel to the direction of the computed eigenvectors, and the apex of the angle is placed at their cross section (see Fig. 13.27).

13.8   SUMMARY

We have discussed requirements for the measurement of distances, angles, areas, and volumes. General applicable tools for these tasks have been presented, with focus on applications in medicine. These tools

---

5   This measure is only reliable for elongated objects in which one eigenvalue is indeed significantly larger than the other two.

can be used to analyze spatial relations in original data without prior image analysis as well as for the analysis of image data with segmentation results available. It is crucial to provide both 2D and 3D visualizations for measurement tasks with a bidirectional synchronization. Measurement tasks are relevant for many clinical questions. In Table 13.1, a selected list of examples is presented. There are many more examples, particularly in orthopedic surgeries such as total knee replacement and total hip replacement, in which measurements are used to assess the defective anatomy and to properly size prosthetic devices.

Segmentation information can be exploited to enhance measurements by providing snapping mechanisms and automatic support for well-defined tasks, such as the definition of object extents and angles between objects. Three-dimensional measurements support diagnosis and pretherapeutic decisions. The design of 3D measurement tools requires careful consideration of 3D visualization and 3D interaction. Three-dimensional measurements in general benefit from 3D input or stereoscopic output. OPEN INVENTOR with its components for 3D interaction provides an appropriate framework for the development of measurement tools.

Outlook For practical use, it is desirable to standardize the use of measurement widgets by defining adjustable measurement styles. The interaction itself might benefit from two-handed interaction. For measurement tasks, bimanual interaction might be used to control both endpoints of a measurement tool or to control the virtual camera and a measurement tool simultaneously. An important aspect for future work is a more in-depth evaluation of the presented measurement functions. It is important to study the precision of interactive measurements and how well users get along with these new facilities using realistic scenarios from the everyday experiences of medical doctors.

Measurement	Anatomic Structure(s)	Consequences for Diagnosis or Treatment
Distance	pathologic structure and risk structure	feasibility and risk of surgical intervention
Diameter	different portions of a vascular structure	severity of a stenosis
Path (polyline)	air- or water-filled structure	length of a catheter
Extent (max. diameter)	tumor	tumor staging, feasibility of tumor ablation
Angle	elongated bony structures	assessment of orthopedic problems
Surface	cross-sectional areas of vascular structures	severity of a stenosis
Volume	pathology (tumor, multiple sclerosis lesions)	treatment planning and evaluation

TABLE 13.1 *Examples for measurement tasks and their clinical applications.*

FURTHER READING

In this chapter, we focused on the quantification of spatial relations in the framework of an interactive 3D visualization based on a segmentation. A related topic is the process of generating quantitative information directly from medical image data (without any interaction). An overview on volumetry is given in [HAHN et al. 2001a] with an application to the cerebrospinal fluid. The quantification for diagnosis of vascular diseases is described in [BOSKAMP et al. 2004]. Other recent examples for algorithms for quantification are focused on the diagnosis of the intrathoracic airway trees and tracheal stenosis [TSCHIRREN et al. 2002, SORANTIN et al. 2002].

PART IV

Advanced Visualization Techniques

Part IV of this book is devoted to advanced and specialized visualization techniques. As its first topic, options for the visualization of vascular structures are described (see Chap. 14). The focus in this chapter is on model-based visualization techniques, which provide reconstructions of vasculature based on simplifying model assumptions and vessel analysis results. Model-based techniques aim at providing smooth easy-to-interpret visualizations, primarily for therapy planning and educational purposes. The accuracy of these methods is carefully studied by combining qualitative and quantitative validation studies.

Virtual endoscopy, a procedure in which a virtual camera is moved through air-filled or fluid-filled structures in the human body, is introduced in Chapter 15. Virtual endoscopy is essential for diagnosis—pathologies, such as polyps, can be detected more efficiently and reliably compared to diagnoses based on axial slices. A second application area is surgery planning and simulation with respect to endoscopic procedures. Similar to the visualization of vascular structures, virtual endoscopy is based on prior image analysis (segmentation and skeletonization of the target structure). The navigation, often a trade-off between a flexible 3D interaction and a guided movement along an automatically generated path, is a crucial aspect of any virtual endoscopy system.

So far, we have considered analysis and visualization techniques to support diagnosis and therapy planning. To support physicians during an intervention, virtual and augmented reality techniques are employed (see Chap. 16). Preoperatively acquired image data and results derived from analyzing these data are integrated from intraoperatively acquired information, either intraoperative imaging (open MRI, ultrasound) or video imaging. This integration allows the projection of preoperatively acquired data onto the patient or the fusion of preoperative and intraoperative information, presented on a screen. Intraoperative visualization is essential to support the transfer of a complex therapy plan in the operating room.

Emphasis techniques and illustrative rendering (see Chap. 17) have become two of the most active research areas in medical visualization in the past few years. Although the primary motivation for these techniques is medical education, first studies indicate that there is also potential for therapy planning, in particular when complex anatomic structures are involved. We describe illustrative rendering techniques, such as silhouette generation and hatching based on surface and volume representations, and discuss the ways these techniques may be combined with conventional rendering techniques (recall Part II). Finally, we discuss strategies to use these additional rendering options, primarily for emphasizing anatomic or pathologic structures.

As the last chapter of Part IV, we describe the acquisition, analysis, visualization, and exploration of MRI Diffusion Tensor Images (MRI-DTI) (see Chap. 18). MRI-DTI represent the anisotropic diffusion of water in human tissue, primarily in the whiter matter of the human brain. Thus, white matter fiber tracts can be reconstructed from these data. The integrity of white matter tracts is important for the diagnosis of neurodegenerative diseases such as Morbus Alzheimer and for planning neurosurgical interventions, particularly brain tumor surgery. We emphasize the different visualization options, ranging from a per-voxel visualization of anisotropy and principal diffusion direction to the visualization of whole fiber tracts after tracking and clustering fiber information. The suitability of the different options for diagnosis, therapy planning, and intraoperative visualization is discussed.

Chapter 14

Visualization of Anatomic Tree Structures

For medical education as well as for many therapy planning tasks it is crucial to understand the branching pattern of tree-like anatomic structures, such as nerves, and vascular, and bronchial trees. For therapy planning, it is of paramount importance to recognize shape features and morphology of vascular structures, as well as spatial relations between vascular and other relevant structures. For a convenient interpretation, the curvature, the depth relations, and the diminution of the diameter towards the periphery should be depicted correctly.

In this chapter, we describe methods to reconstruct, to render, and to explore vascular trees based on medical volume data (CT or MRI angiography). Traditional volume visualization methods, such as direct volume rendering, threshold-based isosurface rendering, or maximum intensity projection (recall Sect. 8.3.1), are not well suited for the above-mentioned goals (see Fig. 14.1). Due to the limited resolution of CT- and MRI-scanners, conventional visualizations show distracting aliasing artifacts, particularly for small vessels in which the diameter varies between slices due to partial volume effects and high-frequency noise. Also, the visual separation of contrast-enhanced vascular structures and other high-intensity structures such as bones might be very difficult with conventional medical visualization techniques. Instead, vascular structures should be reconstructed based on the radiological data of a particular patient and some model assumptions as to the shape of vasculature [GERIG et al. 1993]. In the following, we use the terms *vessel visualization* and *visualization of anatomic tree structures* as synonyms, because vascular structures are the primary application of the discussed visualization techniques.

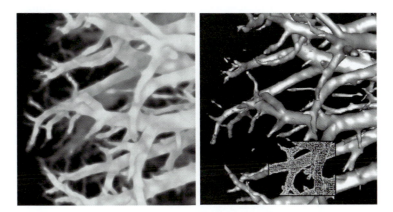

FIGURE 14.1 *Visualization of vasculature by means of direct volume rendering and isosurface rendering. Even with carefully selected transfer functions and isovalues, spatial relations are difficult to extract from such visualizations. The inset in the right image shows the complexity of the geometric model.*

Depending on the quality of the acquired data, vascular systems might be rather complex (with several thousand branchings). Moreover, in some organs, several vascular systems occur (e.g., an arterial tree for blood supply and a venous tree for drainage). The intrahepatic vasculature, for example, consists of the portal veins, the liver arteries, the hepatic veins, and the biliary ducts. Figure 14.2 presents an illustration of these vascular structures from a textbook on surgery which may serve as orientation for computer-generated vessel visualization [MAZZIOTTI and CAVALLARI 1997]. It can be noticed that the branching pattern and geometric properties (vessel diameter, curvature) are easy to interpret with smooth visualizations of vessels. In this chapter, we focus on visualization methods guided by the objective to reconstruct a symbolic vascular model and to visualize this model by emphasizing the topologic and geometric information. For diagnostic purposes, other visualization techniques are required that adhere more closely to the underlying data.

Organization In this chapter, we begin with image analysis (segmentation and centerline extraction) techniques, which are a prerequisite for high-quality vessel visualization (see Sect. 14.1) and with an overview of vessel visualization methods (see Sect. 14.2). The vessel skeleton and the associated diameter information serve as input for the visualization.

After the overview, we describe the explicit reconstruction of polygonal meshes (see Sect. 14.3). These methods either fit graphics primitives (such as cylinder or truncated cones) along the skeleton or generate parametric surfaces to represent the circular cross section of anatomic tree structures. Explicit reconstruction techniques are efficient, but they exhibit artifacts, particularly at branchings.

Therefore, we also describe a radically different approach based on convolution surfaces, a variant of implicit surfaces introduced in [BLOOMENTHAL and SHOEMAKE 1991]. Instead of explicitly describing the geometry, anatomic structures are described by implicit equations and visualized by polygonizing the resulting scalar field. After we discuss the basics of implicit modeling and convolution surfaces in Section 14.4, we discuss vessel visualization with convolution surfaces in Section 14.5.

Implicit modeling is known for the generation of smooth surfaces. However, the smoothness is often achieved at the expense of accuracy. We study the so-called unwanted effects and describe how they are avoided.

For in-depth understanding and practical use of these techniques, we discuss the validation of the resulting visualizations (see Sect. 14.6). In clinical settings, an initial (static) visualization is usually not the ultimate goal. Instead, it is the basis for the exploration of vascular structures. Interaction techniques, such

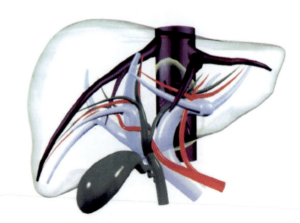

FIGURE 14.2 *Vascular structures of the human liver [MAZZIOTTI and CAVALLARI 1997].*

FIGURE 14.3   *Vascular structures represented as isosurface, as concatenated truncated cones, and as implicit surface* [OELTZE and PREIM 2005]. *(Images courtesy* STEFFEN OELTZE, *University of Magdeburg)*

as focusing on relevant portions, are described in Section 14.8. The visualization of vascular structures is essential for therapy planning as well as for diagnosis. High-quality model-based visualizations are not appropriate for diagnosis tasks. In Section 14.9, we give an overview of visualization techniques for diagnosis of vascular diseases, such as aneurysms. The commonality between all of the discussed methods is the use of image analysis results.

14.1   VESSEL ANALYSIS

For the reconstruction and high-quality visualization of anatomic tree structures, several image processing and analysis steps have to be carried out. In particular, the centerline of these structures and the local diameter are needed to visualize tree structures with circular cross sections. With this information, visualizations may be restricted to branches for which the diameter is above a specific threshold. Such restricted visualizations may support surgeons who try to avoid damage of vascular structures above a certain diameter or—if this turns out to be impossible—consider vascular reconstruction. The exploration of vascular trees is supported with the pipeline of analysis steps in Figure 14.4. The first steps of the pipeline—outside the dotted box—are described in a formal manner in [SELLE et al. 2002]. We briefly repeat the main steps here.

Vessel analysis is an active research area in medical image analysis. Basically, there are approaches in which vessels are first segmented and then skeletonized, and approaches that start by searching for the centerline in each slice and continue by searching the cross section of a vessel for each detected centerline voxel. If it is important to detect small vessels in the periphery, multiscale approaches are often successful in combining segmentation results derived in different resolutions. As with other areas of image analysis, there is a strong trade-off between general methods with a wide scope and highly specialized algorithms that incorporate model assumptions about parts of the human body or particular image acquisition protocols. Such knowledge-based methods have been developed for the analysis of the bronchial tree, for example [SONKA et al. 1994 and BARTZ et al. 2003b].

14.1.1 PREPROCESSING TO ENHANCE VESSEL-LIKE STRUCTURES

The segmentation of vascular structures is often based on a preprocessing step where the signal to noise ratio (recall Sect. 5.2.4) is improved and inhomogeneities due to the irregular distribution of a contrast agent are removed. As a special preprocessing for vascular analysis, a special "vesselness" operator has been proposed by LORENZ et al. [1997] and SATO et al. [1997] and refined by FRANGI et al. [1998]. It is based on the Hessian matrix, which consists of the second-order derivatives of the intensity variations

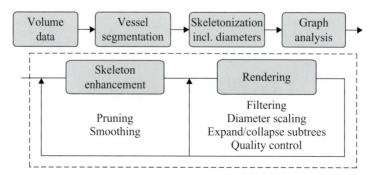

FIGURE 14.4 *Pipeline for vessel visualization and exploration* [HAHN *et al.* 2001b]. (*Image courtesy* HORST HAHN, *MeVis Bremen*)

$(I_{xx}, I_{xy}, I_{xz}, I_{yy}, I_{yz}, I_{zz})$. The symmetric Hessian has three real-valued eigenvalues λ_i that can be used to determine the likelihood of a voxel to belong to a line-shaped structure. The absolute values of the eigenvalues are sorted ($|\lambda_1| \geq |\lambda_2| \geq |\lambda_3|$) and compared. For an ideal line-shaped structure, the following relation holds: $\lambda_1 \gg \lambda_2 \approx \lambda_3$. With appropriate weight parameters, this analysis may be used to enhance vascular structures. This analysis can be carried out at different scales to cope with vessels of a different diameter, on which the scale has an essential effect. FRANGI *et al.* [1998] apply the filter in a multiscale approach. The refined "vesselness" filter is widely used and yields excellent results with respect to improved visualization (MIP, Direct Volume Rendering, Fig. 14.5) as well as better segmentation. This preprocessing step, however, is computationally expensive and often applied as an offline process.

14.1.2 VESSEL SEGMENTATION

After appropriate preprocessing, vessel segmentation is the next step in the vessel analysis pipeline (see Fig. 14.6). For vessel segmentation, region-growing algorithms (recall Sect. 5.3.3) are often used. They are initiated with a user-defined seedpoint and accumulate adjacent voxels that satisfy a homogeneity criterion (often a threshold that should separate contrast-enhanced voxels of vascular structures from surrounding tissue). For vascular structures, region growing may be refined by employing the assumption of elliptical cross sections (recall Sect. 5.4.5 and [HENNEMUTH *et al.* 2005]). Besides a powerful segmentation algorithm, a fast and goal-directed interaction is essential to fine-tune the result (e.g., adjustments of thresholds and definition of additional seedpoints). An encompassing overview on vessel segmentation is given in [KIRBAS and QUEK 2004].

14.1.3 SKELETONIZATION

A variety of algorithms exist to convert the segmentation result to a skeleton (recall Sect. 5.7). With typical radiological data, this requires consideration of the anisotropic shape of voxels. Ideally, the skeleton is located precisely in the center of vascular structures and contains exactly all relevant branches. It must be noted that the results of the widely available skeletonization algorithms particularly differ with respect to their accuracy (deviation to the centerline). KRUSZYNSKI *et al.* [2006] discuss these differences in a quantitative way, which is essential for a morphometric analysis. For pure visualization purposes, the accuracy of known algorithms, such as [DESCHAMPS 2001, NIBLACK *et al.* 1992, NAEF *et al.* 1997, PALÁGYI and KUBA 1999], is sufficient, since the deviation is usually very small compared to the voxel size.

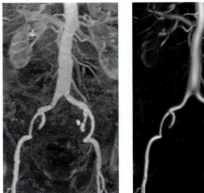
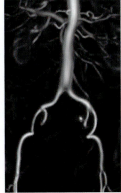

FIGURE 14.5 *An MIP image of an MRA dataset is generated (left). The "vesselness" filter is applied to suppressing other structures (right)* [FRANGI *et al.* 1998]. *(Images courtesy* ALEJANDRO FRANGI, *Universitat Pompeu Fabra)*

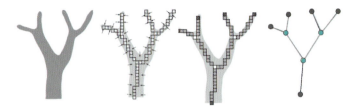

FIGURE 14.6 *Vessel segmentation, skeletonization (construction of a one voxel-width representation in the centerline of the branches), and reconstruction of a branching graph illustrated in the 2D-case. Points in the skeleton with more than two neighbors are considered branching points and form the nodes in the branching graph* [SELLE *et al.* 2000]. *(Image courtesy* DIRK SELLE, *MeVis Bremen)*

Very small side-branches often arise due to noise or partial volume effects. These irrelevant branches should be suppressed (pruning). This can be accomplished by taking into account the length of a side-branch in relation to the branch which is in the hierarchy at the next higher level (recall [MASUTANI *et al.* 1996]). However, care must be taken to prevent relevant branches from being removed.

For the exploration of vascular structures, such as hiding a subtree, it is essential to represent them as a graph. If an anatomic tree structure is correctly identified, it should not contain any cycles (cycles should be removed).

After this step, anatomic trees may be represented as directed acyclic graph $G = (V, E)$, with nodes V representing branching points and edges E representing connections between them. For each edge, a list of the skeleton voxels and vessel diameters along that edge should be represented. It should be noted that the graph analysis step poses some challenges. In 3D, it is often ambiguous which skeleton voxel actually forms the junction, depending on the chosen neighborhood definition (6, 12, or 26 neighborhood for voxels that share a face, an edge, or a vertex). REINDERS *et al.* [2000] discuss this issue and suggest considering the voxel with three face-connected neighbors as the junction node. If no such node exists, a voxel that shares edges or faces with three voxels is chosen. This way, the analysis usually becomes unambiguous.

Enhancement of Skeletons Due to the discrete nature of radiological data, distracting aliasing effects occur if the skeleton is immediately visualized. Jagged lines appear instead of straight lines, and curved line segments are not faithfully represented. To eliminate these effects, skeletons are smoothed with a low pass filter (applied along the skeleton). This smoothing process is an example for the general noise reduction problem discussed in Section 5.2.4.

The classic low pass filter is the Gaussian, which is discretely approximated by the binomial filter (the elements of the filter are the binomial coefficients). A binomial filter of size three ([121]-kernel) or size five ([1 4 6 4 1]-kernel) is appropriate to smooth the edges of the skeleton (see Fig. 14.7). For all voxels of the skeleton with two neighbors (e.g., in the absence of branchings) the resulting skeleton is strongly improved. However, at bifurcations, the simple smoothing causes undesirable effects. In the case of a small bifurcation, the main branch is pulled towards the small bifurcation. If a symmetric bifurcation occurs (at the end of a major vessel where two smaller vessels coincide) it is preferable that both smaller vessels bifurcate with the same angle. Therefore, the smoothing process is modified at branchings, weighting the voxels involved as to their *relevance* (see Fig. 14.8). Different metrics may be used to measure *relevance* of a branch. A simple and efficient method is to consider the total length (in skeleton voxels) of the subtree that depends on a particular branch. With this measure, leaf branches have a low relevance and branches close to the root of a vascular tree have a high relevance. The same filtering technique and the same strategy at branchings can be applied to the local vessel diameter. The appearance of the vascular structures is strongly enhanced by filtering the diameter (see Fig. 14.9).

There are alternative strategies to enhance skeletons. A group of algorithms simplifies skeletons, similar to the way polygonal surface models are smoothed: skeleton nodes that are not essential for the topology (endpoints and junctions) are evaluated with respect to their influence on the accuracy. If they are not crucial (e.g., they are located almost at the straight line between their neighbors), they are removed [REINDERS et al. 2000].

Identification of Different Vessel Systems In some organs of the human body, several vascular systems occur. Usually, the vessel segmentation yields voxels of all these systems. Figure 14.10 illustrates locations where

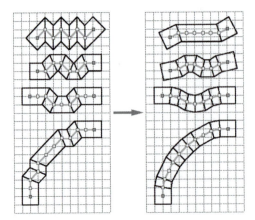

FIGURE 14.7 *Smoothing with a binomial filter. The jaggy skeleton with all elements located at grid positions (left) is smoothed whereas skeleton elements are no longer forced to be located at grid positions. Small quadrilaterals represent the center of voxels. Note that the start- and endpoints of the skeleton are not affected [HAHN et al. 2001b]. (Images courtesy HORST HAHN, MeVis Bremen)*

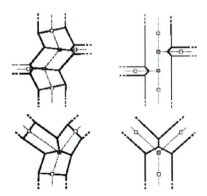

FIGURE 14.8 Undesired effects on branching structures (left) are corrected by considering the relevance of voxels (right). In particular, small side branches (leaf nodes in the tree representation) with low relevance do not influence major branches significantly (images in the top row), and at symmetric Y-shaped bifurcations, two branches with similar relevance are correctly smoothed (images in the bottom row) [HAHN et al. 2001b]. (Images courtesy HORST HAHN, MeVis Bremen)

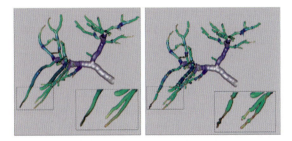

FIGURE 14.9 Smoothing the local diameter with a binomial filter. The diameter is color-coded to reveal the differences between the smoothed variant (left) compared to the original information. In particular, in the periphery, where the diameter changes between 1 and 2 voxels, the smoothing step is essential [HAHN et al. 2001b]. (Images courtesy HORST HAHN, MeVis Bremen)

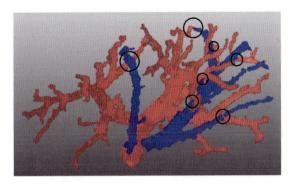

FIGURE 14.10 The vessel segmentation result was automatically decomposed into two vascular trees. At the encircled points, the trees touch each other. Based on model assumptions with respect to the diameter, the trees are separated [SELLE et al. 2000]. (Image courtesy DIRK SELLE, MeVis Bremen)

two vascular systems touch each other, due to the limited resolution of the acquired data, in which a voxel of one vascular structure might be in the adjacency of a voxel belonging to another structure. Vessels may be separated in the *graph analysis* step. Different model assumptions may be employed for this purpose. One assumption is that the vessel diameter is reduced from the root of the tree to the periphery. Points of the skeleton where this assumption is not valid are candidates for the separation of vascular structures. Another assumption concerns the angles measured at bifurcations and the type of branchings. Some branching types are typical candidates for the separation—for example, where branches touch each other with an X-shape at the branching.

After the separation of vessel systems, there is one graph per vessel system. The root of each graph represents the root of the corresponding vascular tree. With this data structure top-down and bottom-up traversal of vascular structures is possible. A review of vessel analysis methods is presented in [SELLE *et al.* 2002].

It must be noted that the vessel graphs resulting from this process are not always reliable and correct. In particular, the graphs may contain loops, which are undesirable if some kind of local hierarchical filtering (collapse subtrees) is attempted. Therefore, systems for the exploration of vascular structures should provide facilities to tackle this problem. On the one hand, automatic strategies can be used to select edges due to certain criteria, with the consequence that the removal of these edges avoids cycles. However, these methods are also prone to errors, due to the underlying data. Ideally, an interactive solution should also be provided where loops are emphasized and edges can be interactively selected to remove the loops [KRUSZYNSKI *et al.* 2006].

14.2   OVERVIEW OF VESSEL VISUALIZATION

Conventional methods for the visualization of anatomic structures from volume data do not reconstruct vascular structures. Isosurface rendering results in artifacts: either vessels appear disconnected in the periphery, or structures that do not belong to the vessels but exhibit similar intensity values are included in the visualization. This problem can be reduced by analyzing and postprocessing the resulting surfaces. As an example, the connected component analysis reveals whether one connected surface was generated or whether several components without a connection arose. Using this information, the visualization can be restricted to the largest component [SCHROEDER *et al.* 2001]. Smoothing techniques for polygonal meshes may also improve isosurface renderings of vascular structures (see Fig. 14.11). But even these approaches do not ensure that the topology of the resulting tree structures can be easily recognized.

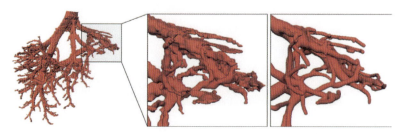

FIGURE 14.11 *Comparison of a raw isosurface and a strongly smoothed isosurface of a vascular tree. Smoothing was accomplished by means of a Laplacian smoothing filter, applied six times. Further smoothing did not change the visual quality. (Image courtesy* STEFFEN OELTZE, *University of Magdeburg)*

For the visualization of vascular structures, maximum intensity projections (MIPs) are used frequently. However, MIP projections do not correctly reflect depth relations, because voxels might be displayed even though other voxels with high opacity are nearer to the camera. Moreover, small vessels tend to disappear completely.

As a modification of the MIP, closest vessel projections (CVPs) have been introduced [ZUIDERVELD 1995b]. The CVP scheme is as follows: for each ray, the first local maximum with an intensity above a user-defined threshold is projected to the image. Thus, small vessels in front of large vessels (with higher intensities) are visible. With the methods described thus far, the interaction for exploring vascular structures is restricted (see Fig. 14.12). For example, it is not possible to selectively hide or emphasize vessels.

14.2.1 RECONSTRUCTION OF VESSELS FOR VISUALIZATION

The benefit of the reconstruction of vascular structures for a visualization that emphasizes the connectivity and shape of features was recognized early [GERIG et al. 1993, EHRICKE et al. 1994]. Meanwhile, several attempts have been made to develop special visualization techniques for anatomic tree structures in general and vascular trees in particular. In another early work, abstract visualizations have been generated that highlight the topology of vessels but ignore vessel diameters [ZAHLTEN et al. 1995]. Frequently, a visualization less abstract than the right image in Figure 14.13 is desired. Ideally, the level of abstraction can be interactively modified.

The reconstruction and visualization are based on the model assumption that the cross section of non-pathologic vessels has a circular shape. This model assumption is discussed (e.g., in [MASUTANI et al. 1996]).

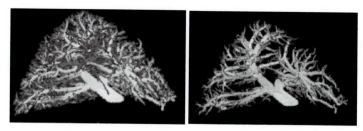

FIGURE 14.12   *Closest vessel projection of a corrosion cast of the human liver. Left: a low threshold; right: a higher threshold.* (*Image courtesy* SVEN KOHLE, *MeVis Bremen*)

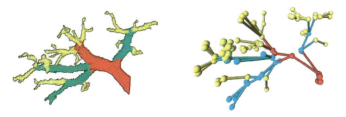

FIGURE 14.13   *A "realistic" surface-based vessel visualization (left) and abstract vessel visualization consisting of tubes and spheres* (right). *Colors represent the hierarchy of the vessels* [ZAHLTEN et al. 1995]. (*Image courtesy* CORNELIA ZAHLTEN, *University of Bremen*)

This assumption turned out to be appropriate for therapy planning procedures in which vascular structures are not pathologic themselves but represent important anatomic context.

An advanced method for vessel visualization is curved planar reformation (CPR) [KANITSAR et al. 2002b]. Given the vessel skeleton, a curved plane is generated by moving a line—aligned parallel to the horizontal axis of the viewing plane—along the skeleton. A 2D image of the vessel is eventually obtained by flattening the curved plane and displaying all voxels located close to it. A comprehensive survey of methods for vessel analysis and visualization is given in [BÜHLER et al. 2004].

14.2.2 RECONSTRUCTION OF VESSELS FOR INTERACTION

The reconstruction of vascular structures also enables essential interaction facilities. For example, the local vessel diameter might be used to restrict the visualization of a vascular tree to the parts that are above a specific threshold. The exploration is crucial, because modern imaging devices allow the extraction of complex vascular trees that are difficult to understand at a glance. In [NIESSEN et al. 1999], vessels were segmented and analyzed to selectively hide them. The subdivision of vessels by placing and moving balloons with the goal of interacting with parts of vascular structures is described in [BARTZ et al. 1999c]. MARTINEZ-PEREZ et al. [2000] deal with the geometrical and morphological analysis of retinal blood images. Although interaction facilities are not directly addressed, they describe the determination of measurements that are useful for interaction.

14.2.3 EXPLICIT AND IMPLICIT SURFACE RECONSTRUCTION

In the following sections, we consider two principally different approaches to vessel visualization:

- *Explicit surface reconstruction.* This category of methods explicitly generates a polygonal mesh of a vascular system based on the detected centerline and the associated diameter information.
- *Implicit surface reconstruction.* These methods generate a scalar field based on implicit equations. A polygonal mesh arises by thresholding the scalar field.

Most of the explicit reconstruction techniques employ a *generalized cylinder*, with the skeleton as a 3D curve representing the centerline and a closed circular cross section perpendicular to it defining the local diameter of the generalized cylinders. Tubes, truncated cones, and parametric surfaces are specific examples of explicit surface reconstruction techniques.

14.3   EXPLICIT SURFACE RECONSTRUCTION

In this section we describe explicit surface reconstruction methods. MASUTANI et al. [1996] fitted cylinders along the skeleton to visualize vascular structures. However, severe discontinuities occur at branchings where cylinders with different diameters coincide.

A special problem, the visualization of cerebral structures, has been tackled in [PUIG et al. 1997]. They modeled typical bifurcations and pathologic situations, such as aneurysms and stenosis, and fitted these models to the patient specific data at hand. In total, five different graphics primitives are used to reconstruct the vascular tree. The focus of their work is on the geometric continuity and on realistic shading.

A semitransparent visualization of the segmented vessels overlaid with an opaque visualization of the skeleton inside the vessels was suggested in [HERNANDEZ-HOYOS et al. 2000]. This method is based on a sophisticated vessel segmentation and targets the quantification of blood vessels to detect stenosis.

14.3.1 VISUALIZATION WITH PARAMETRIC SURFACES

HÖHNE et al. [2000] built a geometric model for anatomy education based on the Visible Human dataset. Small vessels and nerves that could be detected only in part (or not at all) have been modeled by placing ball-shaped markers connected with b-splines, resulting in smooth visualizations (see Fig. 14.14) even at branchings. The splines allow local changes to the shape of the modeled tree structures through modifying the size or position of the markers. Figure 14.15 shows how these modeled anatomic tree structures are integrated in a visualization of the Visible Human dataset.

14.3.2 VISUALIZATION WITH TRUNCATED CONES

The visualization technique described in this subsection was developed for exploring vascular structures from corrosion casts (very large vascular trees with several thousand branches are involved). Efficiency was therefore an essential requirement [HAHN 1998]. The visualization is based on truncated cones (TC), which are able to represent the constriction of the vessel diameter appropriately. The method is therefore referred to as TC visualization. It is another example for a generalized cylinder technique.

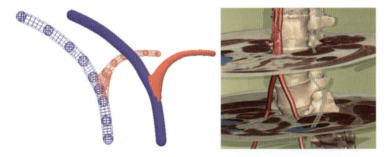

FIGURE 14.14   *Small anatomic tree structures are modeled by placing ball-shaped markers and represented as a special variant of splines* [POMMERT et al. 2001]. *(Image courtesy* ANDREAS POMMERT, University Hospital Hamburg-Eppendorf)

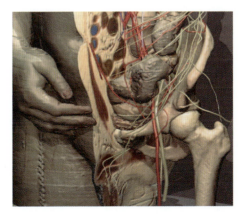

FIGURE 14.15   *Modeled nerves and vascular structures as part of a body model based on the Visible Human dataset* [POMMERT et al. 2001]. *(Image courtesy* ANDREAS POMMERT, University Hospital Hamburg-Eppendorf)

For the visualization, a vascular tree must be mapped to a set of lists L_i that comprise sequential edges of a vascular tree. The edges of each list represent a path at which the TC are extruded. Along one path, surface normals and colors are interpolated such that a smooth appearance results. At the touching points between two paths, visible discontinuities arise. To minimize these distracting artifacts, it is desirable to assign as many edges as possible to one list. As a second criterion, at branchings a list should be continued in the direction that deviates least from the last branch. Figure 14.16 illustrates the mapping of a 2D tree to sequential lists.

Quality

The accuracy of the visualization, which we refer to as quality, depends on two parameters:

- The accuracy of the polygonal approximation of cones (the number of vertices per TC)
- The sampling rate along the path (the number of cones generated)

Minimum accuracy for the first parameter means that the circular cross section of cones is represented via a triangle. With the minimum sampling rate, one TC is generated to represent the complete path between two bifurcations. With the maximum sampling rate, one cone is generated between two voxels along the path. In Figure 14.17, the influence of the sampling rate on the resulting visualizations is shown.

A reasonable trade-off between quality and speed is to employ eight to twelve vertices to approximate the circular cross-section of each TC and to use the maximum sampling rate (one TC represents the vascular tree between two subsequent voxels).

One problem with a straightforward TC visualization is the appearance of endpoints. Without special care, vessels seem to end abruptly instead of coming to a natural, smooth end. To improve this, the end of each path is capped by a half-sphere (see Fig. 14.18).

Examples

The visualization technique described above has been extensively used for preoperative planning in liver surgery. As one example, the improved vessel visualization is used for oncologic liver surgery, in which it is essential to recognize the spatial relations around a malignant tumor and to estimate how the destruction or removal of this tumor will affect the blood supply [PREIM et al. 2000].

The second example concerns live donor liver transplants (LDLT). These operations are motivated by the lack of organs required for transplantation. In this procedure, the liver is split into two parts; one remains in situ while the other is given to a recipient. Vascular anatomy is crucial in the evaluation of potential donors (see Fig. 14.19 and Fig. 14.20). The TC visualization is widely used for surgery planning. It is part of a commercial software assistant called MeVis Liver Explorer, which is used at various hospitals.

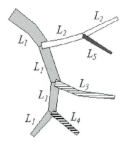

FIGURE 14.16 *Sequential edges of the vascular tree are mapped to different lists as prerequisite for the visualization* [HAHN et al. 2001b]. *(Image courtesy* HORST HAHN, *MeVis Bremen)*

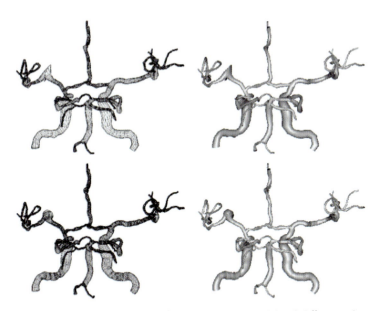

FIGURE 14.17   *Cerebral blood vessels are reconstructed from MRI data and sampled with different resolutions along the skeleton. The wire-frame visualizations (left) correspond to the Gouraud shaded visualizations (right). In the top row, a moderate sampling rate is chosen, whereas in the bottom row, the maximum sampling rate results in a fine-grained mesh and a smooth surface visualization. (Images courtesy HORST HAHN, MeVis Bremen)*

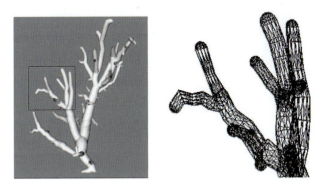

FIGURE 14.18   *The right image presents a close-up view of the left image as wire-frame visualization. A (triangulated) half-sphere leads to a smooth appearance at the endpoints of vessels [HAHN et al. 2001b]. (Image courtesy HORST HAHN, MeVis Bremen)*

14.3.3 VISUALIZATION WITH SUBDIVISION SURFACES

The most advanced explicit reconstruction technique is based on subdivision surfaces; it was developed at the VRV research center in Vienna [FELKL et al. 2002, FELKL et al. 2004, Bühler et al. 2004]. This method is also an instance of the generalized cylinder approach relying on the vessel skeleton derived with the methods described in [KANITSAR et al. 2002b].

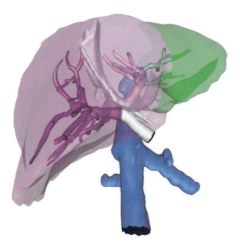

FIGURE 14.19 *Planning of live donor liver transplants. The plane in the central part reflects the intended splitting position. The large aorta is visualized with (traditional) surface-based rendering. The intrahepatic vessels are visualized by means of the TC method [SELLE et al. 2000]. (Image courtesy WOLF SPINDLER, MeVis Bremen)*

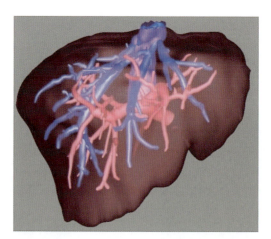

FIGURE 14.20 *Visualization of the intrahepatic vascular anatomy (hepatic vein and portal vein) inside the semitransparent liver [SELLE et al. 2000]. (Image courtesy WOLF SPINDLER, MeVis Bremen)*

An initial base mesh is constructed along the vessel centerline. This base mesh consists of quadrilateral patches and can be subdivided and refined according to the Catmull-Clark subdivision technique described in [DEROSE et al. 1998]. The smoothness of the final model depends on the iteration depth of the refinement step.

The algorithm can handle different branching types in a uniform way and is very efficient. A problem of this algorithm is that it requires nonoverlapping cross sections not only along vessel segments but also at joints. Base meshes and their initial refinements are shown in Figure 14.21. The application to "real" clinical data is illustrated in Figure 14.22.

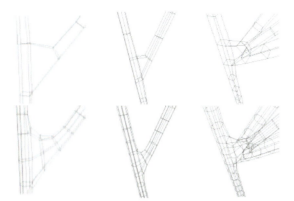

FIGURE 14.21   *Visualization of tree structures by means of subdivision surfaces. In the top row, three base meshes are shown, whereas the bottom row shows the corresponding meshes after the first refinement. The refinement leads to considerably smoother representation at the expense of an increased polygon site* [FELKEL *et al.* 2004]. *(Image courtesy* PETR FELKEL, *Czech Technical University)*

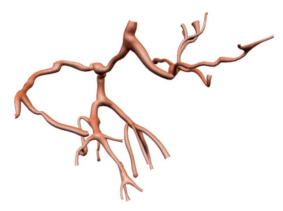

FIGURE 14.22   *Subdivision surfaces applied to a vessel tree derived from clinical data. (Image courtesy* PETR FELKEL, *Czech Technical University)*

Branchings are treated separately to avoid rendering discontinuities and the construction of objectionable structures inside the geometric model. Reliable avoidance of objectionable structures is essential for virtual endoscopy applications, in which the virtual camera is moved inside a vascular system[1] to assess the vessel wall [BARTZ *et al.* 2001d].

14.4   MODELING TREE STRUCTURES WITH IMPLICIT SURFACES

The previously described methods are fast and produce fairly smooth visualizations. However, some artifacts cannot be avoided, due to the construction process, in which graphics primitives are explicitly connected.

---

1   This particular kind of virtual endoscopy is referred to as *angioscopy*.

14.4.1 INTRODUCTION

Implicit surfaces offer an alternative to explicitly constructing the surface of an object by polygons or parametric patches. They describe the surface by an equation that is often more compact than its parametric counterpart. Especially in modeling smooth, deformable objects, implicit surfaces unfold their full strength. BLINN [1982b] introduced implicit surfaces in computer graphics. He developed *Blobby Molecules* to visualize electron density fields: points in space represent energy sources, and the resulting energy fields are visualized by means of isosurfaces connecting points with the same energy.

Later, the pioneering work of Jules Bloomenthal made it possible to efficiently visualize skeletal structures (such as vascular trees) with implicit surfaces. However, care must be taken to ensure that the structures are visualized faithfully. Some effects of implicit modeling in particular, such as bulging and blending between skeleton parts, must be controlled.

Before we describe the visualization by means of convolution surfaces we introduce some concepts of implicit modeling (see [BLOOMENTHAL et al. 1997] for an in-depth discussion).

14.4.2 IMPLICIT SURFACES: A BRIEF INTRODUCTION

An example for an implicit equation is the description of a sphere with radius r: $x^2 + y^2 + z^2 - r^2 = 0$. This formula represents all points $p(x, y, z)$ in space that are on the surface of a sphere with radius r centered at the origin. The above equation can be generalized as:

$$F(p) - Iso = 0 \qquad (14.1)$$

$F(p)$ is called the *scalar field function* because a scalar value may be computed for each point p. *Iso* denotes an *isovalue* used for generating an *isosurface* that represents all points for which the implicit equation is zero. The function employed by BLINN [1982b] is given in Equation 14.2:

$$F(p) = be^{-\sigma\|c-p\|^2} \qquad (14.2)$$

where c is the center of an electron. Equation 14.2 describes a Gaussian bump centered at c, with height b and standard deviation σ. For several energy sources, the scalar value at p can be calculated as Equation 14.3:

$$F(p) = \sum_i b_i e^{-\sigma_i \|c_i - p\|^2} \qquad (14.3)$$

Other popular field functions were presented by [NISHIMURA et al. 1985] (metaballs) and [WYVILL et al. 1986] (soft objects). Note that only scalar fields around point primitives had been considered so far.

14.4.3 CONVOLUTION SURFACES

BLOOMENTHAL and SHOEMAKE [1991] extended implicit descriptions to surfaces defined by skeletal primitives (e.g., line segments or polygons). This enhancement allows the generation of smooth generalized cylinders, which is essential to visualize vascular structures. They introduced *convolution surfaces* to model the surface of an object around its skeleton. In the following, S denotes a skeleton, and s refers to a single point on the skeleton. Convolution surfaces (CS) avoid bulges and creases for nonbranching skeletal structures. The scalar value is calculated according to Equation 14.4:

$$F(p) = f(S, p) = \int_S e^{\left(\frac{-\|s-p\|^2}{2} \right)} ds \qquad (14.4)$$

in which $f(S, p)$ is the convolution of a skeleton S with a 3D Gaussian filter. In contrast with other implicit surfaces, the value is computed considering *all* points of the skeleton by integration.

Convolution surfaces utilize a concept that is well known from signal processing: namely, the modification of a signal by a filter (recall Sect. 5.2.4 where noise reduction with convolution filters was discussed). For a Gaussian filter, Equation 14.4 may be rewritten as:

$$F(p) = f(S, p) = (h \otimes S)(p) \qquad (14.5)$$

where S is the signal, h is the filter function, and $\otimes$ denotes the convolution operator.

For the visualization of vasculature, the skeleton corresponds to the signal. The selected filter function should smooth this signal and thereby suppress high frequencies. A low pass filter is most suitable for that purpose. The resulting field around the skeleton corresponds to the scalar field mentioned above. By constructing an isosurface through this field, the CS is formed.

For the understanding of bulge-free blending, it is necessary to elaborate on the superposition property of convolution:

$$h \otimes (S_1 + S_2) = (h \otimes S_1) + (h \otimes S_2) \qquad (14.6)$$

This guarantees that two abutting segments produce the same convolution as does their union [BLOOMENTHAL 1995]. Furthermore, superposition has an impact on implementation issues and the modeling process. It permits the convolution of a complex object primitive by primitive in an arbitrary order, instead of considering the skeleton as a whole.

Filter Selection   For vessel visualization, the underlying filter function should be continuous and monotonic. Furthermore, it should have finite support (or be negligible beyond a certain distance). These requirements restrict the filter selection to low pass filters. The Gaussian is a prime example for this type of function. Numerous other kernels have been published [SHERSTYUK 1998]. However, the scope of eligible filter functions is strongly reduced when a CS faithfully represents a given local radius information. In [BLOOMENTHAL 1995], a Gaussian function (see Eq. 14.7) is used for convolution.

$$h(p) = e^{-d(p,S)^2 \omega}, \quad \omega = \ln 2, \ d(p, S) > 0 \qquad (14.7)$$

ω is referred to as the *width coefficient* and equals $1/(2\sigma^2)$, where σ is the standard deviation. The distance between point p and the line segment skeleton S is denoted by $d(p, S)$. In [HORNUS et al. 2003], two other filter functions are discussed to correctly represent a radius information. However, these descend more slowly towards zero compared to the Gaussian.

The choice of a filter function must also consider computational speed, because large datasets are involved. By definition of a CS (see Eq. 14.4), the entire skeleton needs to be considered when calculating the scalar value at a point p. For the visualization of vascular structures, this means a prohibitively high computational effort. To improve performance, the computation of the scalar field might be restricted to bounding volumes along line segments (parts of the vessel skeleton between two branchings). The tightness of a suitable bounding volume depends on the filter function (particularly on the distance from the center to where the function value is negligible). The Gaussian allows the employment of tight bounding volumes, because it drops much more quickly toward zero than many other kernels, such as those described by [HORNUS et al. 2003], which is unfavorable for a fast computation.

The computation of the convolution integral in Equation 14.4 may be simplified by separating it into the product of an *integration filter* and a *distance filter* [BLOOMENTHAL 1995]. Whereas the first term requires solving a 1D integral, the second is simply a single evaluation of the kernel (see Eq. 14.8):

$$h(p) = e^{-(d(p,H))^2 \omega} \tag{14.8}$$

where $d(p, H)$ is the distance between point p and its projection H on the line that proceeds through the considered line segment (if p is near the end of the segment H might be beyond the segment).

Correct Representation of the Radius Information   The separation of the computation into two filters is crucial for an efficient evaluation of the implicit function. Instead of the 3D integration (see Eq. 14.4), a 1D integral has to be solved. It can be precomputed and stored in a lookup table. For adapting the radius of the resulting CS, $d(p, H)$ is divided by radius $r(H)$, which is linearly interpolated between the radii at the segment endpoints.

To let the CS converge against a given radius, appropriate isovalues and width coefficients ω must be selected. Bloomenthal employed an isovalue of $1/2$ so as to let the CS pass through the segment endpoints. Now, let us consider the CS of a sufficiently long cylinder and a point p that is located exactly on the surface and in the middle of it. Here, the integration filter equals 1, as the kernel is fully subtended by the segment. With the constraint that $d(p, H) = r(H)$ for point p on the CS, it follows from Equation 14.8 and Equation 14.1:

$$F(p) = e^{-(r(H)/r(H))^2 \omega} - 1/2 = e^{-\omega} - 1/2 = 0 \tag{14.9}$$

Thus, $\omega = \ln 2 \approx 0.6931$. ω might be used as parameter to control the amount of blending.

14.4.4   BLENDING

The ability to create smooth transitions between simple objects to form a complex organic shape is a strength of implicit surfaces. Here, so-called *blends* are used instead of parametric freeform surfaces.

For a CS, blending corresponds to an integration of the filter along the entire skeleton. At the skeleton joints, the scalar fields of adjacent primitives overlap. The CS constructed through the resulting field forms a smooth envelope of the underlying joint. In an implementation, each primitive may be convolved separately, due to the superposition property of convolution. Blending may have negative effects on the visualization of vascular structures; these effects are discussed in the following.

Blending Strength at Branchings   With the initial filter design [BLOOMENTHAL and SHOEMAKE 1991], the transitions at branchings were very smooth but deviated strongly from the skeleton (see Fig. 14.23 (middle)). This is undesirable, and in some cases, the radiologist's interpretation of the topology is hampered. Therefore, a narrower filter kernel should be used to produce a surface that tracks the skeleton more faithfully.

Unwanted Blending   For precise modeling of complex shapes, it is essential to control the blending between different parts. Concerning anatomic tree structures, segments with skeletons that are not connected should not blend with each other. OPALACH and MADDOCK [1993] use a *restricted blending graph* to solve this problem. Based on the topology of the given skeleton, primitives are classified into blendable and unblendable primitives. This manual classification, however, is not suitable for vessel visualization. Also, this solution does not ensure C^1 continuity of the shape.

FIGURE 14.23 *Blending strength, left: skeleton; middle: high blending strength; right: reduced blending strength [OELTZE and PREIM 2005]. (Images courtesy STEFFEN OELTZE, University of Magdeburg)*

FIGURE 14.24 *Bulging problem, left: skeleton;middle: convolution surface; right: bulge at the branching in horizontal view [OELTZE and PREIM 2005]. (Images courtesy STEFFEN OELTZE, University of Magdeburg)*

Bulging Convolution surfaces are bulge-free for nonbranching line segment skeletons, due to the super-position property of convolution. However, as shown in [BLOOMENTHAL 1995], they do exhibit bulges at branchings. This effect is disturbing for the visualization of vascular structures, because a bulge might be easily mistaken for a pathological variation (e.g., an aneurysm). Even though model-based visualization methods are not targeted at supporting vascular diagnostics, this drawback should be minimized.

Consequences The Gaussian is the preferred filter for the convolution of vascular structures. In particular, the Gaussian is the only filter function that allows the correct visualization of the radius information and provides a parameter, the width coefficient ω, that can be used to control the amount of blending. However, a modification of the original kernel is advisable to reduce the blending strength at branchings [OELTZE and PREIM 2004]. The same modification also reduces the other unwanted effects (unwanted blending and bulging). Furthermore, the polygonization of scalar fields might be accelerated by using tighter bounding volumes. These aspects are discussed and illustrated in the following Section 14.5.

14.5   VISUALIZATION WITH CONVOLUTION SURFACES

In this section, we describe how a modified width coefficient ω affects the undesired effects. We continue by discussing a preprocessing of the data to reduce the effort required to compute the CS. This section is based on [OELTZE and PREIM 2004].

14.5.1 FILTER MODIFICATION

An evaluation of different ω values yielded that a value of $5ln(2) \sim 3.5$ is suitable to prevent the undesired effects by still maintaining the desired effects (smooth blending). With considerably larger width coefficients, blending would be avoided, and the CS visualization leads to almost exactly the same result as the TC visualization, except for the construction of polygons inside the vascular surface at branchings. Note, that ω has been increased with the effect that the filter function is narrower (see Fig. 14.25).

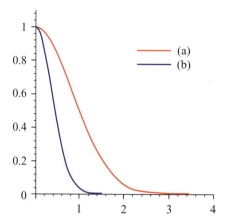

FIGURE 14.25 *Gaussian function from Bloomenthal (a) compared to the modified version with increased width coefficient and narrower shape (b)* [OELTZE *and* PREIM 2005]. *(Image courtesy* STEFFEN OELTZE, *University of Magdeburg)*

To correctly represent the radius information along a line segment, a recalculation of the isovalue is required. With respect to the new ω value, the isovalue (Iso) is evaluated as follows (recall Eq. 14.9):

$$F(p) = e^{-(r(H)/r(H))^2 5 \ln 2} - Iso = e^{-5 \ln 2} - Iso = 0 \qquad (14.10)$$

Hence, $Iso = 1/32 = 0.03125$.

To evaluate this filter function, a simple skeleton with a trifurcation (four coinciding branches) might be employed. In vascular trees, primarily bifurcations and trifurcations occur. Figure 14.26 (a) and (b) show how the blending strength is reduced for the simple skeleton. Also, bulging is avoided with the modified filter function (see Fig. 14.26 (c) and (d)). To study unwanted blending, an S-shaped skeleton with 3-mm distance between the horizontal lines is useful. The radius was increased until blending occurred. The ratio between the distance of the CS and the distance of the centerlines determines the occurrence of unwanted blending. With the modified width coefficient, the ratio could be reduced from 29% to 9% (see Fig. 14.27).

14.5.2 COMPUTATIONAL COMPLEXITY

For the construction of a CS, it is necessary that the scalar value can be evaluated at every point in space. Without special care, all parts of the skeleton are considered for the evaluation of the implicit equation at each point. For large anatomic tree structures with more than 1000 branchings, the computational effort is prohibitive.

To accelerate the computation, it should be restricted to the *significant range* of the *scalar field* (SSF) about each line segment. For a point p located outside this range, $F(p)$ is smaller than a given threshold T (e.g., $T = 0.001$). To store the SSF, a partitioning of space is necessary. The voxel grid of the underlying data may be used as a basis for the partitioning.

The following preprocessing turned out to be useful. While iterating over all line segments, a cylindrical bounding volume (CBV) was constructed. The cylindrical shape of the bounding volume allows a close approximation of the shape of the convolution surface and the underlying scalar field. The radius of the CBV is based on the SSF, which in turn is determined by the maximum radius along the line segment

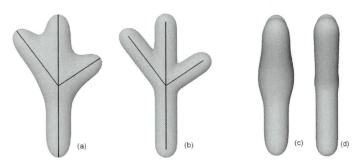

FIGURE 14.26   Transitions at branching, (a): convolved with original filter function ($\omega = ln(2)$), (b): convolved with modified filter ($\omega = 5ln(2)$). The semitransparent visualization reveals the underlying skeleton. (c):side view of the same skeleton convolved with original Gaussian filter. (d) side view of the skeleton convolved with modified filter avoids bulging [Oeltze and Preim 2005]. (Images courtesy Steffen Oeltze, University of Magdeburg)

FIGURE 14.27   Distance between the branches of the S-shapes is 3 mm. The radius of all branches is 1.37 mm. Unwanted blending (left) is considerably reduced with the narrower filter (right) [Oeltze and Preim 2005]. (Images courtesy Steffen Oeltze, University of Magdeburg)

multiplied by a factor *fac*. The latter is computed with respect to the width of the convolution filter. The width influences the extension of the SSF. Although the Gaussian has infinite support, it exhibits values close to 0 for points beyond a certain distance from the center. This distance is adapted to T:

$$e^{-fac^2\omega} < T \qquad (14.11)$$

For $T = 0.001$ and $\omega = 5 \ln 2$, a factor of $fac = 1.5$ is adequate to identify those voxels contained in the SSF of the current line segment (see Fig. 14.28).

For the realization of the CBV test, two problems must be solved:

- Efficiently check whether a point (the center of a voxel) is inside a cylinder
- Restrict the voxels that undergo the inclusion test

Concerning the first problem, an implicit description of a cylinder is appropriate for a convenient test of inclusion. With respect to the second problem, for each line segment an axis-aligned bounding box (AABB) is computed in voxel coordinates (see Fig. 14.28). The test of inclusion in the CBV is performed only for all voxels inside the AABB of the current line segment (see Fig. 14.29). In [Oeltze and Preim 2004], it is described how these data structures are actually employed for a fast computation.

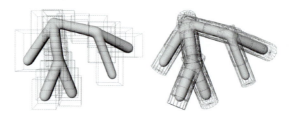

FIGURE 14.28 *Acceleration of polygonization by means of axes-aligned bounding boxes (left) and cylindrical bounding volumes (right) for an artificial tree [OELTZE and PREIM 2005]. (Images courtesy STEFFEN OELTZE, University of Magdeburg)*

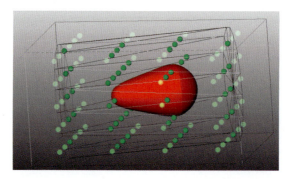

FIGURE 14.29 *Voxel selection for a single line segment. Green spheres mark midpoints of voxels that are within the AABB of this segment. Dark green spheres mark midpoints of voxels that passed the CBV test [OELTZE and PREIM 2005]. (Image courtesy STEFFEN OELTZE, University of Magdeburg)*

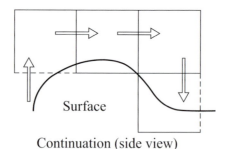

FIGURE 14.30 *Functionality of the implicit polygonizer. (From [BLOOMENTHAL 1994])*

14.5.3 CONSTRUCTION OF A GEOMETRIC MODEL

For the visualization of the vascular structures, the CS is transformed into a triangle mesh, which might be accomplished with the *implicit polygonizer* [BLOOMENTHAL 1994].

The implicit polygonizer partitions the space about the surface based on a continuation scheme presented in [WYVILL et al. 1986]. An initial cube is centered at an arbitrary point on the convolution surface (see Fig. 14.30). The root of an anatomic tree may serve as the seedpoint for computing the position of the initial cube. The size of the cube should be derived from the voxel size of the underlying data to reflect the resolution of the data and to prevent small details of the vessel tree from being ignored.

The implicit function f is evaluated in the neighborhood of the seedpoint, and a point with opposite polarity of f in the neighborhood of the root is determined. The zero-crossing of f—determined by binary subdivision between the two points with different signs of f—represents a point on the desired surface. The initial cube is translated so that it is centered around the point on the surface.

In the next stage, f is evaluated for all vertices of a cube, and faces consisting of vertices with opposite polarity are identified. Continuation proceeds by generating new cubes (with the same size) across any such face; this process is repeated until the surface is closed (for each cube, an adjacent cube with respect to the 6-neighborhood is generated). Inside these cubes, triangles are generated to reflect the surface.

14.6   VALIDATION AND EVALUATION

A crucial aspect for any visualization technique intended for clinical use is its validation. A general discussion of validating visualization algorithms was presented in Section 9.8. We extend this discussion here and focus it on the visualization of vasculature.

The validation attempts the assessment of a method's accuracy. Sufficient accuracy is the prerequisite for the usefulness of a method studied in the evaluation subsection. Validation must be accomplished for all stages, from the original image data to visualizations. With respect to the visualization of anatomic tree structures, validation is essential for filtering approaches, segmentation, skeletonization, skeleton enhancement, and the actual visualization techniques, which include trade-offs between accuracy and rendering speed.

We discussed validation strategies for image analysis in Section 5.8. As an example, the segmentation and skeletonization approach that produces the underlying data for the visualization of vasculature (skeleton and vessel diameter) is described in [SELLE et al. 2002]. We focus here on the validation of the visualization techniques and regard the underlying data as correct. The validation of the visualization should answer the following questions:

- Are (small) branches of the tree structure suppressed in the visualization?
- Are there occurrences of small branches that are not represented in the data?
- Are there occurrences in which separate branches appear as one branch?
- Is the vessel diameter represented correctly?

These questions are relevant, because the implicit modeling approach is more prone to such visualization errors than explicit methods in which graphics primitives are fitted along the skeleton. This validation has been described in more detail in [OELTZE and PREIM 2005].

14.6.1 QUALITATIVE VALIDATION

To answer these questions, the visualization of artificial data with different branching types (e.g., with a trifurcation—recall Fig. 14.26) should be explored. Over and above, the different visualizations should be compared with respect to clinical data. A comparison between the CS visualization and the TC visualization is shown in Figures 14.31 and 14.32. Comparisons of the CS visualization with the corresponding isosurfaces showed that the isosurface completely encloses the convolution surface, which leads to the conjecture that the vessel tree is slightly underestimated with a convolution surface. The tests with artificial data showed that unwanted effects (bulging, unwanted blending) could be strongly reduced. The unwanted blending problem may occur in rare cases (recall Sect. 14.4.4).

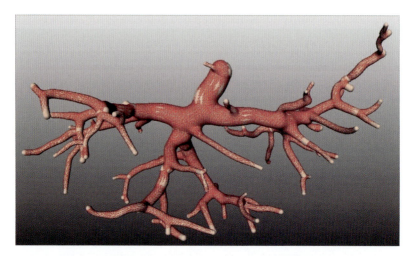

FIGURE 14.31   *The visualization method described in [HAHN et al. 2001b] (concatenated truncated cones) and the visualization by means of convolution surfaces are combined. The convolution surfaces are rendered as wire-frame, while the results of theother method are shaded [OELTZE and PREIM 2005]. (Image courtesy STEFFEN OELTZE, University of Magdeburg)*

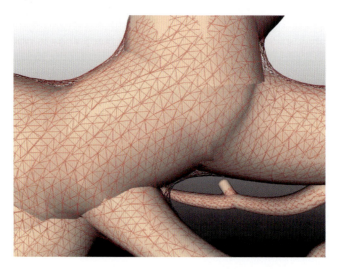

FIGURE 14.32   *A closeup of the visualization from Fig. 14.31 [OELTZE and PREIM 2005]. (Image courtesy STEFFEN OELTZE, University of Magdeburg)*

14.6.2 QUANTITATIVE VALIDATION

Beyond the visual inspection, a quantitative analysis is necessary to judge whether the underlying data (centerline and local diameter) are faithfully represented. Distance measures, such as the surface distances between isosurfaces (rendering of the segmentation result), TC, and CS visualization are most relevant because these visualizations are often used to assess distances (e.g., from a lesion to a vessel). In Section 9.8, we introduced the normal error as another general criterion for validating visualization algorithms. However, for vascular structures, we do not employ this metric, as no acceptable ground

	Ø	σ	Rms	Min	Max	Med	Area
CS→Iso	0.37	0.32	0.49	0	3.21	0.29	8.74
CS→TC	0.09	0.11	0.14	0	1.13	0.05	0.56

TABLE 14.1 *Averaged results of the quantitative comparison of surfaces based on 10 different datasets. Measures were computed from CS to isosurface (Iso) and from CS to TC. All length measures are in mm, whereas "Area" is measured in %. The distance threshold for the "Area" determination is between 1.6 mm and 2.2 mm, depending on the resolution of the dataset.*

truth is available. The jaggy surfaces created by the direct transformation of vessel segmentation results to a surface are certainly not "correct."

For the analysis of surface distances, the software platform AMIRA (© Mercury Computer Systems Inc.) provides dedicated support. A comparison of the CS with both the isosurface and the TC was accomplished, using the width coefficient set to $5ln(2)$ for the CS (recall Sect. 14.5.1). A comparison is usually realized on a per-vertex basis (for each vertex of one surface, the closest point on the other surface is computed). From the histogram of these values, the following statistical measures are calculated:

- Mean and standard deviation of the distance (Ø, σ)
- Root mean square distance (Rms)
- Minimum and maximum distance (Min, Max)
- Median of the distance (Med)
- Area deviation: percentage of area that deviates more than a given threshold (Area)

In Table 14.1, the averaged results of the surface distance measurements concerning ten datasets based on CT of the human liver are presented. It is reasonable to choose half the diagonal voxel size (*VoxDiag*2) as the threshold for computing the area deviation (last column in Table 14.1).[2] Boxplots illustrating the distribution of measured distances for each dataset are presented in Figure 14.33.

With an average of 0.37 mm, deviations between CS and isosurface are below a typical value for *VoxDiag*2. Note also the average area overlap of 91.26%, which refers to the respective value of *VoxDiag*2. It could be observed that high deviations (>3 mm) occur in all datasets only close to the root of the vessel tree as illustrated in Figure 14.34. This effect is negligible because the root does not pertain to the intrahepatic vessel system and is therefore of less interest for surgery planning. Inside the vascular trees, even distance measurements are reliable with the CS. The deviations along the whole vessel tree are to be expected, as the CS constantly underestimates the segmentation result as described in Section 14.6.1. It could be further ascertained that smoothing the vessel skeleton has a negligibly small effect on the measurements. The CS based on their corresponding nonsmoothed skeletons yielded almost the same results. Pruning of small side branches had no significant effect.

The validation focused on a comparison between model-based visualization techniques and (raw) isosurfaces. For some datasets, the effect of Laplacian mesh smoothing on the distance measurements was investigated. It turned out that even strong mesh smoothing (six iterations) has a very low effect on all metrics for directional distances. A bit to our surprise, the distances between CS and isosurface rendering increased slightly, but monoton with more iterations of the smoothing operation. This leads to the conclusion that polygonal smoothing does not converge against a model-based visualization. The major difference between model-based visualizations and (raw or smoothed) isosurfaces is the circular cross section.

---

2 As an example, for a voxel size of 0.7 × 0.7 × 3 mm, *VoxDiag2 is 1.6 mm.*

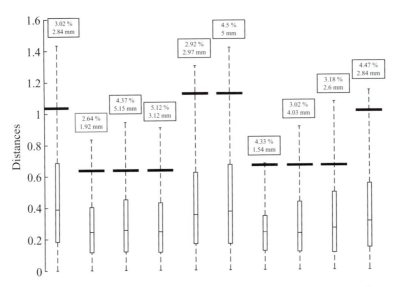

FIGURE 14.33 Boxplots of the distance measures (in mm) carried out for a comparison of CS and isosurface based on 10 vascular trees. Each box has lines at the lower quartile, median, and upper quartile values. The whiskers extend from each end of the box to show the extent of the rest of the data. Their length equals the interquartile range multiplied by 1.5. The upper value within each text box represents the percentage of data values beyond the ends of the whiskers. The lower value is the maximum distance. Thick lines indicate the VoxDiag2 values. Note that each upper quartile is consistently below its corresponding value [OELTZE and PREIM 2005]. (Image courtesy STEFFEN OELTZE, University of Magdeburg)

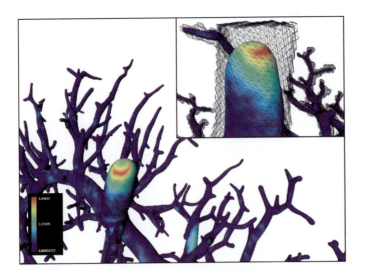

FIGURE 14.34 Color-coded visualization of the deviation from CS to isosurface. Each vertex of the CS is assigned a color with respect to the corresponding distance. The legend represents the correlation between color and magnitude of the deviation. The strongest deviations occur at the root of the vessel tree as depicted in the inset showing the superimposed isosurface in wire-frame mode [OELTZE and PREIM 2005]. (Image courtesy STEFFEN OELTZE, University Magdeburg)

Figure 14.33 shows boxplots that refer to the comparison of 10 isosurfaces with the corresponding convolution surfaces. In Figure 14.34, we relate the distance values to the convolution surface of vascular structures by color-coding distance values.

As could be expected, there is a better correspondence between the two model-based approaches (TC and CS visualization). More than 99% of the directional distances are below *VoxDiag2*. The average maximum deviation between CS and TC is 1.13 mm, which is less than typical values for *VoxDiag2*. The low deviations indicate that strong blending, unwanted blending, and bulging are effectively avoided. Minor deviations occur at branchings, which results from the smooth transitions of the CS. Along straight parts of the vessel tree, no deviations can be noticed. The highest deviations occur at the vessel ends, since the TC visualization produces longer branches at the leaves of the vessel tree (recall Sect. 14.6.1).

14.6.3 DETERMINATION OF THE WIDTH COEFFICIENT

We also investigated the effect of different ω values based on the same vascular tree, as the ω value determines the accuracy of the CS visualization. For ω, multiples of the original ω value were used for a surface comparison between the CS and the corresponding TC (see Fig. 14.35).

With an increasing ω value, the distances between the CS and the TC decrease on average. This can be expected, as increasing ω reduces the blending strength. However, with $\omega > 10 \ln 2$, the effect of smoothing is almost leveled, and the resulting surface exhibits creases at branchings (see Fig. 14.36 right). $\omega = 5 \ln 2$ turns out to be an appropriate default value, because mean, median, and standard deviation hardly decrease for higher values.

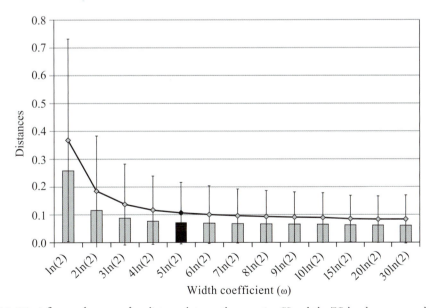

FIGURE 14.35 *Influence of ω on surface distances between the respective CS and the TC based on one vascular tree. Mean (diamonds), median (bars), and standard deviation (vertical lines) of the distance measures (in mm) hardly decrease for values higher than $\omega = 5 \ln 2$ [OELTZE and PREIM 2005]. (Image courtesy STEFFEN OELTZE, University of Magdeburg)*

FIGURE 14.36 *Influence of varying ω on the blending strength at branchings. The close-ups of the trifurcation from Figure 14.26 were generated using $\omega = 2\ln 2$, $\omega = 5\ln 2$, and $\omega = 30\ln 2$ (from left to right). With $\omega = 2\ln 2$, the blending strength is barely reduced. Using $\omega = 30\ln 2$ the surface exhibits creases at the skeleton joint [OELTZE and PREIM 2005]. (Images courtesy STEFFEN OELTZE, University of Magdeburg)*

14.6.4 EVALUATION

In the following, we briefly describe a user study carried out to evaluate the benefit of model-based visualizations (see [OELTZE and PREIM 2005] for a detailed description). This description should serve as an orientation on how to run visualization-related user studies.

In the study, a collection of visualization results was rated by six experienced surgeons and five radiologists. All participants in the study had experience with 3D visualizations and in particular with the TC visualization [HAHN et al. 2001b]. The collection represented three different liver vessel trees from CT data and consisted of ten images per tree: one context view for better orientation showing the tree within the liver lobe, and three different close-ups generated by isosurface rendering, TC, and CS visualization respectively. The viewing direction and all other visual parameters were identical (see Fig. 14.37).

The evaluation focused on close-up views because these are relevant for therapy and surgery planning. The evaluation criteria were:

- Clarity of the visualization
- Comprehensibility of spatial relations
- Similarity to operative views
- Visual quality

For each criterion, users were asked to rate it from 1 (unsatisfactory) to 5 (excellent). The CS consistently achieves the best results. However, the difference between CS and TC is not statistically significant. Above all, the similarity to operative views and the visual quality were emphasized by doctors in discussion. The model-based visualization clearly outperforms isosurface rendering.

We have also investigated the effect of smoothing isosurfaces in comparison with model-based visualizations. For this purpose, all widespread smoothing techniques, such as variants of Laplacian smoothing, low pass filtering, mesh fairing based on diffusion, and curvature flow were applied to vascular structures (recall Sect. 7.3.3 and [BADE et al. 2006a]). It turned out that even careful selection of these general smoothing techniques does not improve the visual quality considerably. In Figure 14.38, an isosurface, a strongly smoothed isosurface, and a convolution surface are compared with each other.

14.6.5 VISUALIZATION OF THE ERROR

For the user of a model-based visualization technique, it is crucial to know how precisely the visualization depicts the data of a specific case. Such an analysis needs to be carried out locally, enabling the user to see exactly where strong deviations occur and to explore the corresponding regions in detail—for example, in slice-based visualizations. Color-coding the distance between the visualization and the borders of the

FIGURE 14.37   *Close-ups of a liver vessel visualizations generated by isosurface rendering, TC, and CS visualization (from left to right) [OELTZE and PREIM 2005]. (Images courtesy STEFFEN OELTZE, University of Magdeburg)*

FIGURE 14.38   *Comparison of a smoothed isosurface (after six iterations of a Laplacian smoothing filter) and a convolution surface. More iterations of the smoothing filter did not change the visual result. It turns out that there are clear differences between strongly smoothed isosurfaces and convolution surfaces. (Images courtesy STEFFEN OELTZE, University of Magdeburg)*

segmentation result (recall Fig. 14.34) is a viable approach. A better approach is to restrict the visualization of the error to regions where this error is noticeable. This can be achieved by comparing the minimum and maximum diameters along the skeleton. If these measures deviate strongly for several adjacent voxels, the model-based visualization is not precise there. It must be noted that the determination of a maximum diameter is not reliable close to branchings. Therefore, the analysis should be restricted to portions of the vascular tree that are not immediately adjacent to a branching point. The images in Figure 14.39 are based on the analysis of minimum and maximum diameters along the skeleton.

In regions where the visualization is classified as less reliable, voxels representing the segmentation can be included. An alternative is to map the deviation of minimum and maximum diameters to the length of a line drawn on top of the convolution surface. Both visualizations could be used to focus the user to these portions of a vascular tree and to explore them in the original data.

14.7   EXAMPLES

The visualization with convolution surfaces has been applied to a large variety of clinical datasets. The quality of the visualization can be seen in Figures 14.40 through 14.42. In Figures 14.43 and 14.44, we illustrate the use of vessel visualizations for surgery planning.

We carefully examined the surfaces near branchings and noted that geometric continuity was achieved for all kinds of branchings and branching angles. The surfaces are terminated at leaves of the anatomic trees with a rounded appearance, which is a consequence of the construction method. To give an idea of the complexity of the resulting geometry and the timings involved in the computation, we present the results for four anatomic tree structures in Table 14.2. The first three lines represent the datasets shown in Figures 14.40 through 14.42.

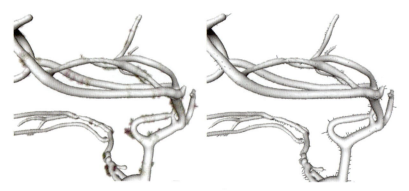

FIGURE 14.39   *Different visualizations convey the error involved in a model-based visualization of vascular structures. In the left image, voxels of the segmentation that result where the convolution surface is not precise are included in the visualization. The criterion for not being precise is that the relation between maximum and minimum diameters exceeds 1.5 and that these measurements are not closer than 3 voxels to a branching point. In the right image, lines perpendicular to the surface convey regions where the maximum and minimum vessel diameters are strongly different from each other. (Images courtesy* CHRISTIAN SCHUMANN, *University of Magdeburg)*

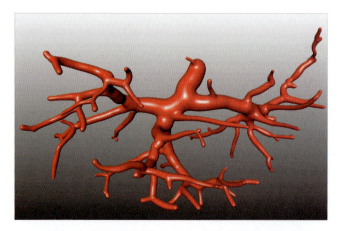

FIGURE 14.40   *Visualization of the portal vein derived from a clinical CT dataset with 136 edges* [OELTZE and PREIM 2005]. *(Image courtesy* STEFFEN OELTZE, *University of Magdeburg)*

14.8   EXPLORATION OF VASCULATURE

In educational settings, as well as in therapy planning systems, it is often necessary to explore anatomic tree structures—for example, to restrict the visualization or to focus it on subtrees. For example, in tumor surgery, vessel segments around the tumor are more important than more distant parts. In general, surgeons would like to know which vessel segments have such a large diameter that they must be reconstructed if they have to be cut. Small vessels might be irrelevant for them and might be hidden or visualized in a less pronounced manner. The results of the image analysis allow interactions that support such visualization goals. Based on the branching graph, vessel segments that depend on a user-selected branch might be identified and highlighted or removed from the visualization. Using a region-selection (called lasso selection) or picking a subset of vessels might be selected based on their position in the

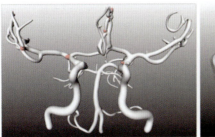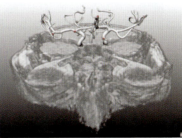

FIGURE 14.41 *Visualization of cerebral blood vessels derived from a clinical MRI angiography with 149 edges. In the right image, vessel visualization is combined with direct volume rendering and interactive clipping to explore the spatial relations* [OELTZE and PREIM 2005]. *(Images courtesy* STEFFEN OELTZE, *University of Magdeburg)*

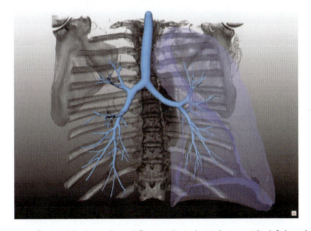

FIGURE 14.42 *Visualization of a bronchial tree derived from a clinical CT dataset. The left lung lobe (right part of the image) is presented as a semitransparent surface and other structures are included by means of direct volume rendering to provide anatomic context* [OELTZE and PREIM 2005]. *(Image courtesy* STEFFEN OELTZE, *University of Magdeburg)*

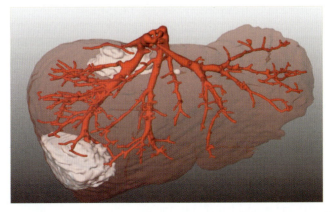

FIGURE 14.43 *Visualization of vascular structures inside the liver together with liver metastasis and liver parenchyma for liver surgery planning* [OELTZE and PREIM 2005]. *(Image courtesy* STEFFEN OELTZE, *University of Magdeburg)*

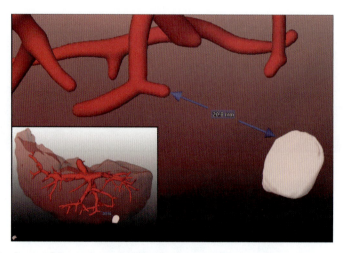

FIGURE 14.44   *Visualization of the portal vein together with a liver metastasis. Since the visualization is accurate, reliable distance measurements may be integrated. (Image courtesy* STEFFEN OELTZE, *University of Magdeburg)*

Edges	Triangles (*1000)		Setup Time (s)	
	CS	**Cones**	**CS**	**Cones**
136	125	55	6.14	0.11
149	253	74	8.12	0.12
1504	1126	599	53.24	1.30
3461	2366	907	52.01	2.11

TABLE 14.2   *Performance measurements for different anatomic tree structures. The measurements are taken on a Pentium IV CPU (3.06GHz, 1 GB RAM, ATI Radeon 9600).*

viewport. Instead of completely removing the selected edges, it is often useful to show them as less focused by using gray colors and/or transparency (see Fig. 14.45).

Often, two or more vascular structures are displayed together. In these cases, it is often preferable to show one tree in detail and others defocused. Several visualization techniques can be employed for this purpose. The obvious way to defocus 3D objects is to render them semitransparently. As an interaction facility, it might be appropriate to reduce the vessel diameter for defocused trees. This reduction has a similar effect to transparency, because it is easier to look through this reduced tree. In Figure 14.46, both visualization techniques are compared.

14.9   VESSEL VISUALIZATION FOR DIAGNOSIS

The diagnosis of vascular diseases, such as coronary heart disease, cerebral or abdominal aneurysms, or stenotic changes, is an important aspect of the clinical routine in radiology departments. We have focused so far on therapy planning and model-based visualizations, which are not suitable for the diagnosis of vascular diseases. For diagnostic purposes, precise visualizations, as well as quantitative information such

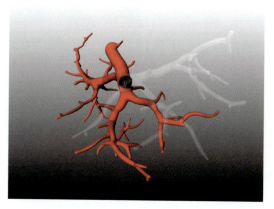

FIGURE 14.45 *Lasso selection and defocused visualization of the selected vessel segments. Inside the semitransparent vessels the centerline is presented. (Image courtesy* STEFFEN OELTZE, *University of Magdeburg)*

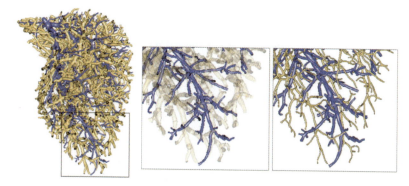

FIGURE 14.46 *To explore the complex visualization of two vascular systems (left), two methods are compared. Transparency is employed in the middle image to defocus one tree. In contrast, in the right image the radius is scaled uniformly for the defocused tree. (Images courtesy* HORST HAHN, *MeVis Bremen)*

as cross-sectional areas, are essential. Support for these tasks requires integrated visualizations that present the relevant information in different views that are carefully synchronized with each other. An important ingredient for such a system is an MPR view, which presents the original data orthogonal to the local vessel centerline. This cross-sectional view, however, must be mentally integrated in an overview of the vascular tree (see Fig. 14.47). The 3D visualization in this context serves to verify the image analysis results and to locate the detailed information in the overall structure [BOSKAMP et al. 2004].

For the evaluation of plaques and stenotic changes, a stretched MPR is desirable, as it shows the course of the vessel in the original data in one view. For a quantitative analysis the change of the (minimal or average) diameter in all slices should be visualized (see Fig. 14.48).

For diagnosis of a vascular tree, the visualization techniques presented in Figures 14.47 and 14.48 need to be refined. The user should be able to specify two points in a vascular tree that indicate the path analyzed in a *stretch view*. As an example, the visual analysis of coronary vessels is shown in Figure 14.49. All visualizations in this section are screenshots of the VASCUVISION system developed at the Center for

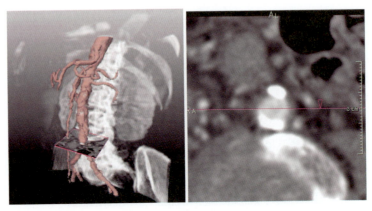

FIGURE 14.47   Left: direct volume rendering of bony structures combined with isosurface rendering of segmented vessels. Right: a small oblique MPR view is displayed. This view is centered at the skeleton and oriented perpendicular to the current direction of the skeleton. The position of the MPR view is displayed in the 3D visualization (left) to support the mental integration of both views. (Images courtesy TOBIAS BOSKAMP, MeVis Bremen)

FIGURE 14.48   For a quantitative analysis of vascular diseases, a stretch view (left) and the corresponding cross-sectional measurement diagram (right) are useful. (Image courtesy TOBIAS BOSKAMP, MeVis Bremen)

Medical Diagnosis Systems and Visualization (MeVis), Bremen. This software is in regular clinical use; a clinical evaluation is described in [GERHARDS et al. 2004].

Visualization for Computer-Aided Detection   The most advanced support for diagnostic purposes is the computer-aided detection (CAD) and subsequent visualization of regions that are suspected of having

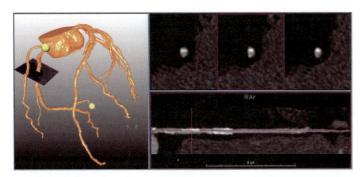

FIGURE 14.49   *Integrated visualization for the diagnosis of coronary vessels. In the 3D overview, the user marked two points in the tree to which the detailed analysis relates. The stretch view (bottom part) contains calcifications (appearing bright). The upper right views show cross-sectional slice views in the neighborhood of the current position of the cross-sectional view in the left view. (Images courtesy* ANJA HENNEMUTH, *MeVis Bremen)*

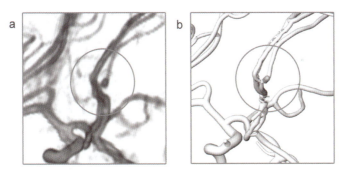

FIGURE 14.50   *Visualization of a sac-like cerebral aneurysm. Comparison of direct volume rendering and isosurface rendering. The aneurysm is located in the encircled region. The visualizations are based on MRI angiography data (time of flight sequence). (Images courtesy* MILO HINDENNACH, *MeVis Bremen)*

a vascular abnormality. Model assumptions with respect to expected sizes of vascular branches, as well as expected changes of the vessel diameter in adjacent slices, are a suitable basis for a CAD system.[3] Once suspicious regions are determined, an appropriate visualization is needed that emphasizes the corresponding regions and supports a detailed investigation. In principle, isosurface and direct volume rendering may be used as basic 3D techniques (see Fig. 14.50). The surface visualization is often better suited to recognize an aneurysm. For the actual diagnosis, however, slice views must also be considered. CAD, in general, is useful for screening purposes, such as when patients without any symptoms are investigated in a limited time.

14.10   SUMMARY

We have discussed methods for visualizing vasculature that adhere to the underlying data (skeleton and local vessel diameter) while producing smooth transitions at branchings. These model-based

---

3   A CAD example described in BOSKAMP *et al.* [2006] relates to clinically relevant cerebral aneurysms.

visualizations are generated primarily for therapy planning. For the diagnosis of vascular diseases, such as stenosis or aneurysms, these visualizations are not appropriate. Image analysis is essential for the visualization of vasculature. Potential inaccuracy might be introduced at all levels (segmentation, skeletonization, graph analysis). The idea of reconstructing branching structures based on a skeleton is not bound to vascular structures. As a very different example, REINDERS et al. [2000] employed this idea to characterize and visualize turbulent flow.

We described explicit surface reconstruction methods based on the concept of a generalized cylinder. Specific examples of this concept include the simple cylinder (which does not convey the change of the vessel diameter in a vessel segment), truncated cones, and subdivision surfaces as the most recent and advanced explicit reconstruction techniques.

While explicit techniques either exhibit artifacts or are very complex in the construction process, implicit surface reconstruction was also discussed. In particular, convolution surfaces are appropriate to visualize skeletal structures. The filter design, however, has to be fine-tuned to prevent bulges, to control blending, and to represent the course of the vessel diameter faithfully. The explicit technique of truncated cones, as well as the convolution surfaces, have been compared and analyzed with respect to the surface distances. Similar to the validation of image segmentation techniques, distance metrics are an essential means to validate model-based visualization techniques.

Outlook Despite recent advances in the visualization of vascular structures, there is still room for further improvements. Interaction techniques for focusing on parts of vascular trees are desirable for surgery planning—for example, to emphasize the region near the tumor. A hybrid combination of isosurface rendering and convolution surfaces would allow applications in diagnostics. Isosurfaces could be used for those parts of a vascular tree in which the assumption of a circular cross section is strongly violated. As an alternative, it should be explored whether the visualization with convolution surfaces can be generalized to structures that do not exhibit a circular cross section.

It will be interesting to investigate more advanced surface smoothing techniques with respect to isosurfaces of the segmentation results. With topology and feature-preserving smoothing techniques, it might be possible to achieve renderings with a quality similar to convolution surfaces.

Often, it is desirable to convey more information than just the shape and topology of vascular structures—for example, the distance to a tumor. Colors might be used for this purpose, in principle. An alternative is to use hatching lines. The advantage of such illustration techniques is that more than one attribute can be presented and that the visualization is also appropriate for output media without color. As a first step, RITTER et al. [2006] developed such techniques to convey information for surgery planning.

FURTHER READING

While we attempted at an encompassing overview of vessel visualization methods, we only touched on the segmentation, skeletonization, and separation of vascular trees from 3D datasets. With respect to the segmentation, QUEK and KIRBAS [2001], BULLITT and AYLWARD [2002], AYLWARD and BULLITT [2002], AVANTS and WILLIAMS [2000], FRIDMAN et al. [2003] provide other approaches that have been carefully tested. Methods for the separation of vascular trees are described, for example, in [LEI et al. 2001, and VAN BEMMEL et al. 2003]. There are, of course, alternative methods for smoothing skeletons. As an example, the moving square filter [ZHUKOV and BARR 2002] for smoothing fibers detected in DTI data (see Chap. 18) is also applicable to skeletons. However, this filter is rather slow and should be only used for small amounts of data. BORNIK et al. [2005] presented a reconstruction technique for vascular trees based on simplex meshes. LLUCH et al. [2004] carefully investigated continuity problems at bifurcations and superpositions of geometry. Smooth transitions without superposition are achieved by using L-systems—a technique that is widely used to visualize botanical trees. A similar problem to the visualization of vascular structures is the exploration of coral structures. KRUSZYNSKI et al. [2006] describe this process with a focus on image analysis (segmentation, skeletonization, graph analysis) and quantifying spatial relations.

We have not explored volume rendering for the visualization of segmented vascular structures. In a series of publications at the University of Erlangen-Nürnberg, volume rendering for neuroradiological diagnosis, particularly for visualizing cerebral aneurysms, arteriovenous malformations, and neurovascular compression syndromes, has been investigated [HASTREITER and ERTL 1998, ISERHARDT-BAUER et al. 2002, VEGA et al. 2003, HIGUERA et al. 2005]. High-quality rendering of segmentation results and multidimensional transfer functions are used to present vascular structures so that the diagnosis and the therapy decisions are supported. An intersting combination of direct volume rendering and curved planar reformation is the *VesselGlyph*, described in [STRAKA et al. 2004].

Much research effort was spent on the reconstruction of vascular structures from 2D data, such as Biplane Angiography. The interested reader is referred to [WAHLE et al. 1998, 1999, KEHL et al. 2000].

Chapter 15

Virtual Endoscopy

Minimally invasive procedures are of increasing importance in medicine because they have less deleterious effects on the patient. In particular, these procedures are used in gastroenterology, surgery, neurosurgery, and (interventional) radiology, but also in many other fields.

The typical instruments for these procedures are endoscopes, which in essence consist of a fiber optic that is moved to the target area. The fiber optic itself can be flexible or stiff, depending on the size and other requirements of the endoscope. For instance, a typical endoscope for neurosurgery has a quite small diameter to minimize the impacted brain tissue. The small diameter reduces the capability to transport sufficient light through the fiber to the endoscope head. Building a stiff fiber to allow a maximum of light [DUFFNER et al. 1994] compensates for this effect. Beside the light source, an endoscope consists of the optic for a camera to transport the acquired image to a monitor, as well as one or more "working tubes" that are used to move tools such as pliers to the target area. Lenses at the tip of the endoscopes usually have a large opening angle to provide a sufficient overview. Unfortunately, this also aggravates optical effects such as the fish eye view [FREUDENSTEIN et al. 2001].

Other tools for minimally invasive interventions include catheters, which are moved to the target area using a guidance wire and fluoroscopy/X-ray control. The wire gives the very flexible catheter stiffness, and the imaging provides an overview of the current localization of it. A specific application area of catheters are interventions on (usually arterial) blood vessels. In the past few years, medical engineering companies have also come up with angioscopes to examine blood vessels. Due to their small size, however, they have some limitations concerning the number of working channels.

Several drawbacks are associated with minimally invasive procedures. In several cases (e.g., colonoscopy), minimally invasive procedures can be quite unpleasant for patients. Furthermore, they are expensive (although they are still cheaper than "traditional" open surgery), and some areas of interest cannot be reached by the endoscope or catheter due to folds and plaits. Especially in (neuro-) surgery, these procedures lack the fast access for open surgery in case of serious complications, such as strong

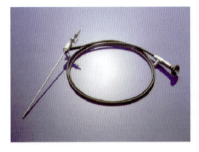 

FIGURE 15.1 *Neuroendoscope with one working channel. Left: neuroendoscope; left is the trochar that guides the actual endoscopic optic (right) to the target area. On the right side is the occular, which is used to acquire the endoscopic image. Right: endoscope with one working channel containing a plier. (Images courtesy FRANK DUFFNER, University of Tübingen)*

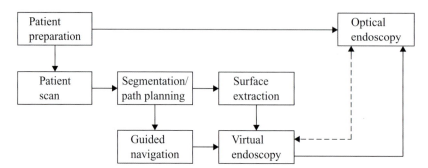

FIGURE 15.2 *Processing pipeline of virtual endoscopy: after the preparation, the patient is scanned. The target cavities are segmented and a path planning is performed. Based on the segmentation, the data structures for the guided navigation system are built, and data structures for rendering are computed. Finally, a virtual endoscopy is performed on the generated data. Depending on the application scenario, an optical endoscopy may follow the virtual endoscopy (diagnosis and intervention planning), or optical and virtual endoscopy are employed to benefit each other (intraoperative navigation). Optical endoscopy may not be part of the training scenario.*

bleeding. Therefore, careful planning and realization of these procedures is essential to avoid such complications. This problem aggravates, because handling and control of many of these endoscopes is very difficult, mainly due to limited flexibility of and limited field of view through the endoscope, a very limited depth perception, and the sensitive nature of brain tissue.

In contrast, virtual endoscopy is a convenient alternative. It is based on a 3D scan of the respective body region. Examples of these scans include CT or MRI scans of the abdominal area, the heart, the head, or the lungs, or rotational angiographies of blood vessels in various body parts. Based on the resulting volumetric data, the organs of interest are visualized and inspected from interior ("endo") viewpoints.

Figure 15.2 shows the typical processing pipeline for virtual endoscopy. After a proper patient preparation (which might be also necessary for the respective optical endoscopy), the patient is scanned and afterwards the generated datasets are processed. Succeeding the segmentation of the relevant anatomical structures, path planning for the virtual camera is done. This step typically involves the generation of a centerline or a skeleton of the segmentation data. If a guided navigation scheme is used, auxiliary data is computed based on that information. Furthermore, data structures for volume rendering are prepared; for example, the surface is extracted, or space-traversal structures are set up. Finally, the virtual endoscopy application is initiated. Depending on the application scenario (see next section), an optical endoscopy might follow the virtual endoscopy, or both might be combined. Note that depending on the employed techniques and the target area, some processing steps might be skipped.

Organization We start this chapter by introducing the application scenarios for virtual endoscopy. Afterwards the technical issues that must be addressed for virtual endoscopy are discussed in Section 15.2. The following sections describe a variety of clinical applications of virtual endoscopy used in clinical practice. Note, however, that the presented applications by no means represent a complete list, and several other applications have been discussed before. A more comprehensive overview of virtual endoscopy applications can be found in [ROGALLA et al. 2000].

15.1 APPLICATION SCENARIOS FOR VIRTUAL ENDOSCOPY

Virtual endoscopy can be applied with a variety of different goals. These goals depend largely on the clinical questions of the respective original endoscopic procedure being mimicked by virtual endoscopy.

Some of the goals are aimed at reducing costs in the clinical routine, a topic of almost permanent relevance in modern health care; others are aimed at improving the intervention quality by reducing the risks of complications. Another possible goal is the reduction of the training costs for medical specialists.

Diagnosis and Screening   Commercially, the most interesting goal is the replacement of the optical endoscopic procedure by the virtual endoscopic pendant. Particularly as a diagnostic alternative, virtual endoscopy has the potential to reduce the costs of assessing the colon significantly. The typical application in this context is colonoscopy, in which the interior colon wall is inspected for pathologies such as polyps (see Sect. 15.3). If no suspicious areas are found, assuming a sufficient sensitivity and specificity (see Sect. 2.3), no further intervention is necessary. In the other case, however, a surgical intervention may be necessary to acquire additional information through an endoscopic biopsy or to remove an identified pathology. Next to the diagnostic applications in a specific case, virtual endoscopy is also discussed in the context of screening examinations, in which a whole age or risk group is examined—a process that is too costly to perform with optical endoscopy.

Training and Teaching   For this kind of application scenario, virtual endoscopy combined with a tissue simulation model allows the training of physicians without the necessity of employing animals or patients. Unfortunately, no available tissue model allows accurate simulations at sufficient simulation speed of a complex organ system. This is still an active research topic (see Sect. 20.6.2). With respect to teaching, virtual endoscopy can be used to instruct students on the anatomy of patients from interior viewpoints. Note, however, that virtual endoscopy applications are based on volumetric patient datasets. No texture and color information of the organ is acquired; hence, it cannot be properly represented. This can be a substantial flaw for a training application.

Intervention and Therapy Planning   Currently, the most frequently employed scenario is intervention and therapy planning, in which a virtual endoscopy application is used to explore access ways, potential complications, or the specific patient's anatomy. A clear advantage of virtual endoscopy–based planning is the possibility of visualizing anatomic structures that are not visible through optical endoscopy. This includes risk structures, such as blood vessels, but also areas that are not accessible to optical endoscopy. If this information can be used to improve the quality of the intervention through a better diagnosis or better access planning, it is worthwhile to consider. In this chapter, Sections 15.4 through 15.6 describe such applications.

Intraoperative Navigation   Finally, virtual endoscopy can be applied in connection with image-guided surgery (see Chap. 16) to provide an additional intraoperative navigation aid for a minimally invasive intervention. The basic concept behind this scenario is the fact that optical endoscopy is often limited to inside views of the visited cavity.[1] All anatomical structures beyond the cavity wall are usually not visible. With virtual endoscopy, this can be different (see Sect. 15.5.2) when additional information is provided. Consequently, a combination of optical and virtual endoscopy can provide valuable information to significantly reduce the complication rate of modern minimally invasive surgery. The major advantage of intraoperative navigation to intervention planning is that the virtual endoscopy presentation of the anatomy is tightly connected with the optical endoscope via the patient with him- or herself as common reference frame.

---

[1]   By far, most endoscopy applications explore body cavities, which are also called preformed areas. Some applications of optical endoscopy also describe interventions within body tissue, not preformed areas, but they are typically not explored with virtual endoscopy.

15.2   TECHNICAL ISSUES

Several technical issues need to be addressed for virtual endoscopy. The first issue concerns the rendering of the virtual endoscopy view, and the second issue relates to the navigation of the virtual camera through the visual representation of the respective body cavity. Furthermore, the user-interface and the functionality must be carefully integrated to provide a seamless workflow.

15.2.1 RENDERING FOR VIRTUAL ENDOSCOPY

Virtual endoscopy mimics the visual representation of an optical endoscope. Hence, the optical properties of the endoscopes must be mapped to the parameters of the virtual camera. Next to the camera distortion (fish eye and barrel distortion), this requires the perspective rendering of the dataset, which is not always possible for all rendering algorithms. The two basic alternatives are indirect and direct volume rendering, which are discussed in this section.

Note that most examples in this chapter use indirect volume rendering based on the Marching Cubes algorithm and an occlusion-culling approach. Only Section 15.5.3 describes an application that employs direct volume rending.

Indirect Volume Rendering

With indirect volume rendering (see Chap. 7), a polygonal surface representation of the respective body cavities is generated and subsequently rendered. This approach has several advantages and disadvantages to be considered. First, a polygonal representation offers good control over the visual result of the rendering. Transparencies can be specified easily in a way that allows a concise visualization of the participating anatomical structures. Furthermore, many methods are available to improve the appearance and quality of the polygonal meshes that represent the body organs. Finally, graphics hardware allows fast and flexible rendering of polygonal objects; perspective transformations in particular come at no extra cost.

On the downside, the visual quality of most indirect volume rendering methods is not as good as that of many direct volume rendering approaches. In particular, the standard Marching Cubes approach (see Sect. 7.2.3) does not provide trilinear interpolation of the triangle vertices, which results in *diamond* artifacts (see Fig. 7.15) for zoomed views close to the voxel resolution.

Furthermore, the two-stage process of surface extraction and subsequent rendering allows no flexible refinement of the isovalue that describes the surface. However, this issue sounds worse than it actually is, since most virtual endoscopy applications use an already carefully determined surface classification.

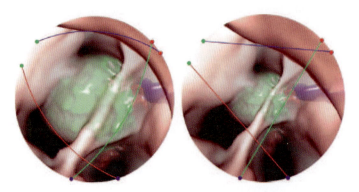

FIGURE 15.3   *Barrel distortion of a simulated endoscopic camera. Left: distorted camera image; right: undistorted camera image* [NEUBAUER 2005]. *(Images courtesy* ANDRÉ NEUBAUER, *VRVis Wien)*

Finally, the number of (often small) triangles generated by the surface extraction algorithms can be very large, overwhelming the abilities of many graphics accelerators. In those cases, methods such as geometry culling and surface simplification (see Sect. 7.3) may be applied. In particular, geometry culling, specifically occlusion culling, is worthwhile to consider, since virtual endoscopy inherently has a high occlusion potential due to the interior viewpoints. Surface simplification, in contrast, only has a low user acceptance, due to the potential loss of visual fidelity.

Direct Volume Rendering

Direct volume rendering (see Chap. 8) computes the visual contribution of the current scene without generating an intermediate polygonal representation. The advantage of this approach is that no preprocessing step has to be performed before the renditions can address changes of the classification.[2] This enables more flexibility for the exploration of the appropriate classification. However, as we have pointed out above, this flexibility is not required for most virtual endoscopy applications.

Most virtual endoscopy systems that use direct volume rendering employ a special version of ray casting (see Sect. 9.1). This ray casting is called *first-hit ray casting* and it searches the viewspace for the first sample that indicates the isosurface of a respective organ representation [NEUBAUER et al. 2002, NEUBAUER 2005].[3] In general, ray casting approaches have the advantage that endoscopic views almost by definition have viewpoints close to or at least not far away from the surface, and hence the first-hit sample is usually found quite rapidly. To further accelerate this sampling process, *space leaping* (empty space traversal methods) is applied to skip large parts of the cavity itself (see Sect. 9.1.2). Note, however, that even in these relatively small spaces, *perspective ray divergence* must be addressed to provide sufficient sampling (see Sect. 9.1.1).

Since some virtual endoscopy applications require the visual representation of anatomical objects behind the surface of the currently visited cavity, first hit ray casting must be adapted to include those objects. NEUBAUER et al. [2004a] split the respective rendering elements into foreground and background objects and rendered them into a foreground and background image. Based on the depth information computed during ray casting, the background image is blended with the foreground image. Figure 15.4 demonstrates the fusion of fore- and background in the context of pituitary gland surgery (see Sect. 15.5.3). While the left image shows the blending of fore- and background with a fixed blending parameter, the right image considers the depth distance between fore- and background for the pixel-wise blending. Note that if background objects are rendered semi-transparently, regular ray casting (not first-hit) must be used.

15.2.2 NAVIGATING THROUGH BODY CAVITIES

Another important aspect that needs to be addressed by a virtual endoscopy system is the navigation paradigm used. HONG et al. [1997] pointed out that in the context of such a system, three different options are available: automatic navigation, manual or free navigation, and guided navigation.

Automatic or planned navigation relies on a predefined camera path through the representation of the respective body cavity. This camera path must specify positions and view directions (orientations) of the virtual camera. Afterwards, a fly-through is computed based on that path. While this option offers a good overview of the target area, it requires the refinement of the camera path—and the subsequent

---

2   While this statement is correct for the general approaches, many acceleration and classification data structures do require some preprocessing.

3   Neubauer's approach is actually an object-space order, cell-based ray casting method that composes ray segments from different voxel bricks ("macro cells").

FIGURE 15.4 *Blended fore- and background images for first-hit ray casting. Left: The images are blended with a constant blending parameter. Right: The images are blended considering the distance between fore- and background* [NEUBAUER et al. 2004b]. *(Images courtesy ANDRÉ NEUBAUER, VRVis Wien)*

regeneration of the fly-through—to capture details that were previously not sufficiently visible. In essence, it offers only VCR-like functionality to examine an animation. One of the drawbacks of this approach is that one fly-through may cover only up to 70% of the cavities' surface. This coverage can be improved up to 95% by a fly-through in both directions, as DACHILLE *et al.* [2001] pointed out. A specific variation of the planned navigation approach is *reliable navigation* [HE and HONG 1999], in which viewing of all interior surface parts is guaranteed. This, however, can also result in an over-coverage of parts of the cavity, and thus in a lower examination efficiency. Note that planned navigation does not require an interactive volume rendering, since no user interaction is immediately involved.

The second possibility is **manual or free navigation**, where the camera is transformed freely. This navigation paradigm is particularly popular for viewing computer graphics models from the outside. For virtual endoscopy applications, however, free navigation poses severe difficulties due to the high complexity of many body cavities. Furthermore, the lack of collision avoidance mechanisms, and the difficulties of adding those to a free navigation system, worsen this issue. Since free navigation relies on the direct interaction of the user with the system, it also requires interactive rendering speed; lags between interaction and the resulting rendering accumulate and cannot be tolerated.

The best option for virtual endoscopy combines navigation flexibility with guidance and is hence called **guided navigation** [GALYEAN 1995]. It combines a set of constraints that guide the user to a predefined target area. Note that this target area must be specified, but does not need to be an identified feature. Instead, it typically indicates the distal end of a body cavity. HONG *et al.* [1997] implemented a guided navigation system by employing a set of distance fields that are interpreted as potential fields. One type of distance field (see Fig. 15.5 left) implements a current towards the target area (blue), and another type (middle) implements a collision avoidance system (see HONG *et al.* [1997] for details). If these fields are combined (right) and explored with a physically-based camera model, this system realizes a very intuitive navigation system. They compare their combined navigation model with a microfield submarine traveling through a bloodsteam inside the body, a scenario of the Academy Award–winning movie *Fantastic Voyage* (20th Century Fox, 1966).

An alternative, more restricted guided navigation system was presented by VILANOVA *et al.* [1999]. Instead of allowing the location of the camera to move through the cavities only limited by the constraints, the movement of the guided camera in their system is limited to a predefined camera path. Only the camera's orientation can be selected freely.

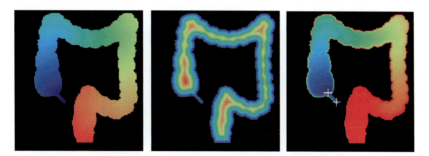

FIGURE 15.5 *Distance fields for guided navigation. Left: distance to target (blue). Middle: distance to surface. Right: combined distance field. The distance-to-surface influence is only visible at the surface boundary [HONG et al. 1997]. (Images courtesy SHIGERU MURAKI, AIST Japan)*

Guided navigation clearly benefits from interactive rendering. However, the constraints can compensate for potential interaction lags, thus allowing also for only near-interactive framerates.

15.2.3 USER INTERFACE

Research systems and systems for clinical practice vary in their functionality and user interfaces. While research systems are typically proof-of-concepts, they are often a starting point for commercial systems. The critical difference between the available commercial systems, however, is often not their available rendering speed or quality, but the careful arrangement of their functionality. In particular, the adaptation of the system to the clinical routine of a hospital or any other doctor's practice is important. Note, however, that too much adaption may lead to a limited innovation that does not enable the full potential of a specific technique. One example of such a situation was documented by PICKHARDT [2003], who compared different virtual colonoscopy systems. One system mimicked the standard CT viewing mode of radiologists by representing the 3D colon surface based on an axial CT view. The other system provided a full 3D rendering together with the standard slice views. As it turned out, the traditional approach performed significantly worse than a full 3D system in supporting the physicians to locate polyps in the colon.

15.3   VIRTUAL COLONOSCOPY

Cancer of the colon (see Fig. 15.6) and rectum is the second leading cause of cancer deaths in the United State of America. Approximately 150,000 new cases of colorectal cancer are diagnosed every year [COHEN et al. 1995], and similar numbers are assumed for western Europe and parts of Asia. Consequently, it is imperative that an effective diagnostic procedure be found to detect colonic polyps or tumors at an early stage. Currently, optical colonoscopy and barium enema are the major procedures available for examining the entire colon to detect polyps larger than 5 mm in diameter, which are clinically considered to have a high probability of being malignant. In optical colonoscopy, a fiber optical probe is introduced into the colon through the rectum. By manipulating the tiny camera attached to the tip of the probe, the physician examines the inner surface of the colon to identify abnormalities. This invasive procedure takes about one hour and requires intravenous sedation, resulting in high costs. Barium enema, in contrast, requires a great deal of physical cooperation from the patient when the X-ray radiographs of the colon are taken at different views. Additionally, its sensitivity can be as low as 78% in detecting polyps in the range of 5 mm to 20 mm [MOROSI et al. 1991].

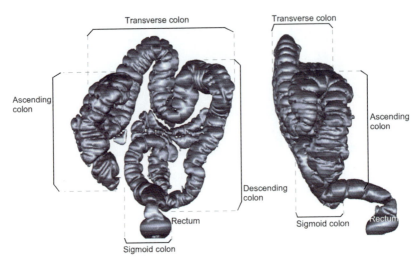

FIGURE 15.6 *Colon dataset; the colon is composed of ascending colon, transverse colon, and descending colon. After the sigmoid colon, it exits through the rectum. The left image shows a coronal view, the right image shows a sagittal view of an isosurface representing the inner colon wall.*

Both methods are either too expensive or too circumstantial for prophylactic screening examinations and result in a low patient acceptance. Consequently, virtual colonoscopy was proposed to limit optical colonoscopy to cases in which either a suspicious polyp was found (which induced a biopsy or removal of the polyp) or results were inconclusive in virtual colonoscopy [VINING et al. 1994]. The latter happens if (shape) defects of the graphical representation of the inner colon surface cannot be identified as polyps or residual stool.

After cleansing and inflating of the colon (both actions are also required for optical colonoscopy), a CT scan (or alternatively an MRI scan) is performed. The resulting image stack is preprocessed and examined using the virtual endoscopy system.

Optical and Virtual Endoscopy

HONG et al. [1997] compared the results of optical and virtual endoscopy based on polyps found in both procedures. In particular, they compared snapshots of two polyps (see Fig. 15.7). The first polyp (see Fig. 15.7 left) is located in the descending colon, close to the sigmoid colon (lower arrow). It is 8 mm in size, and hence of high clinical relevance. Figure 15.7 top row images show the information provided by optical colonoscopy, while bottom row images show the information provided by virtual colonoscopy. The shape information of the polyp is well represented by the virtual technique. However, textual information is not available, although it is very helpful in optical colonoscopy (though not obvious in Fig. 15.7 top row) to identify false positive polyps, which often are remaining stool and residual fluids.

The second polyp is 4 mm in size and is located in the transverse colon, not too far away from the hepatic (right) flexure (upper left arrow). Similar to the previous polyp, the actual location is quite different from the rough estimation in the overview image of optical colonoscopy, which locates the polyp in the ascending colon (see Fig. 15.7 middle).

A study on the advantages of virtual colonoscopy compared to optical or conventional colonoscopy has been presented by FENLON et al. [1999]. The authors found that the performance of virtual colonoscopy is comparable to optical, as long as the data resolution is sufficient to detect polyps of the respective size.

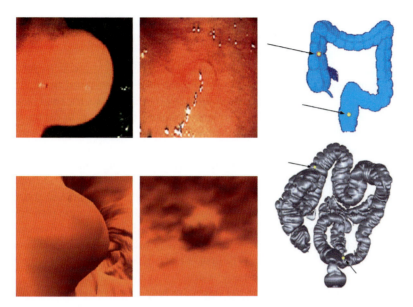

FIGURE 15.7 *Polyps in optical and virtual colonoscopy. Top row optical colonoscopy, bottom row virtual colonoscopy. Left: A 8-mm polyp; middle: a 4-mm polyp; right: colon overview. The top arrow (yellow marker) indicates the 4-mm polyp, the bottom arrow (yellow marker) indicates the 8-mm polyp [HONG et al. 1997]. (Images courtesy LICHAN HONG, Palo Alto Research Center)*

Problems arose from residual stool, which often was the cause of a false positive finding. More recently, PICKHARDT et al. [2003] presented an even larger study[4] that essentially confirmed the findings by FENLON et al. Interestingly, they found several positively identified polyps in virtual colonoscopy that were not seen in the initial optical colonoscopy. After a re-examination that took into account the virtual colonoscopy information, these polyps were identified by optical colonoscopy.

PICKHARDT et al. also pointed out that the result of virtual colonoscopy depends significantly on the dataset preparation and the way virtual colonoscopy is applied. Digital cleansing of the data (tagging of identified stool and residual fluids) enabled a better surface representation of the colon. Furthermore they showed that a full 3D representation enables better polyp identification than an examination of the axial slices only. Overall, virtual colonoscopy achieved a sensitivity of more than 88% for polyps larger than 6 mm, and a specificity of close to 80%.

To summarize, virtual colonoscopy is an alternative procedure for the diagnosis of polyps in the human colon. However, it does not replace optical colonoscopy, which is still required to remove a found polyp or to identify a suspicious structure with additional information, such as texture, color, and histological information, through a biopsy, which is generally not available through volume scanning methods.

15.4 VIRTUAL BRONCHOSCOPY

Among the most important organ systems of the human body is the respiratory system, which transports air into the body (inhaling) and removes exhausted air from the body (exhaling). The exchange of the air

---

4 A large subset of datasets used for that study can be found at nova.nlm.nih.gov/WRAMC. Every approach on identifying polyps should be benchmarked with these datasets to get comparable results.

takes place in the lungs, which are a complementary system of airways and blood vessels. Both systems are supplied through large pipe-like structures which split successively into smaller ones, thus creating the tracheo-bronchial (airways) and blood vessel tree.

The tracheo-bronchial tree is connected to the outside through the trachea, which splits into the main bronchi (left and right lungs) at the main bifurcation. Inhaled air is distributed through the bronchial tree down to the alveoli, where the oxygen/carbon-dioxide exchange between air and blood takes place. The exhausted air (enriched with carbon dioxide) is then transported back up to the trachea during the exhale. The tracheo-bronchial tree is complemented by a system of pulmonary venous and arterial blood vessels that transports the blood to and from the heart into the lungs.

Several pathologies can jeopardize a sufficient lung function. Among them are tumors, pulmonary embolism, collapse of the lungs (atelectasis), pneumonia, emphysema, asthma, and many more. For a proper diagnosis and treatment, the respective pathologies need to be identified and in some cases quantified. In the case of lung surgery, this information is necessary for intervention planning in situations for which the anatomical relation of affected bronchi to non-affected areas is required preoperatively (e.g., to provide a safe distance from essential structures and to determine resectability). However, the usage of virtual bronchoscopy as a diagnostic tool is limited, since detailed information on the mucosa is not available; thus, tumors limited to that area cannot be detected easily [ROGALLA 1999].

The current gold standard for identifying the respective lung parenchyma and airways is computed tomography (CT). A CT scan is performed prior to a bronchoscopy, a tool for inspecting the trachea and central bronchi and deriving tissue samples. Due to the recent technical development improving resolution and scan velocity, multislice CT—in connection with virtual bronchoscopy—became a promising alternative to bronchoscopy in cases for which tissue samples are not required. This is amplified by the fact that optical bronchoscopy is limited by smaller, lower airways (third generation and up) or by obstructions. Nevertheless, even smaller structures of the lower airways are extremely difficult to segment from CT datasets, due to leakages caused by the notorious partial volume effect and due to the lack of sufficient contrast to surrounding tissue or air. BARTZ et al. [2003b] presented a segmentation approach that also enables the segmentation of small airways. Here, we concentrate on the virtual endoscopy of the airways, the virtual bronchoscopy to visualize airways, blood vessels, and tumors (see Fig. 15.8).

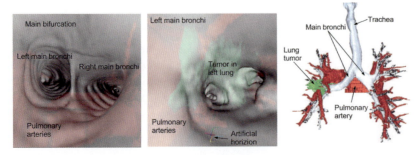

FIGURE 15.8 *Virtual bronchoscopy: the left image shows a semitransparent rendering of view in trachea at main bifurcation. The pulmonary arteries (red) are visible through the inner surface of the tracheo-bronchial tree. The middle image shows a similar situation farther down the left bronchi. Straight ahead is a large tumor (green) of the left lung, which eventually will obstruct the left bronchi. The right image shows an annotated outside representation with the tracheo-bronchial tree (gray), pulmonary arteries (red), and a tumor (green) in the left lung (view from behind the patient) [BARTZ et al. 2003b].*

Methods for Virtual Bronchoscopy

Virtual bronchoscopy requires data of a high spatial and temporal resolution, since the structures of interest can be quite small. Furthermore, breathing artifacts can reduce the quality of the data. Hence, datasets of approximately 250 to 300 images of 512 × 512 voxels with a submillimeter spacing are acquired using a multislice CT scanner. Unfortunately, the data resolution does not allow a simple region-growing segmentation of the airways, blood vessels, and possible tumors with sufficient quality. Instead, a complex multistage segmentation pipeline selects the respective voxels and allows the reconstruction of a surface representation of the lungs. Details of this segmentation pipeline and the quality of the segmentation can be found in [BARTZ et al. 2003b, MAYER et al. 2004].

Figure 15.8 shows two snapshots from a virtual bronchoscopy. The left image shows the endo-view from the trachea looking down to the main bifurcation, where the tracheo-bronchial tree splits into the left and right lungs. Figures 15.8 (middle) and (right) show a tumor in green in the left lung of a different patient dataset. At the same time, poor contrast and beam hardening artifacts of the voxels of the pulmonary arteries expose segmentation difficulties; the blood vessel tree is only incompletely segmented (see Fig. 15.8 (right)).

With the segmentation approach presented in [BARTZ et al. 2003b, MAYER et al. 2004], virtual bronchoscopy achieved a sensitivity of 85% up to the fifth generation of the inner airways, and more than 58% for the sixth generation. Beyond the sixth generation, the sensitivity drops below 30%.

15.5 VIRTUAL NEUROENDOSCOPY

One of major fields of application for virtual endoscopy is the central nervous system (CNS), which essentially consists of the brain itself, the cerebral nerves, and the spine. This interest in virtual endoscopy is mostly due to the complex anatomical configuration of nerve tissue, blood vessels, and other organ tissue in a relatively small space. Furthermore, the sensitive nature of the CNS often indicates the use of minimally invasive procedures, such as endoscopy. This basically determines the two closely connected types of applications of virtual neuroendoscopy: planning of a complex intervention and intraoperative navigation support. Here, we examine two application areas within the CNS; the *cerebral ventricular system* (see Sect. 15.5.1), and the *pituitary gland* (see Sect. 15.5.3). Because in both cases multiple data modalities are used to represent the different tissue types in the head, we will also discuss how they can be combined in Section 15.5.2.

15.5.1 CEREBRAL VENTRICULAR SYSTEM

The focus of (optical and virtual) ventriculoscopy is the ventricular system of the human brain [AUER and AUER 1998], where the CSF (cerebrospinal fluid) is produced and resorbed (see Fig. 15.9 (left)). Specifically, the CSF is produced in the lateral (upper two) ventricles. Due to respiration and other metabolistic activity, the CSF flows through the *foramen of Monro* into the third ventricle (which is also producing CSF), and via the narrow connection of the ventricular (cerebral) aqueduct to the lower fourth ventricle. From this ventricle, the CSF is distributed to other cavities inside of the skull.

Unfortunately, the drain of the third ventricles into the fourth ventricles can be blocked, due to occlusion or a stenosis of the *cerebral aqueduct*. This can be caused by a tumor, an accident, meningitis, or a congenital defect. The result of such a blockage is a serious disturbance of the natural flow of the CSF, which frequently leads to a dangerous increase of pressure inside the skull and can damage the brain severely (see Fig. 15.9 (right)).

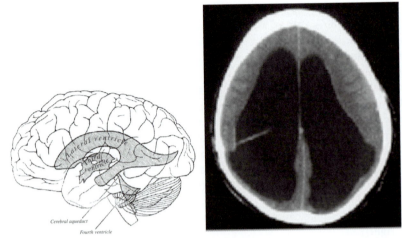

FIGURE 15.9 *Ventricular system of the human head* [GRAY 1918]: *Left: A ventricles, B ventricular (cerebral) aqueduct,* *Right: Hydrocephalus in an image from a* CT *scan. (Right image courtesy* DIRK FREUDENSTEIN, *University of Tübingen)*

The standard procedure for hydrocephalus is the external drainage of the ventricular system into the abdominal cavity using a shunt. Unfortunately, this external drainage system is frequently the cause of complications—such as obstructions and degenerative processes—that result in a needed neurosurgical replacement of the shunt. Furthermore, the missing natural flow of CSF may lead to degenerative processes of CSF-producing structures, as well as the disintegration of the septum between the lateral ventricles. The treatment of the basic cause of the occlusion is usually not possible, because of the inaccessibility of the aqueduct for any neurosurgical instruments. In the past 10 years, a new endoscope—small enough to pass through one of the foramina of Monro and with enough luminous intensity—was developed; it allows interventions inside the ventricular system [DUFFNER et al. 1994]. Considering the inaccessibility of the cerebral aqueduct—even with the new endoscope—several neurosurgeons are performing a (third) ventriculostomy, where the natural drain via the aqueduct and the fourth ventricle is bypassed by a new drain in the floor of the third ventricle. To access the ventricles, a hole is drilled through the skull and a tube is placed through this hole, through the brain, into the posterior horn of the left or right lateral ventricle. Thereafter, the endoscope is introduced through the tube, which is used as a stable guide for the endoscope. It proceeds forward through one of the foramina of Monro to the floor of the third ventricle.

Because of the water-like optical property of the CSF, which fills the ventricular system, viewing of the surrounding tissue is possible. Movement of the endoscope—guided by video-control via the small field of view of the endoscope—is limited by the tube and the surrounding tissue. Microinstruments, introduced through an additional canal inside the endoscope, can then be used to perform the actual minimally invasive procedure (e.g., removing accessible mass lesions). In the case of a ventriculostomy, the thin membrane of the *lamina terminalis* is perforated, thus realizing a new CSF perfusion balance.

Other indications for minimally invasive procedures include the formation of a CSF-filled cyst, which also introduces pressure on blood vessels, nerves, or the ventricular aqueduct. To avoid these dangerous increases of pressure inside the skull, the cyst is drained using the endoscope.

Virtual Ventriculoscopy

The major problem of the procedures described above is the limited view and orientation throughout the intervention, which increases the necessary time of the intervention and, consequently, the inherent risks of serious complications. To overcome these drawbacks, a virtual endoscopy system can be used to improve the planning of and orientation during this procedure [AUER and AUER 1998, BARTZ and SKALEJ 1999, BARTZ et al. 1999b].

Based on preoperatively acquired MRI/3D CISS (Constructive Interference in Steady States) scans of the patient's head, the respective ventricular system is reconstructed and examined by the virtual endoscopy system. In particular, the access ways to the target areas (e.g., the floor of the third ventricle) are explored to optimize the optical neuroendoscopic procedure. Besides the planning of neuroendoscopic interventions, virtual neuroendoscopy can also be applied to explore the stenosis of the cerebral aqueduct, an area that is not accessible with an optical endoscope. In Figure 15.10 the top row shows various snapshots from virtual ventriculoscopy; the position and orientation of the virtual camera is represented in the bottom row of Figure 15.10.

Each snapshot visualizes important anatomical structures, such as the *choroid plexus*, which is responsible for the production of CSF, and the *choroid plexus vein*, which supplies the choroid plexus in Figure 15.10 top/left. The entry point for the endoscope into the third ventricle, one of the foramina of Monro, is shown in Figure 15.10 top/middle. The pipe-like structure of the *adhesio interthalamica* connects the *thalamus* through the third ventricle. The upper bending of the foramina of Monro contains the *fornix*, which belongs to the *limbic system*. The limbic system is involved in the learning process, which means that the fornix is a very sensitive part of the body. If it is injured by the endoscope as it enters the third ventricle, a severe learning disability can be the result. The *mamillary bodies* in the floor of the third ventricle also belong to the limbic system. Figure 15.10 top/right shows a view from a viewpoint that is not accessible for an optical endoscope. It visualizes another important structure in the floor of the third ventricle, the

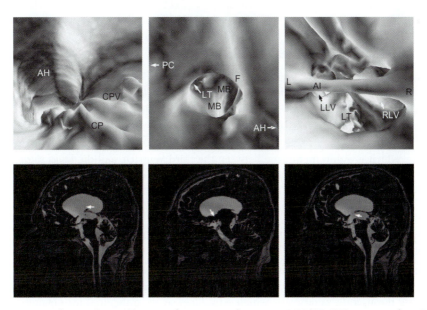

FIGURE 15.10 *Virtual ventriculoscopy. Top row: endoscopic views; bottom row: MRI/3D CISS orientation slices. Left: left lateral ventricle, approach from posterior horn via pars centralis (PC) to anterior horn (AH); Middle: foramina of Monro, approach via right lateral ventricle; Right: foramina of Monro, approach from third ventricle. CP = choroid plexus, CPV = choroid plexus vein, F = fornix, AI = adhesio interthalamica, MB = mamillary bodies, LT = lamina terminalis, LLV = entrance to left lateral ventricle, RLV = entrance to right lateral ventricle [BARTZ et al. 1999b].*

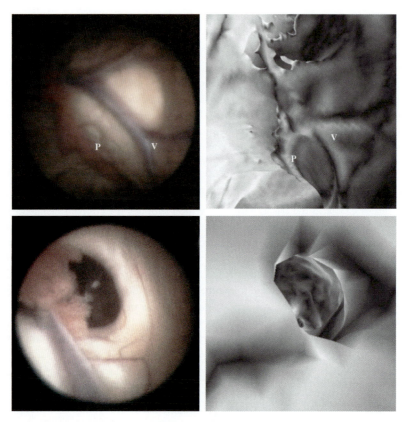

FIGURE 15.11 *Manually matched views from optical (left) and virtual (right) ventriculoscopy. The top row images show the thalamostriate vein (V) and choroid plexus (P) from the right lateral ventricle. The bottom row images show the right foramina of Monro, including the choroid plexus vein (see Fig. 15.10 (top/left)) and the choroid plexus structure [Bartz 2001]. (Optical endoscopy images courtesy Dirk Freudenstein, University of Tübingen)*

lamina terminalis, which is a thin membrane between the third ventricle and the *basilar cistern* (sometimes also referred to as cistern of the lamina terminalis). This membrane is the target area for the new CSF drain of the ventricular system.

15.5.2 MULTIMODAL VISUALIZATION FOR NEUROENDOSCOPIC INTERVENTIONS

One of the most dreaded complications of minimally invasive neurosurgery is lesions of blood vessels. Even if only a small blood vessel is injured, the resulting bleeding ("red-out") causes a sudden loss of optical visibility through the endoscope, which introduces severe difficulties for obtaining the desired results of the interventions. A more dangerous situation arises if a major blood vessel is injured. A lesion of an artery may result in a fatal mass bleeding, a usually lethal outcome of an intervention.

Unfortunately, the major basilar artery is located directly below the floor of the third ventricle, without optical visibility from the third ventricle. To avoid traumas of such blood vessels, a virtual endoscopy system should be able to represent different anatomical information of the patient from multiple datasets using different 3D scanning techniques [BARTZ et al. 2001c]. This approach typically requires the registration of the respective datasets and the fusion of the visual representations. BARTZ et al. [2001c] showed in such a context that registration may be relatively easy if the datasets are acquired by the same MRI scanner, thus introducing virtually no patient movement. In this case, they acquired an MRI angiography (time-of-flight (TOF) sequence) for the angio-architecture, and an MRI T2-weighted sequence (turbo-spin-echo (TSE)) for the ventricular system. Furthermore, they showed that visual fusion could be achieved by the semitransparent rendering of the inner surface, and the opaque and red rendering of the blood vessels [BARTZ et al. 2001c].

Figure 15.12 shows the rendered result of such a combination, where the vascular topography is combined with the information of the anatomical structures of the CSF-filled ventricular cavities. This information is successfully used to represent the location of the blood vessels to carefully plan the neuroendoscopic intervention. Lesions of the respective arteries can be avoided, resulting in a substantial reduction of the risk of serious complications. Next to the planning of third ventriculostomies, this approach was also used to plan the treatment of a *trigeminal neuralgia* caused by an ectatic *basilar artery* [FREUDENSTEIN et al. 2002].

15.5.3   MINIMALLY INVASIVE SURGERY OF THE PITUITARY GLAND

The pituitary gland is an important part of the endocrine system of the body. It regulates the production and distribution of many hormones for many different tasks such as growth; milk production (for females); stimulation of the adrenal and thyroid glands, ovaries, and testes; and skin pigmentation. It is located in a small bone cavity, the *sella turcica* (near the base of the skull, and next to the brain and important blood vessels).

An endoscopic intervention of the pituitary gland is usually performed in cases of a (typically benign) pituitary tumor. This tumor can cause headaches, impaired vision due to the compression of the optical nerve by the tumor, and, most importantly, the excessive production of hormones, which in turn causes a severe imbalance of the endocrine system [NEUBAUER 2005].

One of the standard interventional approaches is endonasal transsphenoidal pituitary surgery, which uses a rigid endoscope that accesses the target area through the nose (endonasal), the *sphenoid ostium* to the *sphenoid sinus* (transsphenoidal, see Fig. 15.13). Since the sphenoid ostium is usually too small to provide enough space for the endoscopic approach of the sphenoid sinus, it must be enlarged by a bone puncher,

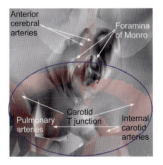
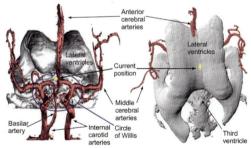

FIGURE 15.12 *Multimodal representation of ventricular system: Left: Frontal view from the cerebral aqueduct entrance in the third ventricle. The floor of the third ventricle—the potential location for a new CSF drain—is bounded by the arterial circle of Willis (blue ellipse), a potential cause for mass bleeding. Right: Frontal and top overview of ventricular system.*

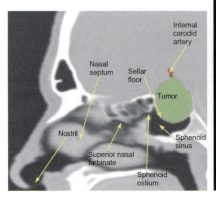 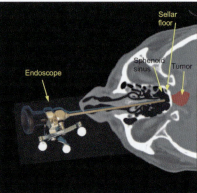

FIGURE 15.13 *Location of and approach to pituitary tumors. The endoscope approaches the pituitary gland through the nose and the sphenoid sinus. Sagittal (left) and axial (right) slice with segmented tumor (green) [NEUBAUER 2005]. (Images courtesy ANDRÉ NEUBAUER, VRVis Wien)*

a process that is called a *sphenoidotomy*. The same applies to septa located in the sphenoid sinus. Next, to provide sufficient access for the intervention, this step is also used to assess size and location of the pituitary gland and other important anatomical structures behind the floor of the *sella turcica* [NEUBAUER et al. 2004b]. The pituitary gland, and hence the tumor, is located behind the floor of the *sella turcica*, which must be opened using a drill or a chisel. The bone puncher is again used to enlarge the opening for a full access of the tumor. Subsequently, the tumor can be removed. If the tumor is located within the pituitary gland, the gland must be dissected to provide access to the tumor. After the removal of the tumor, the new cavity must be filled with body tissue of the patient, such as fat and muscular tissue from the abdomen. The sella floor is reconstructed using available parts of the bone and fibrinous glue.

Due to the complex anatomy of paranasal sinus, nearby arterial blood vessels, the pituitary gland, and the brain tissue, careful planning of the intervention is needed. NEUBAUER et al. [2004b] presented a system, STEPS, for the planning of this intervention.

Virtual Endoscopy of the Pituitary Gland

Virtual endoscopy of the pituitary gland requires the identification of the important anatomical structures for a proper visualization. Since this planning requires the representation of structures of the skull and a good soft-tissue contrast, CT and MRI scans of the patients are performed and registered to each other. Smooth segmentations of the relevant structures in both scans are computed (see Sect. 5.6.2) [NEUBAUER et al. 2004a]. Note that tumors of the pituitary gland can be quite small and may be difficult to segment.

Direct volume rendering is performed as described in Section 15.2.1. The surface of the endonasal structures and of the sphenoid structures is handled as a foreground object, while the tumor, pituitary gland, blood vessels, and optical nerve are treated as background objects. Figure 15.14 shows two examples from virtual endoscopy of the pituitary gland. The left image shows a fused visualization of the sphenoid sinus, where the sella floor and the surrounding bone structure are rendered semitransparent, thus exposing the tumor (bright green), the internal carotid arteries (red), and the optical nerve (blue). The pituitary gland is completely occluded by the tumor. The right image shows a similar situation, where only the tumor is visible in front of the pituitary gland. Next to the endoscopic view, three multiplanar slice projections (red, green, and blue) are visible. These slice projections show the intersection of the slices with the segmented dataset from the current endoscopic viewpoint.

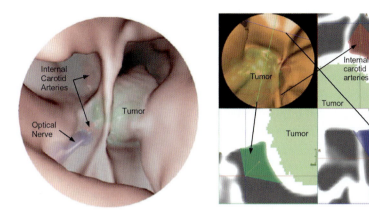

FIGURE 15.14   *Left: view from the sphenoid sinus to the pituitary gland (green) behind the sella floor. The segmented optical nerve (blue) and the internal carotid arteries (red) are also shown [NEUBAUER 2005]. Right: endoscopic view of the tumor (bright green) of the pituitary gland, with multiplanar reconstruction of the standard slices that contain the current viewpoint. The slices also represent their view contribution to the endoscopic view by representing the respective intersection of the slices with the endoscopic view in all four representations: sagittal (green), axial (red), coronal (blue) [NEUBAUER et al. 2004b]. (Images courtesy ANDRÉ NEUBAUER, VRVis Wien)*

Next to the endoscopic visualization of the virtual procedure, STEPS also provides the functionality to simulate steps of the minimally invasive procedure. In particular, it simulates several cutting tools that remove tissue during the procedure, such as the bone puncher. These tools actually change the data volumes of the respective tissue behind the impact region. This impact region is defined by a circular projection onto the surface of the tissue and the depth of the tissue before it enters the underlying tissue. Note, however, that a real tool defines the impact depth by the applied force and the material properties, not just by geometric means.

15.6   VIRTUAL ANGIOSCOPY

The blood circulation system is of special interest for physicians, since many injuries and diseases of this organ system can result in serious, potentially life-threatening conditions. Many of the diseases cause stenosis or aneurysms of the blood vessels. Both developments can be assessed using virtual endoscopy methods. These methods can be particularly useful in diagnostic applications, in which interior explorations using "real" endoscopic tools are not possible.

15.6.1 ANGIOSCOPY OF CEREBRAL BLOOD VESSELS

To acquire the angio-architecture of a target region, several angiography modalities can be used. In this example, a rotational angiography (see Sect. 3.1.2) is used. It allows a high spatial resolution with isotropic voxel spacing and represents the respective blood vessels (if a contrast agent is injected) and other anatomical structures. However, the relatively short scanning times of up to 13 seconds make rotational angiography still too slow for fast movements (e.g., the heartbeat).

A common procedure in neuroradiology is the examination of extra- and intracranial blood vessels. The major motivation behind these examinations is the diagnosis of cerebral aneurysms. Clinically, two major forms of aneurysms are distinguished; the *fusiform aneurysm* and the *non-fusiform or other aneurysms*. The fusiform aneurysm is an expansion of an arterial blood vessel through all of its wall layers (see Fig. 15.15 (left)). The basic criterion is that no *neck of the aneurysm* can be determined, which renders the aneurysm effectively as nontreatable. In contrast, a neck or exit can be identified for *non-fusiform aneurysm* (see Fig. 15.15 (right)). From an anatomic point of view, other distinctions are possible according to the shape and location of the aneurysms. Furthermore, some aneurysms include a rupture of the inner arterial wall layers, the intima and media. The remaining adventitia layer forms a saccular deformation that is very sensitive to pressure. However, these differences cannot be easily identified, which results in no clinical relevance of this distinction.

The expansion of the aneurysms can introduce pressure on other blood vessels—possibly resulting in the occlusion of those vessels—or on surrounding commissures (nerve fibers). This pressure can result in severe headache, partial paralysis, or a stroke. Furthermore, strong blood flow vortices and swirls at the neck and in the aneurysms increase the risk of a highly dangerous rupture of the artery, particularly if the blood pressure is increasing due to physical exercise. This rupture in turn results in the serious destruction or necrosis of the surrounding brain tissue, or in a lethal mass bleeding.

The usual procedures to treat aneurysms include neurosurgical and neuroradiological interventions. The major neurosurgical procedure is the exclusion of the aneurysm from the blood flow by positioning a clip on the neck of the aneurysm. In neuroradiology, tiny platinum spirals ("coils") are introduced into the dome of the aneurysm using a microcatheter, which is usually inserted via one of the femoral

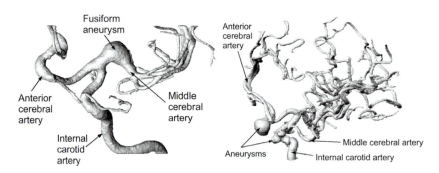

FIGURE 15.15   *Cerebral aneurysms; fusiform aneurysm (left), non-fusiform (saccular) aneurysm (right).*

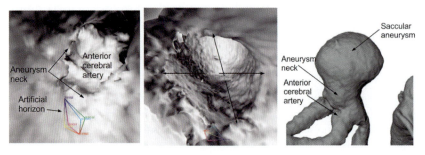

FIGURE 15.16   *Non-fusiform (saccular) aneurysm. Left: view from anterior cerebral aneurysm into anterior cerebral artery. Middle: view from anterior cerebral artery into aneurysm. Measurements show the size of the aneurysm neck. Right: anterior cerebral artery with saccular aneurysm from outside.*

arteries of the legs. Together with the clotting of the thrombocytes, the coils close the aneurysm from the bloodstream. All these interventions require the identification of the neck and exit of the aneurysms. These tasks, however, frequently cannot be achieved with standard 2D angiographies, MIPs, or slicing through the volume dataset. Three-dimensional geometry reconstructions using direct or indirect volume rendering techniques have been recently introduced into the clinical practice of research hospitals [GÜRVIT et al. 2000] to provide a better understanding of the angio-architecture of aneurysms in complex blood vessel trees. In particular, endovascular inspections of the blood vessel can provide valuable information on the position, orientation, and connection (neck) of the aneurysm [MARRO et al. 1997].

15.6.2 ANGIOSCOPY OF CORONARY BLOOD VESSELS

The human heart is responsible for circulating the blood through the blood vessels of the human body; it is organized into four chambers, the atria and ventricles (see Fig. 15.17 (left)). One atrium and one ventricle each belong to the *right heart* and *left heart* respectively. The heart is connected with the blood vessel system through veins (leading towards the heart) and arteries (leading away from the heart). The venous blood from the various body parts arrives in the *right atrium* through the *great veins*, the *superior* and *inferior vena cava*. It enters through the right *atrioventricular valve*, the *tricuspid valve*, into the *right ventricle*, where it is pumped via the *pulmonary valve* into the *pulmonary artery* to the lungs. After the blood is refreshed with oxygen in the lungs, it arrives through the *pulmonary veins* in the left atrium. It is passed via the *left atrioventricular valve*, the *mitral valve*, into the *left ventricle* and is pumped via the *aortic valve* into the *aorta*, which distributes the blood to all body parts. Directly after the aortic valve are the entrances to the *left* and *right coronary arteries*, which supply the heart muscle with blood. The left coronary artery bifurcates into the *anterior interventricular branch* and the *circumflex branch*, which supplies most of the left heart, and it is the main source of supply of the interventricular septum (which separates the left and right ventricles) that includes most of the conducting system of the heart. The right coronary artery extends over the right heart. It supplies this part of the heart, the interatrial septum (which separates the left and right atria) and, additionally, the interventricular septum, including the sinuatrial and atrioventricular nodes, which are the important parts of the conduction system of the heart [HOLLINSHEAD and ROSSE 1985].

Cardiac diseases are among the number one causes of life-threatening situations in Europe and North America. Usually, the under-supply of the heart muscle with oxygen through the blood leads to severe arrhythmia. This arrhythmia can cause an electromechanic decoupling of the conduction of the heart, resulting in a dangerous reduction of pumping performance, a possible collapse of blood circulation, and finally the death of the patient. Even if the arrhythmia does not lead to a fatal decoupling of the conduction, the missing supply of oxygen leads to the necrosis of that part of the heart muscle if the

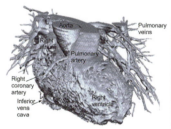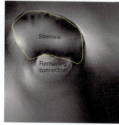

FIGURE 15.17 Left: front/top view on contrast media–filled cavities of the heart. Middle: outside reconstruction of stenosis of right coronary artery. Right: endoscopic view on stenosis [BARTZ et al. 2001a].

necessary medical procedures are not applied in time. The actual cause of the under-supply of the heart muscle is usually a stenosis or an occlusion of a coronary artery.

For the diagnosis of these malfunctions, several clinical and laboratory tests are applied. For imaging, echo cardiography, coronary angiography, or nuclear medicine methods are used. However, only 3D scanning methods are able to generate volumetric data of the heart. Unfortunately, most modalities are too slow to avoid motion artifacts of the fast moving heart. More or less only ECG-triggered (electrocardiogram) spiral CT provides scanning that captures volumetric data of the heart that is widely motion artifact–free. With the introduction of multislice CT, enough spatial resolution is also available for 3D coronary angiography.

Based on an anisotropic dataset from multislice CT coronary angiography, the heart can be explored by using virtual endoscopy for a virtual angioscopy of the coronary arteries [BARTZ et al. 2001a]. The dataset consists of 150 slices at a slice distance of 1.25 mm. Each of the slices has a resolution of 512 × 512 pixels at a pixel distance of 0.59 mm. Outside views of the reconstructed, contrast media–filled cavities of the heart can be seen in Figure 15.17 (left). The reconstructed surface geometry of the heart is very complex (more than two million polygons); thus, occlusion culling techniques are required to accelerate rendering.

The coronary valves, which open and close at a high speed, cannot be reconstructed completely, due to motion artifacts in the scanned dataset. In particular, the right atrium of the heart is subject to artifacts due to the injection of the contrast agent; they can be seen in the respective slices of the CT dataset. However, other important features of the anatomy of the patient's heart are visible, such as the aorta, the pulmonary artery, the great veins, the pulmonary veins, and the coronary arteries. Of special interest are the latter ones, since most cardiac emergencies result from a stenosis of these arteries. Figure 15.17 (middle) and (right) shows such a stenosis of the right coronary artery, which supplies the right heart and important parts of the conduction system of the heart.

One of the key application for cardiac imaging in general is the noninvasive assessment of coronary arteries for coronary artery diseases. This includes the assessment of calcifications and non-calcified plaques in those vessels, which may lead to a stenosis or even an occlusion of the respective coronary artery. Virtual cardioendoscopy enables the interior measurement of blood vessels at those stenoses and thus provides a quantitative evaluation of the stenosis.

The identification of stenoses in coronary arteries can be difficult from outside in cases where the respective blood vessel is occluded by other heart structures. Such a situation is visible in Figure 15.18. The left image shows a close-up view of a stenosis of the LAD artery that is occluded by the pulmonary artery from an outside view (right image). While it was possible to visualize this stenosis from the outside, it was originally detected through virtual cardioendoscopy of the left coronary artery.

Another advantage of virtual cardioendoscopy is the possibility of accurate measurements. The traditional axial (or otherwise oriented) image slice view may not properly represent the stenosis, thus leading to inaccurate size measurements (see Sect. 13.2). Other measurements include the volume of the ventricles, which can provide valuable information of the performance of the heart. Therefore, virtual cardioendoscopy provides valuable information for the assessment of a stenosis.

15.7   SUMMARY

The different objectives of virtual endoscopy applications impose specific requirements on the virtual endoscopy system. For an educational objective, the system should focus more on the visual quality that demonstrates the general topologic and geometric aspects of the specific patient anatomy. In contrast, the

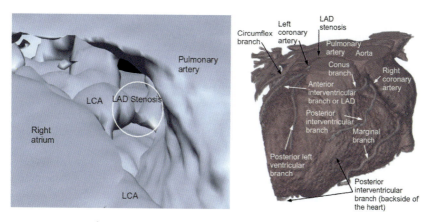

FIGURE 15.18 *LAD stenosis of the heart. Left: a surface-rendered visualization of a stenosis of the left anterior descent (LAD) branch of the left coronary artery (lCA). Right: volume-rendered representation of the dataset from a frontal (anterior) right view* [BARTZ *and* LAKARE 2005].[5]

accuracy of fine details is only of limited importance if the details are not the subject of the examination. However, it is different for a clinical objective, for which accurate rendering is one of the major factors that determine usability, because an incorrectly represented blood vessel connection might have a fatal impact on the medical intervention. If virtual endoscopy is used for planning an intervention, it is important that relevant anatomical structures are represented appropriately, since otherwise the planned access path (e.g., in virtual ventriculoscopy) might be occluded in the "real world" anatomy. Similarly, the visual representation must be highly accurate for intraoperative navigation to provide usable information to the surgeon.

There are several sources of errors that can lead to an inaccurate visual representation of anatomical structures in virtual endoscopy. Most notorious are partial volume effects and undersampling, which generate false connections between various caverns that are actually not connected. Furthermore, motion artifacts can reduce the visual quality severely or distort the actual anatomical geometry during a (long) medical scanning procedure or scans of fast-moving organs (e.g., the heart). In essence, all issues of poor data processing (e.g., due to insufficient data acquisition or poor segmentation quality) are likely to reduce the quality of the virtual endoscopic exploration significantly as well. Validation methods must be used in this context to determine the influence of improperly represented anatomical structures on the visualization, and, in the last consequence, on a treatment decision.

Finally, for all procedures that require a histological examination of a tissue sample under a microscope, virtual endoscopy is not able to compete. The data resolution of modern 3D scanners does not reach anywhere near the resolution of a microscope, although it is already in a submillimeter range, thus rendering a *virtual biopsy* insufficient. Furthermore, texture information—such as structure, color, and reflections—is also not captured by 3D scanners. Similarly, if the medical procedure includes the removal of tissue (e.g., lesions or tumors), or other objects, invasive or minimally invasive procedures cannot be replaced by virtual endoscopy, since it does not interact with the actual body of a patient.

---

5   Note that the rendered heart is mirrored, which is inherent to CT scans. Figure 15.17 shows a rendered heart model, in which the mirroring is corrected.

Virtual endoscopy has by now gone a long way from its first proposition in the early 1990s to today. However, most applications focus on small niches in the clinical routine; hence, they have not drastically changed modern health care, while they still provide valuable information for a better diagnosis. The only commercially successful application is virtual colonoscopy, which actually has the potential to replace optical colonoscopy in many cases. This is particularly true for screening examinations in which a whole age group with specific preconditions is examined.

The major issue that hinders the wide application of virtual endoscopy for intervention planning is the added time that needs to be spent on the planning. This additional time, however, can only be justified in clinical practice if the added value is clearly communicated. This situation aggravates, because these planning costs are typically not covered by the various health insurance plans. With respect to training applications, virtual endoscopy suffers from insufficiently realistic tissue modeling. This limits the training effect to the overall workflow and handling techniques, but it does not teach the operation of an optical endoscope on a patient.

The future of virtual endoscopy probably lies in a tight integration with optical endoscopy during the actual intervention. An image-guided surgery system (IGS) provides a common reference frame, the patient, which enables the mapping of computed information to the patient itself. The major challenge here lies in strategies to deal with tissue deformation (see Chap. 16) that can render the preoperatively acquired patient datasets as no longer accurate enough.

FURTHER READING

An overview of virtual endoscopy systems and applications can be found in [BARTZ 2005]. More discussions of the specifics of volume rendering for virtual endoscopy are available in the respective section of rendering and virtual endoscopy in [BARTZ et al. 2005a].

WEGENKITTL et al. [2000] presented a virtual bronchoscopy application that combines six Quicktime movies in a cube map to provide the rendered image. A similar technique based on ray casting was presented by SERLIE et al. [2001]. Details on fast CPU-based direct volume rendering are presented by GRIMM [2005] for the general case, and by NEUBAUER [2005] for virtual endoscopy.

An alternative approach for the examination of colon datasets has been presented by HAKER et al. [2000] and was further developed in [VILANOVA et al. 2001b, c]. Instead of an interior inspection of the colon surface mimicking an optical endoscope, this approach mimics a pathology approach to examination. The colon surface is cut, stretched, and unfolded into a flat representation. The most algorithmic effort is invested to provide geometric mapping that preserves the size and shape of surface features like polyps. Unfortunately, the unfolding approach does not allow the mapping of more complex organ systems, like blood vessels or airways.

Various image analysis techniques have been proposed in the context of virtual endoscopy. BARTZ and LAKARE [2005] discussed an interactive segmentation approach for coronary arteries employing virtual endoscopy, and LAKARE et al. [2000] presented a digital cleansing method for virtual colonoscopy. For more details on centerline generation and skeletonization of segmentations, refer to Section 5.7.

Chapter 16

Image-Guided Surgery and Virtual Reality

In the chapters so far, we learned about the different image analysis, visualization, and interaction techniques used in the context of medical volume datasets. All these approaches have one concept in common; they are applied before an actual medical intervention. In contrast, this chapter focuses on techniques that are used during an intervention. Hence, they are called *intraoperative*, in contrast to the previous *preoperative* techniques.

One of the most intriguing aspects of intraoperative techniques is that they directly interact with the patient lying (or sometimes sitting) on the operating room (OR) table. This aspect, however, requires several prerequisites to be met, such as an appropriate dataset of the patient, sufficiently prepared and pre-processed data (e.g., segmentations), and last but not least a sufficiently accurate registration procedure. This registration procedure maps the patient's dataset to the patient him- or herself. Once this registration is achieved, and after proper testing has shown that the mapping is good enough, visual output from the dataset can be mapped to the patient. Based on this registration, surgical instruments can be mapped to the patient datasets as well, if these instruments are tracked by a *navigation system*. This creates an *image-guided system* or IGS; there is a direct correlation between the patient's dataset and the patient. Instruments are tracked and thus, we can locate them on the patient (with our eyes) and in the dataset (through the registration mapping).

Typical IGS setups provide a view of the patient (through the surgeon's eyes) and of the patient's datasets (through the screen of the navigation system). If a surgeon positions a tracked or navigated instrument (e.g., a scalpel) on the patient, an abstract representation of that instrument is displayed on the multiplanar reconstructions (recall Sect. 7.1). Such a setup, however, has two disadvantages. First, the flexibility of how the patient is seen is limited. Second, reality and virtuality (the presentation of the virtual or computer-graphically rendered objects) are represented in two different reference frames; the OR table for reality, and the screen for virtuality. Hence, the surgeon must move her or his head away from the patient to look at the screen, and back. To reduce this cumbersome situation, virtual reality techniques are used to combine reality and virtuality to an *augmented* or *mixed reality*.

Organization In this chapter, we will examine the different techniques and setups that were briefly introduced in the previous paragraphs. Section 16.1 will look into general boundary conditions for intraoperative techniques. Afterwards, image-guided surgery is examined in Section 16.2, and finally, virtual reality techniques are discussed in Section 16.3.

16.1 PREREQUISITES FOR INTRAOPERATIVE VISUALIZATION

As mentioned above, interacting with data in an intraoperative setup requires several preconditions that must be carefully considered. The most important precondition is the choice of an **appropriate dataset**. This dataset should be able to represent the specific target anatomy of the patient; a dataset of the left leg will not be able to provide much information about the abdominal area. Another aspect is the

time between acquisition of the dataset and the intervention; this time should be as short as possible. Metabolic activity will change the local anatomy of the patient. If, for example, the brain changes its volume, the usability of earlier datasets will be limited. Typically, we can directly correlate the time between image acquisition and intervention and changes of the anatomy; the longer the time between, the larger the local change will be. Note, however, that change and **movements** are intrinsic to several body parts: the heart is beating, the lungs and the abdominal area are moved through breathing, the extremities move. While this movement, and the respective change, means that some body parts are extremely difficult to handle in intraoperative visualization, it can be dealt with in many situations. Head movement, for example, can be addressed if only the head alone is examined. The preoperatively scanned head is rigid enough to limit changes. Nevertheless, this does not compensate for the movement between neck and head, which also involves deformations.

16.1.1 TISSUE DEFORMATION AND BRAIN SHIFT

Deformations of the anatomy are one of the most difficult topics in intraoperative visualization, since changes of the anatomy are very difficult to predict. Furthermore, these deformations will happen whenever the surgeon is interacting with the body; repositioning the patient may change the anatomy, as might cutting through the skin, the muscles, or the bones. If the skull is opened for a neurosurgical procedure, the pressure situation within will change once the *dura*, the leather-like skin of the brain, is cut (see Fig. 16.1). Hence, the shape and the position of the brain will slightly change, a phenomena which is known as *brain shift*. Moreover, the removal of tissue from the body (e.g., a tumor) represents a significant change. Fortunately, these changes may be limited to a local region or can be compensated for by a variety of techniques. If a sufficient compensation is achieved, the preoperative dataset is still usable in areas away from the origin of change. In the other cases, the surgeon cannot rely on the preoperatively acquired datasets. One option for this situation is the use of intraoperative imaging (recall Chap. 3), where up-to-date data are acquired intraoperatively after the anatomy has changed. The advantage of intraoperative imaging lies in its repeatability; it can be applied after every changing action of the surgeon. The downside is that the devices must be registered and accommodated in a typically already cramped OR.

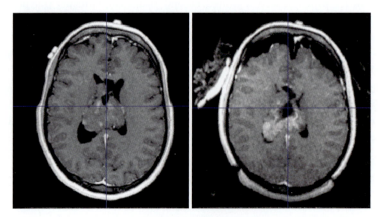

FIGURE 16.1 *Tissue deformation due to brain shift. Left: preoperative image of MRI head scan. Right: intraoperative image of MRI head scan after opening of the skull. The brain has shifted due to the changes of pressure inside of the skull [LÜRIG et al. 1999].* (Images courtesy PETER HASTREITER, University of Erlangen-Nürnberg)

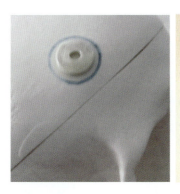 

FIGURE 16.2   *Fiducials and bolts as external markers. Left: fiducial glued to a skull model. Right: bolt to be screwed into the skull.* (*Right image courtesy* Jürgen Hoffmann, *University of Tübingen*)

16.1.2 REGISTRATION

Once an appropriate dataset has been acquired, it is transferred to the OR computer system and mapped to the patient lying on the OR table. This mapping is called *registration* and requires the identification of specific features in the dataset and on the patient. These features are typically identified through *fiducials*, a type of marker that is glued to the skin of patients (see Fig. 16.2 (left)) and that is visible in MRI or CT datasets. Alternatively, some surgical disciplines use bolt heads that are screwed into the bone (see Fig. 16.2 (right)).[1] Anatomical landmarks are also used, albeit rarely for registration. While they do not rely on extrinsic fiducials, they are difficult to identify and even more difficult to identify with a constant quality.

An alternative way of defining the relationship between dataset and patient is a *stereotactic frame*, an apparatus that spans a coordinate system. The stereotactic frame is attached (drilled) to the head before scanning and is then registered to the patient. Surgical instruments can be attached to the frame and thus can be navigated during the intervention. The advantages of frame-based stereotactic surgery are the high navigation accuracy, while the drawbacks are the more elaborate and cumbersome setup—which renders it unsuitable for certain interventions—and the more invasive attachment of the frame to the head. With the advent of reliable fiducial-based navigation, frame-based stereotactic surgery became less common. Hence, we will focus in the following on fiducial-based navigation.

The minimum number of markers for a pose (position and orientation) is three. In most cases, however, six markers are matched to optimize registration errors. Once all markers are identified within the dataset and on the patient, the actual optimization process to compute the transformation between these points is started (recall Sect. 5.9). The quality of the registration—which is basically its accuracy in the workspace[2]—depends largely on how the markers are arranged on the patient. For a good registration, they should span an as large as possible space around the respective body part. In case of the head, for example, markers are frequently positioned on the frontal, back, and lateral (sideways) parts of the head. Furthermore, markers are positioned on the upper and lower parts (see Fig. 16.3). If a more or less

---

1   While screwing of bolts into the bone sounds a bit terrifying, it inflicts only minor lesions, but provides superior accuracy. This situation exposes a common trade-off in surgery; accuracy versus invasiveness.

2   The workspace is the area of the intervention in which the navigation system tracks the instruments. Outside the workspace, the cameras of the navigation system do not see the instruments, or the accuracy is greatly reduced.

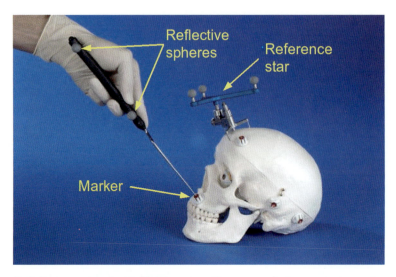

FIGURE 16.3 *Tracked pointer tool to identify fiducial positions. The pointer tool selects one marker on the maxilla of the skull. A reference star (see Sect. 16.2.2) is connected to the forehead. (Image courtesy JÜRGEN HOFFMANN, University of Tübingen)*

uniform arrangement cannot be achieved, the accuracy of the registration in the less-covered areas will be significantly lower, a fact that must be considered during the intervention.

Recently, an alternative registration method that employs the ICP registration algorithm[3] has become common. This registration method acquires a point cloud on the skin of the patient (e.g., the facial skin), which is then matched with a surface representation of the patient's dataset. This point cloud can be generated through a laser point projected on the skin, which in turn is measured through an already registered camera. BrainLAB's z-touch®, for example, is such a laser pointer and is measured through an infrared camera of the navigation system (see Fig. 16.4 left and next section).

The registration accuracy of the ICP-based method depends on how the point cloud is selected. The larger the space included by the convex hull of the points, the better the registration accuracy will be. Unfortunately, the location of the points for this method is limited to the areas visible to the cameras that measure them. This means that backfacing body areas (e.g., the back of the head) or areas hidden by hair or other body parts cannot be used. This is different from landmark- or fiducial-based registration, where only the relevant parts of the pointing device that are seen by the cameras (see Fig. 16.3) must be visible. For surgery around the head, the area of the forehead and around the orbits (eye sockets) is frequently used to acquire the point cloud, since they provide firmness and some spatial extent at the same time (see Fig. 16.4 (right)). HOFFMANN et al. [2005] showed that the accuracy of the ICP-based registration is not as good as fiducial-based registration, but can be sufficient for specific interventions. The major advantage of this approach, however, lies in the contactless registration, which can be helpful if that region is injured.

As described in the previous paragraphs, the arrangement or localization of the data acquired for the registration (fiducial position, point cloud distribution) strongly influences the accuracy and quality of the registration. Other important factors depend on the tracking device used by the navigation system.

---

3   Iterative closest point [BESL and McKAY 1992].

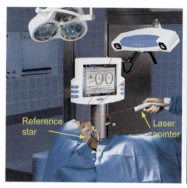
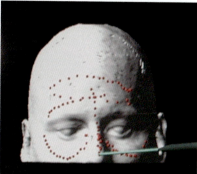

FIGURE 16.4 *ICP-based registration of a point cloud. Left: a laser pointer (BrainLAB's z-touch®) is used to indicate points on the facial skin that are seen by the infrared light cameras of a navigation system (BrainLAB's VectorVision®). The red lines indicate the path from the laser pointer to the skin, and the line-of-sights from the cameras to the position on the skin indicated by the laser. Right: acquired point cloud on the facial skull. A pointer tool points to the tip of the nose. (Left image courtesy JÜRGEN HOFFMANN, University of Tübingen; right image courtesy BrainLAB AG, Feldkirchen)*

These devices typically need a warm-up time of up to one hour, during which it slightly changes its shape (physical deformations due to temperature changes). Furthermore, measurement interferences with the tracking device reduce the quality of the tracking. This can be scattered light (mostly daylight) for optical tracking systems, or magnetic or metallic objects for electromagnetic tracking systems. More details on the tracking technology will be provided in the next section.

16.2   IMAGE-GUIDED SURGERY

As mentioned above, image-guided surgery allows the localization of surgical instruments and hence their mapping to the patient's dataset. Before this mapping can be achieved, the patient's dataset must be registered to the patient through the identification of markers on the patient and in the patient's dataset. The identification itself is performed by a pointing device that essentially consists of a calibrated long needle with a handle (see Fig. 16.3). This pointer must be localized through a tracking device, which we will examine more closely now.

16.2.1 TRACKING SYSTEMS

Tracking systems have the task of localizing objects in space. For that purpose, they must measure the positions and orientations (the poses) of these objects. While the field of virtual reality has seen many different tracking approaches, here we will focus only on electromagnetic and optical tracking. Later, we will also briefly look into vision-based tracking approaches.

Electromagnetic Tracking

Electromagnetic tracking is based on measuring the magnetic field strength at a certain location [SHERMAN and CRAIG 2003]. This magnetic field (actually three orthogonal fields) is generated by a field generator, the *transmitter*, at a fixed location. Sensors, the *receivers*, consist of three orthogonal coils in which voltage is induced by the magnetic field. They are connected to moving objects (e.g., surgical instruments) and thus measure the pose of these objects.

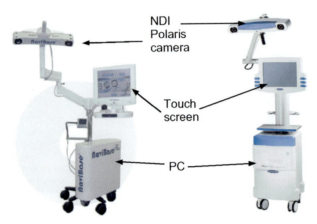

FIGURE 16.5 *Two navigation systems with optical tracking. Left: a NaviBase system from ROBODENT. Right: a VectorVision-Compact system by BrainLAB. (Left image courtesy ROBODENT GmbH, Berlin; right image courtesy BrainLAB AG, Feldkirchen)*

A major advantage of electromagnetic tracking is that it does not require a line of sight between transmitter and receiver. This allows the localization of the sensors in instruments that are moved inside a body cavity, which is a very important feature for image-guided surgery. Unfortunately, these sensors typically are not wireless and are hence connected with the tracking systems through a cable. Since this cable runs through the sterile area of the intervention, it must be wrapped in sterile drapes and may annoy the surgeons at the OR table. Furthermore, electromagnetic tracking suffers from two major causes of artifacts: if instruments/objects of conducting material are introduced into the magnetic field, eddies in the field are generated that disturb the magnetic field and hence the measurements. Moreover, if a magnetic field is generated nearby (e.g., by an intraoperative MRI scanner) electromagnetic tracking will be very difficult to use. Second, objects of ferromagnetic material will also disturb the measurements and hence cannot be used.

Overall, electromagnetic tracking provides reasonable accuracy if the magnetic field is not disturbed by other magnetic fields or by conducting and ferromagnetic materials. Since most surgical instruments are typically made from metal, this is a problem in the OR. However, electromagnetic tracking in the OR has made progress, and several companies provide solutions specifically for the OR. It remains to be seen whether sufficient accuracy has been achieved in specific situations.

Optical Tracking

Optical tracking identifies the pose of a tracked object by measuring light transmitted from or reflected by this object. Cases where light is transmitted from the object—typically through LEDs—are referred to as *active optical tracking*. Cases where light is reflected are referred to as *passive optical tracking*. Since active tracking requires cables running to the LEDs, it is no longer used in the OR, or indeed for medical applications in general. Hence, we will focus on passive tracking.

Passive tracking is achieved through specific markers connected to the surgical instruments. These markers are typically spherical and consist of infrared light reflecting material. This light is transmitted from an infrared light source at the optical tracking system, reflected by the markers, and finally measured by two cameras positioned at a defined distance from each other. Most optical tracking systems ("navigation systems") use NDI's Polaris®, its successor the Polaris Spectra™, or the smaller Polaris Vicra™ cameras (see Fig. 16.6).

FIGURE 16.6 *Polaris Spectra*^{TM} *(left) and Polaris Vicra*^{TM} *(right) optical infrared camera system. (Images courtesy NDI)*

Optical tracking provides a high measurement accuracy and is not influenced by any conducting or metallic objects nearby. Furthermore, passive optical tracking does not require any cables between the tracked instruments and the tracking system. However, passive optical tracking requires that the infrared light reflected by the markers be seen by the cameras. If this line of sight is blocked, that respective object cannot be localized. For surgical instruments, this means that we cannot see the parts of the instrument that are located inside the body; only outside parts can be tracked, hence the markers are typically located at the distal end of the instrument. Since the relation between tip and distal end of the instrument cannot be measured by the cameras either, this must be a fixed relationship that was measured in a calibration step. Consequently, flexible instruments like catheters or flexible endoscopes cannot be used in this type of setup. Furthermore, any scattered infrared light from a different source (e.g., the sun) will disturb the optical tracking. Hence, care must be taken to block out such light sources.

16.2.2 NAVIGATING INSTRUMENTS IN THE OR

As mentioned in Section 16.1.2, the patient's dataset is mapped to the patient through the registration step. Technically, the patient on the OR table is first located in the OR room coordinate system, whose origin is typically located right on the OR table. However, before the OR table is recognized by the navigation system, it also must be tracked by it. Hence, a sensor (for electromagnetic tracking) or infrared-reflecting markers (for optical tracking) must be fixed to the OR table in such a way that it remains in a constant relationship to the OR table. In the following, we assume an optical tracking technology, which is the standard approach in most cases.[4] The typical configuration of such markers consist of three markers arranged in a star shape, hence the name *reference star*.

In the second step, the actual registration step, the dataset is mapped to the OR coordinate system, which in essence maps the dataset to the patient. Note that the patient must remain in a constant relationship to the OR table and hence to the reference star. If the patient is moved on the OR table, the registration procedure must be repeated.

Similar to the OR table, every tracked (navigated) instrument is identified through a specific configuration of markers (a *reference array*) connected to the instrument by a *marker clamp*. Each instrument is uniquely identified by the configuration of markers (e.g., number of markers, distance and angles between markers). The physical distance and direction of the tip of the instrument to the markers is measured in a calibration step and typically stored afterwards (see Fig. 16.7).[5]

Each reflective marker is now seen by the two infrared cameras. Hence, the position of the markers can be computed by measuring the distance to the cameras through triangulation with basic trigonometry (see Fig. 16.8). If the configuration of markers is recognized, the orientation of the respective instrument is computed from the marker positions. Otherwise, the user will be requested to calibrate the new instrument.

---

4   An electromagnetic tracking approach actually does not differ significantly from this setup.

5   If the relationship between markers and instrument is changed (e.g., by moving the marker clamp), the calibration step has to be repeated.

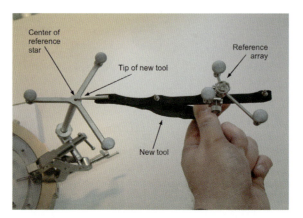

FIGURE 16.7 *The reference star on the left is to identify the OR table (patient), while reference arrays (right) identify tools. A new pointer tool is calibrated by attaching a reference array to the tool (right) and by pointing with the tip to the center of the reference star (left). (Image courtesy JAN FISCHER, University of Tübingen)*

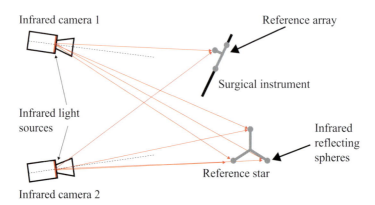

FIGURE 16.8 *Marker triangulation: infrared is emitted from the infrared light sources and is reflected by the reflecting spheres. The infrared cameras measure the direction of the reflection and compute the distance and then the position by triangulating the measured information. Note that all spheres are measured; only one measurement is shown for the reference array of the surgical instrument, for clarity only. (Image courtesy MARKUS NEFF, BrainLAB AG, Feldkirchen)*

Note that for a full pose, three markers are required. However, some instruments (e.g., the pointer tool in Fig. 16.3) are only tracked by two markers. In this case, the navigation system cannot compute the complete pose; a rotation around the axis of these two markers will not be recognized. Furthermore, the navigation system cannot tell if the tip or the distal end of the instrument points towards the patient. In most cases, the system will then make a reasonable assumption, which may nevertheless be wrong.

Typical navigated instruments include the pointer to identify anatomical structures of the patient (see Fig. 16.3), electrodes for EEGs (electroencephalograms) to measure the electric activity of the brain, and intraoperative image devices such as ultrasound probes (see Fig. 16.9) or endoscopes. For all these instruments, the position of the calibrated instrument tip and the orientation of the instrument are indicated in the multiplanar reconstructions, and possibly in the 3D reconstruction (see Fig. 16.10).

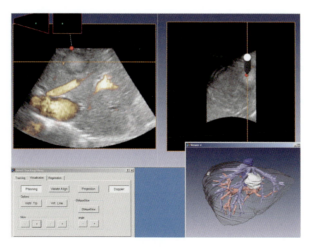

FIGURE 16.9   *Intraoperative imaging in the OR. Intraoperative 3D ultrasound data is acquired with a tracked ultrasound probe. The surgeon examines the liver with a tracked pointing tool to plan the resection of the liver. (Image courtesy THOMAS LANGE, Clinic for Surgery and Surgical Oncology, Charité-Universitätsmedizin Berlin)*

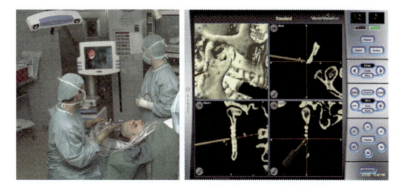

FIGURE 16.10   *Tracked screwdriver for maxillo-facial surgery. Left: overview of OR setup. Right: representation on the navigation system. Top/left shows a 3D reconstruction, and the other panels show the multiplanar reconstruction. The brown object shows the visual representation of the tracked screwdriver. (Images courtesy JÜRGEN HOFFMANN, University of Tübingen)*

A special variation of this approach, Navigated Control® [HEIN and LUETH 1999], limits an active tool to a specific area of the dataset. A navigated surgical drill, for example, stops drilling if its position and orientation does not satisfy specified conditions. This helps to mitigate complications and to increase the quality of the intervention.

16.3   VIRTUAL AND MIXED REALITY IN THE OR

So far, we have the patient lying on the OR table and the patient's data in the computer visualized on its screen. This means that the surgeon has to turn her or his head to look at the patient and the dataset with the representations of the navigated instruments. To provide a single view of the patient and his/her dataset, specific virtual reality techniques must be employed.

Virtual reality, in general, is the simulation of a world consisting of virtual objects with which the user can interact. The results of the interaction are then presented to the user, thus creating a closed interaction/reaction loop. Traditionally, virtual reality describes only virtual objects in a virtual space (virtuality). Therefore, the term *virtual environments* is used to describe such setups. In another type of virtual reality, a representation of the reality is combined with the representation of the virtuality. Theses scenarios are then called *augmented reality* or, more recently, *mixed reality*. In a mixed reality scenario, the representation of the reality is then enriched with objects from the virtuality. However, it is necessary to align the virtual objects to the reality representation, which is achieved through registration of the virtuality to the reality. In our IGS scenario, the virtuality of the dataset is registered to the reality of the patient on the OR table.

The position and orientation of the virtual objects are either fixed to the virtual space or to marker or *prop* objects [SHERMAN and CRAIG 2003]. The latter prop objects are physical representations of the virtual objects. These props are usually significantly less modeled than the virtual objects. Alternatively, every physical object has a virtual representation. Figure 16.11, for example, shows the virtual representation (yellow) of a pointing tool. The necessary alignment information is provided through the calibration of the tool and the tracking by the navigation system.

The display systems of mixed realities can be classified into two different groups [AZUMA 1997]. **Optical see-through displays** project the virtual objects onto a view of the reality, either through a mirror that maps the virtual objects onto a semitransparent view screen (e.g., most head-mounted displays—HMD) or through a semitransparent display that allows the user to see the reality through the screen itself (e.g., MEDARPA's semitransparent LCD screen, see Fig. 1.4 left). The other alternatives are **video see-through devices** that capture reality through a camera and enrich the video stream with virtual objects.

16.3.1 THE OCCLUSION PROBLEM OF MIXED REALITY

The main issue with mixed reality is that only a small amount of information about the reality is captured in a 2D image (or video stream). Hence, the virtual information is simply drawn over the 2D image of the reality in many mixed reality systems. However, this approach will not generate a proper depth for both worlds; due to the lack of depth information for reality, we cannot properly sort the virtual objects according to their depth position. Hence, they are drawn on top of real objects, even if they should be located behind them (see Fig. 16.11 (left)). This can severely disturb the user's immersion and interpretation of the position of the objects in the scene [FISCHER et al. 2004a].

FIGURE 16.11 *Virtual occlusion of reality. Left: the pointer tool vanishes behind the skull model, but its virtual representation is rendered still in front of the skull. Middle: virtual representation of tool behind the skull is correctly occluded. Right: detail of the cheek bone correctly occludes part of tool. (Images courtesy JAN FISCHER, University of Tübingen)*

One approach to solve that situation is to represent relevant parts of reality with computer graphic models. The resulting geometry is then used to set up the depth buffer to provide the correct depth information for the rendering of the virtual objects. Unfortunately, the modeling of a whole OR is too complex and tedious to be a realistic option. However, the actual focus during the intervention is solely on the patient. If we can recover the depth information of the patient, we can use this information for a proper depth representation (see Fig. 16.11 (middle)). Luckily, detailed information about the patient is available through the patient's dataset. The respective 3D information can be computed by reconstructing an isosurface representing the body part, thus creating a *shadow geometry* which is only rendered into the depth buffer, but not into the framebuffer. Hence it will be taken into account for the depth sorting, but it will not be visible on the screen. FISCHER et al. [2004a] described such a system, in which CT or MRI datasets are used to extract the shadow geometry. Note, however, that a straightforward extraction of the isosurface of the skin or skull will frequently generate a shadow volume with too many polygons. In these cases, FISCHER et al. suggest that one could compute a visual hull of the polygons outside, reducing the complexity roughly by a factor of two. Note that the accuracy of such a shadow geometry must also be considered, since any reduction is accompanied with a certain loss of fidelity. Fortunately, most applications can get away with a shadow representation that is significantly less accurate than the original reality [FISCHER et al. 2004a].

16.3.2 ALIGNMENT OF THE MIXED REALITY CAMERA

In Section 16.2, we pointed out the need for calibrated instruments for their successful tracking. In a mixed reality application, the camera capturing reality must also be tracked, and hence, it must be calibrated. If we again assume passive optical tracking, a reference array of markers must be connected to the camera (see Fig. 16.12 (left)) and the geometric relationship between the camera image and the reference array must be determined. Once this is the case, the virtual information from the patient's dataset can be aligned with the camera image (see Fig. 16.13).

Establishing the relationship between camera image and reference array is not an easy task. If the tedious and unreliable measurement of the relationship with a ruler is to be avoided, a special calibration step must be devised. FISCHER et al. [2004b] describe such a calibration step using the well-known ARToolkit [KATO and BILLINGHURST 1999]. The ARToolkit is a vision-based tracking toolkit that searches for a specific pattern in an image, the camera image, to estimate the pose of the camera. In the approach

FIGURE 16.12 *Calibrating the new camera. Left: a reference array is attached to a simple Web camera. Right: the corners of the marker pattern (black frame with "Hiro" written in it) of the vision-based tracking system are referenced with a pointer tool. (Images courtesy JAN FISCHER, University of Tübingen)*

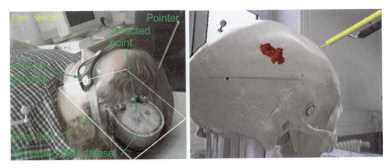

FIGURE 16.13 *Aligned virtual and real information. Left: point selection in patient's dataset with pointer tool and oblique slice tool overlaid on camera image. The registration goggles are carrying the fiducials. Right: overlaid segmented tumor (red) and tool (yellow) representation. (Images courtesy* ANGEL DEL RÍO *and* JAN FISCHER, *University of Tübingen)*

by FISCHER et al. the camera is positioned over such a marker pattern (a video marker) and the pose of the camera relative to that marker is computed by the ARToolkit. At the same time, the camera and its reference array are located in the workspace of the navigation system, hence the navigation system "sees" the camera (its reference array, actually). If the video marker (its corners) is now also referenced with a tracked pointer tool to the navigation system (see Fig. 16.12 (right)), the transformation is now completely determined.[6] This chain of individual transformations connects the camera image via the video marker and the reference array to the navigation system, and the camera is now calibrated for the navigation system. Note that this is a one-time calibration procedure and must be repeated only if the reference array of the camera is moved afterwards [FISCHER et al. 2004b].

16.3.3 INTERACTION IN THE OR

Once camera alignment and occlusion of virtual objects are addressed, the system can be used in an OR setting. The mixed reality is presented on one screen (see Fig. 16.13), and the surgeon no longer needs to change view direction to see the patient and the dataset. The system described in [FISCHER et al. 2004a, b] provides the mixed view on a screen mounted near the OR table. Consequently, the surgeon is not looking at the patient while interacting with the system. This is the typical scenario of endoscopic interventions, where the surgeon follows the endoscopic images on a video screen. For non-endoscopic surgery, however, the surgeon typically prefers to keep her or his view on the patient (see Fig. 16.10 (left)). For such situations, a tracked semitransparent LCD screen mounted on a swivel arm was introduced by SCHWALD et al. [2002]. In an OR setting, this device is positioned between surgeon and patient so that the surgeon looks through the device (see Fig. 16.14). A somewhat similar device introduced by WEBER et al. [2003] provides a tracked display with a camera on the patient's facing side to capture a video stream of the patient. In contrast to the mounted MEDAPRA display, this display is held in the hands of a surgeon (see Fig. 16.14 (right)).

A typical interaction in a medical mixed reality is the examination of the patient enriched with virtual information of target or risk structures. This information can then be used to plan the access path, to

---

6 For the computation of the transformation, the information of the navigation system must be exchanged with the vision-based tracking system. This requires an interface between components that may not be always available.

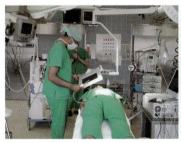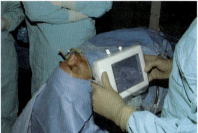

FIGURE 16.14   *Display options that direct the view at the patient. Left: semitransparent LCD mounted on a swivel arm. Right: tracked LCD with a camera on the other side. (Left image courtesy* BERND SCHWALD *of the MEDARPA project, ZGDV Darmstadt; right image courtesy* TIM LUETH *and* STEFAN WEBER, *MiMed, University of Technology München)*

navigate the surgical instruments to the target, or to avoid risk structures. However, these instruments can also be used to interact with the navigation system to modify parameters or to trigger specific operations such as special rendering styles. Figure 16.13 (left) shows an example of a medical mixed reality setup which used the pointer tool and a cutting plane tool to identify specific structures in the head to be used for a tissue classification [DEL RÍO et al. 2005, 2006].

FISCHER et al. [2005] introduced an interaction device, the *interaction sticker*, based on stickers that can be printed on sterilizable material and hence attached in the immediate proximity of the surgeon. This way, the surgeon can interact with the navigation system without directing personnel to modify the system parameters directly at the user-interface of the navigation system. Typical tasks can be the repositioning of the datasets, the application of clip planes, or the activation of a screen shot. Also possible is the drawing of an intervention plan directly on the representation of the patient (see Fig. 16.15). Currently, this is either only shown in the patient's dataset, or alternatively drawn with color markers directly on the target organ.

Before the interaction sticker can be used, it must be registered to the system by calibrating its respective activation fields with the pointing tool before the intervention. If a predefined interaction sticker is used, the calibration can be simplified by using video markers that are recognizable and differentiable by the ARToolkit (see Fig. 16.16).

Calibrated Mixed Reality Endoscope

As pointed out above, the setup in which the surgeon sees both the patient and the features from the patient's dataset on a screen resembles the setup of an endoscopic intervention. Hence, it is a natural step to combine a navigated conventional optical endoscope with a virtual endoscope (see Chap. 15). This scenario was already described in [BARTZ et al. 2002, 2003a] for applications in neurosurgery and maxillofacial surgery. Once the optical endoscope is calibrated as an instrument through the optical infrared tracking system and as a camera[7] through the vision-based tracking system, the virtual objects can be embedded into the endoscopic image. Note that we assume here that the video stream from the endoscopic camera is already digitized. While this is provided by a fully digital endoscope, it does require framegrabbing for standard analog endocopes.

---

7   Endoscopes have special optical properties that distort the image. This distortion needs to be considered when the virtual objects are mixed with the camera image (see Sect. 15.2.1).

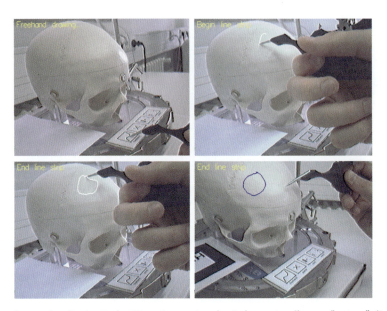

FIGURE 16.15 *Intervention planning in the OR: an intervention plan is drawn virtually on a "patient." (Images courtesy* JAN FISCHER, *University of Tübingen)*

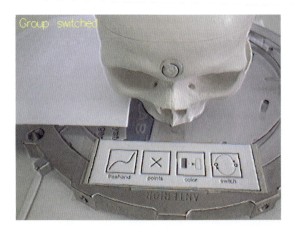

FIGURE 16.16 *Interaction sticker: calibrated fields on a sterilizable sticker act as interaction buttons activated through the pointing device. (Image courtesy* JAN FISCHER, *University of Tübingen)*

16.4   SUMMARY

Prior to this chapter, image analysis, visualization, and interaction techniques were applied only in settings outside of the OR. In contrast, this chapter discussed the foundations for applying these techniques in the intraoperative setting. Major prerequisites for an intraoperative application are appropriate dataset acquisition and registration of the patient and the respective datasets (see Sect. 16.1). Together with a tracking system, instruments interacting with the patient can be mapped to the dataset, comprising an image-guided surgery system or intraoperative navigation system. Finally, virtual information computed from the dataset can be combined with a view of the patient into one display, creating a medical mixed reality system. The advantage of such a system is clear; previously hidden targets (e.g., lesions and tumors) or risk structures (nerves or blood vessels) can be seen while interacting with the patient.

Many mixed reality setups use standard virtual reality components, in particular standard tracking technology. However, the use of such technology in a medical setting, in particular an OR, requires special certification of all components. Furthermore, ORs are typically small rooms that do not easily accommodate the extra equipment. In addition, extra special equipment often requires tedious setup procedures that can a take significant amount of time, which is largely not available before an intervention. We also described an IGS configuration that employs an already certified navigation system, minor additional components, and a simplified setup, thus removing most of the issues that obstructed mixed reality from being a successful application in the OR. Up to now, intraoperative navigation and image-guided surgery became a standard in many clinical disciplines including neurosurgery, maxillo-facial surgery, or ear-neck-throat surgery. In contrast, they are still at a research state for abdominal surgery. Futhermore, most mixed reality application scenarios are research projects and are not yet ready for clinical use, although several research activities are getting close to a clinical evaluation.

FURTHER READING

Various medical mixed reality scenarios have been proposed in the past. Among the first was the ultrasound-guided needle biopsy of BAJURA et al. [1992] and STATE et al. [1996]. SCHEUERING et al. [2003a] introduced a mixed reality system for liver surgery, which they combined with video sequences in [SCHEUERING et al. 2003b]. More information on this system is provided in [SCHEUERING 2003]. Another mixed reality system for liver surgery planning was described by BORNIK et al. [2003b]. This system, however, was not designed as an intraoperative application. BIRKFELLNER et al. [2000] introduced Varioscope AR, which used a very compact head-mounted display (HMD) and optical tracking to mimic a surgical microscope. A similar approach was also described by EDWARDS et al. [1999]. Closely related to the endoscopy application above is the work of [DEY et al. 2000], which matches virtual and optical view. However, both views were not combined into one view. OLBRICH et al. [2005] proposed a partial and periodic combination of virtual and video-endoscopic images for endoscopic liver surgery. Related techniques were also used for robot-assisted port placement for heart surgery [FEUERSTEIN et al. 2005].

Various solutions have been proposed for the occlusion problem of mixed reality. BREEN et al. [1996] proposed a model-based approach for static occlusion, which was later extended by FUHRMANN et al. [1999] for the user's body. A variation of the latter approach for marker occlusion of the user's hand was presented by MALIK et al. [2002]. Dynamic occlusion with static backgrounds on basis of textures for the background objects was addressed by FISCHER et al. [2003]. Finally, BERGER [1997] and LEPETIT and BERGER [2000] examined occlusion in stored video sequences.

As mentioned above, the ARToolkit [KATO and BILLINGHURST 1999] is the standard, but not the only vision-based tracking solution. ARTag [FIALA 2004] is more reliable and provides a more robust vision-based tracking solution. However, in contrast to ARToolkit, it is not available in source code; hence its integration may be difficult or even impossible.

One solution to tissue deformation is the acquisition of new image data intra-operatively. A popular approach is to integrate data from tracked ultrasound scanner [SAUER et al. 2001, VOGT et al. 2003] and register it to preoperatively acquired CT or MRI datasets [LANGE et al. 2002, 2004]. Alternatively, calibrated and tracked intraoperative X-ray systems are an option proposed by NAVAB et al. [1999]. Another alternative for intraoperative imaging is MRI with an open low-field MRI scanner [KETTENBACH et al. 2000] or with a full-field MRI scanner [NIMSKY et al. 2006, 2003].

Chapter 17

Emphasis Techniques and Illustrative Rendering

Visualizations in medicine are generated to "answer" a diagnostic question or to support an intervention planning scenario. In these scenarios, it is essential to adapt the appearance of objects or regions to their relevance for the specific task. As an example, it is often useful to focus on certain anatomic structures, and therefore other objects or regions only serve as orientation aids that might be displayed in a less pronounced manner. A medical visualization system might "know" what is relevant after the user selected an object, either immediately within the visualization or indirectly via its name in a list. Emphasis techniques modify the visualization of a selected object or other objects so that their shapes can be clearly recognized and their locations in the overall model become obvious. Research in visual perception indicates that emphasis techniques indeed support our ability to perceive and interpret complex visualizations (recall Sect. 2.4.1). In a medical illustration guide, the following advice is given: "A drawing of surgery removes inessentials. It eliminates distracting background and simplifies and emphasizes information." [BRISCOE 1996].

In this chapter, we discuss a variety of techniques inspired by conventional illustrations. These techniques are not only targeted at educational systems but also at intervention planning. In particular, we discuss visualization techniques that emphasize certain objects while de-emphasizing others. Two-dimensional as well as 3D visualizations are considered in which emphasis techniques should be applied simultaneously to both visualizations. The design of emphasis techniques for 3D visualizations is challenging, because relevant objects might be far away (and thus too small) or even occluded. As SELIGMANN and FEINER [1991] pointed out, visibility and recognizability must be ensured to emphasize an object.

As a family of visualization techniques suitable for emphasis in medical visualization, we discuss so-called non-photorealistic rendering techniques in which points and lines are employed to display and augment objects. These are inspired by traditional illustration techniques in scientific and medical applications. The potential of these techniques is to emphasize important features and to remove extraneous detail [HODGES 1989].

Local, Regional, and Global Emphasis Techniques To support a structured view on emphasis techniques and meaningful combinations of them, we provide a classification. Basically, we differentiate between *local*, *regional*, and *global* emphasis techniques. While local techniques only influence the currently selected object (CSO), regional and global techniques also have an influence on nearby objects or even the whole dataset. As an example for regional techniques, objects or regions in the (geometric or functional) neighborhood might be rendered transparently or completely removed to ensure the visibility of the CSO. An example of a global technique is the adaptation of the viewing direction to show the CSO unoccluded.

The use of regional and global techniques is justified to emphasize occluded objects. Therefore, it is useful to perform an analysis concerning the visibility of the CSO to decide whether to apply such a technique. In particular, emphasis techniques that affect the whole visualization might be difficult to interpret. To improve the comprehensibility of global emphasis techniques, dynamic techniques that animate the change of a visualization are useful. The application of potentially useful emphasis techniques for medical volume data is manifold. The discussion in this chapter is by no means complete. We shall give examples of viable and appropriate solutions, discuss their limitations, and, we hope, inspire new research concerning the evaluation of existing or the development of novel techniques.

Focusing with Emphasis Techniques Emphasis techniques have to fulfill the visualization task of *focusing* (i.e., showing and highlighting important objects effectively). Therefore, "importance" must be computed. This can be implemented by deriving importance from the interaction of the user (e.g., distance to the mouse cursor, objects selected by the user) or by taking into account the *a priori* importance of certain objects [FURNAS 1986]. A combination of *a priori* importance and parameters derived from user interaction is also feasible.

Research in visual perception indicates that there are visualization parameters that are recognized independent of the number of competing objects "at a glance" (*preattentive vision* [TREISMAN 1985]). As an example, a few objects shown with highly saturated colors are recognized immediately in a large set of objects. Another effective emphasis technique is blurring, in which only important objects are rendered sharply, whereas others appear blurred, similar to unfocused regions in photographs [KOSARA et al. 2002]. In conventional medical volume rendering, this is addressed by the opacity transfer function (OTF), which specifies the range of intensity values that are important (and rendered opaque) and the values that are less relevant (and more or less rendered transparently). The general concept here is to support multiple levels of importance (focus).

Organization This chapter has the following structure: we start with a discussion of non-photorealistic rendering techniques and their potential to improve shape perception. In Section 17.1, we focus on techniques applied to surfaces and volumes. In Section 17.2, we discuss hybrid combinations of volume, surface, and line renderings. As a prerequisite for the selection of appropriate emphasis techniques, we describe visibility analysis techniques (see Sect. 17.3). These methods determine whether the CSO is occluded and which objects eventually occlude it. Based on this discussion, local (see Sect. 17.4) and regional (see Sect. 17.5) emphasis techniques are presented. A short section discusses dynamic emphasis techniques (see Sect. 17.6). In Section 17.7, we describe how emphasis techniques can be applied simultaneously to 2D and 3D visualizations, an essential feature for relating 3D objects to their representation in the underlying data. Finally, a classification of emphasis techniques is introduced in Section 17.8.

17.1   ILLUSTRATIVE SURFACE AND VOLUME RENDERING

For a long time, computer graphics has been focused on photorealistic rendering, in which the goal is to compute an image from a description of the geometry by simulating optical effects such as reflection, absorption, and refraction as closely as possible. A high degree of visual realism on one hand and acceptable frame rates on the other are traded carefully. Photorealistic renderings are typically intensively illuminated and brisk visual representations. This, however, is often inappropriate for visualization, since this also implies an exactness that is misleading in cases of incomplete models or uncertainty in data acquisition and processing.

In 1990, a new direction emerged and meanwhile gained much acceptance—non-photorealistic rendering (NPR). Basically, NPR aims at a stylization of the visual representation, which is the opposite direction of photorealistic rendering. A rendering style that does not attempt at high realism, NPR provides a wide range of different rendering techniques to express various effects and to simulate styles from traditional scientific and medical illustration.

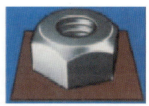

FIGURE 17.1   *Silhouettes are computed to enhance shape recognition. The combination of shading and silhouettes provides even more cues* [SAITO and TAKAHASHI 1990]. *(Image courtesy TAKAFUMI SAITO, Tokyo University)*

Although the term "non-photorealistic" is widespread in computer graphics, it is misleading for visualization, in which the typical rendering is not photorealistic.[1] Due to their inspiration by traditional illustrations, these methods are also called *illustrative rendering, stylized rendering,* or in some cases *artistic rendering*. In our experience, illustrative rendering is a better term for the communication between computer scientists and medical doctors. Application specialists often have an intuitive understanding of illustrative rendering. Using the term non-photorealism in a discussion with application specialists requires an explanation of photorealistic rendering and its limitations first. In the remainder of this chapter and this book, we will use the term *illustrative rendering* to emphasize this situation. However, we will continue to use the abbreviation NPR interchangeably with *illustrative rendering*, due to its widespread usage in computer graphics.

The driving idea behind illustrative rendering for visualization is the emphasis on relevant features and the removal of unimportant details. Hence, attention is directed to the relevant features. This can be achieved by rendering strokes and points instead of shaded polygons.

Another set of techniques focusing on 3D shapes was proposed in the pioneering work of SAITO and TAKAHASHI [1990] (see Fig. 17.1). These techniques generated silhouettes and feature lines to emphasize the shape of objects. These characteristics were computed by analyzing discontinuities in the depth buffer and visualized through lines. Silhouettes and feature lines are in particular important for the recognition of shapes, since they provide cues for object-to-ground distinction.[2] These techniques were complemented by hatching, which is employed to highlight the curvature and orientation of objects.

It is interesting and worthwhile to note that the goals of scientific visualization and NPR are very similar: to convey information effectively and to emphasize features in the data. Therefore, it is not surprising that NPR techniques have been adopted in visualization in general and in medical visualization in particular [NAGY et al. 2002].

Shape Perception   Psychological studies clearly revealed that silhouette and hatching lines might improve the comprehensibility of images. As an example, KIM et al. [2003a, b] investigated the effect of textured lines superimposed on shaded surfaces. In their study, users had to estimate surface normals. The results of the study showed that the 3D shape was better perceived with hatching lines in the direction of maximum curvature (see Fig. 17.2). Slightly better results were achieved with hatching lines in the direction of the two principal curvatures (see Fig. 17.2 (right)). These and other studies reveal that texture may improve shape perception. While NPR has many subareas and applications, such as artistic applications or games, we focus on techniques to improve the perception of anatomic structures.

---

1   As Craig Reynolds commented on the name, with a quote that is attributed to Stanislam Ulam (www.red3d.com/cwr/npr): "The study of non-linear physics is like the study of nonelephant biology."

2   Further discussion of silhouettes and feature lines can be found in Section 17.1.2.

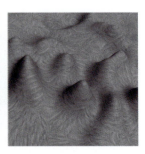

FIGURE 17.2   *Three examples from a study testing shape perception. Left: Phong shading; middle: lines representing one principal direction; and right: lines in two principal directions* [KIM et al. 2003b]. *(Images courtesy* VICTORIA INTERRANTE, *University of Minnesota)*

17.1.1 EMPHASIS AND ILLUSTRATIVE RENDERING

NPR provides a wide range of techniques that might be employed for emphasis purposes. In photorealistic rendering, emphasis might be achieved by adapting the position of the virtual camera or by placing a spotlight source. The rendering process itself, however, regards all edges and faces as similarly important. Nothing is left blank, even if it is less relevant. Partial visibility of an outer object to reveal inner structures can only be achieved by semitransparent rendering or clipping. This method, however, strongly degrades shape perception.

NPR offers more degrees of freedom to emphasize objects or regions. The CSO might be enhanced by silhouette and hatching lines, while others are not. As has been pointed out by VIOLA et al. [2004b, 2005], NPR permits *sparse visual representations* of objects, which consumes less screen space than shading surfaces. Outlines or silhouettes are probably the sparsest meaningful visualization that can roughly convey the object shape. The addition of prominent feature lines or hatching lines leads to a denser representation, which reveals more detail on the object shape. Finally, the combination of such illustration techniques with conventional rendering techniques results in a dense representation that depicts an object clearly, at the expense of the obstructed objects behind. The adjustment of the level of sparseness is probably an essential aspect of emphasis techniques.

The negative side of this freedom is that appropriate choices for many parameters are needed. More degrees of freedom make it more difficult to adjust a visualization. While artists may take hours to produce expressive images, medical visualizations are often generated under strict time limits. However, medical visualizations should still be precise, reliable, and interactive. Our view of NPR is focused on these aspects. Techniques that require considerable and nontrivial input by the user (for example, specification of hatching directions) are not considered. Also, rendering styles that are more artistic than precise are omitted. For a broad overview on NPR, we refer to [GOOCH and GOOCH 2001, STROTHOTTE and SCHLECHTWEG 2002].

Useful rendering styles for use in medical education and intervention planning can be inspired by traditionally drawn medical illustrations (see Fig. 17.3). The left image of Figure 17.3 uses silhouettes and points to convey the shape of the liver. The local density of points is adapted to the curvature of the organ and simulates a lighting effect. This rendering style is called *stippling*. Small dots of ink are placed onto paper in such a way that their density gives the impression of tone. Besides its expressive power, stippling is attractive, because the rendering of points is very fast, facilitating interactive exploration. Stippling is closely related to dithering and half-toning, in which patterns of black points are used to convey different gray tones. The major difference is that dithering is accomplished in a high resolution, so that usually individual points are not recognized. In contrast to dithering, stippling does not necessarily involve a fixed pattern.

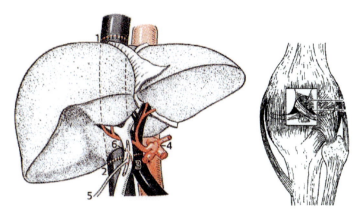

FIGURE 17.3 *Illustration techniques in traditional textbook illustrations. Left: an illustration to explain vessel reconstruction techniques in liver surgery. Silhouette lines and stippling are used to depict the liver. Right: a cutaway view shows hidden anatomic structures* [SCHUMPELICK *et al.* 2003]. *(Images courtesy* VOLKER SCHUMPELICK, *RWTH Aachen)*

In Figure 17.3 (right), lines are used exclusively. In addition, *cutaway views* are included. Computer-generated cutaway views are discussed later in this chapter (see Sect. 17.5.1).

17.1.2 SILHOUETTE AND FEATURE LINES FROM POLYGONAL MODELS

Before we look into the techniques for the specification of silhouettes and feature lines, we briefly discuss the definition of silhouettes. The term silhouettes can be traced back to Étienne de Silhouette, a French finance minster in the 18th century. To decorate his home, he cut portraits of his friends and relatives that outlined only the outer shape of the subject to differentiate it from the background. Hence, the silhouette looks like the shadow of the person and does not include inner feature lines. Note that this standard definition of a silhouette differs significantly from the widely used definition of a silhouette in NPR, in which a silhouette separates front- and backfacing graphic objects (e.g., polygons). This definition of a silhouette is similar to the daily life definition of a contour. But since the term contour is used in computer graphics to specify an isosurface (or isocontour), we refrain from using it in this context.

Note that there are feature lines other than silhouettes. Ridge lines or creases denote discontinuities of the object (such as edges in the depth or normal space in the framebuffer or angles beyond a threshold between polygons) but do not yet satisfy the NPR definition of a silhouette. In Figure 17.1 (left), silhouettes are rendered as black lines, while ridge lines are rendered in white. Furthermore, note that feature lines are typically view-dependent. Consequently, they need to be determined for every viewing direction [ISENBERG *et al.* 2003].

Polygonal (surface) models in medical visualization are generated by thresholding medical volume data or by transforming segmentation information into (polygonal) surfaces. For continuously differentiable surfaces, such as b-spline surfaces, the silhouette S is defined as the set of points on the object's surface where the surface normal is perpendicular to the vector from the viewpoint [HERTZMANN and ZORIN 2000]. At these points p_i, the dot product of the normal $\vec{n_i}$ with the view vector $\vec{v} = (p_i - c)$ is zero, with c being the camera position for perspective projections (see Eq. 17.1):

$$\{S\} = \{P | \vec{n_i} \times \vec{v} = 0\} \qquad (17.1)$$

For Gouraud-shaded polygonal models, the definition above cannot be directly applied, because normals are only defined for faces and vertices but not for arbitrary points. However, silhouettes can be found along edges in a polygonal model that lie on the border between changes of surface visibility. Thus, silhouette edges of a polygonal model are edges that share a front- and a backfacing polygon. Note that silhouettes are often computed based on discrete data (voxels or polygonal mesh vertices). Thus, the scalar product of normal $\vec{n_i}$ and viewing direction $\vec{n_i}$ are rarely exactly zero. Therefore Equation 17.1 is usually replaced with Equation 17.2, which evaluates the scalar product in an ϵ-neighborhood:

$$\{S\} = \{P | \vec{n_i} \times \vec{v} < \epsilon\} \qquad (17.2)$$

Silhouette algorithms solve two tasks: they determine silhouette edges and determine the visible subset of them. In general, *image-* and *object-space* methods are available for these tasks (see [ISENBERG et al. 2003] for a survey). While object-space methods evaluate every vertex/edge (or other graphics primitive) of the model, image-space methods typically compute the silhouettes within the framebuffer. In the following, we focus on image-space methods. Object-space methods will be discussed in the context of volumetric data in Section 17.1.4.

As mentioned above, image-space methods operate on the different buffers of the framebuffer, which contain per pixel information. In particular, the z-buffer (depth buffer) and the normal-buffer (representing the z-coordinate and the normal of the polygon rendered at each pixel) are useful for finding silhouette edges. Strong discontinuities in these buffers indicate the boundaries between objects and, thus, silhouettes. Edge detection methods from conventional image processing are employed for this purpose (recall [HERTZMANN and ZORIN 2000]). An alternative approach exploits the depth-buffer of OpenGL [RASKAR and COHEN 1999, LANDER 2000b]. After rendering the frontfacing polygons in a chosen shading style (flat white for silhouette rendering only), the depth-buffer function is changed from LESS to LEQUAL (less equal) and the backfacing polygons of the same object are rendered in a wire-frame mode. Since the rasterized pixels of the silhouette have the same depth value for the front- and the backfacing polygons, they are rasterized twice (depth function is LEQUAL) and hence appear on the rendering. Image-space methods efficiently compute silhouettes, because they are based on fast framebuffer operations typically performed on graphics hardware. Figure 17.4 illustrates the use of image-space silhouettes and feature lines to convey the shape of context objects.

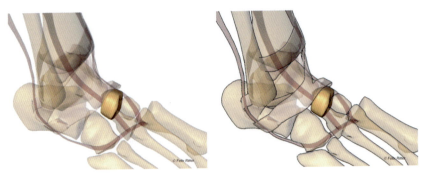

FIGURE 17.4 *An anatomic illustration with emphasis on a user-selected bone. The context objects are rendered highly transparent (left). On the right, transparent objects are enhanced with silhouette and feature lines to better convey their shape. (Images courtesy* FELIX RITTER, *MeVis Bremen)*

Subpolygon Silhouettes   If we compute the silhouette using Equation 17.2, we only evaluate the normals of the vertices. A silhouette will be in a polygon with vertices that exhibits a sign change of the scalar product in Equation 17.2. Depending on the local curvature of these polygons, the scalar product at the vertices has a varying magnitude. If we further consider varying polygon sizes, the polygon edges might be poor silhouette approximations and exhibit interpolation or staircasing artifacts. Instead, we can compute a refined silhouette by computing a piecewise linear approximation of the silhouette (see Fig. 17.5) within the respective polygons [HERTZMANN and ZORIN 2000].

Suggestive Contours   An interesting extension of the more traditional silhouettes are the so-called *suggestive contours* introduced by DECARLO *et al.* [2003]. They include contours derived from closely related viewpoints to generate expressive renderings that convincingly convey complex shapes with concavities. Suggestive contours are computed based on Equation 17.1. Instead of composing a silhouette of points in which the dot product of surface normal and view vector is zero, the silhouette is composed of points where the dot product represents a local minimum.

   An essential advantage of suggestive contours is their temporal coherence. While conventional silhouettes may strongly change after small rotations, suggestive contours are more constant [DECARLO *et al.* 2004]. Temporal coherence is an advantage for animations as well as for interactive 3D renderings.

Smoothing Polygonal Models   In general, silhouette and feature line detection algorithms assume that the underlying polygonal meshes are sufficiently smooth. However, this is not generally the case for isosurfaces extracted from medical volume data, particularly if the volume dataset is highly anisotropic or if the isosurfaces are based on a segmentation (see Sect. 7.2.3).

   If silhouettes and feature lines are generated on the basis of high frequency noise and other aliasing artifacts, distracting and erroneous lines are generated. This can be avoided by interpolating additional slices with a higher order interpolation scheme, such as cubic b-splines. This strategy, however, is combined with substantial additional memory and time consumption. As an alternative, the polygonal meshes can be smoothed (recall Sect. 7.3.3).

   In Figure 17.6 and Figure 17.7, the effect of smoothing a surface on the resulting silhouettes and feature lines is shown. In both cases, the same filter was applied. However, the two parameters had to be selected differently to cope with the specifics of these structures.

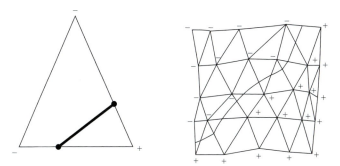

FIGURE 17.5   *Computation of a subpolygon silhouette for an isolated triangle (left) and a polygonal mesh (right). (Images courtesy* AARON HERTZMANN, *1999 ACM)*

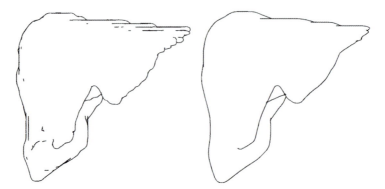

FIGURE 17.6   *Silhouette generation of the liver. Left: the isosurface representing the original segmentation result is employed. The resulting staircase artifacts are distracting and confusing since they have no anatomical basis. Right: the triangle mesh of the isosurface was smoothed with a relaxation filter. (Images courtesy* CHRISTIAN TIETJEN, *University of Magdeburg)*

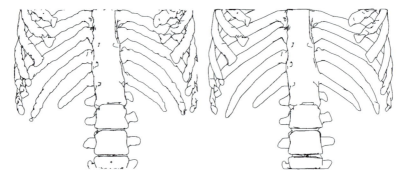

FIGURE 17.7   *Silhouette generation of skeletal structures. The unprocessed isosurface leads to noisy artifacts, which can be corrected by appropriate smoothing. (Images courtesy* CHRISTIAN TIETJEN, *University of Magdeburg)*

Data Structures for Silhouette and Feature Line Determination   To efficiently extract lines and strokes from 3D meshes, it is essential to use a data structure that provides local connectivity information. For conventional surface rendering, it is sufficient to represent the affiliation of vertices to polygons. For silhouette and feature line determination, it is essential to access adjacent polygons (polygons that have a common edge or a common vertex). This information is represented, for example, in a Winged Edge data structure [BAUMGART 1975], a direct graph that is a suitable basis for object-oriented rendering methods. As the name suggests, it is based on a global edge list and consists of locally linked edges. For every object, the data structure additionally stores a list of polygons and vertices. As an example, the Winged Edge data structure allows the selection of adjacent polygons with strong deviation in the surface normal efficiently. This data structure is typically created in a preprocessing step.

17.1.3 HATCHING SURFACE MODELS

Feature lines may effectively convey prominent features of a surface, such as ridges and valleys in the shape of the human brain. In the absence of such prominent features, they are not applicable. The surface of organs, for example, has only a very few landmarks that might be emphasized with feature lines. For such smooth objects, hatching may convey shape information. Hatching techniques support a continuous perception of a surface, encompassing rapidly changing as well as relatively constant areas.

Hatching may be used in isolation or in combination with surface rendering, particularly with strongly transparent surfaces that are often used in medical visualization to show the boundaries of an organ as well as inner structures of interest, such as vasculature or tumors, simultaneously. The drawback of this strategy is that most of the depth-cues to convey shape have a minimal effect (at best) for transparent surfaces. This is well known in psychophysics as well as in computer graphics and visualization [INTERRANTE et al. 1996].

The challenge, however, is to develop algorithms for the optimal placement and scaling of hatching lines and strokes to convey shape information best. While hatching techniques designed for artists rely on many parameters that have to be supplied by the user, in medical visualization an easy or even automatic parameterization is essential. Artists have recognized that the direction of strokes has a strong influence on our perception of surfaces. A uniform direction is not preferable, as shapes tend to be perceived as flattened. INTERRANTE et al. [1995] found that medical illustrators often use the curvature of surfaces to guide hatching: strokes are oriented along the principal curvature direction. The driving application for their work is radiation treatment planning, in which isosurfaces represent equal intensity of radiation dose [INTERRANTE et al. 1995]. For treatment planning, the radiation beams and several of the surfaces are shown as transparent isosurfaces together with the opaquely rendered tumor to be destroyed. Hatching techniques enhance the interpretation of the transparent isointensity surfaces. Figure 17.8 reveals the potential of this technique. However, if the placement of lines is not adapted to the inner object, the view on it might be compromised (see Fig. 17.8 (right)). The project on radiation treatment planning started early [LEVOY et al. 1990] and represents one of the first applications of NPR techniques in medical visualization.

17.1.4   ILLUSTRATIVE RENDERING OF MEDICAL VOLUME DATA

For medical applications, volume data such as CT and MRI are employed for the visualization. This raises the question of whether NPR visualizations might be generated directly based on volume data. Such

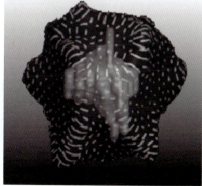

FIGURE 17.8   *Semitransparent isointensity surface for radiation treatment planning and a tumor inside. In the right image, strokes along the principal curvature are added* [INTERRANTE et al. 1996]. *(Images courtesy VICTORIA INTERRANTE, University of Minnesota)*

techniques are referred to as *Volume Illustration*, a term coined in [EBERT and RHEINGANS 2000, RHEINGANS and EBERT 2001], which describes its main goals as enhancing the expressiveness of volume rendering through emphasizing important features, similar to an illustration.

In volumetric data, material interfaces between different objects are usually specified by the gradient; a high gradient magnitude indicates such a material interface, while a small gradient magnitude indicates a more or less homogenous material. Methods for the approximation of a gradient were discussed in Section 6.3.2. If we connect the voxels with a high gradient magnitude, the resulting edges form the object boundary.

Silhouette lines are generated from these edges where, in addition to the large gradient magnitude, we also get a scalar product of view vector and the gradient direction (normal) that is close to 0 (recall Eq. 17.1). A threshold ϵ must be supplied to state precisely what is regarded "as close to zero." ϵ actually controls the thickness of the silhouette. A useful default value is 0.2 [SALAH et al. 2005c]. Another threshold for the gradient magnitude must be supplied to restrict the generation of silhouettes to regions with strong transitions that may represent edges. An example of this kind of silhouette generation is shown in Figure 17.9, in which the large gradient magnitude between air and skin is employed for silhouette generation. However, for many regions in the human body, contrasts in CT and MRI data are considerably lower than at the air-skin boundary, and correct silhouettes cannot be identified easily. In MRI data, with its inherent inhomogeneity, feature lines might pronounce irrelevant discontinuities.

Better results are achieved if segmentation results are available and can be used to restrict silhouette generation to certain objects (see Fig. 17.10). With segmentation information available, the first step of illustrative rendering is usually to identify the set of surface voxels S of a particular object O. This can be easily accomplished by a morphologic erosion with a 3×3 kernel, yielding an eroded version O_E. The surface voxels S are yielded by the difference $O - O_E$ [SALAH et al. 2005c]. If the above described scalar product of gradient magnitude at these voxels (voxel normals) and the viewing direction is smaller than the selected threshold ϵ, these surface voxels become silhouette candidates depending on their visibility. SALAH et al. [2005c] describe an approach where an oriented disc is rendered at every surface voxel that is not a silhouette candidate. If the density of these discs is high enough—which is easily the case for discs at

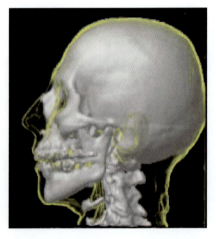

FIGURE 17.9 *Contours combined with isosurface rendering* [CSÉBFALVI et al. 2001]. *(Image courtesy* BALÁZS CSÉBFALVI, *Technical University of Budapest)*

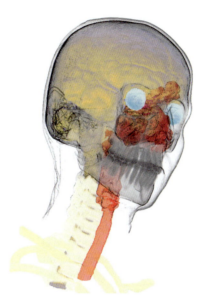

FIGURE 17.10 *Combination of rendering styles. The skin is shown as silhouette rendering, the eyes as shaded direct volume rendering, and the trachea as maximum intensity projection [HADWIGER et al. 2003b]. (Image courtesy MARKUS HADWIGER, VRVis Wien)*

voxel positions—they will occlude the silhouette candidate voxels behind them. All true silhouette surface voxels will not be occluded, since the orientation of the discs according to the voxel normal (gradient) ensures that their visible surface approximates zero towards the silhouette.

Context-Preserving Volume Rendering   An essential of the interactive use of volume-rendered images is a lack of context. It is crucial that some structures, such as those with a clear boundary, remain visible after rotations to provide the context necessary to understand the current view. The position of specular highlights is another aspect that supports the orientation of the viewer if it remains constant after rotation.

BRUCKNER *et al.* [2005] recently introduced a variant of volume-rendered images that retains the context based on a function that considers, among others, gradient magnitude and shading intensity. With this technique, opacity is reduced for regions that receive a high shading intensity (since these appear flat) and increased for regions with lower intensity, which could be better recognized. Illustrative techniques are also used for context-preserving volume rendering.

17.1.5 HATCHING VOLUME MODELS

One of the first volume illustration approaches addressed hatching of volumetric data [TREAVETT and CHEN 2000]. A slightly different approach was proposed by DONG *et al.* [2003], who used segmentation information to reliably calculate silhouettes and principal curvature directions. With volume hatching, strokes are generated that take into account the intensity values of the volume data. Also, in contrast to surface hatching, interior voxels close to the surface make a contribution to the hatching. Based on gradient estimation schemes, the local orientation of a surface in the volume data is approximated to calculate lighting information. Thus, the depth cues provided by shadings are also provided.

Hatchings based on volume information produce smoother hatching lines compared to purely surface-based methods. Dong et al. [2003] describe a method where smooth patches are fitted to the intensity values of eight adjacent voxels. In contrast to a polygonal isosurface, with its discontinuities in the surface normal, these patches provide smooth transitions of the orientation (see Fig. 17.11 for an example).

While hatching lines guided by the principal curvature direction are very general, special hatching techniques are needed for particular structures such as muscles, which are hatched by medical illustrators according to their fiber orientation. Dong et al. [2001] describe methods for approximating the muscle fiber orientation to guide hatching lines (see Fig. 17.11). The general principle here is to derive material properties to guide hatching directions.

For the application of hatching techniques in medical visualization systems, frame coherence is crucial. Frame coherence refers to a consistent display of surfaces, lines, and points in consecutive frames of an animation or interactive movement. For many illustrative techniques, it is a challenge to provide frame coherence, because random number generation is often involved in the placement and parameterization of graphics primitives. With the method described by Dong et al. [2001], this is achieved by an object-space approach (using illuminated 3D strokes as rendering primitives). The stroke generation is currently rather slow, and the techniques are not widely evaluated, but they indicate the great potential of hatching techniques for medical visualization applications.

17.1.6 ILLUSTRATIVE SHADING STYLES

The typical shading methods in standard computer graphics are based on Gouraud and Phong shading [Foley et al. 1995]. While these shading methods can be used in the context of illustrative rendering, other more illustrative shading techniques may be preferred. In this section, we will discuss two of them: half-tone shading and cool-to-warm tone shading. Note, however, that the strokes of hatching and the points of stippling already provide shading similar to half-toning.

FIGURE 17.11 *Volumetric hatching of the muscles of a human thigh guided by the muscle fiber orientation* [Dong et al. 2003]. *(Image courtesy* Feng Dong, *Brunel University)*

Half-Tone Shading

Half-toning is a technique that was originally developed for printing, where it was used to simulate brightness variations. The typical half-toning approach uses different bitmap patterns to compose the half-toned image. These bitmap patterns essentially consist of enabled (black) and disabled (white) bits to define the *half-tone patterns*.

An alternative half-toning approach varies the size of the shading primitives. APPEL [1968] used different sizes of a "+" symbol to mimic shading effects by half-toning. Today, the typically used primitive is a filled circle [STROTHOTTE and SCHLECHTWEG 2002]. A variation of this half-toning approach was recently presented by SALAH et al. [2005c], who use a 2D disc oriented in 3D space as a half-toning primitive (see Sect. 17.1.4). The actual size of the discs is computed by Equation 17.3, where L_i represents the diffuse light intensity of that disc (using Phong's illumination model) and S_{total} is a global intensity scaling parameter.

$$S_{shd} = I_{shd} \cdot \left(\frac{A_{shd} - L_i}{S_{total}} \right)^n \tag{17.3}$$

The important parameters are $A_{shd} \in [0, 2]$, which controls the influenced area of the half-toning, and I_{shd}, which determines the darkness of the half-toning (see in Figure 17.12 how these parameters influence the half-toning method). Note that half-tone shading realizes an inverted representation; an area of intensive lighting will receive little or no half-toning contributions, while a dark area will receive significantly more contributions. Hence, the normalized light intensity L_i is subtracted from the area

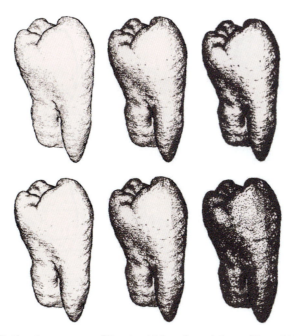

FIGURE 17.12 *Effect of half-toning parameters of Equation 17.3 on the tooth dataset [SALAH 2006]. Top row shows increasing values of I_{shd} of 1, 3, and 5. The bottom row shows increasing values of A_{shd} of 0.7, 0.9, and 1.1. (Image courtesy ZEIN SALAH, University of Tübingen)*

factor. From the numerator $A_{shd} - L_i$ only the non-negative values are considered; if they become negative (e.g., for $A_{shd} = 0, L_i > 0$), the result is clamped to zero. For a large area factor (e.g., $A_{shd} > 1$), a half-toning contribution even in bright areas is achieved.

The overall size transition, or the transition from bright to dark, is controlled by the exponent n. As SALAH et al. [2005c] showed, a value of $n = 1$ generates a good half-toning effect for objects with only small curvature changes.

Cool-to-Warm Tone Shading

One approach to illustrative shading aims at the use of colors to emphasize the structure of objects. However, varying different colors (hues) over an object might lead to undesired visual effects, since varying hue is perceptually not isometric, as we discussed in Section 2.4.2. Hence, a more limited color variation scheme was proposed by GOOCH et al. [1998]: *cool-to-warm tone shading*.

Alternative color variation schemes (*color scales*) are brightness variations and variations between two colors. Both methods are more perceptually uniform than hue variations, hence they are more suitable for the interpretation of that variation. In the context of tone shading, we use the object's color and combine that color either with white [LUM and MA 2001] or with black to generate a different tone of the color. Depending on the chosen object color and the chosen combination (white or black), this scale generates large (dark color with white, bright color with black) or little (dark color with black, bright color with white) brightness variations [STONE 2003]. In Figure 17.13, we see examples of these tone scales. In Figure 17.13 (top/middle), we see a little brightness variation where we combine red with black, while

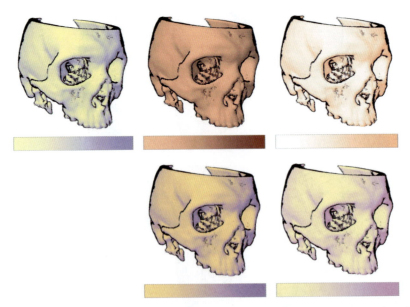

FIGURE 17.13 Cool-to-warm tone shading of skull model [SALAH 2006]. *The respective color scales are shown below the shaded images. Top row: cool-to-warm shading (left), tone shading with object color and black (black tone, middle), tone shading with object color and white (white tone, right). Bottom row: combined shading with black tone (middle) and white tone (right). (Images courtesy ZEIN SALAH, University of Tübingen)*

we see a large brightness variation in Figure 17.13 (top/right), where we combine red with white. This brightness variation is also called a *luminance shift* [GOOCH *et al.* 1998].

The second aspect of combining two colors is represented in a temperature scale, which combines a color perceived as cool (e.g., blue, violet, green) with a color perceived as warm (e.g., yellow, orange, red). Figure 17.13 (top/left) shows an example that combines blue as cool color with yellow as warm color. This color variation is also called a *hue shift* [GOOCH *et al.* 1998]. If we combine both scales—the tone scales and the temperature scales—with a bilinear interpolation, we get a color scale that nicely emphasizes silhouettes and contours through the tone scale and surface orientation through the temperature scale (see Fig. 17.13 bottom).

The combined color scale is indexed by the normalized diffuse light component of the used Phong lighting model. While the typically used scales are continuous (within the bounds of the accuracy of the number representation), a discrete representation can be chosen by indexing the scale through a discrete and potentially non-uniform lookup table to generate a cartoonish shading style [LANDER 2000a] (see Fig. 17.14).

17.1.7 STYLE SPECIFICATION FOR ILLUSTRATIVE VOLUME RENDERING

The incorporation of enhancing effects and advanced shading techniques increases the expressiveness of volume rendering. On the other hand, the optimal use of these techniques requires the adjustment of many parameters, which is tedious and requires considerable experience. This situation is very similar to transfer function design, in which the expressiveness could be strongly enhanced with multidimensional transfer functions (recall Sect. 11.2). Similar to transfer function design, the user interface is crucial for illustrative volume rendering. Although fine-grained control on the parameters is essential, more high-level interactions that summarize individual parameters and intent-based interactions that are more closely related to the users' goals are required.

SVAKHINE *et al.* [2005] suggest an architecture of an interactive volume illustration system with *low-level, mid-level,* and *high-level interfaces* designed for different categories of users. While low-level interaction is targeted at experienced illustrators and system builders, mid-level interaction is designed with experienced end users in mind. At the highest level, interaction techniques are provided for average end users, such as surgeons or medical students. At the highest level, rendering parameters that define an illustrative technique are summarized. An essential but simple feature at the highest level is the selection of a focal region. Based on this selection, different emphasis techniques might be selected (see Fig. 17.15).

FIGURE 17.14 *Discrete cool-to-warm shading with three steps (left), four steps (middle), and eight steps (right).* (*Image courtesy* ZEIN SALAH, *University of Tübingen*)

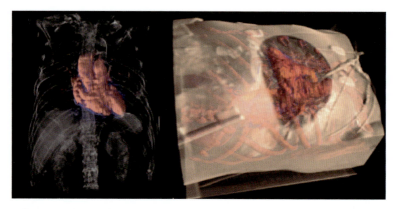

FIGURE 17.15 *Illustrative volume renderings created with the three-level interface described in [SVAKHINE et al. 2005]. Left: the anterior view of the heart; right: a surgical view of the heart. (Images courtesy NICHOLAI SVAKHINE, Purdue University)*

17.2 COMBINING LINE, SURFACE, AND VOLUME VISUALIZATION

The combination of different rendering styles is a challenging problem, as discussed for surface and volume rendering in Section 9.7. Hybrid surface and volume renderings can be generated either by converting surface data to volume data (voxelization) and subsequently creating a combined volume rendering, or by applying a two-pass rendering, in which surfaces and volume data are rendered independently and combined in a final step, considering depth values of surface and volume data. Similarly, there are two different strategies for integrating line rendering into surface and volume rendering:

1   Integrate lines and surfaces in the volume rendering process
2   Apply different rendering passes to render lines, surfaces, and volume data

The first strategy is computationally faster and easier to implement. An example for this approach is given in [VIOLA et al. 2004b].

17.2.1 HYBRID RENDERING WITH OBJECT-BASED METHODS

The second strategy of combining different rendering passes leads to an object-space method where line strips are considered as individual graphics primitives that might be parameterized in a flexible way. This strategy was suggested by NAGY et al. [2002] and realized in [TIETJEN et al. 2005], in which silhouettes line, surface, and volume rendering are integrated in an extended OpenInventor scenegraph.[3] This object-space approach, however, poses some technical problems to achieving a correct rendering with respect to the depth-order and the visibility of lines, surfaces, and volume data. We address these difficulties by separating the visibility computation based on the depth-buffer from the correct rendering order. Note that employing transparency increases the complexity of the visibility and depth order computation.

To achieve the proper ordering of the three rendering elements (lines, surfaces, volume data), we first need to consider their influence on the depth-buffer. *Volume data* rendered with Direct Volume Rendering methods (DVR) represent the whole space of the dataset. Hence, they will fill the whole depth-buffer with their frontmost elements, blocking all other elements. Therefore, volume data must be rendered

---

3   OpenInventor is a 3D toolkit designed for interactive 3D applications. It is built on top of OpenGL and described in [WERNECKE 1994].

last. *Surfaces* are rendered with the regular depth-buffering, so no special care has to be taken except that they must be rendered before the data rendered through DVR. Finally, our *stylized line elements* will share similar depth-values as the surface elements, which essentially means that they must be rendered without depth-buffering against the surface elements. Furthermore, we need to provide some kind of hidden-line-removal that is not achieved through the depth-buffer of line elements. Consequently, we separate their visibility computation from the rendering process by first filling the depth-buffer with the depth information of the objects and then computing the visibility based on that information [ISENBERG et al. 2002]. One advantage of this approach of separating visibility computation from rendering is that stylized line objects behind transparent surfaces can now be treated in the same framework without influencing the actual rendering—particularly the rendering order.

Specifically, we combine the information in the following order; for the first stage of visibility computation, we extract all necessary geometry information for the surfaces and the stylized lines (and silhouettes, Fig. 17.16a) from the data and render it into the depth-buffer (see Fig. 17.16b). We use that information to determine the visibility of the line elements (see Fig. 17.16c) and clear the framebuffer (particularly the depth-buffer afterwards). In the second stage, we render our scene elements into the framebuffer. First, the surface elements are rendered into the cleared framebuffer (see Fig. 17.16d) and the stylized line elements are added (see Fig. 17.16e). Finally, the remaining volume data is directly rendered into the framebuffer (see Fig. 17.16f).

17.2.2 EMPHASIS WITH HYBRID VISUALIZATIONS

Different rendering styles will be used to depict different structures according to their relevance for the visualization. With respect to relevance in the following we will refer to four types of structures or objects:

- *Focus Objects* (FO): objects in the center of interest, emphasized in a particular way.
- *Near Focus Objects* (NFO): important objects for understanding functional interrelation or spatial location. Their visualization depends on the particular problem and supports the FO.
- *Context Objects* (CO): all other objects.
- *Container Objects* (CAO): one object that contains all other objects.

The combination of different rendering styles provides facilities to adapt a visualization to the importance of anatomical and pathologic structures. NPR might be used to depict the anatomical context, either in single rendering mode or in combination with strongly transparent surface rendering. As an alternative, volume rendering might be employed for the anatomical context. Surface rendering and full opaqueness might be used for FOs. In Figures 17.17 and 17.18, we show some combinations of rendering styles designed for a medical education system. Focus objects are the liver and the intrahepatic vascular structures; the skeleton serves as anatomical context.

A relevant yet difficult question concerns the appropriateness of the images in Figures 17.17 and 17.18. Many options have been discussed with surgeons, and the four images displayed in Figures 17.17 and 17.18 have been regarded as suitable. But is there any best image? An encompassing user study might give some hints. Different viewers will probably differ strongly in their choice. As a consequence, it should be easy to generate such images, and it should be easy to save parameters as individually preferred styles to be reused for other images.

Another example of silhouette and surface rendering is shown in Figure 17.19. This image was generated for surgical planning in the neck region. This kind of image is considered useful and appropriate by medical experts.

Silhouettes may also be used to discriminate two classes of objects: those that exhibit a certain feature are rendered with silhouettes enabled, whereas the remaining objects are drawn without silhouettes.

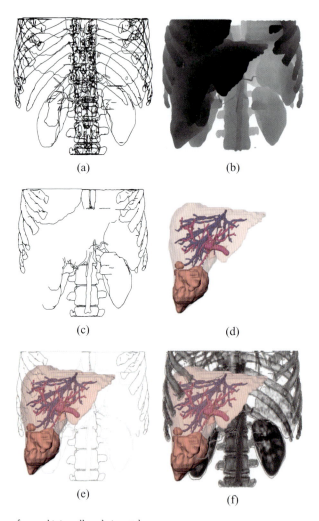

FIGURE 17.16   *Sequence for combining all rendering styles.*

A reasonable use of this strategy is to enable silhouettes for objects that are more "interesting," because silhouettes direct the user's attention. Alternatively, signaling colors such as red can be used to direct the user's focus to the focus object. This is shown in Figure 17.20, where the (red) colon is the focus object in the left image, and the paranasal sinus is the focus object in the right image.

Line stylization may be used to control whether objects are conceived as FO or CO. An interesting type of stylization refers to the visibility of lines. Hidden lines may be depicted in a different manner from visible lines to better convey the spatial relationships (see Fig. 17.21). This is only feasible with the object-space approach to the visualization of lines.

Default Values   Hybrid visualizations consisting of lines, surfaces, and volume data provide rich possibilities for fine-tuning visualizations of medical volume data. However, the huge space of possible renderings is due to many parameters. To make hybrid visualizations feasible, it is essential to carefully select appropriate default values for the visualization of categories of anatomical and pathologic structures, such as organs,

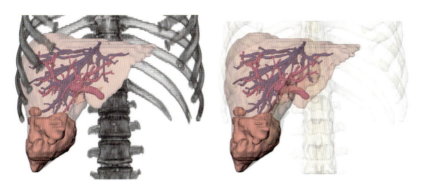

FIGURE 17.17   Important structures as surface rendering. Bone context shown as opaque direct volume rendering (left) and as highly transparent surfaces (right). (Images courtesy CHRISTIAN TIETJEN, University of Magdeburg)

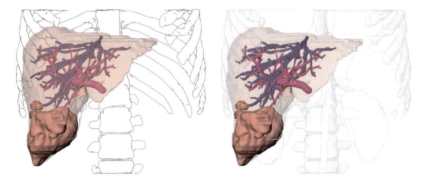

FIGURE 17.18   Important structures as surface rendering with silhouettes. Context displayed exclusively with silhouettes (left) and as highly transparent surfaces combined with silhouette rendering (right). (Images courtesy CHRISTIAN TIETJEN, University of Magdeburg)

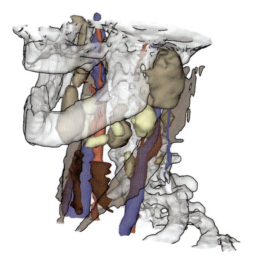

FIGURE 17.19   Illustrative rendering for neck dissection planning. Silhouettes are generated for the bones, which serve as anatomic context. (Image courtesy CHRISTIAN TIETJEN, University of Magdeburg)

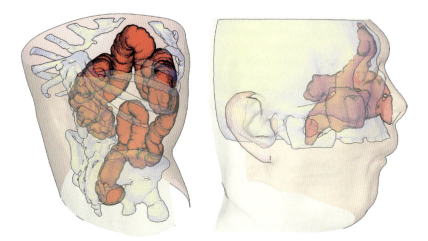

FIGURE 17.20 *Mixed rendering styles for multiple objects. Left: Abdominal dataset from CT with colon (FO with red color, half-tone shading, point-based rendering with silhouette), skeleton (NFO, semi-transparent cool-to-warm shading, mesh, silhouette), and skin (CAO, highly transparent Gouraud shading). Right: Head dataset from CT with paranasal sinus (FO with red color, half-tone shading, point-based rendering with silhouette), skull (NFO, with semi-transparent cool-to-warm shading, rendered mesh with silhouette), and skin (CAO, highly transparent Gouraud shaded mesh). (Images courtesy* ZEIN SALAH, *University of Tübingen)*

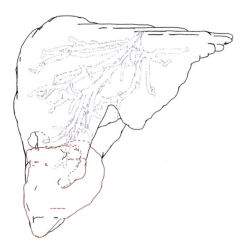

FIGURE 17.21 *Hidden feature lines are rendered as dashed lines. With this technique, additional information concerning a tumor and the intrahepatic vasculature are included in a visualization. (Image courtesy* ANGELA BRENNECKE, *University of Magdeburg)*

lesions, or vascular structures. Users should be able to modify these values, but in general the interaction effort should be reduced.

For most applications, the following guidelines for default settings are useful [SALAH et al. 2005a]: the focus object (FO) should be rendered with a strong emphasis by applying silhouettes and a fully opaque rendering. Near focus objects (NFO) should have a reduced opacity (compared to FOs), but may still employ a silhouette. Container objects may have a very low opacity and no silhouettes. Context objects (CO) may have an opacity that varies between those of the NFO and the CAO and may have no silhouette or only a silhouette. Examples for using these guidelines can be found in Figure 17.20.

17.3   VISIBILITY ANALYSIS

A visibility analysis of the CSO (currently selected object) should compute which portion of the CSO is visible and also give an estimate of the size of the visible portion. These values may be used to decide whether local techniques are sufficient.

Visibility analysis is a wide area of research in which methods can be classified either as image-based methods that are computed on-the-fly, or as from region methods that are typically precomputed. In most cases, however, some kind of hierarchical data structure is used to accelerate visibility queries (see Sect. 7.2.5). Furthermore, visibility algorithms can be classified into conservative approaches (which ensures that all visible objects are determined as not occluded) or non-conservative or approximating approaches [BARTZ et al. 1999a]. The latter approaches trade accuracy for performance and take small visibility errors into account. In the context of medical visualization applications, we restrict ourselves to static scenes, although some medical visualization problems involve dynamic data (recall Chap. 10). For more details on the various visibility and occlusion algorithms, please refer to the survey paper of COHEN-OR et al. [2003].

One purpose of the visibility analysis is to determine the visibility of specific objects or regions. One particularly interesting question is whether the view on the CSO is obstructed by any object. If this is the case, this obstructing object, which is called the *occluder*, must be removed or at least modified so that the viewer can see through it. Occluded objects in that context are called *occludees*.

As mentioned above, the various visibility algorithms trade accuracy for time until the visibility query is answered. Therefore, the choice of an algorithm depends on the available time. In applications that aim at interactive (>10 frames per second (fps)) or even real-time (>20 fps) rendering performance, the allotted time for such a query is obviously much smaller than in non-interactive applications [BARTZ et al. 1999a, BARTZ and SKALEJ 1999]. Therefore, the queries do not test the full object geometry, which might consist of many thousands of polygons and vertices, but only a rough approximation of it. Typically, axis-aligned bounding boxes (AABBs) are used as such an approximation, which is a minimum/maximum rectangle of the object aligned with the coordinate system. For a detailed discussion on AABBs and other bounding volumes, please refer to Section 7.2.5. Section 7.3.1 provides a detailed discussion of image-space on-the-fly occlusion culling, which can be used for the visibility analysis.

If high accuracy of the visibility query is important (e.g., to determine the visibility status of the FO or CSO), the full geometry of that object can be tested against the already fully rendered scene (without the FO/CSO).

Discussion

We did not consider the current transparency of objects for their impact as occluders. This, however, is an important consideration, as VIOLA et al. [2004b] showed by modeling the occluder's transparency. Furthermore, the traversal orders of correctly dealing with transparency (back-to-front) and optimally handling occlusion (front-to-back) pose several challenges.

For medical visualization, a combination of precomputed visibility and on-the-fly estimation can be very effective, as BARTZ and SKALEJ [1999] showed for virtual endoscopy, which benefits from interior viewpoints. Often, large objects (container objects like skin or the skull) limit the visibility of other objects. These objects are thus occluders for all internal objects, independent of the viewing direction, and might be computed in a preprocess.

17.4   LOCAL EMPHASIS TECHNIQUES

Local emphasis techniques change only the appearance of the CSO. With local emphasis techniques, visible objects might be pronounced without any side effect on other objects. For objects that are hidden or that appear as tiny spots in the image, local emphasis techniques are insufficient. In Section 17.5, we discuss techniques appropriate in these cases.

Local changes might influence an object in several ways. The object color might be adapted; e.g. a texture might be applied. NPR techniques such as feature lines, silhouettes, and hatching lines might be invoked to emphasize an object. Also, additional symbols might be included to emphasize the CSO. Arrows might point towards the CSO, or a cross-hair cursor might indicate the position of the object center. The bounding box might be included to reveal the extent of the CSO. There are many other techniques applicable in principle. In the following sections, we discuss some of them.

17.4.1 EMPHASIS USING COLOR

The use of a color for emphasis is probably the most obvious and simple emphasis technique. It might be effective if the color guides the user's attention. Saturated colors, in particular reddish colors, serve well for this purpose. As a local technique, only the CSO's color is influenced. Therefore, adjacent objects might have similar colors, resulting in low contrasts that would compromise the emphasis of the CSO. As a solution, a single color—clearly distinctive from all other colors—may be "reserved" for emphasizing objects.

The drawback of this approach is that in an emphasized state, the object color might strongly differ from its color in a non-emphasized state. Whatever the object's color was before, in an emphasized state it is rendered in the global highlight color. While this color might be appropriate for muscles and vascular structures it might look very unnatural for tumors, bones, or organs. This leads to the idea of taking the object's original color into account for highlighting purposes. If the object's color is represented in HSV-color mode (hue, saturation, value), the color's hue- and value-component remain unchanged, and the saturation is increased to emphasize the CSO. In general, the modification of the object color is more appropriate than the use of a global highlight color; however, it assumes that all strongly saturated colors are avoided for rendering objects in their normal state.

17.4.2 FOCUS AND CONTEXT VIEWS

In the exploration of traditional visualizations, such as maps or radiologic films, lenses are employed to enlarge interesting regions for better analysis. In a similar way, detailed views with an enlarged display of a particular object or region may complement a context view. In city maps, detail views are often used to show the city center enlarged and with additional information.

Detail views, also called insets, represent a simple, general, and effective facility for emphasis. The detailed view might be used to show the CSO in isolation, so that its shape can be assessed. It can also be used for an enlarged volume rendering of a particular region [ZHOU et al. 2004]. The user should have full control over the content of the detail view, either by selecting an object or by moving a box through the context view. In the case of volume rendering, it is useful to support a different transfer function for the detail view (recall the discussion of local transfer functions in Sect. 11.5). The detail view might show finer inner structures, compared to the same region in the context view (see Fig. 17.22 and

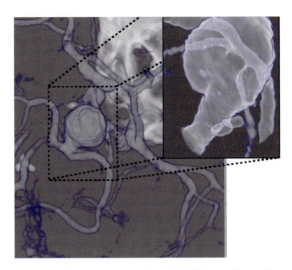

FIGURE 17.22 *Detail and context views for the exploration of cerebral MRI data. The detail view shows a region enlarged where an aneurysm is supposed. With a different transfer function, the structure might be better explored. The position of the detail view is indicated with a rectangle in the context view. (Image courtesy* PETER HASTREITER, *University Erlangen-Nürnberg)*

[HASTREITER et al. 1998]). Synchronization facilities between both views should be provided. It is conceivable to regard both views as equal, with the effect that manipulations (such as a rotation) carried out in the detail view are also applied in the context view.

A problem with the use of detail and context views is the mental integration of both views. To support this mental process, the context view should indicate which part or region is shown in the detail view. Also, the user should be able to place the detail view. If a few objects are selected, the user might have the choice to open and close detail views. The exploration of several metastasis or aneurysms are examples where multiple detail views might be essential.

An alternative to the use of two separate views would be to integrate them in one view with smooth changes of the scale between detail and context view. These are called *fisheye views* [FURNAS 1986, DILL et al. 1994]. There are successful applications of this strategy in 2D graph and network visualization where abstract shapes are involved. However, in clinical applications, non-linear scales are in general not appropriate.

17.4.3 EMPHASIS WITH ARROWS

Arrows are commonly used in traditional illustrations to emphasize objects. The use of arrows to emphasize arbitrary objects in 3D illustrations is challenging. As an example, a larger number of arrows is necessary to emphasize the shape of long and branching structures. Hence, we restrict the following discussion to compact objects with a rather simple shape, where it is sufficient to employ one arrow. Emphasis with arrows also requires that the CSO is visible. Finally, the arrow itself should be visible.

Several parameters of an arrow have to be determined:

- The start- and endpoint, or the startpoint, the direction, and the length
- The linewidth
- The line color

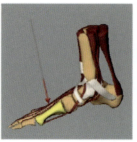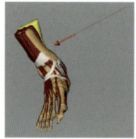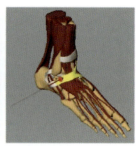

FIGURE 17.23 *Use of an arrow to support emphasis with color. (Images courtesy* CHRISTINA DÖRGE, *University of Bremen)*

Concerning the startpoint, there are several reasonable strategies: the arrow may start in a corner (or near the corner) of the viewer, or it may be chosen so that a vertical or horizontal line arises starting at or near the border of the image. It is essential that the arrow starts outside the rendered objects.

To define a horizontal or vertical line, the endpoint must be defined first. The endpoint might be a vertex of the CSO—for example, the vertex closest to the center of gravity (COG) or closest to the center of a bounding box face. As an alternative to specifying the endpoint explicitly, the startpoint and the direction might be specified, with a criterion that terminates the arrow in the given direction. The direction might be the vector between the startpoint and the COG of the CSO. The line might be terminated at the first intersection with the CSO or at the first intersection with the CSO's bounding box. The linewidth must be chosen in a way that the resulting size of the arrow is sufficient. In Figure 17.23, examples of emphasis with arrows are shown.

When an arrow is partially occluded, modifications of other objects might be accomplished to ensure the arrow's visibility. In this case, the emphasis with arrows is no longer a local technique, because the appearance of other objects or regions is affected. As an alternative, the overlay buffer of the graphics hardware might be employed to draw arrows on top of the rendered image.

The assignment of an appropriate color is difficult, because the arrow has to be visible on top of varying background colors (recall a similar discussion concerning measurement facilities, Sect. 13.1). As a general strategy, a dark arrow surrounded by a light outline (or vice versa) always provides a good contrast.

17.4.4 EMPHASIS WITH SHADOW VOLUMES

Shadows may be used to highlight objects. Because the relation between the CSO in the rendered image and its shadow projection is important, a shadow volume for the selected object is useful. Shadow volumes are semi-infinite regions identified by extruding silhouette edges (with respect to the light source).[4] To emphasize an object with shadow volumes, the shadow projection should be adapted for this object, for example, by using a different color (see Fig. 17.24). Among the discussed local emphasis techniques, this is the first one that makes the CSO—at least in the shadow projection—visible. Similar to the emphasis by means of additional symbols, the shadow volume might compromise the visibility of some objects—in a very narrow sense, therefore, it is not a local technique.

---

4   Shadow volumes were introduced in [CROW 1977]. BRABEC [2003] and BRABEC and SEIDEL [2003] surveyed shadow volume generation algorithms and described an up-to-date hardware-accelerated algorithm.

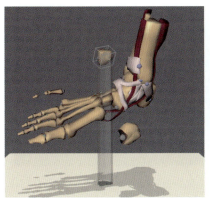
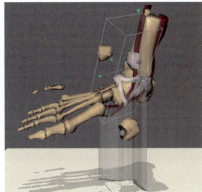

FIGURE 17.24 *Shadow volumes (65% transparent) combine the selected object and its shadow projection. The shadow color is adapted for the selected object to delineate it. (Images courtesy* FELIX RITTER, *MeVis Bremen)*

17.5   REGIONAL AND GLOBAL EMPHASIS TECHNIQUES

The discussion of emphasis techniques so far has focused on local techniques. With these techniques, the CSO is emphasized with an appropriate color, with additional lines superimposed, or by placing symbols that direct the viewer to the CSO. Local techniques might also be successful if parts of the CSO are hidden. If, however, larger portions (or the CSO as a whole) are hidden, local techniques are insufficient. In this section, we discuss cutaway and ghost views that ensure the visibility of the CSO. We also discuss regional techniques for color selection; in particular, we consider contrasts between the CSO and adjoined objects.

17.5.1 CUTAWAY AND GHOST VIEWS

There are several possibilities for employing the visibility analysis results. If the CSO is sufficiently visible, a local technique should be used. If the CSO is heavily occluded, objects in front of the CSO might be rendered transparently, or a combination of semitransparent rendering and silhouette rendering might be employed. Instead of objects, occluding regions may be removed. Such visualizations are called cutaway illustrations (recall Fig. 17.3). A slightly different illustration technique is referred to as *ghost view*. In these views, a region is rendered semitransparently. Compared to ghost views, cutaway views lead to a sharp contrast between foreground and background objects. Thus, ambiguities with respect to spatial ordering are avoided [DIEPSTRATEN et al. 2003]. Cutaway views were introduced by FEINER and SELIGMANN [1992] in computer-based illustration systems with applications in maintenance.

To indicate that an illustration technique is applied, the shape of the cut regions should differ strongly from the shape of anatomical or pathologic structures. While technical illustrators often create zigzag-shaped cutaway views (these differ from shapes in technical domains), regular shapes, such as prisms or cylinders, are useful for medical visualization. Cutaway views may be generated in the context of volume rendering as well as in the context of surface rendering. Cutaways in volume rendering require voxelizing the clip geometry. Based on a voxel representation, volume rendering is modified so that voxels in the clip region are discarded (recall Sect. 12.4).

Figure 17.25 shows a ghost view based on a cylindrical cutaway in a volume visualization that emphasizes enlarged lymph nodes relevant for neck dissection planning. The circular cross section is parallel to the view plane and located around the tumor. The cylinder height is chosen such that the lymph nodes

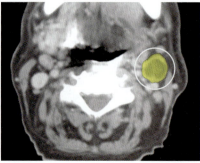

FIGURE 17.25 *Ghost view of enlarged lymph nodes for neck dissection planning. The ghost view is applied simultaneously to the 2D and 3D visualization [KRÜGER et al. 2005]. (Image courtesy ARNO KRÜGER, University of Magdeburg)*

become completely visible. Together, the circular clip region is scaled so that the tumor itself, as well as an appropriately sized margin in x-, y-, and z-direction, is cut out. The borderline of the cut is depicted to be clearly recognizable. For surgical users, it is useful to relate the ghost view to the 2D slices of the original data (see Fig. 17.25 (right)).

Cutaway views of small pathologic lesions may be combined with an interaction to systematically explore them. With a special key—for example, the tab key—the user may step through emphasized visualizations of these objects. Additional information such as size and volume might be included for the currently selected object.

Realization of Cutaway and Ghost Views   In the context of medical visualization, we often experience large models. Hence, an efficient approach is necessary to compute the cutaway region and to adapt it immediately to a changing viewing direction. A useful intermediate result is the convex hull ch of an object o. The convex hull of a 3D pointset P is the smallest convex polygon that contains all points of P. If the enclosing cut-region has a convex shape (e.g., a cylinder), the enclosing cut-region of the $ch(o)$ is the same as the cut-region of o itself. The convex hull $ch(o)$ has considerably less vertices than o and may be further geometrically simplified, as the accuracy requirements are not distinctive. Note, however, that the complexity of the computation of a convex hull is already $O(|P| \cdot log|P|)$ and may require substantial computation time itself.

The convex hull is projected into the viewing plane, and the position and size of the cut shape in the viewing plane are determined in a second step. In the case of cylindrical cut-regions, an algorithm that determines minimally enclosing circles of a pointset is necessary. After a rotation, only the second step has to be carried out.

Convex hull determination is one of the most essential problems studied in computational geometry. BERG et al. [2000], for example, provide a chapter on convex hull algorithms. Minimally enclosing circle determination (or, more generally minimally enclosing discs) are also discussed in computational geometry books [SCHNEIDER and EBERLY 2002, BOISSONNAT et al. 1998]. The latter problem can be solved in $O(n)$ time, which means that the computational effort only linearly increases with the number of points involved.

Importance-Driven Volume Rendering   Recently, cutaway views have been generalized to importance-driven volume rendering [VIOLA et al. 2004b]. Here, less important parts of the data are suppressed, for example, by employing transparency. The general concept here is to transform *importance* to *visibility*.

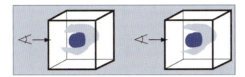

FIGURE 17.26   *Maximum importance projection to expose the dark inner object. Left: a cylindrical countersink. Right: an enlarged conical countersink [VIOLA et al. 2004b].* (Image courtesy IVAN VIOLA, Vienna University of Technology)

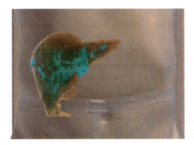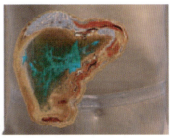

FIGURE 17.27   *Importance-driven volume rendering is employed to highlight the liver and intrahepatic structures. The conical shape of the countersink (right) renders the spatial relations more clearly [VIOLA et al. 2004b].* (Image courtesy IVAN VIOLA, Vienna University of Technology)

Importance-driven rendering is based on a visibility priority assigned to each object. It is thus more general than an emphasis technique for the CSO only. Similar to cutaways, importance-driven rendering is most suitable to focus on smaller objects (see Fig. 17.27). If objects with high priorities occlude each other, the object with maximum priority is drawn (maximum importance projection). The straight-forward application of this concept leads to a cylinder-shaped countersink for an important object. This approach suffers from similar problems as the maximum intensity projection (recall Sect. 8.3.1) where the depth relations are difficult to recognize. As a refined version, a conical shape of the countersink is employed. Both variants are compared in the sketch in Figure 17.26 and in the screenshots in Figure 17.27. While the emphasis of small compact objects is certainly the major application for cutaway views, other objects might be emphasized as well. As an example, the course of elongated or branching structures might be shown clearly with cutaway views (see Fig. 17.28). A considerable speed-up of importance-driven rendering was achieved recently [ROPINSKI et al. 2005].

17.5.2   DEFINING CONTRASTS FOR EMPHASIS

In Section 17.4.1, we discussed the modification of the CSO's color and stated that no contrast can be achieved this way. As a regional or global emphasis technique, the colors of other objects might be modified as well to ensure a certain contrast between the CSO and adjacent objects. ITTEN [1961] gives a good survey on different kinds of contrast. For emphasis, two of them seem very suitable:

- Saturation contrast, where the CSO is strongly saturated while the saturation of adjacent objects is reduced.
- Darkness contrast, where the CSO's brightness is increased and the brightness of adjacent objects is reduced.

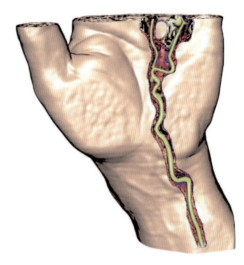

FIGURE 17.28   *A cutaway view ensures the visibility of vascular structures. (Image courtesy* STEFAN BRUCKNER, *Vienna University of Technology)*

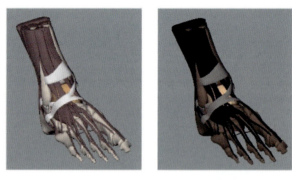

FIGURE 17.29   *Selected objects are highlighted by contrast. Left: saturation contrast (the CSO strongly saturated). Right: lightness contrast (the CSO appears floodlit with a spotlight). (Images courtesy* CHRISTINA DÖRGE, *University of Bremen)*

Figure 17.29 illustrates these two kinds of contrast used to emphasize the CSO [DÖRGE 2002]. While in the images above all objects were modified to achieve a contrast to the CSO, regional techniques are also possible. Taking the visibility analysis into account (the list of objects that partially occlude or are adjoined to the CSO), the change of colors might be restricted to adjacent objects.

17.6   DYNAMIC EMPHASIS TECHNIQUES

Time as presentation variable is very useful for emphasis techniques. If the visualization changes considerably for the emphasis of an object, it is often difficult to understand the changes. It requires less cognitive effort if the changes are continuously animated and the viewer observes how the previous visualization is transformed. Changes of transparency or object colors might be interpolated. Cutaway regions and arrows might be faded in.

An alternative dynamic change for emphasis purposes is to employ dynamics as a means of expression, instead of using it purely as an aid for interpretation. The most obvious type is blinking. Dynamics is very well suited to guide the user's attention. However, it is obtrusive and should therefore be used with care.

17.7   SYNCHRONIZED EMPHASIS

It has been discussed several times in this book that the interpretation and analysis of medical volume data requires 2D cross-section views as well as 3D visualizations. Measurements and virtual resections are examples of frequent tasks in which synchronized 2D and 3D views are employed (recall Chap. 12 and 13). Two-dimensional and 3D views, as well as the synchronization between them, are also essential for the emphasis of objects. If an object is selected in a 3D visualization, the 2D view should be adapted to make the selected object visible and recognizable. And vice versa, an object selected in a 2D visualization or by its name on a list should be emphasized in a 3D visualization. The use of colors and silhouettes should be synchronized in 2D and 3D visualizations. However, this approach is insufficient if the CSO is not visible in the other view.

In the following, we discuss methods for adapting the 2D view to make the CSO visible. If an object is selected that is not included in the current 2D view, different slice(s) must be selected. This can be achieved by choosing one slice—representative for the CSO—or by splitting the 2D view into several subviews to accommodate all slices to which the CSO belongs. As with every emphasis technique, the splitting of the 2D view is only applicable under certain circumstances—for example, if the CSO is small (a few slices).

The realization of this strategy raises a number of questions:

- What is a good slice to display the CSO in a 2D visualization?
- What is the best way to emphasize the CSO in that slice?
- What is the best way to indicate the location of the particular slice with respect to other slices that include the selected object? Or, in other words, how should we convey the range of slices to which the CSO belongs?

Each of these questions is difficult to answer, and good strategies strongly depend on the size and shape of selected objects. In general, textbooks on cross-sectional anatomy are inspiring to look for expressive slice-based illustrations. The following discussion is based on [PREIM et al. 2005].

17.7.1 SLICE SELECTION

The slice selection can be accomplished by calculating the center of the object's bounding box (BB).[5] The slice that contains this point is selected. There are some arguments against this strategy. First, the BB center might not be a representative point if, for example, the CSO has an elongated long bulge in a certain direction. Second, the BB center does not necessarily belong to the CSO. This situation is frequent in cases with branching or concave objects, such as vascular trees. Concerning the first problem, the center of gravity (COG) is a better candidate to guide the slice selection. The computational effort is similar to

---

5   In the following, we simply use the term *bounding box*. For a discussion of the different kinds of bounding volumes used as BB, please refer to Section 7.2.5.

the BB computation. However, the COG too may be outside the selected object. As a suggestion, a vertex may be searched with minimal distance to the COG, and the slice containing this vertex is included.

17.7.2 EMPHASIS IN 2D SLICES

A wide range of opportunities exists to emphasize an object in a 2D slice view. Our choice should consider that similar emphasis techniques should be applicable in both the 2D and 3D view. The following list presents just some examples:

- Draw a crosshair cursor through a representative point (COG, BB center) of the object.
- Draw the outline of the object (the intersection of the silhouette with a slice).
- Draw a halo—an enlarged silhouette.
- Draw a rectangle indicating the object's bounding box.
- Use a special texture to emphasize an object.
- Use a special highlight color to depict the object's silhouette.
- Fill the object with a special highlight color.

Any of these techniques might be combined. While the first two techniques support the understanding of the CSO's size and position, the last two techniques convey the shape of the CSO. Since correlation with the underlying data is essential, the lines (techniques 1–3) should be thin and filling (technique 4) and should be used as a semitransparent overlay, thus blending the fill color with the original data. Each of these techniques can be applied or easily extended to a 3D emphasis technique. Figure 17.30 presents some emphasis techniques applied to 2D slice views.

17.7.3 RANGE VISUALIZATION

The selected object belongs to a certain range of slices. For simplicity, we assume that the CSO is included in sequential slices only (which is often the case, but exceptions may occur). Assume that our object starts at slice s_1, proceeds to slice s_2 with some intermediate slice $s_{selected}$ ($s_1 <= s_{selected} <= s_2$) that is currently displayed. The 2D view should indicate the location of $s_{selected}$ with respect to s_1 and s_2.

One technique for indicating the position of $s_{selected}$ and the range of slices is to enhance the 2D viewer with a vertical bar that contains a rectangle representing the range of slices (s_1; s_2) and a horizontal line indicating the current slice. A drawback of this technique is that the vertical bar might be far away from

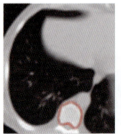 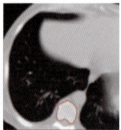 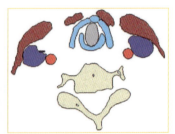

FIGURE 17.30 *Emphasis in slice views. A halo and a silhouette are added to emphasize the spine (left and middle image). In the right image, colors, silhouettes, and textures for skeletal structures are used to show structures in the neck region* [TIETJEN et al. 2006]. *(Images courtesy CHRISTIAN TIETJEN, University of Magdeburg)*

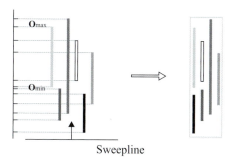

Sweepline

FIGURE 17.31 *Generation of an overview for the ranges of segmented objects. Each bar represents the interval of slices to which one segmented object belongs. By analyzing the slice numbers of each object, the necessary horizonal space may be reduced [TIETJEN et al. 2006]. (Image courtesy CHRISTIAN TIETJEN, University of Magdeburg)*

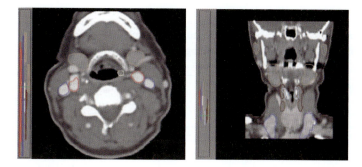

FIGURE 17.32 *Emphasis in 2D slices. A vertical bar attached to the 2D viewer indicates the position of segmented objects. Left: an axial slice view; right: a coronal slice view of CT neck data [TIETJEN et al. 2006]. (Images courtesy CHRISTIAN TIETJEN, University of Magdeburg)*

the CSO, forcing the user to focus on another area on the screen. This technique may be enhanced to give a better overview of the data by presenting the range of all segmented objects instead of just the selected one. To reduce the space for such a visualization, two objects that do not overlap in their slice numbers may share a vertical line (see Fig. 17.31). This principle is used to generate the images in Figure 17.32.

As an alternative, the range visualization might be included close to the CSO, immediately in the display of the radiological data. This could be accomplished by using a rectangle around the respective object with a modified vertical line. This line should be subdivided so that it reflects the distance from $s_{selected}$ to s_1. In Figure 17.33 (right), a thick line is drawn from the rectangle's left border representing $dist(s_{selected}, s_1)$ and a thin line representing $dist(s_{selected}, s_2)$. This technique could be easily extended to layouts with three orthogonal views and one 3D view—the typical layout for computer-assisted surgery.

17.8 CLASSIFICATION OF EMPHASIS TECHNIQUES

After discussing many individual emphasis techniques, we try to provide a structured view of these techniques. Table 17.1 summarizes the most important emphasis techniques for medical visualization.

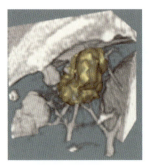 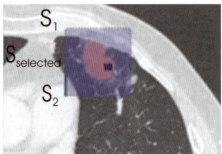

FIGURE 17.33 *Synchronized emphasis of a lung tumor. Left: local volume rendering combined with surface rendering of the tumor. Right: the range of slices is indicated by the blue semitransparent rectangle around the tumor. The size of the thick lines on the left conveys how many slices before the selected slice also contain the tumor. (Images courtesy VOLKER DICKEN, MeVis Bsremen)*

Emphasis Technique	Suitability for Multiple Objects	Degree of Changes	Implemen-tation Effort	Remarks
Local color	yes	local	minimal	saturation and lightness to support emphasis
Regional color	yes	regional	moderate	modify local color and colors of adjacent objects to achieve contrasts
Local silhouette	yes	local	high	silhouette lines (in addition to surface shading) for the CSO
Regional silhouette	yes	regional	high	silhouette lines to visualize context objects
Transparency of occluding objects	partial	regional	high	
Transparency of all objects (except CSO)	yes	global	low	
Cutaway views	yes	regional	high	for small and compact objects

TABLE 17.1 *Emphasis techniques and their applications*

Emphasis Technique	Suitability for Multiple Objects	Degree of Changes	Implementation Effort	Remarks
Detail view	yes	local	moderate	synchronization with context view required
Shadow volumes	yes	local	high	
Arrows	yes	local	high	for small and compact objects

TABLE 17.1 *(continued)*

Although the discussion so far was focused on the emphasis of a single object, we also mention whether or not the technique is applicable to several objects. The degree of change (local, regional, or global) is the most important criterion. The implementation effort (column four) typically varies greatly between these techniques.

The techniques in rows one to six do not add new objects or views, but change the appearance of objects. The following techniques add or remove objects or include additional symbols. We marked some techniques as particularly suitable for small and compact objects. The size of an object in relation to the overall size of the 3D model is thus an essential parameter and the AABB may be used to assess the size of an object. To estimate the compactness of an object, its skeleton may be computed. Branching skeletons indicate structures that are not compact.

17.9 SUMMARY

We presented a variety of 3D emphasis and focus techniques applicable and viable for medical visualization. We deliberately excluded emphasis techniques that change relative sizes or positions of objects, such as 3D fisheye views, because these are in general inappropriate for medical visualizations (at least for clinical applications). So far, most work on illustrative medical visualization primarily targets at medical education, since this domain is not characterized by severe time constraints in the way routine medical diagnosis and intervention planning are. However, most of the techniques described in this chapter are relevant for clinical applications, too. Some of these techniques, such as silhouettes and ghost views, are already integrated in research prototypes for intervention planning and are currently evaluated [KRÜGER et al. 2005]. Illustrative techniques are not only relevant for displaying complex spatial relations but also have potential to encode additional information onto the anatomy.

Outlook Illustrative rendering of medical volume data is one of the most active research areas in medical visualization. We discussed only emphasis and illustration for static volume data. An extension and adaption of such techniques to dynamic data is left open for future work. We briefly described the idea by VIOLA et al. [2004b] to adjust visualization parameters to the importance of objects. This idea can be extended in many ways; in particular, the importance may be different for different parts of objects (e.g., the shape of a long muscle near a tumor is highly important, whereas other areas are less important).

The most important work to be done concerns an evaluation of emphasis techniques by means of controlled user studies (see [KOSARA et al. 2003] for a discussion of issues in the preparation, execution, and analysis of user studies of visualization techniques). More insight is necessary to automatically choose and combine emphasis techniques.

We restricted the discussion in this chapter to the emphasis of individual objects. Some of these techniques, in particular local techniques, can also be applied to multiple objects. However, some of them need to be refined for multiple objects.

FURTHER READING

For an overview on NPR, two dedicated books can be recommended: STROTHOTTE and SCHLECHTWEG [2002] and GOOCH and GOOCH [2001]. Since 2000, the Non-Photorealistic Rendering and Animation (NPAR) conference has been established as a biannual event (see the conference Web site, www.npar.org). Concerning hatching, PRAUN et al. [2001], ZANDER et al. [2004], and JODOIN et al. [2002] are recommended; concerning silhouettes and feature lines, we refer to RASKAR and COHEN [1999], and ISENBERG et al. [2002]. ISENBERG et al. [2002] give an overview discussing requirements and appropriate silhouette detection methods. XU et al. [2004] describe high-quality silhouette rendering based on point-based models. Some papers are dedicated to fast object-space detection of silhouettes. Hierarchical data structures [SANDER et al. 2000], precomputed information [BUCHANAN and SOUSA 2000, GOOCH et al. 1999], or probabilistic methods [MARKOSIAN et al. 1997] are employed to accelerate the computation.

NAGY et al. [2002] describe interactive volume illustration in which expressive hatchings are generated based on the estimated curvature, transparency, and lighting. The placement of hatchings is guided by seedpoints specified by the user, which are used as starting points for tracking lines with high curvature. KINDLMANN et al. [2003] designed curvature-based transfer functions that make it possible to emphasize regions with large values for the major curvature κ_1 and κ_2. With this approach, ridges and valleys can be emphasized effectively, and silhouettes with a constant strengths can be computed. In [RÖSSL et al. 2000a, b], the approximation of curvature information in polygonal meshes is used to guide the extraction of feature lines. The use of line-based illustrations for displaying several isosurfaces and the value of line-based illustration for emphasis is discussed in [TREAVETT and CHEN 2000].

We omitted a discussion of stippling techniques, although these techniques are relevant for emphasis. Stippling is based on points or small filled circles as rendering primitives. Meanwhile, complex objects can be stippled sufficiently quickly, and they can be easily parameterized. Stippling techniques are described, for example, in [DEUSSEN et al. 2000, SECORD 2002, PASTOR and STROTHOTTE 2002]. LU et al. [2002] and LU et al. [2003] also considered stippling techniques for the visualization of medical volume data (see Fig. 17.34). Gradient direction and gradient magnitude are estimated to adjust the local resolution of points so that silhouettes and local features are highlighted. For medical visualization, the combination of stippling with other rendering techniques is needed (see Fig. 17.35). Integrated approaches to stippling and silhouette generation and stippling are described in [YUAN et al. 2005 and SALAH et al. 2005c]. Expressive visualizations arise particularly if shading effects are integrated to control the density of points. LUM et al. [2002] presented a novel visualization technique—kinetic visualization—that uses particle systems to add motion cues that can aid in the perception of shape and spatial relationships of static objects.

It is recommended to look at applications of illustrative renderings in other application areas, such as illustration of terrain data [WHELAN and VISVALINGAM 2003] and illustration in technical areas [GOOCH et al. 1999]. Shape perception by means of computerized line drawings has been investigated—among others—by KOENDERINK [1984] and KOENDERINK et al. [1996].

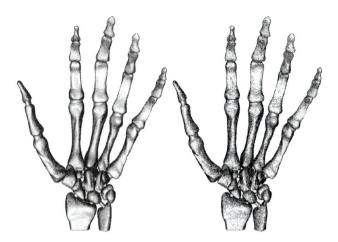

FIGURE 17.34 *Different stipplings of a human hand. Shape information and object borders are clearly visible [LU et al. 2003]. (Image courtesy AIDONG LU, University of North Carolina at Charlotte)*

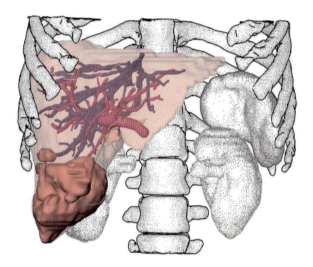

FIGURE 17.35 *Stippling, silhouette, and surface rendering combined. Stippling is applied to context objects only, whereas focus objects are rendered as surfaces. (Image courtesy ALEXANDRA BAER, University of Magdeburg)*

Visibility analysis is important for the selection of emphasis techniques. For conventional computer graphics, this topic is also essential for accelerating the rendering of very large scenes with a small portion of visible polygons. A tutorial from the ACM SIGGRAPH conference gives an overview [COHEN-OR et al. 2000]. A more recent survey can be found in [COHEN-OR et al. 2003]. Also in this survey, the majority of the algorithms estimate visibility by using hierarchies of bounding volumes. In contrast to the visibility analysis discussed here, individual polygons are considered in computer graphics instead of (high-level) objects such as anatomic structures. Despite this difference, fast computer graphics algorithms can be modified to be useful for emphasis techniques.

Many of the emphasis techniques discussed here have been used for an educational system based on the metaphor of a 3D jigsaw puzzle [RITTER et al. 2000]. The generation of cutaway illustrations is discussed in [DIEPSTRATEN et al. 2003].

Chapter 18

Exploration of MRI Diffusion Tensor Images

The characterization of fiber tracts plays a crucial role in cognitive science, diagnosis, and treatment planning. Neurodegenerative diseases, such as multiple sclerosis and Alzheimer's, or tumor infiltration lead to changes or disruptions of neural fiber tracts that might be used to detect the disease at an early stage and also to evaluate the effect of a therapy. The knowledge of an individual patient's fiber tracts may also be employed for neurosurgery and radiotherapy planning, in which damage of such tracts has to be avoided.

Gray matter in the human brain is responsible for processing information. The *activation areas* may be depicted with functional MRI after stimulating visual, auditory, or motor functions (recall Sect. 3.3.3). White matter, on the other hand, connects functional regions in the brain. The white matter consists of neural pathways, called fiber tracts. Within fiber tracts, diffusion is strongly anisotropic, due to the presence of cell membranes and myelin sheaths surrounding the axons. Due to their low permeability, cell membranes restrict the diffusion.

Magnetic resonance diffusion tensor imaging (DTI) measures the diffusion of water molecules, which is characterized by random Brownian motion [WESTIN et al. 1999]. The diffusion velocity in different directions depend on the tissue type. Fluid-filled compartments are characterized by a very high isotropic diffusion (i.e., the diffusion is similar in all directions). Some structured tissues, such as the spinal cord and muscles, are inhomogeneous and *anisotropic*—diffusion occurs primarily in a distinguished direction and is restricted in transverse directions. DTI is carried out to characterize the anisotropy in certain tissues and thus to investigate diffusion directions and connectivity, primarily of neurological structures.

Fiber tracts, consisting of parallel nerve fibers, are therefore identified by DTI as areas of a highly anisotropic diffusion. The fiber tract axis coincides with the direction of highest diffusion.

Diffusion tensor imaging is a relatively new MRI modality (introduced by BASSER et al. [1994]). It is based on diffusion-weighted MRI, which records the *amount of diffusion*. DTI generalizes this concept and allows the characterization of the *direction of diffusion*, which indicates the fiber tract architecture. Since DTI is a variant of MRI, patients are not exposed to ionizing radiation. Before the advent of DTI [BASSER et al. 1994], investigation of brain anatomical connectivity was only obtained through postmortem studies.

As a result of DTI, the diffusion rate at every sample point in a 3D volume is determined by a series of diffusion-weighted MRI images (each dataset is acquired with a different gradient). DTI data are challenging to process, to visualize, and to explore. The spatial resolution of the data is lower than in conventional MRI. DTI data are even more sensitive to noise and exhibit stronger geometric distortions compared to conventional MRI. The low spatial resolution and the artifacts do not allow depiction of small nerve tracts. Instead, only larger fiber bundles can be located with DTI.

From the visualization point of view, we have to consider a new class of visualization techniques: *tensor visualization* methods, which convey the properties of a second-order tensor[1] and indicate coherency

---

1 A tensor of rank zero is a scalar value, a tensor of rank one is a vector, and a tensor of rank two is a matrix.

between adjacent voxels representing similar diffusion characteristics such as principal direction and level of anisotropy. The eigenanalysis of the tensor matrix is the primary tool for analysing and representing of second-order tensor data.

Diffusion tensor imaging and analysis has experienced tremendous development in recent years. Many research groups investigate DTI data to come up with reliable and intuitive visualization methods. Medical researchers take the opportunity to investigate neuroanatomical differences and variants as well as clinically relevant diagnostic procedures. More and more, DTI data is being employed for neurosurgery planning to avoid damage to important white matter tracts.

Tensors and Eigenanalysis Tensor fields occur in a variety of applications in engineering and physical sciences. Visualization of tensor fields plays a crucial role in data analysis of large-scale finite element models of physical phenomena. Such simulations are frequently carried out in mechanical and civil engineering, resulting in stress and strain tensor fields. Tensor data are somehow incomprehensible compared to scalar or vector data, which occur in many real-world problems. Therefore, a variety of visualization techniques, used to analyze tensor fields, originates from scalar and vector visualization. These techniques allow the depiction of certain aspects of tensor data comprehensibly. However, the full information of a tensor cannot be conveyed with a single visualization of scalar- or vector-valued quantities.

Diffusion tensors are second-order tensors that describe linear transformations between vectors by means of 3×3 matrices T_{ij}. Diffusion tensors are symmetric ($T_{ij} = T_{ji}$) and positive definite. Diffusion tensor matrices are therefore similar to covariance matrices, which were employed for virtual resection (see Sect. 12.3) and measurement tasks (see Sect. 13.7.1). From these sections, we know that symmetric matrices of dimension n have n eigenvalues λ_i and n orthogonal eigenvectors e_i, which fulfill Equation 18.1.

$$T e_i = \lambda_i e_i \qquad\qquad (18.1)$$

Eigenvectors and eigenvalues that fully characterize a diffusion tensor are independent of the coordinate system of the scanner. Eigenvectors characterize the direction of diffusion, and eigenvalues represent the amount of diffusion in the corresponding direction. The eigenanalysis is the basis for most analysis methods of diffusion tensors, as well as for their visualization.

Organization We start this chapter with a discussion of the medical background, which includes neuroanatomy, the interpretation of diffusion tensor data, their relationship to diseases and abnormalities, and a survey of image acquisition variants (see Sect. 18.1). We continue and explain image processing techniques that support the visualization and exploration of diffusion tensor data by smoothing, removing outliers, and fitting continuous functions to the discretely sampled data (see Sect. 18.2). Visualization attempts to convey anisotropy in various regions of the brain; therefore, we discuss expressive metrics for anisotropy in Section 18.3.

We introduce and discuss a variety of visualization techniques. In Section 18.4, we start with slice-based visualizations. We continue with more advanced and more abstract visualization techniques. First, we discuss iconic or glyph-based visualization techniques that depict graphics primitives for each measured value (see Sect. 18.5). Afterward, we present volume rendering techniques that provide a better overview of diffusion tensor data (see Sect. 18.6). In Section 18.7, we describe a variety of techniques from flow and tensor visualization that convey the direction of diffusion and thus, indirectly, the fiber tracts. Most of the techniques are based on *streamlines*, a well-known technique in the visualization of vector fields. The visualization of individual tensor values and the visualization of fiber tracts complement each other. We proceed by describing an even more high-level visualization based on the identification of

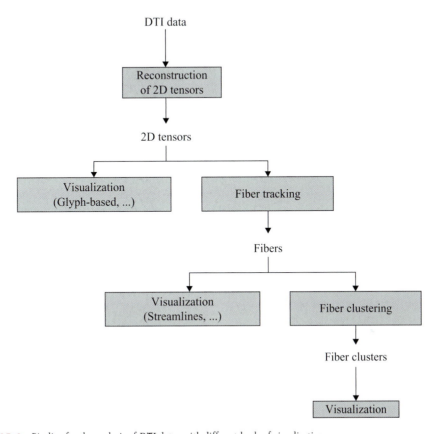

DTI data

Reconstruction
of 2D tensors

2D tensors

Visualization
(Glyph-based, ...)

Fiber tracking

Fibers

Visualization
(Streamlines, ...)

Fiber clustering

Fiber clusters

Visualization

FIGURE 18.1 *Pipeline for the analysis of DTI data, with different levels of visualization.*

clusters of fibers (see Sect. 18.8). The relation between DTI data and various processing and visualization tasks is illustrated in Figure 18.1, which serves as a graphic organization chart of this chapter.

18.1   MEDICAL BACKGROUND AND IMAGE ACQUISITION

In this section, we describe the acquisition and interpretation of tensor data to motivate the design of algorithms for the exploration of DTI data. DTI is based on different diffusion properties and primarily applied to discriminate and analyze brain tissues. The diffusion rate is highest for the ventricles, lower for gray matter, and lowest for white matter. The directional dependence of diffusion is very low for ventricles and gray matter, where diffusion is basically isotropic. Strong anisotropic diffusion occurs in white matter only. The course of fibers strongly differs from patient to patient. In the presence of a brain tumor, there is a wide variety of different courses, and it is essential to assess the fiber tract architecture preoperatively [MERHOF et al. 2004].

18.1.1 NEUROANATOMY

To understand the examples presented in this chapter and to understand the clinical applications, we shall briefly describe neuroanatomic fundamentals, based on [GUYTON 1987 and WÜNSCHE 2004b].

The brain is part of the central nervous system and is responsible for reacting to sensory information from the environment. Information is received from the endings of sensory nerves and is transmitted via the spinal cord to the brain. The principal functions of the brain are:

- Sensory function (information from the body to the brain)
- Integrative function (information from brain to brain—for example, thinking processes)
- Motor function (information from the brain to the body for controlling movements)

Different areas in the brain are "responsible" for these functions. These areas are connected with each other via nerve fiber tracts (often abbreviated as fiber tracts). Brain tissue consists of nerve cells (*neurons*) and supporting cells (*neuroglia*). Neurons have a cell body, as well as structures for the exchange of information, namely axons (long structures) and dendrites. Nerve fibers are only found in white matter. Fiber tracts are bundles of nerve fibers with a common origin and destination. According to [MAMATA et al. 2002], the major fiber tracts can be differentiated into:

- Commissural fibers
- Association fibers
- Projection fibers
- Fibers of the brain stem and cerebellum

Commissural fibers cross over or join the two brain hemispheres, connecting identical cortical areas in both hemispheres. The largest of these fiber tracts is the *corpus callosum*. It consists of densely packed and coherent fibers. In publications relating to the exploration of DTI data, this region is often employed to discuss the presented solutions.

Association fibers connect areas in the same hemisphere. Projection fibers transmit sensory information from the body to the cortex (sensory fibers) and motor information from the cortex to the spinal cord (motor fibers). Many projection fibers originate from the internal capsule. These structures are illustrated in Figure 18.2.

Neuroanatomy and DTI An interesting question is how the different amounts of anisotropy can be explained. Most tissues are made of different compartments, at least an extracellular and an intracellular compartment. These compartments have strongly different diffusion properties; intracellular compartments restrict water motion with more strength than do extracellular compartments. Considering this fact, diffusion measurements indicate the fraction of extracellular space in certain regions. Pathologic changes, such as those occurring in the acute stage of an ischemic stroke, change the portion of extracellular space and thus the diffusion properties.

Figure 18.3 illustrates functional regions and their connectivity via white matter bundles. The location of a lesion in the vicinity of white matter bundles is shown in Figure 18.4 to illustrate diagnostic questions relevant for DTI. As an example, we present a sketch of white matter tracts and a lesion that damages these tracts, and show the effects on diffusion using diffusion ellipsoids derived by means of DTI (see Fig. 18.5).

18.1.2 IMAGE ACQUISITION

Diffusion tensor imaging (DTI) is related to diffusion-weighted MRI imaging (DWI), introduced by BIHAN et al. [1986]. The latter modality is more established and widespread. DWI is based on a single gradient

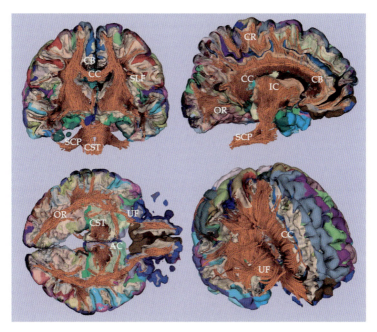

FIGURE 18.2 *Important neuroanatomical structures. CC—corpus callosum, CR—corona radiate, SLF—superior longitudinal fasciculus, OR—optic radiation, CB—cingulum bundle, SCP—superior cerebellar peduncle, CST—corticospinal tract, UF—uncinate fasciculus, AC—anterior commissure [PARK et al. 2004]. (Image courtesy HAE-JONG PARK, Yonsei University)*

FIGURE 18.3 *Connectivity of functional regions (FR) by means of white matter tracts. This information is essential for the diagnosis of cognitive disorders. (Image courtesy RAGNAR BADE, University of Magdeburg)*

pulse applied during image acquisition.[2] The diffusion of water molecules causes randomization of the nuclear magnetic resonance spin. The amount of reduction provides a quantitative measure of diffusion in the gradient direction [KUBICKI et al. 2002]. Diffusion is a stochastic process that can be modeled by a Gaussian probability distribution. Due to the stochastic nature of the process, even measurements under exactly the same conditions would lead to slightly different signal intensities. To improve the signal-to-noise ratio, several measurements are often carried out and averaged.

---

2   MORI and BARKER [1999] provide an introduction to MRI with a focus on DWI and DTI.

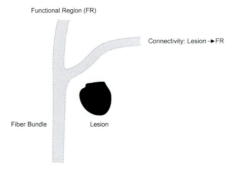

FIGURE 18.4 Connectivity of fiber bundles close to a lesion. Such visualizations are employed for neurosurgery and radiotherapy planning to evaluate the safety margin around a lesion. (Image courtesy RAGNAR BADE, University of Magdeburg)

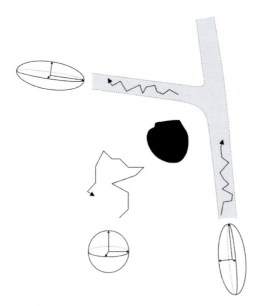

FIGURE 18.5 White matter tracts (long bars) are damaged by a lesion, leading to a measurable anisotropy loss of the diffusion indicated by less elongated diffusion ellipsoids. (Image courtesy RAGNAR BADE, University of Magdeburg)

Technical constraints hamper clinical use. DWI characterizes molecular displacements on a very small scale, and any movement, such as brain perfusion, interferes with the measurement.[3] Therefore, fast image acquisition is a priority to limit the amount of motion.

Diffusion-Weighted MRI Imaging Diffusion is measured through the Stejskal-Tanner imaging sequence [STEJSKAL and TANNER 1965]. To eliminate the influence of other imaging parameters, two measurements

---

3   The relation between perfusion and diffusion and the separation of both effects is described in [BENGER et al. 2006].

are accomplished, one with diffusion weighting and one without, to determine the apparent diffusion coefficient (ADC) with Equation 18.2, in which S is the signal with and S_0 is the signal without diffusion weighting; b is the diffusion weighting factor.

$$S = S_0 * e^{-bADC} \qquad (18.2)$$

The diffusion weighting factor b depends on the duration of intervals between gradient pulses and on the gradient. b is non-negative and measured in s/mm^2. S_0 is often referred to as baseline image data. Equation 18.2 describes how the signal without diffusion (S_0) is attenuated in the presence of diffusion. High diffusion leads to a low signal intensity.

The most important parameter of DWI is the diffusion weighting factor b, which determines the weight of the diffusion component. With $b = 0$, a T2-weighted MRI image results. With high values, such as $b = 1000 \ s/mm^2$, diffusion has a major influence on the images, resulting in a bright appearance for areas with high diffusion magnitude. The product of b and the diffusion coefficient is roughly of order one. The diffusion coefficients of brain tissues are between $0.7 * 10^{-3} \ s/mm^2$ (for gray matter) and $3 * 10^{-3} \ s/mm^2$ (for water).

Because diffusion-weighted imaging cannot distinguish between perfusion and diffusion, the diffusion values resulting from the subtraction are not perfectly reliable. Therefore, the diffusion values are referred to as the *apparent diffusion coefficient* (ADC). The direction of diffusion cannot be assessed through DWI.[4]

Diffusion Tensor MRI Imaging   Diffusion tensor data is acquired by applying consecutive magnetic field gradient pulses. Each gradient is applied for some milliseconds, during which the water molecules move some 10 micrometers [KUBICKI et al. 2002].

For DTI, it is not sufficient to derive a base image S_0 and a diffusion-weighted image S. Instead, diffusion is measured along different gradient directions. For DTI, at least six gradients are required. These gradients must be non-coplanar. As mentioned before, averaging of repeated measurements increases the reliability (not the signal-to-noise ratio). Therefore, many studies are based on (often four times) repeated acquisitions. Frequently, the following gradients, representing the optimum distribution of six gradients, are employed [WESTIN et al. 2002]:

$g_1 = (1, 1, 0)^T$
$g_2 = (0, 1, 1)^T$
$g_3 = (1, 0, 1)^T$
$g_4 = (0, 1, -1)^T$
$g_5 = (1, -1, 0)^T$
$g_6 = (-1, 0, 1)^T$

Each image dataset S_i corresponds to the gradient direction g_i. Together with the base image at least seven images ($s_0, \ldots, s_6$) are acquired.

Calculation of the Diffusion Tensor   The calculation of the diffusion tensor D is based on Equation 18.2, which can be reformulated as:

$$S_i = S_0 * e^{-b\bar{g}_i^T D \bar{g}_i} \qquad (18.3)$$

---

4   WESTIN *et al.* [2002] describe the fundamentals of DWI and DTI in detail.

The scalar value ADC in Equation 18.2 is replaced by the diffusion tensor, where $\bar{g}_i$ is the i-th gradient. In Equation 18.3, $\bar{g}_i$ is the i-th normalized gradient ($\bar{g} = g/|g|$) and S_i represents the signal intensity according to gradient i. Equation 18.3 employs that for any set of normalized and orthogonal vectors $\bar{g}_i$ the following equation holds: $D = \bar{g}_i * D * \bar{g}_i^T$. Equation 18.3 may be transformed to:

$$ln(\frac{S_i}{S_0}) = -b\bar{g}_i^T D\bar{g}_i \qquad (18.4)$$

For N non-coplanar gradients, a least-square formulation of Equation 18.4 leads to Equation 18.5.

$$\bar{D} = (\bar{G}^T G)^{-1}\bar{G}^T \bar{B} \qquad (18.5)$$

$$\bar{B}_i = -(1/b)ln(\frac{S_i}{S_0}) \qquad (18.6)$$

$$\bar{G}_i = (g_1^i * g_1^i, 2g_1^i * g_2^i, g_2^i * g_2^i, 2 * g_1^i * g_3^i, 2 * g_2^i * g_3^i, g_3^i * g_3^i) \qquad (18.7)$$

$$\bar{D} = (D_{11}, D_{12}, D_{13}, D_{22}, D_{23}, D_{33}) \qquad (18.8)$$

$$i = 1, \dots, N \qquad (18.9)$$

If six gradients are used, Equation 18.5 describes a linear system of six equations for the six unknown parameters $D_{11}, D_{12}, D_{13}, D_{22}, D_{23}, D_{33}$ that can be uniquely solved. A quadratic 6×6 matrix GM is constructed based on the components of the $\bar{G}$ vector in Equation 18.5. The off-diagonal elements of GM are zero, and the diagonal elements GM_{ii} correspond to G_i. The calculation of D can now be simplified to $D = GM^{-1}\bar{B}$.

Due to image noise, the regression schemes may lead to diffusion tensors with negative eigenvalues. Physically, diffusivity in each principal direction cannot be negative. Therefore, it has been suggested that this property be incorporated as a constraint in the calculation of the diffusion tensor and that negative values be set to zero.

The accuracy of the diffusion tensor and the signal-to-noise ratio is increased if data are collected from more directions to avoid sampling direction biases [BIHAN et al. 1986, JONES et al. 1999]. The directions should be uniformly distributed. In a case with perfectly isotropic diffusion, the diagonal elements of D (D_{xx}, D_{yy}, D_{zz}) are non-zero and equal, whereas all off-diagonal elements are zero.

Resolution and Quality of DTI Data DTI has a low spatial resolution (e.g., a 128×128 matrix and about 30 to 60 slices). Typical voxel spacings are $2 \times 2 \times 2$ mm. Note that with this resolution, individual voxels are considerably larger than the cross section of a nerve. Slice thickness is sometimes even larger, which makes it impossible to reliably extract small fiber bundles. As we have discussed in Section 3.3.1, there is a trade-off between acquisition time, spatial resolution, and image quality. In general, image acquisition times are larger for high-resolution images, and the signal-to-noise ratio is decreased with more spatial resolution.

The quality of DTI data is compromised by a variety of factors. Movements, such as eye movements, may cause motion artifacts. More severe artifacts are due to eddy currents, which arise because the magnetic field gradients are frequently switched. Eddy currents generate additional unwanted magnetic fields that are superimposed on the intended magnetic field. As result, the gradients of the samples differ from the gradients prescribed by the b-matrix [BASSER and JONES 2002]. Several attempts have been made to reduce the effect of eddy currents at the image acquisition stage and to correct for them in the postprocessing stage. BASSER and JONES [2002] give an overview of these investigations.

Another severe problem with DTI is the occurrence of artifacts due to strong discontinuities in the magnetic susceptibility—for example, at the tissue-air interface. These artifacts lead to additional local gradients, which cause the *b*-matrix to vary locally [BASSER and JONES 2002]. The amount of this particular artifact is related to the strength of the magnetic field. While most of the investigations described in the literature are carried out with 1.5 Tesla scanners, currently 3 Tesla scanners are used more often, particularly for research projects. In the 3 Tesla scanners, it is even more important to model and account for these artifacts.

Diffusion Tensor Imaging Techniques   Basically, two different imaging techniques are clinically used [KUBICKI *et al.* 2004]:

- Echo-planar imaging (EPI)
- Line scan diffusion imaging (LSDI)

EPI is fast and therefore robust against motion artifacts. However, it provides less spatial resolution and is very sensitive to variations in magnetic susceptibility, as well as induced eddy currents. LSDI, on the other hand, is based on the sequential acquisition of parallel columns lying in the image plane. Compared to EPI, in which complete images are acquired, the acquisition time is four to six times slower. Increased spatial resolution and strongly reduced magnetic field artifacts are the benefits of LSDI, introduced by GUDBJARTSSON *et al.* [1996].

Recently, KUBICKI *et al.* [2004] compared both imaging methods by applying them to the same subjects and by analyzing the same white matter regions. They came to the conclusion that with LSDI, better reproducibility and accuracy is achieved. The reliability of the anisotropy characterization was severely reduced with EPI, particularly for the temporal lobe, which is essential for assessing Alzheimer's disease and schizophrenia. The accuracy of EPI may be increased by averaging several measurements. However, this process increases acquisition times and thus reduces the major advantage of this imaging technique.

18.1.3 CLINICAL APPLICATIONS

DTI is very useful for exploring fibrous structures such as white matter in the brain and muscle. Diffusion tensor imaging has a variety of clinical applications. We differentiate between diagnostic purposes and surgery planning.

Diagnostic Value of DTI   For diagnostic purposes, the degree of anisotropy loss is characteristic for white matter tract pathology, such as swelling and infiltration [KUBICKI *et al.* 2002]. Such pathologies lead to axonal loss and degeneration of fiber tracts, which become indirectly measurable with DTI. It must be noted, however, that normal conditions such as age, handedness, and gender also influence anisotropy characteristics.

Because, DWI turned out to be the most sensitive method for detecting ischemic strokes, it was natural to complement it with DTI. The anisotropy loss derived from DTI correlates well with the clinical status and allows evaluation of the fiber tract reorganization following an acute stroke. MUKHERJEE *et al.* [2000] showed that white matter damage after a stroke is observed earlier in DTI (compared to DWI). Also, in case of traumatic brain injury, DTI is more and more often replacing diffusion-weighted images [KUBICKI *et al.* 2002]. DTI enables new perspectives on the investigation of neurodegenerative diseases. Clinical studies indicated an influence of Morbus Alzheimer [STAHL *et al.* 2003], multiple sclerosis [TIEVSKY *et al.* 1999], and brain tumors [PRICE *et al.* 2004, SCHLUETER *et al.* 2005b, TROPINE *et al.* 2004] on white matter connectivity. Alzheimer's disease is particularly interesting, due to the large and growing number of patients. While it affects primarily gray matter, DTI studies also indicated significant connectivity disruptions of the association fibers and in the corpus callosum in an early stage of multiple sclerosis [KUBICKI *et al.* 2002].

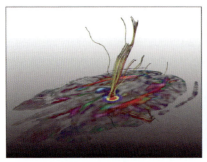 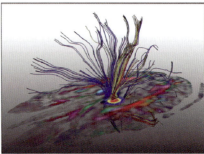

FIGURE 18.6 Risk analysis for neurosurgery planning based on DTI data. In the left image, a small safety margin has been selected and the fibers within this margin are tracked. In the right image, due to a larger margin, considerably more fiber tracts are involved, leading to very different areas in the brain. (Images courtesy MATHIAS SCHLUETER, MeVis Bremen)

KUBICKI et al. [2002] give an overview of 35 studies investigating diagnostic applications of DTI. Twelve diseases are involved, with six studies relating to ischemic stroke and five to schizophrenia and multiple sclerosis. Most of these studies are small- to medium-sized, with patient numbers between 10 to 50. Thus, it is too early to come to definite conclusions about the diagnostic value of DTI. However, the results achieved so far are promising and strongly encourage further research.

For routine diagnosis by means of DTI, reproducible procedures are required. Currently, most evaluations of anisotropy are based on manually selected ROIs, for example in a brain tumor, which limits the reproducibility. Model assumptions with respect to probability distributions of diffusion properties within fiber bundles and the background may be employed for a more reproducible evaluation [SCHLUETER et al. 2005b]. Due to the age dependency, such model-based techniques have to consider age-normalized values.

DTI for Surgery Planning and Intraoperative Use For neurosurgery planning, particularly in tumor surgery, it is valuable to identify functional brain areas and to estimate their connectivity in order to save important fiber tracts. Complete tumor resection on one hand, and optimal preservance of healthy structures to avoid postoperative deficits on the other, are the contradictory goals of neurosurgery [NIMSKY et al. 2005a, 2006].

If a brain tumor has been reliably identified in shape and volume, fiber tracts within different safety margins around the tumor may be determined and visualized. This kind of analysis would allow assessment of the risks involved in different variants of a surgical procedure (see Fig. 18.6 and [BENTER et al. 2006]). It should be noted that the visualization of white matter tracts is just one component of preoperative planning; other components include morphological information derived from anatomic data and information concerning eloquent brain areas derived from functional MRI data. The analysis and visualization techniques applied in Figure 18.6 are discussed later. Recently, DTI visualization was integrated in surgical navigation systems and used intraoperatively. First experiences indicate that this integration leads to resections with lower morbidity [KAMADA et al. 2005, NIMSKY et al. 2005b].

18.2   IMAGE ANALYSIS OF DTI DATA

DTI data are noisy and exhibit various artifacts. To visualize and explore these data, appropriate image processing and image analysis techniques are indispensable. In particular, the visualization of fiber tracts benefits from adequate preprocessing. The enhancement of DTI data is based on some assumptions and observations concerning the anatomy of fiber tracts. Fiber tracts are smooth: frequent and strong changes of their direction do not appear.

18.2.1 INTERPOLATION OF DTI DATA

A first step in the processing of DTI data is often to interpolate a continuous tensor field based on the discrete measurements of tensor data. The reconstruction of a continuous field is a prerequisite for fiber tracking, which is based on the computation of integral lines of the eigenvector field and thus requires tensor data at arbitrary locations [BENGER et al. 2006].

Classic Interpolation Methods Interpolation is a basic task in image processing. Linear, cubic, or radial basis functions are frequently employed (see [LEHMANN et al. 1999, 2001] for an overview). Nearest neighbor interpolation is too coarse and does not lead to valuable information [BENGER et al. 2006]. Approximation techniques consider noise in the computation of continuous image data and achieve a smoother result. In Section 10.4, we discussed such a filter to smooth perfusion data based on a simulation of diffusion processes [LYSAKER et al. 2003].

The application of these general techniques to the individual elements of diffusion tensor data is questionable, as these techniques do not consider the characteristics of tensor fields.[5] In particular, interpolating a new tensor based on interpolations of individual elements may result in a tensor that is no longer positively definite (although all sampled tensors are).

The most commonly used interpolation scheme is trilinear interpolation, which was introduced in Section 2.1. With trilinear interpolation, the interpolation of a tensor $T(x, y, z)$ is a linear combination of the 8-adjacent tensors $T(x_i, y_j, z_k)$, $T(x_{i+1}, y_j, z_k)$, $\ldots T(x_{i+1}, y_{j+1}, z_{k+1})$ weighted by their distances to (x, y, z).

Trilinear interpolation of tensor data is accomplished by interpolating all components of a tensor independently. This approach is viable, as symmetric tensors are closed under linear interpolation (any linear combination of symmetric tensors yields a symmetric tensor). A disadvantage of trilinear interpolation is that eigenvalues along a path are not perfectly preserved. Despite its disadvantages, component-wise interpolation is superior to a direct interpolation of eigenvectors and eigenvalues [ZHUKOV and BARR 2002].

Advanced Interpolation Methods Trilinear interpolation is a simple but crude interpolation method, since it does not consider relevant features in the surroundings. Taking into account that anisotropy should be evaluated through DTI, it is essential that the anisotropy within the data is not jeopardized in the interpolation process [CASTANO-MORAGA et al. 2004].

BASSER and JONES [2002] describe higher order interpolation schemes borrowed from differential geometry. With these higher order schemes, continuous tensor fields (with smooth gradients at any point) are generated. Moreover, measures such as mean curvature may be derived. Such measures are essential to characterize the shape of tensor fields and have been used, for example, to evaluate structures in the heart.

Advanced *anisotropic* interpolation techniques are based on a local analysis around the unsampled point P and attempt to preserve edges (points on opposite sides of a strong edge should not be combined by interpolation). Such a local analysis is based on the assumption that high gradient magnitudes indicate an edge. To reliably calculate gradients in tensor data, a local structure tensor is fitted to the data in the

---

5   Note, however, that it is the standard technique for the interpolation of scalar voxel data.

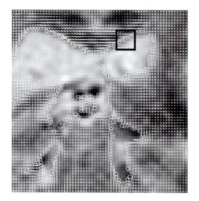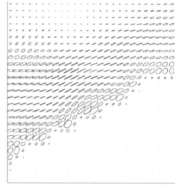

FIGURE 18.7 *Anisotropic interpolation in a slice of DT MRI data (64 × 64 resolution) in the border of the corpus callosum. The DTI data are superposed over T2 data (left). The zoomed image on the right with many interpolated tensors correctly reflects the border of the corpus callosum [CASTANO-MORAGA et al. 2004]. (Image courtesy CARLOS CASTANO MORAGA, Universidad de las Palmas de Gran Canaria)*

vicinity of P. For a detailed description of linear anisotropic interpolation, we refer to [CASTANO-MORAGA et al. 2004]. Figure 18.7 presents an example of anisotropic interpolation in a region with strong changes in diffusivity.

Preservation of anisotropy is certainly desirable; however—as BENGER et al. [2006] point out—even preserving a certain property does not guarantee that the interpolated values are correct or at least more correct than those of simpler interpolation techniques.

18.2.2 FILTERING DTI DATA

Standard noise reduction filters, such as Gaussian or median (recall Sect. 5.2.4), are not sufficient, because most of the directional information in the data is blurred by these filters [ZHUKOV and BARR 2002]. Filtering should be adaptive and consider:

- The principal direction of diffusion
- The amount of diffusion
- Sharp features, such as ridges

The first requirement means that smoothing should be reduced between fibers and increased along fibers. Smoothing should also depend on the diffusivity. The last requirement can be fulfilled by integrating filtering with fiber tracking and thus considering the original course of a fiber.

ZHUKOV and BARR [2002] introduce a filtering technique that fulfills the requirements stated above through a moving least squares filter. The idea behind this technique is to fit a polynomial to the data in a small region around the current voxel position V_p. The parameters of the polynomial are determined by minimizing the sum of the least square distances involved in the approximation. The least square distance computation is applied to the trilinearly interpolated tensor data.

The value at V_p is then replaced by applying the polynomial to V_p. The orientation and size of a region considered in the polynomial approximation depends on the value of the tensor at V_p. Unfortunately, the moving window filter is computationally highly demanding, even for polynomials with a low degree. Due to the extremely high computational effort, the filter can only be applied in a preprocess. An implementation of the 1D moving least squares filter is described in [PRESS et al. 1992].

18.2.3 DISCUSSION

A severe problem in the interpolation and filtering of tensor data is the correct handling of regions that correspond to converging and diverging fiber tracts. Another problem is the correct handling of bifurcations, such as crossings and T-junctions. In general, interpolation and filtering of noisy, rather low-resolution data leads to results with limited reliability. Particularly in regions with (almost) isotropic tensors, the principal eigenvector (corresponding to the largest eigenvalue λ_i) is not well defined [BENGER et al. 2006]. Therefore, fiber tracking that relies on the results of denoising and interpolation should be restricted to regions with strong and consistent anisotropy.

A principal limitation of the tensor model is the representation of fiber tract crossings. If fiber tracts with strongly different directions coincide within a voxel, the average directional information is measured and later visualized. If anisotropy is used to guide a filtering process, tensor glyphs representing crossings may even be omitted, since the average anisotropy is low.

18.3   QUANTITATIVE CHARACTERIZATION OF DIFFUSION TENSORS

The exploration of DTI data is based on quantitative characterizations of diffusion measurements. For this purpose, a variety of metrics has been developed and refined. A first group of metrics characterizes the diffusivity (amount of diffusion) without regarding the direction. A second group of metrics characterizes anisotropy in the diffusion of individual voxels. While these groups of measures are derived for individual diffusion tensors, there is a third group of measurements that refers to the intervoxel coherence of diffusion properties.

The analysis and visualization is primarily based on the eigenanalysis of the diffusion tensor. The eigenvectors at a particular location characterize the frame of reference in which diffusion occurs. In this frame, diffusion is characterized by a tensor with the three eigenvalues as diagonal elements and zero in the off-diagonal elements.

18.3.1 DIFFUSIVITY METRICS

Diffusivity metrics are essential for the assessment of the direction-independent component of diffusion. Such a metric may be used as a filter to select which voxels should be visualized. Often, the mean diffusivity λ_{mean} is used for this purpose. λ_{mean} is simply the average of the three eigenvalues λ_i. Alternatively, the maximum of the λ_i values may be used as a measure for the diffusivity at a particular location.

18.3.2 ANISOTROPY METRICS

A variety of anisotropy metrics is discussed in the literature. Most of them are based on the eigenanalysis of the tensor matrix T. Since T is a symmetric real valued matrix, it has three real and non-negative eigenvalues, denoted λ_i, and three orthogonal eigenvectors, denoted e_i. A widespread characterization of anisotropy is based on the sorted eigenvalues, with $\lambda_1 \geq \lambda_2 \geq \lambda_3$. This leads to the barycentric space depicted in Figure 18.8. A barycentric space is a coordinate system related to a triangle. All points in this space have coordinates (here c_p, c_l, and c_s) with components between 0 and 1. At the vertices of the triangular space, one component equals 1 and the other two components equal 0. At the edges of the triangle, one component equals 0, and the sum of the two other components equals 1.

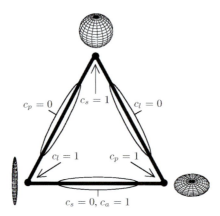

FIGURE 18.8   *Barycentric space of anisotropies with linear and planar anisotropy as well as spherical isotropy at the corners* [KINDLMANN *et al.* 2000]. *(Image courtesy* GORDON KINDLMANN, *Brigham and Women's Hospital Boston)*

The variance of the eigenvalues is a natural anisotropy metric (see Eq. 18.10). The variance does not depend on the order of the eigenvalues and is a relatively stable metric.

$$c_{var} = (\lambda_1 - \lambda_{mean})^2 + (\lambda_2 - \lambda_{mean})^2 + (\lambda_3 - \lambda_{mean})^2 \qquad [18.10]$$

To determine whether the diffusion is primarily oriented along a line (a neural pathway) or within a plane, or whether diffusion is primarily isotropic, three related measures are derived (see Eqs. 18.11 to 18.13). These measures, in contrast to the variance, depend on the order of the eigenvalues.

$$c_l = \frac{\lambda_1 - \lambda_2}{\lambda_1 + \lambda_2 + \lambda_3} \qquad [18.11]$$

$$c_p = \frac{2 * (\lambda_2 - \lambda_3)}{\lambda_1 + \lambda_2 + \lambda_3} \qquad [18.12]$$

$$c_s = \frac{3 * \lambda_3}{\lambda_1 + \lambda_2 + \lambda_3} \qquad [18.13]$$

These metrics were introduced in [WESTIN *et al.* 1999] and are now widely used. A primarily linear diffusion occurs if c_l is the largest of these values. Planar diffusion occurs if $\lambda_1 \approx \lambda_2$ and $\lambda_2 \gg \lambda_3$, which leads to a large c_p value. High planar diffusion might indicate very different situations that cannot be discriminated due to the small size of fibers compared to the resolution of DTI data. Fibers may "kiss," cross, or diverge (see Fig. 18.9) [MOBERTS *et al.* 2005]. Moreover, bending fibers lead to high planar diffusion, too.

If all eigenvalues are similar, the largest c_s value corresponds to isotropic diffusion. The factors 2 and 3 in Equation 18.12 and 18.13 have been inserted to ensure that c_p and c_s are in the range from zero to one and that all measures sum up to one. Based on these properties, a single anisotropy measure, the *anisotropy index* (see Eq. 18.14), can be derived:

$$c_a = 1 - c_s \frac{\lambda_1 + \lambda_2 - 2 * \lambda_3}{\lambda_1 + \lambda_2 + \lambda_3} \qquad [18.14]$$

In Figure 18.10, c_l, c_p, and c_s for a coronal brain section are compared.

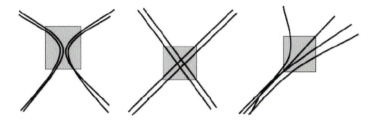

FIGURE 18.9 *High planar diffusion might have different reasons: fibers "kiss" (left), cross (middle), or diverge (right)* [BERENSCHOT 2003]. *(Image courtesy ANNA VILANOVA, Technical University of Eindhoven)*

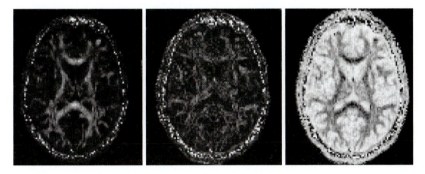

FIGURE 18.10   Linear, planar, and spherical component of diffusion (from left to right) in a coronal brain section. White indicates a high level of the respective component of diffusion. The area outside of the brain has been set to black [BENGER et al. 2006]. (Image courtesy WERNER BENGER, Zuse-Institute Berlin)

Fractional Anisotropy   Another frequently used anisotropy measure is *fractional anisotropy*. It is also computed based on the eigenvalues. Fractional anisotropy (see Eq. 18.15) characterizes the amount of anisotropy but cannot distinguish between linear and planar anisotropy.

$$FA = \frac{\sqrt{(\lambda_1 - \lambda_2) + (\lambda_2 - \lambda_3) + (\lambda_1 - \lambda_3)}}{\sqrt{2}\lambda_1 + \lambda_2 + \lambda_3}$$

(18.15)

18.3.3 COHERENCE METRICS

A group of measurements relates to the intervoxel coherence of adjacent voxels. They are essential for fiber tracking algorithms that aim at detecting coherent fibers and bundles of fibers.

One approach to quantifying coherence is to consider the relation of the principal eigenvectors and eigenvalues of adjacent voxels (v_i, v_j). With this approach, the similarity between two tensors is evaluated. The cosine of the angle between e_i^1 and e_j^1 is a natural choice to quantify directional similarity.

As has been pointed out by FRANK [2001], coherence metrics are particularly important for locations in which several (small) fiber locations occupy the same voxel. The tensor derived from the averaged sample is not expressive in such cases. Taking measurements from adjacent voxels into account may lead to an improved characterization.

18.3.4 DISCUSSION

There are many more measures used to characterize anisotropy of individual voxels. PIERPAOLI and BASSER [1996], for example, defined a simple *anisotropic ratio* as λ_1 / λ_3, which evaluates the relative magnitude of diffusivities along fiber tracts and along traverse directions. For an overview of such metrics, see [KUBICKI et al. 2002, SKARE et al. 2000, and VILANOVA et al. 2005]. These measures have in common that they are independent of the orientation of the diffusion ellipsoid.

18.4   SLICE-BASED VISUALIZATIONS OF TENSOR DATA

The exploration of DTI data requires dedicated visualization techniques. A naïve approach to presenting the raw data (six datasets with different information concerning directional diffusion) is not expressive at all. Appropriate visualization techniques for such data integrate the measurements of different datasets and assess the anisotropy in various regions.

As we discussed in Chapter 4, radiologists are accustomed to exploring volume data with slice-based 2D visualizations. The main advantage of 2D visualization is that every voxel contributes to the visualization and can be selected to inquire quantitative values. A slice-based visualization with the usual interaction functionality, such as browsing through the slices (cine mode) and interactive modification of the presentation lookup table (mapping of anisotropic measures to gray values or colors), is an appropriate starting point for our discussion of visualization techniques.

Color-Coding Diffusivity and Anisotropy The metrics discussed in Section 18.3 are useful for designing color-mapping schemes that indicate the amount of diffusion and the anisotropy [WÜNSCHE 2004b]. For color mapping, it is crucial to get rid of background voxels through an appropriate threshold for mean diffusivity λ_{mean}. As usual, with MRI data, absolute values are not appropriate. Instead, thresholds must be adapted to the image histogram. The design of color-mapping schemes that convey the quantitative nature of tensor data unambiguously is a complex and challenging task.

Non-linearity in the output device, as well as in human color perception, must be considered. The human visual system tends to interpret separate regions with similar colors as belonging to the same object or structure. Therefore, care has to be taken to avoid ambiguities [PAJEVIC and PIERPAOLI 1999]. Color is usually represented as an element of a 3D color space, using RGBα (red, green, and blue) or HSV (hue, saturation, and value) triples. Thus, color may represent up to three independent scalar data. Diffusion tensors, however, have six elements and cannot be directly mapped to a color space. Therefore, color is primarily used to convey a subset of the tensor information, such as the principal diffusion direction. A perceptually oriented color scale, such as the heated body scale, may be applied for this purpose (recall color perception, see Sect. 2.4.2).

Color-Coding Directional Information The directional information encoded in the diffusion tensor may be color-coded in various ways. To avoid confusion, directional information should not be combined with other parameters such as diffusivity. An important aspect of encoding the principal diffusion direction is that the orientation of diffusion is meaningless: parallel and antiparallel vectors (e_1 and $-e_1$) convey the same information with respect to the diffusion direction. To compare and evaluate color schemes, some requirements are discussed. According to [PAJEVIC and PIERPAOLI 1999], color schemes should:

- Be perceptually linearized
- Be independent of the reference frame in which the data are acquired

- Use principal colors (red, green, blue, cyan, magenta, and yellow) for principal directions (along the x-, y-, and z-directions, as well as along directions bisecting the xy-, the xz-, and the yz-planes).

In addition, an anisotropy metric should be used as a filter to avoid visualizing directional information in isotropic regions, where it is meaningless and confusing.

The first requirement is very general and holds for any kind of color-coding, (as an example, recall Sect. 10.5 where colors are employed to explore time-varying data). There are color spaces such as the HSV space where the Euclidean distances roughly correspond to the perceived distances of humans with normal color vision. However, whether the difference between perceived colors at particular locations corresponds to the distance of the underlying data is difficult to predict. Complex interactions with colors at adjacent locations strongly influence color perception. In particular, contrasts are enhanced by our human visual system. Despite these limitations, the HSV color space is a good choice to convey directional information.

The second requirement is crucial to compare DTI data from different patients or scanners. To fulfill this condition, an anatomical coordinate system is required, based on landmarks that can be reliably identified in each dataset. If DTI data are analyzed, the landmarks have to be selected and the data aligned with the coordinate system. PAJEVIC and PIERPAOLI [1999] suggest a coordinate system with the yz-plane corresponding to the sagittal plane aligned with the interhemispheric fissure, and the y-axis corresponding to the anterior-posterior intercommissural line.

Based on an appropriate coordinate system, colors may be assigned by considering the polar coordinates of the principal diffusion direction. A normalized vector is uniquely characterized by a polar θ and an azimuthal angle ϕ. PAJEVIC and PIERPAOLI [1999] suggest encoding the polar angle with the hue component and the azimuthal angle with the saturation component of the HSV color space. This is a viable strategy. However, the hue-component of the HSV space is not (nearly) perceptually linear. Brightness may be used to encode anisotropy. To avoid encoding too much information, a few discrete brightness values may be employed [SCHLUETER et al. 2005b].

A widespread color scheme is to map the x-, y-, and z-components of the normalized e_1 vector to the red-, green-, and blue-components of a color. WÜNSCHE [2004b] found that linear mappings of diffusion metrics to colors are not optimal for the interpretation of fiber tracts. Instead, he used exponential color maps for visualizing anisotropy and a cylindrical color map for mean diffusivity, which made subtle differences more recognizable and enabled high contrasts to arise (see Fig. 18.11). There is probably no optimal color-coding scheme for all users and tasks. Therefore, users should be able to select among (a few) perceptually oriented color maps.

A general limitation of slice-based visualizations is that the full tensor information is not visualized. Instead, scalar values are derived and visualized.

Combining Color and Transparency to Convey Directional Information   A common extension of color-coding is to employ transparency. Since DTI data are primarily analyzed with respect to the direction of principal diffusion, it is reasonable to use transparency to convey the amount of anisotropy. As an example, the amount of linear anisotropy may be mapped to transparency (maximum linear anisotropy is mapped to zero transparency). With this strategy, directional information is only pronounced if it is reliable. The use of transparency requires some background information—either a constant background color or anatomic information such as a T2-weighted image (see Fig. 18.12).

Gabor Patches as Tensor Icons   An interesting approach for tensor visualization was recently introduced by BENGER et al. [2006]. It is based on the human shape perception capability, which allows excellent

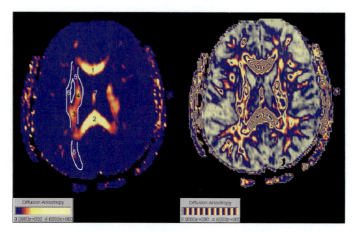

FIGURE 18.11 Left: an exponential color map is used for anisotropy. Right: a cylindrical color map indicates mean diffusivity. *Such a color map is not unique (different values are mapped to the same color), but the frequency of changes may be observed well* [WÜNSCHE 2004b]. *(Image courtesy* BURKHARD WÜNSCHE, *University of Auckland)*

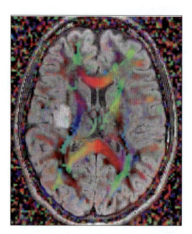

FIGURE 18.12 *The components of the principal eigenvector are mapped to the red-, green- and blue-components of color. Transparency indicates linear anisotropy. In regions with low linear anisotropy, the T2-weighted image is displayed. A malignant tumor in the left half becomes obvious as a bright region with very low linear anisotropy* [BENGER et al. 2006]. *(Image courtesy* WERNER BENGER, *Zuse-Institute Berlin)*

discrimination of patterns. As a general strategy, they suggest mapping tensorial quantities to texture patterns. More specifically, they employ the Gabor filter (see Fig. 18.13 and [GABOR 1946]), which conveys directional information well. A Gabor patch is mapped to the plane formed by the principal and median eigenvector (the y-direction of the Gabor patch is aligned with the principal eigenvector). Mapping tensor information to Gabor textures is optionally combined with the previously defined mapping to color and transparency. Thus, directional information is only visualized if it is assessed as reliable based on the relation between the eigenvalues. In summary, anisotropy characteristics are mapped to color, transparency, and texture (see Fig. 18.13).

FIGURE 18.13 *Semitransparent colored Gabor patches are used to depict anisotropy from tensor data. If the tensor is isotropic (top corner of the triangle), transparency is 100%. Red indicates that planar anisotropy dominates, whereas green indicates that the tensor exhibits predominantly linear anisotropy. The texture indicates direction in case of strong linear anisotropy [BENGER et al. 2006]. (Image courtesy WERNER BENGER, Zuse-Institute Berlin)*

18.5   VISUALIZATION WITH TENSOR GLYPHS

Glyphs convey second-order tensor data by mapping their eigenvalues and eigenvectors to the orientation and shape of a geometric primitive, such as a cylinder or a cuboid. Glyph-based visualizations transform a glyph geometry G into a tensor glyph G_T through Equation 18.16:

$$G_T = R^{-1}ERG \qquad (18.16)$$

E is a diagonal matrix that consists of the eigenvalues λ_i, and R is a rotation matrix that transforms the coordinate system of the dataset to the basis formed by the (orthogonal) eigenvectors [KINDLMANN 2004b].

Since the diffusion tensor has three non-negative real-valued eigenvalues, glyph geometries such as cubes, generalized cylinders (with ellipsoidal cross sections), and ellipsoids are typical choices. For such glyph geometries, the principal, medium, and minor axes correspond to the eigenvectors e_i, and the glyphs are scaled in each dimension according to the eigenvalues λ_i. Among these geometries, cubes have the advantage that only a few polygons need to be rendered for each of them. A disadvantage of cubes is the limited spatial perception due to the flat surfaces.

Tensor glyphs must be able to depict all possible tensor shapes. To evaluate tensor glyphs, the barycentric space (recall Fig. 18.8) with linear, planar, and spherical isotropy as its corners is appropriate, as this space contains all tensor shapes. The evaluation of tensor glyphs is guided by the following criteria [KINDLMANN 2004b]:

- **Continuity.** Small changes in the tensor shape should not lead to discontinuous changes in the resulting tensor geometry.
- **Uniqueness of the tensor geometry.** Each tensor shape should be uniquely mapped to one tensor geometry.
- **Unambiguous visualization of the tensor geometry.** The differences between tensor geometries should be recognizable in image-space. This property should hold for each viewing direction.

KINDLMANN [2004b] demonstrated that cylinders fail with respect to the first requirement: small changes of the tensor shape may lead to a switch of the orientation of the cylinder in cases in which planar and linear anisotropy have similar values. Cuboids do not exhibit such discontinuous behavior. However, they are not uniquely defined in case of zero planar anisotropy. Among the simple 3D shapes, ellipsoids are most frequently used as tensor glyphs. Ellipsoids, which are presented in the next sub-section, fulfill the first and second requirements. As we will discuss later in more detail, they fail with respect to the third requirement, which gives rise to more advanced tensor glyphs based on the concept of superquadrics.

18.5.1 ELLIPSOIDS AS TENSOR GLYPHS

The orientation and size of an ellipsoid conveys the space in which water molecules, originating at the ellipsoid's center, diffuse. The ellipsoid has the advantage of depicting all information of the diffusion tensor in a simple shape.

Limitations The major problem of ellipsoidal tensor glyphs is their ambiguity in image-space: Under certain viewing directions, different tensor shapes are hard to discriminate. Depending on the projection direction, the extent of the ellipsoid in the z-direction is difficult to assess (see Fig. 18.14). Only shading provides cues to differentiate a sphere from an ellipsoid with small extent in the viewing direction. In principle, some information loss in the projection from 3D to 2D cannot be avoided. However, as WESTIN et al. [2002] showed, the information loss may be reduced with more advanced geometric shapes.

18.5.2 SUPERQUADRIC TENSOR GLYPHS

With superquadric surfaces as tensor glyphs, all requirements discussed at the beginning of this section may be fulfilled. Superquadric surfaces have been widely used in visualization and graphics since their introduction by BARR [1981]. The use of superquadrics for visualizing DTI data has been suggested by KINDLMANN [2004b]. Superquadrics may be represented implicitly by Equation 18.17.

$$q(x, y, z) = (x^{\frac{2}{\alpha}} + y^{\frac{2}{\alpha}})^{\frac{\alpha}{\beta}} + z^{\frac{2}{\beta}} - 1 = 0 \qquad (18.17)$$

The angles α and β control the shape of superquadrics. Ellipsoids are special variants of superquadrics. If α equals β, Equation 18.17 can be strongly simplified and results in the implicit representation of a sphere. For use as tensor glyphs, the space of superquadrics is restricted to a subset defined by $\beta \leq \alpha \leq 1$. Superquadric tensor glyphs can now be defined with respect to the anisotropy measures c_l and c_p and a user-controlled sharpness parameter γ [KINDLMANN 2004b], according to Equation 18.18 and 18.19.

$$\alpha = (1 - c_p)^{\gamma} \qquad (18.18)$$
$$\beta = (1 - c_l)^{\gamma} \qquad (18.19)$$

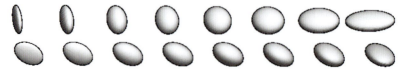

FIGURE 18.14 Ellipsoids in the lower image are perceived as similar, although they are actually quite different. The same ellipsoids are depicted in the upper image. Due to a different viewing direction, the ellipsoids can be better discriminated [KINDLMANN 2004b]. (Image courtesy GORDON KINDLMANN, Brigham and Women's Hospital Boston)

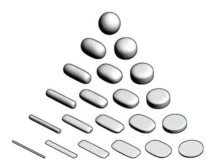

FIGURE 18.15   *Superquadric tensor glyphs in the barycentric space with sharpness factor 1.5 [KINDLMANN 2004b]. (Image courtesy GORDON KINDLMANN, Brigham and Women's Hospital Boston)*

The edge sharpness parameter γ controls how pronounced edges occur with growing values of c_p and c_l (see Fig. 18.15). The edge sharpness parameter is user-defined; however, some heuristics may be employed to come to a reasonable adjustment. Lower values for γ are appropriate in noisier regions of the data.

So far, no user study has been carried out to prove an advantage of this kind of tensor glyph. However, theoretical observations (recall the criteria discussed at the beginning of this section), as well as studies on the perception of differences in rendered superquadrics, make it very likely that superquadrics represent very good tensor geometries [SHAW et al. 1999].

18.5.3 VISUALIZATION OF TENSOR GLYPHS

For the visualization of tensor information in a selected slice, a 2D array of tensor glyphs is created.

Controlling Density   An important aspect of the visualization of tensor glyphs is their placement and scaling. Without special care, elongated glyphs in areas of high diffusion may overlap, resulting in visual clutter. On the other hand, if the glyphs are too sparsely spaced to ensure that no overlap occurs, the connection between them will be difficult to recognize. LAIDLAW et al. [1998] suggested normalizing the glyphs so that their largest extent is equal. This normalization gives a better overview of the anatomy and pathology. However, with this normalization, the magnitude of the diffusion tensor is no longer visually represented.

Jittered Placement   If tensor glyphs are rendered at node positions of the regular grid of the underlying DTI data, the structure of the grid becomes obvious and compromises image interpretation. Image interpretation may be considerably improved by slightly (randomly) disturbing tensor glyphs' positions. This technique is called *jittering* and is used, for example, in vector visualization with arrow-shaped glyphs. Figure 18.16 illustrates the effect of jittering for an easier interpretation of DTI data with ellipsoids.

3D Visualization   Glyphs are well suited for 2D visualization. However, for the investigation of the whole 3D data, additional or completely different visualization techniques are desirable. Glyphs fail to convey complex 3D data because they occlude each other and their connectivity is not visually represented. Taking into account the metrics defined in Section 18.3, the display of tensor glyphs may be restricted,

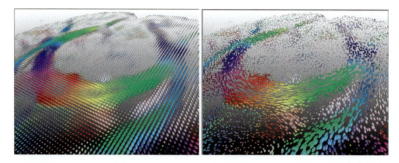

FIGURE 18.16   *In the left image, ellipsoids are centered at the original grid positions, thus highlighting the regular grid. By slight random translations (jittering), the distracting effect of the grid is removed. Glyphs are colored according to the principal eigenvector described in [SCHLUETER et al. 2005b]. (Images courtesy MATHIAS SCHLUETER and OLAF-KONRAD VERSE, MeVis Bremen)*

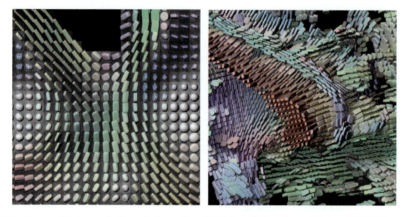

FIGURE 18.17   *Superquadric tensor glyphs applied to a slice of DTI data (left) and to a 3D view (right) [KINDLMANN 2004b]. (Images courtesy GORDON KINDLMANN, Brigham and Women's Hospital Boston)*

for example, to those regions with high mean diffusivity and strong anisotropy. Figure 18.17 illustrates the use of superquadrics for depicting a slice of DTI data of the human brain.

18.5.4 COLOR SCHEMES FOR TENSOR GLYPHS

Tensor glyphs are usually color-coded. Color may represent the orientation of the principal eigenvector as described in Section 18.4. It is desirable that the perceived difference of colors for adjacent glyphs are small if the major orientation differs only slightly. As we have discussed earlier in this chapter, the HSV color space is appropriate for this purpose. SCHLUETER et al. [2004] derived a color scheme that is very effective for the analysis of slices. This color scheme allows the encoding of anisotropy—for example, the anisotropy index (see Eq. 18.14)—as well as the projection of the largest eigenvector e_1 onto the current slice. The orientation of e_1 is mapped to the hue component, whereas the length of the projection is mapped to the saturation. Finally, the brightness further conveys the anisotropy. Figure 18.18 presents ellipsoidal tensor glyphs colored according to the described color scheme. Particularly for distant or partially occluded ellipsoids, color is welcome as an additional visualization parameter, although it does not present more information than the ellipsoid.

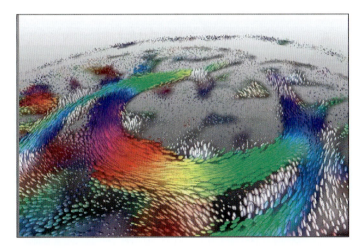

FIGURE 18.18 *Ellipsoids represent diffusion tensors in a selected oblique plane. The HSV color model is employed to color-code the major orientation of the data, its projection to the selected plane, and fractional anisotropy. (Image courtesy MATHIAS SCHLUETER, MeVis Bremen)*

18.6   DIRECT VOLUME RENDERING OF DIFFUSION TENSOR FIELDS

The visualization techniques discussed so far display the whole tensor information for a discrete set of locations. Direct volume rendering (DVR) conveys the continuous structure formed by varying attributes of the continuous scalar field [KINDLMANN 2004b]. As we have seen earlier, DVR also provides sophisticated facilities to explore 3D data. The use of clipping planes and slab rendering in particular allows a focused evaluation of arbitrary subvolumes. With appropriate opacity transfer functions, the visible portion of the data is adjusted so that the investigation of relevant data is feasible (recall Chap. 11). Moreover, transfer functions for gray values and opacity determine the contrast in the resulting visualizations. Transfer function design in traditional volume rendering refers to the scalar intensity values of the data. For DTI data, it is useful to provide a 1D domain as well. KINDLMANN et al. [2000] explored the applicability of volume rendering for DTI data and found that anisotropy measures are an appropriate basis for determining what is relevant in a visualization. Figure 18.19 illustrates the effectiveness of such visualizations. In the left part, the transfer functions (color and opacity) are shown, which guide the volume rendering.

18.7   FIBER TRACT MODELING

The extraction and visualization of fiber tracts is an essential feature of software assistance for the exploration of DTI data, since the investigation of fiber tract integrity and the connectivity of different functional regions are the principal motivation for DTI acquisition.

Before we describe approaches towards this goal, we need to stress the still experimental nature of these approaches. Fiber tract modeling is based on coarsely and discretely sampled data that exhibits considerable noise, and is exposed to various artifacts, as discussed in Section 18.2.1. Fiber tract modeling requires continuous tensor fields resulting from interpolation and approximation. As shown by BENGER et al. [2006], the derived directional information is only reliable in a rather small portion of the data.

Fiber tract extraction may lead to incoherent pathways and may pretend connectivity between brain regions that does not exist in reality. Therefore, any clinical application of these methods is only justifiable

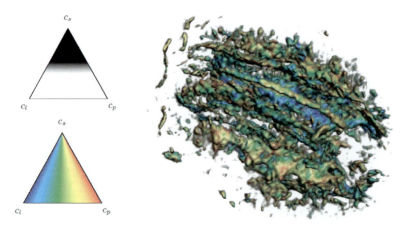

FIGURE 18.19 *Direct volume rendering of MRI DTI data. Opacity and color TF specification is based on anisotropy measures* [KINDLMANN et al. 2000]. *(Images courtesy GORDON KINDLMANN, Brigham and Women's Hospital Boston)*

if users with long-term experience carefully interpret these "connectivity" data and correlate them to the original data and to other, less abstract visualization techniques.

The principal diffusion directions are employed to compute the contiguous pathways of nerve fiber tracts. Fiber tracking usually starts by selecting a region of interest from which seedpoints are selected by the user or determined automatically. Starting from these seed voxels, adjacent voxels with similar principal diffusion direction are looked for. Fiber tracts are reconstructed by interpolating directions between voxels in the neighborhood of the current tracking position. Finally, fiber tracts are visualized by either *streamlines* or some kind of stream polygons. Streamlines and polygons have their origin in vector field analysis and visualization. These visualization techniques summarize information and provide a more abstract view than the glyph-based visualizations of DTI data, which depict each individual tensor. In the context of DTI visualization, streamline tracing is also referred to as *fiber tracking* [MORI and BARKER 1999] or *tractography* [BASSER and JONES 2002].

18.7.1 STREAMLINE COMPUTATION AND VISUALIZATION

Streamlines are based on directional tracking in vector fields. For tensor visualization, streamline computation is usually applied to the principal eigenvector e_1. Streamlines that follow the principal eigenvector in a tensor field are called *tensorlines* [DICKINSON 1989]. It should be noted that streamlines do not completely represent tensor information. Streamlines can be thought of as the trace of massless particles that are advected through the vector field V. Mathematically, streamlines are computed by integrating the vector field along a path s (see Fig. 18.20).

$$s = \int \vec{V} ds \qquad (18.20)$$

Integration is carried out along a path in forward and backward directions starting from an initial seedpoint (see Eq. 18.20). At each grid location, the streamline corresponds to the local vector $\vec{V}$. There is only one streamline at each position in V except at singularities, so-called critical points where the magnitude of the vector is zero. Such singularities represent sources, sinks, or center points of the vector fields enclosed by streamlines.

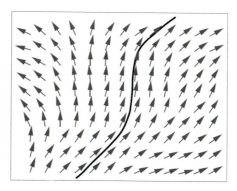

FIGURE 18.20 Sketch of a vector field and a particular streamline computed by numerical integration [HEGE and STALLING 1997]. (Image courtesy CHRISTIAN HEGE, Zuse-Institute Berlin)

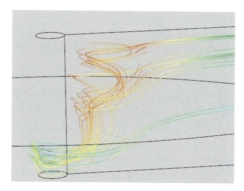

FIGURE 18.21 Example of a streamline visualization depicting airflow [SCHROEDER et al. 2001]. (Image courtesy WILL SCHROEDER, Kitware Inc., New York)

Due to the discrete nature of the data, the integral (see Eq. 18.20) is numerically approximated, for example, by Runge-Kutta or Euler schemes. Numerical approximations are based on a certain step size, in which higher accuracy is achieved with smaller step sizes. As usual, increased accuracy is achieved at the expense of higher computational effort; therefore, a reasonable trade-off is needed. An appropriate step size depends on the expected frequency of sudden changes.

The visualization of streamlines does not indicate the magnitude of a vector, which is often an essential feature. A common technique is to color-code streamlines, for example with low magnitudes corresponding to green and high magnitudes to red (see Fig. 18.21). In case of DTI data, color-coding could be applied to reveal the amount of diffusion along the direction of maximum diffusion. As a variant of this strategy, brightness can be employed to convey diffusion anisotropy. SCHLUETER et al. [2005a] used this variant to explore fiber tracts near malignant brain tumors. With this strategy, dark fiber tracts indicate fiber destruction.

For visualization with streamlines, different integration limits that affect the length of the resulting streamlines are used. In general, longer streamlines are preferred, since a few longer streamlines are easier to interpret than many small streamlines. On the other hand, longer streamlines exhibit larger errors, due to the accumulation of errors along the path. Streamlines are terminated either when the integration limits are reached, when a critical point with a very low magnitude of the local vector is encountered, or when the curvature of the streamline exceeds a defined threshold.

Adaptation of Streamlines for Tensor Data   DTI data have a low resolution. Therefore, numerical integration is accomplished with small step sizes, such as a quarter of a voxel cell size [MERHOF *et al.* 2005a]. A small step size is chosen to prevent important features (e.g., turn-offs), from being omitted. The evaluation of the tensor field with subvoxel accuracy requires proper interpolation schemes (recall Sect. 18.2.1).

For the visualization of fiber tracts, it is essential that only tensor values that exhibit strong anisotropy are combined (low anisotropy indicates an absence of fibers). Therefore, the diffusion anisotropy is a useful criterion to determine whether a fiber should be further tracked or terminated. Also, it is essential that maximum diffusivity exceeds a certain limit at any step of integration. According to ZHUKOV and BARR [2002], we can integrate these considerations in Algorithm 18.1.

In line 3, the diffusion tensor at point P is determined by interpolating the tensor field T with a filter kernel that corresponds to the diffusion ellipsoid. In line 4, a linear anisotropy measure is derived and compared with some threshold *epsilon* (line 5) to assess whether a significant linear diffusion occurs. If this is the case, the principal eigenvector e_1 of the tensor T_p at P is determined. Tracking is performed in forward and backward directions (opposing direction of e_1). A numerical integration scheme such as Runge-Kutta is employed to approximate the integrals. The two traces are connected with each other.

Below, the *fibertracking* procedure is outlined. Filtering again considers the ellipsoid of the tensor P. As an additional parameter, the current direction e_1 is considered. If the anisotropy at the new point P_n is above the threshold, it is added to the trace and fibertracking continues. The termination criterion of fibertracking may be a sophisticated combination of several measurements. At least a linear anisotropy measure should be taken into account.

Usually, fibertracking is modified to avoid very short fibers, because they are less reliable and are distracting in the visualization. These modifications are performed as a correction step after an initial determination of fibers. Also, some constraints with respect to the curvature are often included to avoid sudden changes of the fiber direction. These constraints are reasonable, as sudden changes often represent a wrong path.

ALGORITHM 18.1   Control fibertracking

```
 1. Region R ⇐ selected by user
 2. for all P in R do
 3.     Tₚ ⇐ filter(T, P, ellipsoid)
 4.     cₗ ⇐ anisotropy(Tₚ)
 5.     if cₗ > eps then
 6.         e₁ ⇐ direction(Tₚ)
 7.         trace₁ ⇐ fibertrace(P, e₁)
 8.         trace₂ ⇐ fibertrace(P, −e₁)
 9.         trace ⇐ trace₁ + trace₂
10.     end if
11. end for
```

Seeding Strategies   A crucial issue for visualizing tensor data with streamlines or any derived fibertracking is the appropriate seed strategy. Fibertracking easily results in visual clutter if the number and density of tensorlines is not controlled appropriately. Very simple strategies include regular seeding (tracing is started at regularly spaced locations) or random seeding (a predefined number of lines is traced at randomly selected positions). A trade-off between both is jittered regular seeding, in which the positions of regularly sampled seed voxels are slightly (randomly) disturbed. None of these simple techniques guarantees that the selected seeding points are in some way particularly relevant. Another strategy is manual seeding, in which the user decides where tracking starts. With this method, the user has fine-grained control. However, in case of patients with strongly abnormal anatomy (often due to pathologic changes), it might be very difficult to select appropriate seed regions.

With respect to assessing fiber directions and fiber connectivity, a desirable strategy is one based on anisotropy metrics. SHEN and PANG [2004] introduced this strategy and employed anisotropy measures, such as c_l, and a certain threshold value. The threshold is used to compute an isosurface that represents portions of the DTI data with the corresponding anisotropy level. Seedpoints are selected on these surfaces with some additional rules—for example, to ensure that the lines are not traced too close to each other.

Streamlines with Controlled Density   An essential aspect of streamline-based visualization is the density of the resulting streamlines. Since fiber tracts are diverging, very sparse as well as cluttered regions arise when the density is not controlled. In sparse regions, essential features might be omitted, whereas in cluttered regions, relevant features are hard to recognize.

In flow visualization, streamline density is controlled in the following way: an initial streamline is tracked and new seedpoints are chosen in a certain distance d_{seed}. Starting from these new seedpoints, streamlines are tracked forward and backward until the distance to an existing streamline falls below the desired minimum distance d_{sep} [JOBARD and LEFER 1997]. While d_{sep} is provided by the user, d_{seed} is automatically determined and must be higher than d_{sep}.

These techniques have been adapted for fibertracking [VILANOVA et al. 2004, MERHOF et al. 2005b]. With respect to efficiency and accuracy, distances may be computed in different resolutions along the streamlines. An efficient 3D implementation of evenly spaced streamlines was presented in [MERHOF et al. 2005b] (see Fig. 18.22). Instead of a global distance, the streamline density might be automatically adapted to an anisotropy metric with higher density in regions with major white matter tracts (see Fig. 18.23).

ALGORITHM 18.2   Fibertrace (P, e_1)

1. $trace \Rightarrow add(P)$
2. repeat
3. $P_n \Leftarrow integrate_{forward}(P, e_1, step_{size})$
4. $T_p \Leftarrow filter(T, P_n, ellipsoid, e_1)$
5. $c_l \Leftarrow anisotropy(T_p)$
6.   if $c_l > eps$ then
7. $trace \Rightarrow add(P_n)$
8. $P \Leftarrow P_n$
9. $e_1 \Leftarrow direction(P)$
10.   end if
11. until $c_l < eps$

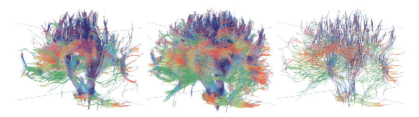

FIGURE 18.22 *Comparison of standard fibertracking (left) with even streamline placement. In the middle, d_{sep} equals 1.5 mm, and in the right image, d_{sep} equals 5 mm* [MERHOF et al. 2005b]. *(Image courtesy DORIT MERHOF, University Erlangen-Nuremberg)*

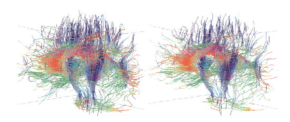

FIGURE 18.23 *Adaptive streamline placement with higher density in regions with higher fractional anisotropy. In the left image, the distance varies from 0.5 to 3 mm; in the right image from 0.5 to 5 mm* [MERHOF et al. 2005b]. *(Image courtesy DORIT MERHOF, University Erlangen-Nuremberg)*

Evaluating Fiber Segments Instead of Individual Voxels Due to the noisy character of DTI data, fibertracking can unreliably terminate because at a single voxel the computed linear diffusion is very low. This low diffusion may be due to the averaging property of the partial volume effects and does not reliably represent an area with low diffusion. As an example, if diverging fibers meet in the volume represented by a voxel, the average diffusion may be low although there is actually strong diffusion.

Instead of single voxels, moving averages for anisotropy and curvature should be evaluated in a small *fiber window* (a portion of the fiber centered at the current position). In Algorithm 18.1, the anisotropy test of the current voxel should be replaced by considering a fiber window. SCHLUETER et al. [2005a] demonstrate that this leads to more robust tracking, especially in the vicinity of white matter lesions.

Illumination of Streamlines Streamlines, representing fiber tracts, are usually color-coded. The color-coding strategies are similar to the strategies described for encoding directional information in slice-based visualizations (recall Sect. 18.4). There is some debate as to whether the visualization of fibers benefits from applying a light model to the streamlines. A light model changes the brightness of colors and makes the relation between colors and the depicted anisotropy values more difficult to recognize. On the other hand, shading information is usually thought of as improving spatial orientation. An example of both options is shown in Figure 18.24, which compares the visualization of fibers with and without illumination. As a consequence of this debate, it might be the best strategy to allow the user to turn lighting on and off.

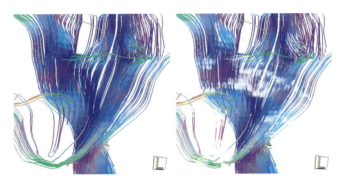

FIGURE 18.24   *Comparison of fiber visualization without (left) and with (right) illumination* [MERHOF *et al. 2005a*]. *(Image courtesy* DORIT MERHOF, *University Erlangen-Nuremberg)*

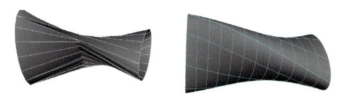

FIGURE 18.25   *Without subdividing the path, linear interpolation between cross-sectional profiles may lead to self-intersections (left). With appropriate subdivision, this can be effectively avoided (right)* [REINA *et al. 2006*]. *(Image courtesy* GUIDO RAINA, *University of Stuttgart)*

18.7.2 HYPERSTREAMLINES AND STREAM SURFACES

Hyperstreamlines are developed to convey more information on the tensor data than streamlines that actually restrict the information presented to the direction of the principal eigenvector. Features such as torsion or minor eigenvalues are not conveyed with streamlines.

Hyperstreamlines owe their name to the analogy of streamlines and were designed as a special visualization technique developed for second-order tensor fields [DELMARCELLE and HESSELINK 1992]. Similar to streamlines, hyperstreamlines follow the diffusion from some seedpoints. Instead of connecting the points determined by integration with a line, hyperstreamlines sweep a polygon along the detected path. The polygon is stretched in a transverse plane to reflect the magnitude of the other eigenvalues. Different graphics primitives may be used to encode the magnitude of the minor eigenvalues (λ_2 and λ_3) in the cross section. DELMARCELLE and HESSELINK [1992] consider stretching a circle at every point to form an ellipse and rendering a cross with the length of the two lines conveying the related magnitudes. The first variant leads to tube-shaped hyperstreamlines, whereas the latter leads to a helix. An appropriate trade-off between quality and speed has to be made when the graphics primitive is mapped to a polygon. REINA *et al.* [2006] suggest using 16 vertices to represent the cross section at each sampling point. It might be necessary to subdivide the hyperstreamline (computation of additional profiles along the path) in cases where there is strong torsion (see Fig. 18.25). The number of the required additional profiles can be derived from the angle between the two major eigenvectors at consecutive points.

If the hyperstreamline diameters vary strongly, they may overlap each other. It is therefore reasonable to normalize the diameters or to scale the diameters such that a certain limit is not exceeded.

Streamsurfaces Streamsurfaces are primarily used to depict tensor information in case the diffusion is predominantly planar. In such regions, λ_1 and λ_2 define a plane. Streamlines and streamsurfaces can be combined in a natural way to indicate linear as well as planar diffusion (see Fig. 18.26). In a seed region, streamlines are tracked. If the streamlines reach voxels with primarily planar diffusion, streamline tracking is not terminated. Instead, a streamsurface is generated. Streamline tracking is continued behind the region with primarily planar diffusion.

Streamlines Versus Streamtubes The visualization of fibers through streamlines has the advantage of being a fast method, due to low geometric complexity. However, lines with more than one pixel suffer from gaps in highly curved areas. Depth perception is not supported when lines with a constant density are employed [MERHOF et al. 2006]. Streamtubes, on the other hand, provide a better visual quality with the depth cues of a shaded surface visualization at the expense of higher rendering load. MERHOF et al. [2006] presented a new technique that combines the quality of streamtubes with the performance of streamlines. They employed triangle strips with only two triangles per segment to represent the fiber (see Fig. 18.27 (left)). The triangles are textured so that they appear as shaded surfaces (see Fig. 18.27 (right)).

Multimodal Visualization Often DTI data are explored together with other anatomical data. The visualization of information derived from several datasets requires restriction of the visualization to relevant portions or properties. With respect to DTI data, an abstract or aggregated visualization, such as fibertracking results, is a viable option.

Anatomical image data are also used for the diagnosis, since they provide a higher spatial resolution. The integration of fused multimodal visualizations requires *a priori* registration. Instead of discussing all

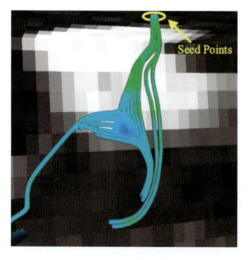

FIGURE 18.26 *Combining streamlines and streamsurfaces to visualize primarily linear and planar diffusion [VILANOVA et al. 2004]. (Image courtesy ANNA VILANOVA, Technical University of Eindhoven)*

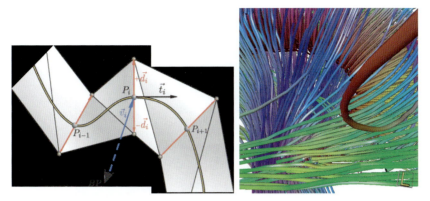

FIGURE 18.27 *Efficient visualization of DTI fibers with triangle strips. Instead of representing a tube (with eight triangles), two textured triangles oriented towards the viewer are used to represent each segment of the fiber* [MERHOF et al. 2006]. *(Image courtesy* DORIT MERHOF, *University Erlangen-Nuremberg)*

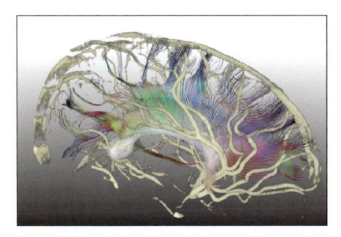

FIGURE 18.28 *DTI fibertracking combined with vascular structures extracted from MRI data. (Image courtesy* MATHIAS SCHLUETER *and* HORST K. HAHN, *MeVis Bremen)*

options to integrate DTI-based visualizations with other data, we present two examples to illustrate the expressiveness of such visualizations. Figure 18.28 integrates MRI angiography data with the results of fibertracking from DTI data. Figure 18.29 integrates fibertracking results with a volume rendering of T1-weighted MRI data.

Integration of Anatomical Landmarks   Three-dimensional visualizations of diffusion tensor data might benefit from the integration of some landmarks that serve as anatomical context. The eyes as well as the ventricles are appropriate landmarks for brain images. WÜNSCHE [2004b] showed that eyes and ventricles could be identified and delineated robustly by means of their diffusion characteristics. In Figure 18.30, these landmarks enhance a visualization of fiber tracts.

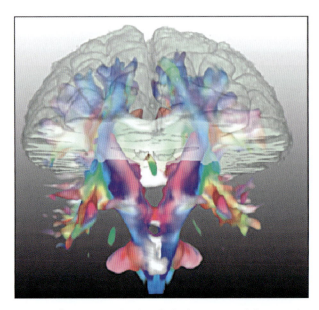

FIGURE 18.29 *Color-coded data from DTI combined with the brain extracted from T1 data. (Image courtesy* MATHIAS SCHLUETER, *MeVis Bremen)*

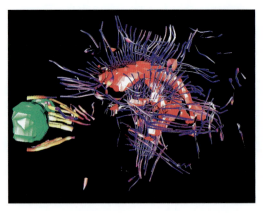

FIGURE 18.30 *Integration of eyes and ventricles as landmarks to support the evaluation of the fiber tracts* [WÜNSCHE 2004b]. *(Image courtesy* BURKHARD WÜNSCHE, *University of Auckland)*

18.8   EXPLORATION OF FIBER TRACTS THROUGH CLUSTERING

So far, we have discussed how individual tensorlines are determined and visualized as representations of fiber tracts. Tensorlines are more aggregate compared to visualizations of individual measurements. From a surgical point of view, single streamlines are still of minor interest. Instead, whole fiber bundles are essential for surgical planning [NIMSKY et al. 2005a].

The computation of clusters of tensorlines yields an even more abstract visualization. With clustering information, DTI data can be explored at different levels of detail: a global view includes the clusters and local views show the fibers of selected clusters [MOBERTS 2005]. With respect to the problems of tracking fibers in noisy low-resolution data, the major problem of any clustering technique is its dependency on fibertracking results.

Clustering or *bundling* is motivated by knowledge of neuroanatomy and driven by clinical applications. Reliable assessments of white matter connectivity and fiber disruption are very difficult to achieve by exploring individual tensorlines alone [GERIG et al. 2004]. Fiber bundles that correspond to known structures, such as the corpus callosum or the pyramidal tract, are the basis for further analysis, such as the exploration of anisotropy measures along a fiber bundle.

Clustering fiber tracts is a special example of the general clustering task, where n-dimensional data are grouped to support a further analysis. Clustering data includes a metric to evaluate the proximity of data. The core of clustering is an algorithm that summarizes elements to clusters and lower level clusters to higher level clusters. The special clustering problem considered here has some characteristic features that are essential in the selection of proximity metrics and clustering algorithms. Fiber bundles occur in various shapes and sizes. Some fiber bundles are composed of a few long fibers forming a tube structure, whereas other fiber bundles contain more smaller bundles that diverge.

Based on Figure 18.31, some observations essential for clustering fibers can be derived [MOBERTS 2005]:

- A pair of fibers from the same bundle that are direct neighbors are separated by a small distance and have a similar shape.
- A pair of fibers from the same bundle that are not direct neighbors can have very different shapes. However, between dissimilar and distant fibers from the same bundle, there are other bundles with intermediate shapes. As a consequence, there is a smooth shape transition between fibers from the same bundle.

It must also be considered that clinical DTI data are noisy, thus exhibiting other problems. These problems include missing parts of bundles, whereas other pathways detected in the fibertracking stage are erroneous.

18.8.1 PROXIMITY METRICS FOR CLUSTERING

Clustering fibers is based on a proximity metric that allows the assessment of the similarity of pairs of fibers. Proximity metrics either quantify similarity (high values indicate that the fibers are almost equal) or dissimilarity (high values indicate that the fibers differ strongly). They are applied to individual fibers or to bundles to decide whether they should be merged. Since the tensor lines represent fibers, we refer to them by F.

FIGURE 18.31   *Schematic picture depicting white matter bundles of the brain. The right view presents a closeup of the left view. Fibers of one anatomic structure might differ considerably in shape and size* [BRUN et al. 2003]. *(Image courtesy* ANDERS BRUN, *Linköping University)*

All proximity metrics that have been evaluated for fiber clustering are symmetric, yielding the same value for the pairs of fibers (F_i, F_j) and (F_j, F_i). Each tensorline F_i is a 3D curve represented by a set of points p_k. With distance-based metrics, F_i and F_j are regarded as belonging to the same bundle if a distance $d(F_i, F_j)$ is below a threshold d. There are many metrics to characterize the distance between two 3D curves. Some of them were introduced in Section 5.8 and used to validate segmentation and vessel visualization techniques.

The closest distance between bundles F_i, F_j relates to a pair of points $(p_{ik} \in F_i, p_{jl} \in F_j)$ for which the distance is minimal. In general, this metric is not appropriate as the proximity metric for DTI clustering, as the closest distance between two bundles is zero if they converge, diverge, or cross. Figure 18.31 contains several distinct bundles in which individual fibers overlap. These fibers would act as a "bridge," and the bundles would be erroneously merged. Other global distance measures are the mean of closest point distances and the Hausdorff distance. The Hausdorff metric is relevant here, because it allows to remove outliers (where the Hausdorff distance is large). All global distance measures result in large distances for fibers of different lengths and for diverging fibers. The Hausdorff distance between fibers of different lengths or between fibers that are very close but diverge at some point are large, although such fibers might well belong to the same cluster. The closest distance is not expressive for clustering, since fibers may diverge strongly even if their closest distance is small. The average closest distance has the advantage that information concerning the whole fibers F_i and F_j is considered.

Advanced Proximity Metrics   Due to the problems of simple proximity metrics, more advanced metrics have been explored. DING et al. [2001b] suggested a metric based on a subdivision of fibers into segments. These segments of the fibers F_i and F_j are then analyzed to find corresponding segments, and distance metrics are applied to pairs of corresponding segments. As GERIG et al. [2004] showed, a suitable metric integrates several criteria instead of using a single one. It cannot be expected that one (composed) similarity metric is appropriate in all cases. Therefore, a tool to assist in the exploration of DTI data should also allow the user to adjust the weights of all criteria that are part of the similarity metric.

In addition to applying distance measurements between points on the curve, similarity is also based on some parameters that characterize the fibers as entire curves. Examples are the distances between the center of gravity, and length or curvature information (average mean curvature along a path).

18.8.2 CLUSTERING ALGORITHMS

Clustering imposes a classification on the data. Based on a proximity metric, fibers are clustered. The evaluation of the metric leads to a *proximity matrix*, where for each pair of items the proximity is recorded.

Clustering algorithms differ with respect to their result. *Hierarchical clustering* algorithms generate a nested hierarchy of partitions. At different levels of the hierarchy, different numbers of clusters arise. *Partitioning algorithms*, on the other hand, produce a single partitioning of the data. Clustering algorithms may assign each element to exactly one cluster (hard clustering) or compute a membership probability. The latter class of algorithms is referred to as *fuzzy clustering*. For the analysis of fiber tracts, hierarchical and partitioning algorithms have been explored. Fuzzy clustering, however, is not particularly useful, neither for the subsequent visualization nor for the quantitative analysis. Hard clustering algorithms assign a label to each item in the data to represent the (low level) cluster to which it belongs.

Hierarchical Clustering   The basic strategy for hierarchical clustering is as follows:

1   Each item is regarded as an individual cluster.
2   The two most similar clusters (with respect to the proximity metrics) are merged.
3   The second step is repeated until only one cluster remains.

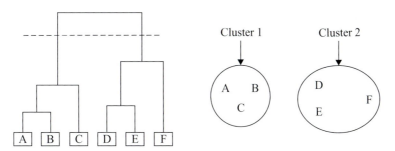

FIGURE 18.32 *A graph represents the results of hierarchical clustering (left image). With a cut (see the dotted line) a particular classification with two cluster results (right)* [MOBERTS 2005]. *(Image courtesy* ANNA VILANOVA, *Technical University of Eindhoven)*

Figure 18.32 illustrates hierarchical clustering.

Two simple and popular methods for the merge step are *single linking* and *complete linking*. Single linking considers the closest pair of items, whereas complete linking considers the maximum distance between a pair of items. Despite its problems with noisy data, single linking has been used in most cases for clustering fiber tracts [ZHANG *et al.* 2003].

Partitional Clustering This class of clustering algorithms is also relevant for the analysis of fiber data because the known fiber pathways are not hierarchically organized. COROUGE and GOUTTARD [2004] presented an algorithm that propagates cluster labels to closest neighbors. The algorithm assigns each unlabeled fiber to the cluster of its closest neighbor if the proximity metric is above a specific threshold. This algorithm is well suited for the properties of DTI fibers, because it can in principle collect all fibers of a bundle, even if distant fibers are strongly different. The selection of the threshold determines how many clusters are actually generated.

MOBERTS *et al.* [2005] recently evaluated *shared nearest neighbor clustering* [ERTÖZ *et al.* 2003] for clustering fiber data. This algorithm is particularly useful for clustering items of different size and shape, even in noisy data. It works as follows [MOBERTS *et al.* 2005]:

1 A k nearest neighbor graph (kNNG) is constructed from the proximity matrix. In this graph, nodes represent items (individual fibers) and edges connect nodes with their k nearest neighbors.
2 A shared nearest neighbor graph (SNNG) is a weighted graph constructed from kNNG. Edges in SNNG exist only between items that belong to each others' shared neighbors. More precisely, if p belongs to the k closest neighbors of q, and q belongs to the k closest neighbors of p, they are connected through an edge. Depending on the position of p in q's nearest neighbor list and q in p's nearest neighbor list, a weighting factor is computed to differentiate between close and far nearest neighbors.
3 Clusters are obtained by removing edges from SNNG if their weight is below a threshold. This threshold determines the number of resulting clusters.

18.8.3 VISUALIZATION AND QUANTIFICATION OF FIBER BUNDLES

Clustering may be used for a variety of purposes. With respect to visualization, it might be useful to restrict the visible fibers to those that belong to a bundle with a certain minimum number of fibers. This restriction is motivated by the fact that fibers without adjacent similar fibers have a high probability of being erroneously detected. Figure 18.33 compares tensorlines and clustering results.

FIGURE 18.33 *Clustering of sets of tensorlines (left) to fiber bundles (right) in the area of the corticospinal tract. It was specified that two clusters (left and right corticospinal tract) should be looked for. Tensorlines that were not considered as members of the two largest clusters were removed. The curve distance metric introduced by DING et al. [2001a] has been modified in this particular cluster algorithm [GERIG et al. 2004]. (Image courtesy GUIDO GERIG, University of North Carolina at Chapel Hill)*

Besides the visualization, fiber bundles may be analyzed with respect to their anisotropy properties. GERIG et al. [2004] found that anisotropy significantly changes along bundles but crosses them.

A quantitative analysis of fiber bundles is often more interesting than the quantification of individual fibers. Diffusion parameters such as mean diffusivity along and perpendicular to the major fiber direction, as well as geometric properties such as mean curvature, are relevant for neuroanatomic studies [COROUGE and GOUTTARD 2004].

Visualization of Fiber Bundles   There are different strategies for visualizing fiber bundles. The general strategy is to generate some kind of hull to "wrap" a bundle [DING et al. 2001a]. The hull representing a bundle may be derived by computing a centerline and cross sections at different locations on the centerline. In principle, different geometries may be employed to visualize the hull. Graphics primitives, such as cylinders or ellipsoids, may be fitted along the centerline—very similar to model-based visualizations of vascular structures (recall Sect. 14.3). The resulting visualizations, however, may strongly differ from the detected fibers.

Another, more accurate visualization was recently introduced [ENDERS et al. 2005]. In Figure 18.34, the visualization of the optical and nerve tract are shown. Instead of graphics primitives, boundary polygons are defined in planes orthogonal to the skeleton. Boundary polygons are defined by connecting the intersections of fibers with the cross-sectional area perpendicular to the centerline at a particular sampling point. These boundary polygons may be immediately visualized as lines or connected with adjacent polygons to form surfaces. As ENDERS et al. [2005] pointed out, these boundary polygons should not be directly used for the visualization. Instead, the convex hull, as a simpler representation, should be employed. For each tract, two visualizations have been generated, comprising different portions of the fibers.

Ideally, the visualization of a fiber bundle should reflect the uncertainty involved in fiber tract determination. This can be achieved by visualizing results generated with slightly different anisotropy thresholds in fibertracking or slightly modified parameters of the clustering algorithm. A transparent overlay of two or three such surfaces is an expressive visualization of such an analysis. In addition, a combination of individual fibers and a transparent hull is expressive, since it conveys how individual lines have been summarized to clusters (see Fig. 18.35). While these visualization options are certainly valuable, validation studies and more experience are needed to provide a technical and clinical definition of safety margins [NIMSKY et al. 2006].

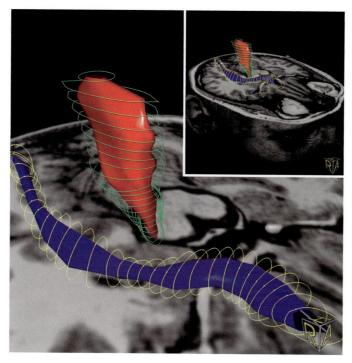

FIGURE 18.34 *Combination of direct volume rendering of high-resolution MRI T1 data with pyramidal (red) and optic tract (blue). The rings around the surface represent more defensive approximations. For surgical planning, more safety is achieved if the region inside the rings is preserved [ENDERS et al. 2005]. (Image courtesy FRANK ENDERS, University Erlangen-Nuremberg)*

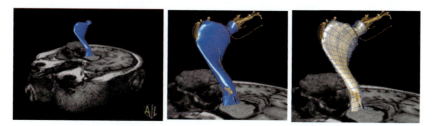

FIGURE 18.35 *A fiber bundle is shown as an opaque surface (left), as an opaque surface combined with individual fibers (middle), and as a combination of a transparent surface and rings with individual fibers [ENDERS et al. 2005]. (Images courtesy FRANK ENDERS, University Erlangen-Nuremberg)*

Discussion   The convex hull, however, might overestimate the fiber strongly—for example, if it exhibits a banana shape. Tighter (nonconvex) hulls, such as alpha shapes [EDELSBRUNNER and MÜCKE 1994], are a better choice. Alpha shapes are generalizations of the convex hull of the point set. Alpha shapes formalize the notion of shape, and for a varying parameter α, they range from crude to fine shapes. The crudest shape is the convex hull itself, which is obtained for large values of α. As α decreases, the shape shrinks and develops cavities. Another problem of the described hulls is their restriction to nonbranching fibers.

It is not clear how the visualization can be generalized to faithfully represent the shapes of fibers near branchings.

18.8.4 VALIDATION OF FIBER CLUSTERING

Validation is a crucial issue, in particular if fiber clustering is to be used for neurosurgery planning and monitoring. As a first step towards validation, two terms are essential to characterize the quality of a clustering technique: *completeness* and *correctness* [MOBERTS et al. 2005]. Maximum completeness is achieved if all fibers that belong to a particular nerve tract are assigned to this nerve tract. Correctness characterizes whether all fibers assigned to a particular nerve tract really belong to that nerve tract. Incorrect fibers might be composed of parts that belong to different anatomic structures. The relation between correctness and completeness is exactly the same as the relation between sensitivity and specificity that characterizes diagnostic processes. Maximum completeness could be easily achieved by considering all fibers as one cluster; correctness in this case is very low. The other extreme would be to assign each fiber to a different cluster—resulting in maximum correctness but very low completeness. Figure 18.36 compares a correct, an incorrect, and an incomplete clustering result. Incorrectness and incompleteness should not be weighted equally. Incomplete but correct results can be easily improved by marking clusters that belong together. Incorrect results, on the other hand, are difficult to correct, since many individual fibers have to be selected and assigned to another cluster [MOBERTS 2005].

Validation of clustering algorithms requires a gold standard. Similar to the gold standard used for the validation of segmentation algorithms, the classification of an expert is used. The goal of validation processes is to characterize proximity metrics and clustering algorithms with respect to their influence on completeness and correctness. Most of these algorithms have parameters that allow adjustment of the trade-off between completeness and correctness. If one parameter, such as the number of desired clusters, is considered, a curve arises that depicts the influence of this parameter on completeness and correctness. These curves allow comparisons between different algorithms and metrics.

Recently, MOBERTS et al. [2005] presented a framework for validating clustering algorithms and compared basic proximity metrics and clustering algorithms by means of this framework. Besides correctness and completeness, they discussed a variety of other metrics to evaluate clustering approaches. The shared nearest neighbor clustering turned out to be the best algorithm. Their results should be regarded as preliminary, as they are based on only a few neuroanatomic structures. Nevertheless, their framework is sound and substantial.

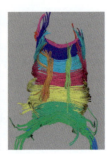

FIGURE 18.36 *The correct clustering result provided by a physician (left) compared with an incorrect (middle) and an incomplete (right) clustering. While the incomplete result could be easily modified in the correct result, the correction of the incorrect result requires considerably more interaction* [MOBERTS et al. 2005]. *(Image courtesy ANNA VILANOVA, Technical University of Eindhoven)*

18.9   SOFTWARE TOOLS FOR THE EXPLORATION OF DTI DATA

Software for effectively supporting DTI data exploration has to provide a broad spectrum of functionality. The computation of the tensor data from the series of diffusion-weighted image data must be supported, and image filtering and interpolation techniques must be provided. With respect to analyzing and visualizing the tensor data, the following features should be available [GERIG et al. 2004]:

- Selection of orthogonal and oblique slices
- Integration of anatomic data (base image) and DTI-based color maps, such as fractional anisotropy maps
- Appropriate color scales to convey diffusivity and anisotropy measures
- Numeric evaluation of different diffusion parameters

The last requirement is motivated by the desire to analyze the relation between major white matter tracts and a tumor, in order to understand the amount of tumor invasion [NIMSKY et al. 2006]. With respect to fibertracking, some additional features are necessary:

- Selection of an ROI in oblique and orthogonal slices as well as in 3D, which comprises seedpoints for fibertracking
- Adjustment of termination criteria for fibertracking
- Statistical analysis of fiber tracts with respect to diffusion properties, e.g., fractional anisotropy and ADC

For fiber clustering, another set of features is essential:

- Selection of a proximity metric
- Selection of a clustering algorithm
- Interactive manipulation of clustering results
- Visualization of fiber clusters
- Quantification of anisotropy along fiber bundles

A few years ago, the analysis and visualization of DTI data was a pure research topic. Currently, modern MRI scanners support DTI acquisition with predefined image sequences. Commercial software for surgery planning, such as those from the SIEMENS SYNGO family, provide *task cards* dedicated to the analysis of DTI data [NIMSKY et al. 2006] and provide roughly the functionality discussed above.

18.10   SUMMARY

In this chapter, we discussed the acquisition, processing, quantification, and visualization of diffusion tensor images. These types of MRI images record directional information with respect to the diffusion of water molecules. DTI is able to provide unique information concerning the architecture and microstructure of tissue, which turned out to be essential for assessing abnormalities in case of a variety of relevant neurologic diseases. However, many theoretical studies underlined "how much care is necessary to interpret DTI data properly and infer accurate information" [BIHAN et al. 2001].

We encountered a new class of techniques related to the visualization of symmetric 3 × 3 tensors. To illustrate the relevance of these visualizations, we discussed neuroanatomy and applications of DTI. Glyph-based visualization techniques and techniques based on streamlines have also been presented. Both families of visualization techniques have their merits and applications. Glyph-based techniques are superior for the local assessment of white matter integrity, which is essential for the diagnosis of neurodegenerative diseases and for evaluating tumor infiltration. On the other hand, streamline-based visualizations of fiber tracts give a better overview. For surgery planning, for example in the vicinity of brain tumors, fiber clustering and visualization of appropriate hull representations is even more useful. In intraoperative settings, time for the exploration of images is strongly limited. Therefore, the most abstract visual representation, namely 3D hull representations, is favored. Detailed representations such as fractional anisotropy maps are simply not usable [NIMSKY et al. 2006].

The exploration of DTI data is not a pure visualization problem. Instead, image analysis plays a crucial role in preprocessing the data to support appropriate visualization techniques. Diffusion tensor imaging is usually complemented by other modalities that better depict the morphology and anatomy. Software assistants for the exploration of DTI data, therefore, should support the integration of such data.

Clinical experiences indicate that much care is necessary to avoid presenting too much information simultaneously. The user study carried out by NIMSKY et al. [2006] indicated that neurosurgeons want to see only the most important fiber tract for a particular intervention. This is in contrast to the images produced by visualization researchers, in which many fiber tracts are shown simultaneously.

Outlook Despite the promising results, there are plenty of open research questions in DTI acquisition, analysis, and visualization. Such improvements will permit DTI identification of some relevant nerve tracts that are currently missed due to their small size.

Further research will likely improve image quality with respect to resolution, distortion, and signal-to-noise ratio. Several aspects of DTI, including the selection of gradient directions and the b-factor, need more thorough investigation. Currently, it is extremely difficult to carry out investigations that include multiple scanners from different sites, due to the amount of artifacts in DTI data. As BASSER and JONES [2002] point out, phantoms that are well characterized are essential in developing imaging techniques that lead to comparable image data.

An essential step towards quality measurements of tensor fits has been achieved by BENGER et al. [2006]. They derived methods to evaluate the reliability of the major diffusion direction that underlies most visualization techniques. Thus, they can encode uncertainty directly into the visualization or restrict the use of visualization techniques relying on the major direction to subsets of the data.

Validation is a crucial issue, in particular for fibertracking algorithms. Robust fibertracking in the vicinity of fiber tracts' bifurcations is an essential problem. The whole pipeline of analysis steps needs to be rigorously analyzed with respect to the errors that occur. Clinical research will focus on a better understanding of the role of DTI in diagnosis and monitoring. Finally, dedicated software assistants that support the exploration of DTI data with respect to specific diagnostic questions or treatment decisions are required. Higher order tensor representations will be likely explored to disambiguate areas where no major diffusion direction can be reliably identified. First studies on higher order tensor fields are described in [HLAWITSCHKA and SCHEUERMANN 2005].

FURTHER READING

For complex diagnostic questions and therapy decisions, DTI data are complemented by conventional (anatomic) MRI data and functional MRI. To support neurosurgical interventions, intraoperative MRI may be fused with DTI [TALOS et al. 2003]. VILANOVA et al. [2005] gave a broad overview of visualization techniques and applications of DTI, providing many additional references in particular for neuroanatomic studies and diagnostic procedures based on DTI.

Pajevic et al. [2005] and Weickert [2005] described dedicate interpolation techniques based on NURBS (non-uniform rational b-splines) and partial differential equations respectively. Schlueter et al. [2005a] discussed brain tumor phantoms and their application to DTI. We chose only a selection of visualization techniques for this chapter. It might be inspiring to look at some other techniques, such as anisotropy modulated line integral convolutions [Wünsche, 2004a], or slice-based visualization based on concepts from oil-paintings, as introduced in [Laidlaw et al. 1998]. Furthermore, a large variety of tensor icons has been developed; they differ in shape and color mapping, as an example, see Westin et al. [1999].

Impressive visualizations might be generated by segmenting fiber tracts. Segmentation of tensor data is a challenging task that can be regarded as a clustering problem. Promising results are documented in [Brun et al. 2004]. As an example for a general textbook on cluster analysis, we recommend [Jain and Dubes 1988].

Merhof et al. [2004] applied nonlinear registration techniques to fuse diffusion tensor data with a standard MRI dataset in order to support neurosurgery planning. Neuroanatomy is relevant for understanding DTI applications. Mamata et al. [2002] provided a detailed relation between DTI and neuroanatomy. Readers with more interest in neuroanatomy are referred to in [DeArmond et al. 1989, Carpenter 1996]. Tensor field visualization is based on tensor field and vector field analysis. Readers interested in these fundamentals are referred to in [Kendall 1977, Young 1978].

In this chapter, we focused on diffusion tensor data to assess brain tissue and fiber tract connectivity. There is also a growing interest in diffusion tensor imaging for diagnosis of heart diseases (see [Wünsche 2004b]). DTI is employed in particular for characterizing cardiac muscle tissue architecture.

PART V

Application Areas and Case Studies

The last part of the book is devoted to a comprehensive case study and special application areas. In Chapter 19, we describe liver surgery planning by means of carefully designed computer support. We decided to discuss a special example instead of giving general overview on intervention planning. Intervention planning is usually highly specialized, and only a few aspects are general across many different examples. The imaging modalities on which the planning process is based are different; the segmentation target structures, which guide the selection of image analysis methods, are strongly different; and the therapeutic decisions in particular are highly specialized and complex. At an abstract level, we can only state, "The relevant surgical decisions should be carefully analyzed and directly supported." The chapter on liver surgery planning discusses the whole process of designing, evaluating, and refining computer support for a group of related surgical interventions.

We also discuss medical education as a special application area (see Chap. 20). In particular, anatomy and surgery education benefits from 3D visualizations of medical volume data and related symbolic information. The integration of image data with symbolic information, such as labels and anatomic classification, is a challenge for educational systems. Beside static images and interactive manipulation of 3D visualizations and knowledge bases, predefined image sequences have a role in medical education. We discuss the efficient authoring of such animations.

Chapter 19

Image Analysis and Visualization for Liver Surgery Planning

In this chapter, we do not introduce further visualization techniques. Instead, we present an encompassing case study and describe how a variety of the techniques introduced in previous chapters are combined to solve clinically relevant problems in intervention planning. These problems are related to liver surgery, which is a demanding surgical discipline because the liver is characterized by a complex vascular architecture that surgeons have to consider.[1] Similar to other areas of computer-assisted surgery planning, image analysis, visualization, and interaction techniques have to be carefully combined. In this chapter, the reader is confronted with many details of surgical strategies. This may be surprising; however, it is necessary to understand which aspects have to be considered for developing appropriate computer support. We discuss image analysis and visualization with respect to the following clinical questions:

- **Treatment of liver carcinoma.** If patients suffer from a malignant liver disease (e.g., primary tumors or metastases from colorectal cancer), the question arises whether they may be treated by a surgical resection or by thermoablation (tumor destruction by local application of heat, e.g., by laser beams). The feasibility of these treatments depends primarily on the spatial relations between the tumors and major hepatic vessels.
- **Live-donor liver transplantation (LDLT).** A healthy voluntary donor gives a part of his or her liver to a recipient who is in urgent need of a transplant due to a severe liver disease. These transplantations require careful planning to decide on appropriate resection strategies for splitting the liver, as well as volumetric calculations to find out whether both parts of the liver will work properly.

Many aspects of the necessary computer support are similar for the two applications; however, slight differences must be considered for a successful and clinically acceptable solution. With respect to the first question, it is essential and sometimes very difficult to find out whether a tumor is resectable. Concerning the second problem, the most important question is whether a person is appropriate as a donor, which means that the risk for the donor must be kept low. The risk depends strongly on the vascular architecture and on volumetric considerations that predict the portion of functional liver parenchyma that remains in the patient. Often, several persons are evaluated concerning their suitability as a donor. Supporting this donor selection process is the most important goal of computer support for these interventions.

Computer support for liver surgery planning has to consider the radiological data of an individual patient and has to start with image analysis. Fast and robust segmentation of the relevant intrahepatic structures are of primary importance. Based on the image analysis results, a 3D model of the individual patient is created and employed for intervention planning. Among the techniques relevant for liver surgery planning are: image analysis (see Chap. 5), virtual resection (see Chap. 12), measures (see Chap. 13),

---

1 Liver surgery developed later than other parts of abdominal surgery due to severe problems from hemostasis.

and high-quality visualization of vasculature (see Chap. 14). The focus of this chapter is the integration of algorithms in software systems to support pretherapeutic decisions.

The research described in this chapter was initiated by the mathematician Prof. PEITGEN and the radiologist Prof. KLOSE in 1992 and was carried out at the Center for Medical Diagnosis Systems and Visualization Bremen. After careful refinement of the algorithms and the related user interfaces, the software for liver surgery planning is regularly used, primarily as an out-of-hospital service.

Organization This chapter has the following structure: in Section 19.1, we describe the medical background with respect to liver anatomy and liver surgery. We continue by describing the image analysis based on CT data (see Sect. 19.2). Noise reduction, image segmentation, and skeletonization are important aspects of this section.

In Section 19.3, we discuss an important aspect of tumor surgery planning, which we call *risk analysis*. With this term, we emphasize that a surgeon is supported in his or her assessment of the short-term risk (postoperative liver function) and the long-term risk (progress of the disease). Visualization aspects for donor selection and planning liver transplants are discussed in Section 19.4. In the case of inoperable liver carcinoma, thermoablation of metastases has become a viable option in the last few years. The placement of applicators and the simulation of the thermoablation with respect to the resulting temperature distribution are important aspects of planning these interventions. In Section 19.5, we show how this process can be supported by appropriate visualizations. Computer support for therapy planning requires not only sophisticated algorithms but also a well-designed user interface that hides the complexity of the underlying algorithms and supports the clinical workflow—for example, by seamless management of segmentation results. In Section 19.6, we briefly discuss software concepts. Liver surgery planning serves as an example for a real and complex task that may be supported by the techniques described in this book. Section 19.7 discusses surgeons' experiences with the use of software. It is worthwhile to note how surgical decisions are refined based on image analysis results and 3D visualization. Liver surgery planning has many similarities to planning pancreatic and renal surgery. In Section 19.8, we briefly show how the analysis and visualization techniques developed for liver surgery can be used for tumor surgery planning in other abdominal organs.

19.1 MEDICAL BACKGROUND

19.1.1 LIVER ANATOMY

Due to the complex vascular anatomy of the liver, surgical interventions are challenging. Four different vessel systems supply and drain the liver: the portal vein, the hepatic vein, the hepatic artery, and the biliary ducts (see Fig. 19.1). Usually, the portal vein, the hepatic artery, and the biliary ducts proceed in parallel. The portal vein is the largest of these three and can be displayed in radiological data in more detail.

To enable surgeons to resect parts of a liver, a schematic model of the liver was introduced by a French liver surgeon [COUINAUD 1957]. Following this model, the human liver can be divided into different segments according to the branching structure of the portal and hepatic vein. Basically, Couinaud's model assumes a binary ramification of the portal vein. A liver segment is defined by the supplied territory of a third-order branch of the portal vein, thus defining nine segments (segment IV is divided into subsegments IVa and IVb, see Fig. 19.2). The hepatic veins proceed between these segments. The Couinaud scheme is well established for radiological diagnosis and for communication between radiologists and surgeons. In particular, the localization of tumors is described in terms of Couinaud segments. The Couinaud scheme serves as a liver-specific coordinate system.

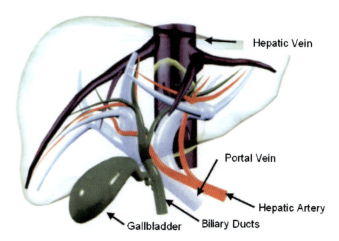

FIGURE 19.1   *Vascular structures of the human liver.* [MAZZIOTTI *and* CAVALLARI *1997*]

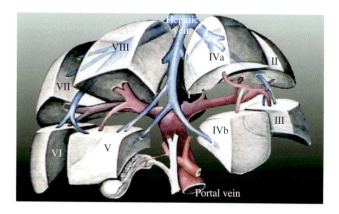

FIGURE 19.2   *The liver segments according to the scheme from Couinaud.* [PRIESCHING *1986*]

Since these segments are supplied independently, segment-oriented surgery avoids affecting the blood supply of the remaining liver segments. Applying the widespread model by Couinaud directly, however, is questionable from an anatomical point of view, since the liver segments are highly variable from patient to patient in shape, size, and number [FASEL *et al.* 1998]. Therefore, an important goal is to identify, visualize, and analyze individual liver segments that are not bound by planes.

Particularly for living-donor liver transplantation (LDLT), an in-depth understanding of vascular anatomy is necessary. To keep the discussion short, we restrict our discussion to typical variants of the hepatic artery and their influence on LDLT planning (the hepatic and portal vein anatomy also exhibit typical variants that must be considered).

Hepatic Artery   The hepatic artery is assessed in relation to the arteria gastroduodenalis (GDA) because the take-off of the common hepatic artery at the GDA varies strongly. The hepatic artery that supplies segment IV is important for LDLT planning. Usually, there is a take-off at the left hepatic artery (LHA) where the

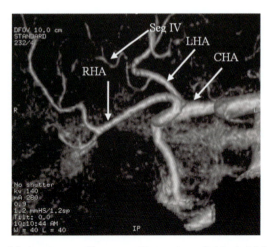

FIGURE 19.3 *Visualization of the hepatic artery. The segment IV artery is supplied by the left hepatic artery (LHA), which is the normal case. The right hepatic artery (RHA) and the common hepatic artery (CHA) are also recognizable in this surface visualization. (Image courtesy* CHRISTOPH WALD, *Lahey Clinic, Boston)*

segment IV artery begins (see Fig. 19.3). In rare cases, however, the segment IV (recall Fig. 19.2) artery starts at the right hepatic artery (RHA). This variant would be an argument to reject a donor, because a vessel reconstruction would be necessary. An additional criterion is the distance from the LHA to the segment artery (in case of an abnormality). The shorter the distance, the easier it would be to reconstruct the artery. In Figure 19.3, the hepatic artery in a clinical dataset is depicted.

The interesting aspect of this discussion is how different the topology of vascular structures actually is, even if no pathology is involved.

19.1.2 PREOPERATIVE IMAGING

Standardized and high-quality radiological data are a prerequisite for high-quality visualizations, as well as for the determination of reliable measures. For liver surgery planning, contrast-enhanced CT data (see Fig. 19.4) are primarily employed. The contrast agent highlights vascular structures (providing a high vessel-to-tissue contrast) and also increases the intensity of the liver parenchyma, which makes it easier to delineate it from surrounding structures. Often, biphasic or even triphasic CT data are used. With bi- and triphasic data, two or three datasets are acquired at slightly different times so that the contrast agent is located in different vascular structures. This allows analysis of the vascular anatomy in more detail; however, it requires alignment of the datasets. In many cases, it is sufficient to manually align the datasets with a global affine transformation. However, if breathing artifacts are involved, more sophisticated registration techniques are required.

Data resolution has increased in the last few years with modern multislice CT data. Currently, the slice distance is between 0.5 and 3 mm, resulting in some 100 to 600 slices with a 512 × 512 matrix per slice. A higher resolution is technically feasible. However, data with very low slice distances exhibit a considerable noise level unless the radiation is strongly increased.

As imaging modalities CT, MRI, or angiographies are employed. Because healthy persons are examined for donor evaluation, it is highly desirable to avoid ionizing radiation. LEE *et al.* [2001] showed

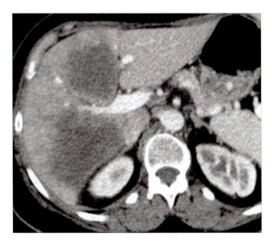

FIGURE 19.4 *A region of interest of a CT slice for liver surgery planning. The applied contrast agent provides a high vessel-to-tissue contrast and reveals the highlighted portal vein. The dark regions inside the liver represent two liver metastases. (Data courtesy MICHAEL GALANSKI, Medical School Hannover)*

that MRI alone might be employed to evaluate donors routinely. Computer support and image analysis, however, are more challenging with MRI data due to inhomogeneities and reduced resolution compared to CT data.

19.1.3 LIVER SURGERY

The central issue of modern liver surgery is to take into account the individual intrahepatic vessel and segment anatomy. The Couinaud scheme was developed to guide oncologic surgery and to foster segment-oriented resections. The same scheme is also widely used to guide the split process in split-liver transplants.

Liver surgery is challenging, since the boundaries of the individual liver segments can neither be localized by external landmarks on the liver surface nor be made visible by any radiological procedure. Therefore, a mathematical model is required to compute the localization and extent of the individual liver segments and tumors directly from the rather coarse information in the medical image data.

Surgical Treatment of Liver Carcinoma

Liver carcinoma belongs to the most common malignant diseases worldwide. Among the well-established therapies, only surgical intervention has a substantial curative effect (a five-year survival rate of about 30%). Long-term survival depends on whether all lesions have been removed entirely with a sufficient tumor-free margin (a tumor-free margin of at least 10 mm has a confirmed positive prognostic effect). Therefore, it is essential to decide on a reliable basis whether a tumor can be treated surgically and which region should be resected. Currently, this decision is made on the basis of planar slices of CT and MRI images. This raises several problems: the spatial relationships between major vessels and lesions are difficult to judge. The volume of lesions, the vessels involved in the resection of a lesion, and the region supplied by the involved vessels can only be roughly estimated. Furthermore, it is often difficult to decide whether multiple lesions should be resected separately.

Ablation of Liver Metastases

If a surgical resection turns out to be impossible as a result of either a tumor's location, its size, or the patient's constitution, the destruction of a tumor by minimally invasive thermal interventions, such as laser-induced interstitial thermotherapy (LITT) or radio-frequency ablation (RF), is often a viable alternative. A significant prolongation of life can be achieved if all metastases are completely removed [SOLBIATI et al. 1997]. There are several benefits to minimally invasive ablation therapy, compared to conventional surgery. It can lead to reduced morbidity and improved quality of life and can be performed without hospitalization. This gentle therapy is appropriate for example, for very old patients, who cannot undergo major surgical intervention. The technology of ablation is still changing fast; therefore, few substantial studies discuss their value [GOLDBERG and DUPUY 2001].

Ablation of liver metastases urgently needs image guidance, which can be achieved by contrast-enhanced CT, MRI, or ultrasound. While CT and MRI guidance limit the access to the patient and are very expensive, ultrasound is cheap and can be easily performed—however the quality is reduced [BLACKALL et al. 2001]. The intervention is carried out as follows: the thin needle electrode is pushed through the skin and directed to the center of the tumor (using image guidance). The needle delivers energy through a part of the probe tip that is conductive and causes tissue heating. Image guidance is necessary not only to direct the needle in the center of the tumor but also to ensure that damage to critical structures, such as major blood vessels, is avoided [BLACKALL 2003]. There are several parameters of thermoablation: applicators differ slightly in their performance (and consequently in the thermolesion, which might be created). Ablation might be carried out at one position or at several positions (translating the applicator). Also, in rare cases, two applicators are combined to produce the required thermolesion. An appropriate choice of these parameters is the goal of computer support.

Profound planning is even more important for thermoablation compared to conventional surgery. On the one hand, vascular territories have to be respected; on the other hand, there is a lack of visual control of the ongoing therapy due to limitations of intraoperative imaging.

Strategies for Live Donor Liver Transplants

For many liver diseases, liver transplants are needed to cure patients. Among them are hepatitis C, liver cirrhosis, and cases of inoperable liver carcinoma. Patients who could benefit from a liver transplant are included in a waiting list (managed by Eurotransplant for many European countries and by the United Network for Organ Sharing (UNOS) in the USA).[2] Due to the lack of organs, patients in need have to wait a rather long time until an appropriate donor is selected. Often, the state of patients aggravates severely in that time. This is particularly relevant for small children, because fitting organs for them are difficult to find and often urgently needed. To overcome these problems, the split-liver technology was introduced in 1989 [BROELSCH et al. 1990, RAIA et al. 1989]. Split-liver transplants (LX transplants) are viable due to the regenerative power of the liver and the fact that some 30% of the liver parenchyma suffices to ensure liver function. Two variants of split-liver transplants exist:

- The cadaver transplant, in which the organ of a dead person is divided into two grafts
- LDLT, in which a healthy volunteer donor gives a part of his or her liver to a recipient

These splitting techniques are demanding procedures that require—apart from surgical excellence—careful preoperative planning. The challenge of both kinds of operations is to split the liver in two parts in such a way that the blood supply by the portal vein and hepatic artery is ensured and that the other vascular structures (biliary ducts and hepatic veins) fit together.

---

2   See www.eurotransplant.nl and www.unos.org.

Between the two kinds of split-liver transplants, we concentrate on live-donor liver transplantation. A major advantage of LDLT is that an operation can be scheduled as regular surgical intervention and is not considered as an emergency case. Another benefit is that LDLT is usually applied between relatives, resulting in less frequent rejections of the liver. However, LDLT means that a healthy person undergoes a major surgical intervention. This requires, from an ethical point of view, that the donor selection and the preoperative planning are carried out with excellence.

Donor Selection for LDLT

A potential donor must be in good physical condition and his or her liver must be functioning (e.g., persons with a high grade of liver fattiness cannot be considered). An important criterion for donor selection is whether a graft can be obtained with a size and volume compatible to that required by a recipient. In the preoperative planning process, it is essential to assess the hepatic vascular anatomy. Surgeons try to avoid operations that carry a high risk for complications (e.g., operations that require extended vessel reconstructions and operations, in the case of variants of the vascular anatomy).

In addition to the liver volume, the shape of the organ must be considered. This is particularly important for small children, for the simple reason that the graft must fit in the child's body.

Since donor safety is a primary concern, great care must be taken to minimize damage to the remaining liver segments of the donor as well as to the liver graft. An appropriate visualization and reliable quantitative analysis of the hepatic vasculature make it easier for the transplantation team to decide which person is the most appropriate donor.

19.2   IMAGE ANALYSIS FOR LIVER SURGERY PLANNING

Segmentation target objects for liver surgery planning are lesions, the liver parenchyma, and intrahepatic vessels.

Liver Segmentation

Liver segmentation is an important aspect in liver surgery planning because it serves different purposes:

- **Visualization.** It allows the user to selectively hide or show the liver tissue.
- **Segmentation of intrahepatic structures.** Subsequent segmentation of intrahepatic vasculature or tumors can be restricted to the liver segmentation result, which serves as a barrier. In particular, region-based algorithms benefit from such a barrier.
- **Quantification.** Volumetric calculations of liver lobes, liver segments, or other resection areas require liver segmentation.
- **Approximation of vascular territories.** The liver segmentation is the prerequisite for the approximation of vascular territories.

The last two aspects require that liver segmentation be performed accurately. For the segmentation of the liver, a combination of the contour-oriented, two-dimensional livewire algorithm and subsequent shape-based interpolation was found to be effective [SCHENK et al. 2000] (recall Sect. 5.3.5). With the livewire algorithm, piecewise optimal boundary paths between user-defined contour points are computed and displayed. Users verify contours determined through interpolation and may correct them locally by translating seedpoints.

In this way, even the delimitation between the heart and liver, which exhibit similar gray values in CT images, can be defined with little user interaction. Thus, the required interaction time is kept low, while full manual control is still available.

Alternative model-based approaches have also been investigated and successfully evaluated for liver segmentation [LAMECKER et al. 2002, SOLER et al. 2001]. LAMECKER et al. [2002] introduced an active shape model (recall Sect. 5.4.3) for the liver. SOLER et al. [2001] designed a strategy in which most of the abdominal organs are segmented automatically. The liver segmentation is the last step in this pipeline and benefits from previously derived segmentation results.

In many cases, the segmentation time can be reduced considerably with a carefully adapted automatic approach (according to [SOLER et al. 2001], in some 80% of cases). However, there is still a significant number of cases in which automatic segmentation fails. A combination of automatic segmentation (for the majority of the cases) and a semi-interactive approach for the remaining cases is recommended.

Tumor Segmentation

Lesions are very different with respect to shape, variation of gray values, and contrast to liver tissue. On the one hand, there are metastases from colorectal carcinoma; on the other hand, primary liver tumors (hepatocellular carcinoma). Primary liver tumors are usually segmented manually, because the contrast with normal liver tissue is too low. For the segmentation of liver metastases, a variety of methods has been explored. Watershed transformation is often used (recall Sect. 5.3.4) and performs well with high-contrast metastases (one include and one exclude marker may be sufficient). In more difficult cases, a method originally developed for the segmentation of lung nodules was adapted and successfully tried [KUHNIGK et al. 2004] (see Fig. 19.5). This method is based on an initial region growing, in which a threshold is determined based on a histogram analysis of the region around the user-specified seedpoint. This initial result is refined with morphologic operators, which allow separation of the lesion from the vasculature using the assumption that the lesion is larger than the connection to vasculature.

Segmentation and Analysis of the Intrahepatic Vasculature

The segmentation of the various vascular trees is based on a region growing method, which aggregates all highlighted voxels of the intrahepatic systems (see Sect. 5.3.3 for an introduction to region growing). An optimal threshold is suggested automatically by taking into account how the number of accumulated vessels changes with respect to the threshold. If necessary, a fast manual manipulation of the threshold with 2D and 3D visual control is possible. A good suggestion for a threshold is crucial, because otherwise users have to guess an initial threshold and use trial and error to find a good value, which is tedious and also not reproducible.

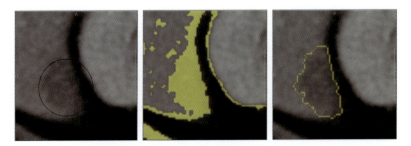

FIGURE 19.5 *The tumor in the encircled region (left image) is segmented with the method described in [KUHNIGK et al. 2004]. After an initial region growing (middle image), the segmentation is automatically refined with morphologic operators (right image). (Images courtesy LARS BORNEMANN, MeVis Bremen)*

The quality of the results can be improved by using filters for noise reduction (blurring, median filter) and additionally for background compensation (Laplacian-like filters). Background compensation is useful if the contrast agent is not equally well distributed in the liver—resulting in different intensity values of liver parenchyma in different parts of the image. To analyze the morphology and the ramification pattern of the vascular systems, the segmented vessels are skeletonized (recall Sect. 5.7). The skeleton is also the basis for a transformation of the vessel systems into a mathematical graph. Graph theoretical algorithms are applied to separate and distinguish arteries and portal and hepatic veins, as well as to analyze the hierarchical structure of the portal vein and hepatic vein. The separation of intrahepatic vasculature is necessary, because vascular systems cannot be segmented separately. This problem and possible solutions have been described in the context of vessel visualization (recall Sect. 14.1). Based on the identification and graph representation of vascular trees, vascular territories are determined. Third-order branches of the portal vein define territories roughly corresponding to the Couinaud segments. With respect to the hepatic vein, the territories drained by the left, middle, and right hepatic vein are determined.

Although the vessel analysis pipeline is carried out automatically [SELLE et al. 2002], interactive manipulation of the results is essential to allow radiologists to bring in their knowledge if necessary.

Prediction of the Anatomy of the Liver Segments
The segmental anatomy of the liver is defined by the branching structure of the portal vein. Within corrosion casts, a very detailed branching structure can be segmented (see Fig. 19.6). It has an accumulated

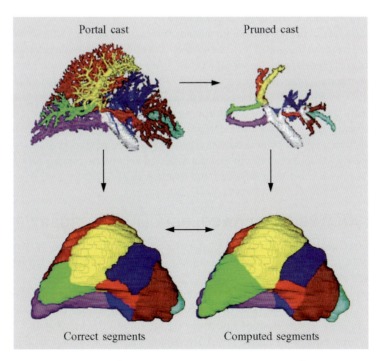

FIGURE 19.6 *High-resolution CT scan of a corrosion cast allows the segmentation of the portal vein branches (upper left). Associated liver segments (lower left). Pruned portal tree simulating clinical data (upper right). Model-based predicted segments (lower right). (Image courtesy* DIRK SELLE, *MeVis Bremen)*

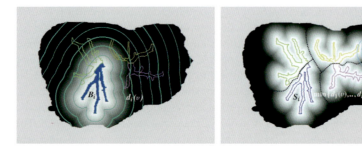

FIGURE 19.7 *Nearest neighbor segment approximation (NNSA) using the Euclidean metric. Left: Euclidean distance for the branch B_i: the darker the liver voxels, the greater their distance from the branch B_i. The indicated lines are equidistant from B_i. Right: the minimum of the distance functions for all branches reveals the segment boundaries. (Images courtesy DIRK SELLE, MeVis Bremen)*

length of about 2000 m, clearly revealing the shape of the liver segments. In clinical data, as shown in Figure 19.4, the accumulated length of the segmented portal vein is only about 2 to 4 m.

To compensate for this lack of information and to predict the segmental anatomy, various models have been developed and evaluated. These models are based on different distance metrics (Euclidean distance, potential fields) and predict the segmental territories just using third-order portal branches and the segmented liver (both have been determined in previous image analysis steps). The segment approximation using the Euclidean distance metric is illustrated in Figure 19.6. This approximation can also be described as a Voronoi decomposition of the liver.

To improve the accuracy of the prediction, further anatomical information (radii of the portal branches and the hepatic vein) has been integrated into the models. The effectiveness of these models was evaluated on studies of corrosion preparations (recall Fig. 19.6). With corrosion casts, the portal vein could be reconstructed up to the sixth branching order—the overall length of the extracted vessels is an order of magnitude larger than in clinical data. The corrosion casts have been kindly supplied by the anatomist Prof. FASEL (University Genf, Department for Morphology).

To this end, the authentic segments were determined and the portal tree was pruned to simulate a portal vein derived from a typical clinical dataset. The models were used to predict segments based on the pruned tree (see Fig. 19.7). It turned out that the expected volumetric overlap between the authentic and the predicted segments is between 80% and 90% [SELLE et al. 2002].

19.3   RISK ANALYSIS FOR ONCOLOGIC LIVER SURGERY PLANNING

With virtual resection functions (recall Chap. 12), the user has full control to flexibly develop and explore resection strategies. In particular, the deformable cutting plane (recall Sect. 12.3) has been developed to support liver surgery planning.

For tumor surgery, there is an alternative and more reproducible approach to preoperative planning: to let the system emphasize which portion of the liver parenchyma should be removed. Such a resection proposal should consider the position and size of a tumor and the location and branching structure of vascular systems. Finally, the influence of a resection on the blood supply and the drainage of the remaining liver parenchyma must be considered. Such a high-level support was developed based on the following scenario: starting from a selected lesion and a given tumor-free margin (5 or 10 mm), the involved parts of the vessel system are identified and the supplied liver parenchyma is calculated.

A principal sketch is presented in Figure 19.8. This approach was investigated first by working with CT images of corrosion casts (recall Sect. 19.2). In these models, a sphere with a 1 cm diameter was included as a model of a focal lesion and calculated the liver parenchyma to resect for different security margins (see Fig. 19.9). The calculation of resection regions also respects large hepatic veins that should not be damaged. It turned out that the resection proposals correspond well to surgical practice in shape and size.

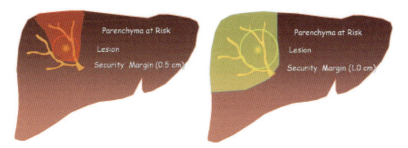

FIGURE 19.8 *Schematic drawing to illustrate the principle underlying resection proposals. For security margins of 5 and 10 mm, different parts of the vasculature and of the liver parenchyma are affected. (Images courtesy* HEINZ-OTTO PEITGEN, *MeVis Bremen)*

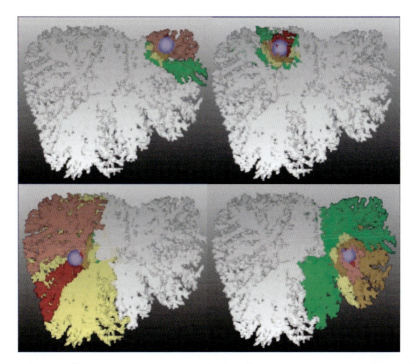

FIGURE 19.9 *Illustration of resection proposals based on vascular data of a corrosion cast and a simulated tumor. (Images courtesy* DIRK SELLE, *MeVis Bremen)*

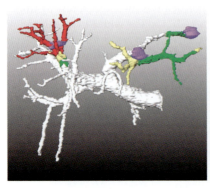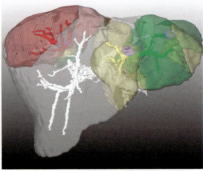

FIGURE 19.10 *Risk analysis for tumor surgery with respect to the portal vein: three liver metastasis. Red, yellow, and green indicate vascular structures and the affected vascular territories in the 5-, 10-, and 15-mm security margin. (Images courtesy MILO HINDENNACH, MeVis Bremen; data courtesy HUBERTUS FEUSSNER, Technical University Munich)*

In the large majority of the cases, the highlighted regions could have been resected in principle, although their shape is sometimes rather complex. Surgeons would prefer a smoothed version of the shape with reduced area, because it is easier to realize and reduces the number of small blood vessels that would be hurt.

The appearance of a tumor in a CT image, and thus the size and shape of the segmented tumor, is not perfectly reliable. Moreover, the surgeon cannot exactly follow a planned resection. Resection proposals have to consider the limited accuracy of the data and the procedure. Therefore, the calculation is carried out for different margins: the red one is the inner region, which must definitely be resected; the other colors (orange, yellow, green) represent more distant zones. This visualization thus indicates the risk involved in the procedure for the damage of major blood vessels (which are in the orange or yellow region). The resection regions suggested can be fine-tuned interactively with the virtual resection methods described in Chapter 12.

To validate resection proposals and to assess their feasibility, it is essential that the results are also displayed in a 2D slice view. For this purpose, the approximation of vascular territories is transparently overlaid with the original radiological data.

Exploration of Resection Proposals

A typical sequence of interactions is as follows. The user starts the analysis with the metastasis that is probably the most difficult to resect and performs the analysis of security margins for the portal vein (see Fig. 19.10). Following this step, the analysis for the hepatic vein is separately carried out (see Fig. 19.11),and subsequently both results are integrated in one visualization, with the vascular trees pruned appropriately. Risk analyses for the portal vein and the hepatic vein yield similar but not identical territories. The distance between them might well be 1 cm. Therefore, it is essential that both vascular systems are considered. Liver arteries are less important, because the portal vein ensures the largest portion (some 80%) of the blood supply. The visualization of the vascular territory is usually restricted to one such territory. However, the volumetric analysis is carried out simultaneously for all security margins that have been considered. If other metastases have to be treated, the analysis is carried out for these lesions afterwards and finally an overall visualization and volumetric analysis is carried

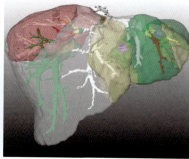

FIGURE 19.11   *Risk analysis for tumor surgery with respect to the hepatic vein carried out for the same case as in Figure 19.10. (Images courtesy* MILO HINDENNACH, *MeVis Bremen; data courtesy* HUBERTUS FEUSSNER, *Technical University Munich)*

out. A detailed description of risk analysis for tumor surgery and its application to six clinical cases can be found in [PREIM *et al.* 2002a].

19.4   RISK ANALYSIS FOR LIVE DONOR LIVER TRANSPLANTATION

In the previous sections, we discussed which particular image analysis and visualization techniques are required for donor selection and preoperative planning. In this section, we describe specific aspects of LDLT planning and a case study with a potential donor based on a multislice CT dataset of Lahey Clinic, Boston.

19.4.1 GRAFTS WITH OR WITHOUT MIDDLE HEPATIC VEIN

There are two rather difficult situations in which LDLT is applied. For small children, often infants with congenital defects, small grafts are needed. In these cases, the smaller left liver lobe is used as a graft and more than half of the liver remains with the donor. The majority of persons who need an organ, however, are adults, who need considerably larger portions of the liver volume. LDLT for adults is more challenging, because careful volumetric analysis is necessary to ensure that both the donor and the recipient have sufficient functional liver parenchyma. The resection line for adult recipients is near the middle hepatic vein (MHV). The key question is whether the MHV should remain with the donor or be given to the recipient. In both cases, a certain part of the liver parenchyma is not drained because the draining branch of the MHV is resected. To support the decision of which way to resect, a reliable approximation of the volume of these areas is essential. Figure 19.12 illustrates the two situations. The volumetric approximation is accomplished again by predicting the vascular territories of the MHV branches, taking into account the Euclidean distance of liver voxels to branches of the hepatic vein. Based on a comparison with intraoperative images, it could be shown that the area predicted to lose drainage is reliable (see Fig. 19.13).

To support the decision as to whether the MHV should remain on the donor side or be transplanted, the volume of the territories for their branches are calculated. For the donor, the percentage of the liver that remains is crucial, while for the recipient, the absolute volume is essential. An appropriate graft volume is estimated based on the patient's weight.

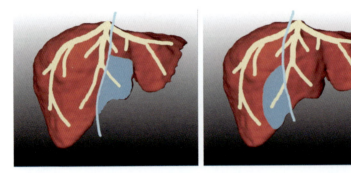

FIGURE 19.12   *Different resection lines with respect to the MHV. If the MHV is part of the graft (left), a portion of the remaining liver volume will be damaged. On the other hand, the functional graft volume is reduced if the MHV remains in the donor's liver. Volumetric calculations are performed to predict the functional liver volume and to assess the feasibility of a resection. (Images courtesy* HEINZ-OTTOPEITGEN, *MeVis Bremen)*

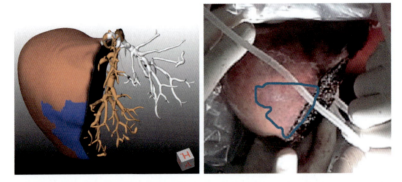

FIGURE 19.13   *Comparison of preoperative planning (left) to the intraoperative situation. It turns out that the devascularized territory could be correctly predicted (intraoperatively, this area becomes light blue). (Images courtesy* HOLGER BOURQUAIN, *MeVis Bremen)*

If it turns out that a substantial portion of the remaining liver tissue is at risk with respect to venous outflow, transplantation is still possible. However, vascular reconstructions will be necessary. Very similar considerations are required for extended liver tumor surgery. LANG et al. [2005a] reported on their experiences of using volumetric calculations for tumor surgery planning and recommended carrying out vascular reconstructions to improve venous outflow if more than 20% of the remaining tissue is at risk.

19.4.2 CASE STUDY

In this case study, we discuss how the image analysis results of a particular case are used for donor evaluation and preoperative planning. For preoperative planning, each individual vascular system is shown in two animation sequences (rotation around an axial and sagittal axis) without any additional structures. These visualizations are used to depict the branching pattern of each individual vascular system.

In addition, they define how the liver will be split: which parts of the liver remain *in situ* and which parts will be used as a graft. The volume of the graft and its percentage with respect to the total liver volume are calculated.

Different visualization options are available to explore the results: either the segments are rendered semitransparently, with the vessels inside visible, or they are rendered opaquely (see Fig. 19.14). In the preoperative planning stage, it turned out that the potential donor is a suitable candidate for LDLT. Due to the large diameter of the accessory vein (larger than 5 mm), a reconstruction of this vascular structure was required. Because of the large distance between the accessory vein and the confluence of the hepatic vein, there is enough space for a vessel reconstruction (see Fig. 19.16).

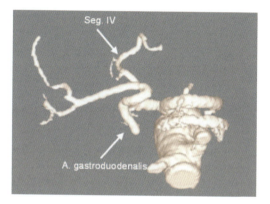

FIGURE 19.14   *Surface rendering of the segmented hepatic artery. The medial part of the lienal artery and parts of the gastroduodenal artery are also visible. (Data courtesy* CHRISTOPH WALD, *Lahey Clinic, Boston)*

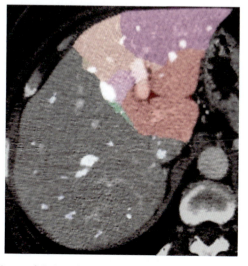

FIGURE 19.15   *The color-coded parts of the liver that are to be used as a graft. (Data courtesy* CHRISTOPH WALD, *Lahey Clinic, Boston)*

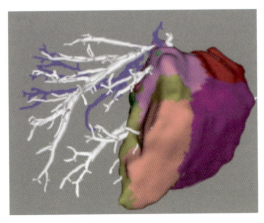

FIGURE 19.16 *Visualization of the hepatic vein. An accessory vein is highlighted. The segments in the remaining part of the liver are included.* (Data courtesy CHRISTOPH WALD, Lahey Clinic, Boston)

19.5   SIMULATION AND VISUALIZATION FOR PLANNING OF THERMOABLATIONS

Thermoablation is often an attractive therapeutic option if patients are not resectable, due for example to their general condition or to liver cirrhosis (recall Sect.19.1.3). Having segmented the intrahepatic structures, one can support the physician in deciding whether the given case can be treated with thermotherapy or not. Thermotherapy is carried out with radiofrequency energy (RF) or by means of laser beams (LITT, laser-induced interstitial thermotherapy).

A single LITT applicator can coagulate a volume with a diameter of up to 5 cm if hepatic perfusion is maintained. Coagulation means that the tissue is irreversibly destroyed—the volume destroyed in this manner is called thermolesion. Coagulation requires a temperature of at least 42 degrees Celsius for at least one minute. Larger tumors, therefore, require additional applicators, especially since it is generally attempted to coagulate a volume consisting of the visible tumor and a security margin of 1 cm around it. Tumors with a diameter larger than 5 cm generally cannot be treated successfully with thermoablation.[3] By automatically measuring the tumors' sizes, the decision as to whether thermoablation is feasible is supported.

The LITCIT (laser-induced temperature calculation in tissue) is a research prototype developed by ROGGAN et al. at the LMTB[4] that simulates each intervention individually (see [VOGL et al. 1998] for a discussion of the clinical evaluation of LITCIT). A similar system for the simulation of RF ablation has been developed by the same group [DESINGER et al. 1998, STEIN et al. 1999].

19.5.1 APPLICATOR POSITIONING

To completely destroy the tumor while preserving surrounding healthy tissue, is the overall goal of applicator placement and other aspects of thermoablation. For applicator placement, the user is

---

3   Thermoablation and coagulation are synonyms.

4   Institute for Laser and Medicine Technology Berlin, www.lmtb.de.

provided with synchronous 2D and 3D views of the segmented data as well as of the applicators. In 2D, the original data is transparently overlaid with the segmentation results, and the same colors are employed in 2D and 3D to communicate the relationship. Because it is also possible to combine the surface-rendered 3D scene with volume rendering of the original dataset, one can easily check whether any bony structures or main vascular branches lie within any applicator's path (see Fig. 19.17). This evaluation is additionally supported by presenting the user with a histogram showing the gray value distribution along the applicator's path. Prominent peaks are a reliable hint either on bones or on contrast-enhanced vessels. Automatic positioning is supported in the previously described way, but if this setting does not meet the physician's requirements, the position and orientation can interactively be modified, either through a mouse-driven interface or incrementally with the keyboard. Applicator positioning in 2D and 3D views using the image analysis results is described in [LITTMANN et al. 2003].

19.5.2 PHYSICAL EFFECTS OF THERMOABLATION

To reliably predict the shape and location of the damaged tissue, it is necessary both to segment all intra-hepatic structures and to specify these structures' thermal and physical characteristics. Having defined the applicators' properties, such as energy and application time, a simulation of the therapy that precalculates the damaged tissue can be performed. The simulation is carried out by the previously mentioned LITCIT, which was modified so that the segmentation results could be directly used as an anatomical basis for the simulation of the heating. The distribution of the photons emitted by the laser applicator is approximated with a Monte-Carlo simulation. Based on the simulation, the temperature distribution is determined. Heat transport within the tissue is calculated with finite differences. An important aspect of the simulation is the cooling effect of perfusion close to larger vascular structures. Large blood vessels reduce the heating effect of a nearby thermoablation (see Fig. 19.18). Eventually, it turns out that perfusion has to be stopped—as in open surgery. This is a more extended intervention in which some of the advantages of thermoablation, such as reduced trauma and hospital stay, do not exist. However, it might be the only potentially curative treatment.

For the evaluation, the damage distribution is visualized both in 2D and 3D in the described synchronous way. Analogous to resection proposals, the territory being affected by the necrosis of the damaged tissue is determined as additional decision support.

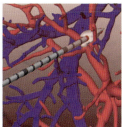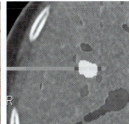

FIGURE 19.17 *Synchronous 2D and 3D views enable the user to quickly check whether either bony structures or important vessels lie on an applicator's path. (Images courtesy ARNE LITTMANN, MeVis Bremen)*

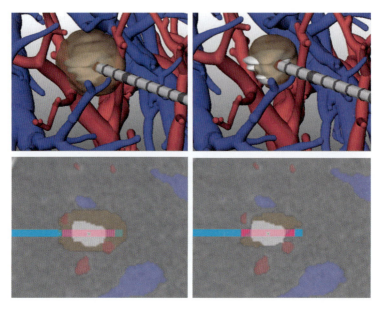

FIGURE 19.18   *The thermolesion that will be irreversibly destroyed by a LITT intervention is shown as a 3D object (surrounding the applicator). In the 2D visualization, the relation between a metastasis and the thermolesion is shown. Neglecting intrahepatic vessels in the LITT simulation (left) results in a lesion that fully encloses the tumor (outlined black), whereas the simulation that takes vascular structures into account shows that more energy is necessary to completely destroy the tumor, due to the cooling effect of surrounding vessels. (Images courtesy* ARNE LITTMANN, *MeVis Bremen)*

19.6   SOFTWARE ASSISTANTS FOR LIVER SURGERY PLANNING

Computer support for liver surgery planning as described in this chapter has two aspects:

- The reconstruction of the relevant parts of the patient's anatomy
- The exploration of a 3D model of the patient's anatomy

The image analysis requires experience in the processing of image data and in the parameterization of various image analysis methods. In general, this process takes one to two hours for experienced users. The users of this software are either radiologists or their technical assistants. Coping with the large variety of datasets and anatomic variations requires dedicated training (several days) and considerable experience.

On the other hand, the exploration of the individual patient model is targeted at surgical users to support their therapy decisions. An effective use of these functions can be learned within hours. It turned out to be useful to provide two software assistants for these different target user groups:

- HEPAVISION, a dedicated software assistant for image analysis in CT liver data
- INTERVENTIONPLANNER, a general software assistant for 3D visualization, resection and access planning, and documentation

The term *software assistant* refers to highly specialized applications tailored for specific tasks with carefully chosen default values for parameters and a support for the particular workflow. Instead of providing mere toolboxes with all necessary algorithms and unlimited flexibility in their combination and use, software assistants are streamlined for a very specific application.

One of the reasons for separating the software assistants is to support the idea of a service center for image analysis: a service center provides the highly specialized image analysis and produces results that can be explored by customers with dedicated software. In fact, such an out-of-hospital service has been established at the Center for Medical Diagnosis and Visualization Systems (MeVis) in Bremen, and it has been used by 36 hospitals in almost 2000 cases (692 cases relate to oncologic liver surgery, 952 to LDLT, and 178 to other situations, primarily pancreatic and renal surgery, until September 2006).

19.6.1 IMAGE ANALYSIS WITH HEPA VISION

The image analysis software is designed to support the typical workflow, starting with importing DICOM data (up to three datasets if triphasic CT data was acquired). Usually, the size of the data is reduced to a region of interest in the next step. Liver segmentation, tumor segmentation, and the different steps of vascular segmentation and analysis follow. All these subapplications have a unified layout, with as much space as possible allocated to the display of the data and all user interface elements placed at the right. Typical interactions, such as slicing through the data or changing brightness and contrast, are accomplished with mouse-based interaction directly in the image data. An important aspect of the image analysis is to support the user in managing and structuring resulting data. The names assigned in the image analysis stage are later used in the INTERVENTIONPLANNER to select objects and adjust their appearance. All image analysis steps need an input image of a certain type (e.g., raw data, segmentation result, vessel skeleton). It is crucial to offer only data that are appropriate for the current step. Often, exactly one image dataset of the appropriate type exists—to load this dataset automatically is a welcome support. In general, the user may only carry out these tasks if the necessary prerequisites have been fulfilled. For example, risk analysis requires that all vessel analysis steps have been carried out before.

19.6.2 SURGERY PLANNING WITH THE INTERVENTION PLANNER

The INTERVENTIONPLANNER is the software assistant targeted at surgical users. The image analysis results are put into this system, which allows users to create flexible arrangements of the intrahepatic structures.

Segmented objects might be selectively displayed or hidden to customize the visualization to the questions related to the therapeutic process at hand. However, the mere visualization of important structures is often insufficient. The lack of surrounding tissue, particularly of skeletal structures, makes it difficult to understand the current view. Therefore, medical doctors appreciate the visual integration of bony structures (see Fig. 19.19). The volume visualization of bony structures serves as the anatomic context that supports the interpretation of other structures. For each object, additional information (annotations, volumetric results) is available to be presented in the context of 3D visualizations. For vascular structures, the INTERVENTIONPLANNER allows the user to choose between an isosurface rendering of the segmentation result or a reconstruction of vasculature with truncated cones (recall Sect. 14.3.2). In most cases, the high-quality visualization is chosen (see Fig. 19.17 to Fig. 19.19).

Beside the mere visualization functionality, the exploration of the data is supported by providing clipping planes (which might be used selectively, recall Sect. 12.1.1) and by providing all the measurement functions described in Chapter 13. The automatic measurement functions are particularly welcomed by surgeons for tumor surgery planning (determination of tumor size and minimal distances to vasculature are essential).

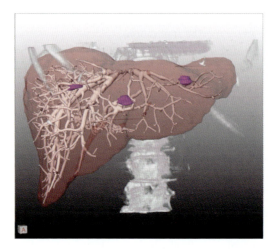

FIGURE 19.19 *Direct volume rendering of bony structures and surface rendering of intrahepatic structures (liver, vascular systems, tumors). The cube in the lower left corner indicates the viewing direction. (Data courtesy Michael Galanski, Medical School Hannover)*

Documentation facilities allow the creation of annotated screenshots as well as certain animation sequences (rotations of defined subsets of the structures). Besides these rather general functions, there is dedicated functionality to support thermoablations: applicator placement is supported (recall Sect. 19.5.1) and the INTERVENTIONPLANNER might control the LITCIT to simulate the thermoablation achieved with certain parameters in combination with LITT applicators.

Two general aspects are crucial for the use of the INTERVENTIONPLANNER:

- Default values for visualization parameters. Taking into account the severe time pressure in hospitals, it is reasonable to provide mechanisms to standardize aspects of the visualization.
- Synchronization between 3D and 2D views.

Default Values Visualizations such as that shown in Figure 19.19 are controlled by a variety of parameters. These include object colors, transparency values, and the viewing direction, as well as smoothness and quality parameters (resolution used for the rendering). It is essential that these parameters be available via the graphical user interface. However, it is tedious if they have to be specified again and again for individual objects. Hence, meaningful default values that can be accepted in the majority of the cases are crucial. How can these be specified? First, it is important to classify objects, because classification provides a useful base for the assignment of default values. Examples of object classes are organs, bony structures, vascular structures, and tumors. Organs are large structures; usually, it is desirable to see details of the organ interior. Therefore, by default, they are rendered semitransparently, whereas lesions and vascular structures are not. Note that different transparency values are useful for 2D and 3D visualizations. In 2D visualizations, the original data should be visible to some extent. Therefore, even lesions and vascular structures are not displayed fully opaque. Large compact structures, such as organs, can be displayed with lower resolution compared to thin elongated structures. Finally, the initial viewing direction should be a natural one, preferably the surgeon's view.

Individual users have slightly different preferences. Therefore, it is possible to customize visualizations by storing personalized default values. Well-selected default values not only save time, but also result in a visualization with better quality and reproducibility. Default values are also useful for integrating measurements and annotations. Here, colors, fonts, linestyle parameters, and measurement units should be adjustable on the one hand but carefully preconfigured on the other.

In Section 1.3 we discussed the general value of 2D and 3D visualization for diagnosis and therapy planning, as well as the need to closely integrate both kinds of visualization. Three-dimensional visualizations were found to be intuitive, providing a good overview of spatial relations. Two-dimensional visualizations, on the other hand, allowed more precise investigation and interaction. Therefore, the synchronization between 2D and 3D views is a core design issue of the INTERVENTIONPLANNER. The basic layout consists of a 2D and a 3D view. Initially, the 3D view is larger than the 2D view, but both can be easily exchanged by the user.

Synchronization   Synchronization between both views is applied consequently to all interactions. For example, 2D and 3D visualizations are employed for the placement of an applicator (recall Sect. 19.5.2). The precise definition of the target point (the point where the applicator produces a maximum of energy to destroy the pathology around it) is usually selected in 2D. The entry point (where the applicator penetrates the skin) might also be selected in a 2D visualization. It becomes more obvious in 3D visualizations whether important structures are hurt by this access path.

In a similar manner, 2D and 3D visualizations are combined for measurements, such as distances and angles, for the quantitative analysis of spatial relations (recall Sect. 13.2.1 and Sect. 13.3). Another task supported by the INTERVENTIONPLANNER is the specification of resection areas (the parts of the body that should be removed in surgery). Resection specification can be accomplished in 2D (by drawing on selected slices and interpolating between them) and in 3D by moving surgical tools that virtually remove tissue through the data. Again, it is crucial to evaluate the virtual resection in the other view (recall Sect. 12.3). If the resection area was specified in 2D, the 3D view is important to assess the resulting shape. On the other hand, if the resection was specified in 3D, the 2D view is useful to assess the affected regions.

19.7   CLINICAL APPLICATION

The methods described here are used routinely in various hospitals, primarily in the United States and in Japan. In several research cooperations, the impact of improved planning on surgical strategy and outcome has been documented and discussed in journal publications. The surgeons using the described software support appreciate its ability to investigate the consequences of different resection planes on the blood supply and hepatic venous drainage.

So far, the most detailed description of the clinical use of the described methods can be found in [FRERICKS et al. 2004]. The authors discuss the value of computer support with respect to 56 cases of LDLT planning and evaluation. In particular, the correspondence between preoperative planning and intraoperative findings is considered. The accuracy of volumetric calculations and the improved understanding of vascular abnormalities are considered major advantages compared to conventional planning.

RADTKE et al. [2005] report on their experiences with computer support for 55 patients for whom different LDLT strategies were planned and performed. They refined surgical strategies based on the results of volumetric calculations. HEPAVISION and the INTERVENTIONPLANNER were used at the University of Leipzig to evaluate 13 LDLT candidates and three LDLT recipients. Related experiences are discussed by HARMS et al. [2004].

LANG et al. [2005a] and LANG et al. [2005b] describe experiences in oncologic liver surgery planning. LANG et al. [2005a] report on a series of 25 patients, out of which four were regarded as not resectable.

They compared conventional planning based on 2D CT images with improved surgical planning and documented how improved planning altered the surgical strategy. The resection line was first drawn in 2D slices and then analyzed with respect to the risk of devascularization and venous congestion. In seven of the 21 patients, a large deviation (more than 20%) between remaining liver volume and functional liver volume was computed. In these cases, either the amount of the resection was reduced or vascular reconstructions were performed. Based on their experiences, smaller devascularized territories are better tolerated by patients.

It turns out that computer-assisted planning is essential for repeated hepatectomies in which the vascular anatomy is altered due to previous vascular dissection. The authors regard precise preoperative knowledge of the distribution pattern of hepatic veins and their depending territories as essential for assessing functional resectability.

19.8   PLANNING PANCREATIC AND RENAL SURGERY

Image analysis and visualization methods, as well as the software assistants for liver surgery planning, are also useful for surgery planning in related areas, particularly for pancreatic and renal surgery. Also in these abdominal organs, the analysis of different vascular trees (arteries and veins), as well as the spatial relation between a tumor and its surroundings, is essential to evaluate a resection strategy. While the pancreas does not exhibit special vascular territories, the kidney consists of four vascular territories that are relevant for surgery planning. The overall goal of tumor surgery in these organs is to completely remove the tumor and to preserve as much functional tissue as possible. In the following, we illustrate one case of pancreatic surgery as well as one case of renal surgery.

Figure 19.20 illustrates the anatomy of the pancreas, and Figure 19.21 presents results from the risk analysis for the pancreatic artery and vein. Similarly, for renal surgery planning, we present the anatomy (see Fig. 19.22) and risk analysis results (see Fig. 19.22). For both renal and pancreatic surgery planning, vascular territories for both vascular systems are computed, displayed, and quantitatively analyzed.

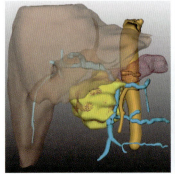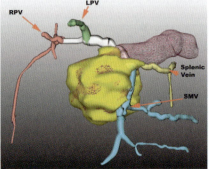

FIGURE 19.20 *Pancreatic surgery planning. The yellow object represents a tumor in the pancreas (wire-frame object). In the left image, the liver (large object) and the aorta (large vertical structure) are displayed for orientation. RPV and LPV represent the right and left portal vein, whereas SMV represents the superior mesenteric vein. (Images courtesy HOLGER BOURQUAIN, MeVis Bremen)*

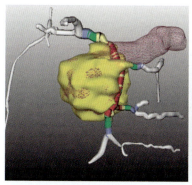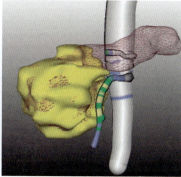

FIGURE 19.21   *Risk analysis for pancreatic surgery planning. A large tumor (100 ml) occupies large portions of the pancreas (128 ml). Left image: The red area on the pancreatic vein represents the regions that touch the tumor. The yellow, green, and blue areas are within the 2-mm, 5-mm, and 10-mm security margin. Right image: the distance of the pancreatic vein to the tumor is color-coded with the same colors for the same distances. Finally, a wedge resection of the tumor was considered the optimal choice. (Images courtesy* HOLGER BOURQUAIN, *MeVis Bremen)*

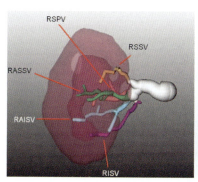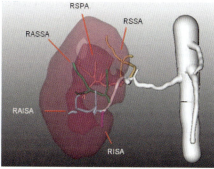

FIGURE 19.22   *For renal surgery planning the vascular anatomy is presented. The R refers to right, S to segmental or superior, A to anterior or artery, V to vein, and I to inferior. As an example, RPSA refers to the right posterior segmental artery. (Images courtesy* HOLGER BOURQUAIN, *MeVis Bremen)*

19.9   SUMMARY

Common tools for preoperative visualization (e.g., 2D slices, MIP) only support a very limited comprehension of the patient's complex and individual anatomy and pathology. Applying the described image analysis steps provides a flexible 3D visualization of the relevant structures and facilitates an easier interpretation of diagnostic findings. Abnormalities and variants of the vascular architecture appear much more pronounced in high-quality smoothed visualizations compared to the original axial slices. Intrahepatic vasculature can be assessed quantitatively. In particular, the risk for devascularization or venous congestion can be identified prior to liver resection [LANG et al. 2005b].

Interactive planning of resections and quantitative analysis, such as estimating the volume of tumors, the individual liver segments, and the remaining liver parenchyma, make it possible to estimate the risk of surgical strategies. The software described here serves as a basis for discussions on the planning of resections

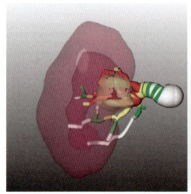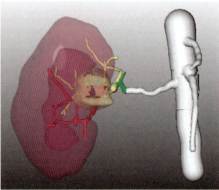

FIGURE 19.23   *Risk analysis applied to renal surgery planning (red indicates vascular structures the 5 mm safety margin around a tumor, yellow the 10 mm margin and green the 15 mm margin. In the left image, the analysis is applied to venous structures and in the right image to the arteries. (Images courtesy* HOLGER BOURQUAIN, *MeVis Bremen)*

within the radiological and surgical team. Clinical evaluations have shown that the preoperative results correlated well with the intraoperative findings [FRERICKS et al. 2004]. For complex resections and LDLT, in which healthy patients are involved, the additional expenses of computer-aided planning are highly accepted for use in clinical routine.

Computer support for liver surgery planning involves a great deal of image analysis and visualization issues. This situation is typical for therapy planning applications, which should not be regarded as pure image analysis or as pure visualization problems.

The image analysis techniques have great potential; however, they are demanding to accomplish. Even experienced users take approximately one hour to carry out all the subtasks. Much effort has been spent to make the algorithms as efficient as possible from the user's view. In this vein, automatic suggestions for the threshold in the vessel segmentation, automatic separation of vessel systems, and sophisticated shape-based interpolation for liver segmentation have been developed.

The methods described in this chapter are inspired by liver surgery planning and evaluated for planning these interventions. However, many individual steps are also required for similar interventions. Several organs within the human body—for example, the lung, the kidney, and the pancreas—are characterized by vascular trees. The planning of resections in these organs also requires vessel analysis and the approximation of the supplied territories. Many concepts realized in the INTERVENTIONPLANNER are relevant for other therapy planning tasks as well. Default visualization parameters, synchronization between 2D and 3D visualization for major interactions, high-quality visualization of vascular systems, and easy-to-use measurement functions are general aspects for therapy planning software.

Outlook   It might be surprising that after so many years, still more research and development efforts are required to optimize computer support for liver surgery planning. An important research goal is to combine the use of different image data for diagnosis and treatment planning. In particular, the use of MRI data and the combination of several MRI sequences are desirable. Because MRI sequences for liver surgery planning are an active research area, software to analyze these data need future adaptations. Fast, precise, and robust registration are among the challenges to cope with. Another direction left open for future work is a better integration of simulation and visualization for planning thermoablation and the planning of combined therapies (e.g., open surgery to interrupt the blood supply during thermoablation). Finally, intraoperative support is a great challenge left open for future work. The development of these algorithms is one challenge; their evaluation is another, even more long-term goal.

FURTHER READING

Concerning the clinical background, the overview by TANAKA and KIUCHI [2002] is highly interesting for LDLT (the authors' clinic has by far the most experience worldwide with LDLT surgery). An extensive review concerning techniques for ablation of liver metastases is given in [DESANCTIS et al. 1998]. There are alternative strategies to simulate the heat distribution in LITT and RF ablation. As an example, more accurate results at the expense of higher computational demands can be achieved with Finite Element methods [VERHEY et al. 2003, VERHEY et al. 2005].

First attempts to provide intraoperative support during liver surgery were described in [SCHEUERING et al. 2003c, VETTER et al. 2003]. Both systems, however, have only been evaluated with animal cadavers so far. More promising results are achieved for thermoablation, as the amount of intraoperative deformation is considerably less. In addition to the appropriate use of navigation and intraoperative visualization technology, the correlation between preoperative and intraoperative images is challenging. Bifurcations of vascular structures are well suited as landmarks to guide the registration [AYLWARD et al. 2003]. BORNIK et al. [2003a] developed an encompassing augmented-reality system for liver surgery planning at the University of Graz.

An encompassing and dedicated effort to image-guidance in ablation of liver metastases was carried out by BLACKALL [2003]. She measured and modeled the respiratory motion and deformation of the liver by analyzing MRI scans from volunteers. Her analysis of the motion during the life-cycle has been incorporated in a nonrigid registration algorithm to correlate intraoperative ultrasound with preoperative imaging (see also [PENNEY et al. 2004]).

BUTZ et al. [2001] described planning of applicator placement, but instead of simulating the heating or cooling on an individual basis, they determined the destroyed tissue by merely transferring standardized shapes of lesions won from previous interventions into the new planning dataset. BRICAULT et al. [2004] described computer-aided monitoring after radiofrequency ablation to detect local recurrences as early as possible. NICOLAU et al. [2005a] and NICOLAU et al. [2005b] introduced an augmented reality system for training thermoablation as well as for evaluating its results.

There are alternative approaches to the image analysis problems involved in liver surgery planning, in particular with respect to liver segmentation [LAMECKER et al. 2002]. A promising approach is to build and employ statistical models of the liver. Since liver segmentation is still the most time-consuming step, a reduced interaction time in this part is highly desirable.

The impact of 3D visualization for liver surgery planning has been investigated in [LAMADÉ et al. 2000]. Dedicated support for liver surgery planning has also been described in [GLOMBITZA et al. 1999, SOLER et al. 2001].

Chapter 20

Visualization for Medical Education

This chapter is dedicated to educational applications of medical visualization techniques. Interactive 3D visualizations have a great potential for anatomy education as well as for surgery education, with potential users ranging from high school students and physiotherapists to medical doctors who want to rehearse therapeutical interventions. Many techniques that have been described in earlier chapters are crucial for educational purposes: high-quality and efficient surface and volume visualization, as well as interaction facilities to explore medical volume data such as clipping and virtual resection (see Chap. 12), are essential ingredients for educational systems. Most of the illustrative rendering techniques described in Chapter 17 are motivated by applications in educational systems. Educational systems benefit from low-level illustration techniques, such as silhouette enhancement, as well as high-level techniques, such as cutaways and ghost views. However, the design of educational systems poses new challenges and requires additional visualization techniques that have not been discussed so far. Textual explanations and relations between anatomic objects have to be assigned and efficiently represented to allow users to explore symbolic knowledge and spatial relations in a coherent manner. We focus on three problems:

- The integration of labels in 3D visualizations
- The specification of animation sequences and the integration of animation with interactive exploration of anatomic structures
- The design and realization of educational systems in surgery. Challenging aspects of such systems include haptic feedback and soft tissue simulation.

The integration of labels is important in particular for anatomy education, in which labels convey the terminology in relation to graphical realizations of anatomic objects. Since the number of labels to be integrated in a 3D visualization might be large, challenging layout problems have to be tackled.

The discussion of animation sequences is motivated by observations from high-quality video material developed for medical education. Such video material may effectively convey knowledge about anatomic variants as well as about therapeutic interventions. Particularly for educational purposes, interactive manipulation of 3D visualizations should be added through well-prepared animation sequences comprising smooth transitions between appropriate views.

Although we introduce labeling and animation generation in the chapter on educational purposes, they are also relevant for some diagnostic tasks and therapy planning. For the documentation of diagnostic findings, automatic labeling may be useful if, for example, information concerning several nodules must be included in a visualization. Animation sequences may be more effective than interactive exploration to present a case in interdisciplinary discussions—for example, in tumor boards. The generation of animation sequences takes an *author* additional time but may considerably reduce the time for all participants of an interdisciplinary discussion.

Dealing with educational systems in medicine requires at least an introduction to the broader topic of computer-based training (CBT). Researchers in CBT have gained much knowledge regarding general interaction strategies, appropriate feedback for learners, and last but not least motivational aspects that are crucial for the success of any educational system. One consequence of this discussion is the exploration of metaphors that guide the development of educational systems. To round off the picture, we discuss specific examples of anatomy education systems.

The last part of this chapter is dedicated to the emerging area of surgical simulators. Many challenging tasks have to be solved to provide a realistic virtual environment for practicing complex surgical interventions. Surgical simulation is of paramount importance for endoscopic (or minimally invasive) interventions. These interventions have many advantages for the patient, including reduced trauma and postoperative pain, but they exhibit inherent problems and pitfalls for the surgeon due to the small incision size through which all actions have to be performed. These problems include the lack of dexterity due to the loss of two degrees of freedom (instruments can only be moved forward or backward), the lack of fine manipulation, and the degradation of force feedback in the interaction with human tissue, which is essential for the palpation of the patient [TAVAKOLI *et al.* 2006]. We describe some of the general problems, such as modeling elastic tissue properties, simulating soft tissue deformation, and adequate haptic feedback.

We primarily discuss applications in anatomy and different surgical disciplines. This is motivated by the benefit of interactive rendering of volume data and derived 3D models in these areas. Computer support may enhance education in selected medical disciplines. However, traditional forms of learning, such as lectures, dissections of cadavers, and assistance during surgical interventions, shall not be replaced by any software solution.

Organization This chapter starts with a brief review of visualization and interaction techniques relevant for educational purposes and discusses the data on which educational systems are based (see Sect. 20.1). Afterward, the methodological aspects of integrating labels in 3D visualizations and generating animations are discussed in Section 20.2 and Section 20.3. As a basis for the discussion of case studies, we introduce general concepts of computer-based training (see Sect. 20.4) and metaphors for educational systems. Case studies in anatomy education (see Sect. 20.5) and surgery education (see Sect. 20.6) complete the chapter.

20.1   DATASETS AND KNOWLEDGE REPRESENTATION FOR MEDICAL EDUCATION

CBT systems for anatomy and surgery education require appropriate image data and segmentation results. Based on these data, high-quality renderings can be generated and interactively explored as an essential component of such CBT systems. Direct volume rendering as well as surface rendering techniques may be employed. While clinical applications require fast segmentation and visualization, educational systems require primarily high-quality results. By the way, the accuracy of visualizations is less important. Smooth surfaces without distracting features are preferred.

20.1.1 DATASETS FOR MEDICAL EDUCATION

As a source for anatomy education, commercial 3D model catalogues can be employed. A leading vendor is Viewpoint Datalabs; their catalogue is provided by Digimation (www.digimation.com). The surface models have an excellent quality, and we will see a variety of illustrations derived from these models throughout this chapter.

The most widely used data sources for anatomy education are the Visible Human datasets from the National Library of Medicine Visible Human project. These 3D datasets originate from two bodies that were given to science, frozen, and digitized into horizontally spaced slices. A total number of 1871 cryosection slices were generated for the Visible Man (1-mm slice distance) and even more for the Visible

Woman (0.33-mm slice distance). Besides photographic cryosectional images, fresh and frozen CT data have been acquired. The total volume of all slices represents 13 GB of data for the male dataset and 40 GB for the female dataset. The project was carried out at the University of Colorado (headed by DR. VICTOR SPITZER) under contract with the National Library of Medicine, Bethesda, Maryland [SPITZER et al. 1996].

The Visible Human datasets have a high quality that was unprecedented at that time. CT data were acquired with high radiation—resulting in an excellent signal-to-noise ratio—and without breathing and other motion artifacts. However, the quality of the data is not perfect: the frozen body was cut in four blocks prior to image acquisition, leaving some noticeable gaps in the data. The Visible Human datasets are employed for a variety of educational systems; a prominent example is the VOXELMAN system [HÖHNE et al. 2001, 2003].

An alternative source of data is high-quality clinical data. As an example, the first versions of the VOXELMAN were based on a cerebral MRI dataset [HÖHNE et al. 1992]. For anatomy education, some care is necessary in using data from a healthy person with normal anatomic relations. If anatomic differences are to be compared, the selection of cases should be representative with respect to typical variants. Surgery education systems are often also based on one particular dataset that is carefully enhanced with the necessary information, such as elastic properties of different portions.

The segmentation of these datasets is a normal task that can be accomplished with general segmentation techniques (recall Sect. 5.3). A special aspect is the segmentation of the photographic datasets of the Visible Human project. These datasets represent colored voxels (24 bits per voxel, representing red, green, and blue components). The segmentation of colored data represents new challenges and opportunities, as regions in RGB-space are separated [SCHIEMANN et al. 1997].

For anatomy education, in principle all anatomic structures that can be derived from the image data are relevant. Therefore, considerably more objects are segmented compared to clinical applications. The VOXELMAN, for example, is based on the segmentation of 650 objects (clinical applications often require the segmentation of less than 10 objects). A challenge is the identification and delineation of functional areas—for example, in the brain—because these areas are not represented as recognizable objects in the image data. Considerable expert knowledge is necessary to delineate these features.

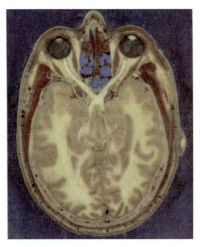 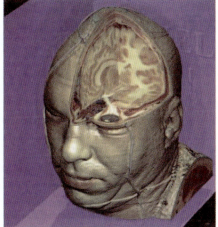

FIGURE 20.1 *Photographic data from the Visible Human Male dataset. Left: a slice view, right: a volume rendering with clipping enabled [TIEDE et al. 1996]. (Image courtesy ULF TIEDE, University Hospital Hamburg-Eppendorf)*

20.1.2 KNOWLEDGE REPRESENTATION

Although interactive visualizations are the primary components of medical education systems, they are not sufficient to effectively support learning processes. The mental integration of visual elements and related symbolic knowledge is an essential learning goal. Symbolic knowledge relates to concepts, names, and functions of anatomic objects and the various relations between them—for example, which area is supplied by a certain vascular structure. Knowledge representation schemes employ segmentation information and allow the addition of various relations between individual objects. Before we actually discuss knowledge representations, it should be noted that anatomy is studied under different aspects. Essential aspects of anatomy are found www.netanatomy.com (accessed January 15, 2007):

- *Clinical anatomy*: the study of anatomy that is most relevant to the practice of medicine.
- *Comparative anatomy*: the study of the anatomy of different organisms, drawing contrasts and similarities between the structure and function of the anatomies.
- *Cross-sectional anatomy*: anatomy viewed in the transverse plane of the body.
- *Radiographic anatomy*: the study of anatomy as observed with imaging techniques, such as conventional X-ray, MRI, CT, and ultrasonography. Images that relate to cross-sectional and radiographic anatomy are shown in Figure 20.2.
- *Regional anatomy*: the study of anatomy by regional parts of the body (e.g., thorax, heart, and abdomen). In regional anatomy, all biological systems (e.g., skeletal, circulatory, etc.,) are studied, with an emphasis on the interrelation of the systems and their regional function.
- *Systemic anatomy*: the study of anatomy by biological systems (e.g., the skeletal, muscular, or circulatory system). In systemic anatomy, a single biological system is studied concurrently across all body regions.
- *Macroscopic anatomy*: the study of anatomy with the unaided eye, essentially visual observation. Typically, macroscopic anatomy is explored using dissected cadavers.
- *Microscopic anatomy*: the study of anatomy with the aid of the light microscope as well as electron microscopes that provide subcellular observations. Microscopic anatomy is based on very high-resolution images and provides insight at a level that is not possible with either tomographic image data or dissecting cadavers.

These different aspects of anatomy form different "views" of the anatomy. For example, the kidney is part of the abdominal viscera in the *regional anatomy* and part of the urogenital system in the *systemic anatomy* [POMMERT *et al.* 2001].

Ideally, CBT systems for anatomy comprise and integrate all aspects, for example by smoothly blending data in different resolutions. Currently, such an ideal system does not exist, probably due to many technical problems inherent in acquiring and analyzing a large variety of image data and adapting visualization techniques. Clinical anatomy and radiographic anatomy can be explored with medical volume data and derived information. As an example of combining different aspects of anatomy, the DIGITAL ANATOMIST [BRINKLEY and ROSSE 1997] provides 3D overviews in which the positions of certain slabs are marked (see Fig. 20.2 (left)). For each slab, the related information is shown as a CT slice, as photographic data, and as a clipped 3D visualization (see Fig. 20.2 (right)).

CBT for the study of comparative anatomy requires a variety of different datasets (along with segmentation results) that represent at least the typical anatomic variants. Most CBT systems do not support this important aspect of anatomy. CBT systems that do support microscopic anatomy require appropriate image data from microscopes, as well as image analysis results.

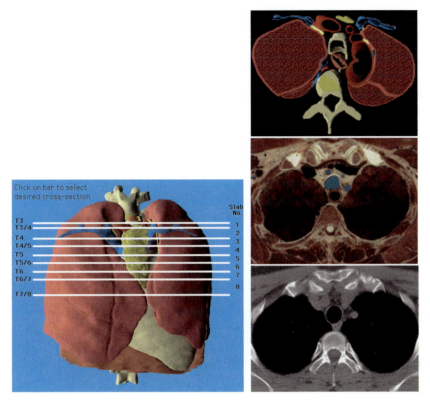

FIGURE 20.2   *A 3D overview (left) is used to show different levels for which cross-sectional and radiographic images are provided. The images on the right relate to the T1-level in the left image. (Screenshot from the DIGITAL ANATOMIST)*

Many anatomy education systems focus on regional anatomy and represent the relation between labels and segmentation results. Some systems provide textual labels and related textual explanations with facilities to explore them, along with the graphical representation [PREIM et al. 1997]. A sophisticated representation of symbolic anatomic knowledge, however, goes far beyond this, effectively building an ontology composed of different views (e.g., different kinds of relations between anatomic objects). The first advanced (digital) knowledge representation for anatomy was developed by SCHUBERT et al. [1993]. Among others, they represent:

- *Part of relations* (one object belongs to a larger object, for example, a functional brain area)
- *Is a relations* (groups anatomic objects into categories)
- *Supplied by relations* (characterizes the blood supply)

This knowledge is integrated in a *semantic net*—a flexible knowledge representation (see Fig. 20.3). The relation between variably labeled volumes and the symbolic knowledge is referred to as *intelligent voxel*. This relation provides the basis for interactive interrogation of parts of graphical representations. Similar concepts for knowledge representation were used later for the DIGITAL ANATOMIST [BRINKLEY and ROSSE 1997] and the ANATOMYBROWSER [KIKINIS et al. 1996] (see Sect. 20.5).

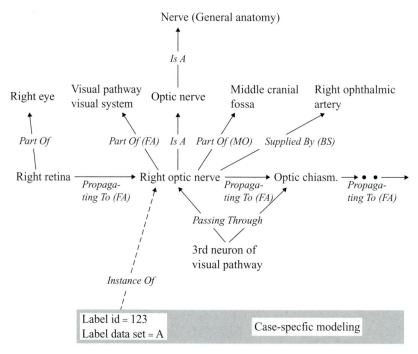

FIGURE 20.3 *A semantic net describes anatomic knowledge and serves as a basis for interactive interrogation* [SCHUBERT *et al.* 1993]. (*Image courtesy* RAINER SCHUBERT, *University Hospital Hamburg-Eppendorf*)

20.2   LABELING MEDICAL VISUALIZATIONS

Textual annotations, such as labels, captions, and legends, are important to coordinate visual and related symbolic information. In this section, we describe the integration of labels in interactive illustrations. Labels are used to establish a bidirectional link between visual representations of anatomic structures and their textual names (in a certain language). On one hand, students should learn how visual objects are named. On the other hand, they should learn where an object—characterized by a certain name—is located, and which characteristic features determine its shape.

The annotation of anatomic objects via labels is a relevant and challenging task in educational systems. Given that the relevant objects are segmented and that a textual label (and optionally additional information) is assigned to each object, the task is to define which objects should be labeled and which strategy (or labeling style [ALI *et al.* 2005]) should be used. Labeling is relevant for 2D as well as for 3D visualizations. We focus on labeling 3D visualizations, which is the more challenging aspect.

Labeling is related to the integration of measurement facilities in 3D illustrations, which we discussed in Chapter 13. Again, appropriate layout decisions are necessary to unambiguously convey the way symbolic information relates to visual information. Since 3D visualizations are interactively explored, the relation between annotations and visual information has to be maintained. However, there are also major differences: measures often relate to two objects (e.g., minimal distance, angle between the major axis of two objects) whereas the relation between a label and a visual object is a 1:1 relation. Usually, only a few measures are integrated in a visualization, whereas when more labels are considered, it increases the complexity of layout decisions.

Interactive Labeling   The simplest and most general solution is to leave the labeling task to the user; he or she might select a position, initiate a label command, and then interactively place that label. The label name corresponds to the object visible at the position selected by the user. A connection line is generated to connect the textual label with an anchor point—the position the user selected. If more labels should be included, it is the user's task to make sure that labels do not overlap and that the overall layout is not confusing. Interactive labeling is incorporated in the VOXELMAN (see Fig. 20.4). This simple strategy has obvious drawbacks: it puts a burden on the user and is not appropriate in interactive scenarios where the objects are rotated and zoomed in, since the labels might simply disappear.

Automatic Labeling   Therefore, we discuss automatic labeling strategies in the following. Automatic labeling strategies can be classified as *internal* or *external* [GÖTZELMANN et al. 2005]. Internal labels overlap with the objects to which they refer, whereas external labels are arranged in the background and connected to the graphical representation of their *reference object*. The most salient advantage of internal labels is that the relation between a visual object and its label is easy to perceive.

The use of external labels requires *anchor points* and *connection lines* as additional graphical elements. The selection of anchor points is crucial to establish a clear correlation between a label and its reference object. Despite the problems of providing a correlation between a textual label and related visual objects, we regard *external labels* as the more promising approach for CBT systems in medicine and discuss them in more detail. The most obvious advantage of external labels is better legibility, because external labels are placed on top of a background in uniform color. Moreover, external labels do not restrict the perception of the shape of visual objects, which is essential in medicine because object shapes are irregular and may be very complex.

20.2.1 PLACEMENT OF EXTERNAL LABELS

The placement of external labels involves several tasks. For each object, at least one anchor point needs to be defined. All labels must be placed and connected with their anchor points. We discuss several labeling

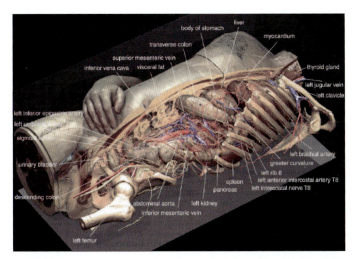

FIGURE 20.4   *Interactive labeling with the VOXELMAN [POMMERT et al. 2001]. (Image courtesy ANDREAS POMMERT, University Hospital Hamburg-Eppendorf)*

strategies based on the following requirements [PREIM and RAAB 1998, BRUCKNER and GRÖLLER 2005, HARTMANN et al. 2004]:

1 Anchor points should be visible.
2 The projection of an anchor point in screen space should be inside the projection of the reference object.
3 Labels must not hide any graphical representation.
4 Labels must not overlap.
5 A label should be placed as close as possible to its reference object. In particular, connection lines should not cross.

These requirements are very general, and each configuration may be easily checked to determine whether they are actually fulfilled. The list above represents a minimal subset of requirements discussed by various authors. HARTMANN et al. [2005] grounded their work on an advanced labeling technique with similar requirements. In addition, they claim that:

• Anchor points should ease the identification of the reference object.
• Connection lines should be orthogonal to a main axis.
• Label placement should be coherent in dynamic and interactive illustrations.

We agree with them, but consider these requirements to be minor compared with the previous list. Anchor point determination is indeed a crucial issue, which will be discussed. However, it is not easy to tell whether a given configuration of graphical objects and anchor points fulfills the requirement. Orthogonal connection lines dominate in manual illustrations, which probably explains HARTMANN's second requirement. However, we regard this requirement as too rigid (taking into account the constraints imposed by the list of general requirements) and therefore would relax it. The last requirement is the only one related to interactive illustrations. "Coherent" basically means that strong and sudden changes of anchor point and label positions should be avoided. We will discuss the interactive scenario later.

For the moment, we assume that each object is characterized by exactly one anchor point. This point might be the center of gravity or the bounding box center. To ensure that the anchor point is actually visible (Req. 1), it is smart to analyze the projection of an object in screen space and select a point on a visible segment of that object. In object space, rays between the camera position and the anchor point candidate should be evaluated. If other vertices of the reference object are in front of the anchor point candidate and close to the viewing ray, the closest of them should be selected. An alternative is to render all faces (strongly) transparent if they block the side of the reference object. For elongated or branching anatomic objects, it might be difficult to define an anchor point that belongs to the object (Req. 2). Later, we discuss appropriate strategies for such objects.

To fulfill requirements 3 through 5, some general layout strategy is necessary. Observations in medical illustrations reveal two typical strategies: either labels are arranged in vertical columns to the left and right of the drawing, or they are placed close to the silhouette of the drawing. For an automatic algorithm, it is difficult to place labels in concave notches. Therefore, HARTMANN et al. [2004] and BRUCKNER and GRÖLLER [2005] suggest using the projection of the convex hull of the drawing instead (see Fig. 20.5).

In Figure 20.6, the vertical arrangement of labels is employed. For a static illustration, the layout in Figure 20.5 is more appropriate, since it leads to shorter connection lines and an easier understanding of the relation between labels and anatomic objects. In an interactive scenario, however, the area occluded by the illustration changes considerably and therefore the label positions have to be adapted. The layout in Figure 20.6 considers the 3D bounding box of the underlying model and places labels outside. After rotations, the second requirement is still fulfilled.

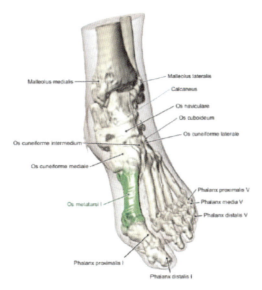

FIGURE 20.5 External labeling for an anatomic illustration of a foot. Labels are arranged close to the convex hull of the whole model. Labels do not overlap each other, and connection lines do not cross [BRUCKNER and GRÖLLER 2005]. (Image courtesy STEFAN BRUCKNER, Vienna University of Technology)

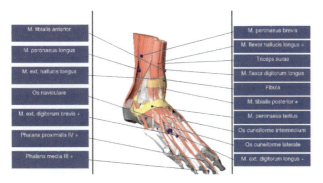

FIGURE 20.6 Initial layout of labels arranged in columns left and right of an illustration.

The third requirement relates to the distribution of labels in the area "reserved" for labels. A layout algorithm that manages occupied space is necessary. The algorithm described in [HARTMANN et al. 2004] is briefly explained as follows. Starting from initial labels close to the silhouette lines, labels are exchanged or slightly translated to prevent overlaps and crossing connection lines. A maximum number of iterations ensures that the algorithm terminates. BRUCKNER and GRÖLLER [2005] also employed this algorithm (see Fig. 20.5).

A simple strategy for the placement of external labels is described in [PREIM et al. 1995]: the positions of anchor points in screen space are analyzed to decide which labels are placed on the left and which on the right. The number of labels in both regions should be roughly equal (the interpretation of "roughly equal" is controlled by a parameter), and the assignment of labels to one of the two regions is based on proximity (labels relating to anchor points with low x-coordinates are labeled on the left, others on the right). In the second step, the position of each label is guided by sorting the corresponding anchor points according to their y-coordinates. With this strategy, crossing connection lines are unlikely; however, they are not completely excluded. In a final step, it may be explored whether two lines cross each other, and should this occur, the two labels are exchanged (provided that no other lines cross as a consequence of the change). A result of this algorithm is shown in Figure 20.6.

Anchor Point Determination

While simple strategies such as using an object's center of gravity are sufficient for labeling compact and visible objects, they may be inappropriate or even fail for other objects. Anchor points might not be enclosed by the reference object's outline, or they might be obscured by other objects. In case of branching objects, which are only partially visible, one anchor point is simply not enough to convey the relation between a label and a graphic object.

The first problem is that anchor points should be inside the projection of an object to screen space (Req. 2). If the anchor point is determined with a simple strategy, it should be tested whether this condition is fulfilled. If this is not the case, a vertex of the object that is close to the original anchor point position should be chosen. This strategy is successful in the case of a completely visible object. Otherwise, a visibility analysis is necessary (recall Sect. 17.3) to select—if possible—a visible anchor point.

Using Potential Fields and Distance Transforms to Guide Label Placement The most advanced general labeling algorithm is based on potential fields and their applications in robot motion planning [HARTMANN et al. 2005]. The requirements for a good configuration of labels lead to the definition of attractive forces (between a label and a related anchor point) and repulsive forces (between different labels, or between a label and anchor points that do not belong to the reference object). This algorithm starts from an initial configuration of labels and moves them through the potential field. Figure 20.7 illustrates how the initial configuration of labels improves due to the forces of the potential field.

A fast approach to anchor point determination was introduced more recently [GÖTZELMANN et al. 2006a]. The whole computation is carried out in screen space, which makes sense because the relation between an anchor point position and the projection of a visual object determines the quality of a labeling process. This approach is based on object-ID-buffers—2D structures representing each pixel of

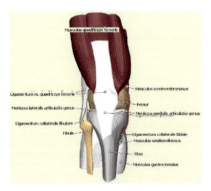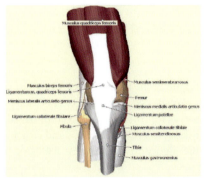

FIGURE 20.7 *Labeling anatomic objects with potential fields. The initial layout (left) is improved (right). In particular, overlapping labels are effectively avoided [HARTMANN et al. 2005]. (Image courtesy KNUT HARTMANN, University of Magdeburg)*

a rendered image that contains a unique number (the ID) for each object. The number looked up at the pixel $id(x, y)$ in the ID-buffer represents the object that is visible at the corresponding location $r(x, y)$ in the rendered image—represented in the frame buffer. The ID-buffer is employed to determine silhouettes of each object that should be labeled in 2D. A distance transform is applied to these silhouettes, resulting in an integer value for each pixel that indicates the pixel's distance from the silhouette. Ideal anchor points are placed at the local maxima of the distance transform (see Fig. 20.8). This strategy can be modified, for example, if anchor points were placed too close to each other.

Grouping External Labels

So far, we have discussed labeling as a process in which as many individual labels as possible should be placed in an illustration guided by some layout styles. We did not consider that the information is perceived and interpreted in chunks, as research in visual perception clearly indicates (see, for example, [SIMON 1974]). Individual elements of a visualization are perceived as a chunk:

- If they are located close to each other
- If they are enclosed or otherwise visually summarized (e.g., with a bracket)
- If they have the same visual attributes, such as foreground and background color

These properties allow elements to be visually grouped, a process that has been known for a long time and is formalized as the Gestalt laws. The number of individual elements forming a chunk should be between four and eight. For labeling, it is therefore desirable to make them form recognizable groups primarily by placing labels of a group close to each other [GÖTZELMANN et al. 2006b]. The assignment of labels to groups must be pursued by the author of an illustration; the process may consider spatial proximity (e.g., muscles of the eye) as well as other relations discussed in the knowledge representation. Figure 20.9 presents an illustration in which external labels form clearly recognizable groups to support their perception.

20.2.2 PLACEMENT OF INTERNAL LABELS

Internal labels are placed on top of the graphic representation of an object. The use of internal labels is only feasible for objects that are large enough to accommodate a label and that are not partially obscured by

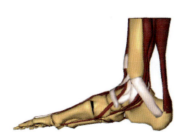

FIGURE 20.8 *A distance transform in image space is accomplished to search for anchor point candidates. The right image presents the distance transform of the rendered image on the left. Dark areas represent large distances from the silhouette of a particular object* [GÖTZELMANN et al. 2006a]. *(Image courtesy* TIMO GÖTZELMANN, *University of Magdeburg)*

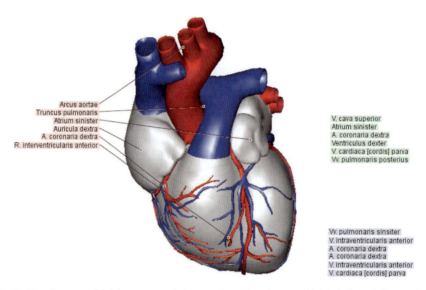

Arcus aortae
Truncus pulmonaris
Atrium sinister
Auricula dextra
A. coronaria dextra
R. interventricularis anterior

V. cava superior
Atrium sinister
A. coronaria dextra
Ventriculus dexter
V. cardiaca [cordis] parva
Vv. pulmonaris posterius

Vv. pulmonaris sinsiter
V. intraventricularis anterior
A. coronaria dextra
A. coronaria dextra
V. intraventricularis anterior
V. cardiaca [cordis] parva

FIGURE 20.9 *Grouping external labels to support their perception. The red group of labels is focused (lines and anchor points related to this group are shown with high contrast)* [GÖTZELMANN *et al.* 2006b]. *(Image courtesy* TIMO GÖTZELMANN, *University of Magdeburg)*

other objects. With respect to legibility, it is preferable to present labels horizontally. If this is not possible, GÖTZELMANN *et al.* [2005] suggest to place a label along the centerline. If the centerline branches, a path needs to be selected that is long enough. The skeleton path is smoothed to gently accommodate a label. Figure 20.10 illustrates the principle approach. The readability of internal labels has been improved by computing individual spacing between any two letters (instead of monospacing) and by incorporating thresholds on the allowable curvature of the path [GÖTZELMANN *et al.* 2006a].

While internal labels are quite common in manually created illustrations, they are less appropriate when read on a conventional monitor with its relatively low resolution. In interactive scenarios, internal labels have a role when graphical representations are strongly zoomed in (see Fig. 20.11).

Labeling of Interactive Illustrations

Labeling interactive 3D illustrations poses some challenges and requires careful decisions. When a 3D model is zoomed in, the visibility of objects and their relative positions do not change. With an external labeling strategy, only the connection lines need to be updated. Labels may, however, occlude part of the geometry. Therefore, it is reasonable to switch to internal labeling for such objects (see Fig. 20.11).

More problems occur when the 3D model is rotated. The visibility of objects, as well as their relative position in screen space, will change. Different strategies are viable to account for this situation: labels relating to objects that are no longer visible are hidden or rendered more transparent to indicate that they are somehow "invalid." The labels may be rearranged in vertical and horizontal positions to reflect the new screen space position of their anchor points. As a consequence, connection lines may get long and cross each other (see Fig. 20.12). "Rearranging" labels yields consistency between labels and graphical elements. However, it is highly distracting when labels "fly" around a 3D model. Assuming that the user's focus during a rotation is on the graphical elements, automatically rearranging labels cannot be

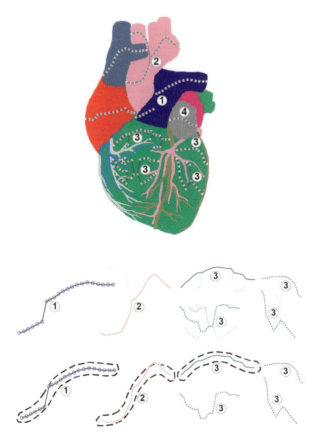

FIGURE 20.10 *Internal label placement based on skeletons of reference objects (top image), selecting one path per object, and smoothing the path. (Images courtesy* TIMO GÖTZELMANN, *University of Magdeburg)*

recommended. Better strategies are to rearrange labels after a rotation is finished or to provide a command that allows the user to enforce a nice label layout [PREIM et al. 1995].

20.2.3 LABELING BRANCHING AND PARTIALLY VISIBLE OBJECTS

For branching objects, it is reasonable to determine several anchor points, as is common in handmade illustrations. Implementation of this principle requires analysis of the shape of reference objects. A general approach for this kind of analysis is skeletonization, which allows assessment of the branching pattern. As a rule of thumb, one anchor point for each branch should be determined. The skeleton may also be used to select the anchor points: as the skeleton represents the medial axis, points on the skeleton are good candidates for anchor points. Since branching objects may be partially hidden, the visibility of anchor point candidates has to be considered as well. Figure 20.13 illustrates the anchor point determination for a branching muscle that is partially occluded.

Generation of Intermediate Connection Points   Once the anchor points for an object have been defined, the label may be connected to each of them directly. This is a viable and simple approach; however, it is not

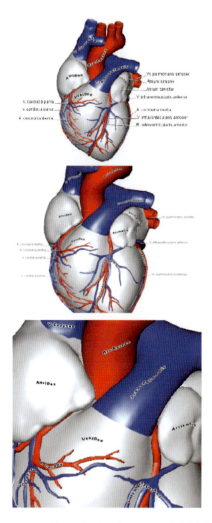

FIGURE 20.11 *Adapting labels after zooming. Objects that have been externally labeled are internally labeled after magnification* [GÖTZELMANN et al. 2005]. *(Image courtesy* TIMO GÖTZELMANN, *University of Magdeburg)*

visually pleasing and can be observed rarely in manual illustrations. Basically, there are two problems of the simple strategy: if the anchor points are far away from each other, connection lines may cross with connection lines from other labels. The second problem occurs if the angle between two connection lines is very small and the lines are hard to distinguish.

Instead, intermediate connection points are typically computed. An analysis of handmade illustrations reveals different strategies, shown in Figure 20.14. All these labeling strategies can be applied automatically (see [PREIM and RAAB 1998] for details). None of these strategies has a general advantage over others; the selection should consider other constraints, such as avoiding crossing connection lines. In general, the strategies should not be mixed so that there will be a consistent layout.

Discussion The determination of one anchor point for each visible segment of a reference object may cause problems—particularly when their number is large. Therefore, it is also useful to develop a strategy

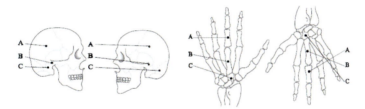

FIGURE 20.12   *Adapting labels after rotation. In the left image, anchor points are farther away from the labels after a rotation. In the right image, connection lines cross each other after a rotation. In both cases, the labels should be adapted to reflect the new positions of the anchor points.*

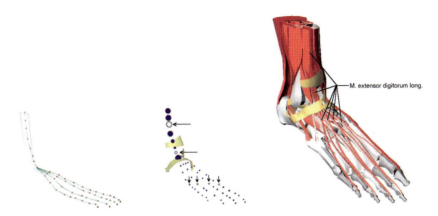

FIGURE 20.13   *Analyzing the shape and visibility of a muscle to determine appropriate anchor points. First, the skeleton of a muscle's surface model is defined (left). A visibility analysis follows (the two yellow objects partially hide the muscle). Based on the visibility, six anchor points are selected, each representing one visible segment. The analysis results are used to label the object (right).*

to choose one visible segment for a reference object. HARTMANN et al. [2005] suggested using an anchor point in the largest visual segment or in the visual segment closest to the label (provided that the label position is already known).

20.2.4 LABELING CROSS-SECTIONAL IMAGES

For radiographic and cross-sectional anatomy, it is essential that cross-sectional images are appropriately labeled. Basically, the strategies discussed so far also apply to 2D visualizations. An appropriate layout strategy is necessary to avoid labels that occlude each other or hide relevant portions of the graphical representation. Usually, external labels are preferred. Anchor point determination is also challenging in 2D; the number and shape of visual segments must be analyzed to select an appropriate anchor point (or points). Figure 20.15 presents a CT slice with external labels arranged at all borders of the image.

20.2.5 PRESENTATION VARIABLES FOR LABELING

Besides the geometric aspects (where to place anchor points and labels in relation to reference objects), labeling is characterized by several presentation variables, such as the font size and style as well as the style,

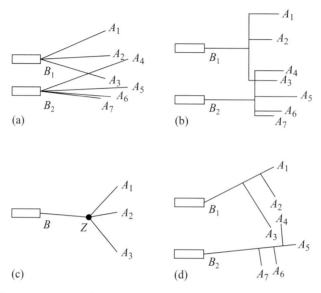

FIGURE 20.14 Labeling strategies in case of multiple anchor points. The labels B_1 and B_2 should be connected with the anchor points A_1 to A_5. (a) No connection points are computed. (b) For both labels, one connection point is determined on the halfway from the label to the anchor points. The lines are connected so that all lines are parallel to a main axis. (c) Only one label with anchor points is shown. A connection point is computed as in (b). The label image in the right image of Figure 20.13 was created with this strategy. The connection point is directly connected to the label and to all anchor points. (d) The most distant anchor point is directly connected with the label. All other anchor points are connected with lines orthogonal to the (long) line.

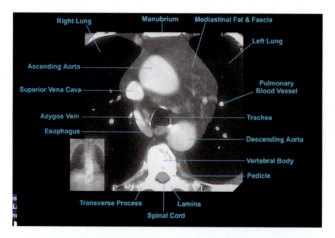

FIGURE 20.15   Labeled cross-sectional views of CT thorax data. (From www.netanatomy.com)

width, and color of connection lines. We do not want to go into detail here. As a general remark, sans serif fonts are preferred. Solid lines visually separate regions of the illustration. This might be avoided with dashed lines. It is difficult to achieve a good contrast between the connection line and the background of an illustration. Illustrators often use parallel lines with different colors for this purpose (a small dark line

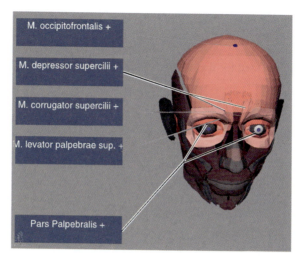

FIGURE 20.16   *Embedding dark connection lines in light surrounding lines to ensure a high contrast with varying backgrounds.*

inside a wider bright line). With this technique, the connection line is very recognizable at all positions (see Fig. 20.16).

20.3   ANIMATING MEDICAL VISUALIZATIONS

Animations may effectively convey complex spatial relations between anatomic objects. As an example, a large series of educational animations was generated in the DIGITAL ANATOMIST project (see Sect. 20.5).

Compared to static illustrations, animations offer additional degrees of freedom for emphasizing objects and clarifying their spatial configuration by performing gradual frame-to-frame changes. The observation of gradual changes between visualizations is mentally easier than the interpretation of two static images. The space of meaningful animation techniques depends on the data and derived information. Most anatomy education and surgical education systems are based on medical volume data and derived information, particularly segmentation information. Typical animation techniques include the rotation of the whole dataset, zooming towards relevant structures, the movement of clipping planes, the movement of the camera along a certain path (for example, through tubular structures), and gradual changes of the transparencies of objects. The design of animations that are successful in educational settings has to take into consideration findings from perceptual psychology. As an example, the number of movements that take place simultaneously should be limited [TVERSKY *et al.* 2002].

Animations are specified by an *author*, for example with recording facilities in an interactive system. The specification of animations by recording the interactive use of a 3D visualization is the most general form of specification. However, it has some limitations.

- Manual specification of animations without dedicated support is a laborious task.
- The content and structure of the animation is not formally represented. A formal representation would allow easy modification of an animation—for example, by specifying that a certain part should be faster. Without formal representation, modification of an animation usually requires redoing the whole animation.

- Animations strongly depend on the author. They are not easily reproducible for a similar case. For comparative anatomy, surgical planning, and training, similar portions of the anatomy from different patients should be visualized and animated. To effectively generate such animations, one description should be reused for the different cases and, if necessary, slightly fine-tuned to adapt to the peculiarities of a case.

These drawbacks gave rise to the development of script-based specification methods for animation design.

20.3.1 SCRIPT-BASED SPECIFICATION OF ANIMATIONS

Effective specifications of animations may be accomplished by means of *scripts*—textual descriptions of an animation. This idea arose in the 1970s at the MIT Artificial Intelligence Lab and is described in a PhD thesis [KAHN 1979].

Scripting languages have been known for a long time as parts of advanced 3D modeling systems and as part of multimedia authoring systems. Scripting can be performed at different levels: at a high level, the intent of an animation may be specified, whereas at lower levels, the movement of specific objects along specific trajectories is specified [KARP and FEINER 1993]. At the lowest level, everything necessary to actually render the animation (e.g., precise coordinates, timings, etc.) is specified. The highest level is called the *task level* [ZELTZER 1990]. Examples of task level specifications are "*show object*" and "*show relation between object₁ and object₂.*"

The intent-based approach to animation design requires built-in rules (*decomposition rules*) that define the mapping of high-level specifications to low-level commands. This principle was first realized in the context of technical documentation, in which animations are intended to support people using and maintaining technical devices [KARP and FEINER 1993, BUTZ 1997].

For authoring educational animations, dedicated support at different levels is also required. A first scripting language for this purpose was presented in [PREIM et al. 1996]. The central command of the task level is "*explain*" followed by the name of an anatomic object or a group of objects. The decomposition of this high-level command was guided by optional parameters, as well as by an analysis of the object's shape and visibility. If the object is currently not visible, occluding objects are gradually made transparent or a clipping plane is translated to the data to remove them. For explanations of elongated and branching objects, pointing devices follow the centerline of the objects. Some screenshots from an example animation are shown in Figures 20.17 and 20.18.

Animations for Anatomy and Surgery Education The basic principle of specifying animations through scripts is also feasible for anatomy and surgery education. However, several aspects are special in medical visualization and have to be considered. Animations in medical visualization should consider slice-based visualizations and direct volume rendering in addition to surface visualization. Slice-based visualizations are essential for supporting the study of cross-sectional and radiographic anatomy. Similar to the cine-mode provided by radiology workstations, smooth transitions between adjacent slices are useful to understand spatial relations. Direct volume rendering is essential to visualize structures that have not been segmented in advance. The movement of clipping planes and the change of transfer function parameters allows gradual changes to the visibility of structures in volume renderings. With respect to these special requirements, the scripting facilities described so far are not sufficient. Finally, for surgery education and for studying comparative anatomy, it is essential that animations be *reusable* for different cases in which similar aspects should be visualized. As a consequence, it should be possible to flexibly combine a script with image data (see Fig. 20.19).

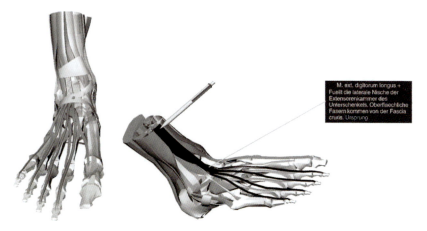

FIGURE 20.17   *Screenshots of an example animation. A 3D model (left) is transformed to emphasize a muscle. A pointing device points towards the upper end of this muscle and a short explanation is presented, along with a label.*

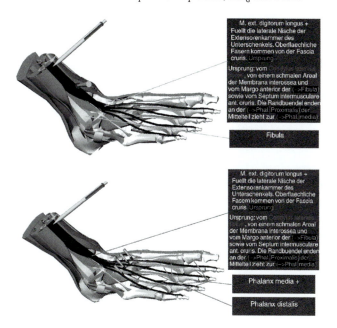

FIGURE 20.18   *Screenshots of an example animation (continued). Arrows as abstract pointing devices clarify the path of a muscle. A corresponding (more detailed) explanation is included, and objects mentioned in the textual explanation are automatically labeled. After the arrow reaches a branching point it splits into four small arrows that are moved along the branches. The textual explanation is updated accordingly.*

A first attempt to generate dedicated animations of medical volume data is described in [MUEHLER et al. 2006]. This scripting language supports slice-based visualizations and movements of clipping planes. It can be tailored to clinical tasks, such as evaluating the infiltration of a risk structure by a tumor or evaluating the resectability of a tumor patient. The efficient generation of animations requires standardization of object

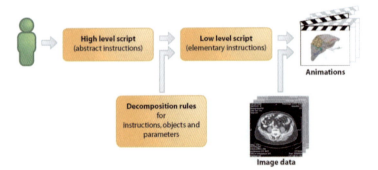

FIGURE 20.19 *Translation of a high-level script to a low-level script based on decomposition rules. The low-level script is applied to image data (and related segmentation results) to generate an animation* [MUEHLER *et al.* 2006]. *(Image courtesy* KONRAD MUEHLER, *University of Magdeburg)*

```
[0,9]   'Liver'   objectOverview
[9,18]  'Remnant' showResection
[18,25] 'Graft'   sceneOverview
[25,60] 'Graft'   showSegments
[60,70] 'All'     sceneOverview
```

FIGURE 20.20 *At the high level, an animation is specified that conveys an intended live-donor liver transplant. The numbers in brackets relate to the timing. Instead of fixed numbers, variables may be used to allow easier modification. "Remnant" relates to the remaining portion of the donor's liver and "Graft" to the portion that is transplanted to the recipient* [MUEHLER *et al.* 2006]. *(Image courtesy* KONRAD MUEHLER, *University of Magdeburg)*

names and employment of anatomic knowledge for the mapping of high-level specifications to low-level scripts. Decomposition rules are stored in a text file in a declarative manner (instead of being hard-coded in an animation system). Thus, the rules may be refined or new rules might be added to support further diagnostic processes. Default techniques to emphasize different categories of anatomic structures are employed. As an example, a camera movement along an object's centerline is appropriate for elongated objects, such as vascular structures. For compact structures, such as tumors, cutaway views are better suited (recall Sect. 17.5.1).

A simple script to support planning of living-related liver transplants is shown in Figure 20.20. Based on standardized object names, the script may be applied to different cases (an example is shown in Fig. 20.21). The camera movement is guided by the center of gravity and the axis-aligned bounding box of a tumor.

Discussion Despite nice examples, the generation of educational animations is still in its infancy. None of the scripting languages described has been extensively tested, evaluated, and refined. Mechanisms to fine-tune animations flexibly and intuitively are required. Authoring facilities that hide the scripting language are desirable. Ideally, a medical expert could generate such animations easily. Standardized animations are also useful for regular intervention planning. TOMANDL *et al.* [2003] described the use of standardized animations for neurosurgery planning. They employed a standardized "flight" path to locate intracranial aneurysms, as well as unique rendering parameters to achieve reproducible results.

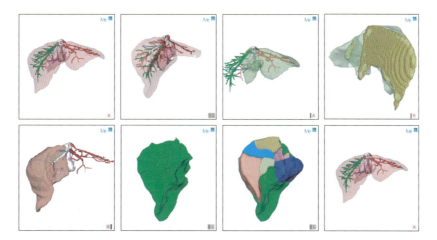

FIGURE 20.21   *Different stages of the animation generated with the script shown in Figure 20.20. After an overview of the liver and the relevant vasculature, the intended resection is shown by presenting the remnant and finally vascular territories* [MUEHLER *et al.* 2006]. *(Image courtesy* KONRAD MUEHLER, *University of Magdeburg)*

20.3.2 CHANGING THE OBJECT FOCUS WITH ANIMATIONS

Educational systems may benefit from a tight coupling of interactive exploration and animations. In particular, animations may be generated on-the-fly to gradually change a 3D visualization from the situation where one object is emphasized to the state where another object is emphasized. Gradual changes of the objects' transparency or colors may be performed in this way. In a case in which optimal viewing directions for objects are defined, the camera can be moved along a sphere surrounding the scene to the optimal viewpoint for the currently selected object.

Interactive Control of Animations   With conventional media players, the animation may be interrupted and played back. More interaction facilities—particularly rotation and zooming—are required to adequately support the mental understanding of complex anatomic shapes and their relations. If the output format of an animation only represents the generated 2D images, such interaction facilities are not possible. An alternative is to generate 3D descriptions of an animation, such as VRML files, in which viewpoint changes during runtime are possible.

20.4   BASICS OF COMPUTER-BASED TRAINING

CBT systems have been used for more than 40 years [OWEN *et al.* 1965]. Due to the widespread availability of appropriate computers and the enhanced use of multimedia presentation capabilities, the interest in and popularity of CBT has grown in recent years. Many experiments showed that presenting knowledge simultaneously with audio and video materials increases the retention of knowledge considerably [MEHRABI *et al.* 2000]. For education in medicine, one advantage of CBT is that clinical pictures are represented graphically.

General concepts and rules of thumb for CBT systems should be considered in the design and evaluation of educational systems for anatomy and surgery. The most essential aspect is that CBT systems should be based on a clear understanding of *learning objectives* and the *target user group*. Theses processes are also known as *task analysis* and *audience analysis* [LEE and OWENS 2000]. The design of CBT systems is a special aspect of interactive system design. Therefore, textbooks on this topic, such as SHNEIDERMAN [1997] and PREECE et al. [2001], are relevant here. In particular, the scenario-based approach to user interface design advocated by ROSSON and CARROL [2001] is highly recommended and has been proven successful in larger CBT projects. The core idea of this approach is that developers and users agree on essential scenarios, sequences of user input and system output described informally in natural language. These scenarios should guide the analysis stage, the prototyping activities, and the user evaluations as well as the documentation of interactive systems. Computer scientists usually prefer formal specifications such as state-transition diagrams, which can be unambiguously interpreted and lend themselves to an automatic analysis. However, formal specifications are not a suitable basis for discussions with users.

CBT systems should provide a self-steered and directed method of learning. With CBT systems, users can "pick an individual learning pace" [MEHRABI et al. 2000]. The overall design goal is to convey the maximum amount of relevant information in the least amount of time. Achieving this goal requires a path to a learning environment that can be followed, left and re-entered freely. It is essential that users be able to explore the material—for example, by interrogating graphical representations, answering multiple-choice questions, or solving tasks that involve the manipulation of graphic objects.

Examples for learning objectives in anatomy are: students should be able to locate certain structures, know the functional relation between certain structures, and know about typical variations of certain structures. Learning objectives should be explicitly specified and guide the design and development of CBT systems. Learning objectives can be decomposed in a hierarchy of more elementary goals. The analysis and understanding of learning objectives may serve as a basis to guide the user through a process that represents a learning experience. In summary, to enable successful learning, CBT systems should:

- Provide realistic and appealing examples
- Support active participation in which users not only observe prepared sequences of images, textual description, and animation, but have to make decisions and solve tasks
- Provide adequate feedback, particularly when the user has solved a task
- Allow the user to flexibly explore tasks and materials with navigation aids that tell the user what has been done and what could be done next

Finally, the success of CBT systems also depends on the motivation of learners. If the use of a CBT system is perceived as diligent work only, few users will fully exploit its capabilities. The study of techniques from the area of computer games may inspire solutions that combine learning with an entertainment experience.

20.5 ANATOMY EDUCATION

In the following, we briefly describe computer support for anatomy education. We restrict the discussion to systems that employ 3D models and do not consider systems based on scanned drawings. Some systems based on scanned drawings are very popular and successful; however, for visualization researchers, these are not very interesting. Moreover, a potential advantage that computer systems hold over books and other modes of learning is not fully exploited. Our discussion is by no means comprehensive; we focus on middle- and long-term project systems carried out at research institutions, as these are well documented in the literature. We start this section with the VOXELMAN—the pioneering 3D anatomy teaching system.

20.5.1 VOXELMAN

The first version of the VOXELMAN was based on a labeled MRI head dataset [HÖHNE *et al.* 1992]. The system supports a flexible exploration of the data, labeling of anatomic structures, and inquiry of a sophisticated knowledge base (recall Sect. 20.1.2). The knowledge base is employed to "interrogate" the graphical representation using context-sensitive pop-up menus (see Fig. 20.22). Direct volume rendering was employed for the 3D visualization, which was unusual at that time due to the high demands for system performance. The VOXELMAN of the brain and skull was completed and publicly released in 1995.

The second generation of the VOXELMAN supports regional, systematic, and radiographic anatomy based on the Visible Human dataset and segmentation information, as well as an advanced knowledge base. Six hundred and fifty anatomic constituents, as well as 2000 relations between them, are represented in the knowledge base [POMMERT *et al.* 2001]. The VOXELMAN provides many interaction facilities for exploring the Visible Human data and the correspondence between the different datasets. Clipping and cutting facilities are included to virtually dissect the patient. For example, a clipping plane may be moved through a 3D volume rendered image, and simultaneously, corresponding slices of CT and photographic data are shown (see Fig. 20.23). With respect to radiographic anatomy, it is essential that X-ray images be simulated (as an average projection of the CT data, see Fig. 20.24 (left)) and that cross sections of CT data can be integrated with 3D surface renderings (see Fig. 20.24 (right)).

20.5.2 DIGITAL ANATOMIST

The DIGITAL ANATOMIST is a long-term project carried out at the Structural Informatics Group in the Department of Biological Structure at the University of Washington. The knowledge base underlying the system is huge. Already in 1999 26,000 anatomic concepts and 28,000 semantic links were represented. The DIGITAL ANATOMIST represents probably the most comprehensive digital knowledge base on

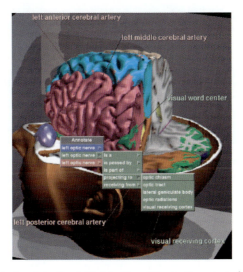

FIGURE 20.22 *Interrogating the knowledge base behind the VOXELMAN in the context of a visual representation. Based on the stored relations (e.g., object is a category) hierarchical pop-up menus are created. (Image courtesy KARL-HEINZ HÖHNE, University Hospital Hamburg-Eppendorf)*

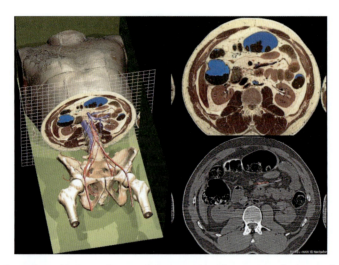

FIGURE 20.23 *Exploring the Visible Human dataset with the VOXELMAN. The movement of a clipping plane in the 3D visualization is shown, along with the corresponding slices of CT and photographic data.* [HÖHNE 2003]. *(Image courtesy KARL-HEINZ HÖHNE, University Hospital Hamburg-Eppendorf)*

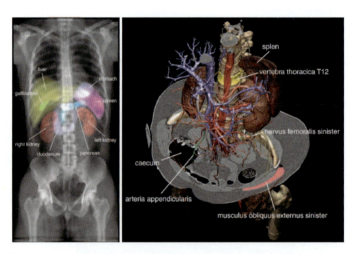

FIGURE 20.24 *Different viewing modes used in the VOXELMAN. Left: simulated X-ray; right: CT slices combined with surface rendering of selected objects* [POMMERT et al. 2001]. *(Image courtesy ANDREAS POMMERT, University Hospital Hamburg-Eppendorf)*

anatomy. The links are explored with a hypertext functionality; the represented relations are very similar to those used in the VOXELMAN (recall Sect. 20.1.2). Basic concepts are described in [BRINKLEY and ROSSE 1997, BRINKLEY et al. 1999]. (www.sig.biostr.washington.edu/projects/da). The DIGITAL ANATOMIST covers a wide variety of anatomy; its focus, however, is on neuroanatomy [BRINKLEY et al. 1997]. The concepts of knowledge representation and the assignment of information to different spatial properties, such as point, line, and area features, are detailed in [ROSSE et al. 1998]. The DIGITAL ANATOMIST is available as a Web service.

A particularly interesting aspect of the system is the wide availability of animation sequences. In these animations, objects are incrementally included, rotated, zoomed, exploded (outer objects are moved away), and finally labeled. The DIGITAL ANATOMIST contains a quiz in which people point to objects and guess their names. In some animations, vascular structures grow along a path. Often, structures are clipped to reveal the insides. All drawings can be modified by adding outlines and labels (see Fig. 20.25). An external labeling scheme is used, with labels arranged in vertical columns. The system may be used in different modes—for example, as a tutorial or in question-and-answer mode. The interaction facilities for exploring the 3D models, however, are limited.

20.5.3 ANATOMYBROWSER

The ANATOMYBROWSER, developed at Brigham and Women's Hospital in Boston, is also a comprehensive system representing a wealth of anatomic relations. It was probably the first system available on standard PCs and later as a Web service. The focus of the ANATOMYBROWSER is also on neuroanatomy. Labeled MRI data have been used as the major data source for the system. Since a variety of datasets, particularly of the brain, are included, comparative anatomy can be explored. The comprehensive knowledge base provides the basis for the exploration. State-of-the-art rendering techniques and flexible annotations are incorporated. The design of the ANATOMYBROWSER is described in a series of excellent publications [SHENTON et al. 1995, KIKINIS et al. 1996, GOLLAND et al. 1998, 1999].

20.5.4 ZOOMILLUSTRATOR AND 3D PUZZLE

The ZOOMILLUSTRATOR is an educational system that closely integrates interactive 3D models and related textual information. It was developed at the University of Magdeburg between 1994 and 1998. The basic architecture of the system is shown in Figure 20.26. Flexible zoom techniques are used to integrate explanations within 3D visualizations (see Fig. 20.27). The system is based on polygonal surface models provided by Viewpoint Datalabs. The ZOOMILLUSTRATOR incorporates external labeling (recall Sect. 20.2). Figures 20.6, 20.13, and 20.14 were generated with the ZOOMILLUSTRATOR. Animation facilities (recall Figs. 20.17 and 20.18) were also included. The design and use of ZOOMILLUSTRATOR is described in [PREIM et al. 1995, 1996, 1997].

An informal evaluation of the visualization and interaction techniques with 12 students of medicine showed that the system is usable and useful, in the sense that additional knowledge is gained

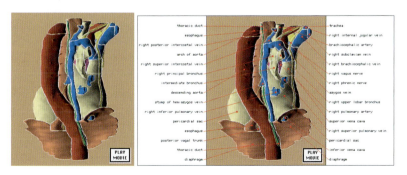

FIGURE 20.25   *Anatomy education with the DIGITAL ANATOMIST. All drawings can be generated with outlines (left) and labels added (right). A 3D model containing structures in the thorax region is shown. Predefined animation sequences are available that show the thorax regions from different viewpoints. (Screenshots of the DIGITAL ANATOMIST)*

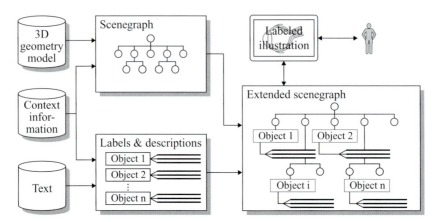

FIGURE 20.26 *Basic architecture of the ZOOMILLUSTRATOR. The 3D geometry model and context information, such as labels and the classification of anatomic structures, are integrated in a 3D scenegraph. This scenegraph is extended with more detailed descriptions. Labeled illustrations present a subset of this extended scenegraph and serve as a basis for the exploration of the user [SCHLECHTWEG and WAGENER 1998]. (Image courtesy STEFAN SCHLECHTWEG, University of Magdeburg)*

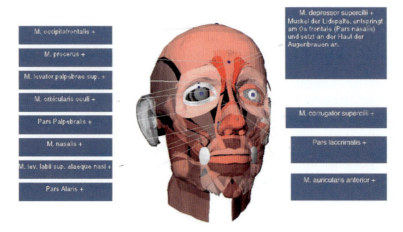

FIGURE 20.27 *Integration of labels and textual explanations with the 3D model. The face muscle that is textually explained is emphasized in the 3D model.*

[PITT *et al.* 1999]. After a limited introductory period, students had to solve predefined tasks, such as locating and naming individual anatomic structures as well as groups of related structures. Questionnaires and video recordings were employed to gain insight into the actual use of the system. It turned out that the zoom techniques were used frequently and adequately. However, the 3D interaction facilities were not used extensively by some users, whereas others regard them as too limited.

From a practical point of view, the system has many limitations. The ZOOMILLUSTRATOR supports the exploration of regional anatomy; other important aspects, such as radiographic anatomy, are not even considered. The interaction facilities with the 3D models are limited, which is partly due to the fact that no volume data have been incorporated.

3D Puzzle A second educational system developed at the University of Magdeburg is based on the metaphor of a 3D jigsaw puzzle [RITTER *et al.* 2000, 2001]. The design of this system was motivated by some observations during the evaluation of the ZOOMILLUSTRATOR. In particular, it was designed to get users more involved in 3D interaction.

Other anatomy education systems are based on the atlas-metaphor—the goal being to provide a tool that resembles the classical anatomy atlas with high-quality images. The problem of the atlas-metaphor is that neither developers nor users are forced to think about the new 3D interaction facilities that can be realized with a computerized system. The metaphor of a 3D jigsaw puzzle influenced many design decisions: users should partially compose a 3D model themselves, putting anatomic structures in predefined positions together. Substantial help enables the user to accomplish this task.

The 3D puzzle basically used the same polygonal models and related textual information as the ZOOMILLUSTRATOR, but provided more advanced visualization and interaction techniques to enable the user to put together 3D models. The major hypothesis underlying this system was that the motivation and the ability to understand spatial relations are increased via the task of composing subsets of the human anatomy. Stereo rendering, shadow projections, 3D input devices, and collision detection are among the techniques used to amplify the user's ability to explore the spatial relations (see Fig. 20.28). A controlled user study was carried out to evaluate the progress of the user's knowledge compared to other educational tools [RITTER *et al.* 2002]. In conclusion, some drawbacks of the ZOOMILLUSTRATOR could be overcome; however, from a practical point of view, the 3D puzzle is not comprehensive enough to support a larger variety of learning objectives.

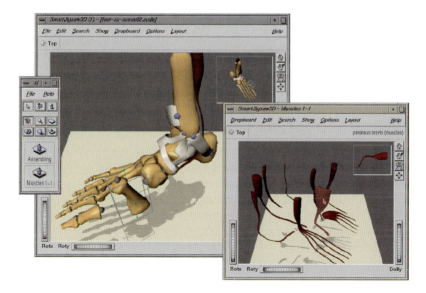

FIGURE 20.28 *Anatomy education with the 3D puzzle. The left view contains the skeletal structures of the foot, where one object is currently placed in the model. The right view contains all muscles at arbitrary positions. The user's task is to move each muscle in the right view and place it correctly at the skeletal structures. (Image courtesy FELIX RITTER, MeVis Bremen)*

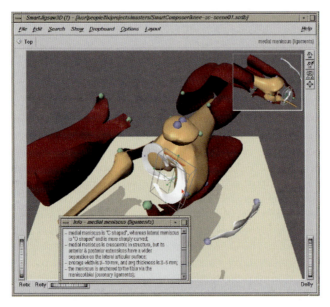

FIGURE 20.29 *Composing the anatomic structures of a knee. Shadow projections, a detail view (with other viewing direction), and textual explanations help the user. (Image courtesy* FELIX RITTER, *MeVis Bremen)*

Summary We discussed a variety of systems offering different features, visualizations, and interaction techniques. These systems are focused on presenting the morphology of anatomic structures and their spatial relations. In addition to the systems and concepts discussed in the scientific literature, a commercial company should be mentioned: PRIMAL PICTURES[1] presents a well-known suite of anatomy education tools. The next-generation anatomy education tools will likely incorporate realistic movements and functional information, for example with respect to blood flow and metabolism. Anatomy education tools may also be extended to provide case studies of pathologies. PRIMAL PICTURES also provides large sets of interactive 3D visualizations that present important sports injuries.

20.6 SURGERY EDUCATION AND SIMULATION

The design of CBT systems for surgery must consider the different constituents of surgery education [MEHRABI et al. 2000]. *Surgical theory* relates to factual knowledge as a basis for decision-making processes. *Clinical surgery* is based on surgical theory and comprises pathologic variations, differential diagnosis, and therapeutic alternatives. In clinical surgery, students should critically reflect on the solution of surgical problems. The study of *operative techniques* requires knowledge in the former areas and aims at skills development. Frequent assistance during operations is the most important learning mode for developing surgical skills. A related but somewhat different classification is presented by WAXBERG et al. [2004] based on earlier and more general work by FITTS [1964]. They regard the acquisition of surgical skills as a special instance of the general process of the acquisition of motor skills. This process consists of three stages:

- *The cognitive phase*, in which a novice becomes familiar with the process to be performed and learns how to attempt first trials

---

1 See www.primalpictures.com.

- *The associative phase*, in which the subject learns to perform the skill and is taught subtle adjustments
- *The autonomous phase*, which begins after months of practice and relates to the time where the skill can be performed largely automatically

CBT systems for studying surgical theory and clinical surgery are rare. In Section 20.6.1, we briefly review such systems and discuss one of them in more detail. This system is dedicated to oncologic liver surgery. Surgical simulators support the *cognitive phase*.

Most research on surgery education and simulation was carried out with respect to the study of operative techniques. Surgery simulators have been developed to simulate the behavior of soft tissue, the interaction of surgical devices with soft tissue, and different surgical techniques, secondary effects, and complications. A brief review of these systems and the challenging tasks that must be solved is given in Section 20.6.2. With respect to the stages described above, such systems support the *associative phase*, often without supporting the cognitive phase.

20.6.1 CBT SYSTEMS FOR STUDYING CLINICAL SURGERY

The potential and necessity of CBT systems for surgery education were recognized early [KLAR and BAYER 1990]. MEHRABI et al. [2000] argued that CBT systems for clinical surgery were necessary to cope with the rapid growth of relevant knowledge in the surgical disciplines. Although the initial costs of CBT development are considerable, these systems can be updated more flexibly than traditional media. Also, the mode of presentation used in state-of-the-art CBT systems is considered superior. In a case study related to the special problem of treating the distal radius fracture, the acceptance of a CBT system and the performance of students were evaluated. It turns out that the large majority considered CBT as a substantial help in self-study and exam preparation. Despite this evidence, the impact of CBT in this field is still very limited.

LiverSurgeryTrainer The LIVERSURGERYTRAINER is an educational system dedicated to *clinical surgery*. Clinical cases of patients with liver tumors are presented with a wealth of information comprising the anamnesis and initial diagnosis, radiological diagnosis, and image analysis results. Therapeutic decisions such as resectability and resection strategy can be trained. Expert opinions are integrated and used to provide feedback to the learning surgeon. The system uses the planning functionalities (e.g., virtual resection, applicator placement) described in Chapter 19, and offers additional multimedia presentation options. In particular, intraoperative video sequences are employed to show how the planned resection was actually performed. In cooperation with experienced surgeons, learning objectives and more elementary goals are determined. Based on this discussion, the LIVERSURGERYTRAINER provides a path, starting from the diagnosis. Operability (based on clinical parameters) and resectability (based on the individual liver anatomy) should be evaluated based on the patient's anatomy. Each step consists of substeps related to more elementary goals (see Fig. 20.30). The LIVERSURGERYTRAINER employs advanced vessel visualization techniques (recall Chap. 14) and illustrative rendering techniques (see Chap. 17). A description of the system can be found in [BADE et al. 2006b].

20.6.2 TASKS AND CONCEPTS FOR SURGERY SIMULATION

Computer support for the study of operative techniques is motivated by the desire to avoid damage to patients early in a surgeon's learning curve. The need for computer support in this area has strongly increased in the last several years, with the introduction of new minimally invasive and endoscopic interventions. In these procedures, endoscopic instruments and a camera are inserted into the patient's body through natural or artificial orifices. These procedures reduce the trauma for the patient and lead to faster

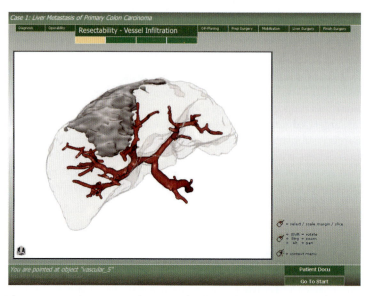

FIGURE 20.30 *The LiverSurgeryTrainer provides support for therapy decisions in oncologic liver surgery. A predefined path guides the learner through the environment. In the current step, the resectability should be evaluated. As a first substep, the vessel infiltration should be assessed. Later, the user is engaged in "OP Planning" and can then watch several sequences of an annotated intraoperative video. (Image courtesy* Ragnar Bade, *University of Magdeburg)*

recovery. The surgeon, however, no longer has the direct view to the operating situs and must learn the handling of new instruments developed for minimally invasive use.

Even experienced surgeons have to obtain new skills, particularly with respect to eye-hand coordination. It is documented for many interventions that the rate of complications is strongly related to the experience of the operator with this particular intervention. Therefore, a risk-free learning environment as well as training on a wide range of clinical cases is required [Sierra et al 2003a]. Providing realistic tactile sensations is one of the major challenges in this endeavor.

Without computer support, surgeons either use dedicated mechanical systems (referred to as "endo trainers"), animals, or cadaveric material. The same elongated instruments as used in real interventions are used in these settings. However, the mechanical systems are restricted to the manipulation of plastic objects that do not provide the elasticity of living tissue. The use of animals and cadaveric material is more realistic, but also not as realistic as desired—in particular, the perfusion of living tissue makes a strong difference. Moreover, the use of animals poses ethical problems and is expensive. These drawbacks are the primary motivation for the development of surgery simulators [Delingette and Ayache 2005].

Computer support for studying operation techniques requires surgery simulators that provide a look and feel that is close to real interventions on the living patient. "For the acceptance of a surgery simulation system, the completeness and correctness of surgical interactions . . . are essential" [Çakmak and Kühnapfel 2000]. Correct (visually realistic) organ models and textures are an important prerequisite. This requirement, however, also yields for anatomy education and relates to models and datasets (recall Sect. 20.1.1). A general decision in the design of surgical simulators is whether surface or volume representations should be used. Speed of rendering and collision detection are advantages of surface models [BRODLIE et al. 2000]. More accurate physical simulation is in general achieved with volume representations.

One essential aspect of realism in surgery simulators is the ability to perform arbitrary freeform cuts. This particular aspect was discussed in Section 12.4, since it is also essential for surgery planning. However, we did not consider soft tissue deformation of the manipulated tissue, which will be discussed in the following list along with other requirements essential for surgery simulation [ÇAKMAK and KÜHNAPFEL 2000]:

- *Soft tissue deformation.* Soft tissue should behave naturally when forces are applied and when the tissue is torn or cut.
- *Variable training scenarios.* Effective training requires variable scenarios with anatomic variants as well as pathologic variations, complications that need to be handled, etc.
- *Haptic interaction.* Realistic training with haptic devices is essential for the learning objectives of surgery simulators, in particular to support eye-hand coordination. Appropriate force-feedback devices are required and a fast update (>1000 Hz) is necessary, since the tactile sense has a very high temporal resolution.
- *Collision detection.* If surgical instruments touch anatomic structures (or other instruments), these collisions need to be detected very quickly to initiate a physically plausible response.
- *Realization of surgical devices, procedures, and effects.* In surgical interventions, various devices (e.g., drill tools and scalpels) are employed in a well-defined manner. These devices need to be modeled with respect to geometry and behavior. The resulting effects—e.g., bleeding if vasculature is hurt, irrigation, and coagulation smoke—must be modeled and implemented with adequate levels of realism.

Most of these requirements are not solved sufficiently well from an applications point of view; therefore, substantial research efforts are ongoing to achieve progress. In the following, we briefly review the state-of-the-art with respect to these requirements and describe selected surgical simulators.[2] ÇAKMAK and KÜHNAPFEL [2000] also considered the simulation of physiology, such as pulse and hemodynamics, to be essential. We agree on this requirement; however, we shall not discuss the current state-of-the-art with respect to this requirement. In general, not enough progress has been made to simulate physiology convincingly. FUNG's book [1993] is a valuable source of information concerning biomechanic properties of human tissue.

Soft Tissue Deformation

Real-time and precise simulation of soft tissue deformation is still a major challenge. Different methods are used to accomplish the simulation, resulting in a different speed and accuracy. No mattar which method is employed, a realistic estimation of stiffness parameters (Young modulus, shear modulus, bulk modulus, viscosity) is required as a basis for the simulation models. The reliable approximation of these parameters still represents a challenge. Ex vivo measurements are not reliable, since the degree of perfusion of an organ has a strong influence on its elastic properties [DELINGETTE and AYACHE 2005]. Noninvasive in vivo measures may be accomplished by employing the fact that the elasticity of a sample is related to the velocity of sound waves, which can be measured with ultrasound [MAASS and KÜHNAPFEL 1999].

---

2 A serious discussion of model assumptions, algorithms, implementation, and validation of surgery simulators would require a book of its own.

Soft tissue deformation in surgery simulators is in general based on the theory of continuum mechanics (more precisely elasticity theory), which has been used for a long time to analyze and predict deformations of elastic bodies. The method of reference for computationally handling elasticity theory is the finite element method (FEM). We therefore start with a discussion of this method.

Simulation with FEM   Building on the work of elasticity theory, the behavior of soft tissue can be described by the Navier-Stokes equations—systems of nonlinear partial differential equations [CIARLET 1988]. In general, these systems cannot be solved analytically. Instead, numerical solutions based on an appropriate discretization are computed through FEM. Finite element modeling is a complex issue. Parameters, such as the selected grid type (e.g., a hexagonal grid or a tetrahedral grid), the actual configuration of the mesh, the boundary conditions that restrict the deformation, and the selection of appropriate time steps for the numerical solution, critically influence the stability, speed, and accuracy of the solution. The typical grid structure is a tetrahedral grid that fills the entire (deformable) structure. To prevent instabilities in the simulation, these grids have to fulfill some quality requirements. Basically, thin and elongated tetrahedra should be avoided—or, in other words, low aspect ratios between the edge lengths should be realized. An overview of 3D mesh generation is given in [BERN and PLASSMANN 1999].

FEM allows precise modeling of soft tissue deformation. The deformations resulting from manipulations such as poking, tearing, pulling, and cutting might be represented realistically. FEM has been used for surgery simulation for a decade (first described in [BRO-NIELSEN and GRAMKOW 1996] and in [KOCH et al. 1996]). In general, precise FEM simulations are very slow and still far from being interactive. This gave rise to a number of variations and completely different simulation methods.

For cutting, it is common to subdivide the affected tetrahedra [BIELSEN et al. 1999]. However, this may also introduce an increased stiffness of the system, due to the increased element number. As an alternative, the nodes are repositioned in [NIENHUYS and VAN DER STAPPEN 2001] to prevent the complexity of the grid from increasing considerably. A simplified version of FEM solutions (considering only linear elasticity) is presented in [NIENHUYS and VAN DER STAPPEN 2001]. For small deformations (less than 10% of the organ size), linear elasticity is considered a valid approximation [DELINGETTE and AYACHE 2005].

Simulation with Mass-Spring Models   Mass-spring models are based on a mesh consisting of masses (nodes) and springs that connect the masses. Strut springs are often added to help the mass-spring surface maintain its shape. The topology of the mesh and the spring parameters determine the behavior of a mass-spring model in a simulation. To simulate the dynamics of a mass-spring system, the relation between position, velocity, and acceleration for the mass m_i at point p_i at time t can be described as [WATERS and TERZOPOULOS 1990]:

$$F_i^{ext}(t) = m_i \frac{d^2 p_i(t)}{dt^2} + \gamma \frac{dp_i(t)}{dt} + F_i^{int}(t) \tag{20.1}$$

γ denotes a damping factor, $F_i^{int}(t)$ denote the internal elastic force caused by strains of adjacent springs of p_i. $F_i^{ext}(t)$ is the sum of all external forces. The dynamics is thus described by a system of second-order ordinary differential equations. For an efficient numerical solution, Equation 20.1 is typically reduced to two coupled first-order differential equations. Either Euler's method or a higher order Runge-Kutta method is employed to solve the equation system (recall [WATERS and TERZOPOULOS 1990]). Figure 20.31 illustrates the use of mass-spring models for simulating deformations and cutting procedures.

Simulations based on mass-spring models are generally faster than simulations based on FEMs, at the expense of accuracy. In general, it is difficult to derive spring constants so that a realistic behavior results. The majority of surgery simulators are based on these models (for example, see [BRO-NIELSEN et al. 1998, DE CASSON and LAUGIER 1999, KÜHNAPFEL et al. 2000, WAGNER et al. 2002b]). BRO-NIELSEN et al. [1998]

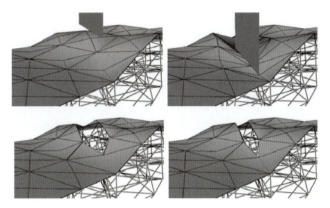

FIGURE 20.31 *Simulating soft tissue deformation with a surgical instrument using mass-spring models (images above). Also, cutting procedures may be simulated in a plausible manner with mass-spring models (images below)* [Teschner *et al.* 2000]. *(Image courtesy* Mattias Teschner, *University of Freiburg)*

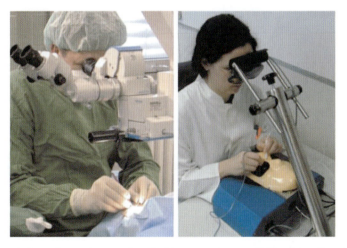

FIGURE 20.32 *A surgical procedure on the eye performed with a stereo microscope (left) and virtually trained within a simulation (right)* [Wagner *et al.* 2002b]. *(Image courtesy* Clemens Wagner, *University of Mannheim)*

used mass-spring models for an abdominal trauma surgery simulator. Wagner *et al.* [2002b] developed an eye-simulator for training microsurgical interventions at the orbita. The handling of the devices and the visualization were close to real surgery (see Figs. 20.32 and 20.33), while the tactile sensation was realistic, within limits. We shall not discuss all the issues of determining appropriate parameters; for more detail see [Bianchi *et al.* 2004].

Discussion Soft tissue deformation is also relevant for a variety of surgery planning tasks. In cranio-maxillofacial surgery, for example, physicians reconstruct massively destroyed tissue caused by a disease or a trauma. The idea of estimating soft tissue deformation due to bone realignment was formulated by Vannier *et al.* [1983]. The planning process is aimed at achieving an optimal aesthetic and functional

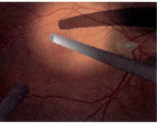

FIGURE 20.33 *View through a stereo microscope of a real surgical procedure (left) view through a virtual microscope (right)* [WAGNER et al. 2002b]. (Image courtesy CLEMENS WAGNER, University of Mannheim)

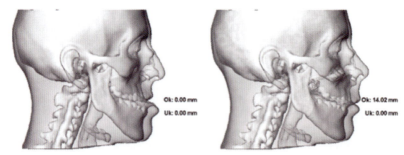

FIGURE 20.34 *For a craniofacial intervention, an osteotomy, the postoperative result is predicted through soft tissue simulation (muscles, skin). The displacement of the upper jaw leads to a satisfying aesthetic result* [ZACHOW et al. 2006]. (Image courtesy STEFAN ZACHOW, Zuse-Institute Berlin)

result. Soft tissue deformation is the core technique for predicting the postoperative result. Thus various surgical procedures can be explored and discussed with colleagues and the patient to support the therapeutic decision. A variety of software systems have been developed in this field. An advanced and carefully evaluated system is described by ZACHOW et al. [2006]. It is based on a FEM simulation applied to tetrahedral data derived from geometric models of the individual patient anatomy. Figure 20.34 illustrates this work: the left image shows the preoperative situation, whereas the right image shows the prediction of the soft tissue appearance after a certain displacement of the upper jaw.

Variable Training Scenarios

The need for variable training scenarios is described by SIERRA et al. [2004]. They compare surgical training with flight training and argue that flight training with an invariable landscape and constant weather conditions would not be effective. Similarly, repeated surgical training with the same organ "obscures training because the user adapts to this special anatomy." Currently, almost no surgery simulators adequately consider the need for varying anatomy. Three strategies are possible to develop variable training scenarios:

- A large amount of individual patient data is selected and analyzed to represent the variety of anatomic and pathologic variations.
- The data are generated with dedicated modeling tools instead of reconstructing models from clinical data.

- Based on clinical datasets, parameterizable models of the anatomy and pathology are developed to generate individual cases flexibly. The problems of reconstructing, simplifying, and smoothing surface models must be solved within this strategy.

All three strategies have their merits and pitfalls. The first, more conventional strategy requires the analysis of a large variety of medical volume data, which involves laborious segmentation tasks. Even a larger selection might be considered too restrictive by surgical users. The advantage of this method is that all examples are realistic with respect to the morphology of the relevant objects and the spatial relations between them. The second strategy requires an enormous modeling effort to provide sufficiently realistic models. Freeform modeling with variants of b-spline and Bézier patches is not only time-consuming but requires considerable experience. An advantage of this strategy is that the problems of correcting and smoothing reconstructed models may be avoided.

The alternative is to employ either one or only a few models and adjust parameters to vary anatomic shapes and pathologic variations. This strategy requires the study and representation of the variability of anatomic structures, as well as an understanding of the growth process of pathologic variations. Care is necessary to avoid the generation of unrealistic models.

The use of parameterizable models has been suggested by SIERRA et al. [2004]. They use active shape models (ASM), often employed for model-based image segmentation (recall Sect. 5.4.3 and [COOTES et al. 1994]) to represent anatomic variations. By adjusting the major modes of variation, they can thus generate an arbitrary number of different instances of an organ. For pathologic variations, the use of statistical models is regarded as not feasible, because the number and range of pathologic cases varies too strongly. Instead, they attempted to model the growth processes and came up with a model of tumor growth. Different simulation techniques, such as cellular automaton and particle-based methods, have been employed (see Fig. 20.35 and [SIERRA et al. 2003b]). Cellular automatons are based on a simple set of rules that allow simulation of a large variety of growing phenomena, including aspects of tumor growth [QI et al. 1993]. The combination of special instances of anatomic variants and pathologic variations is the task of a supervisor or *author* of a training scenario. This combination is not a mere overlay of anatomy and pathology; instead it considers that a pathology arises in a certain organ and is adapted to it [SIERRA et al. 2003a]

Towards Automatic Mesh Generation   The use of variable training scenarios also has consequences for other aspects of surgery simulation. It is no longer feasible to generate the meshes for soft tissue simulation with a large amount of manual work. Instead, the meshes have to be generated in a fully automatic

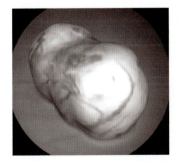 

FIGURE 20.35   *Artificially generated example pathologies for surgery simulation. Left: a myoma created with a cellular automaton; right: an artificial polyp generated with a particle system* [SIERRA et al. 2004]. *(Image courtesy* RAIMUNDO SIERRA, *ETH Zürich)*

fashion, which represents a serious difficulty because the meshes have to fulfill a variety of requirements to allow an efficient and numerically stable simulation. Such an automation is feasible for the generation of tetrahedral meshes based on a given triangulation of the surface. However, for the model generation process described above, this prerequisite is not fulfilled and new 3D mesh generation strategies are required. First attempts towards this goal are described in [SIERRA et al. 2004].

Collision Detection

Collision detection is the general term for algorithms that detect objects that touch or penetrate each other. These algorithms compute the pair of involved objects and also optionally the area of contact or the depth of a penetration. This information is essential, for example, to provide realistic haptic feedback. There are different categories of collision detection problems and consequently different algorithms and data structures that are appropriate to perform the necessary computations quickly and precisely enough.

A comprehensive and up-to-date review of collision detection is given in [TESCHNER et al. 2005]. In general, it discriminates between *rigid body* and *deformable object* collision detection. The latter class of problems is more challenging. In particular, self-occlusions may occur when deformable objects are considered. Unfortunately, simulating soft tissue in surgery simulators falls into the latter class of collision detection problems. Volumetric as well as surface models are employed for surgical simulation and collision detection. With both kinds of models, a general strategy is to adapt the resolution of the surface or volume mesh by retesselating around the region of the cut. Collision detection in surgical simulators considers surgical tools as either static or dynamic, which means that changes to the tools are also considered.

Algorithms for collision detection fall into two categories: *deterministic algorithms*, which precisely compute collisions and related information, and *stochastic algorithms*, which employ probabilistic assumptions and approximate the required information. We do not consider stochastic algorithms here, although they are potentially useful for surgery simulation because they balance real-time requirements with accuracy. The interested reader is referred to [KLEIN and ZACHMANN 2003, GUY and DEBUNNE 2004].

Hierarchic Data Structures for Collision Detection   The core idea to efficiently detect collisions is to employ space partitioning schemes that lead to a hierarchical scene decomposition (recall Sect. 7.2.5). Axis-aligned bounding boxes (AABB), oriented bounding boxes (OBB), k-dimensional discrete orientation polytops (k-dops), and bounding spheres are among the widely used data structures for efficient collision detection. In Section 13.6, we described the modification of a collision detection algorithm for determining minimal distances, based on a bounding sphere's hierarchy. With appropriate hierarchic data structures, the necessary tests and computations can be restricted to a subset of leaves of a hierarchy. However, the use of hierarchic data structures requires additional setup time to construct the hierarchy and additional time to update and adapt the hierarchy as a consequence of motions and collisions. For the nonrigid soft tissue objects considered in surgery simulation, the update process is considerably more complex than for rigid objects. TESCHNER et al. [2005] argue that for this task, AABBs are the most appropriate data structure. Here the structure of replace a with an AABB tree can be kept, but the extent of the nodes has to be corrected. However, other structures (e.g., k-dops and OBBs) enclose the geometry more tightly (see also [VANDENBERGEN 1997, KLOSOWSKI et al. 1998]).

Haptic Feedback

The tactile sense plays an essential role for any task in which objects should be grasped in virtual reality. Movement times are reduced and the perceived level of difficulty decreases simultaneously. These aspects are particularly relevant in many surgical tasks [MASON et al. 2001] in which the tactile sensations play a very important role. Research indicates that haptic feedback is crucial for needle placement tasks in which the puncturing of different tissue types needs to be perceived [GEROVICHEV *et al.* 2002]. Blunt dissection is another important surgical task in which haptic feedback leads to lower error rates and reduced task completion times [WAGNER *et al.* 2002a]. Finally, palpation benefits from adequate haptic feedback. Without appropriate feedback, excessive forces may be applied, leading to tissue damage [SUNG and GILL 2001].

Haptic or tactile feedback is based on computing forces representing the interaction between surgical devices and the patient's anatomy. This computation must be very efficient, since an update rate of more than 1 KHz is required to provide realistic feedback. The user interacts with a tactile device that provides tactile sensation. TAVAKOLI *et al.* [2006] provide an in-depth discussion of haptic interaction issues for endoscopic surgery training.

Tactile Input Devices   A variety of tactile input devices are available. Due to high demands on accuracy, low-cost devices primarily developed for computer games are not appropriate for surgery education. Most surgery simulators are based on the rather expensive PHANToM® devices from SensAble Technologies [MASSIE and SALISBURY 1994]. There are devices providing three degrees of freedom (3-DOF), representing translations in the x-, y-, and z- directions. More advanced devices provide 6-DOF haptics, allowing the transformation of objects in three translational and three rotational directions. Three degrees of freedom devices are adequate to represent point-based interactions between surgical devices and the anatomy (the surgical device or, more generally, the manipulator is represented as a point). If more advanced interactions, such as line-surface interactions, should be represented, 6-DOF devices are required. To actually provide an application with tactile feedback not only requires an appropriate input device, but also software to control the device. Research work in surgery simulation is typically based on one of the following commercial solutions:

- The GHOST library provided by SensAble Technologies to control the PHANToM® devices
- The Open Haptics toolkit, also provided by SensAble
- The open source Chai3D software[3]
- Systems based on hardware from Immersion Medical, Xitact, and Force Dimension

Haptic Rendering   Haptic rendering is the process of calculating a reaction force (the collision response) for a specified position of the haptic input device. Usually, this position is represented as a point indicating the endpoint of the haptic device [LAYCOCK and DAY 2003b]. This first step of a haptic rendering algorithm is collision detection, discussed above. For haptic rendering, the instruments and tools are usually reduced to a few representative points. The second step involves the determination of the intersected area of the manipulated object and the determination of the penetration depth. Based on this information, a force is computed and applied to the arm of the tactile input device.

Due to the significant computational effort and the necessary high update rate, most haptic rendering systems are still very restricted. Usually, the surgical instrument itself is regarded as static. While this is a reasonable assumption in most cases, there are surgical interventions in which the flexibility of the tool is crucial. One example is root canal surgery, an important surgical intervention in dentistry. A first prototype for the simulation of deformable tools is presented by [LAYCOCK and DAY 2003b].

Moreover, soft tissue deformation and haptic rendering is usually restricted to a single organ. In reality, deformations of one organ affect neighboring organs, and the deformation of one organ depends on the neighboring organs.

---

3   www.chai3d.org.

20.6.3 CBT SYSTEMS FOR STUDYING OPERATIVE TECHNIQUES

The design and development of CBT systems to train surgical procedures is a complex endeavor. A careful user and task analysis, including an understanding of the context of use, is required as input in the early design process. The task analysis is based on several actions, including observations, video recordings of surgical procedures, and close-ups of the most relevant actions [JOHN et al. 2001]. In the following, we briefly describe some prominent and long-term efforts in surgical simulator development.

Endoscopic Surgery Simulation A long-term effort on endoscopic surgery simulation has been carried out at the Research Center of Karlsruhe. Many aspects of real laparoscopic interventions have been carefully modeled in their KISMET (kinematic simulation, monitoring and off-line programming environment for telerobotics) system [KÜHNAPFEL et al. 2000, MAASS et al. 2003]. Anatomic objects are represented as surface models and soft tissue deformation is realized with mass-spring models. Many effects, such as bleeding and coagulation, are faithfully simulated in their system. A special modeling system was developed to generate the underlying geometric and kinematic models. The system has been refined; in particular, haptic feedback had been added. The system is now commercially available by the Select IT VEST Systems AG as VEST-VSOne. Figure 20.36 gives a photo of the VEST-VSOne system (see also [CAKMAK et al. 2005]).

Hepatic Surgery Simulator A simulator for hepatic surgery was developed at INRIA, primarily to train laparoscopic interventions [COTIN et al. 2000, DELINGETTE and AYACHE 2005]. Laparoscopic interventions are also accomplished through small incisions in the human body, and similar to the learning objectives addressed in the KISMET-development, the eye-hand coordination is regarded as essential. The trade-offs between simulation realism and simulation cost have been investigated thoroughly. FEM was used as general computation method and tetrahedra as the grid type. As a consequence of the realism-versus-cost trade-off, one mode was developed for which deformations are precomputed and actual deformations are computed as linear deformations of the precomputed values [DELINGETTE and AYACHE 2005]. This fast method was used to generate Figure 20.37. This approach, however, is restricted to situations in which the topology of the mesh is not changed. Therefore, a second mode was developed for situations in which the fast method produces too-crude approximations. Besides soft tissue deformation, various interactions of surgical tools with the anatomy are simulated (see Fig. 20.38).

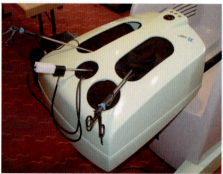

FIGURE 20.36 *The Virtual Endoscopic Surgery Training (VEST) system "VSOne" and its realistic haptic interface. Left: an overview with a display that resembles the "real" endoscopic view. Right: detailed display of the haptic surgical devices. (Image courtesy HÜSEYIN ÇAKMAK, Forschungszentrum Karlsruhe and Select-IT VEST Systems AG)*

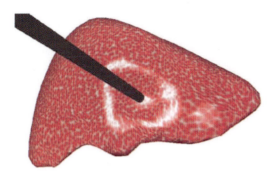

FIGURE 20.37   *Liver deformation in the hepatic surgery simulator. The deformation is computed very quickly using precomputed deformations. The lightning simulates the situation in laparoscopic liver surgery [DELINGETTE and AYACHE 2005]. (Image courtesy INRIA—Asclepios team)*

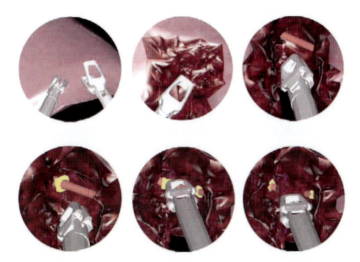

FIGURE 20.38   *A simulated liver resection including clipping and cutting the portal vein [DELINGETTE and AYACHE 2005]. (Images courtesy INRIA—Asclepios team).*

Petrous Bone Surgery Simulation   Petrous bone surgery (or middle ear surgery) is accomplished primarily to attach cochlear implants such as hearing aids or to remove tumors (mastoidectomy) [JOHN et al. 2001]. For this purpose, it is necessary to drill through the mastoid bone (see Fig. 20.39) without hurting relevant structures nearby. Petrous bone surgery involves a surgical site with complex anatomy. Key anatomic features—derived by the task analysis—include the facial nerve, other neuronal features, and the jugular bump. The task analysis also provides information related to the most important instruments and materials, as well as to the preferred display type. Three types of instruments are primarily used:

- A burr reducing tracebular bone in fine dust
- An irrigator to introduce water
- A sucker that removes bone dust and water

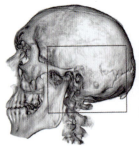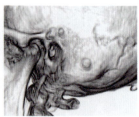

FIGURE 20.39 *Overview of the skull and a closeup view of the mastoid region [AGUS et al. 2002a]. (Image courtesy MARCO AGUS, CRS4-ViC, Pula)*

Virtual petrous bone surgery has attracted much research in the last years. The IERAPS (Integrated Environment for the Rehearsal and Planning of Surgical Intervention) project represents the second large-scale effort to create virtual petrous bone surgery [JOHN et al. 2001, JACKSON et al. 2002]. This process is performed by the surgeon who holds a high-speed burr in one hand and a suction device in the other. The latter is used to remove the mixing of bone dust with water [JOHN et al. 2001]. The primary learning objectives are to teach access to the middle ear and to teach the drilling process itself. It is important that all the above-mentioned effects are simulated. Otherwise, important aspects such as the need for regular irrigation and suction are not perceived [AGUS et al. 2002a].

The Ohio Virtual Temporal Bone dissection simulator [WIET and BRYAN 2000, BRYAN et al. 2001, STREDNEY et al. 2002] focused on bone removal. The bone removal is accomplished by extending virtual resection techniques described in Chapter 12 (recall [GALYEAN and HUGHES 1991]). Multiresolution approaches, such as octrees, are essential to effectively localize the voxels which are affected by the movement of the virtual tool. Voxels that are removed become transparent, whereas voxels affected by local bleeding become reddish. Whereas in virtual resection the removal of voxels is just a Boolean operation, in surgery simulation it is necessary to provide adequate haptic feedback. A physically motivated simulation of the burr/bone interaction is feasible but rather complex [AGUS et al. 2002b]. The secondary effects caused by the irrigator and the sucker were not considered in the Ohio Virtual Temporal Bone dissection simulator.

A long-term effort to simulate petrous bone surgery has also been accomplished at the University Hospital Hamburg-Eppendorf [PETERSIK et al. 2002, PFLESSER et al. 2002] by the same group that pioneered anatomy education with voxel-based models (recall Sect. 20.5). They focused, among other things, on a high-quality visual representation of all relevant anatomic structures. The system employs high-quality volume visualization at subvoxel accuracy and haptic rendering based on a volume representation. The spatial accuracy of the data, as well as of the rendering, supports the tactile sense of small anatomic structures (e.g., nerves), which are essential for the trainee's learning process. The drill is represented as a sphere-shaped tool; 26 positions at the sphere's surface are sampled to detect collisions. Soft tissue deformation is not considered, since drilling the temporal bone does not cause significant elastic deformations.

The trainee may choose different kinds of drills or perform drilling while watching the scene displayed in stereoscopic mode. Much effort was spent on mimicking the real situation in particular with respect to the patient's orientation and the surgeon's viewing direction and hand orientation. The trainee uses the stylus of the force feedback device (Phantom 1.0 from SensAble Technologies), which mimics the drill. He thus gets the haptic feeling of the real procedure. Even drilling vibrations and sounds have been faithfully simulated. An example of the visual impression of the trainee can be seen in Figure 20.40. As a result of this development, the VOXEL-MAN TEMPOSURG is now commercially available.

Validation of Surgical Simulators

Once surgical simulators are designed, developed, and refined after gathering initial feedback from the first users, validation becomes an important issue. Many questions are relevant for validating surgical simulators. Among other issues, it is important to ensure that the use of the simulator provides a substantial learning effect and that this learning effect can be transferred to real surgery. To validate a surgical simulator, users with different levels of experience with the respective surgical intervention are needed. One aspect of quality of a surgical simulator relates to the differences between novices and experienced users in their results (error rates, task completion times) within a simulator. In the following, we briefly describe two studies to give examples for viable and reliable methods of validation.

One of the earliest validation studies related to the minimally invasive virtual reality simulator for laparoscopic surgery (MIST-VR) [TAFFINDER et al. 1998, 1999]. They defined a score for various aspects of psychomotor skill and conducted two studies related to the simulator: the first study assessed surgeons of different surgical experience to validate the scoring system, and the second study investigated the effect of a standard laparoscopic surgery training course. Experienced surgeons (those who had performed more than 100 laparoscopic cholecystectomies) were significantly more efficient, made less correctional submovements, and completed the tasks faster than trainee surgeons. The training course caused an improvement in efficiency and a reduction in errors for trainee surgeons. The MIST-VR simulator can objectively assess a number of desirable qualities in laparoscopic surgery and can distinguish between experienced and novice surgeons.

Another study related to the MIST-VR simulator explored the accuracy of the simulation models. The aim of this study was to validate a simulation model with six tasks commonly used in clinical practice for the acquisition of psychomotor skills in minimally invasive surgery. These tasks included, for example, the clipping and dividing of a vessel, the excision of a lesion, suturing perforation, and hand-sewn anastomosis. A prospective study was accomplished to compare the effects of different training procedures prior to using the simulator with the results achieved with the simulator. One group trained for all six procedures; the control group practiced only three of them. It turned out that the improved training led to better results in the use of the simulator. A variety of criteria were registered in this study: accuracy

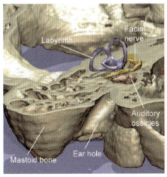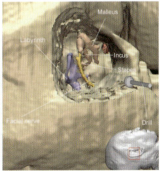

FIGURE 20.40   *Left: detailed view of the inner ear. Right: the result of the simulation of a particular mastoidectomy. This image is similar to the surgeon's view during the operation. A drill-like tool has been used to uncover the internal structures* [PFLESSER et al. 2002]. *(Images courtesy* BERNHARD PFLESSER, *University Hospital Hamburg-Eppendorf)*

error, tissue damage, operating time, and dangerous movements. However, the advantages of surgical simulation trainers are still debated, due to the limited simulation accuracy.

Discussion Despite the efforts to create and refine advanced surgery simulators, these are still not commonly integrated into the medical curriculum. Integration with other modes of learning is essential for the widespread use of surgery simulators. SIERRA et al. [2004] compared this integration with the current state in the use of flight simulators. These are fully accepted as training tools and are evaluated and certified by official authorities such as the U.S. Federal Aviation Administration. Pilots are allowed to register simulation hours as flight times. A better understanding of the required surgical skills, about the necessary degree of realism as well as refined models and convincing evaluations, is required to achieve a similar acceptance of surgery simulators.

There are some first encouraging examples. The minimally invasive virtual reality simulator (MIST-VR) was recently used for a *competency-based training curriculum*—a structured virtual reality training program aimed at achieving previously defined competency levels [AGGARWAL et al. 2006].

We discussed surgical planning, primarily with respect to specific examples in liver surgery and surgery simulation as separate topics motivated by different target users and different methods necessary to provide adequate support. In the future, there might be a closer link between surgical planning and simulation. In particular, younger surgeons might benefit from simulating the intervention based on the data of their patients.

20.7 SUMMARY

In this chapter, we described educational systems and the visualization techniques and strategies that characterize them. Labeling and animation specification are important ingredients of educational systems in anatomy and surgery. Educational systems are based on high-quality datasets, reliable segmentation results, and symbolic knowledge bases carefully linked to the corresponding portions of medical volume data. Although many technical problems have been solved, computer support still plays a minor role in medical education. It is necessary to fine-tune educational systems to the relevant learning objectives, to create stimulating experiences using these systems, and to increase the awareness of instructors. Currently, educational systems are used as stand-alone software without clear and explicit relations to conventional forms of education, such as lectures and surgical practice courses. It is preferable that educational systems be carefully integrated into traditional courses and curricula.

Outlook Despite the success of anatomy education systems, much work lies ahead. Even the leading systems of the VOXELMAN family only support some aspects of anatomy education. Computer support is also feasible and desirable for studying comparative anatomy, in which anatomic variants are explored. Educational systems in general are based on only one level of spatial resolution—usually the resolution of medical image data. The incorporation of higher resolution medical image data (MicroCT, microscopic data) and the development of interaction facilities to explore data at different levels is one of the remaining challenges.

More effective and comprehensive scripting facilities are necessary for the generation of animations. Computer support for surgery education is still in its infancy. Surgeons are not fully satisfied with the level of realism of soft tissue deformation achieved in surgery simulators so far. A particular limitation is the focus on single organs, or to a small extent on limited organ systems; whole body parts are not considered, due to the enormous complexity.

Much work is necessary to understand the learning objectives of different interventions and to develop appropriate computer support. The evaluation of educational systems is another important area for future work. Finally, surgery simulators today do not consider functional aspects. In the future, physiologic modeling of organic systems, such as cardiovascular and digestive systems, will be included in surgery simulation. Since physical and physiologic properties are coupled, new challenges must be solved to provide comprehensive and realistic models [DELINGETTE and AYACHE 2005].

FURTHER READING

With respect to labeling, it is interesting to look into labeling problems in cartography. Most of this work is based on cartographic principles introduced in [IMHOF 1975]. These principles were transformed in an optimization task that can be efficiently solved [CHRISTENSEN et al. 1995, EDMONDSON et al. 1996]. The placement of axis-aligned labels without overlaps, as well as aesthetic aspects (particularly consistency of labeling styles), is discussed in cartography. It is also considered essential for the navigation of virtual and augmented environments [BELL et al. 2002, FEKETE and PLAISANT 1999]. The dynamic computation of space available for labeling is an essential ingredient for such applications [BELL et al. 2001]. Labeling is a special aspect of the more general problem of generating layouts for presentations. A survey on layout generation and evaluation strategies for automatic layout generation is given in [LOK et al. 2004]. LEE and OWENS [2000] described major types of media, showing the benefits and drawbacks of each. In particular, the didactic effectiveness of media and media combinations is essential to guide CBT development.

We have discussed the generation of animation sequences in which material properties of static models are changed and camera positions are moved. A related topic is the generation of animations that convey movements, such as a walking man. The design of such animations based on medical volume data (e.g., the Visible Human datasets), was discussed in [GAGVANI and SILVER 2001].

Visualizations for, medical education may be enhanced by figure captions that describe the current view. Text generation strategies to generate initial figure captions and to update them after interactions are described in [PREIM et al. 1998]. As a general link to study aspects discussed in this chapter in more depth, the *Journal of Medical Education* is recommended.

LIN and GOTTSCHALK [1998b] provide a comprehensive survey on collision detection. Haptic rendering with 3-DOF based on a volume representation was pioneered by AVILA and SOBIERAJSKI [1996]. Haptic rendering with 6-DOF and a sufficiently fast update rate for modestly complex polygonal surface model was reported by MCNEELY et al. [1999]. A good survey on haptic devices is given in [LAYCOCK and DAY 2003a].

A variety of interesting concepts for the fast realization of soft tissue deformation, along with an application in craniofacial surgery, was presented in [KOCH et al. 1996]. Another system for craniofacial surgery simulation was described in [KEEVE et al. 1999]. ZACHOW et al. [2003a] developed a craniofacial planning and simulation system that is in regular use for planning complex osteotomies. SZÉKELY et al. [1998] presented a framework for the full-scale, real-time, finite element simulation of elastic tissue deformation and considered scalable parallel algorithms and special-purpose parallel hardware to be key components. Another specific view on soft tissue simulation was given by HAUTH [2004].

RADETZKY et al. [2000] introduced a neuro-fuzzy model that allows description of the visual and haptic deformation behavior of the simulated tissue through expert knowledge in the form of medical terms. With respect to the surgical simulation, we want to point to the MISTELS system (McGill Inanimate System for Training and Evaluation of Laparoscopic Skills). A series of publications describes its development, its use, and its validation, with respect to the ability to assess surgical skills reliably [DEROSSIS et al. 1998, DAUSTER et al. 2005, FELDMAN et al. 2004].

Chapter 21

Outlook

Image acquisition has made tremendous progress in the last few years and will continue to do so in the years to come. The advent of CT scanners with multiple rows of detectors (multislice CT) in 1998 led in a rapid sequence to devices with 2, 4, 16, and currently 64 rows of detectors. New devices that are not commercially available at the moment are in the clinical trial stage: flat-panel detector CTs [KALENDER 2003] improve the spatial resolution to isotropic voxels of the size 0.2 mm, and Dual Source CTs improve the temporal resolution. Similar developments can be observed for MRI, ultrasound, and other acquisition techniques. New diagnostic procedures and improved accuracy within existing procedures are becoming reality. As an example, the diagnosis of the beating heart strongly benefits from an increased spatial and temporal resolution. These developments offer new chances and raise new challenges for the analysis and visualization of such data.

At the same time, many new therapy options have been developed and existing options have been refined. To name a few examples, minimally invasive and endoscopic interventions, focused ultrasound, and radiofrequency ablation have been introduced. Driven to a large extent by the development of new instruments and other devices, interventional radiology, radiation treatment, and many surgical disciplines have made substantial progress in recent years. The variety of therapy options leads to increased requirements with respect to diagnosis, therapy planning, and intraoperative monitoring. Many challenges for the analysis, integration, visualization, and exploration of medical image data are directly related to these new treatment options.

In this book, we described a variety of techniques for analyzing and visualizing the patient's anatomy based on medical image data. We focused on static 2D and 3D image data. With respect to visualizing higher dimensional data, such as time-varying data, diffusion tensor data, and fused image data, many research problems are not solved or at least are not solved sufficiently for routine applications. Higher dimensional data pose many challenges with respect to filtering, segmentation, registration, and visualization. In addition to visualizing the anatomy, exploring functional information, such as vessel wall thickness, is essential for diagnosis and treatment planning. Illustrative visualization techniques, which were described in Chapter 17, should be explored with respect to their ability to convey relations in higher dimensional data. Illustrative visualization may be also useful for mapping quantitative information onto the patients' anatomy. Throughout this book, we primarily discussed algorithms that produce static images, as well as the interaction facilities with which to explore them. The generation of animation sequences was only briefly discussed (recall Sect. 20.3), as it has not been investigated very well. Animation generation will likely play a more important role in the future. Animation sequences can convey a wealth of information in a limited amount of time—medical education and collaborative intervention planning may strongly benefit from appropriate animations.

Visualization strongly benefits from research in visual perception. Whether something can be perceived at all, whether color differences can be discriminated, and whether objects can be discriminated at a glance (preattentive vision) is dependent on the selection of visualization parameters. A variety of user studies have been carried out and provide a valuable source for information [WARE 2000, LAIDLAW et al. 2005].

Finally, task knowledge can be exploited to determine which objects are essential for certain tasks and to guide the selection of visualization parameters.

Most of the visualization techniques and systems developed so far are primarily based on an informal task analysis and on the intuition of the respective authors. Later, the techniques were fine-tuned after informal user studies with qualitative feedback. While this represents a good starting point, more systematic analysis is required. Controlled psychophysical experiments would allow the systematic comparison of different visualization options as to their influence on the viewer's accuracy and speed. In addition, eye-tracking may reveal patterns of viewing behavior and thus help explain differences. Designing and accomplishing user studies so that the results can be generalized is a complex challenge. Many user studies in visualization are biased in some way or overly simplified, relying on too-simple geometric models or tasks that do not represent the user's goals very well. But there are also excellent examples, which may serve as an orientation. The series of experiments on the influence of visualization parameters on shape perception carried out by V. INTERRANTE and her group is highly recommended [INTERRANTE et al. 1995]. Other inspiring examples include the comparison of 2D vector field visualizations [LAIDLAW et al. 2005] and of color scales [RHEINGANS and EBERT 2001]. KOSARA et al. [2003] discussed the role of user studies in visualization in general, providing a useful starting point for designing evaluation studies related to visualization techniques in general.

Eventually, perceptually based guidelines for designing medical visualizations may be developed. A couple of questions might inspire further research: What is the best way to visualize nested anatomic surfaces, such as a tumor inside an organ, or a vascular system inside an organ? What is the best way to show the spatial relation between a tumor and surrounding risk structures?

Another venue for future work is to establish collaborations between designers and computer scientists for the further development of medical visualizations and the interfaces to explore them. Industrial software and, in particular, user interface development are often based on the joint effort of mathematicians, computer scientists, and designers. Companies such as Tiani Medgraph (now a part of Agfa) and BrainLAB have a reputation not only for the functionality of their products but also for the high quality of their visual design and the exciting experience of working with them. In scientific settings, this component is usually missing. Figure 21.1 presents a user interface design accomplished by a professional designer. This design was employed as the starting point for the actual system design and development and turned out to be successful in first clinical trials. Good visual design—which, from a scientific point of view, may be regarded as less relevant—makes a strong difference in the acceptance of software systems. The scientific relevance of such a collaboration lies in the improved motivation and feedback of medical doctors, which is essential to evaluate and fine-tune initial solutions.

The design of user interfaces for special workplaces (e.g., the operating room), the layout of different views and interaction facilities, and the definition of all the default values for colors and other visual properties are tasks for which people trained in visual design might provide valuable hints. In the following, we briefly describe some topics where substantial research is necessary.

21.1   INTEGRATING SIMULATION AND VISUALIZATION

A great potential for future work lies in a closer integration of numerical simulations with appropriate visualizations. Numerical simulations play an essential role in a variety of diagnostic tasks, as well as in therapy planning. We have presented an example of these applications in the context of the simulation of soft tissue deformation for craniofacial surgery planning. Recent work deals with the stress and strain simulation of vascular structures as an additional aid to determining the risk of rupture for an aneurysm

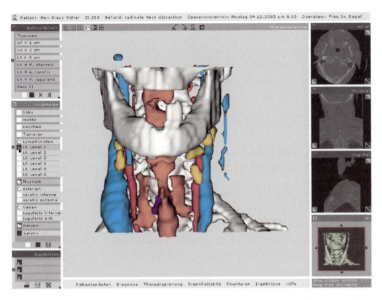

FIGURE 21.1   *Visual design of an application for neck dissection planning. A prototyping tool (Macromedia Director) was employed by a design student to create the visual design. A focus of this design is the workflow (buttons at the bottom line) and sorting criteria relating to the selection of relevant subsets of anatomic structures (left). (Image courtesy* CLAUDIA JANKE, *University of Applied Sciences, Magdeburg)*

[DE PUTTER et al. 2006]. The optimal visualization of such simulation results has not been investigated so far. Another example is the numerical simulation of the effect of thermoablations and, thus, the feasibility of thermoablation for a particular tumor (see Sect. 19.5.2). Visualization plays an essential role in such settings: on one hand, visualization should convey the results of the simulation, usually integrated with the visualization of anatomic information. As soon as more than one scalar parameter has to be mapped on the representation of the anatomy, the visualization is challenging. On the other hand, visualization may be used to validate simulation results qualitatively. For this purpose, it is essential that the simulation results are visualized along with the underlying grid. Whether or not the results are reliable eventually becomes obvious for an expert with an appropriate visualization. If the results are regarded as not reliable, the underlying mesh may be refined or the time-step reduced and a new visualization started.

21.2   INTEGRATED VISUALIZATION OF PREOPERATIVE AND INTRAOPERATIVE VISUALIZATION

Preoperative planning of complex interventions is often based on careful image analysis and visualization. Appropriate computer support may help physicians define an optimal therapy or an optimal combination of therapies. However, therapy planning has only a limited effect on the actual realization of the treatment plan. During an intervention, the spatial relationships and locations of organs can change significantly, due to the deformation imposed by the surgeons (through instruments or by their hands) and to removed or cut tissue. An ideal intraoperative visualization would be updated according to these changes. The intraoperative situation might lead to new findings, such as an additional tumor detected by palpation or intraoperative ultrasound. This raises the question whether an efficient process can be designed to adapt the preoperative planning to the new findings.

The transfer of preoperatively analyzed information to the operating room is a challenge for many application areas. While a lot of work dealt with the problems of registration, tracking, and intraoperative navigation, the use of image analysis results and advanced visualization techniques in the operating room is not handled well so far.

21.3 INTEGRATED VISUALIZATION OF MORPHOLOGIC AND FUNCTIONAL IMAGE DATA

Medical diagnosis of complex and serious pathologies can rely on scanned datasets of the morphology (anatomy) with a high spatial resolution and a high spatial-to-noise ratio. Often, additional image data, such as functional MRI, PET, or SPECT data, are acquired to study neural activation patterns, and metabolistic processes. However, *functional* image data are typically acquired at a significantly lower temporal and spatial resolution and are often hampered by artifacts, such as geometric distortion. The integrated interpretation of morphologic and functional images is one of the most challenging tasks for radiologists. The integration of such images in a fused visualization is therefore highly desirable. Considerable work has been done in image registration (the transformation of one image dataset in the coordinate system of another to provide an optimal information correspondence; recall Sect. 5.9). However, the visualization problems occurring once the data have been aligned have not been addressed with the same intensity. While the registration problems are reduced by technical developments such as joint acquisition of combined acquisition devices (e.g., PET/CT, PET/SPECT, or PET and MRI data), the visualization challenges remain.

21.4 MODEL-BASED VISUALIZATION

For this concept, we must look back into *model-based* segmentation techniques used to reduce the interaction effort and increase the reproducibility (recall Sect. 5.4). Statistical models, such as Active Shape Models and Active Appearance Models, employ *a priori* knowledge with respect to the expected shape and gray value distributions (model assumptions). With increasingly more visualization options, users must adjust many parameters to generate expressive visualizations. Surface models may be smoothed using a variety of techniques and parameters. Surface visualization and illustrative rendering techniques are controlled by a large set of additional parameters. Although interactive 3D visualizations should be flexible and support individual planning tasks, appropriate selection of visualization techniques and presets for their parameters is needed. In this chapter, we discusss this kind of visualization support. Here, we briefly outline this kind of *model-based visualization* to denote the selection and parameterization of visualization techniques based on *a priori* knowledge concerning visual perception, shapes of anatomical objects, and intervention planning tasks.

Based on image analysis results, visualization parameters can be locally adapted to individual objects or certain categories of anatomic structures, such as nerves or lymph nodes. Since visualizations should provide insights into spatial relations, there is an argument for visualization techniques that "idealize" anatomic structures to some extent to render them more comprehensibly.

The design of "idealized" visualizations requires assumptions with respect to geometric properties. This gives rise to the term *model-based visualization*. A variety of sources can be exploited to derive such automatic selections. Similar to the model generation process in image segmentation, experience with the visualization of a variety of similar datasets is an essential source of information.

Illustrative visualization has a great potential for intervention planning. However, for practical use, the selection and parameterization of illustrative rendering techniques must be supported. An informal user study indicated that silhouette rendering is useful for large structures, such as organs, but not for small structures such as small nodules [TIETJEN et al. 2005]. Depending on the visualization goal, silhouette rendering may be used as the only rendering mode or combined with surface rendering. "Model-based" techniques are also needed for a variety of other applications, such as the visualization of diffusion tensor data.

Similar to segmentation problems, the suitability of visualization techniques depends on the object shape and size and on the attributes of other objects in the neighborhood. Visualization can benefit from the substantial work on representing *a priori* knowledge for image segmentation.

In Table 21.1, model-based segmentation and visualization are compared. While the distribution of gray values of the target structures in CT and MRI data is valuable information for model-based segmentation, this information is not relevant for model-based visualization. Derived information such as gradient magnitude or curvature metrics is essential for edge-based segmentation. Primary tumors, for example, often have weak borders, and their precise extent is uncertain. This information can be employed to select a visualization technique that conveys this uncertainty (for example, a semitransparent volume rendering instead of a "perfect" shiny isosurface). We regard as geometric shape any shape descriptor, such as compactness or anisotropy. Assumptions related to shape descriptors are useful to identify the target structure and to visualize it appropriately. Similarly, topology information, such as connectedness and the number of holes, is essential for segmentation and visualization.

Despite the similarities between model-based segmentation and visualization, there are also fundamental differences. Model-based segmentation is employed to automatically segment one target structure, whereas model-based visualization refers to whole classes of anatomic structures.

While there is one correct segmentation, there are potentially many appropriate visualization settings for a particular set of anatomic structures. The suitability of visualization parameters depends on user preferences, experiences, and visual capabilities.

Information	Model-based Segmentation	Model-based Visualization
Gray value distribution	×	—
Gradient magnitude/curvature metrics	×	×
Geometric shape	×	×
Topology	×	×
Structural relation between objects	×	×
Visual perception	—	×
Task knowledge	—	×

TABLE 21.1 *Model-based segmentation and visualization.*

Appendix A

Systems for Visualization in Medicine

Research and development for visualization in medicine requires a substantial investment in software. The field has become so complex that it is usually not feasible to start developments from scratch. In particular need is software support for basic file handling, low-level image processing (filtering), high-level image processing (segmentation, registration), and viewing, visualization, and interaction options.

In the following, we briefly discuss a variety of systems and toolkits that support these tasks, and that in part can be used as basis for further implementations. We focus on general purpose systems that support more than one aspect, such as loading and viewing DICOM data. For each system, we discuss the specialties, the kind of support provided, and whether the system is freely available or not. For commercial systems, we do not discuss pricing in detail, as it frequently changes and may be subject to individual agreements. The possibility of generating applications with appropriate user interfaces is also described for all systems.

We consider OpenSource software not only as a viable basis for software development, but also as an urgently needed vehicle to distribute scientific results in medical image analysis and visualization, as well as their applications in computer-assisted medicine. Hence, we will focus in particular on freely available OpenSource software. As pointed by WOLF et al. [2005], scientific publications often have an immediate value, for example in medicine and biology. In medical image analysis and visualization, however, algorithms and methods described in a scientific paper must be reimplemented and carefully tested for those who want to use them. Therefore, it is important and necessary to advance the field that new achievements are not only published as a scientific paper, but also disseminated as part of OpenSource software.

To give an overview of software is not an easy task. An extensive evaluation of all toolkits is a huge effort and the results would still be strongly subjective. While comprehensive information on software toolkits is available, almost all of this information is provided by the institutions who developed the software. Consequently, the strengths of the respective toolkits are emphasized and the success stories presented; problems are usually mentioned less often. This is partially also true if toolkits are presented in scientific publications that were subject to peer reviews. Ideally, high-quality information independent of the creators of the software should be used as the basis for an overview. Recently, such a comparison was performed and published [BITTER et al. 2007]. Because of this reliable and independent source of information, three of these four systems (MITK, SciRun, MeVisLab) are described in more detail. VolView, although included in the comparison, is only briefly mentioned here because it is a compact system that does not provide broad support.

We tried to include the important and mature toolkits, but we do not claim that this overview is complete. It is not even completely balanced, which is due to the different amount of available and reliable information and the fact that much research described in this book was realized on the basis of either Amira or MeVisLab, which are therefore described with more detail. Hence, the level of detail in the following descriptions should not be regarded as an indicator of the quality.

A.1   CONCEPTS OF GENERAL PURPOSE VISUALIZATION SOFTWARE

The toolkits currently used for visualization in medicine have a lot of similarities with respect to their software approach. Most of them are consequently realized as object-oriented systems with a clear modular design that lends them flexibile for future extensions. An advantage of flexible object-oriented systems is the ease of integrating them in larger applications. The dominant programming language of these toolkits is still C++. Although other languages such as Java and Smalltalk have many advantages over C++ in general, they are not widespread in medical image processing and visualization, primarily due to the better performance of C++-based toolkits with dedicated memory and thread management.

Since the very first visualization systems, AVS [UPSON et al. 1989] and Iris Explorer [FOULSER 1995], most toolkits follow a dataflow metaphor: modules have inputs and outputs and can be connected with each other by specifying that an output parameter of one module should be connected to the input parameter of another module (sometimes these interface elements of a module are referred to as "ports"). Some modules import and read image data from an external file. The modules are *sources* in the visualization network; they have no input parameters and provide an internal representation of the image data as output. Other modules save results or allow exploration of the data in a 2D or 3D viewer. These modules—also called *sinks*—have no output parameters. The solution of a visualization problem in such systems is provided by an appropriate network—a graph structure that might include branchings and loops.

Textual Versus Visual Programming   While the dataflow metaphor is widely used, there is a strong difference in the way visualization networks are actually created. In some systems, this is accomplished in an intuitive way through visual programming; modules are placed at a canvas, and lines represent connections between inputs and outputs (see Fig. A.3). With other systems, the connection of operators and the definition of networks is performed by traditional (textual) programming, which is more demanding for beginners. Visual programming should be supported by a carefully designed graphic editor. Interaction tasks, such as selection of a module, grouping, and ungrouping to support the placement of modules, as well as adding, translating, and removing connection lines, should be supported in a convenient way. Once visualization networks get larger, hierarchical solutions (macros, subnetworks) are essential. In general, the creation and modification of large networks poses a problem with visual programming.

Interaction Support   The creation of solutions for diagnosis support and intervention planning requires more than image processing and visualization parameters. Such applications have to be highly interactive; parameters for a segmentation are specified, polygonal models are modified, and finally viewing parameters are changed. Usually, multiple views are needed, and consistency must be ensured. Therefore, functionality is needed that synchronizes the execution of visualization networks and triggers changes once a certain parameter has been changed. Usually, multiple views, e.g., 2D and 3D views, are needed, and consistency must be ensured. Again, object-oriented concepts such as the subject/observer pattern support the management of large, highly interactive applications. The integration of such interaction support in dataflow-oriented systems is not straightforward, and the systems differ in their ability to handle complex interaction patterns.

Scripting   Visualization networks provide an appropriate level for expert users; they integrate modules into existing networks or parameterize the available modules. For medical doctors, more high-level support is necessary; the complexity of the underlying networks should be effectively hidden from them. For this purpose, scripting languages are used to realize graphic user interfaces with appropriate window management and workflow support. The availability and expressiveness of scripting languages is thus another important criterion in the selection of a software toolkit.

Memory Management and Persistent Data   Due to the large size of medical image datasets, memory management is a serious issue that affects the performance of applications and the productivity of programmers. Most of the systems described below provide memory management that supports the tracking of errors and memory leaks and increases performance compared to standard C++ new/delete methods. To maximize their usefulness, all software systems must be able to store data to disk at the end of execution and retrieve that data later for additional processing. Advanced image analysis and visualization toolkits, such as SciRun and MeVisLab, provide dedicated support to work with persistent data. Synchronization functionality that supports multiple consistent views to the same data is an essential feature, as it is extremely difficult to achieve consistency in complex applications without dedicated and general mechanisms. Fortunately, the toolkits described below provide such mechanisms. In addition to the mentioned methods, error handling and debugging support is needed.

Documentation   Another important aspect in the selection of a suitable software toolkit is the quality of the documentation. Most of the toolkits described below provide not only reference documentation targeted at experienced users, but also "how to get started" documents, example datasets, example networks, a list of frequently asked questions, and wizards to aid in the development of new modules. Since the quality of the documentation rapidly changes, the information given here will be outdated soon. Therefore, we direct interested readers to the respective mentioned Web sites, where hopefully up-to-date information will be available.

A.2   TOOLKITS AND OTHER SOFTWARE SYSTEMS FOR VISUALIZATION IN MEDICINE

The first systems we describe are VTK and ITK. They are of particular importance because they are frequently used as solid foundation for many other systems.

VTK   The visualization toolkit (www.vtk.org) is a general OpenSource visualization software toolkit that provides, among other services, support for isosurfacing, mesh smoothing, and mesh decimation. It is available on all frequently used software platforms, such as most Windows platforms, Mac OS X, and UNIX platforms. Direct volume rendering, vector, and tensor visualization, relevant for the visualization of DTI data, are also provided. High-level modeling algorithms, such as implicit modeling, are supported. Overall, VTK consists of more than 700 classes of C++-code. VTK can process and generate many different file formats. Image data is processed by the *Reader* classes; *Writer* classes produce the output in the selected file format, such as VRML and Open Inventor. The file formats of modeling tools such as 3D Studio and Alias Wavefront are also supported. The viewer classes of VTK are convenient and support the interactive viewing and exploration of 3D visualizations with intuitive 3D interaction. VTK directly employs OpenGL and can therefore be used as a direct access to graphics hardware. Other systems employ graphics libraries at a higher level, such as Open Inventor, for which this is not possible.

VTK is a mature and robust system with a very large user group and many successful applications in real-world applications. It is maintained and further refined by Kitware (www.kitware.com). Similar to other image analysis and visualization systems, it is based on a *dataflow metaphor*. VTK filters process the input values and output the result values. A great advantage is that the underlying concepts are documented very well in a book [SCHROEDER et al. 2001]. An elegant and easy-to-understand object-oriented design is a strong advantage of VTK. The methods realized in VTK are general, but not fine-tuned with respect to performance. VTK is not tailored to medical applications. Therefore, some of the specialties of VTK, e.g., the support of various grid types, are often not needed in medical applications. On the other hand, dedicated support for special tasks in diagnosis and therapy planning is not available.

User interfaces on top of the VTK functionality can be generated with Tcl/Tk, Python, and Java. VTK provides support for interactive applications, but for complex (clinical) applications, this support is not sufficient. VTK is used as a basis for more specialized libraries, such as MeVisLab [HAHN et al. 2003] and MITK [WOLF et al. 2004, 2005] which are described later in this section. The use of VTK in specialized libraries is facilitated by the OpenSource character of VTK.

ITK The Insight Segmentation and Registration toolkit is mainly designed as image processing toolkit. ITK not only has a similar name as VTK, it is also maintained by Kitware, and its development is led partially by the same people as the VTK development (www.itk.org). It is an OpenSource software system, originally started to support the Visible Human Project.

ITK was developed by six principal organizations: three commercial (Kitware, General Electrics Corporate R&D, and Insightful) and three academic (University of North Carolina at Chapel Hill, University of Utah, and University of Pennsylvania).

ITK provides general methods for image processing, segmentation, and registration in two, three, and more dimensions. The functionality of ITK is impressive; basic as well as advanced segmentation methods, such as levelsets and fast marching methods, are available. Bayesian minimum error classifiers for classes of Gaussian distributions and advanced registration methods are provided. ITK is often combined with VTK, a combination that is supported very well. ITK has an excellent documentation: the extensive ITK *Software Guide* [IBANEZ and SCHROEDER 2005] describes many of the features of the toolkit and contains information for both users and developers. The book is available in a printed version that includes a CD-ROM with source, documentation, and data. A fully hyperlinked version of the text is available on the CD-ROM as well. The ITK theory book [YOO 2004] provides another rich source of documentation and discussion. Due to its quality, its broad availability, and its substantial documentation, ITK has a broad user basis and can be regarded as the standard library in medical image analysis. However, ITK does not support visual programming and is therefore not appropriate for users without programming skills. This gave rise to combinations with other systems, such as MITK and MeVisLab, that incorporate ITK.

SciRun SciRun is a powerful and complex simulation and visualization system developed at the University of Utah. It is based on the paradigm of computational steering, in which simulations are accomplished, results are visualized, and immediate changes of parameters influence the simulation. In medical applications, biomechanic simulations are an example that demonstrates the essential power of the SciRun concepts.

Similar to other toolkits, SciRun is based on a dataflow model and provides visual programming mechanisms. SciRun uses Tcl/Tk as its GUI front end. It provides high-level support such as scene graph and widget libraries, and math and geometry libraries, as well as low-level support—particularly thread and memory management.

SciRun is provided with a variety of Tcl/Tk applications. For medical scenarios, two of them are particularly relevant:

- The BioImage application is designed to support the exploration of medical volume data. In addition to powerful support for loading, resampling, and viewing medical image data, it provides many color scales and well designed user interfaces for all modules. The work of KNISS and KINDLMANN on specifying multidimensional transfer functions is also included [KNISS et al. 2002].

- The BioTensor application processes and visualizes diffusion tensor images (recall Chap. 18). It includes sophisticated support for the reconstruction of tensor data from individual diffusion weighted images. The analysis and visualization of diffusion tensor data is supported very well. In particular, Gordon Kindlmann's work on visualizing diffusion tensor images is included [KINDLMANN et al. 2000], [KINDLMANN 2004a].

More information on SciRun can be found at the Web site www.software.sci.utah. edu/, as well as in PARKER et al. [1997].

Amira Amira (www.amiravis.com) was originally developed by the scientific visualization group of the Zuse-Institute Berlin and is now commercially available through Mercury systems. Amira incorporates the OpenInventor library [WERNECKE 1994] with its powerful set of 3D viewer classes, its scenegraph concept, and many classes that support 3D interaction.

There are several similarities between Amira and VTK; both are object-oriented extensible toolkits, and both provide a similar functionality. Tcl is used as scripting language to provide dedicated user interfaces for end users. In contrast with VTK, Amira supports visual programming.

Amira provides all general visualization techniques for scalar, vector, and tensor data. Some more sophisticated algorithms, particularly methods for geometry reconstruction from volume data, surface simplification, surface smoothing, and surface editing, are also included. Geometry reconstruction is performed by an algorithm that effectively avoids cracks and holes even if multiple (more than two) different materials touch each other [STALLING et al. 2005] (recall Sect. 7.2 for surface generation from volume data). Surface smoothing may be accomplished with different methods, including a constrained smoothing method that provides a good trade-off between accuracy and smoothness.

Although Amira is a general purpose visualization toolkit with successful applications in different application areas, it also provides dedicated support for the medical applications that are briefly described in the following. A strength of Amira in medical applications is its ability to import many variants of DICOM data, including tilted datasets. A powerful component of Amira is its segmentation editor, which provides access to a variety of fundamental segmentation methods, such as thresholding, region growing, and LiveWire. Editing of segmentation results is possible in 2D as well as 3D views, which supports a fast segmentation very well. The generation of grid structures for numerical simulations based on segmentation results is an essential feature for surgery simulation and advanced surgery planning. Many aspects of the grid quality must be considered in this process to avoid numerical instabilities. Based on long-term research in this area, Amira provides advanced support for the generation of tetrahedral grids for finite element simulation [STALLING et al. 2005], [ZACHOW et al. 2003a]. This includes the definition of boundary conditions on the surfaces, as well as various smoothing and relaxation facilities, to improve the grid quality.

Amira provides support for rigid and elastic registration methods. A *landmark editor* may be employed to specify corresponding positions in two datasets. Either a rigid registration, which optimizes the position overlap of landmarks, or elastic registration, which matches the landmarks precisely, can be applied. Since elastic registration requires a resampling of the data, various resampling filters are available to support this task. For multimodal image registration, voxel-based techniques are also available. Many more rather basic functions are provided and are often useful in medical applications: arithmetic and boolean operations can be performed on image data, and various statistics can be computed either with respect to the whole image data or to a subset of it.

In general, Amira provides very useful features for the comparison of visualization results and thus for the validation of visualization methods. Figure A.1 and A.2 present two examples of Amira's analysis of surface meshes with respect to local curvature and triangle quality. Other examples are described in Section 14.6.

Amira is a commercial software, and its price depends on the required license and number of additional packages that extend the core functionality. New modules can be added with the developer's license.

A large variety of successful applications, for example in surgery planning and simulation, shows that Amira is indeed a good choice for many tasks in medical visualization, particularly for tasks that involve numerical simulations. The advanced support for grid generation is a unique feature of Amira. Beside the commercially available version, other versions of Amira are used at the ZIB-institute. The research carried out there will be part of future Amira versions.

MeVisLab MeVisLab (www.mevislab.de) [HAHN *et al.* 2003, REXILIUS *et al.* 2005] was developed at the Center for Medical Diagnosis Systems and Visualization (MeVis, Bremen). Similar to Amira, MeVisLab is based on long-term research and development by a large research group (approximately 40 people) and on the development of the MeVisLab predecessor ILab, which began in 1993. There is a broad overlap of functionality between MeVisLab and Amira, since both incorporate the full functionality of OpenInventor. Furthermore, the functionality of loading and processing medical image data is very similar; several segmentation and registration methods are available in both systems. Both systems provide a powerful visual programming environment and extensive documentation (see www.mevislab.de). MeVisLab's graphic editor for visual programming is convenient to use and designed very well. Three kinds of ports are provided: triangular ports transfer image data, rounded ports transfer 3D graphics data such as polygonal meshes, and quadrilateral ports transfer other datastructures, such as a graph description of some shapes. Only ports of the same type can be connected (see Fig. A.3).

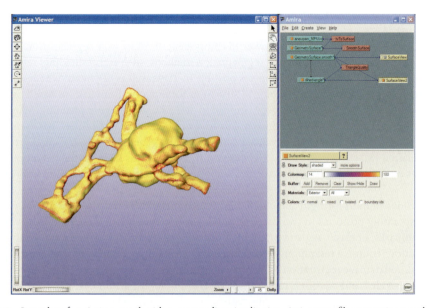

FIGURE A.1 *Screenshot of an Amira network with a corresponding visualization. An inventor–file representing a cerebral aneurysm is loaded, visualized, and analyzed with respect to the triangle quality. The result of this analysis is mapped onto the surface with the color scale shown in the lower right part. (Image courtesy CHRISTIAN SCHUMANN, University of Magdeburg)*

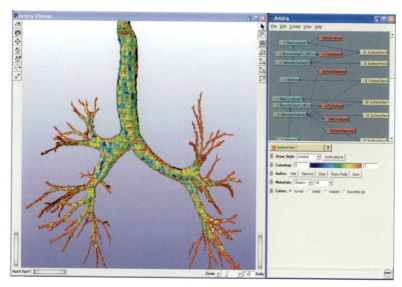

FIGURE A.2   *Curvature analysis and visualization with Amira. Two versions of a bronchial tree surface are loaded and their curvature is analyzed, resulting in a variety of SurfaceViews that are superimposed. The maximum curvature values are color-coded. (Image courtesy* CHRISTIAN SCHUMANN, *University of Magdeburg)*

Since visualization networks tend to grow very quickly, a hierarchical solution is available using macros that hide the complexity of a subnetwork in one node. An example is the View2DExtensions macro in Figure A.3, which hides the complex network shown in Figure A.4. This image also indicates that visual programming is limited to small- or moderate-sized networks; visual programming with large networks becomes inconvenient even with an advanced graphics editor.

The scripting facilities are comprehensive. The MeVisLab IDE is based on Qt (Trolltech, www.trolltech.com), a modern and portable user interface toolkit [BLANCHETTE 2006]. An abstract hierarchical definition language allows the design of module panels and efficient user interfaces.

Javascript and Python can be used to implement dynamic functionality on network and user interface levels. With these functionalities, many software assistants have been realized that are in routine clinical use. An example for liver surgery planning was described earlier in Section 19.6.

A strong, robust, and highly efficient part of MeVisLab is the image processing library ML. Multithreading and efficient memory management (paging) that avoids the recomputation of a whole dataset and instead processes tiles of the data are important characteristics. Segmentation in MeVisLab is not accomplished with a segmentation editor; instead, many individual segmentation modules are available. For example, advanced watershed and LiveWire segmentation (recall Sect. 5.3) are useful for a variety of segmentation tasks. In general, powerful image processing and analysis functions are available. MeVisLab also contains a powerful volume renderer, the *Gigavoxelrenderer*, which is dedicated to the efficient exploration of very large datasets. The graphics hardware support of different modern GPUs is exploited if available.

Many visualization and interaction techniques described in this book have been developed within the MeVisLab platform. Interactive and automatic measurement functionality (recall Chap. 13) are part of MeVisLab. Simple and advanced methods for virtual resection are realized as MeVisLab modules. The

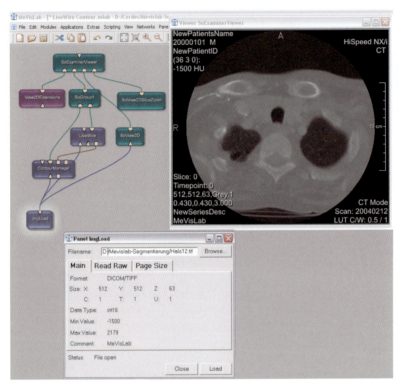

FIGURE A.3 MeVisLab network with basic image loading, segmentation, and viewing functionality. The dataflow is from bottom (ImgLoad) to top (SoExaminerViewer). The ImgLoad-panel is open to specify the file to be read from. The ContourManager handles multiple contours on multiple datasets and is employed for all edge-based segmentation methods. Here, it is used in combination with LiveWire segmentation. (Image courtesy JEANETTE CORDES, University of Magdeburg)

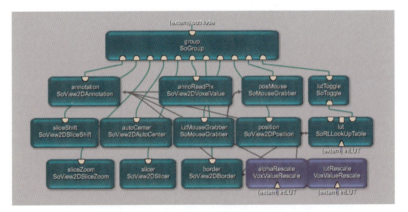

FIGURE A.4 Internal network of the Macro View2DExtensions. The individual operators provide the functions for different aspects of a 2D slice viewer, such as the placement and layout of the annotation, the selection of a voxel to inquire its value, the specification of the lookup table through mouse movements, and the border of the viewer.

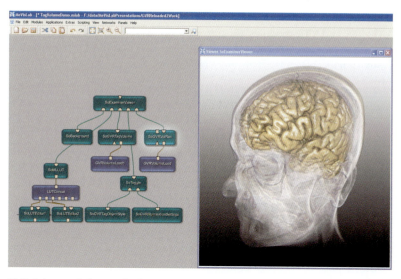

FIGURE A.5 *MeVisLab network for tagged volume rendering. Two transfer functions are created and combined (LUTConcat). A volume data set and related segmentation information are loaded and connected with the rendering modules. All data are displayed in a 3D viewer. (Image courtesy FLORIAN LINK, MeVis Bremen)*

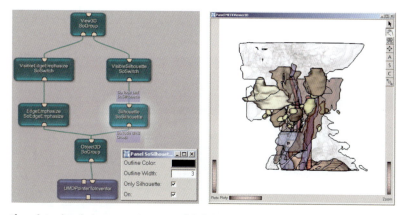

FIGURE A.6 *If a node is selected, the input and output are labelled. By subclassing from the OpenInventor library, SoEdgeEmphasize and SoSilhouette nodes were developed as parts of MeVisLab (left image). With these nodes, silhouette rendering is accomplished (right image). (Images courtesy KONRAD MÜHLER, University of Magdeburg)*

visualization of vascular structures with truncated cones and with convolution surfaces (recall Chap. 14) is implemented as MeVisLab operators. Illustrative rendering techniques are also part of MeVisLab (Fig. A.6).

MeVisLab has a free basic version for noncommercial use; the developers' version which allows the extension of MeVisLab, is only free of charge with restricted functionality. Similar to Amira, an extended version of the public MeVisLab is employed and constantly extended at MeVis, with the goal of distributing the research results once they have achieved a stable state.

The value of MeVisLab has strongly increased for many users due to the integration of ITK (180 modules) and VTK. ITK and VTK modules are automatically wrapped as MeVisLab modules. With this feature, MeVisLab users benefit from future developments of ITK and VTK. MeVisLab is available on Windows and Linux systems.

MITK   The Medical Image Processing Toolkit (MITK) is another advanced toolkit built on top of ITK and VTK. It is an OpenSource software, developed and maintained by the German Cancer Research Center (DKFZ) and available via a Web site: www.mitk.org. Most MITK classes are realized as subclasses of ITK base classes. Therefore, the fundamental mechanisms of ITK are available in MITK too. On one hand, MITK provides a frontend to ITK functionality, for example a registration frontend. On the other hand, dedicated new functions are provided. A unique feature is the integration with the PACS system Chili (MITK applications can be realized as plugins into the Chili system, www.chili-radiology.com). This aspect is particularly important for applications that are intended to run in a hospital environment. The design considerations, the architecture, and the representative applications are described in WOLF et al. [2004, 2005]. A strong aspect of MITK is its support for highly interactive applications; a sophisticated mechanism for undo/redo at multiple levels is provided, and advanced synchronization functionality is available. The images in Figures A.7 and A.8 provide an impression of MITK and the applications that can be generated with this toolkit.

VolV   VolV is a framework for VOLume Visualization of medical data developed at the University of Tübingen in the context of the DFG Focus Program 1124, "Medical Robotics and Navigation" http://gris.uni-tuebingen.de/projects/volv/index.html. VolV provides methods for reading a large variety of image data, including DICOM data, through the OFFIS dcmtk (DICOM toolkit). Furthermore,

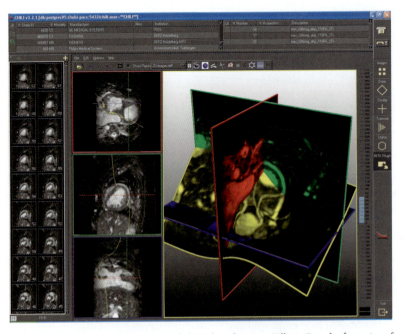

FIGURE A.7   *Integration of MITK as a plugin into a radiological workstation. Yellow: Curved reformation of coronary arteries.* (Image courtesy IVO WOLF, DKFZ Heidelberg)

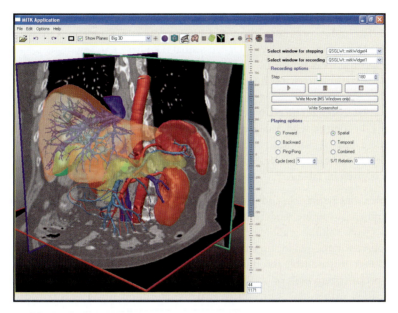

FIGURE A.8 *Preoperative decision support for pancreatic surgery: Visualization of abdominal organs and vasculature. Arteries and veins are extracted from two different CT datasets and registered for visualization. (Image courtesy* MAX SCHÖBINGER, DKFZ *Heidelberg)*

the data can be visualized using numerous methods, including the standard methods for medical data such as MIP, Pseudo X-ray, CVP, and indirect and direct volume rendering. In addition, several volume processing and conversion methods are provided. While VolV provides all these general visualization and processing methods, its actual focus is on intraoperative visualization.

The modular architecture of VolV allows the integration of new modules into the system. Currently under development are modules for segmentation, medical mixed reality, image-guided surgery, and a wizard system to create specific applications. VolV is based on OpenGL, with Qt as an interface toolkit, and on VTK. It is provided as free OpenSource system (for noncommercial applications) and supported under Linux, although the general architecture is portable to other platforms too.

Julius   The development of Julius (www.julius.caesar.de) is centered at the Caesar Institute in Bonn. Julius, similar to the aforementioned systems, supports many tasks in medical image analysis and visualization. It is implemented using the Qt system as its event and windowing API and can be extended flexibly through a plugin mechanism. However, the focus and specialty of Julius are biomechanical simulations. Julius can be used free of charge in noncommercial settings. More information on Julius can be found at the Web site and in KEEVE *et al.* [2001, 2003].

Extensible Base Applications   The description above focused on modular software libraries, which provide a high degree of flexibility. An alternative and more classical variant of software support for medical image analysis and visualization is the use of an extendable base application.

A well known example and pioneering work is the *Analyze* software (AnalyzeDirect, Lenexa, USA, www.analyzedirect.com). It is based on long-term biomedical imaging research and development at the Mayo Clinic. Analyze is a commercial system with a core and several additions, for example for the analysis of DTI data. It provides access to the comprehensive AVW (A Visualization Workshop) library with a Tcl/Tk user interface and incorporates advanced DICOM support. ITK functionality was integrated into the Analyze/AVW environment at two levels. First, essential ITK filters, e.g., segmentation and registrations functions, are wrapped as AVW functions, making them directly accessible to developers. Second, custom Analyze modules are available to enable interactive use of ITK algorithms. Analyze is available on all major platforms.

Another well known and advanced system of this category is the *3D Slicer* (www.slicer.org [GERING *et al.* 1999, 2001]). In contrast with Analyze, 3D Slicer is free OpenSource software. The focus of the 3D Slicer is the segmentation, registration, and quantification of medical image data. The user interface is also realized in Tcl/Tk and can be extended. The visualization core functions use VTK. A summary of the essential systems is given in Table A.1.

Specialized Volume Rendering Systems In addition to general purpose systems for medical visualization, there are dedicated commercial volume rendering systems, such as the *VolumeGraphics Library* (VGL) provided by Volume Graphics (www.volume graphics. com) and *Voxar 3D* (www.barco.com) provided by Barco. An advanced OpenSource volume-rendering system is OpenQVis, developed by DR. REZK-SALAMA, DR. ENGEL, and DR. VEGA HIGUERA. It is available through SourceForge at www.openqvis. sourceforge.net.

VolView is a special system built on top of VTK and ITK, which thus supports advanced volume rendering in combination with sophisticated image analysis algorithms. VolView is provided by Kitware as a commercial solution for high-end volume rendering (see Fig. A.9).

Further Software for Medical Image Analysis and Visualization Two additional widespread and general systems should also be mentioned.

- IDL (Visual Information Solutions, www.ittvis.com/idl) is available on all common platforms, and provides an integrated development platform and an interpretative programming language. The focus of IDL is image processing and image analysis.
- MatLab (The MathWorks, www.mathworks.com/products/matlab) has gained widespread acceptance as a prototyping, data analysis, and visualization tool. MatLab can process data of various formats, and many packages are available to extend the core functionality. As an example, the SPM package has evolved as the standard tool to analyze functional MRI data.

Software	Availability	Scripting Language	Extensibility	Visual Programming
VTK	open source	Tcl/Tk	C++ API	No
ITK	open source	Tcl and Fltk	C++ API	No
MeVisLab	free basic version	Python	C++ API	Yes
MITK	open source	Plugin	No	No
Amira	commercial	Tcl	C++ API	Yes
SciRun	open source	Tcl/Tk	Yes	Yes
3D Slicer	open source	Tcl/Tk	Plugin	Yes
Analyze	commercial	Tcl/Tk	C++ API	No

TABLE A.1 *Toolkits for medical visualization and their basic properties*

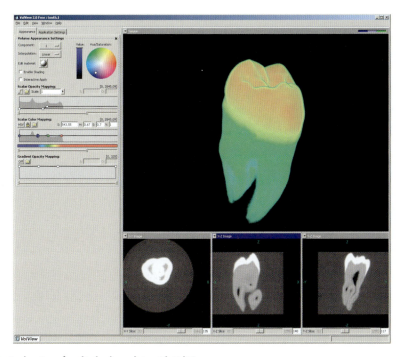

FIGURE A.9   *Exploration of medical volume data with VolView.*

OFFIS dcmtk   The OFFIS dicom toolkit (dicom.offis.de) is an important foundation library that manages reading and writing of DICOM datasets. Although it is by itself no visualization or image analysis toolkit, it is used by most packages described in this chapter as an interface to DICOM datasets.

A.3   SUMMARY

The selection of software toolkits is a crucial and challenging decision. In a recent paper [BITTER et al. 2006], four of the above described systems—VolView, MITK, MeVisLab, and SciRun—were systematically compared. Functional requirements should be the primary criteria to guide the selection while avoiding the reimplementation of things that already available in a good quality. OpenSource or freely available software is of primary interest in academic settings, since it allows the distribution of new methods in an optimal way. Table A.1 includes important criteria for a selection of tools. A checklist for evaluating toolkits should also include:

- Design concepts, particularly with respect to interactive applications
- Memory and thread management
- Debugging and diagnosis facilities
- Quality and quantity of documentation
- Support
- Supported platforms

We hope that this discussion provides a useful orientation for the selection of appropriate software.

Bibliography

R. ADAMS and L. BISCHOF. Seeded region growing. *IEEE Transactions on Pattern Analysis and Machine Intelligence*, 16(6):641–647, 1994.

R. AGGARWAL, T. GRANTCHAROV, K. MOORTHY, J. HANCE, and A. DARZI. A competency-based virtual reality training curriculum for the acquisition of laparoscopic psychomotor skill. *American Journal of Surgery*, 191(1):128–133, 2006.

M. AGUS, A. GIACHETTI, E. GOBBETTI, G. ZANETTI, N. W. JOHN, and R. J. STONE. Mastoidectomy simulation with combined visual and haptic feedback. In J. D. WESTWOOD, H. M. HOFFMANN, G. T. MOGEL, and D. STREDNEY, editors, *Proc. of Medicine Meets Virtual Reality*, pp. 17–23, IOS Press, Amsterdam, 2002a.

M. AGUS, A. GIACHETTI, E. GOBBETTI, G. ZANETTI, and A. ZORCOLO. Real-time haptic and visual simulation of bone dissection. In *Proc. of IEEE Virtual Reality*, IEEE Computer Society Press, pp. 209–216, February 2002b. (Conference held in Orlando, Florida, USA).

K. AKELEY. Reality engine graphics. In *Proc. of ACM SIGGRAPH*, pp. 109–116, 1993.

H. AKIBA, N. FOUT, and K.-L. MA. Simultaneous classification of time-varying volume data based on the time histogram. In *Data Visualization (Proc. of Eurographics/IEEE Symposium on Visualization)*, pp. 171–178, 2006.

N. AL-SAADI, M. GROSS, A. BORNSTEDT, B. SCHNACKENBURG, C. KLEIN, E. FLECK, and E. NAGEL. Comparison of various parameters for determining an index of myocardial perfusion reserve in detecting coronary stenosis with cardiovascular magnetic resonance tomography. *Z Kardiol*, 90(11):824–834, November 2001.

N. AL-SAADI, E. NAGEL, M. GROSS, A. BORNSTEDT, B. SCHNACKENBURG, C. KLEIN, W. KLIMEK, H. OSWALD, and E. FLECK. Noninvasive detection of myocardial ischemia from perfusion reserve based on cardiovascular magnetic resonance. *Circulation*, 101(12):1379–1383, March 2000.

M. ALDER, T. DEAHL, and S. MATTESON. Clinical usefulness of two-dimensional reformatted and three-dimensionally rendered computerized images: literature review and a survey of surgeon's opinions. *Journal of Oral Maxillofacial Surgery*, 37:375–386, 1995.

K. ALI, K. HARTMANN, and T. STROTHOTTE. Label layout for interactive 3D illustrations. *Proc. of WSCG*, 13(1):1–8, 2005 (13th Conference in Central Europe on Computer Graphics, Visualization and Computer Vision WSCG).

F. ALLAMANDRI, P. CIGNONI, C. MONTANI, and R. SCOPIGNO. Adaptively adjusting Marching Cubes output to fit a trilinear reconstruction filter. In *Proc. of Eurographics Workshop on Visualization in Scientific Computing*, pp. 25–34, 1998.

A. APPEL. Some techniques for shading machine renderings of solids. In *Proc. of Spring Joint Computer Conference*, pp. 37–45, 1968.

S. G. ARMATO, G. MCLENNAN, M. F. MCNITT-GRAY, C. R. MEYER, D. YANKELEVITZ, D. R. ABERLE, C. I. HENSCHKE, et al. Lung image database consortium: developing a resource for the medical imaging research community. *Radiology*, 232(3):739–748, 2004.

K. ASSMANN and K. H. HÖHNE. Investigations of structures and operations for medical image data bases. In *Proc. of the 2nd Conference on Picture Archiving and Communication Systems*, pp. 282–286, 1983.

D. AUER and L. AUER. Virtual endoscopy—a new tool for teaching and training in neuroimaging. *International Journal of Neuroradiology*, 4:3–14, 1998.

B. B. AVANTS and J. P. WILLIAMS. An adaptive minimal path generation technique for vessel tracking in CTA/CE-MRA volume images. In *Proc. of Medical Image Computing and Computer-Assisted Intervention (MICCAI)*, volume 1935 of *Lecture Notes in Computer Science*, pp. 707–716, 2000.

R. AVILA, L. SOBIERAJSKI, and A. KAUFMAN. Towards a comprehensive volume visualization system. In Proc. of IEEE Visualization, pp. 13–20, 1992.

R. AVILA and L. M. SOBIERAJSKI. A haptic interaction method for volume visualization. In Proc. of IEEE Visualization, pp. 197–204, 1996.

L. AXEL. Cerebral blood flow determination by rapid-sequence computed tomography: theoretical analysis. Radiology, 137:679–686, 1980.

S. R. AYLWARD and E. BULLITT. Initialization, noise, singularities, and scale in height-ridge traversal for tubular object centerline extraction. IEEE Transactions on Medical Imaging, pp. 61–75, 2002.

S. R. AYLWARD, J. JOMIER, S. WEEKS, and E. BULLITT. Registration of vascular images. International Journal of Computer Vision, 55(2/3):128–138, 2003.

F. S. AZAR, D. N. METAXAS, and M. D. SCHNALL. Methods for modeling and predicting mechanical deformations of the breast under external perturbations. Medical Image Analysis, 6:1–27, 2002.

R. AZUMA. A survey of augmented reality. Presence: Teleoperators and Virtual Environments, 6(4):355–385, 1997.

R. BADE, J. HAASE, and B. PREIM. Comparison of fundamental mesh smoothing algorithms for medical surface models. In Proc. of Simulation and Visualization, pp. 289–304, 2006a.

R. BADE, I. RIEDEL, L. SCHMIDT, K. J. OLDHAFER, and B. PREIM. Combining training and computerized planning of oncologic liver surgery. In Proc. of Workshop Bildverarbeitung für die Medizin, Informatik Aktuell, 2006b.

J. BAERENTZEN. Robust generation of signed distance fields from triangle meshes. In Proc. of Volume Graphics, pp. 167–175, 2005.

C. L. BAJAJ, V. PACUCCI, and D. R. SCHIKORE. The contour spectrum. In Proc. of IEEE Visualization, pp. 167–173, 1997.

M. BAJURA, H. FUCHS, and R. OHBUCHI. Merging virtual objects with the real world: seeing ultrasound imaginary within the patient. In Proc. of ACM SIGGRAPH, pp. 203–210, 1992.

D. BANKS and S. LINTON. Counting cases in Marching Cubes: toward a generic algorithm for producing substitopes. In Proc. of IEEE Visualization, pp. 51–58, 2003.

J. F. BARBARA ZITOVÁ. Image registration methods: a survey. Image and Vision Computing, 21:977–1000, 2003.

E. L. BARBIER, L. LAMALLE, and M. DECORPS. Methodology of brain perfusion imaging. Journal of Magnetic Resonance Imaging, 13:496–520, 2001.

C. BARILLOT, B. GIBAUD, L. M. LUO, and J. M. SCARABIN. 3D representation of anatomic structures from CT examinations. In Proc. of Biostereometrics, volume 302, pp. 307–314, 1985.

A. BARR. Superquadrics and angle-preserving transformations. IEEE Computer Graphics and Applications, 1:11–23, 1981.

W. A. BARRETT and E. N. MORTENSEN. Interactive live-wire boundary extraction. Medical Image Analysis, 1(4):331–341, 1997.

D. BARTZ. Large Model Visualization: Techniques and Applications. Ph.D. thesis, Dept. of Computer Science (WSI), University of Tübingen, 2001.

D. BARTZ. Virtual endoscopy in research and clinical practice. Computer Graphics Forum, 24(1):111–126, 2005.

D. BARTZ, J. FISCHER, A. DEL RÍO, J. HOFFMANN, and D. FREUDENSTEIN. VIRTUE: A navigated virtual endoscopy system for maxillo-facial and neurosurgery. In 3D Modelling, 2003a.

D. BARTZ, R. GROSSO, T. ERTL, and W. STRAßER. Parallel construction and isosurface extraction of recursive tree structures. In Proc. of WSCG, volume III, pp. 479–486, 1998.

D. BARTZ, Ö. GÜRVIT, D. FREUDENSTEIN, H. SCHIFFBAUER, and J. HOFFMANN. Integration von navigation, optischer und virtueller endoskopie in der neurosowie mund-, kiefer- und gesichtschirurgie. In *Jahrestagung der Deutschen Gesellschaft für Computer-und Roboterassistierte Chirurgie e. V. (CURAC)*, 2002.

D. BARTZ, Ö. GÜRVIT, M. LANZENDÖRFER, A. KOPP, A. KÜTTNER, and W. STRAßER. Virtual endoscopy for cardio vascular exploration. In *Proc. of Computer Assisted Radiology and Surgery*, pp. 960–964, 2001a.

D. BARTZ, G. KINDLMANN, K. MUELLER, B. PREIM, and M. WACKER. Visual medicine: advanced applications of medical imaging. In *IEEE Visualization Tutorial T3*, 2005a.

D. BARTZ, J. KLOSOWSKI, and D. STANEKER. Tighter bounding volumes for better occlusion performance. In *Visual Proc. of ACM SIGGRAPH*, p. 213, 2001b.

D. BARTZ and S. LAKARE. Scaffolding-based segmentation of coronary vascular structures. In *Proc. of Volume Graphics*, pp. 47–54, 2005.

D. BARTZ, D. MAYER, J. FISCHER, S. LEY, A. DEL RÍO, S. THUST, C. HEUSSEL, H. KAUCZOR, and W. STRAßER. Hybrid segmentation and exploration of the human Lungs. In *Proc. of IEEE Visualization*, pp. 177–184, 2003b.

D. BARTZ and M. MEIßNER. Voxels versus polygons: a comparative approach for volume graphics. In *Proc. of Volume Graphics*, pp. 33–48, 1999.

D. BARTZ, M. MEIßNER, and T. HÜTTNER. OpenGL-assisted occlusion culling of large polygonal models. *Computers & Graphics*, 23(5):667–679, 1999a.

D. BARTZ, J. ORMAN, and Ö. GÜRVIT. Accurate volumetric measurements of anatomical cavities. *Methods of Information in Medicine*, 43(4):331–335, 2004.

D. BARTZ and M. SKALEJ. VIVENDI — a virtual ventricle endoscopy system for virtual medicine. In *Data Visualization (Proc. of Eurographics/IEEE Symposium on Visualization)*, pp. 155–166, 324, 1999.

D. BARTZ, M. SKALEJ, D. WELTE, W. STRAßER, and F. DUFFNER. A virtual endoscopy system for the planning of endoscopic interventions in the ventricle system of the human brain. In *Proc. of BiOS'99: Biomedical Diagnostics, Guidance and Surgical Assist Systems*, volume 3514, pp. 91–100, 1999b.

D. BARTZ, D. STANEKER, and J. KLOSOWSKI. *Tighter Bounding Volumes for Better Occlusion Culling Performance*. Technical Report WSI-2005-13, Dept. of Computer Science (WSI), University of Tübingen, 2005b.

D. BARTZ, W. STRAßER, Ö. GÜRVIT, D. FREUDENSTEIN, and M. SKALEJ. Interactive and multi-modal visualization for neuroendoscopic interventions. In *Data Visualization (Proc. of Eurographics/IEEE Symposium on Visualization)*, pp. 157–164, 2001c.

D. BARTZ, Ö. GÜRVIT, M. LANZENDÖRFER, A. KOPP, A. KÜTTNER, and W. STRAßER. Virtual endoscopy for cardio vascular exploration. In *Proc. of Computer Assisted Radiology and Surgery*, pp. 1005–1009, 2001d.

D. BARTZ, D. MAYER, J. FISCHER, S. LEY, A. DEL RIO, S. THUST, C. P. HEUSSEL, H. U. KAUCZOR, and W. STRAßER. Hybrid segmentation and exploration of the human lungs. In *Proc. of IEEE Visualization*, pp. 177–184, 2003c.

D. BARTZ, M. SKALEJ, D. WELTE, and W. STRAßER. 3D-virtual angiography. In *Proc. of Computer Assisted Radiology and Surgery*, pp. 44–48, 1999c.

P. J. BASSER and D. K. JONES. Diffusion-tensor MRI: theory, experimental design and data analysis. *NMR in Biomedicine*, 15:456–467, 2002.

P. J. BASSER, J. MATTIELLO, and D. LE BIHAN. Estimation of the effective selfdiffusion tensor from NMR spin echo. *Journal of Magentic Resonance*, 103(3):247–254, 1994.

B. G. BAUMGART. A polyhedral representation for computer vision. In *Proc. of AFIPS National Computer Conference*, volume 44, pp. 589–596, 1975.

U. Behrens, J. Teubner, C. J. G. Evertsz, M. Walz, H. Jürgens, and H.-O. Peitgen. Computer-assisted dynamic evaluation of contrast-enhanced MRI. In *Proc. of Computer Assisted Radiology*, pp. 362–367, 1996.

B. Bell, S. Feiner, and T. Höllerer. View management for virtual and augmented reality. In *Proc. of ACM Conference on User Interface Software and Technlogy (UIST)*, pp. 101–110, 2001.

B. Bell, S. Feiner, and T. Höllerer. Information at a glance. *Computer Graphics and Applications*, 22(4):6–9, 2002.

W. Benger, H. Bartsch, H.-C. Hege, H. Kitzler, A. Shumilina, and A. Werner. Visualizing neuronal structures in the human brain via diffusion tensor MRI. *International Journal of Neuroscience*, pp. 461–514, 2006.

M. Bentum, B. Lichtenbelt, and T. Malzbender. Frequency analysis of gradient estimators in volume rendering. *IEEE Transactions on Visualization and Computer Graphics*, 3(2):242–254, 1996.

G. Berenschot. *Visualization of diffusion tensor imaging*. Master's thesis, Dept. of Mathematics and Computer Science, Technische Universiteit Eindhoven, 2003.

M. Berger. Resolving occlusion in augmented reality: a contour-based approach without 3D reconstruction. In *Proc. of the IEEE Conference on Computer Vision and Pattern Recognition*, pp. 91–96, 1997.

L. D. Bergmann, B. E. Rogowitz, and L. A. Treinish. A rule-based tool for assisting colormap selection. In *Proc. of IEEE Visualization*, pp. 118–125, 1995.

M. Bern and P. Plassmann. "Mesh Generation," chapter in *Handbook of Computational Geometry*. Elsevier Science, 1999.

P. Besl and N. McKay. A method for registration of 3D shapes. *IEEE Transactions on Pattern Analysis and Machine Intelligence*, 14(2):239–256, 1992.

G. Bianchi, B. Solenthaler, G. Székely, and M. Harders. Simultaneous topology and stiffness identification for mass-spring models based on FEM reference. In Christian Barillot, editor, *Proc. of Medical Image Computing and Computer-Assisted Intervention (MICCAI)*, volume 3216 of *Lecture Notes in Computer Science*, pp. 293–301, 2004.

D. Bielsen, V. A. Maiwald, and M. H. Gross. Interactive cuts through 3-dimensional soft tissue. *Computer Graphics Forum*, 18(3):31–38, 1999. Proc. of Eurographics.

E. A. Bier, M. Stone, K. Pier, W. Buxton, and T. DeRose. Toolglass and magic lenses: the see-through interface. In *Proc. of ACM SIGGRAPH*, pp. 73–80, 1993.

W. Birkfellner, M. Figl, K. Huber, F. Watzinger, F. Wanschitz, R. Hanel, A. Wagner, D. Rafolt, R. Ewers, and H. Bergmann. The varioscope AR—a head-mounted operating microscope for augmented reality. In *Proc. of Medical Image Computing and Computer-Assisted Intervention (MICCAI)*, in volume 1935, *Lecture Notes in Computer Science* pp. 869–877, 2000.

I. Bitter, R. van Uitert, I. Wolf, L. Ibanez, J. Kuhnigk. Comparison of four freely available frameworks for image processing and visualization that use ITK. *IEEE Transactions on Visualization and Computer Graphics*, 13(3): 483–493, 2007.

J. Bittner, M. Wimmer, H. Piringer, and W. Purgathofer. Coherent hierarchical culling: hardware occlusion queries made useful. In *Proc. of Eurographics*, pp. 615–624, 2004.

J. M. Blackall. *Respiratory Motion in Image-Guided Intervention of the Liver*. Ph.D. thesis, Department of Imaging Sciences, Guy's, King's, and St. Thomas' School of Medicine, 2003.

J. M. Blackall, A. P. King, G. P. Penney, A. Adam, and D. J. Hawkes. A statistical model of respiratory motion and deformation of the liver. In *Proc. of Medical Image Computing and Computer-Assisted Intervention (MICCAI)*, volume 2208 of *Lecture Notes in Computer Science*, pp. 1338–1340, 2001.

A. Blake and M. Isard. *Active Contours*. Springer, 1998.

J. BLANCHETTE. C++ GUI Programming with Qt 4. Prentice Hall, 2006.

J. BLINN. Light reflection functions for simulation of clouds and dusty surfaces. In Proc. of ACM SIGGRAPH, pp. 21–29, 1982a.

J. BLINN. Return of the jaggy. Computer Graphics and Applications, 9(2):82–89, 1989.

J. F. BLINN. A generalization of algebraic surface drawing. ACM Transactions on Graphics, 1(3):235–256, 1982b.

J. BLOOMENTHAL and K. FERGUSON. Polygonization of non-manifold implicit surfaces. In Proc. of ACM SIGGRAPH, pp. 309–316, 1995.

J. BLOOMENTHAL. An implicit surface polygonizer. In Graphics Gems IV, pp. 324–349. Academic Press, Boston, 1994. URL: www.unchainedgeometry.com/jbloom/misc/polygonizer.c.

J. BLOOMENTHAL. Skeletal Design of Natural Forms. Ph.D. thesis, Univerity of Calgary, Calgary, Alberta, Canada, 1995.

J. BLOOMENTHAL, C. BAJAJ, J. BLINN, M.-P. CANI, A. A. ROCKWOOD, B. WYVILL, and G. WYVILL, editors. Introduction to Implicit Surfaces. Morgan Kaufmann, 1997.

J. BLOOMENTHAL and K. SHOEMAKE. Convolution surfaces. Proc. of ACM SIGGRAPH, 25(4):251–256, 1991.

J. BOGAERT, S. DYMARKOWSKI, and A. M. TAYLOR, editors. Clinical Cardiac MRI: with Interactive CD-ROM. Springer, 2005.

J.-D. BOISSONNAT, M. YVINEC, and H. BRONNIMA. Algorithmic Geometry. Cambridge University Press, New York, 1998.

A. BORNIK, R. BEICHEL, B. REITINGER, G. GOTSCHULI, E. SORANTIN, F. LEBERL, and M. SONKA. Computer-aided liver surgery planning: an augmented reality approach. In Proc. of SPIE Medical Imaging, pp. 395–405, 2003a.

A. BORNIK, R. BEICHEL, B. REITINGER, G. GOTSCHULI, E. SORANTIN, F. LEBERL, and M. SONKA. Computer-aided liver surgery planning based on augmented reality techniques. In Proc. of Workshop Bildverarbeitung für die Medizin, Informatik Aktuell, 2003b.

A. BORNIK, B. REITINGER, and R. BEICHEL. Reconstruction and representation of tubular structures using simplex meshes. In Proc. of WSCG 2005—Short Papers, pp. 61–65, 2005.

T. BOSKAMP, H. K. HAHN, M. HINDENNACH, S. ZIDOWITZ, H.-O. PEITGEN, S. OELTZE, and B. PREIM. "Geometrical and Structural Analysis of Vessel Systems in 3D Medical Datasets," chapter in Medical Imaging Systems: Technology and Applications, volume 5. World Scientific Press, pp. 1–60, 2006.

T. BOSKAMP, D. RINCK, F. LINK, B. KUEMMERLEN, G. STAMM, and P. MILDENBERGER. A new vessel analysis tool for morphometric quantification and visualization of vessels in CT and MRI datasets. Radiographics, 24:284–297, 2004.

C. P. BOTHA. Techniques and Software Architectures for Medical Visualization and Image Processing. Ph.D. thesis, Technical University Delft, 2005.

C. P. BOTHA and F. H. POST. New technique for transfer function specification in direct volume rendering using real time visual feedback. In Proc. of SPIE Medical Imaging, volume 4681, pp. 349–356, 2002.

C. P. BOTHA and F. H. POST. ShellSplatting: interactive rendering of anisotropic volumes. In Data Visualization (Proc. of Eurographics/IEEE Symposium on Visualization), pp. 105–112, 2003.

H. BOURQUAIN, A. SCHENK, F. LINK, B. PREIM, and H.-O. PEITGEN. HepaVision 2: a software assistant for preoperative planning in LRLT and oncologic liver surgery. In Proc. of Computer Assisted Radiology and Surgery. pp. 341–346, 2002.

K. W. BOWYER. "Validation of Medical Image Analysis Techniques," Chapter 10 of Handbook of Medical Imaging, volume 2, pp. 567–607. SPIE Press, 2000.

Y. BOYKOV and M.-P. JOLLY. Interactive graph cuts for optimal boundary and region segmentation of objects in N-D images. In *International Conference on Computer Vision*, volume 1, pp. 7–14, 2001.

Y. BOYKOV and O. VEKSLER. "Graph Cuts in Vision and Graphics: Theories and Applications," chapter in *The Handbook of Mathematical Models in Computer Vision*. Springer, 2005.

S. BRABEC. *Shadow Techniques for Interactive and Real-Time Applications*. Ph.D. thesis, Department of Computer Science, University Saarbrücken, December 2003.

S. BRABEC and H.-P. SEIDEL. Shadow volumes on programmable graphics hardware. In *Proc. of Eurographics*, pp. 433–440, 2003.

C. BRECHBUEHLER, G. GERIG, and O. KÜBLER. Parameterization of closed surfaces for 3D shape. *Computer Vision and Image Understanding*, 62(2):154–170, 1995.

D. BREEN, R. WHITAKER, E. ROSE, and M. TUCERYAN. Interactive occlusion and automatic object placement for augmented reality. *Computer Graphics Forum*, 15(3):11–22, 1996

J. BREITENBORN. *Ein System zur automatischen Erzeugung untersuchungsspezifischer Hängungen und zur Unterstützung verteilten kooperativen Arbeitens in der klinischen Radiologie*. Ph.D. thesis, Department Mathematics and Computer Science, University Bremen, Germany, June 2004.

J. BRESENHAM. Algorithm for computer control of a digital plotter. *IBM Systems Journal*, 4(1):25–30, 1965.

J. BRESENHAM. A linear algorithm for incremental digital display of circular arcs. *Communications of the ACM*, 20(2):116–120, 1977.

A. D. BRETT, M. F. WILKINS, and C. J. TAYLOR. A user interface for 3D statistical model building of anatomical structures. In *Proc. of Computer Assisted Radiology and Surgery*, pp. 246–251, 1997.

I. BRICAULT, R. KIKINIS, E. VAN SONNENBERG, K. TUNCALI, and S. G. SILVERMAN. 3D analysis of radiofrequency-ablated tumors in liver: a computer-aided diagnosis tool for early detection of local recurrences. In *Proc. of Medical Image Computing and Computer-Assisted Intervention (MICCAI)*, volume 3216 of *Lecture Notes in Computer Science*, pp. 1042–1043, 2004.

J. F. BRINKLEY, L. M. MYERS, J. S. PROTHERO, G. H. HEIL, J. S. TSURUDA, K. R. MARAVILLA, G. A. OJEMANN, and C. ROSSE. A structural information framework for brain mapping. In S. H. KOSLOW and M. F. HUERTA, editors, *Proc. Neuroinformatics: An Overview of the Human Brain Project*, pp. 309–334, 1997.

J. F. BRINKLEY and C. ROSSE. The Digital Anatomist distributed framework and its applications to knowledge based medical imaging. *Journal of the American Medical Informatics Association*, 4(3):165–183, 1997.

J. F. BRINKLEY, B. WONG, K. P. HINSHAW, and C. ROSSE. Design of an anatomy information system. *Computer Graphics and Applications*, 19(3):38–48, 1999.

M. H. BRISCOE. *Preparing Scientific Illustrations: A Guide to Better Posters, Presentations, and Publications*. Springer, 1996.

M. BRO-NIELSEN, D. HELFRICK, B. GLASS, X. ZENG, and H. CONNACHER. VR simulation of abdominal trauma surgery. In *Proc. of Medicine Meets Virtual Reality*, pp. 117–123. IOS Press, 1998.

M. BRO-NIELSEN. *Medical Image Registration and Surgery Simulation*. Ph.D. thesis, Department of Mathematical Modeling, Technical University of Denmark, 1996.

M. BRO-NIELSEN and C. GRAMKOW. Fast fluid registration of medial images. In *Proc. of Visualization in Biomedical Computing*, volume 1131 of *Lecture Notes in Computer Science*, pp. 267–276, 1996.

K. BRODLIE, N. EL-KHALILI, and Y. LI. Using web-based computer graphics to teach surgery. *Computers & Graphics*, 24:157–161, 2000.

C. E. BROELSCH, J. C. EMOND, P. F. WHITINGTON, J. R. THISTLETHWAITE, A. L. BAKER, and J. L. LICHTOR. Application of reduced-size liver transplants as split grafts, auxiliary grafts, and living related segmental transplants. *Annals of Surgery*, 212:368–377, 1990.

S. BRUCKNER. *Efficient Volume Visualization of Large Medical Datasets*. Master's thesis, Institut für Computergraphik und Algorithmen, Technische Universität Wien, 2004.

S. BRUCKNER, S. GRIMM, A. KANITSAR, and M. E. GRÖLLER. Illustrative context preserving volume rendering. In *Data Visualization (Proc. of Eurographics/IEEE Symposium on Visualization)*, pp. 69–76, 2005.

S. BRUCKNER and M. E. GRÖLLER. Illustrative context preserving volume rendering. In *Proc. of IEEE Visualization*, pp. 85–92, 2005.

A. BRUN, H. KNUTSSON, H.-J. PARK, M. E. SHENTON, and C. F. WESTIN. Clustering fiber traces using normalized cuts. In *Proc. of Medical Image Computing and Computer-Assisted Intervention (MICCAI)*, volume 3216 of *Lecture Notes in Computer Science*, pp. 368–375, 2004.

A. BRUN, H.-J. PARK, H. KNUTSSON, and C.-F. WESTIN. Coloring of DTI MRI fibertraces using Laplacian eigenmaps. In *EUROCAST*, volume 2809 of *Lecture Notes in Computer Science*, pp. 518–529, 2003.

C. BRUYNS, S. SENGER, A. MENON, K. MONTGOMERY, S. WILDERMUTH, and R. BOYLE. A survey of interactive mesh-cutting techniques and a new method for implementing generalized interactive mesh cutting using virtual tools. *The Journal of Visualization and Computer Animation*, 13:21–42, 2002.

J. BRYAN, D. STREDNEY, G. J. WIET, and D. SESSANNA. Virtual temporal bone dissection: a case study. In *Proc. of IEEE Visualization*, 2001.

J. BUCHANAN and M. SOUSA. The edge buffer: a data structure for easy silhouette rendering. In *Proc. of Symposium on Non-Photorealistic Animation and Rendering*, pp. 39–42, 2000.

M. M. J. BUDOFF and J. S. SHINBANE, editors. *Cardiac CT Imaging: Diagnosis of Cardiovascular Disease*. Springer, 2006.

K. BÜHLER, P. FELKL, and A. LA CRUZ. "Geometric Methods for Vessel Visualization—a Survey," chapter in *Geometric Modeling for Scientific Visualization*, pp. 399–420. Springer, 2004.

E. BULLITT and S. R. AYLWARD. Volume rendering of segmented image objects. *IEEE Transactions on Medical Imaging*, 22(8):540–549, 2002.

A. BUTZ. Anymation with CATHI. In *Proc. of AAAI/IAAI*, pp. 957–962. AAAI Press, 1997.

T. BUTZ, S. K. WARFIELD, K. TUNCALI, S. G. SILVERMAN, E. VAN SONNENBERG, F. A. JOLESZ, and R. KIKINIS. Pre- and intraoperative planning and simulation of percutaneous tumor ablation. In *Proc. of Medical Image Computing and Computer-Assisted Intervention (MICCAI)*, volume 2208 of *Lecture Notes in Computer Science*, pp. 317–326, 2001.

B. CABRAL, N. CAM, and J. FORAN. Accelerated volume rendering and tomographic reconstruction using texture mapping hardware. In *Proc. of IEEE/ACM Symposium on Volume Visualization*, pp. 91–98, 1994.

H. ÇAKMAK and U. KÜHNAPFEL. Animation and simulation techniques for VR-training systems in endoscopic surgery. In *Proc. of European Workshop on Computer Animation*, pp. 173–185, 2000.

H. ÇAKMAK, H. MAASS, and U. KÜHNAPFEL. VSone; a virtual reality simulator for laparoscopic surgery. *Minimally Invasive Therapy and Allied Technologies (MITAT)*, 14(3):134–144, 2005.

G. CAMERON and P. UNDRILL. Rendering volumetric medical image data on a SIMD architecture computer. In *Proc. of Eurographics Workshop on Rendering*, pp. 135–145, 1992.

M. B. CARPENTER. *Core Text of Neuroanatomy*, 4th ed. WILLIAM and WILKINS, Baltimore, 1996.

C. A. CASTANO-MORAGA, M. A. RODRIGUEZ-FLORIDO, L. ALVAREZ, C.-F. WESTIN, and J. RUIZ-ALZOLA. Anisotropic interpolation of DT-MRI. In *Proc. of Medical Image Computing and Computer-Assisted Intervention (MICCAI)*, volume 3216 of *Lecture Notes in Computer Science*, pp. 343–350, 2004.

S. CASTRO, A. KÖNIG, H. LÖFFELMANN, and E. GRÖLLER. *Transfer Function Specification for the Visualization of Medical Data*. Technical report, Institute of Computer Graphics, Vienna University of Technology, 1998.

E. CATMULL and A. SMITH. 3D transformations of images in scanline order. In *Proc. of ACM SIGGRAPH*, pp. 279–285, 1980.

A. CELLER, T. FARNCOMBE, C. BEVER, D. NOLL, J. MAEGHT, R. HARROP, and D. LYSTER. Performance of the dynamic single photon computed tomography (dSPECT) method for decreasing or increasing activity changes. *Physics in Medicine and Biology*, 45:3525–3543, 2000.

D. CHEN, Z. LIANG, M. WAX, L. LI, B. LI, and A. KAUFMAN. A novel approach to extract colon lumen from CT images for virtual colonoscopy. *IEEE Transactions on Medical Imaging*, 19(12):1220–1226, 2000.

L. S. CHEN, G. T. HERMAN, R. A. REYNOLDS, and J. K. UDUPA. Surface shading in the cuberille environment. *Computer Graphics and Applications*, 5(12):33–43, 1985.

M. CHEN and J. V. TUCKER. Constructive volume geometry. *Computer Graphics Forum*, 19(4):281–293, December 2000.

W. CHEN, L. REN, M. ZWICKER, and H. PFISTER. Hardware-accelerated adaptive EWA volume splatting. In *Proc. of IEEE Visualization*, pp. 67–74, 2004.

E. CHERNYAEV. *Marching Cubes 33: Construction of Topologically Correct Isosurfaces*. Technical Report CN 95–17, CERN, 1995.

Z. CHO, J. JONES, and M. SINGH. *Foundations of Medical Imaging*. Wiley, New York, NY, 1993.

P. L. CHOYKE, A. J. DWYER, and M. V. KNOPP. Functional tumor imaging with dynamic contrast-enhanced magnetic resonance imaging. *Journal of Magnetic Resonance Imaging*, 17:509–520, 2003.

G. E. CHRISTENSEN. *Deformable Shape Models for Anatomy*. Ph.D. thesis, Washington University, August 1994.

G. E. CHRISTENSEN. Consistent linear-elastic transformations for image matching. In *Information Processing in Medical Imaging*, volume 1613 of *Lecture Notes in Computer Science*, pp. 224–237, 1999.

G. E. CHRISTENSEN. Consistent nonlinear elastic image registration. In *IEEE Proceedings of Mathematical Methods in Biomedical Image Analysis*, pp. 37–43. Kauai, Hawaii, 2001.

J. CHRISTENSEN, J. MARKS, and S. SHIEBER. An empirical study of algorithms for point-feature label placement. *ACM Transactions on Graphics*, 14(3):203–232, 1995.

P. G. CIARLET. *Mathematical Elasticity: Threedimensional Elasticity*, volume 20 of *Studies in Mathematics and Its Applications*. North Holland, 1988.

P. CIGNONI, F. GANOVELLI, C. MONTANI, and R. SCOPIGNO. Reconstruction of topologically correct and adaptive trilinear surfaces. *Computers & Graphics*, 24(3):399–418, 2000.

P. CIGNONI, P. MARINO, C. MONTANI, E. PUPPO, and R. SCOPIGNO. Speeding up isosurface extraction algorithm performance. *IEEE Transactions on Visualization and Computer Graphics*, 3(2):158–170, 1997.

H. CLINE, W. LORENSEN, S. LUDKE, C. CRAWFORD, and B. TEETER. Two algorithms for the three-dimensional construction of tomograms. *Medical Physics*, 15(3):320–327, 1988.

D. A. CLUNIE. *DICOM Structured Reporting*. PixelMed Publishing, Bangor, PA, 2001.

L. COHEN, P. BASUK, and J. WAYE. *Practical Flexible Sigmoidoscopy*. Igaku-Shoin, New York, NY, 1995.

D. COHEN-OR, Y. CHRYSANTHOU, C. T. SILVA, and F. DURAND. A survey of visibility for walkthrough applications. *IEEE Transactions on Visualization and Computer Graphics*, 9(3):412–431, 2003.

D. COHEN-OR and Z. SHEFFER. Proximity clouds, an acceleration technique for 3D grid traversal. *The Visual Computer*, 11(1):27–38, 1994.

D. COHEN-OR, Y. CHRYSANTHOU, C. T. SILVA, and G. DRETTAKIS. Visibility problems, techniques and applications. In *SIGGRAPH Course Notes*. ACM, 2000.

D. COLLINS, A. ZIJDENBOS, V. KOLLOKIAN, J. SLED, N. KABANI, C. HOLMES, and A. EVANS. Design and construction of a realistic digital brain phantom. *IEEE Transactions on Medical Imaging*, 17(3):463–468, 1998.

Commission Internationale de l'Eclairage (CIE). CIE recommendations on uniform color spaces–color difference equations psychometric color terms. *CIE Publication*, 15(E-1.3.1), 1978.

D. B. CONNOR, S. C. SNIBBE, K. P. HERNDON, D. C. ROBBINS, R. C. ZELEZNIK, and A. VAN DAM. Three-dimensional widgets. In *Proc. of ACM Symposium on Interactive 3D Graphics*, pp. 183–188, 1992.

T. F. COOTES, G. J. EDWARDS, and C. J. TAYLOR. Active appearance models. In *Proc. of European Conference on Computer Vision*, volume 2, pp. 484–498, 1998a.

T. F. COOTES, G. J. EDWARDS, and C. J. TAYLOR. A comparative evaluation of active appearance model algorithms. In *British Machine Vision Conference*, volume 2, pp. 680–689, 1998b.

T. F. COOTES, G. J. EDWARDS, and C. J. TAYLOR. Active appearance models. *IEEE Transactions on Pattern Analysis and Machine Intelligence*, 23(6):681– 685, 2001.

T. F. COOTES, A. HILL, C. J. TAYLOR, and J. HASLAM. The use of active shape models for locating structures in medical images. *Image and Vision Computing*, 12(6):355–366, 1994.

J. CORDES, J. DORNHEIM, B. PREIM, I. HERTEL, and G. STRAUß. Preoperative segmentation of neck CT datasets for the planning of neck dissections. In *Proc. of SPIE Medical Imaging*, 2006.

I. COROUGE and S. GOUTTARD. A statistical shape model of individual fiber tracts extracted from diffusion tensor MRI. In *Proc. of Medical Image Computing and Computer-Assisted Intervention (MICCAI)*, volume 3217 of *Lecture Notes in Computer Science*, pp. 671–679, 2004.

C. D. CORREA and D. SILVER. Dataset traversal with motion-controlled transfer functions. In *Proc. of IEEE Visualization*, pp. 359–366, 2005.

S. COTIN, H. DELINGETTE, and N. AYACHE. A hybrid elastic model allowing real-time cutting, deformations and force-feedback for surgery training and simulation. *The Visual Computer*, 16(8):437–452, 2000.

S. COTIN, H. DELINGETTE, and N. AYACHE. Real-time elastic deformations of soft tissues for surgery simulation. *IEEE Transactions on Visualization and Computer Graphics*, 5(1):62–73, 1999.

C. COUINAUD. *Le foie—eudes anatomiques et churgicales*. Masson, Paris, 1957.

M. COX and D. ELLSWORTH. Application-controlled demand paging for out-of-core visualization. In *Proc. of IEEE Visualization*, pp. 235–244, 1997.

R. CRAWFIS and N. MAX. Texture splats for 3D scalar and vector field visualization. In *Proc. of IEEE Visualization*, pp. 261–266, 1993.

F. CROW. Summed-area tables for texture mapping. In *Proc. of ACM SIGGRAPH*, pp. 207–212, 1984.

F. CROW. Shadow algorithms for computer graphics. In *Proc. of ACM SIGGRAPH*, pp. 242–248, 1977.

B. CSÉBFALVI, L. MROZ, H. HAUSER, A. KÖNIG, and E. GRÖLLER. Fast visualization of object contours by non-photorealistic volume rendering. In *Proc. of Eurographics*, pp. 452–460, 2001.

Multislice CT. Multislice-CT—From Seeing to Understanding. www.multislice − ct.com, accessed 2005.

T. CULLIP and U. NEUMANN. *Accelerating Volume Reconstruction with 3D Texture Hardware*. Technical Report TR93-027, Dept. of Computer Science, University of North Carolina at Chapel Hill, 1993.

R. ARNEZ CURRY and B. BATES TEMPKIN. *Sonography: Introduction to Normal Structure and Function*. W. B. Saunders, 2004.

F. DACHILLE, K. KREEGER, M. WAX, A. KAUFMAN, and Z. LIANG. Interactive navigation for PC-based virtual colonoscopy. In *Proc. of SPIE Medical Imaging*, 2001.

J. DANSKIN and P. HANRAHAN. Fast algorithms for volume ray tracing. In *Proc. of IEEE/ACM Symposium on Volume Visualization*, pp. 91–98, 1992.

B. DAUSTER, A. P. STEINBERG, M. C. VASSILIOU, et al. Validity of the MISTELS simulator for laparoscopy training in urology. *Journal of Endourology*, 19:541–545, 2005.

M. DE BRUIJNE, B. GINNEKEN, J. B. A. MAINTZ, W. J. NIESSEN, and M. A. VIERGEVER. Active shape model based segmentation of abdominal aortic aneurysms in CTA images. In *Proc. of SPIE Medical Imaging*, volume 4684, pp. 463–474, 2002.

F. BOUX DE CASSON and C. LAUGIER. Modelling the dynamics of a human liver for a minimally invasive surgery simulator. In *Proc. of Medical Image Computing and Computer-Assisted Intervention (MICCAI)*, volume 1679 of *Lecture Notes on Computer Science*, pp. 1156–1165, 1999.

P. DE FEYTER, editor. *Computed Tomography of the Coronary Arteries*. Taylor & Francis, 2004.

S. DE PUTTER, F. N. VAN DE VOSSE, F. A. GERRITSEN, F. LAFFARGUE, and M. BREEUWER. Computational mesh generation for vascular structures with deformable surfaces. *International Journal of Computer Assisted Radiology and Surgery*, 1(1):39–49, 2006.

S. J. DEARMOND, M. M. FUSCO, and M. M. DEWEY. *Structure of the Human Brain: A Photographic Atlas*. Oxford University Press, New York, 1989.

M. DE BERG, M. VAN KREVELD, M. OVERMARS, and O. SCHWARZKOPF. *Computational Geometry*. Springer, 2nd ed., 2000.

D. DECARLO, A. FINKELSTEIN, and S. RUSINKIEWICZ. Interactive rendering of suggestive contours with temporal coherence. In *Proc. of Symposium on Non-Photorealistic Animation and Rendering*, pp. 15–24, 2004.

D. DECARLO, A. FINKELSTEIN, S. RUSINKIEWICZ, and A. SANTELLA. Suggestive contours for conveying shape. In *Proc. of ACM SIGGRAPH*, pp. 848–855, 2003.

H. DEGANI, V. GUSIS, D. WEINSTEIN, S. FIELDS, and S. STRANO. Mapping pathophysiological features of breast tumors by MRI at high spatial resolution. *Nature in Medicine*, 2:780–782, 1997.

A. DEL RÍO, J. FISCHER, M. KÖBELE, D. BARTZ, and W. STRAßER. Augmented reality interaction for semi-automatic volume classification. In *Proc. of Eurographics Symposium on Virtual Environments*, pp. 113–120, 2005.

A. DEL RÍO, J. FISCHER, M. KÖBELE, J. HOFFMANN, F. DUFFNER, M. TATAGIBA, W. STRAßER, and D. BARTZ. Intuitive volume classification in medical AR. *GMS Journal on Current Topics in Computer and Robot Assisted Surgery*, 1(1), 2006.

H. DELINGETTE, and N. AYACHE. Hepatic surgery simulation. *Communications of the ACM*, 48(2):31–36, 2005.

H. DELINGETTE, G. SUBSOL, S. COTIN, and J. PIGNON. A craniofacial surgery simulation testbed. In *Proc. of Visualization in Biomedical Computing*, volume 2359, pp. 607–618, 1994.

T. DELMARCELLE and L. HESSELINK. Visualization of second-order tensor fields and matrix data. In *IEEE Visualization*, pp. 316–323, 1992.

J. A. DEN BOER and P. J. M. FOLKERS. MR perfusion and diffusion imaging in ischaemic brain disease. *Medica Mundi*, 41(2):20–35, 1997.

J. E. DENNIS and R. B. SCHNABEL. *Numerical Methods for Unconstrained Optimization and Nonlinear Equations*. Prentice Hall, 1983.

T. DEROSE, M. KASS, and T. TRUONG. Subdivision surfaces in character animation. In *Proc. of ACM SIGGRAPH*, pp. 85–94, 1998.

A. M. DEROSSIS, G. M. FRIED, M. ABRAHAMOWICZ, *et al.* Development of a model for training and evaluation of laparoscopic skills. *American Journal of Surgery*, 175:482–487, 1998.

J. T. DESANCTIS, S. N. GOLDBERG, and P. R. MUELLER. Percutaneous treatment of hepatic neoplasms: a review of current techniques. *Cardiovascular Interventional Radiology*, 21:273–296, 1998.

M. DESBRUN, M. MEYER, P. SCHRÖDER, and A. BARR. Implicit fairing of irregular meshes using diffusion and curvature flow. In *Proc. of ACM SIGGRAPH*, pp. 317–324, 1999.

T. DESCHAMPS. *Paths and Shapes Extraction in 3D Medical Images, Application to Tubular Shape Segmentation*. Ph.D. thesis, University Paris-9 Dauphine, 2001.

M. DESCOTEAUX, M. AUDETTE, K. CHINZEI, and K. SIDDIQ. Bone enhancement filtering: application to sinus bone segmentation and simulation of pituitary surgery. In *Proc. of Medical Image Computing and Computer-Assisted Intervention (MICCAI)*, volume 3749 of *Lecture Notes in Computer Science*, pp. 9–16, 2005.

P. DESGRANGES, K. ENGEL, and G. PALADINI. Gradient-free shading: a new method for realistic interactive volume rendering. In *Proc. of Vision, Modeling, and Visualization*, pp. 209–216, 2005.

K. Desinger, T. Stein, A. Roggan, G. Mueller, M. G. Mack, and T. J. Vogl. Interstitial bipolar rf-thermotherapy (RFITT): therapy planning by computer simulation and MRI monitoring—a new concept for minimally invasive procedures. In Thomas P. Ryan, editor, *Surgical Applications of Energy, Proc. of SPIE*, volume 3249, pp. 147–159, 1998.

O. Deussen, S. Hiller, C. Van Overfeld, and T. Strothotte. Floating points: a method for computing stipple drawings. In *Proc. of Eurographics*, pp. 40–51, 2000.

D. Dey, P. J. Slomka, D. G. Gobbi, and T. M. Peters. Mixed reality merging of endoscopic images and 3D surfaces. In *proc. of medical Image Computing and Computer-Assisted Intervention (MICCAI)*, volume 1935 of *Lecture Notes in Computer Science*, pp. 796–803, 2000.

A. Dhawan. *Medical Image Analysis*. Wiley-IEEE Press, 2003.

V. Dicken, B. Wein, H. Schubert, J.-M. Kuhnigk, S. Kraß, and H.-O. Peitgen. Novel projection views for simplified reading of thorax CT scans with multiple pulmonary nodules. In *Proc. of Computer Assisted Radiology and Surgery*, pp. 59–64, 2003.

R. R. Dickinson. A unified approach to the design of visualization software for the analysis of field problems. In *Proc. of SPIE Three-Dimensional Visualization and Display Technologies*, volume 1083, pp. 173–180, 1989.

J. Diepstraten, D. Weiskopf, and T. Ertl. Interactive cutaway illustrations. In *Proc. of Eurographics*, pp. 523–532, 2003.

H. Digabel and C. Lantuejoul. Iterative algorithms. In *Proc. of 2nd European Symposium on Quantitative Analysis of Microstructures in Material Science*, pp. 85–99, 1978.

E. W. Dijkstra. A note on two problems in connection with graphs. *Numerische Mathe-matik*, 1:269–271, 1959.

J. Dill, L. Bartram, A. Ho, and F. Henigmann. A continuously variable zoom for navigating large hier-archical networks. In *Proc. of IEEE Conference on Systems, Man and Cybernetics*, pp. 386–390, 1994.

Z. Ding, J. C. Gore, and A. W. Anderson. Case study: classification and quantification of neuronal fiber pathways using diffusion tensor MRI. In *Proc. of IEEE Visualization*, pp. 453–456, 2001a.

Z. Ding, J. C. Gore, and A. W. Anderson. Classification and quantification of neuronal fiber pathways using diffusion tensor MRI. *Magnetic Resonance in Medicine*, 49:716–721, 2001b.

H. Doleisch, M. Meyer, M. Gasser, R. Wanker, and H. Hauser. Case study: visual analysis of complex time-dependent simulation results of a diesel exhaust system. In *Data Visualization (Proc. of Eurograph-ics/IEEE Symposium on Visualization)*, pp. 91–96, 2004.

F. Dong, G. J. Clapworthy, H. Lin, and M. A. Krokos. Volume rendering of fine details within medical data. In *Proc. of IEEE Visualization*, pp. 387–394, October 2001.

F. Dong, G. J. Clapworthy, H. Lin, and M. A. Krokos. Non-photorealistic rendering of medical volume data. *Computer Graphics and Applications*, 23(4):44–52, July–August 2003.

Y. Dor, R. Porat, and E. Keshet. Vascular endothelial growth factor and vascular adjustments to pertur-bations in oxygen homeostasis. *American Journal of Cell Physiology*, 280(6):C1367–C1374, 2001.

C. Dörge. *Techniken zur Hervorhebung von Objekten in medizinischen Visualisierungen*. Master's thesis, Department of Mathematics and Computer Science, University of Bremen, 2002.

J. Dornheim, H. Seim, B. Preim, I. Hertel, and G. Strauss. Segmentation of neck lymph nodes in CT datasets with stable 3D mass- spring models. In *Proc. of Medical Image Computing and Computer-Assisted Intervention (MICCAI)*, *Lecture Notes in Computer Science*, pp. 478–485, 2006.

L. Dornheim, K. D. Tönnies, and K. Dixon. Automatic segmentation of the left ventricle in 3D SPECT data by registration with a dynamic anatomic model. In *Proc. of Medical Image Computing and Computer-Assisted Intervention (MICCAI)*, volume 3749 of *Lecture Notes in Computer Science*, pp. 335–342, 2005a.

L. Dornheim, K. D. Tönnies, and J. Dornheim. Stable dynamic 3D shape models. In *IEEE International Conference on Image Processing ICIP2005*, volume 3, pp. 1276–1279, 2005b.

R. Drebin, L. Carpenter, and P. Hanrahan. Volume rendering. In *Proc. of ACM SIGGRAPH*, pp. 65–74, 1988.

R. O. Duda, P. E. Hart, and D. G. Stork, editors. *Pattern Classification*, 2nd ed. Wiley Interscience, 2001.

F. Duffner, W. Dauber, M. Skalej, and E. Grote. A new endoscopic tool for the CRW stereotactic system. In *Stereotactic and Functional Neurosurgery*, volume 67(3–4), pp. 213–217, 1994.

M. Dürst. Letters: additional references to Marching Cubes. *Computer Graphics*, 22(2):72–73, 1988.

D. S. Ebert, C. J. Morris, P. Rheingans, and T. S. Yoo. Designing effective transfer functions for volume rendering from photographic volumes. *IEEE Transactions on Visualization and Computer Graphics*, 8(2): 183–197, 2002.

D. Ebert and P. Rheingans. Volume illustration: non-photorealistic rendering of volume models. In *Proc. of IEEE Visualization*, pp. 195–202, 2000.

R. R. Edelman. Contrast-enhanced MR imaging of the heart: overview of the literature. *Radiology*, 232(3):653–668, Sep 2004.

H. Edelsbrunner and E. P. Mücke. Three-dimensional alpha shapes. *ACM Transactions on Graphics*, 13(1): 43–72, 1994.

S. Edmondson, J. Christensen, J. Marks, and S. Shieber. A general cartographic labeling algorithm. *Cartographica*, 33(4):13–23, 1996.

P. J. Edwards, A. P. King, C. R. Maurer Jr., D. A. De Cunha, D. J. Hawkes, D. L. G. Hill, R. P. Gaston, M. R. Fenlon, S. Chandra, A. J. Strong, C. L. Chandler, A. Richards, and M. J. Gleeson. Design and evalution of a system for microscope-assisted guided interventions (MAGI). In *Proc. of Medical Image Computing and Computer-Assisted Intervention (MICCAI)*, volume 1679 of *Lecture Notes in Computer Science*, pp. 842–851, 1999.

H. H. Ehricke, K. Donner, W. Koller, and W. Straßer. Visualization of vasculature from volume data. *Computers & Graphics*, 18(3): 395–406, 1994.

F. Enders, N. Sauber, D. Merhof, P. Hastreiter, C. Nimsky, and M. Stamminger. Visualization of white matter tracts with wrapped streamlines. In *IEEE Visualization*, pp. 51–58, 2005.

K. Engel, M. Hadwiger, J. Kniss, A. Lafohn, C. Rezk-Salama, and D. Weiskopf. Real-time volume graphics. In *ACM SIGGRAPH Course 28*, 2004.

K. Engel, M. Hadwiger, J. Kniss, C. Rezk-Salama, and D. Weiskopf. *Real-Time Volume Graphics*. A.K. Peters Ltd., 2006.

K. Engel, M. Kraus, and T. Ertl. High-quality pre-integrated volume rendering using hardware-accelerated pixel shading. In *Proc. of Symposium on Graphics Hardware*, pp. 9–16, 2001.

K. H. Englmeier, J. Griebel, R. Lucht, M. Knopp, M. Siebert, and G. Brix. Dynamische MR-Mammographie—Multidimensionale Visualisierung der Kontrastmittelanreicherung in Virtueller Realität. *Der Radiologe*, 40(3):262–266, 2000.

L. Ertöz, M. Steinbach, and V. Kumar. Finding clusters of different sizes, shapes and density in noisy high dimensional data. In *Third SIAM International Conference on Data Mining*, pp. 967–968, 2003.

R. Fahrig. *Computed Rotational Angiography*. Ph.D. thesis, University of Western Ontario, 1999.

A. X. Falcao, K. Jayaram, J. K. Udupa, and F. K. Miyazawa. An ultra-fast usersteered image segmentation paradigm: live-wire-on-the fly. *Proc. of SPIE Medical Imaging*, volume 3661:184–191, 1999.

A. X. Falcao and J. K. Udupa. Segmentation of 3D objects using live wire. In *Proc. of SPIE Medical Imaging*, volume 3034(1), pp. 228–239, 1997.

A. X. Falcao, J. K. Udupa, S. Samarasekera, S. Sharma, B. E. Hirsch, and R. De Alencar Lofufo. User-steered image segmentation paradigms: live-wire and live-lane. *Graphics Models and Image Processing*, 60(4): 223–260, 1998.

S. Fang and R. Srinivasan. Volumetric CSG—A model-based volume visualization approach. In *Proc. of WSCG*, pp. 88–95, 1998.

S. Fang, T. Biddlecome, and M. Tuceryan. Image-based transfer function design for data exploration in volume visualization. In *Proc. of IEEE Visualization*, pp. 319–326, 1998.

T. Farncombe, A. Celler, C. Bever, D. Noll, J. Maeght, and R. Harrop. The incorporation of organ uptake into dynamic SPECT reconstructions. *IEEE Transactions on Nuclear Science*, 48(1):3–9, 2001.

J. H. D. Fasel, D. Selle, P. Gailloud, C. J. G. Evertsz, F. Terrier, and H.-O. Peitgen. Segmental anatomy of the liver: poor correlation with CT. *Radiology*, 206(1):151–156, 1998.

R. Fattal and D. Lischinski. Variational classification for visualization of 3D ultrasound data. In *Proc. of IEEE Visualization*, pp. 403–410, 2001.

S. Feiner and D. D. Seligmann. Cutaways and ghosting: satisfying visibility constraints in dynamic 3D illustrations. *The Visual Computer*, 8(5&6):292–302, 1992.

J. D. Fekete and C. Plaisant. Excentric labelling: dynamic neighborhood labeling for data visualization. In *Proc. of ACM Conference on Human Factors in Computing Systems*, pp. 512–519, 1999.

L. Feldkamp, L. Davis, and J. Kress. Practical cone-beam algorithm. *Journal of the Optical Society of America A*, 1(6):612–619, 1984.

L. S. Feldman, V. Sherman, and G. M. Fried. Using simulators to assess laparoscopic competence: ready for widespread use? *Surgery*, 135:28–42, 2004.

P. Felkl, A.-L. Fuhrman, A. Kanitsar, and R. Wegenkittl. Surface reconstruction of the branching vessels for augmented reality aided surgery. *BIOSIGNAL 2002*, 16:252–254, June 2002.

P. Felkl, R. Wegenkittl, and K. Bühler. Surface models of tube trees. In *Computer Graphics International*, pp. 70–77, 2004.

H. Fenlon, D. Nunes, P. Schroy, M. Barish, P. Clarke, and J. Ferrucci. A comparison of virtual and conventional colonoscopy for the detection of colorectal polyps. *New England Journal of Medicine*, 341(20):1496–1503, 1999.

M. Ferrant, A. Nabavi, B. Macq, F. A. Jolesz, R. Kikinis, and S. K. Warfield. Registration of 3D intraoperative MR images of the brain using a finite element biomechanical model. *IEEE Transactions on Medical Imaging*, 20(12):1384–1397, 2001.

M. Feuerstein, S. M. Wildhirt, R. Bauernschmitt, and N. Navab. Automatic patient registration for port placement in minimally invasive endoscopic surgery. In *proc. of Medical Image Computing and Computer-Assisted Intervention (MICCAI)*, volume 3750 of *Lecture Notes in computer science*, pp. 287–294, 2005.

M. Fiala. *AR Tag Revision 1—A Fiducial Marker System Using Digital Techniques*. Technical Report, Computational Video Group, Institute for Information Technology, National Research Council Canada, 2004.

M. Fiebich, C. M. Straus, V. Sehgal, B. C. Renger, K. Doi, and K. R. Hoffmann. Automatic bone segmentation technique for CT angiographic studies. *Journal of Computer Assisted Tomography*, 23(1):155–161, 1999.

J. Fischer, D. Bartz, and W. Straßer. Occlusion handling for medical augmented reality using a volumetric phantom model. In *Proc. of ACM Symposium on Virtual Reality Software and Technology*, pp. 174–177, 2004a.

J. Fischer, D. Bartz, and W. Straßer. Intuitive and lightweight user interaction for medical augmented reality. In *Proc. of Vision, Modeling, and Visualization*, pp. 375–382, 2005.

J. Fischer, M. Neff, D. Bartz, and D. Freudenstein. Medical augmented reality based on commercial image-guided surgery. In *Proc. of Eurographics Symposium on Virtual Environments*, pp. 83–86, 2004b.

J. FISCHER, H. REGENBRECHT, and G. BARATOFF. Detecting dynamic occlusion in front of static backgrounds for AR scenes. In *Proc. of Eurographics Symposium on Virtual Environments*, pp. 153–161, 2003.

P. M. FITTS. "Perceptual—Motor Skills Learning," chapter in *Categories of Human Learning*, pp. 243–285. Academic Press, New York, 1964.

J. M. FITZPATRICK, D. L. G. HILL, and C. R. MAURER, Jr. "Image Registration," chapter in *Handbook of Medical Imaging: Medical Image Processing and Analysis*, volume 2, pp. 447–513. SPIE Press, 2000.

S. FLEISHMAN, I. DRORI, and D. COHEN-OR. Bilateral mesh denoising. In *Proc. of ACM SIGGRAPH*, pp. 950–953, 2003.

T. G. FLOHR, C. H. McCOLLOUGH, H. BRUDER, M. PETERSILKA, K. GRUBER, and C. SUSS. First performance evaluation of a dual-source CT (DSCT) system. *European Journal of Radiology*, 16(2):256–68, 2006.

J. D. FOLEY, A. VAN DAM, S. K. FEINER, and J. F. HUGHES. *Computer Graphics: Principles and Practice*, 2nd ed. Addison Wesley, Reading, MA, 1995.

B. D. FORNAGE, N. SNEIGE, M. J. FAROUX, and E. ANDRY. Sonographic appearance and ultrasound guided fine-needle aspiration biopsy of breast carcinomas smaller than 1 cm. *Journal of Ultrasound in Medicine*, 9:559–568, 1990.

D. FOULSER. Iris explorer: a framework for investigation. *ACM Computer Graphics*, 29(2):13–16, 1995.

R. S. J. FRACKOWIAK, K. J. FRISTON, C. D. FRITH, R. J. DOLAN, and J. C. MAZZIOTTA, editors. *Human Brain Function*. Academic Press USA, 1997.

A. F. FRANGI, W. J. NIESSEN, R. M. HOOGEVEEN, T. VAN WALSUM, and M. A. VIERGEVER. Model-based quantitation of 3D magnetic resonance angiographic images. *IEEE Transactions on Medical Imaging*, 18:946–956, 1999.

A. F. FRANGI, W. J. NIESSEN, and M. A. VIERGEVER. Three-dimensional modeling for functional analysis of cardiac images: a review. *IEEE Transactions on Medical Imaging*, 20(1):2–25, 2001.

A. F. FRANGI, W. J. NIESSEN, K. L. VINCKEN, and M. A. VIERGEVER. Multiscale vessel enhancement filtering. In *Proc. of Medical Image Computing and Computer-Assisted Intervention (MICCAI)*, volume 1496 of *Lecture Notes in Computer Science*, pp. 130–137, 1998.

A. F. FRANGI, D. RÜCKERT, J. SCHNABEL, and W. J. NIESSEN. Construction of multiple-object three-dimensional statistical shape models: application to cardiac modelling. *IEEE Transactions on Medical Imaging*, 21(9):1151–1156, 2002.

L. R. FRANK. Anisotropy in high angular resolution diffusion-weighted MRI. *Magnetic Resonance in Medicine*, 45(6):935–939, 2001.

J. FREIXENET, X. MUNOZ, D. RABA, J. MARTI, and X. CUFI. Yet another survey on image segmentation: region and boundary information integration. In *European Conference on Computer Vision*, volume III, pp. 408–422, Copenhagen, Denmark, May 2002.

B. B. FRERICKS, F. C. CALDARONE, B. NASHAN, D. H. SAVELLANO, G. STAMM, T. D. KIRCHHOFF, H. O. SHIN, A. SCHENK, D. SELLE, W. SPINDLER, J. KLEMPNAUER, H. O. PEITGEN, and M. GALANSKI. 3D CT modeling of hepatic vessel architecture and volume calculation in living donated liver transplantation. *European Journal of Radiology*, 14(2):326–333, 2004.

D. FREUDENSTEIN, D. BARTZ, M. SKALEJ, and F. DUFFNER. A new virtual system for planning of neuroendoscopic interventions. *Computer Aided Surgery*, 6(2):77–84, 2001.

D. FREUDENSTEIN, A. WAGNER, Ö. GÜRVIT, and D. BARTZ. Virtual representation of the basal cistern: technical note. *Medical Science Monitor*, 8(9):153–158, 2002.

Y. FRIDMAN, S. PIZER, S. R. AYLWARD, and E. BULLITT. Segmenting 3D branching tubular structures using cores. In *Proc. of Medical Image Computing and Computer-Assisted Intervention (MICCAI)*, volume 2879 of *Lecture Notes in Computer Science*, pp. 570–577, 2003.

G. FRIEDER, D. GORDON, and R. REYNOLDS. Back-to-front display of voxel-based objects. *Computer Graphics and Applications*, 5(1):352–359, 1985.

K. J. FRISTON, A. P. HOLMES, J.-B. POLINE, P. J. GRASBY, S. C. R. WILLIAMS, R. S. J. FRACKOWIAK, and R. TURNER. Analysis of fMRI time series revisited. *NeuroImage*, 2:45–53, 1995.

K. J. FRISTON, C. FRITH, P. F. LIDDLE, R. DOLAN, A. A. LAMMERTSMA, and R. S. J. FRACKOWIAK. The relationship between global and local changes in PET scans. *Journal of Cerebral Blood Flow and Metabolism*, 10:458–466, 1990.

K. J. FRISTON, C. FRITH, P. F. LIDDLE, and R. S. J. FRACKOWIAK. Comparing functional (PET) images: the assessment of significant change. *Journal of Cerebral Blood Flow and Metabolism*, 11:690–699, 1991.

K. J. FRISTON, P. JEZZARD, and R. TURNER. Analysis of functional MRI time-series. *Human Brain Mapping*, 1:153–171, 1994.

T. FRÜHAUF. Raycasting opaque isosurfaces in nonregularly gridded CFD data. In *Proc. of Eurographics Workshop on Visualization in Scientific Computing*, pp. 45–57, 1995.

H. FUCHS, Z. KEDEM, and B. NAYLOR. On visible surface generation by a priori tree structures. In *Proc. of ACM SIGGRAPH*, pp. 124–133, 1980.

H. FUCHS, Z. KEDMEN, and S. USELTON. Optimal surface reconstruction from planar contours. *Communications of the ACM*, 20(10):693–702, 1977.

A. FUHRMANN, G. HESINA, F. FAURE, and M. GERVAUTZ. Occlusion in collaborative augmented environments. *Computers & Graphics*, 23(6):809–819, 1999.

I. FUJISHIRO, T. AZUMA, and Y. TAKESHIMA. Automating transfer function design for comprehensible volume rendering based on 3D field topology analysis. In *Proc. of IEEE Visualization*, pp. 355–362, 1999.

Y. FUNG, editor. *Biomechanics: Mechanical Properties of Living Tissues*. Springer, 1993.

G. FUNKA-LEA, Y. BOYKOV, C. FLORIN, M.-P. JOLLY, R. MOREAU-GOBARD, R. RAMARAJ, and D. RINCK. Automatic heart isolation for CT coronary visualization using graph-cuts. In *IEEE International Symposium on Biomedical Imaging*, April 2006.

E. FURMAN-HARAN, D. GROBGELD, and H. DEGANI. Dynamic contrast-enhanced imaging and analysis at high spatial resolution of MCF7 human breast tumors. *Journal of Magnetic Resonance Imaging*, 128:161–171, 1997.

G. W. FURNAS. Generalized fisheye views. In *Proc. of ACM Conference on Human Factors in Computing Systems*, pp. 16–23. ACM SIGCHI, 1986.

D. GABOR. Theory of communication. *Journal of the Institution of Electrical Engineers*, 93(3):429–457, 1946.

A. GADDIPATTI, R. MACHIRAJU, and R. YAGEL. Steering image generation with wavelet-based perceptual metric. *Computer Graphics Forum*, 16(3):241–248, 1997.

N. GAGVANI and D. SILVER. Animating volumetric models. *Graphical Models*, 63(6):443–458, 2001.

T. GALYEAN. Guided navigation of virtual environments. In *Proc. of ACM Symposium on Interactive 3D Graphics*, pp. 103–104, 1995.

T. A. GALYEAN and J. F. HUGHES. Sculpting: an interactive volumetric modeling technique. In *Proc. of ACM SIGGRAPH*, pp. 267–274, 1991.

M. GARLAND. Multiresolution modeling: survey and future opportunities. In *Eurographics STAR report 2*, 1999.

M. GARLAND and P. HECKBERT. Surface simplification using quadric error metrics. In *Proc. of ACM SIGGRAPH*, pp. 209–215, 1997.

B. GARLICK, D. BAUM, and J. WINGET. Interactive viewing of large geometric databases using multiprocessor graphics workstations. In *ACM SIGGRAPH Course Notes: Parallel Algorithms and Architectures for 3D Image Generation*, 1990.

A. GERHARDS, P. RAAB, S. HERBER, K. F. KREITNER, T. BOSKAMP, and P. MILDENBERGER. Software-assisted CT-postprocessing of the carotid arteries. *Fortschritte auf dem Gebiet der Röntgenstrahlen und der bildgebenden Verfahren*, 176(6):570–577, 2004.

G. GERIG, S. GOUTTARD, and I. COROUGE. Analysis of brain white matter via fiber tract modeling. In *IEEE Engineering in Medicine and Biology (EMB 2004)*, 2004.

G. GERIG, R. KIKINIS, O. KÜBLER, and F. A. JOLESZ. Nonlinear anisotropic filtering of MRI data. *IEEE Transactions on Medical Imaging*, 11(2):221–232, 1992.

G. GERIG, G. KINDLMANN, R. WHITAKER, R. MACHIRAJU, T. MÖLLER, and T. S. YOO. Image processing for volume graphics. *ACM SIGGRAPH Course Notes*, Course 50, 2002.

G. GERIG, T. KOLLER, G. SZÉKELY, C. BRECHBÜHLER, and O. KÜBLER. Symbolic description of 3D structures applied to cerebral vessel tree obtained from MR angiography volume data. In *Proc. of Information Processing in Medical Imaging*, volume 687 of *Lecture Notes in Computer Science*, pp. 94–111, 1993.

D. GERING, A. NABAVI, R. KIKINIS, W. ERIC, L. GRIMSON, N. HATA, P. EVERETT, F. A. JOLESZ, and W. M. WELLS. Integrated visualization system for surgical planning and guidance using image fusion and interventional imaging. In *Proc. of Medical Image Computing and Computer-Assisted Intervention (MICCAI)*, volume 1679 of *Lecture Notes in Computer Science*, pp. 809–819, 1999.

D. GERING, A. NABAVI, R. KIKINIS, N. HATA, L. J. O'Donnell, W. ERIC, L. GKRIMSON, F. A. JOLESZ, P. M. BLACK, and W. M. WELLS III. An integrated visualization system for surgical planning and guidance using image fusion and an open MR *Journal of Magnetic Resonance Imaging*, 13(6):967–975, 2001.

O. GEROVICHEV, P. MARAYONG, and A. M. OKAMURA. The effect of visual and haptic feedback on manual and teleoperated needle insertion. In *Proc. of Medical Image Computing and Computer-Assisted Intervention (MICCAI)*, volume 2489 of *Lecture Notes in Computer Science*, pp. 147–154, 2002.

A. G. GHUNEIM. Contour Tracing, Tutorial in Image Processing Place.www.imageprocess-ingplace.com/DIP/ dip_downloads/tutorials/contour_tracing_Abeer_George_Ghuneim/author.html/, accessed 2005.

S. F. F. GIBSON. Constrained elastic surface nets: generating smooth surfaces from binary segmented data. In W. M. WELLS et al., editors, *Proc. of Medical Image Computing and Computer-Assisted Intervention (MICCAI)*, volume 1496 of *Lecture Notes in Computer Science*, pp. 888–898, 1998.

A. GLASSNER. *An Introduction to Ray Tracing*. Academic Press, London, UK, 1989.

A. GLASSNER. *Principles of Digital Image Synthesis—Volume One*. Morgan Kaufmann Publishers, Inc., San Francisco, USA, 1995.

G. GLOMBITZA, W. LAMADÉ, A. M. DEMIRIS, M. R. GÖPFERT, A. MAYER, M. L. BAHNER, and H. P. MEINZER. Virtual planning of liver resections: image processing, visualization and volumetric analysis. *Journal of Medical Informatics*, 53(2–3):225–237, 1999.

S. N. GOLDBERG and D. E. DUPUY. Image-guided radiofrequency tumor ablation: challenges and opportunities—part I. *Journal of Vascular Interventional Radiology*, 12:1021–1032, 2001.

B. GOLDSTEIN. *Sensation and Perception*, 7th ed. Wadsworth Publishing, Pacific Grove, CA, 2006.

P. GOLLAND, R. KIKINIS, M. HALLE, C. UMANS, W. E. L. GRIMSON, M. E. SHENTON, and J. A. RICHOLT. Anatomybrowser: a novel approach to visualization and integration of medical information. *Computer Aided Surgery*, 4:129–143, 1999.

P. GOLLAND, R. KIKINIS, C. UMANS, M. HALLEAND, M .E. SHENTON, and J. A. RICHOLT. Anatomybrowser: a framework for integration of medical information. In *Proc. of Medical Image Computing and Computer-Assisted Intervention (MICCAI)*, volume 1496 of *Lecture Notes in Computer Science*, pp. 720–731, 1998.

R. C. GONZALES and R. E. WOODS. *Digital Image Processing* 2nd ed. Prentice Hall, 1998.

A. GOOCH, B. GOOCH, P. SHIRLEY, and E. COHEN. A non-photorealistic lighting model for automatic technical illustration. In *Proc. of ACM SIGGRAPH*, pp. 447–452, 1998.

B. GOOCH, P. SLOAN, A. GOOCH, P. SHIRLEY, and R. RIESENFELD. Interactive technical illustration. In *Proc. of ACM Symposium on Interactive 3D Graphics*, pp. 31–38, 1999.

B. GOOCH and A. A. GOOCH. *Non-Photorealistic Rendering*. AK Peters Ltd. July 2001.

D. S. GOODSELL, S. MIAN, and A. J. OLSON. Rendering of volumetric data in molecular systems. *Journal of Molecular Graphics*, 7(1):41–47, 1989.

T. GÖTZELMANN, K. HARTMANN, and T. STROTHOTTE. Agents-based annotation. In *Symposium on Smart Graphics*, pp. 23–25, 2006a.

T. GÖTZELMANN, K. HARTMANN, and T. STROTHOTTE. Contextual grouping of labels. In *Proc. of Simulation and Visualization*, pp. 245–258, 2006b.

T. GÖTZELMANN, K. ALI, K. HARTMANN, and T. STROTHOTTE. Adaptive labeling for illustrations. In *Proc. of Pacific Graphics*, 2005.

C. B. GRANDIN, T. P. DUPREZ, A. M. SMITH, C. OPPENHEIM, A. PEETERS, A. R. ROBERT, and G. COSNARD. Which MR-derived perfusion parameters are the best predictors of infarct growth in hyperacute stroke?— comparative study between relative and quantitative measurements. *Radiology*, 223:361–370, 2002.

H. GRAY. *Anatomy of the Human Body*. Online version: www.bartleby.com/107., 20th ed. 1918.

C. GREGORY. Chickscope: MRI artifact gallery. chickscope.beckman.uiuc.edu/roosts/carl, accessed 2005.

S. GRIMM. *Real-Time Mono- and Multi-Volume Rendering of Large Medical Datasets on Standard PC Hardware*. Ph.D. thesis, Wien university of Technology Fakultät für Informatik, 2005.

S. GRIMM, S. BRUCKNER, A. KANITSAR, and E. GRÖLLER. Memory effcient acceleration structures and techniques for CPU-based volume raycasting of large data. In *Proc. of IEEE/ACM Symposium on Volume Visualization and Graphics*, pp. 1–8, 2004.

R. GRZESZCZUK, C. HENN, and R. YAGEL. Advanced geometric techniques for ray casting volumes. In *ACM SIGGRAPH Course 4*, 1998.

H. GUDBJARTSSON, S. E. MAIER, and R. V. MULKER. Line scan diffusion imaging. *Magnetic Resonance in Medicine*, 36:509–519, 1996.

Y. GUIARD. A symmetric division of labor in human skilled bimanual action: the kinematic chain as a model. *Journal of Motor Behavior*, 19(4):486–517, 1987.

H. GUMPRECHT, G. K. EBEL, D. P. AUER, and C. B. LUMENTA. Neuronavigation and functional MRI for surgery in patients with lesion in eloquent brain areas. *Minimally Invasive Neurosurgery*, 45(3):151–153, 2002.

T. GÜNTHER, C. POLIWODA, C. REINHART, J. HESSER, R. MÄNNER, H. P. MEINZER, and H. J. BAUR. VIRIM: a massively parallel processor for real-time volume visualization in medicine. In *Proc. of Eurographics/SIGGRAPH Workshop on Graphics Hardware*, pp. 103–108, 1994.

Ö. GÜRVIT, M. SKALEJ, R. RIEKMANN, U. ERNEMANN, and K. VOIGT. Rotational angiography and 3D reconstruction in neuroradiology. *electro medica*, 68(1):31–37, 2000.

S. GUTHE and W. STRAßER. Real-time decompression and visualization of animated volume data. In *Proc. of IEEE Visualization*, pp. 349–356, 2001.

S. GUTHE, M. WAND, J. GONSER, and W. STRAßER. Interactive rendering of large volume data sets. In *Proc. of IEEE Visualization*, pp. 53–60, 2002.

S. GUY and G. DEBUNNE. *Monte-carlo Collision Detection*. Technical Report RR-5136, INRIA, March 2004.

A. C. GUYTON. *Basic Neuroscience—Anatomy and Physiology*. W. B. Saunders Company, 1987.

E. HABER and J. MODERSITZKI. Beyond mutual information: a simple and robust alternative. In *Proc. of Workshop Bildverarbeitung für die Medizin*, Informatik aktuell, pp. 1–5, 2005.

E. HABER and J. MODERSITZKI. Volume preserving image registration. In *Proc. of Medical Image Computing and Computer-Assisted Intervention (MICCAI)*, volume 3216 of *Lecture Notes in Computer Science*, pp. 591–598, 2004.

M. HADWIGER, C. BERGER, and H. HAUSER. High-quality two-level volume rendering of segmented data sets on consumer graphics hardware. In *Proc. of IEEE Visualization*, pp. 301–308, 2003a.

M. HADWIGER, C. SIGG, H. SCHARSACH, K. BUHLER, and M. GROSS. Real-time ray-casting and advanced shading of discrete isosurfaces. *Computer Graphics Forum*, 24(3):303–312, 2005.

M. HADWIGER, C. BERGER, and H. HAUSER. High-quality two-level volume rendering of segmented data sets on consumer graphics hardware. In *Proc. of IEEE Visualization*, pp. 301–308, October 2003b.

H. K. HAHN, M. G. LENTSCHIG, M. DEIMLING, B. TERWEY, and H.-O. PEITGEN. MRI-based volumetry of intra- and extracerebral CSF spaces. In *Proc. of Computer Assisted Radiology and Surgery*, pp. 384–389, 2001a.

H. K. HAHN. *Makroskopische Morphometrie und Dynamik der Lebergefäße des Menschen*. Master's thesis, University of Heidelberg, Department of Physics, 1998.

H. K. HAHN. *Morphological Volumetry: Theory, Concepts, and Application to Quantitative Medical Imaging*. Ph.D. thesis, Department of Mathematics and Computer Science, University of Bremen, 2005.

H. K. HAHN, F. LINK, and H.-O. PEITGEN. Concepts for rapid application prototyping in medical image analysis and visualization. In *Proc. of Simulation and Visualization*, pp. 283–298, 2003.

H. K. HAHN and H.-O. PEITGEN. The skull stripping problem in MRI solved by a single 3D watershed transform. In *Proc. of Medical Image Computing and Computer-Assisted Intervention (MICCAI)*, volume 1935 of *Lecture Notes in Computer Science*, pp. 134–143, 2000.

H. K. HAHN and H.-O. PEITGEN. IWT—Interactive Watershed Transform: A hierarchical method for efficient interactive and automated segmentation of multidimensional grayscale images. In *Proc. of SPIE Medical Imaging*, volume 5032, pp. 643–653, 2003.

H. K. HAHN, B. PREIM, D. SELLE, and H.-O. PEITGEN. Visualization and interaction techniques for the exploration of vascular structures. In *Proc. of IEEE Visualization*, pp. 395–402, 2001b.

J. V. HAJNAL, D. L. G. HILL, and D. J. HAWKES. *Medical Image Registration*. CRC Press, 2001.

S. HAKER, A. TANNENBAUM, and R. KIKINIS. Nondistorting flattening maps and 3D visualization of colon CT images. *IEEE Transactions on Medical Imaging*, 19:665–670, 2000.

L. HALLPIKE and D. J. HAWKES. Medical image registration: an overview. *Imaging*, 14:455–463, 2002.

R. HAMMING. *Art of Doing Science and Engineering: Learn to Learn*. Taylor & Francis, CRC Press, 1997.

C. HAND. A survey of 3D interaction techniques. *Computer Graphics Forum*, 16(5):269–281, 1997.

C. HANSEN and C. JOHNSON. *The Visualization Handbook*. Elsevier, 2004.

M. HARDERS and G. SZÉKELY. Enhancing human-computer interaction in medical segmentation. In *Proc. of the IEEE-Special Issue on Multimodal User Interfaces*, volume 91(9), pp. 1430–1442, 2003.

J. HARMS, H. BOURQUAIN, M. BARTELS, H.-O. PEITGEN, T. SCHULZ, T. KAHN, J. HAUSS, and J. FANGMANN. Surgical impact of computerized 3D CT-based visualizations in living donor liver transplantation. *Surgical Technology International*, 13:191–195, 2004.

K. HARTMANN, K. ALI, and T. STROTHOTTE. Floating labels: applying dynamic potential fields for label layout. In A. BUTZ, A. KRÜGER, and P. OLIVIER, editors, *Proc. of International Symposium on Smart Graphics*, volume 3031 of *Lecture Notes in Computer Science*, pp. 101–113, 2004.

K. HARTMANN, T. GÖTZELMANN, K. ALI, and T. STROTHOTTE. Metrics for functional and aesthetic label layouts. In A. BUTZ, B. FISHER, A. KRÜGER, and P. OLIVIER, editors, *Proc. of International Symposium on Smart Graphics*, volume 3638 of *Lecture Notes in Computer Science*, pp. 115–126, 2005.

P. HASTREITER, C. REZK-SALAMA, B. TOMANDL, K. B. W. EBERHARDT, and T. ERTL. Fast analysis of intracranial aneurysms based on interactive direct volume rendering and CTA. In *Proc. of Medical Image Computing and Computer-Assisted Intervention (MICCAI)*, volume 1496 of *Lecture Notes in Computer Science*, pp. 660–669, 1998.

P. HASTREITER and T. ERTL. Integrated registration and visualization of medical image data. In *Computer Graphics International*, pp. 78–85, 1998.

P. HASTREITER, C. REZK-SALAMA, G. SOZA, M. BAUER, G. GREINER, R. FAHLBUSCH, O. GANSLANDT, and C. NIMSKY. Strategies for brain shift evaluation. *Medical Image Analysis*, 8(4):447–464, 2004.

H. HAUSER, L. MROZ, G.-I. BISCHI, and M. E. GRÖLLER. Two-level volume rendering—fusing MIP and DVR. In *Proc. of IEEE Visualization*, pp. 211–218, 2000.

H. HAUSER, L. MROZ, G.-I. BISCHI, and M. E. GRÖLLER. Two-level volume rendering. *IEEE Transactions on Visualization and Computer Graphics*, 7(3):242–252, 2001.

M. HAUTH. *Visual Simulation of Deformable Models*. Ph.D. thesis, Dept. of Computer Science (WSI), University of Tübingen, 2004.

M. D. HAYHURST, W. MACNEE, and D. C. FLENLEY. Diagnosis of pulmonary emphysema by computerized tomography. *Lancet*, 2:320–322, 1984.

T. HE and L. HONG. Reliable navigation for virtual endoscopy. In *Proc. of IEEE Nuclear Science Symposium and Medical Imaging Conference*, 1999.

T. HE, L. HONG, A. KAUFMAN, and H. PFISTER. Generation of transfer functions with stochastic search techniques. In *Proc. of IEEE Visualization*, pp. 227–234, 1996.

P. HECKBERT. *Fundamentals of Texture Mapping and Image Warping*. Master's thesis, Dept. of Electrical Engineering and Computer Science, University of California at Berkeley, 1989.

H. HEGE, T. HÖLLERER, and D. STALLING. *Volume Rendering: Mathematical Models and Algorithmic Aspects*. Technical Report ZIB-93-07, Zuse Institute Berlin (ZIB), 1993.

H.-C. HEGE and D. STALLING. LIC: acceleration, animation, zoom. In *ACM SIGGRAPH Course 8*, pp. 17–49, 1997.

H.-C. HEGE. Enumeration of symmetry classes in mesh generation. In *Proc. of Dagstuhl Workshop on Hierarchical Methods in Computer Graphics*, number 9821, pp. 9–10, 1998.

H.-C. HEGE, M. SEEBAß, D. STALLING, and M. ZÖCKLER. *A Generalized Marching Cubes Algorithm Based on Non-Binary Classifications*. Technical Report ZIB 95-05, Zuse Institute Berlin (ZIB), 1997.

A. HEIN and T. LUETH. Image-based control of interactive robotics systems. In *Proc. of Medical Image Computing and Computer-Assisted Intervention (MICCAI)*, volume 1679 of *Lecture Notes in Computer Science*, pp. 1125–1132, 1999.

A. HENNEMUTH, T. BOSKAMP, D. FRITZ, C. KÜHNEL, S. BOCKA, D. RINCK, M. SCHEUERING, and H.-O. PEITGEN. One-click coronary tree segmentation in CT angiographic images. In *Proc. of Computer Assisted Radiology and Surgery*, pp. 317–321, 2005.

J. HENNIG. The historical documentation of scientific developments: scientists should participate (editorial). *Journal of Magnetic Resonance Imaging*, 19:521–522, 2003.

G. T. HERMAN and H. K. LIU. Three-dimensional display of human organs from computed tomograms. *Computer Graphics and Image Processing*, 9(1):1–21, 1979.

M. HERNANDEZ-HOYOS, M. ORKISZ, P. PUECH, C. MANSARD-DESBLEDS, P. DOUEK, and I. E. MAGNIN. Computer-assisted analysis of three-dimensional MRI angiograms. *Radiographics*, 22:421–436, 2002.

M. HERNANDEZ-HOYOS, A. ANWANDER, M. ORKISZ, J.-P. ROUX, P. DOUEK, and I. MAGNIN. A deformable vessel model with single point initialization for segmentation, quantification and visualization of blood vessels in 3D MRA. In *Proc. of Medical Image Computing and Computer-Assisted Intervention (MICCAI)*, volume 1935 of *Lecture Notes in Computer Science*, pp. 735–744, 2000.

A. HERTZMANN and D. ZORIN. Illustrating smooth surfaces. In *Proc. of ACM SIGGRAPH*, pp. 517–526, 2000.

S. H. HEYWANG-KÖBRUNNER. Contrast-enhanced magnetic resonance imaging of the breast. *Invest. Radiology*, pp. 94–104, 1994.

S. H. HEYWANG-KÖBRUNNER, P. VIEHWEG, A. HEINIG, and C. KUCHLER. Contrast enhanced MRI of the breast: accuracy, value, controversies, solutions. *European Journal of Radiology*, 24:94–108, 1997.

F. V. HIGUERA, R. FAHLBSUCH, P. HASTREITER, and G. GREINER. High performance volume splatting for visualization of neurovascular data. In *Proc. of IEEE Visualization*, pp. 271–278, 2005.

K. HINCKLEY, R. PAUSCH, D. PROFITT, and N. F. KASSEL. Two-handed virtual manipulation. *ACM Transactions on Human Computer Interaction*, 5(3):260–302, 1998.

J. HLADUVKA, A. KÖNIG, and E. GRÖLLER. Curvature-based transfer functions for direct volume rendering. In *Spring Conference on Computer Graphics*, pp. 58–65, 2000.

M. HLAWITSCHKA and G. SCHEUERMANN. HOT-Lines—tracking lines in higher order tensor fields. In *IEEE Visualization*, pp. 27–34, 2005.

E. R. S. HODGES. *The Guild Handbook of Scientific Illustration*. Van Nostrand Reinhold, 1989.

J. HOFFMANN, C. WESTENDORFF, C. LEITNER, D. BARTZ, and S. REINERT. Validation of 3D-laser surface registration for image-guided craniomaxillofacial surgery. *Journal for Cranio-Maxillofacial Surgery*, 33(1):13–18, 2005.

K. H. HÖHNE. Medical image computing at the Institute of Mathematics and Computer Science in Medicine, University Hospital Hamburg-Eppendorf. *IEEE Transactions on Medical Imaging*, 21(7): 713–723, 2002.

K. H. HÖHNE and R. BERNSTEIN. Shading 3D-images from CT using gray-level gradients. In *IEEE Transactions on Medical Imaging*, volume MI-5, pp. 45–47, 1986.

K. H. HÖHNE, M. BOMANS, M. RIEMER, R. SCHUBERT, U. TIEDE, and W. LIERSE. A 3D anatomical atlas based on a volume model. *IEEE Computer Graphics and Applications*, 12(4):72–78, 1992.

K. H. HÖHNE, A. PETERSIK, B. PFLESSER, A. POMMERT, K. PRIESMEYER, M. RIEMER, T. SCHIEMANN, R. SCHUBERT, U. TIEDE, M. URBAN, H. FREDERKING, M. LOWNDES, and J. MORRIS. *VOXELMAN 3D Navigator: Brain and Skull. Regional, Functional and Radiological Anatomy*. Springer Electronic Media, Heidelberg, 2001.

K. H. HÖHNE, B. PFLESSER, A. POMMERT, et al. A realistic model of the inner organs from the visible human data. In *Proc. of Medical Image Computing and Computer-Assisted Intervention (MICCAI)*, volume 1935 of *Lecture Notes in Computer Science*, pp. 776–785, 2000.

K. H. HÖHNE, B. PFLESSER, A. POMMERT, K. PRIESMEYER, M. RIEMER, T. SCHIEMANN, R. SCHUBERT, U. TIEDE, H. FREDERKING, S. GEHRMANN, S. NOSTER, and U. SCHUMACHER. *VOXEL-MAN 3D Navigator: Inner Organs. Regional, Systemic and Radiological Anatomy*. Springer Electronic Media, Heidelberg, 2003.

K. H. HÖHNE, U. OBERMÖLLER, and M. BÖHM. X-ray functional imaging—evaluation of the properties of different parameters. In *Proc. Conference on Digital Radiography*, pp. 224–228, 1981.

K. H. HÖHNE, M. RIEMER, and U. TIEDE. Viewing operations for 3D-tomographic gray level data. In *Proc. of Computer Assisted Radiology*, pp. 599–609, 1987.

M. HOLDEN. *Registration of Serial MRI Brain Images*. Ph.D. thesis, King's College London, University of London, 2001.

W. HOLLINSHEAD and C. ROSSE. *Textbook of Anatomy*, 4th ed. Philadelphia, Pennsylvania: Harper & Row, 1985.

L. HONG, S. MURAKI, A. KAUFMAN, D. BARTZ, and T. HE. Virtual voyage: interactive navigation in the human colon. In *Proc. of ACM SIGGRAPH*, pp. 27–34, 1997.

D. HÖNIGMANN, J. RUISZ, and C. HAIDER. Adaptive design of a global opacity transfer function for direct volume rendering of ultrasound data. In *Proc. of IEEE Visualization*, pp. 489–496, 2003.

H. HOPPE. Progressive meshes. In *Proc. of ACM SIGGRAPH*, pp. 99–108, 1996.

H. HOPPE, T. DEROSE, T. DACHAMP, J. MCDONALD, and W. STÜTZLE. Mesh optimization. In *Proc. of ACM SIGGRAPH*, pp. 19–26, 1993.

S. HORNUS, A. ANGELIDIS, and M.-P. CANI. Implicit modeling using subdivision curves. *The Visual Computer*, 19(2–3):94–104, 2003.

G. N. HOUNSFIELD. A method of and apparatus for examination of a body by radiation such as X-ray or gamma radiation. US Patent, 1972.

G. N. HOUNSFIELD. Computerised transverse axial scanning (tomography) I. Description of system. *British Journal of Radiology*, 46:1016–1022, 1973.

G. N. HOUNSFIELD. Computed medical imaging: Nobel lecture. *Journal of Computer Assisted Tomography*, 4(5):665–674, 1980.

J. HUANG, R. CRAWFIS, N. SHAREEF, and K. MUELLER. FastSplats: optimized splatting on rectilinear grids. In *Proc. of IEEE Visualization*, pp. 219–226, 2000a.

J. HUANG, N. SHAREEF, R. CRAWFIS, P. SADAYAPPAN, and K. MUELLER. A parallel splatting algorithm with occlusion culling. In *Proc. of Eurographics Symposium on Parallel Graphics and Visualization*, pp. 125–132, 2000b.

T. C. HUDSON, M. C. LIN, J. COHEN, S. GOTTSCHALK, and D. MANOCHA. VCOLLIDE: accelerated collision detection with VRML. In *Symposium on the Virtual Reality Modeling Language*, 1997.

L. IBANEZ and W. SCHROEDER. *The ITK Software Guide 2.4*. Kitware, 2005.

E. IMHOF. Positioning names on maps. *The American Cartographer*, 2(2):128–144, 1975.

V. L. INTERRANTE, H. FUCHS, and S. PIZER. Enhancing transparent skin surfaces with ridge and valley lines. In *Proc. of IEEE Visualization*, pp. 52–59, 1995.

V. L. INTERRANTE, H. FUCHS, and S. PIZER. Illustrating transparent surfaces with curvature-directed strokes. In *Proc. of IEEE Visualization*, pp. 211–218, 1996.

T. ISENBERG, B. FREUDENBERG, N. HALPER, S. SCHLECHTWEG, and T. STROTHOTTE. A developer's guide to silhouette algorithms for polygonal models. *Computer Graphics and Applications*, 23(4):28–37, 2003.

T. ISENBERG, N. HALPER, and T. STROTHOTTE. Stylizing silhouettes at interactive rates: from silhouette edges to silhouette strokes. *Computer Graphics Forum*, 21(3):249–258, 2002.

S. ISERHARDT-BAUER, P. HASTREITER, B. TOMANDL, N. KÖSTNER, M. SCHEMPERSHOFE, U. NISSEN, and T. ERTL. Standardized analysis of intracranial aneurysms using digital video sequences. In *Proc. of Medical Image Computing and Computer-Assisted Intervention (MICCAI)*, volume 2489 of *Lecture Notes in Computer Science*, pp. 411–418, 2002.

T. ITOH and K. KOYAMADA. Automatic isosurface propagation using an extrema graph and sorted boundary cell lists. *IEEE Transactions on Visualization and Computer Graphics*, 1(4):319–327, 1995.

T. ITOH, Y. YAMAGUCHI, and K. KOYAMADA. Fast isosurface generation using an extrema skeleton and cell-edge-centered propagation. *IEEE Transactions on Visualization and Computer Graphics*, 7(1):32–46, 2001.

J. ITTEN. *Kunst der Farbe*. Otto Maier, Regensburg, 1961.

A. JACKSON, N. W. JOHN, N. A. THACKER, R. T. RAMSDEN, J. E. GILLESPIE, E. GOBBETTI, G. ZANETTI, R. STONE, A. D. LINNEY, G. H. ALUSI, *et al.* Developing a virtual reality environment for petrous bone surgery: a "state-of-the-art" review. *Journal of Otology & Neurotology*, 23(2):111–121, 2002.

A. K. JAIN and R. C. DUBES. *Algorithms for Clustering Data*. Prentice Hall, 1988.

Y. JANG, M. WEILER, M. HOPF, J. HUANG, D. EBERT, K. GAITHER, and T. ERTL. Interactively visualizing procedurally encoded scalar fields. In *Data Visualization (Proc. of Eurographics/IEEE Symposium on Visualization)*, pp. 35–44, 2004.

B. JOBARD and W. LEFER. Creating evenly-based streamlines of arbitrary density. In *Proc. of Eurographics Workshop on Visualization in Scientific Computing*, pp. 43–56, 1997.

P.-M. JODOIN, E. EPSTEIN, M. GRANGER-PICHÉ, and V. OSTROMOUKHOV. Hatching by example: a statistical approach. In *Proc. of Symposium on Non-Photorealistic Animation and Rendering*, pp. 29–36, 2002.

N. W. JOHN, N. THACKER, M. POKRIC, A. JACKSON, G. ZANETTI, E. GOBBETTI, A. GIACHETTI, R. J. STONE, J. CAMPOS, A. EMMEN, A. SCHWERDTNER, E. NERI, S. S. FRANCESCHINI, and F. RUBIO. An integrated simulator for surgery of the petrous bone. *Studies Health Technology Information*, 81:218–224, 2001.

E. JOHNSON and C. MOSHER. Integration of volume rendering and computer graphics. *State of the Art in Data Visualization, ACM SIGGRAPH Tutorial*, 1989.

H. J. JOHNSON and G. E. CHRISTENSEN. Consistent landmark and intensity-based image registration. *IEEE Transactions on Medical Imaging*, 21(5):450–461, 2002.

I. T. JOLLIFFE. *Principal Component Analysis*. New York: Springer, 1986.

D. K. JONES, M. A. HORSFIELD, and A. SIMMONS. Optimal strategies for measuring diffusion in anisotropic systems by means of MRI. *Magnetic Resonance in Medicine*, 42:515–525, 1999.

M. JONES. The production of volume data from triangular meshes using voxelization. *Computer Graphics Forum*, 15(5):311–318, 1996.

S. C. JOSHI, S. M. PIZER, P. T. FLETCHER, P. A. YUSHKEVICH, A. THALL, and J. S. MARRON. Multi-scale deformable model segmentation and statistical shape analysis using medical descriptions. *IEEE Transactions on Medical Imaging*, 21(5):538–550, 2002.

K. KAHN. *Creating Animations from Story Descriptions*. Ph.D. thesis, Artificial Intelligence Lab, MIT, 1979.

W. A. KAISER and E. ZEITLER. MRI imaging of the breast: fast imaging sequences with and without Gd-DTPA—preliminary observations. *Radiology*, 170:681–686, 1989.

J. KAJIYA. The rendering equation. In *Proc. of ACM SIGGRAPH*, pp. 143–150, 1986.

J. KAJIYA and B. HERZEN. Ray tracing volume densities. In *Proc. of ACM SIGGRAPH*, pp. 165–174, 1984.

W. KALENDER. *Computer Tomography*. München, Germany: Verlag, 2000.

W. KALENDER. The use of flat-panel detectors for CT imaging. *Radiologe*, 43(5):379–387, 2003.

W. A. KALENDER, D. FELSENBERG, O. LOUIS, P. LOPEZ, E. KLOTZ, M. OSTEAUX, and J. FRAGA. Reference values for trabecular and cortical vertebral bone density in single and dual-energy quantitative computed tomography. *European Journal of Radiology*, 18(2):75–80, 1989.

K. KAMADA, T. TODO, Y. MASUTANI, S. AOKI, K. INO, T. TAKANO, T. KIRINO, and A. MORITA. Combined use of tractography integrated functional neuronavigation and direct fiber stimulation. *Journal of Neurosurgery*, 10:664–672, 2005.

K. KANDA, S. MIZUTA, and T. MATSUDA. Volume visualization using relative distance among voxels. In *Medical Imaging 2002: Visualization, Image-Guided Procedures, and Display*, pp. 641–648, 2002.

A. KANITSAR, D. FLEISCHMANN, R. WEGENKITTL, P. FELKL, and E. GRÖLLER. CPR—curved planar reformation. In *Proc. of IEEE Visualization*, pp. 37–44, 2002.

A. KANITSAR, R. WEGENKITTL, P. FELKL, D. FLEISCHMANN, D. SANDNER, and E. GRÖLLER. Computed tomography angiography: a case study of peripheral vessel investigation. In *Proc. of IEEE Visualization*, pp. 477–480, 2001.

A. KANITSAR, R. WEGENKITTL, D. FLEISCHMANN, and E. GRÖLLER. Advanced curved planar reformation: flattening of vascular structures. In *Proc. of IEEE Visualization*, pp. 43–50, 2003.

U. KANUS, G. WETEKAM, and J. HIRCHE. VoxelCache: a cache-based memory architecture for volume graphics. In *Proc. of Symposium on Graphics Hardware*, pp. 76–83, 2003.

P. KARP and S. K. FEINER. Automated presentation planning of animation using task decomposition with heuristic reasoning. In *Proc. of Graphics Interface*, pp. 118–127, 1993.

M. KASS, A. WITKIN, and D. TERZOPOULOS. Snakes: active contour models. *International Journal of Computer Vision*, 1(4):321–331, 1988.

H. KATO and M. BILLINGHURST. Marker tracking and HMD calibration for a video-based augmented reality conferencing system. In *Proc. of IEEE and ACM International Workshop on Augmented Reality*, pp. 85–94, 1999.

H. Kauczor, B. Wolcke, B. Fischer, P. Mildenberger, and M. Thelen. Threedimensional helical CT of the tracheobronchial tree: evaluation of imaging protocols and assessment of suspected stenoses with bronchoscopic correction. *American Journal of Roentgenology*, 167(2):419–424, 1996.

A. Kaufman. An algorithm for 3D scan-conversion of polygons. In *Proc. of Eurographics*, pp. 197–208, 1987a.

A. Kaufman. Effcient algorithms for 3D scan-conversion of parametric curves, surfaces, and volumes. In *Proc. of ACM SIGGRAPH*, pp. 171–179, 1987b.

A. Kaufman, R. Yagel, and D. Cohen. "Intermixing Surface and Volume Rendering," chapter in *3D Imaging in Medicine: Algorithms, Systems and Applications*, pp. 217–227. Springer, 1990.

J. Kautz. Hardware lighting and shading. *Eurographics State-of-the-Art Report* (STAR3), 2003.

K. Kawachi and H. Suzuki. Distance computation between non-convex polyhedra based on Voronoi diagrams. *Geometric Modeling and Processing*, pp. 123–130, 2000.

D. Kay and D. Greenberg. Transparency for computer synthesized images. In *Proc. of ACM SIGGRAPH*, pp. 158–164, 1979.

E. Keeve, S. Girod, R. Kikinis, and B. Girod. Deformable modeling of facial tissue for craniofacial surgery simulation. *Computer Aided Surgery*, 3(5):228–238, 1999.

E. Keeve, T. Jansen, Z. Krol, L. Ritter, B. von Rymon-Lipinski, R. Sader, H.-F. Zeilhofer, and P. Zerfass. JULIUS—an extendable software framework for surgical planning and image-guided navigation. In *Proc. of Medical Image Computing and Computer-Assisted Intervention (MICCAI)*, volume 2208 of *Lecture Notes in Computer Science*, pp.1191–1192, 2001.

E. Keeve, T. Jansen, B. von Rymon-Lipinski, Z. Burgielski, N. Hanssen, L. Ritter, and M. Lievin. An open software framework for medical applications. In *International Symposium on Surgery Simulation and Soft Tissue Modeling*, volume 2673 of *Lecture Notes in Computer Science*, pp. 302–310, 2003.

H. G. Kehl, J. Jäger, N. Papazis, D. Dimitrelos, J. Gehrmann, R. Kassenböhmer, J. Vogt, and G. Sakas. 3D heart modeling from biplane, rotational angiocardiographic X-ray sequences. *Computers & Graphics*, 24(5):731–739, 2000.

D. E. B. P. Kendall. *Vector Analyis and Cartesian Tensors*. Van Nostrand Reinhold, 1977.

E. Keppel. Approximating complex surfaces by triangulation of contour lines. *IBM Journal of Research and Development*, 19(1):2–11, 1975.

J. Kettenbach, D. Kacher, S. Koskinen, S. Silverman, A. Nabavi, D. Gering, C. Tempany, R. Schwartz, R. Kikinis, P. Black, and F. Jolesz. Interventional and intraoperative magnetic resonance imaging. *Annual Review of Biomedical Engineering*, 2(August):661–690, 2000.

R. Kikinis, M. E. Shenton, D. V. Iosifescu, R. W. McCarley, P. Saiviroonporn, H. H. Hokama, et al. A digital brain atlas for surgical planning, model-driven segmentation, and teaching. *IEEE Transactions on Visualization and Computer Graphics*, 2(3):232–241, 1996.

K. Kim, C. Wittenbrink, and A. Pang. Extended specifications and test data sets for data level comparisons of direct volume rendering algorithms. *IEEE Transactions on Visualization and Computer Graphics*, 7(4): 299–317, 2001.

S. Kim, H. Hagh-Shenas, and V. L. Interrante. Conveying shape with texture: an experimental investigation of the impact of texture type on shape categorization judgments. In *Proc. of IEEE Symposium on Information Visualization*, pp. 163–170, 2003a.

S. Kim, H. Hagh-Shenas, and V. L. Interrante. Showing shape with texture: two directions seem better than one. In B. E. Rogowitz and T. N. Pappas, editors, *Human Vision and Electronic Imaging VIII*, volume 5007, pp. 332–339, 2003b.

Y. Kim and S. C. Horli. *Handbook of Medical Imaging: Display and PACS*, volume 3. SPIE Press, 2000.

G. KINDLMANN. Superquadric tensor glyphs. In *Data Visualization (Eurographics/IEEE Symposium on Visualization)*, pp. 147–154, 2004a.

G. KINDLMANN. *Visualization and Analysis of Diffusion Tensor Fields*. Ph.D. thesis, School of Computing, University of Utah, 2004b.

G. KINDLMANN and J. W. DURKIN. Semi-automatic generation of transfer functions for direct volume rendering. In *Proc. of IEEE/ACM Symposium on Volume Visualization*, pp. 79–86, 1998.

G. KINDLMANN, D. WEINSTEIN, and D. HART. Strategies for direct volume rendering of diffusion tensor fields. *IEEE Transactions on Visualization and Computer Graphics*, 6(2):124–138, 2000.

G. KINDLMANN, R. WHITAKER, T. TASDIZEN, and T. MÖLLER. Curvature-based transfer functions for direct volume rendering: methods and applications. In *Proc. of IEEE Visualization*, pp. 513–520, 2003.

K. KINKEL and N. M. HYLTON. Challenges to interpretation of breast MRI. *Journal of Magnetic Resonance Imaging*, pp. 821–829, 2001.

C. KIRBAS and F. QUEK. A review of vessel extraction techniques and algorithms. *ACM Computing Surveys*, 36(2):81–121, June 2004.

R. KLAR and U. BAYER. Computer-asssisted teaching and learning in medicine. *International Journal of Biomedical Computing*, pp. 7–27, 1990.

J. KLEIN and G. ZACHMANN. Time-critical collision detection using an average-case approach. In *Proc. of ACM Symposium on Virtual Reality Software and Technology*, October 2003.

R. KLEIN, A. SCHILLING, and W. STRAßER. Reconstruction and simplification of surfaces from contours. *Graphical Models*, 62(6):429–443, 2000.

J. T. KLOSOWSKI, M. HELD, J. MITCHELL, H. SOWIZRAL, and K. ZIKAN. Effcient collision detection using bounding volume hierarchies of k-DOPs. *IEEE Transactions on Visualization and Computer Graphics*, 4(1): 21–36, 1998.

E. KLOTZ and M. KÖNIG. Perfusion measurements of the brain: using dynamic CT for the quantitative assessment of cerebral ischemia in acute stroke. *European Journal of Radiology*, 30:170–184, 1999.

J. KNISS, P. MCCORMICK, A. MCPHERSON, J. AHRENS, J. PAINTER, A. KEAHEY, and C. HANSEN. Interactive texture-based volume rendering for large data sets. *Computer Graphics and Applications*, 21(4): 52–61, 2001.

J. KNISS, G. KINDLMANN, and C. HANSEN. Multi-dimensional transfer functions for interactive volume rendering. *IEEE Transactions on Visualization and Computer Graphics*, 8(3):270–285, 2002.

J. M. KNISS, S. PREMOZE, M. IKITS, A. E. LEFOHN, C. D. HANSEN, and E. PRAUN. Gaussian transfer functions for multi-field volume visualization. In *Proc. of IEEE Visualization*, pp. 497–504, 2003.

G. KNITTEL. The ULTRAVIS system. In *Proc. of IEEE/ACM Symposium on Volume Visualization and Graphics*, pp. 71–79, 2000.

G. KNITTEL and W. STRAßER. VIZARD—visualization accelerator for realtime display. In *Proc. of Eurographics/ SIGGRAPH Workshop on Graphics Hardware*, pp. 139–146, 1997.

M. V. KNOPP, F. L. GIESEL, H. MARCOS, H. VON TENGG-KOBLIGK, and P. CHOYKE. Dynamic contrast-enhanced magnetic resonance imaging in oncology. *Topics in Magnetic Resonance Imaging*, 12(4):301–308, August 2001.

M. V. KNOPP, E. WEISS, H. P. SINN, J. MATTERN, H. JUNKERMANN, J. RADELAFF, A. MAGENER, G. BRIX, S. DELORME, I. ZUNA, and G. VAN KAICK. Pathophysiologic basis of contrast enhancement in breast tumors. *Journal of Magnetic Resonance Imaging*, 10:260–266, 1999.

R. M. KOCH, M. H. GROSS, F. R. CARLS, D. F. VON BÜREN, G. FANKHAUSER, and Y. I. H. PARISH. Simulating facial surgery using finite element models. In *Proc. of ACM SIGGRAPH*, pp. 421–428, 1996.

J. J. KOENDERINK. What does the occluding contour tell us about solid shape. *Perception*, 13:321–330, 1984.

J. J. KOENDERINK, A. J. VAN DOORN, C. CHRISTOU, and J. S. LAPPIN. Shape constancy in pictorial relief. *Perception*, 25:155–164, 1996.

S. KOHLE, B. PREIM, J. WIENER, and H.-O. PEITGEN. Exploration of time-varying data for medical diagnosis. In *Proc. of Vision, Modeling, and Visualization*, pp. 31–38. Aka, 2002.

A. H. KÖNIG and E. GRÖLLER. Mastering transfer function specification by using VolumePro technology. In *Proc. of Spring Conference on Computer Graphics*, volume 17, pp. 279–286, 2001.

M. KÖNIG, M. KRAUS, C. THEEK, E. KLOTZ, W. GEHLEN, and L. HEUSER. Quantitative assessment of the ischemic brain by means of perfusion-related parameters derived from perfusion CT. *Stroke*, 32: 431–437, 2001.

M. KÖNIG and H.-O. PEITGEN. Visualization of local correlation in image registration. In *Proc. of Simulation and Visualization*, pp. 165–174, 2005.

O. KONRAD-VERSE, B. PREIM, and A. LITTMANN. Virtual resection with a deformable cutting plane. In *Proc. of Simulation and Visualization*, pp. 203–214, 2004.

R. KOSARA, F. BENDIX, and H. HAUSER. Time histograms for large time-dependent data. In *Data Visualization (Proc. of Eurographics/IEEE Symposium on Visualization)*, pp. 45–54, 2004.

R. KOSARA, C. G. HEALEY, V. INTERRANTE, D. H. LAIDLAW, and C. WARE. Thoughts on user studies: why, how, and when. *Computer Graphics and Applications*, 23(4):20–25, 2003.

R. KOSARA, S. MIKSCH, and H. HAUSER. Focus+context taken literally. *Computer Graphics and Applications*, 22(1):22–29, 2002.

F. W. KREMKAU. *Diagnostic Ultrasound*, 6th ed. W. B. SAUNDERS, 2002.

A. KRÜGER, C. TIETJEN, J. HINTZE, B. PREIM, I. HERTEL, and G. STRAUß. Interactive visualization for neck-dissection planning. In *Data Visualization (Proc. of Eurographics/IEEE Symposium on Visualization)*, pp. 295–302, 2005.

J. KRÜGER and R. WESTERMANN. Acceleration techniques for GPU-based volume rendering. In *Proc. of IEEE Visualization*, 2003.

W. KRÜGER. The application of transport theory to visualization of 3D scalar data fields. In *Computers in Physics*, volume 5, pp. 397–406, 1990a.

W. KRÜGER. The application of transport theory to visualization of 3D scalar data fields. In *Proc. of IEEE Visualization*, pp. 273–280, 1990b.

W. KRÜGER. Volume rendering and data feature enhancement. In *Proc. of IEEE/ACM Symposium on Volume Visualization*, pp. 21–26, 1990c.

K. J. KRUSZYNSKI, R. VAN LIERE, and J. A. KAANDORP. An interactive visualization system for quantifying coral structures. In *Data Visualization (Proc. of Eurographics/IEEE Symposium on Visualization)*, pp. 283–290, 2006.

M. KUBICKI, S. E. MAIER, C.-F. WESTIN, H. MAMATA, H. ERSNER-HERSHFIELD, R. ESTEPAR, *et al.* Comparison of single-shot echo-planar and line scan protocols for diffusion tensor imaging. *Academic Radiology*, 11(2):224–232, 2004.

M. KUBICKI, C.-F. WESTIN, S. E. MAIER, H. MAMATA, M. FRUMIN, H. ERSNER-HERSHFIELD, *et al.* Diffusion tensor imaging and its application to neuropsychiatric disorders. *Harvard Review Psychiatry*, 10(6):324–337, 2002.

C. K. KUHL and H. H. SCHILD. Dynamic image interpretation of MRI of the breast. *Journal of Magnetic Resonance Imaging*, 12:965–974, 2000.

U. KÜHNAPFEL, H. K. ÇAKMAK, and H. MAASS. Endoscopic surgery training using virtual reality and deformable tissue simulation. *Computers & Graphics*, 24(5):671–682, 2000.

J.-M. KUHNIGK, V. DICKEN, L. BORNEMANN, D. WORMANNS, S. KRASS, and H.-O. PEITGEN. Fast automated segmentation and reproducible volumetry of pulmonary metastases in CT-scans for therapy monitoring.

In Proc. of Medical Image Computing and Computer-Assisted Intervention (MICCAI), volume 3217 of Lecture Notes in Computer Science, pp. 933–941, 2004.

J.-M. KUHNIGK, H. K. HAHN, M. HINDENNACH, V. DICKEN, S. KRASS, and H.-O. PEITGEN. Lung lobe segmentation by anatomy-guided 3D watershed transform. In Proc. of SPIE Medical Imaging, pp. 1482–1490, 2003.

P. LACROUTE. Fast Volume Rendering Using a Shear-Warp Factorization of the Viewing Transformation. Ph.D. thesis, Department of Electrical Engineering and Computer Science, Stanford University, 1995.

P. LACROUTE and M. LEVOY. Fast volume rendering using a shear-warp factorization of the viewing transformation. In Proc. of ACM SIGGRAPH, pp. 451–458, 1994.

D. H. LAIDLAW, E. T. AHRENS, D. KREMERS, M. J. AVALOS, R. E. JACOBS, and C. READHEAD. Visualizing diffusion tensor images of the mouse spinal cord. In IEEE Visualization, pp. 127–134, 1998.

D. H. LAIDLAW, R. M. KIRBY, C. D. JACKSON, J. S. DAVIDSON, T. S. MILLER, M. DA SILVA, W. H. WARREN, and M. J. TARR. Comparing 2D vector field visualization methods: a user study. IEEE Transactions on Visualization and Computer Graphics, 11(1):59–70, 2005.

S. LAKARE and A. KAUFMAN. Anti-aliased volume extraction. In Data Visualization (Proc. of Eurographics/IEEE Symposium on Visualization), pp. 113–122, 2003.

S. LAKARE, M. WAN, M. SATO, and A. KAUFMAN. 3D digital cleansing using segmentation rays. In Proc. of IEEE Visualization, pp. 37–44, 2000.

R. C. LALOUCHE, D. BICKMORE, F. TESSLER, H. K. MANKOVICH, and H. KANGARALOO. Three-dimensional reconstruction of ultrasound images. In Proc. of SPIE Medical Imaging, pp. 59–66, 1989.

W. LAMADÉ, G. GLOMBITZA, L. FISCHER, P. CHIU, C. E. CARDENAS, M. THORN, et al. The impact of 3-dimensional reconstructions on operation planning in liver surgery. Archives of Surgery, 135(11): 1256–1261, 2000.

E. LaMAR, B. HAMANN, and K. JOY. Multiresolution techniques for interactive texture-based volume visualization. In Proc. of IEEE Visualization, pp. 355–361, 1999.

H. LAMECKER, T. LANGE, and M. SEEBAß. A statistical shape model for the liver. In Proc. of Medical Image Computing and Computer-Assisted Intervention (MICCAI), volume 2488 of Lecture Notes in Computer Science, pp. 422–427, 2002.

H. LAMECKER, M. SEEBAß, H.-C. HEGE, and P. DEUFLHARD. A 3D statistical shape model of the pelvic bone for segmentation. In Proc. of SPIE Medical Imaging, pp. 1341–1351, 2004.

J. LANDER. Shades of Disney: opaquing a 3D world. Graphics Developer Magazine, 7(3):15–20, 2000a.

J. LANDER. Under the shade of the rendering tree. Graphics Developer Magazine, 7(2):17–21, 2000b.

H. LANG, A. RADTKE, M. HINDENNACH, T. SCHROEDER, N. R. FRUHAUF, M. MALAGO, H. BOURQUAIN, H.-O. PEITGEN, K. J. OLDHAFER, and C. E. BROELSCH. Impact of virtual tumor resection and computer-assisted risk analysis on operation planning intraoperative strategy in major hepatic resection. Archives of Surgery, 140(4):629–638, 2005a.

H. LANG, A. RADTKE, C. LIU, G. C. SOTIROPOULOS, M. HINDENNACH, T. SCHROEDER, H.-O. PEITGEN, and C. E. BROELSCH. Improved assessment of functional resectability in repeated hepatectomy by computer-assisted operation planning. Hepatogastroenterology, 52:1645–1648, 2005b.

T. LANGE, S. EULENSTEIN, M. HÜNERBEIN, H. LAMECKER, and P. M. SCHLAG. Augmenting intraoperative 3D ultrasound with pre-operative models for navigation in liver surgery. In Proc. of Medical Image Computing and Computer-Assisted Intervention (MICCAI), volume 3217 of Lecture Notes in Computer Science, pp. 534–541, 2004.

T. LANGE, S. EULENSTEIN, M. HÜNERBEIN, and P.-M. SCHLAG. Vessel-based non-rigid registration of MRI/CT and 3D ultrasound for navigation in liver surgery. Computer Aided Surgery, 8(5):228–240, 2002.

D. Laur and P. Hanrahan. Hierarchical splatting: a progressive refinement algorithm for volume rendering. In *Proc. of ACM SIGGRAPH*, pp. 285–288, 1991.

P. C. Lauterbur. Image formation by induced local interactions: examples employing nuclear magnetic resonance. *Nature*, 242:190–191, 1973.

S. D. Laycock and A. M. Day. Recent developments and applications of haptic devices. *Computer Graphics Forum*, 22(2):117–132, 2003a.

S. D. Laycock and A. M. Day. The haptic rendering of polygonal models involving deformable tools. In I. Oakley, S. O'Modhrain, and F. Newell, editors, *Proc. of EuroHaptics*, pp. 176–192, 2003b.

D. Le Bihan, E. Breton, D. Lallemand, P. Grenier, E. Cabanis, and M. Laval-Jeanetet. MRI imaging of intravoxel incoherent motions: application to diffusion and perfusion in neurologic disorders. *Radiology*, 161:401–407, 1986.

D. Le Bihan, J.-F. Mangin, C. Poupon, C. A. Clark, S. Pappata, N. Molko, and H. Chabriat. diffusion tensor imaging: concepts and applications. *Journal of Magnetic Resonance Imaging*, 13:534–546, 2001.

V. S. Lee, G. R. Morgan, L. W. Teperman, D. John, T. Diflo, P. V. Pandharipande, *et al.* MRI imaging as the sole preoperative imaging modality for right hepatectomy: a prospective study of living adult-to-adult liver donor candidates. *American Journal of Radiolgy*, 176:1475–1482, 2001.

W. W. Lee and D. L. Owens. *Multimedia-Based Instructional Design: Computer-Based Training, Web-Based Training, and Distance Learning*. Jossey-Bass/Pfeiffer, a Wiley Company, 2000.

H. Lefkovitz and G. Herman. The design and evaluation of color scales for image data. *Computer Graphics and Applications*, 12(1):82–89, 1992.

T. Lehmann, W. Oberschelp, E. Pelikan, and R. Repges. *Bildverarbeitung für die Medizin: Grundlagen, Modelle, Methoden, Anwendungen*. Springer, Heidelberg, Germany, 1997a.

T. Lehmann, C. Gönner, and K. Spitzer. Survey: interpolation methods in medical image processing. *IEEE Transactions on Medical Imaging*, 18(11):1049–Â–1075, 1999.

T. Lehmann, C. Gönner, and K. Spitzer. Addendum: spline interpolation in medical image processing. *IEEE Transactions on Medical Imaging*, 20(7):660–Â–665, 2001.

T. Lehmann, J. Bredno, and K. Spitzer. On the design of active contours for medical image segmentation: a scheme for classification and construction. *Methods of Information in Medicine*, 1:89–98, 2003.

T. Lei, J. K. Udupa, P. K. Saha, and D. Odhner. Artery-vein separation via MRA—an image processing approach. *IEEE Transactions on Medical Imaging*, 20(8):689–703, 2001.

B. Lelieveldt, A. Frangi, S. Mitchell, H. van Assen, S. Ordas, J. Reiber, and M. Sonka. "3D Active Shapes and Appearance Models in Cardiac Image Analysis," chapter in *The Handbook of Mathematical Models in Computer Vision*. Springer, 2005.

V. Lepetit and M. Berger. A semi-automatic method for resolving occlusion in augmented reality. In *Proc. of the IEEE Conference on Computer Vision and Pattern Recognition*, 2000.

H. Levkowitz. *Color Theory and Modeling for Computer Graphics, Visualization, and Multimedia Applications*. Kluwer Academic Publishers, 1997.

H. Levkowitz and G. T. Herman. The design and evaluation of color scales for image data. *Computer Graphics and Applications*, 12(1):72–80, 1992.

M. Levoy. Display of surfaces from volume data. *IEEE Computer Graphics and Applications*, 8(3):29–37, 1988.

M. Levoy. A hybrid ray tracer for rendering polygon and volume data. *IEEE Computer Graphics and Applications*, 2(4):33–40, 1990a.

M. Levoy. Effcient ray tracing of volume data. *ACM Transactions on Graphics*, 9(3):245–261, 1990b.

M. Levoy. Volume rendering by adaptive refinement. *The Visual Computer*, 6(1):2–7, 1990c.

M. Levoy, H. Fuchs, S. M. Pizer, J. Rosenman, E. L. Chaney, G. W. Sherouse, V. Interrante, and J. Kiel. Volume rendering in radiation treatment planning. In *Proc. of Visualization in Biomedical Computing*, pp. 4–10, May 1990.

M. Levoy and R. Whitaker. Gaze-directed volume rendering. In *Proc. of ACM Symposium on Interactive 3D Graphics*, pp. 217–223, 1990.

S.-K. Liao, J. Z. C. La, and Y.-C. Chung. A differential volume rendering method with second-order differences for time-varying volume data. *Journal of Visual Languages and Computing*, 14(3):233–254, 2003.

S.-K. Liao, J. Z. C. La, and Y.-C. Chung. Time-critical rendering for time-varying volume data. *Computers & Graphics*, 28:279–288, 2004.

M. Lin and S. Gottschalk. Collision detection between geometric models: a survey. In *Proceedings of IMA Conference on Mathematics of Surfaces*, 1998.

W. C. Lin and S. Y. Chen. A new surface interpolation technique for reconstructing 3D objects from serial cross-sections. *Computer Vision, Graphics, and Image Processing*, 48:124–143, 1989.

C. Lindstroem, P. Ljung, and A. Ynnerman. Extending and simplifying transfer function design in medical volume rendering using local histograms. In *Data Visualization (Proc. of Eurographics/IEEE Symposium on Visualization)*, pp. 263–270, 2005.

C. Lindstroem, A. Ynnerman, P. Ljung, A. Persson, and H. Knutsson. The alpha-histogram: using spatial coherence to enhance histograms and transfer function design. In *Data Visualization (Proc. of Eurographics/IEEE Symposium on Visualization)*, pp. 227–234, 2006.

A. Littmann, A. Schenk, B. Preim, G. Prause, K. Lehmann, A. Roggan, and H.-O. Peitgen. Planning of anatomical resections and in situ ablations in oncologic liver surgery. In *Proc. of Computer Assisted Radiology and Surgery*, pp. 684–689, 2003.

Y. Livnat, H. Shen, and C. Johnson. A near optimal isosurface extraction algorithm using the span space. *IEEE Transactions on Visualization and Computer Graphics*, 2(1):73–84, 1996.

J. Lluch, R. Vivó, and C. Monserrat. Modeling tree structures using a single polygonal mesh. *Graphical Models*, 66(2):89–101, 2004.

G. Lohmann. *Volumetric Image Analysis*. Wiley & Teubner, 1998.

S. Lok, S. K. Feiner, and G. Ngai. Evaluation of visual balance for automated layout. In *Intelligent User Interfaces*, pp. 101–108, 2004.

W. E. Lorensen and H. E. Cline. Marching Cubes: a high resolution 3D surface construction algorithm. In *Proc. of ACM SIGGRAPH*, pp. 163–169, 1987.

W. E. Lorenson. Geometric clipping using boolean textures. In *Proc. of IEEE Visualization*, pp. 268–274, 1993.

C. Lorenz, T. C. Carlssen, T. M. Buzug, C. Fassnacht, and J. Weese. Multiscale line segmentation with automatic estimation of width, contrast, and tangential direction in 2D/3D medical images. In *Proc. of CVRMed/MRCAS*, volume 1205 of *Lecture Notes in Computer Science*, pp. 233–242, 1997.

C. Lorenz and N. Krahnstöver. 3D statistical shape models for medical image segmentation. In *Second International Conference on 3D Imaging and Modeling*, pp. 414–423, 1999.

O. Louis, R. Luypaert, W. Kalender, and M. Osteaux. Reproducibility of CT bone densitometry: operator versus automated ROI definition. *European Journal of Radiology*, 8(2):82–84, 1988.

A. Lu, C. J. Morris, D. S. Ebert, P. Rheingans, and C. Hansen. Non-photorealistic volume rendering using stippling techniques. In *Proc. of IEEE Visualization*, pp. 211–218, 2002.

A. Lu, C. J. Morris, D. S. Ebert, P. Rheingans, and C. Hansen. Illustrative interactive stipple rendering. *IEEE Transactions on Visualization and Computer Graphics*, 9(2):1–12, 2003.

B. LUCAS, G. D. ABRAM, N. S. COLLINS, D. A. EPSTEIN, D. L. GRESH, and K. P. MCAULIFFE. An architecture for a scientific visualization system. In *Proc. of IEEE Visualization*, pp. 107–114, 1992.

D. LUEBCKE, M. REDDY, J. COHEN, A. VARSHNEY, B. WATSON, and R. HUEBNER. *Level of Detail for 3D Graphics*. San Francisco, California: Morgan Kaufmann, 2004.

A. LUFT, M. SKALEJ, D. WELTE, R. KOLB, K. BURK, J. SCHULZ, T. KLOCKGETHER, and K. VOIGT. A new semi-automated, three-dimensional technique allowing precise quantification of total and regional cerebellar volume using MRI. *Magnetic Resonance in Medicine*, 40(1):143–151, 1998.

E. LUM and K.-L. MA. Non-photorealistic rendering using watercolor inspired textures and illumination. In *Proc. of Pacific Graphics*, pp. 322–330, 2001.

E. B. LUM, A. STOMPEL, and K. L. MA. Kinetic visualization: a technique for illustrating 3D shape and structure. In *Proc. of IEEE Visualization*, pp. 435–442, 2002.

C. LÜRIG, P. HASTREITER, C. NIMSKY, and T. ERTL. Analysis and visualization of the brain shift phenomenon in neurosurgery. In *Data Visualization (Proc. of Eurographics/IEEE Symposium on Visualization)*, pp. 285–289, 1999.

J. T. LURITO, M. J LOWE, C. SARTORIUS, and V. P. MATTHEWS. Comparison of fMRI and intraoperative direct cortical stimulation in localization of receptive language areas. *Journal of Computer Assisted Tomography*, 24(1):99–105, 2000.

M. LYSAKER, A. LUNDERVOLD, and X. C. TAI. Noise removal using fourth-order partial differential equation with applications to medical magnetic resonance images in space and time. *IEEE Transactions on Image Processing*, 12(12):1579–1590, 2003.

H. MAASS, B. CHANTIER, H. K. ÇAKMAK, and U. KÜHNAPFEL. How to add force feedback to a surgery simulator. In *International Symposium on Surgery Simulation and Soft Tissue Modeling*, volume 2673 of *Lecture Notes in Computer Science*, pp. 165–174, 2003.

H. MAASS and U. KÜHNAPFEL. Noninvasive measurement of elastic properties of living tissue. In *Proc. of Computer Assisted Radiology and Surgery*, pp. 865–870, 1999.

R. MACHIRAJU and R. YAGEL. Efficient feed-forward volume rendering techniques for vector and parallel processors. In *Proc. of Supercomputing*, pp. 699–708, 1993.

R. MACHIRAJU and R. YAGEL. Reconstruction error characterization and control: a sampling theory approach. *IEEE Transactions on Visualization and Computer Graphics*, 2(4):364–378, 1996.

A. MACOVSKI. Noise in MRI. *Magnetic Resonance Medicine*, 36(3):494–497, 1996.

M. MADDAH, K. H. ZOU, W. M. WELLS III, R. KIKINIS, and S. K.WARFIELD. Automatic optimization of segmentation algorithms through simultaneous truth and performance level estimation (staple). In *Proc. of Medical Image Computing and Computer-Assisted Intervention (MICCAI)*, volume 3216 of *Lecture Notes in Computer Science*, pp. 274–282, 2004.

F. MAES, A. COLLIGNON, D. VANDERMEULEN, G. MARECHAL, and P. SUETENS. Multimodality image registration by maximization of mutual information. *IEEE Transactions on Medical Imaging*, 16(2):187–198, 1997a.

F. MAES, D. VANDERMEULEN, G. MARCHAL, and P. SUETENS. Fast multimodality image registration using multiresolution gradient-based maximization of mutual information. In *Proc. of Image Registration Workshop*, pp. 191–200, Greenbelt, Maryland, USA, 1997b.

J. MAINTZ and M. VIERGEVER. A survey of medical image registration. *Medical Image Analysis*, 2(1):1–36, 1998.

S. MALIK, C. MCDONALD, and G. ROTH. Hand tracking for interactive pattern-based augmented reality. In *Proc. of IEEE and ACM International Symposium on Mixed and Augmented Reality*, 2002.

T. MALZBENDER. Fourier volume rendering. *ACM Transactions on Graphics*, 12 (3):233–250, 1993.

H. MAMATA, Y. MAMATA, C.-F. WESTIN, M. E. SHENTON, R. KIKINIS, F. A. JOLESZ, and S. E. MAIER. High-resolution line scan diffusion tensor MRI imaging of white matter fiber tract anatomy. *American Journal of Neuroradiology*, 23:67–75, 2002.

P. MANSFIELD. Multi-planar image formation using NMR spin echos. *J Physics C: Solid State*, 10:55–58, 1977.

X. MAO, L. HONG, and A. KAUFMAN. Splatting of curvilinear volumes. In *Proc. of IEEE Visualization*, pp. 61–68, 1995.

L. MARKOSIAN, M. A. KOWALSKI, S. J. TRYCHIN, L. D. BOURDEV, D. GOLDSTEIN, and J. F. HUGHES. Real-time nonphotorealistic rendering. In *Proc. of ACM SIGGRAPH*, pp. 415–420, 1997.

J. MARKS, B. ANDALMAN, P. A. BEARDSLEY, W. FREEMAN, S. GIBSON, J. HODGINS T. KANG, B. MIRTICH, H. PFISTER, W. RUML, K. RYALL, J. SEIMS, and S. SHIEBER. Design galleries: a general approach to setting parameters for computer graphics and animation. In *Proc. of ACM SIGGRAPH*, pp. 389–400, 1997.

B. MARRO, D. GALANAUD, C. VALERY, A. ZOUAOUI, A. BIONDI, A. CASASCO, M. SAHEL, and C. MARSAULT. Intracranial aneurysm: inner view and neck identification with CT angiography virtual endoscopy. *Journal of Computer Assisted Tomography*, 21(4):587–589, 1997.

S. MARSCHNER and R. LOBB. An evaluation of reconstruction filters for volume rendering. In *Proc. of IEEE Visualization*, pp. 100–107, 1994.

M. E. MARTINEZ-PEREZ, A. D. HUGHES, A. V. STANTON, S. A. THOM, N. CHAPMAN, A. A. BAHRATH, and K. H. PARKER. Geometrical and morphological analysis of vascular branches from fundus retinal images. In *Proc. of Medical Image Computing and Computer-Assisted Intervention (MICCAI)*, volume 1935 of *Lecture Notes in Computer Science*, pp. 756–765, 2000.

A. H. MASON, M. A. WALJI, E. J. LEE, and C. L. MACKENZIE. Reaching movements to augmented and graphic objects in virtual environments. In *Proc. of the SIGCHI Conference on Human Factors in Computing Systems*, pp. 426–433, 2001.

T. M. MASSIE and J. K. SALISBURY. The phantom haptic device: a device for probing virtual objects. In *Proc. of ASME Haptic Interface for Virtual Environment and Teleoperator Systems*, pp. 295–301, 1994.

Y. MASUTANI, K. MASAMUNE, and T. DOHI. Region-growing-based feature extraction algorithm for tree-like objects. In *Proc. of Visualization in Biomedical Computing*, volume 1131 of *Lecture Notes in Computer Science*, pp. 161–171, 1996.

N. MAX. Optical models for direct volume rendering. *IEEE Transactions on Visualization and Computer Graphics*, 1(2):99–108, 1995.

D. MAYER, D. BARTZ, J. FISCHER, S. LEY, A. DEL RÍO, S. THUST, H. KAUCZOR, W. STRAßER, and C. HEUSSEL. Hybrid segmentation and virtual bronchoscopy based on CT images. *Academic Radiology*, 11(5): 551–565, 2004.

A. MAZZIOTTI and CAVALLARI. *Techniques in Liver Surgery*. Greenwich Medical Media, 1997.

B. H. MCCORMICK, T. A. DEFANTI, and M. D. BROWN. Visualization in scientific computing. *Computer Graphics*, 21(6):1–14, 1987.

T. MCINERNEY and D. TERZOPOULOS. Deformable models in medical image analysis: a survey. *Medical Image Analysis*, 1(2):91–108, 1996.

W. A. MCNEELY, K. D. PUTERBAUGH, and J. J. TROY. Six degree-of- freedom haptic rendering using voxel sampling. In *Proc. of ACM SIGGRAPH*, pp. 401–408, 1999.

E. R. MCVEIGH and M. J. BRONSKILL. Noise and filtration in MRI imaging. *Medical Physics*, 12(5):586–591, 1985.

A. J. MEGIBOW. Three-d offers workflow gains, new diagnostic options. *Diagnostic Imaging*, pp. 83–93, November 2002.

A. MEHRABI, C. GLÜCKSTEIN, A. BENNER, B. HASHEMI, C. HERFARTH, and F. KALINOWSKI. A new way for surgical education-development and evaluation of a computer-based training module. *Computers in Biology and Medicine*, 30:97–109, 2000.

H. MEIRE, D. COSGROVE, K. DEWBURY, and P. WILDE, editors. *Clinical Ultrasound: A Comprehensive Text*, volume 1, 2nd ed. Edinburgh: Churchill Livingstone, 1993.

M. MEIßNER, U. HOFFMANN, and W. STRAßER. Enabling classification and shading for 3D texture mapping based volume rendering using OpenGL and extensions. In *Proc. of IEEE Visualization*, pp. 207–214, 1999.

M. MEIßNER, J. HUANG, D. BARTZ, K. MUELLER, and R. CRAWFIS. A practical evaluation of four popular volume rendering algorithms. In *Proc. of IEEE/ACM Symposium on Volume Visualization and Graphics*, pp. 81–90, 2000.

M. MEIßNER, U. KANUS, and W. STRAßER. VIZARD II: a PCI-card for real-time volume rendering. In *Proc. of Eurographics/SIGGRAPH Workshop on Graphics Hardware*, pp. 61–68, 1998.

M. MEIßNER, U. KANUS, G. WETEKAM, J. HIRCHE, A. EHLERT, W. STRAßER, M. DOGGETT, P. FORTHMANN, and R. PROKSA. VIZARD II: a reconfigurable interactive volume rendering system. In *Proc. of Eurographics/SIGGRAPH Workshop on Graphics Hardware*, pp. 137–146, 2002.

D. MERHOF, F. ENDERS, F. V. HIGUERA, P. HASTREITER, C. NIMSKY, and M. STAMMINGER. Non-linear integration of DTI-based fiber tracts into standard 3D MRI data. In *Vision, Modelling and Visualization (VMV)*, pp. 371–378, 2004.

D. MERHOF, F. ENDERS, F. V. HIGUERA, P. HASTREITER, C. NIMSKY, and M. STAMMINGER. Integrated visualization of diffusion tensor fiber tracts and anatomical data. In *Simulation and Visualization*, pp. 153–164, 2005a.

D. MERHOF, M. SONNTAG, F. ENDERS, V. P. HASTREITER, R. FAHLBUSCH, C. NIMSKY, and G. GREINER. Visualization of diffusion tensor data using evenly spaced streamlines. In *Vision, Modelling and Visualization (VMV)*, pp. 79–86, 2005b.

D. MERHOF, M. SONNTAG, F. ENDERS, C. NIMSKY, P. HASTREITER, and G. GREINER. Streamline visualization of diffusion tensor data based on triangle strips. In *Proc. of Workshop Bildverarbeitung für die Medizin*, Informatik aktuell, pp. 271–275, 2006.

S. MEYER, M. MÜLLER-SCHIMPFLE, H. JÜRGENS, and H.-O. PEITGEN. MT-DYNA: computer assistance for the evaluation of dynamic MRI and CT data in a clinical environment. In *Proc. of Computer Assisted Radiology and Surgery*, pp. 331–334, 1999.

A. B. MILLER, B. HOOGSTRATEN, M. STAQUET, and A. WINKLER. Reporting results of cancer treatment. *Cancer*, 47(5):207–214, 2000.

S. MILLER, editor. *Cardiac Imaging: The Requisites*, 2nd ed. C.V. MOSBY, 2004.

G. S. MINTZ, S. E. NISSEN, W. D. ANDERSON, S. R. BAILEY, R. ERBEL, P. J. FITZGERALD, et al. *American College of Cardiology Clinical Expert Consensus Document on Standards for Acquisition, Measurement, and Reporting of Intravascular Ultrasound Studies (IVUS). A report of the American College of Cardiology Task Force on Clinical Expert Consensus Documents. Journal of American College of Cardiology*, 37:1478–1492, 2001.

S. C. MITCHELL, J. G. BOSCH, J. H. C. REIBER, BOUDEWIJN, P. F. LELIEVELDT, R. J. VAN DER GEEST, and M. SONKA. 3D active appearance models: segmentation of cardiac MRI and ultrasound images. *IEEE Transactions on Medical Imaging*, 21(9):1167–1178, 2002.

M. MLEJNEK, P. ERMES, A. VILANOVA, R. VAN DER RIJT, H. VAN DEN BOSCH, F. GERRITSEN, and M. E. GRÖLLER. Application-oriented extensions of profile flags. In *Data Visualization (Proc. of Eurographics/IEEE Symposium on Visualization)*, pp. 339–346, 2006.

B. MOBERTS. *Hierarchical visualization using fiber clustering*. Master's thesis, Dept. of Mathematics and Computer Science, Technische Universiteit Eindhoven, 2005.

B. MOBERTS, A. VILANOVA, and J. VAN WIJK. Evaluation of fiber clustering methods for diffusion tensor imaging. In IEEE Visualization, pp. 65–72, 2005.

J. MODERSITZKI. Numerical Methods for Image Registration. Oxford University Press, 2004.

T. MÖLLER, R. MACHIRAJU, K. MUELLER, and R. YAGEL. A comparison of normal estimation schemes. In Proc. of IEEE Visualization, pp. 19–26, 1997.

E. MONIZ. Die zerebrale Arteriographie und Phlebographie. Springer, Berlin, 1940.

B. MORA, J. JESSEL, and R. CAUBET. A new object-order ray-casting algorithm. In Proc. of IEEE Visualization, pp. 203–210, 2002.

S. MORI and P. B. BARKER. Diffusion magnetic resonance imaging: its principle and applications. The Anatomical Record, 257(3):102–109, June 1999.

C. MOROSI, G. BALLARDINI, and P. PISANI. Diagnostic accuracy of the double-contrast enema for colonic polyps in patients with or without diverticular disease. Gastrointestinal Radiology, 16:346–347, 1991.

C. J. MORRIS and D. EBERT. Direct volume rendering of photographic volumes using multi-dimensional color-based transfer functions. In Data Visualization (Proc. of Eurographics/IEEE Symposium on Visualization), pp. 115–124, 2002.

D. F. MORRISON. Multivariate Statistical Methods, 4th ed. Thomson Brooks/Cole, 2005.

E. N. MORTENSEN, B. S. MORSE, W. A. BARRETT, and J. K. UPUDA. Adaptive boundary detection using live-wire two-dimensional dynamic programming. IEEE Computers in Cardiology, pp. 635–638, 1992.

MRI-TIP. Magnetic Resonance Technology Information Portal. www.mrtip − com/, accessed 2005.

K. MUEHLER, R. BADE, and B. PREIM. Adaptive script-based design of animations for medical education and therapy planning. In Proc. of Medical Image Computing and Computer-Assisted Intervention (MICCAI), volume 4191 of Lecture Notes in Computer Science, pp. 984–991, 2006.

K. MUELLER and R. CRAWFIS. Eliminating popping artifacts in sheet buffer-based splatting. In Proc. of IEEE Visualization, pp. 227–234, 1998.

K. MUELLER, T. MÖLLER, and R. CRAWFIS. Splatting without the blur. In Proc. of IEEE Visualization, pp. 363–371, 1999a.

K. MUELLER, N. SHAREEF, J. HUANG, and R. CRAWFIS. High-quality splatting on rectilinear grids with efficient culling of occluded voxels. IEEE Transactions on Visualization and Computer Graphics, 5(2):116–134, 1999b.

K. MUELLER and R. YAGEL. Fast perspective volume rendering with splatting by utilizing a ray-driven approach. In Proc. of IEEE Visualization, pp. 65–72, 1996.

P. MUKHERJEE, M. M. BAHN, R. C. McKINSTRY, J. S. SHIMONY, T. S. CULL, E. AKBUDAK, et al. Differences between gray matter and white matter water diffusion in stroke: diffusion tensor MRI imaging in 12 patients. Radiology, 215:211–220, 2000.

H. MÜLLER and M. STARK. Approximation of contours in multi-dimensional regular grid data. The Visual Computer, 9(4):182–199, 1993.

D. MUMFORD and J. SHAH. Optimal approximations by piecewise smooth functions and variational problems. Communication on Pure and Applied Mathematics, 42(5):577–685, 1989.

A. NABAVI, P. BLACK, D. GERING, C. WESTIN, V. MEHTA, R. PERGOLIZZI, Jr., M. FERRANT, S. WARFIELD, N. HATA, R. SCHWARTZ, W. WELLS III, R. KIKINIS, and F. JOLESZ. Serial intraoperative magnetic resonance imaging of brain shift. Neurosurgery, 48(4):787–797, 2001.

M. NÄF, G. SZÉKELY, R. KIKINIS, M. SHENTON, and O. KÜBLER. 3D Voronoi skeletons and their usage for the characterization and recognition of 3D organ shape. Computer Vision and Image Understanding, 66:147–161, 1997.

E. NAGEL, N. AL SAADI, and E. FLECK. Cardiovascular magnetic resonance: myocardial perfusion. *Herz*, 25(4):409–416, Jun 2000.

E. NAGEL, C. KLEIN, I. PAETSCH, S. HETTWER, B. SCHNACKENBURG, K. WEGSCHEIDER, and E. FLECK. Magnetic resonance perfusion measurements for the noninvasive detection of coronary artery disease. *Circulation*, 108(4):432–437, July 2003.

Z. NAGY, J. SCHNEIDER, and R. WESTERMANN. Interactive volume illustration. In *Proc. of Vision, Modeling, and Visualization*, pp. 497–504, 2002.

S. NAPEL, G. D. RUBIN, and R. B. JEFFREY. STS-MIP: a new reconstruction technique for CT of the chest. *Journal of Computer Assisted Tomography*, 17(5):832–838, 1993.

B. NATARAJAN. On generating topological consistent isosurfaces from uniform samples. *The Visual Computer*, 11(1):52–62, 1994.

N. NAVAB, A. BANI-HASHEMI, and M. MITSCHKE. Merging visible and invisible: two camera-augmented mobile C-arm (CAMC) applications. In *Proc. of IEEE and ACM International Workshop on Augmented Reality*, pp. 134–141, 1999.

T. R. NELSON and T. T. ELVINS. Visualization of 3D ultrasound data. *Computer Graphics and Applications*, 13(6):50–57, 1993.

N. NEOPHYTOU and K. MUELLER. Space-time points: 4D splatting on efficient grids. In *Proc. of IEEE/ACM Symposium on Volume Visualization and Graphics*, pp. 97–106, 2002.

N. NEOPHYTOU and K. MUELLER. GPU accelerated image aligned splatting. In *Proc. of Volume Graphics*, pp. 197–205, 2005.

N. NEOPHYTOU, K. MUELLER, and K. MCDONNELL. *A Feature-Driven Data Agglutination Approach for Volume Splatting*. Technical Report USB-CS-2006, Department of Computer Science, Stony Brook University, 2006a.

N. NEOPHYTOU, K. MUELLER, K. MCDONNELL, W. HONG, X. GUAN, H. QIN, and A. KAUFMAN. GPU-accelerated volume splatting with elliptical RBFs. In *Data Visualization (Proc. of Eurographics/IEEE Symposium on Visualization)*, pp. 13–20, 2006b.

F. H. NETTER. *Atlas of Human Anatomy*, 8th ed. Ciba Geigy, Summit New Jersey, 1995.

A. NEUBAUER, M. FOSTER, R. WEGENKITTL, L. MROZ, and K. BÜHLER. Efficient display of background objects for virtual endoscopy using flexible first-hit ray casting. In *Data Visualization (Proc. of Eurographics/IEEE Symposium on Visualization)*, pp. 301–310, 2004a.

A. NEUBAUER, L. MROZ, H. HAUSER, and R. WEGENKITTL. Cell-based first-hit ray casting. In *Data Visualization (Proc. of Eurographics/IEEE Symposium on Visualization)*, pp. 77–86, 2002.

A. NEUBAUER, S. WOLFSBERGER, M. FORSTER, L. MROZ, R. WEGENKITTL, and K. BÜHLER. STEPS—an application for simulation of transsphenoidal endonasal pituitary surgery. In *Proc. of IEEE Visualization*, pp. 513–520, 2004b.

A. NEUBAUER. *Virtual Endoscopy for Preoperative Planning and Training of Endonasal Transsphenoidal Pituitary Surgery*. Ph.D. thesis, Institut für Computergraphik und Algorithmen, Technical University of Vienna, 2005.

L. NEUMANN, B. CSABFALVI, A. KÖNIG, and E. GRÖLLER. Gradient estimation in volume data using 4D linear regression. In *Proc. of Eurographics*, pp. 351–357, 2000.

C. W. NIBLACK, P. B. GIBBONS, and D. W. CAPSON. Generating skeletons and centerlines from the distance transform. *Graphics Models and Image Processing*, 54(5):420–437, 1992.

S. NICOLAU, A. GARCIA, X. PENNEC, L. SOLER, and N. AYACHE. An augmented reality system to guide radio-frequency tumour ablation. *Computer Animation and Virtual World*, 16(1):1–10, 2005a.

S. A. NICOLAU, X. PENNEC, L. SOLER, and N. AYACHE. A complete augmented reality guidance system for liver punctures: first clinical evaluation. In J. DUNCAN and G. GERIG, editors, *Proc. of Medical Image*

Computing and Computer-Assisted Intervention (MICCAI), volume 3749 of Lecture Notes in Computer Science, pp. 539–547, 2005b.

G. NIELSON. Dual Marching Cubes. In Proc. of IEEE Visualization, pp. 489–496, 2004.

G. NIELSON and B. HAMANN. The asymptotic decider: removing the ambiguity in Marching Cubes. In Proc. of IEEE Visualization, pp. 83–91, 1991.

H.-W. NIENHUYS and A. F. VAN DER STAPPEN. A surgery simulation supporting cuts and finite element deformation. In Proc. of Medical Image Computing and Computer-Assisted Intervention (MICCAI), volume 2208 of Lecture Notes in Computer Science, pp. 145–152, 2001.

W. J. NIESSEN, A. D. M. VAN SWIHJNDREGT, and B. H. P. ELSMANN. Improved arterial visualization in blood pool agent MRA of the peripheral vasculature. In Proc. of Computer Assisted Radiology and Surgery, pp. 119–123, 1999.

O. NILSSON, D. BREEN, and K. MUSETH. Surface reconstruction via contour metamorphosis: an Eulerian approach with Lagrangian particle tracing. In Proc. of IEEE Visualization, pp. 407–414, 2005.

C. NIMSKY, O. GANSLAND, F. ENDERS, D. MERHOF, T. HAMMEN, and M. BUCHFELDER. Visualization strategies for major white matter tracts for intraoperative use. International Journal of Computer Assisted Radiology and Surgery, 1(1):13–22, 2006.

C. NIMSKY, O. GANSLAND, P. HASTREITER, R. WANG, T. BENNER, A. G. SORENSEN, and R. FAHLBUSCH. Preoperative and intraoperative diffusion tensor imaging-based fiber tracking in glioma surgery. Neurosurgery, 56(1):130–138, 2005a.

C. NIMSKY, O. GANSLANDT, F. ENDERS, D. MERHOF, and R. FAHLBUSCH. Visualization strategies for major white matter tracts identified by diffusion tensor imaging for intraoperative use. In Proc. of Computer Assisted Radiology and Surgery, pp. 793–797, 2005b.

C. NIMSKY, O. GANSLANDT, B. VON KELLER, and R. FAHLBUSCH. Preliminary experience in glioma surgery with intraoperative high-field MRI. Acta Neurochirurgica, 88:21–29, 2003.

H. NISHIMURA, M. HIRAI, T. KAWAI, T. KAWATA, I. SHIRAKAWA, and K. OMURA. Object modeling by distribution function and a method of image generation. The Transactions of the Institute of Electronics and Communication Engineers of Japan, J68-D(4):718–725, 1985.

K. NOVINS, F. SILLION, and D. GREENBERG. An efficient method for volume rendering using perspective projection. In Proc. of San Diego Workshop on Volume Visualization, pp. 95–102, 1990.

H. NYQUIST. Certain factors affecting telegraph speed. Bell System Technical Journal, 3(3):324–346, 1924.

S. OELTZE, F. GROTHUES, A. HENNEMUTH, A. KUß, and B. PREIM. Integrated visualization of morphologic and perfusion data for the analysis of coronary artery disease. In Data Visualization (Proc. of Eurographics/IEEE Symposium on Visualization), pp. 131–138, 2006.

S. OELTZE and B. PREIM. Visualization of vascular structures with convolution surfaces. In Data Visualization (Proc. of Eurographics/IEEE Symposium on Visualization), pp. 311–320, 2004.

S. OELTZE and B. PREIM. Visualization of vascular structures with convolution surfaces: method, validation and evaluation. IEEE Transactions on Medical Imaging, 25(4):540–549, 2005.

R. OHBUCHI, D. CHEN, and H. FUCHS. Incremental volume reconstruction and rendering for 3D ultrasound imaging. In Proc. of Visualization in Biomedical Computing, pp. 312–323, 1992.

S. D. OLABARRIAGA and A. W. M. SMEULDERS. Interaction in the segmentation of medical images: a survey. Medical Image Analysis, 5(2):127–142, 2001.

H. OLAFSDOTTIR, M. B. STEGMANN, and H. B. W. LARSSON. Automatic assessment of cardiac perfusion MRI. In Proc. of Medical Image Computing and Computer-Assisted Intervention (MICCAI), volume 3216 of Lecture Notes in Computer Science, pp. 1060–1061, 2004.

B. OLBRICH, J. TRAUB, S. WIESNER, A. WICHERT, H. FEUßNER, and N. NAVAB. Respiratory motion analysis: towards gated augmentation of the liver. In *Proc. of Computer Assisted Radiology and Surgery*, pp. 248–253, 2005.

H. OOSTERWIJK and P. T. GIHRING. *DICOM Basics*, 2nd ed. Aubrey, TX: OTech Inc., 2002.

A. OPALACH and S. C. MADDOCK. Implicit surfaces: appearance, blending and consistency. In *Proc. of European Workshop on Computer Animation*, pp. 233–245, 1993.

J. O'ROURKE. *Computational Geometry in C*. Cambridge, UK: Cambridge University Press, 1993.

A. OSBORN. *Diagnostic Cerebral Angiography*, 2nd ed. LIPPINCOTT WILLIAMS and WILKINS, a Wolters Kluwer Company, 1999.

N. A. OTSU. A threshold selection method from gray-level histograms. *IEEE Transactions on Systems, Man, and Cybernetics*, 9(1):62–66, 1979.

M. OTTE. Elastic registration of fMRI data using bezier-spline transformations. *IEEE Transactions on Medical Imaging*, 20(2):193–206, 2001.

S. G. OWEN, R. HALL, J. ANDERSON, and G. A. SMART. A comparison of programmed instruction with conventional lectures in the teaching of electrocardiography to final-year medical students. *Journal of Medical Education*, 40(11):1058–1062, 1965.

A. PAETH. A fast algorithm for general raster rotation. In *Proc. of Graphics Interface*, pp. 77–81, 1986.

S. PAJEVIC, A. ALDROUBI, and P. J. BASSER. "Continuous Tensor Field Approximation of Diffusion Tensor MRI Data," Chapter in *Visualization and Processing of Tensor Fields*. Springer, 2005.

S. PAJEVIC and C. PIERPAOLI. Color schemes to represent the orientation of anisotropic tissues from diffusion tensor data: application to white matter fiber tract mapping in the human brain. *Magnetic Resonance in Medicine*, 42(3):526–540, 1999.

K. PALÁGYI and A. KUBA. A parallel 3D 12-subiteration thinning algorithm. *Graphics Models and Image Processing*, 61:199–221, 1999.

H.-J. PARK, M. KUBICKI, C.-F. WESTIN, I.-F. TALOS, A. BRUN, S. PEIPER, R. KIKINIS, F. A. JOLESZ, R. W. MCCARLEY, and M. E. SHENTON. Method for combining information from white matter tracking and gray matter parcellation. *American Journal of Neuroradiology*, 24:1318–1324, September 2004.

J. O. PARK, S. I. LEE, S. Y. SONG, K. KIM, C. W. JUNG, Y. S. PARK, et al. Measuring response in solid tumors: comparison of RECIST and WHO response criteria. *Japanese Journal of Clinical Oncology*, 33(10):533–537, 2003.

K. J. PARK, C. J. BERGIN, and J. L. CLAUSEN. Diagnosis of pulmonary emphysema by computerized tomography. *Lancet*, 211(2):541–547, 1999.

S. PARKER, P. SHIRLEY, Y. LIVNAT, C. HANSEN, and P. SLOAN. Interactive ray tracing for isosurface rendering. In *Proc. of IEEE Visualization*, pp. 233–238, 1998.

S. G. PARKER, D. M. WEINSTEIN, C. R. JOHNSON. The scirun computational steering software system. In *Modern Software Tools for Scientific Computing*, pp. 5–44. Springer, 1997.

O. M. PASTOR and T. STROTHOTTE. Frame-coherent stippling. In *Proc. of Eurographics*, pp. 145–152, 2002.

V. PEKAR, R. WIEMKER, and D. HEMPEL. Fast detection of meaningful isosurfaces for volume data visualization. In *Proc. of IEEE Visualization*, pp. 223–230, 2001.

G. P. PENNEY, J. M. BLACKALL, M. S. HAMADY, T. SABHARWAL, A. ADAM, and D. J. HAWKES. Registration of freehand 3D ultrasound and magnetic resonance liver images. *Medical Image Analysis*, 8(1):81–94, 2004.

P. PERONA and J. MALIK. Scale-space and edge detection using anisotropic diffusion. *IEEE Transactions on Pattern Analysis and Machine Intelligence*, 12(7):629–639, 1990.

A. PETERSIK, B. PFLESSER, U. TIEDE, and K.-H. HÖHNE. Realistic haptic volume interaction for petrous bone surgery simulation. In *Proc. of Computer Assisted Radiology and Surgery*, pp. 252–257, 2002.

H.-P. PFISTER, J. HARDENBERGH, J. KNITTEL, H. LAUER, and L. SEILER. The volumePro real-time ray-casting system. In *Proc. of ACM SIGGRAPH*, pp. 251–260, 1999.

H.-P. PFISTER, B. LORENSEN, C. BAJAJ, G. KINDLMANN, W. SCHROEDER, L. AVILA, K. MARTIN, R. MACHIRAJU, and J. LEE. The transfer function bake-off. *IEEE Computer Graphics and Applications*, 21(3):16–22, 2001.

B. PFLESSER, A. PETERSIK, U. TIEDE, K.-H. HÖHNE, and R. LEUWER. Volume cutting for virtual petrous bone surgery. *Computer Aided Surgery*, 7(2):74–83, 2002.

B.-T. PHONG. Illumination for computer generated pictures. *Communications of the ACM (CACM)*, 18(6): 311–317, 1975.

P. PICKHARDT. Three-dimensional endoluminal CT colonoscopy (virtual colonoscopy): comparison of three commercially available systems. *American Journal of Roentgenology*, 181(6):1599–1606, 2003.

P. PICKHARDT, J. CHOI, I. HWANG, J. BUTLER, M. PUCKETT, H. HILDEBRANDT, R. WONG, P. NUGENT, P. MYSLIWIEC, and W. SCHINDLER. Computed tomographic virtual colonoscopy to screen for colorectal neoplasia in asymptomatic adults. *New England Journal of Medicine*, 349(23):2191–2200, 2003.

C. PIERPAOLI and P. J. BASSER. Toward a quantitative assessment of diffusion anisotropy. *Medical Image Analysis*, 1:893–906, 1996.

K. K. PINGLE. "Visual Perception by a Computer," chapter in *Automatic Interpretation and Classification of Images*, pp. 277–284. New York: Academic Press, 1969.

U. PINKALL and K. POLTHIER. Computing discrete minimal surfaces and their conjugates. *Experimental Mathematics*, 2(1):15–36, 1993.

I. PITT, B. PREIM, and S. SCHLECHTWEG. An evaluation of interaction techniques for the exploration of 3D-illustrations. In U. AREND, E. EBERLEH, and K. PITSCHKE, editors, *Software-Ergonomie'99. Design von Information-swelten*, pp. 275–286, Stuttgart–Leipzig: B. G. Teubner, 1999.

S. M. PIZER. Intensity mappings to linearize display devices. *Computer Graphics and Image Processing*, 17: 262–268, 1981.

S. M. PIZER, P. T. FLETCHER, Y. FRIDMAN, D. S. FRITSCH, A. G. GASH, J. M. GLOTZER, S. JOSHI, A. THALL, G. TRACTON, P. YUSHKEVICH, and E. L. CHANEY. Deformable M-reps for 3D medical image segmentation. *International Journal of Computer Vision*, 55(2–3):85–106, 2003.

S. M. PIZER and J. B. ZIMMERMANN. Color display in ultrasonography. *Ultrasound in Medicine and Biology*, 9(4):331–345, 1983.

R. POHLE and K. D. TÖNNIES. A new approach for model-based adaptive region growing in medical image analysis. In *Proc. of the 9th Int. Conf. on Computer Analysis and Patterns*, pp. 238–246, 2001.

R. POHLE and K. D. TÖNNIES. Self-learning model-based segmentation of medical images. *Image Processing and Communication*, 7(3–4):97–113, 2002.

R. POHLE, M. WEGNER, K. RINK, K. D. TÖNNIES, A. CELLER, and S. BLINDER. Segmentation of the left ventricle in 4D-dSPECT data using free form deformation of super quadrics. In *Proc. of SPIE Medical Imaging*, volume 5370, pp. 1388–1394, 2004.

A. POMMERT. *Simulationsstudien zur Untersuchung der Bildqualität für die 3D-Visualisierung tomografischer Volumendaten*. Ph.D. thesis, School of Computer Science, University of Hamburg, 2004.

A. POMMERT and K. HÖHNE. Validation of medical volume visualization: a literature review. In *Proc. of Computer Assisted Radiology and Surgery*, pp. 571–576, 2003.

A. POMMERT, K.-H. HÖHNE, B. PFLESSER, E. RICHTER, M. RIEMER, T. SCHIEMANN, R. SCHUBERT, U. SCHUMACHER, and U. TIEDE. Creating a high-resolution spatial/symbolic model of the inner organs based on the visible human. *Medical Image Analysis*, 5(3):221–228, 2001.

T. PORTER and T. DUFF. Compositing digital images. In *Proc. of ACM SIGGRAPH*, pp. 253–259, 1984.

C. POYNTON. *Frequently-Asked Questions about Color*. URL: **www.poynton.com/ ColorFAQ.html**, accessed 2006.

W. PRATT. *Digital Image Processing*, 2nd ed. New York: John Wiley and Sons, 1991.

E. PRAUN, H. HOPPE, M. WEBB, and A. FINKELSTEIN. Real-time hatching. In *Proc. of ACM SIGGRAPH*, pp. 579–584, 2001.

J. PREECE, Y. ROGERS, and H. SHARP. *Interaction Design: Beyond Human-Computer Interaction*. Wiley Textbooks, 2001.

B. PREIM, H. BOURQUAIN, D. SELLE, H.-O. PEITGEN, and K. J. OLDHAFER. Resection proposals for oncologic liver surgery based on vascular territories. In *Proc. of Computer Assisted Radiology and Surgery*, pp. 353–358, 2002a.

B. PREIM, R. MICHEL, K. HARTMANN, and T. STROTHOTTE. Figure captions in visual interfaces. In T. CATARCI, M. F. COSTABILE, S. LEVIALDI, and L. TARANTINO, editors, *Advanced Visual Interfaces: An International Workshop*, *AVI*, pp. 235–246, 1998.

B. PREIM and A. RAAB. Annotation topographisch komplizierter 3D-modelle. In *Proc. of Simulation and Visualization*, pp. 128–140, 1998.

B. PREIM, A. RAAB, and T. STROTHOTTE. Coherent zooming of illustrations with 3D-graphics and text. In *Proc. of Graphics Interface*, pp. 105–113, 1997.

B. PREIM, A. RITTER, D. R. FORSEY, L. BARTRAM, T. POHLE, and T. STROTHOTTE. Consistency of rendered images and their textual labels. In *Proc. of CompuGraphics*, pp. 201–210, 1995.

B. PREIM, A. RITTER, and T. STROTHOTTE. Illustrating anatomic models: a semi-interactive approach. In *Proc. of Visualization in Biomedical Computing*, number 1131 in Lecture Notes in Computer Science, pp. 23–32, 1996.

B. PREIM, D. SELLE, W. SPINDLER, K. J. OLDHAFER, and H.-O. PEITGEN. Interaction techniques and vessel analysis for preoperative planning in liver surgery. In *Proc. of Medical Image Computing and Computer-Assisted Intervention (MICCAI)*, volume 1935 of Lecture Notes in Computer Science, pp. 608–617, 2000.

B. PREIM, W. SPINDLER, K. J. OLDHAFER, and H.-O. PEITGEN. 3D-interaction techniques for planning oncologic soft tissue operations. In *Proc. of Graphics Interface*, pp. 183–190, 2001.

B. PREIM, C. TIETJEN, and C. DÖRGE. NPR, focusing and emphasis in medical visualization. In *Proc. of Simulation and Visualization*, pp. 139–152, 2005.

B. PREIM, C. TIETJEN, M. HINDENNACH, and H.-O. PEITGEN. Integration automatischer abstandsberechnungen in die interventions-planung. In *Proc. of Workshop Bildverarbeitung für die Medizin*, Informatik aktuell, pp. 259–263, 2003.

B. PREIM, C. TIETJEN, W. SPINDLER, and H.-O. PEITGEN. Integration of measurement tools in medical visualizations. In *Proc. of IEEE Visualization*, pp. 21–28, 2002b.

W. H. PRESS, S. A. TEUKOLSKY, W. T. VETTERLING, and B. P. FLANNERY. *Numerical Recipes in C*. Cambridge, UK: Cambridge University Press, 1992.

R. R. PRICE. The AAPM/RSNA physics tutorial for residents. Contrast mechanisms in gradient-echo imaging and an introduction to fast imaging. *Radiographics*, 15(1):165–178, 1995.

S. J. PRICE, A. PEIA, N. G. BURNET, R. JENA, H. A. L. GREEN, T. A. CARPENTER, J. D. PICKARD, and J. H. GILLARD. Tissue signature characterisation of diffusion tensor abnormalities in cerebral gliomas. *European Radiology*, 14(10):1909–1917, 2004.

A. PRIESCHING. *Leberresektionen*. München, Germany: Urban and Schwarzenberg, 1986.

S. PROTHMANN, S. PUCCINI, B. DALITZ, A. KÜHN, L. RÖEDEL, C. ZIMMER, and T. KAHN. Präoperatives mapping der sprachareale mittels fMRI bei patienten mit hirntumoren: ein methodenvergleich. *Fortschritte auf dem Gebiet der Röntgenstrahlen und bildgebenden Verfahren*, 177(11):1522–1531, 2005.

A. PUIG, D. TOST, and I. NAVAZO. An interactive cerebral blood vessel exploration system. In *Proc. of IEEE Visualization*, pp. 443–446, 1997.

T. PURCELL, I. BUCK, W. MARK, and P. HANRAHAN. Ray tracing on programmable graphics hardware. In *Proc. of ACM SIGGRAPH*, pp. 703–712, 2002.

A. S. QI, X. ZHENG, C. Y. DU, and B. S. AN. A cellular automaton model of cancerous growth. *Journal of Theoretical Biology*, 161(7):1–12, 1993.

Z. QIAN, X. HUANG, D. METAXAS, and L. AXEL. Robust segmentation of 4D cardiac MRI-tagged images via spatio-temporal propagation. In *Proc. of SPIE Medical Imaging*, volume 5746, pp. 580–591, 2005.

F. K. H. QUEK and C. KIRBAS. Vessel extraction in medical images by wave propagation and traceback. *IEEE Transactions on Medical Imaging*, 20(2):117–131, 2001.

S. QUINLAN. Efficient distance computation between non-convex objects. In *IEEE International Conference on Robotics and Automation*, pp. 3324–3329, 1994.

A. RADETZKY, A. NÜRNBERGER, and D. P. PRETSCHNER. Elastodynamic shape modeler: a tool for defining the deformation behavior of virtual tissues. *Radiographics*, 20:865–881, 2000.

J. RADON. Über die Bestimmung von Funktionen durch ihre Integralwerte längs gewisser Mannigfaltigkeiten. *Berichte Sächsische Akademie der Wissenschaften, Math.-Phys. Kl.*, 69:262–267, 1917.

A. RADTKE, T. SCHROEDER, G. C. SOTIROPOULOS, E. MOLMENTI, A. SCHENK, A. PAUL, S. NADALIN, H. LANG, F. SANER, H.-O. PEITGEN, C. E. BROELSCH, and M. MALAGO. Anatomical and physiological classification of hepatic vein dominance applied to liver transplantation. *European Journal of Medical Research*, 10(5): 187–194, 2005.

S. RAIA, J. R. NERY, S. MIES, et al. Liver transplantation from live donors. *Lancet*, pp. 497–498, 1989.

G. RAMACHANDRAN and A. LAKSHMINARAYANAN. Three-dimensional reconstruction from radiographs and electron micrographs: application of convolutions instead of fourier transforms. *Proc. of the National Academic of Scienceo of the United States of America*, 68(9):2236–2240, 1971.

R. RASKAR and M. COHEN. Image precision silhouette edges. In S. N. SPENCER, editor, *Proc. of ACM Symposium on Interactive 3D Graphics*, pp. 135–140, 1999.

R. RAU, D. WEISKOPF, and H. RUDER. Special relativity in virtual reality. In *Proc. of Mathematical Visualization*, pp. 269–279, 1998.

G. REINA, K. BIDMON, F. ENDERS, P. HASTREITER, and T. ERTL. GPU-based hyperstreamlines for diffusion tensor imaging. In *Data Visualization (IEEE/Eurographics Symposium on Visualization)*, pp. 35–42, 2006.

F. REINDERS, M. JACOBSON, F. POST, and E. ASSOCIATION. Skeleton graph generation for feature shape description. In *Data Visualization (Proc. of Eurographics/IEEE Symposium on Visualization)*, pp. 73–82, 2000.

J. REXILIUS, J. JOMIER, W. SPINDLER, F. LINK, M. KÖNIG, and H.-O. PEITGEN. Combining a visual programming and rapid prototyping platform with ITK. In *Proc. of Workshop Bildverarbeitung für die Medizin*, Informatik aktuell, pp. 460–464, 2005.

C. REZK-SALAMA. *Volume Rendering Techniques for General Purpose Graphics Hardware*. Ph.D. thesis, Technische Fakultät, University Erlangen-Nürnberg, 2002.

C. REZK-SALAMA, K. ENGEL, M. BAUER, G. GREINER, and T. ERTL. Interactive volume rendering on standard PC graphics hardware using multi-textures and multi-stage rasterization. In *Proc. of Eurographics/SIGGRAPH Workshop on Graphics Hardware*, pp. 109–118, 2000a.

C. REZK-SALAMA, P. HASTREITER, J. SCHERER, and G. GREINER. Automatic adjustment of transfer functions for direct volume rendering. In *Proc. of Vision, Modeling, and Visualization*, pp. 357–364, 2000b.

C. REZK-SALAMA, S. ISERHARDT-BAUER, P. HASTREITER, J. SCHERER, K. EBERHARDT, B. F. TOMANDL, G. GREINER, and T. ERTL. *Automated 3D Visualization and Documentation for the Analysis of Tomographic Data*. Technical Report, Department for Computer Science, Friedrich-Alexander University Erlangen-Nürnberg, July 2000c.

P. RHEINGANS. Color, change, and control for quantitative data display. In *Proc. of IEEE Visualization*, pp. 252–259, 1992.

P. RHEINGANS. Task-based color scale design. In *Proc. of Applied Image and Pattern Recognition*, pp. 35–43, 1999.

P. RHEINGANS and D. EBERT. Volume illustration: nonphotorealistic rendering of volume models. *IEEE Transactions on Visualization and Computer Graphics*, 7(3):253–264, 2001.

M. RICHTSCHEID, M. GRIMM, and G. SAKAS. "Free hand Scanning for Precordial Data Acquisition in Three-Dimensional Echocardiography," chapter in *Three-Dimensional Echocardiography of the Heart and Coronary Arteries*, pp. 31–35, 1999.

F. RITTER, B. BERENDT, B. FISCHER, R. RICHTER, and B. PREIM. Virtual 3D jigsaw puzzles: studying the effect of exploring spatial relations with implicit guidance. In *Mensch & Computer 2002*, pp. 363–372, 2002.

F. RITTER, O. DEUSSEN, B. PREIM, and T. STROTHOTTE. Virtual 3D puzzles: a new method for exploring geometric models in VR. *IEEE Computer Graphics and Applications*, 21(5):11–13, Sept 2001.

F. RITTER, C. HANSEN, B. PREIM, V. DICKEN, and O. KONRAD-VERSE. Real-time illustration of vascular structures for surgery. *IEEE Transactions on Visualization and Computer Graphics*, 12, 2006.

F. RITTER, B. PREIM, O. DEUSSEN, and T. STROTHOTTE. Using a 3D puzzle as a metaphor for learning spatial relations. In *Proc. of Graphics Interface*, pp. 171–178, 2000.

P. K. ROBERTSON and J. F. O'CALLAGHAN. The generation of color sequences for univariate and bivariate mapping. *Computer Graphics and Applications*, 6(2):24–32, 1986.

A. ROCHE, G. MALANDAIN, N. AYACHE, and S. PRIMA. Towards a better comprehension of similarity measures used in medical image registration. In *Proc. of Medical Image Computing and Computer-Assisted Intervention (MICCAI)*, volume 1679 of *Lecture Notes in Computer Science*, pp. 555–566, 1999.

P. ROGALLA. Virtual endoscopy: an application snapshot. *Medica Mundi*, 43(1):17–23, 1999.

P. ROGALLA, J. T. VAN SCHELTINGA, and B. HAMM. *Virtual Endoscopy and Related 3D Techniques*. Heidelberg: Springer-Verlag, 2000.

B. ROGOWITZ and A. D. KALVIN. The "Which Blair Project": a quick visual method for evaluating perceptual color maps. In *Proc. of IEEE Visualization*, pp. 183–190, 2001.

B. ROGOWITZ, L. TREINISH, and S. BRYSON. How not to lie with visualization. *Computers in Physics*, 10(3): 268–274, 1996.

T. ROHLFING, C. R. MAURER, Jr., D. A. BLUEMKE, and M. A. JACOBS. Volume-preserving non-rigid registration of MRI breast images using free-form deformation with an incompressibility constraint. *IEEE Transactions on Medical Imaging*, 22(6): 730–741, 2003.

K. ROHR. *Landmark-Based Image Analysis*. Kluwer Academic Publishers, 2001.

W. RÖNTGEN. Über eine neue Art von Strahlen (vorläufige Mitteilung). *Sitzungsberichte der physikalisch-medizinischen Gesellschaft zu Würzburg*, pp. 132–141, 1895.

T. ROPINSKI, F. STEINICKE, and K. HINRICHS. Interactive importance-driven visualization techniques for medical volume data. In *Proc. of Vision, Modeling, and Visualization*, pp. 273–280, 2005.

C. ROSSE, L. G. SHAPIRO, and J. F. BRINKLEY. The digital anatomist foundational model: principles for defining and structuring its concept domain. In *Proc. of American Medical Informatics Association Fall Symposium*, pp. 820–824, 1998.

C. RÖSSL, L. KOBBELT, and H.-P. SEIDEL. Extraction of feature lines on triangulated surfaces using morphological operators. In *Smart Graphics, Proceedings of the 2000 AAAI Symposium*, pp. 71–75, 2000a.

C. RÖSSL, L. KOBBELT, and H.-P. SEIDEL. Line art rendering of triangulated surfaces using discrete lines of curvature. In *Proc. of WSCG*, pp. 168–175, 2000b.

M. B. ROSSON and J. CARROL. *Usability Engineering: Scenario-Based Development of Human-Computer Interaction*. Morgan Kaufmann, 2001.

S. RÖTTGER, S. GUTHE, D. WEISKOPF, T. ERTL, and W. STRAßER. Smart hardware-accelerated volume rendering. In *Data Visualization (Proc. of Eurographics/IEEE Symposium on Visualization)*, pp. 103–108, 2003.

S. RÖTTGER, M. BAUER, and M. STAMMINGER. Spatialized transfer functions. In *Data Visualization (Proc. of Eurographics/IEEE Symposium on Visualization)*, pp. 271–278, 2005.

F. ROUX, D. IBARROLA, M. TREMOULET, Y. LAZORTHES, P. HENRY, J. SOL, and I. BERRY. Methodological and technical issues for integrating functional magnetic resonance imaging data in a neuronavigational system. *Neurosurgery*, 49(5): 1145–1156, 2001.

D. RUECKERT, L. I. SONODA, C. HAYES, D. L. G. HILL, M. O. LEACH, and D. J. HAWKES. Nonrigid registration using free-form deformations: application to breast MR images. *IEEE Transactions on Medical Imaging*, 18(8):712–721, 1999.

J. RUIZ-ALZOLA, C. F. WESTIN, S. K. WARFIELD, C. ALBEROLA, S. MAIER, and R. KIKINIS. Nonrigid registration of 3D tensor medical data. In *Medical Image Analysis*, volume 6, pp. 143–161, 2002.

E. J. RUMMENY, P. REIMER, and W. HEINDEL, editors. *Ganzkörper MRI-Tomographie*. Thieme, 2002.

G. J. M. RUTTEN, N. F. RAMSEY, P. C. VAN RIJEN, H. J. NOORDMANS, and C. W. M. VAN VEELEN. Development of a functional magnetic resonance imaging protocol for intraoperative localization of critical temporoparietal language areas. *Annals of Neurology*, 51(3):350–360, 2002.

P. SABELLA. A rendering algorithm for visualizing 3D scalar fields. In *Proc. of ACM SIGGRAPH*, pp. 51–58, 1988.

T. SAITO and T. TAKAHASHI. Comprehensible rendering of 3D shapes. In *Proc. of ACM SIGGRAPH*, pp. 197–206, 1990.

F. SAKAI, G. GAMSU, J. G. IM, and C. S. RAY. Pulmonary function abnormalities in patients with CT-determined emphysema. *Journal of Computer Assisted Tomography*, 11:963–968, 1987.

G. SAKAS, L.-A. SCHREYER, and M. GRIMM. Preprocessing and volume rendering of 3D ultrasonic data. *IEEE Computer Graphics and Applications*, 15(4):47–54, 1995.

G. SAKAS and S. WALTER. Extracting surfaces from fuzzy 3D-ultrasound data. In *Proc. of ACM SIGGRAPH*, pp. 465–474, 1995.

Z. SALAH. *Segmentation and Illustrative Visualization of Medical Data*. Ph.D. thesis, Dept. of Computer Science (WSI), University of Tübingen, 2006.

Z. SALAH, D. BARTZ, E. SCHWADERER, F. DAMMANN, and W. STRAßER. *A Segmentation Pipeline for Robot-Assisted ENT-Surgery*. Technical Report WSI-2003-7, Dept. of Computer Science (WSI), University of Tübingen, Sept 2003.

Z. SALAH, D. BARTZ, and W. STRAßER. *Visual Differentiation of Multiple Objects in Illustrative Visualization*. Technical Report WSI-2005-08, Dept. of Computer Science (WSI), University of Tübingen, 2005a.

Z. SALAH, D. BARTZ, and W. STRAßER. Illustrative rendering of segmented Anatomical Data. In *Proc. of Simulation and Visualization*, pp. 175–184, 2005c.

Z. SALAH, J. ORMAN, and D. BARTZ. Live-wire revisited. In *Proc. of Workshop Bildverarbeitung für die Medizin*, Informatik Aktuell, pp. 158–162, 2005b.

H. SAMET. *The Design and Analysis of Spatial Data Structures*. Reading, MA: Addison-Wesley, 1994.

P. V. SANDER, X. GU, S. J. GORTLER, H. HOPPE, and J. SNYDER. Silhouette clipping. In *Proc. of ACM SIGGRAPH*, pp. 327–334, 2000.

Y. SATO, S. NAKAJIMA, H. ATSUMI, T. KOLLER, G. GERIG, S. YOSHIDA, and R. KIKINS. 3D multi-scale line filter for segmentation and visualization of curvilinear structures in medical images. In *Proc. of CVRMed/MRCAS*, volume 1205 of *Lecture Notes in Computer Science*, pp. 213–222, 1997.

F. SAUER, A. KHAMENE, B. BASCLE, L. SCHIMMANG, F. WENZEL, and S. VOGT. Augmented reality visualization of ultrasound images: system description, calibration, and feature. In *Proc. of IEEE and ACM International Workshop on Augmented Reality*, p. 30, 2001.

A. SCHENK, G. PRAUSE, and H.-O. PEITGEN. Efficient semiautomatic segmentation of 3D objects in medical images. In *Proc. of Medical Image Computing and Computer-Assisted Intervention (MICCAI)*, volume 1935 of *Lecture Notes in Computer Science*, pp. 186–195, 2000.

A. SCHENK, G. P. M. PRAUSE, and H.-O. PEITGEN. Local cost computation for efficient segmentation of 3D objects with live wire. In *Proc. of SPIE Medical Imaging*, volume 4322, pp. 1357–1364, 2001.

M. SCHEUERING. *Fusion medizinischer Videobilder mit tomographischen Volumendaten*. Ph.D. thesis, Technische Fakultät, Universität Erlangen-Nürnberg, 2003.

M. SCHEUERING, U. LABSIK, C. VOGELGSANG, and G. GREINER. Fusion von Freihand-Videosequenzen mit triangulierten Oberflächen zur 3D-Szenenexploration in der Medizin. In *Proc. of Simulation and Visualization*, pp. 259–270, 2003b.

M. SCHEUERING, A. SCHENK, A. SCHNEIDER, B. PREIM, and G. GREINER. Intra-operative augmented reality for minimally invasive liver interventions. In *Proc. of SPIE Medical Imaging*, pp. 407–417, 2003a.

M. SCHEUERING, A. SCHENK, A. SCHNEIDER, B. PREIM, and G. GREINER. Intra-operative augmented reality for minimally invasive liver interventions. In *Proc. of SPIE Medical Imaging*, volume 5029, pp. 407–417, 2003c.

T. SCHIEMANN, U. TIEDE, and K.-H. HÖHNE. Segmentation of the Visible Human for high quality volume based visualization. *Medical Image Analysis*, 1:263–271, 1997.

A. SCHILLING, G. KNITTEL, and W. STRAßER. Texram: a smart memory for texturing. *Computer Graphics and Applications*, 16(3):32–41, 1996.

T. SCHINDEWOLF, U. FRESE, and J. MEISSNER. Segmentierung und Volumetrie der Hirnventrikel mit MRT-Datensätzen. In *Proc. of Workshop Bildverarbeitung für die Medizin*, Informatik aktuell, pp. 92–96, 1999.

S. SCHLECHTWEG and H. WAGENER. "Interactive Medical Illustrations," chapter in *Computational Visualization: Images, Abstraction, and Intreactivity*, pp. 295–311. Berlin, Heidelberg, and New York: Springer, 1998.

M. SCHLUETER, O. KONRAD-VERSE, H. K. HAHN, B. STIELTJES, J. REXILIUS, and H. O. PEITGEN. White matter lesion phantom for diffusion tensor data and its application to the assessment of fiber tracking. In *Proc. of SPIE Medical Imaging*, volume 5746, pp. 835–844, 2005a.

M. SCHLUETER, J. REXILIUS, H. K. HAHN, H. PEITGEN, and B. STIELTJES. Unique planar color coding of fiber bundles and its application to fiber integrity quantification. In *Proc. of IEEE International Symposium Biomedical Imaging*, pp. 900–903, 2004.

M. SCHLUETER, B. STIELTJES, H. K. HAHN, J. REXILIUS, O. KONRAD-VERSE, and H. PEITGEN. Detection of tumor infiltration in axonal fiber bundles using diffusion tensor imaging. *International Journal of Medical Robotics and Computer Assisted Surgery*, 1:80–86, 2005b.

J. SCHMITTLER, I. WALD, and P. SLUSALLEK. SaarCOR: a hardware architecture for ray tracing. In *Proc. of Eurographics/SIGGRAPH Workshop on Graphics Hardware*, pp. 27–36, 2002.

M. D. SCHNALL, S. ROSTEN, S. ENGLANDER, S. G. OREL, and L. W. NUNES. A combined architectural and kinetic interpretation model for breast MRI images. *Academic Radiology*, 8:591–597, 2001.

P. SCHNEIDER and D. H. EBERLY. *Geometric Tools for Computer Graphics*. Morgan Kaufmann, 2002.

P. SCHRÖDER and G. STOLL. Data parallel volume rendering as line drawing. In *Proc. of IEEE/ACM Symposium on Volume Visualization*, pp. 25–32, 1992.

W. SCHROEDER. A topology modifying progressive decimation algorithm. In *Proc. of IEEE Visualization*, pp. 205–212, 1997.

W. SCHROEDER, J. ZARGE, and W. LORENSEN. Decimation of triangle meshes. In *Proc. of ACM SIGGRAPH*, pp. 65–70, 1992.

W. SCHROEDER, K. MARTIN, and B. LORENSEN. *The Visualisation Toolkit*, 3rd ed. Kitware, 2001.

R. SCHUBERT, K.-H. HOEHNE, A. POMMERT, M. RIEMER, T. SCHIEMANN, and U. TIEDE. Spatial knowledge representation for visualization of human anatomy and function. In Proc. of Information Processing in Medical Imaging, volume 687 of Lecture Notes in Computer Science, pp. 168–181, 1993.

J. SCHULZE, R. NIEMEIER, and U. LANG. The perspective shear-warp algorithm in a virtual environment. In Proc. of IEEE Visualization, pp. 207–214, 2001.

H. SCHUMANN and W. MÜLLER. Visualisierung—Grundlagen und allgemeine Methoden. Heidelberg: Springer, 2000.

V. SCHUMPELICK, N. M. BLEESE, and U. MOMMSEN. Kurzlehrbuch Chirurgie, 6th ed. Georg Thieme Verlag, September 2003.

B. SCHWALD, H. SEIBERT, and T. WELLER. A flexible tracking concept applied tomedical scenarios using an AR window. In Proc. of IEEE and ACM International Symposium on Mixed and Augmented Reality, pp. 261–262, 2002.

N. SCOTT, D. OLSEN, and E. GANNETT. An overview of the VISUALIZE fx graphics accelerator hardware. The Hewlett-Packard Journal, (May):28–34, 1998.

A. SECORD. Weighted Voronoi stippling. In Proc. of Symposium on Non-Photorealistic Animation and Rendering, pp. 37–43, 2002.

D. D. SELIGMANN and S. FEINER. Automated generation of intentbased 3D illustrations. In Proc. of ACM SIGGRAPH, pp. 123–132, 1991.

D. SELLE, B. PREIM, A. SCHENK, and H.-O. PEITGEN. Analysis of vasculature for liver surgery planning. IEEE Transactions on Medical Imaging, 21(11):1344–1357, November 2002.

D. SELLE, W. SPINDLER, B. PREIM, and H.-O. PEITGEN. "Mathematical Methods in Medical Image Processing: Vessel Analysis for Preoperative Planning in Liver Surgery," Chapter in Mathematics Unlimited–Springer's Special Book for the World Mathematical Year 2000, pp. 1039–1059. Springer, 2000.

P. SEREDA, A. VILANOVA, and F. A. GERRITSEN. Automating transfer function design for volume rendering using hierarchical clustering of material boundaries. In Data Visualization (Proc. of Eurographics/IEEE Symposium on Visualization), pp. 243–250, 2006.

I. SERLIE, F. VOS, R. VAN GELDER, J. STOKER, R. TRUYEN, F. GERRITSEN, Y. NIO, and F. POST. Improved visualization in virtual colonoscopy using image-based rendering. In Data Visualization (Proc. of Eurographics/IEEE Symposium on Visualization), pp. 137–146, 2001.

J. SERRA. Image Analysis and Mathematical Morphology. London, UK: Academic Press, 1982.

J. A. SETHIAN. Level Set Methods and Fast Marching Methods. Cambridge, UK: Cambridge University Press, 1999.

C. SHANNON. Communication in the presence of noise. Proceedings of Institute of Radio Engineers, 37(1):10–21, 1949.

C. SHAW, J. HALL, C. BLAHUT, D. EBERT, I. SOBOROLL, and D. ROBERTS. Using shape to visualize multivariate data. In Proc. of Workshop on New Paradigms in Information Visualization and Manipulation, pp. 17–20, 1999.

H. SHEN, C. HANSEN, Y. LIVNAT, and C. JOHNSON. Isosurfacing in span space with utmost efficiency (ISSUE). In Proc. of IEEE Visualization, pp. 287–294, 1996.

H. W. SHEN, L. J. YEH-CHING CHIANG, and K. L. MA. A fast volume-rendering algorithm for time-varying fields using a time-space partioning (TSP) tree. In Proc. of IEEE Visualization, pp. 371–377, 1999.

H. W. SHEN and C. R. JOHNSON. Differential volume rendering: a fast volume visualization technique for flow animation. In Proc. of IEEE Visualization, pp. 180–187, 1994.

W. SHEN and A. PANG. Anisotropy-based seeding for hyperstreamline. In IASTED Conference on Computer Graphics and Imaging, 2004.

M. E. SHENTON, R. KIKINIS, R. W. MCCARLEY, P. SAIVIROONPORN, H. H. HOKAMA, A. ROBATINO, et al. Harvard Brain Atlas: a teaching and visualization tool. In Proc. of Biomedical Visualization, pp. 10–17, 1995.

L. SHEPP and B. LOGAN. The Fourier reconstruction of a head section. IEEE Transactions on Nuclear Science, 21:21–43, 1974.

W. SHERMAN and A. CRAIG. *Understanding Virtual Reality*. Morgan Kaufmann, 2003.

A. SHERSTYUK. *Convolution Surfaces in Computer Graphics*. Ph.D. thesis, Monash University, Melbourne, Victoria, Australia, 1998.

H. SHIN, B. KING, M. GALANSKI, and H. K. MATTHIES. Development of an intuitive graphical user interface for volume rendering of multidetector CT data. In *Proc. of Computer Assisted Radiology and Surgery*, pp. 264–269, 2003.

P. SHIRLEY and A. TUCHMAN. A polygonal approximationm to direct scalar volume rendering. In *Proc. of San Diego Workshop on Volume Visualization*, pp. 63–70, 1990.

B. SHNEIDERMAN. Direct manipulation—a step beyond programming. *IEEE Computer*, 16(8):42–61, 1983.

B. SHNEIDERMAN. *Designing the User Interface*, 3rd ed. Addison Wesley, 1997.

B. SHNEIDERMAN and B. BEDERSON. *The Craft of Information Visualization*. Morgan Kaufmann, 2003.

J. SIEBERT, T. ROSENBAUM, and J. PERNICONE. Automated segmentation and presentation algorithms for 3D MRI angiography (poster abstract). In *Proc. of 10th Annual Meeting of the Society of Magnetic Resonance in Medicine*, Poster 758, 1991.

R. SIERRA, M. BAJKA, C. KARADOGAN, G. SZÉKELY, and M. HARDERS. Coherent scene generation for surgical simulators. In *Medical Simulation Symposium*, 3078, pp. 221–229. Springer, 2004.

R. SIERRA, M. BAJKA, and G. SZÉKELY. Evaluation of different pathology generation strategies for surgical training simulators. In *Proc. of Computer Assisted Radiology and Surgery*, pp. 376–381, 2003a.

R. SIERRA, M. BAJKA, and G. SZÉKELY. Pathology growth model based on particles. In R. E. ELLIS and T. M. PETERS, editors, *Proc. of Medical Image Computing and Computer-Assisted Intervention (MICCAI)*, volume 2879 of *Lecture Notes in Computer Science*, pp. 25–32, 2003b.

J. SIJBERS. *Signal and Noise Estimation from Magnetic Resonance Images*. Ph.D. thesis, University of Antwerp, 1998.

H. SIMON. How big is a chunk? *Science*, 183:482–488, 1974.

A. SINGH, D. GOLDGOF, and D. TERZOPOULOS. *Deformable Models in Medical Image Analysis*. IEEE Computer Society, 1999.

S. SKARE, T.-Q. LI, B. NORDELL, and M. INGVAR. Noise considerations in the determination of diffusion tensor anisotropy. *Magnetic Resonance Imaging*, 18(6):659–669, 2000.

J. G. SLED, A. P. ZIJDENBOS, and A. C. EVANS. A nonparametric method for automatic correction of intensity nonuniformity in MRI data. *IEEE Transactions on Medical Imaging*, 17(1):87–97, 1998.

L. SOBIERAJSKI and R. AVILA. A hardware acceleration method for volume ray tracing. In *Proc. of IEEE Visualization*, pp. 27–34, 1995.

L. SOBIERAJSKI and A. KAUFMAN. Volumetric ray tracing. In *Proc. of IEEE/ACM Symposium on Volume Visualization*, pp. 11–18, 1994.

P. SOILLE and H. TALBOT. Directional morpholgical filtering. *IEEE Transactions on Pattern Analysis and Machine Intelligence*, 23:1313–1329, 2001.

L. SOLBIATI, T. IERACE, S. N. GOLDBERG, S. SIRONI, T. LIVRAGHI, and R. FIOCCA. Percutaneous US-guided radio-frequency tissue ablation of liver metastases: treatment and follow-up in 16 patients. *Radiology*, 202:195–203, 1997.

L. SOLER, H. DELINGETTE, and G. MALANDIN. Fully automatic anatomical, pathological, and functional segmentation from CT scans for hepatic surgery. *Computer Aided Surgery*, 6(3):131–142, 2001.

M. SONKA and J. M. FITZPATRICK. *Handbook of Medical Imaging*, volume 2. SPIE Press, 2000.

M. SONKA, V. HLAVAC, and R. BOYLE. *Image Processing, Analysis, and Machine Vision*, 2nd ed. Brooks-Cole, 1999.

M. SONKA, G. SUNDARAMOORTHY, and E. A. HOFFMAN. Knowledge-based segmentation of intrathoracic airways from multidimensional high resolution CT images. In *Proc. of SPIE Medical Imaging*, pp. 73–85, 1994.

E. SORANTIN, C. HALMAI, B. ERDHELYI, K. PALAGY, B. GEIGER, G. FRIEDRICH, K. KIESEL, and S. LONCARIC. CT-based assessment of tracheal stenoses using 3D-skeletonization. *IEEE Transactions on Medical Imaging*, 21(3):263–273, 2002.

G. SOZA, M. BAUER, P. HASTREITER, C. NIMSKY, and G. GREINER. Non-rigid registration with use of hardware-based 3D bézier functions source. In *Proc. of Medical Image Computing and Computer-Assisted Intervention (MICCAI)*, volume 2489 of *Lecture Notes in Computer Science*, pp. 549–556, 2002.

V. SPITZER, M. J. ACKERMAN, A. L. SCHERZINGER, and D. WHITLOCK. The Visible Human Male: a technical report. *Journal of American Medical Informatics Association*, 3(2): 118–130, 1996.

R. R. SPRINGMEYER, M. M. BLATTNER, and N. L. MAX. A characterization of the scientific data analysis process. In *Proc. of IEEE Visualization*, pp. 236–242, 1992.

M. SRAMEK and A. KAUFMAN. Object voxelization by filtering. In *Proc. of IEEE/ACM Symposium on Volume Visualization*, pp. 111–118, 1998.

M. SRAMEK and A. KAUFMAN. Alias-free voxelization of geometric objects. *IEEE Transactions on Visualization and Computer Graphics*, 3(5):251–266, 1999a.

M. SRAMEK and A. KAUFMAN. VXT: a C++ class library for object voxelization. In *Proc. of Volume Graphics*, pp. 295–306, 1999b.

R. STAHL, O. DIETRICH, S. TEIPEL, H. HAMPEL, M. F. REISER, and S. O. SCHOENBERG. Assessment of axonal degeneration on Alzheimer's disease with diffusion tensor MRI. *Radiologe*, 43(7):566–575, 2003.

D. STALLING, M. SEEBAß, and S. ZACHOW. Mehrschichtige Oberflächenmodelle zur computergestützten Planung in der Chirurgie. In *Proc. of Workshop Bildverarbeitung für die Medizin*, Informatik aktuell, pp. 203–207, 1999.

D. STALLING, M. WESTERHOFF, and H.-C. HEGE. Amira: a highly interactive system for visual data analysis. In C. D. HANSEN and C. R. JOHNSON, editors, *The Visualization Handbook*, chapter 38, pp. 749–767. Elsevier, 2005.

D. STALLING, M. ZÖCKLER, and C. HEGE. Segmentation of 3D medical images with subvoxel accuracy. In *Proc. of Computer Assisted Radiology*, pp. 137–142, 1998.

D. STANEKER, D. BARTZ, and M. MEIßNER. Improving occlusion query efficiency with occupancy maps. In *Proc. of IEEE Symposium on Parallel and Large Data Visualization and Graphics*, pp. 111–118, 2003.

D. STANEKER, D. BARTZ, and W. STRAßER. Occlusion culling in OpenSG PLUS. *Computers & Graphics*, 28(1): 87–92, 2004.

D. STANEKER, D. BARTZ, and W. STRAßER. Occlusion-driven scene sorting for efficient culling. *Computer Graphics Forum*, 25(4):699–708, 2006.

A. STATE, M. LIVINGSTON, G. HIROTA, W. GARRETT, M. WHITTON, H. FUCHS, and E. PISANO. Technologies for augmented-reality systems: realizing ultrasound-guided needle biopsies. In *Proc. of ACM SIGGRAPH*, pp. 439–446, 1996.

M. B. STEGMANN, B. K. ERSBOLL, and R. LARSEN. Fame—a flexible appearance modeling environment. *IEEE Transactions on Medical Imaging*, 22(10):1319–1331, 2003.

M. B. STEGMANN, R. FISKER, B. K. ERSBOLL, H. H. THODBERG, and L. HYLDSTRUP. Active appearance models: theory and cases. In *Proc. of 9th Danish Conference on Pattern Recognition and Image Analysis*, volume 1, pp. 49–57, 2000.

T. STEIN, K. DESINGER, A. ROGGAN, and G. MUELLER. Interstitial thermotherapy with bipolar RF applicators: computer-aided therapy control and monitoring. In *Surgical Applications of Energy*, volume 3565, pp. 4–17, 1999.

E. O. STEJSKAL and J. E. TANNER. Spin diffusion measurements: spin echos in the presence of a time-dependent field gradient. *Journal of Chemical Physics*, 42:288–292, 1965.

D. STOELZEL. *Entwurf gradientenabhängiger 2D-Transferfunktionen für die medizinische Volumenvisualisierung*. Master's thesis, Department of Computer Science, Otto-von-Guericke University of Magdeburg, 2004.

M. STONE. *A Field Guide to Digital Color*. Natick, MA: A. K. Peters, 2003.

M. STRAKA, M. CERVENANSKÝ, A. LA CRUZ, A. KÖCHL, M. SRÁMEK, E. GRÖLLER, and D. FLEISCHMANN. The VesselGlyph: focus & context visualization in CT-angiography. In *Proc. of IEEE Visualization*, pp. 385–392, 2004.

D. STREDNEY, G. J. WIET, J. BRYAN, D. SESSANNA, J. MURAKAMI, P. SCHMALBROCK, K. POWELL, and D. B. WELLING. Temporal bone dissection simulation—an update. In *Proc. of Medicine Meets Virtual Reality*, pp. 507–513, 2002.

M. STRENGERT, M. MAGALLÓN, D. WEISKOPF, S. GUTHE, and T. ERTL. Hierarchical visualization and compression of large volume datasets using GPU clusters. In *Proc. of Eurographics Symposium on Parallel Graphics and Visualization*, pp. 41–48, 2004.

T. STROTHOTTE and S. SCHLECHTWEG. *Non-Photorealistic Computer Graphics: Modeling, Rendering, and Animation*. Morgan Kaufmann, 2002.

R. STRZODKA and A. TELEA. Generalized distance transforms and skeletons in graphics hardware. In *Data Visualization (Proc. of Eurographics/IEEE Symposium on Visualization)*, pp. 221–230, 2004.

C. STUDHOLME. *Measures of 3D Medical Image Alignment*. Ph.D. thesis, University of London, 1997.

M. STYNER, G. GERIG, C. BRECHBÜHLER, and G. SZÉKELY. Parametric estimate of intensity inhomogeneities applied to MRI. *IEEE Transactions on Medical Imaging*, 19(3):153–165, 1998.

P. SUETENS. *Foundations of Medical Imaging*. Cambridge, UK: Cambridge University Press, 2002.

G. T. SUNG and I. S. GILL. Robotic laparoscopic surgery: a comparison of the Da Vinci and Zeus systems. *Urology*, 58(6):893–898, 2001.

P. SUTTON and C. D. HANSEN. Isosurface extraction in time-varying fields using a temporal branch-on-need tree. In *Proc. of IEEE Visualization*, pp. 147–153, 1999.

N. SVAKHINE, D. S. EBERT, and D. STREDNEY. Illustration motifs for effective medical volume illustration. *Computer Graphics and Applications*, 25(3):31–39, 2005.

E. SWAN, K. MUELLER, T. MÖLLER, N. SHAREEL, R. CRAWFIS, and R. YAGEL. An antialiasing technique for splatting. In *Proc. of IEEE Visualization*, pp. 197–204, 1997.

J. SWEENEY and K. MUELLER. Shear-warp deluxe: the shear-warp algorithm revisited. In *Data Visualization (Proc. of Eurographics/IEEE Symposium on Visualization)*, pp. 95–104, 2002.

J. A. SWETS and R. M. PICKET. *Evaluation of Diagnostic Systems*. Academic Press, 1982.

G. SZÉKELY, C. BRECHBÜHLER, R. HUTTER, A. RHOMBERG, N. IRONMONGER, and P. SCHMID. Modeling of soft tissue deformation for laparoscopic surgery Simulation. In W. M. Wells, III, et al., editors, *Proc. of Medical Image Computing and Computer-Assisted Intervention (MICCAI)*, volume 1496 of *Lecture Notes in Computer Science*, pp. 550–561, 1998.

N. TAFFINDER, S. SMITH, J. HUBER, et al. The effect of a second-generation 3D endoscope on the laparoscopic precision of novices and experienced surgeons. *Surg Endoscopy*, 13:1087–1092, 1999.

N. TAFFINDER, C. SUTTON, and R. J. FISHWICK, et al. Validation of virtual reality to teach and assess psychomotor skills in laparoscopic surgery: results from randomised controlled studies using the MIST VR laparoscopic simulator. *Stud Health Technol Inform*, 50:124–130, 1998.

I. TAKANAHI, S. MURAKI, A. DOI, and A. KAUFMAN. 3D active net for volume extraction. In *Proc. SPIE Electronic Imaging*, pp. 184–193, 1998.

I.-F. TALOS, L. O'DONNELL, C.-F. WESTIN, S. K. WARFIELD, W. M. WELLS, III, S.-S. YOO, et al. Diffusion tensor and functional MRI fusion with anatomical MRI for image-guided neurosurgery. In *Proc. of Medical*

Image Computing and Computer-Assisted Intervention (MICCAI), volume 2879 of *Lecture Notes in Computer Science*, pp. 407–415, 2003.

A. TANAKA, M. KAMEYAMA, S. KAZAMA, and O. WATANABE. A rotation method for raster image using skew transformations. In *Proc. of IEEE Conference on Computer Vision and Pattern Recognition*, pp. 272–277, 1986.

K. TANAKA and T. KIUCHI. Living-donor liver transplantation in the new decade: perspective from the twentieth to the twenty-first century. *Journal of Hepatobiliary Pancreat Surg*, 9:218–222, 2002.

A. TAPPENBECK, B. PREIM, and V. DICKEN. Distance-based transfer function design: specification methods and applications. In *Proc. of Simulation and Visualization*, pp. 259–274, 2006.

G. TAUBIN. A signal processing approach to fair surface design. In *Proc. of ACM SIGGRAPH*, pp. 351–358, 1995.

M. TAVAKOLI, R. V. PATEL, and M. MOALLEM. A haptic interface for computer integrated endoscopic surgery and training. *Virtual Reality*, 9(2):160–176, 2006.

A. TELEA and J. J. VAN WIJK. An augmented fast marching method for computing skeletons and centerlines. In *Data Visualization (Proc. of Eurographics/IEEE Symposium on Visualization)*, pp. 251–259, 2002.

S. TENGINAKAI, J. LEE, and R. MACHIRAJU. Salient iso-surface detection with model-independent statistical signatures. In *Proc. of IEEE Visualization*, pp. 231–238, 2001.

S. TENGINAKAI and R. MACHIRAJU. Statistical computation of salient iso-values. In *Data Visualization (Proc. of Eurographics/IEEE Symposium on Visualization)*, pp. 19–24, 2002.

B. TER HAAR ROMENEY, editor. *Geometry Driven Diffusion*. Dordecht: Kluwer Academic Publishers, 1994.

D. TERZOPOULOS, A. WITKIN, and M. KASS. Constraints on deformable models: recovering 3D shape and nonrigid motion. *Artificial Intelligence*, 36(1):91–123, 1988.

M. TESCHNER, S. GIROD, and B. GIROD. Direct computation of nonlinear soft-tissue deformation. In *Proc. of Vision, Modeling, and Visualization*, pp. 383–390, 2000.

M. TESCHNER, S. KIMMERLE, B. HEIDELBERGER, G. ZACHMANN, L. RAGHUPATHI, and A. FUHRMANN. Collision detection for deformable objects. *Computer Graphics Forum*, 24(1):61–81, 2005.

P. THERASSE, S. G. ARBUCK, E. A. EISENHAUER, J. WANDERS, R. S. KAPLAN, L. RUBINSTEIN, et al. New guidelines to evaluate the response of treatment in solid tumors. *Journal of the National Cancer Institute*, 92(3): 205–216, 2000.

P. THÉVENAZ, T. BLU, and M. UNSER. "Image Interpolation and Resampling," chapter in *Handbook of Medical Imaging, Processing and Analysis*, I. N. Bankman, editor. pp. 393–420. Academic Press, 2000.

N. THUNE and B. OLSTAD. Visualizing 4D medical ultrasound data. In *Proc. of IEEE Visualization*, pp. 210–217, 1991.

U. TIEDE, K.- H. HÖHNE, M. BOMANS, A. POMMERT, M. RIEMER, and G. WIEBECKE. Investigation of medical 3D-rendering algorithms. *IEEE Computer Graphics and Applications*, 10(2):41–53, 1990.

U. TIEDE, T. SCHIEMANN, and K. HÖHNE. High quality rendering of attributed volume data. In *Proc. of IEEE Visualization*, pp. 255–263, 1998.

U. TIEDE, M. BOMANS, and K.-H. HÖHNE. A computerized threedimensional atlas of the human skull and brain. *American Journal of Neuroradiology*, 14(3):551–559, 1993.

U. TIEDE, T. SCHIEMANN, and K.-H. HÖHNE. Visualizing the Visible Human. *Computer Graphics and Applications*, 16(1):7–9, 1996.

C. TIETJEN, T. ISENBERG, and B. PREIM. Combining silhouettes, shading, and volume rendering for surgery education and planning. In *Data Visualization (Proc. of Eurographics/IEEE Symposium on Visualization)*, pp. 303–310, 2005.

C. TIETJEN, B. MEYER, S. SCHLECHTWEG, B. PREIM, I. HERTEL, and G. STRAUß. Enhancing slice-based visualizations of medical volume data. In *Data Visualization (Proc. of Eurographics/IEEE Symposium on Visualization)*, pp. 123–130, 2006.

A. L. TIEVSKY, T. PTAKA, and J. FARKASA. Investigation of apparent diffusion coefficient and diffusion tensor anisotropy in acute and chronic multiple sclerosis lesions. *American Journal of Neuroradiology*, 20(9):1491–1499, 1999.

P. TOFTS and A. KERMODE. Simultaneous MRI measurement of blood flow, blood volume, and capillary permeability in mamma tumors using two different contrast agents. *Journal of Magnetic Resonance Imaging*, 12(6):991–1003, 1991.

B. F. TOMANDL, P. HASTREITER, S. ISERHARDT-BAUER, N. C. KÖSTNER, M. SCHEMPERSHOFE, W. J. HUK, T. ERTL, C. STRAUSS, and J. ROMSTOCK. Standardized evaluation of CT angiography with remote generation of 3D video sequences for the detection of intracranial aneurysms. *Radiographics*, 23:e12, 2003.

C. TOMASI and R. MANDUCHI. Bilateral filtering for gray and color images. In *Proc. of IEEE International Conference on Computer Vision*, pp. 839–846, 1998.

X. TONG, W. WANG, W. TSANG, and Z. TANG. Effciently rendering large volume data using texture mapping hardware. In *Data Visualization (Proc. of Eurographics/IEEE Symposium on Visualization)*, pp. 121–131, 1999.

T. TOTSUKA and M. LEVOY. Fourier domain volume rendering. In *Proc. of ACM SIGGRAPH*, pp. 271–278, 1993.

S. TREAVETT and M. CHEN. Pen-and-ink rendering in volume visualization. In *Proc. of IEEE Visualization*, pp. 203–210, October 2000.

L. TREINISH. Task-specific visualization design. *Computer Graphics and Applications*, 19(5): 272–7732, 1999.

A. TREISMAN. Preattentive processing in vision. *Computer Vision, Graphics, and Image Processing*, 31(2):156–177, 1985.

A. TROPINE, G. VUCUREVIC, P. DELANI, S. BOOR, N. HOPF, J. BOHL, and P. STOETER. Contribution of diffusion tensor imaging to delineation of gliomas and glioblastomas. *Journal of Magnetic Resonance Imaging*, 20(6):905–912, 2004.

J. TSCHIRREN, K. PALAGYI, J. M. REINHARDT, E. A. HOMAN, and M. SONKA. Segmentation, skeletonization, and branchpoint matching—a fully automated quantitative evaluation of human intrathoracic airway trees. In *Proc. of Medical Image Computing and Computer-Assisted Intervention (MICCAI)*, volume 2489 of *Lecture Notes in Computer Science*, pp. 12–19, 2002.

B. TVERSKY, J. MORRISON, and M. BETRANCOURT. Animation: can it facilitate? *International Journal of Human-Computer Studies*, 57:247–262, 2002.

R. TYLER. Visualization multiple fields on the same surface. *Computer Graphics and Applications*, 22(3):6–10, October 2002.

F.-Y. TZENG, E. B. LUM, and K.-L. MA. A novel interface for higher- dimensional classification of volume data. In *Proc. of IEEE Visualization*, pp. 505–512, 2003.

J. K. UDUPA. "Three-Dimensional Visualization: Principles and Approaches," chapter in *Handbook of Medical Imaging*, volume 3, pp. 5–66, 2000.

J. K. UDUPA and G. T. HERMAN. *3D Imaging in Medicine*. CRC Press, 2000.

J. K. UDUPA and D. ODHNER. Shell rendering. *Computer Graphics and Applications*, 13(6):58–67, 1993.

J. K. UDUPA, and S. SAMARASEKERA. Fuzzy connectedness and object definition: theory, algorithms and applications in image segmentation. *Graphics Models and Image Processing*, 58(3):246–261, 1996.

J. K. UDUPA, S. SAMARASEKERA, and W. A. BARRETT. Boundary detection via dynamic programming. In *Proc. of Visualization in Biomedical Computing*, pp. 33–39, 1992.

J. K. UDUPA, L. WEI, S. SAMARASEKERA, Y. MIKI, M. A. VAN BUCHEM, and R. I. GROSSMAN. Multiple sclerosis lesion quantification using fuzzy connectedness principles. *IEEE Transactions on Medical Imaging*, 16: 598–609, 1997.

C. UPSON, T. FAULHABER, JR. D. KAMINS, D. LAIDLAW, D. SCHLEGEL, J. VROOM, R. GURWITZ, and A. VAN DAM. The application visualization system: a computational environment for scientific visualization. *Computer Graphics and Applications*, 9(4):30–42, 1989.

C. UPSON and M. KEELER. VBUFFER: visible volume rendering. In *Proc. of ACM SIGGRAPH*, pp. 59–64, 1988.

C. VAN BEMMEL, L. SPREEUWERS, M. VIERGEVER, and W. NIESSEN. Level-set based carotid artery segmentation for stenosis grading. In *Proc. of Medical Image Computing and Computer-Assisted Intervention (MICCAI)*, volume 2489 of *Lecture Notes in Computer Science*, pp. 36–43, 2002.

C. M. VAN BEMMEL, L. J. SPREEUWERS, M. A. VIERGEVER, and W. J. NIESSEN. Level-set based artery-vein separation in blood pool agent CEMR angiograms. *IEEE Transactions on Medical Imaging*, 22(10): 1224–1234, 2003.

A. VAN GELDER and K. KIM. Direct volume rendering with shading via three-dimensional textures. In *Proc. of IEEE/ACM Symposium on Volume Visualization*, pp. 23–30, 1996.

J. VAN WIJK and A. TELEA. Enridged contour maps. In *Proc. of IEEE Visualization*, pp. 69–74, 2001.

G. VAN DEN BERGEN. Effcient collision detection of complex deformable models using AABB trees. *Journal of Graphical Tools*, 2(4):1–14, 1997.

M. VANNIER. Evaluation of 3D imaging. *Crit. Rev. Diagn. Imaging*, 41(5):315–378, 2000.

M. W. VANNIER, J. L. MARSH, and J. O. WARREN. Three dimensional computer graphics for craniofacial surgical planning and evaluation. In *Proc. of ACM SIGGRAPH*, pp. 263–273, 1983.

F. VEGA, N. SAUBER, B. TOMANDL, C. NIMSKY, G. GREINER, and P. HASTREITER. Enhanced 3D-visualization of intracranial aneurysms involving the skull base. In *Proc. of Medical Image Computing and Computer-Assisted Intervention (MICCAI)*, volume 2879 of *Lecture Notes in Computer Science*, pp. 256–263, 2003.

F. VEGA, N. SAUBER, B. TOMANDL, C. NIMSKY, G. GREINER, and P. HASTREITER. Automatic adjustment of bidimensional transfer functions for direct volume visualization of intracranial aneurysms. In *Proc. of SPIE Medical Imaging*, pp. 275–284, 2004.

J. F. VERHEY, Y. MOHAMMED, A. LUDWIG, and K. GIESE. Implementation of a practical model for light and heat distribution using laser-induced thermotherapy near to a large vessel. *Physiology in Medicine and Biology*, 48(1):3595–3610, 2003.

J. F. VERHEY, Y. MOHAMMED, A. LUDWIG, and K. GIESE. A finite element method model to simulate laser interstitial thermotherapy in anatomical inhomogeneous regions. *BioMedical Engineering OnLine*, 4(1), 2005.

M. VETTER, I. WOLF, P. HASSENPFLUG, M. HASTENTEUFEL, R. LUDWIG, L. GRENACHER, G. M. RICHTER, W. UHL, M. W. BÜCHLER, and H.-P. MEINZER. Navigation aids and real-time deformation modeling for open liver surgery. In *Proc. of SPIE Medical Imaging*, volume 5029, pp. 58–68, 2003.

A. VILANOVA, G. BERENSCHOT, and C. VAN PUL. DTI visualization with stream surfaces and evenly-spaced volume seeding. In *Data Visualization (Eurographis/IEEE Symposium on Visualization)*, pp. 173–182, 2004.

A. VILANOVA, A. KÖNIG, and E. GRÖLLER. VirEn: virtual endoscopy system. *Machine Graphics & Vision*, 8(3):469–487, 1999.

A. VILANOVA, R. WEGENKITTL, and E. GRÖLLER. Projected slabs: approximation of perspective projection and error analysis. *Journal of Visualization and Computer Animation*, 12(5):253–262, 2001a.

A. VILANOVA, R. WEGENKITTL, A. KÖNIG, and E. GRÖLLER. Nonlinear virtual colon unfolding. In *Proc. of IEEE Visualization*, 2001b.

A. VILANOVA, R. WEGENKITTL, A. KÖNIG, E. GRÖLLER, and E. SORANTIN. Virtual colon flattening. In *Data Visualization (Proc. of Eurographics/IEEE Symposium on Visualization)*, pp. 127–136, 2001c.

A. VILANOVA, S. ZHANG, G. KINDLMAN, and D. LAIDLAW. "An Introduction to Visualization of Diffusion Tensor Imaging and Its Applications," chapter in *Visualization and Processing of Tensor Fields*. Springer, 2005.

L. VINCENT and P. SOILLE. Watersheds in Digital Spaces: an Effcient Algorithm Based on Immersion Simulations. *IEEE Transactions on Pattern Analysis and Machine Intelligence*, 13(6):583–598, 1991.

D. VINING, R. SHIFRIN, E. GRISHAW, K. LIU, and R. CHOPLIN. Virtual colonoscopy (abstract). In *Radiology*, volume 193(P), p. 446, 1994.

I. VIOLA, A. KANITSAR, and E. GRÖLLER. Importance-driven volume rendering. In *Proc. of IEEE Visualization*, pp. 139–145, 2004a.

I. VIOLA, A. KANITSAR, and E. GRÖLLER. Importance-driven volume rendering. In *Proc. of IEEE Visualization*, pp. 139–145, 2004b.

I. VIOLA, A. KANITSAR, and E. GRÖLLER. Importance-driven volume rendering. *IEEE Transactions on Visualization and Computer Graphics*, 11(4):408–418, 2005.

P. A. VIOLA. *Alignment by Maximization of Mutual Information*. Technical Report, MIT, 1995.

T. J. VOGL, M. MACK, P. MÜLLER, A. ROGGAN, V. JAHNKE, and R. FELIX. Laser ablation of tumors of the head and neck. In F. A. JOLESZ, editor, *Interventional MR: Techniques and Clinical Experience*, pp. 239–254, 1998.

S. VOGT, A. KHAMENE, F. SAUER, A. KEIL, and H. NIEMANN. A high performance AR system for medical applications. In *Proc. of IEEE and ACM International Symposium on Mixed and Augmented Reality*, pp. 270–271, 2003.

J. VOLLMER, R. MENCEL, and H. MÜLLER. Improved Laplacian smoothing of noisy surface meshes. In *Proc. of Eurographics*, pp. 131–138, 1999.

W. VOLZ. Gigabyte volume viewing using split software/hardware interpolation. In *Proc. of IEEE/ACM Symposium on Volume Visualization and Graphics*, pp. 15–22, 2000.

C. WAGNER, N. STYLOPOULOS, and R. HOWE. Force feedback in surgery: analysis of blunt dissection. In *Proc. of the 10th Symposium on Haptic Interfaces for Virtual Environment and Teleoperator Systems*, pp. 68–74, 2002a.

C. WAGNER, M. A. SCHILL, and R. MÄNNER. Intraocular surgery on a virtual eye. *Communications of the ACM*, 45(7):45–49, 2002b.

A. WAHLE, G. P. M. PRAUSE, S. C. DEJONG, and M. SONKA. 3D fusion of biplane angiography and intravascular ultrasound for accurate visualization and volumetry. In *Proc. of Medical Image Computing and Computer-Assisted Intervention (MICCAI)*, volume 1496 of *Lecture Notes in Computer Science*, pp. 146–155, 1998.

A. WAHLE, G. P. M. PRAUSE, S. C. DEJONG, and M. SONKA. Geometrically correct 3D reconstruction of intravascular ultrasound images by fusion with biplane angiography—methods and validation. *IEEE Transactions on Medical Imaging*, 18(8):686–699, 1999.

I. WALD, P. SLUSALLEK, C. BENTHIN, and M. WAGNER. Interactive rendering with coherent ray tracing. *Computer Graphics Forum*, 20(3):153–164, 2001.

L. WANG, Y. ZHAO, K. MÜLLER, and A. KAUFMAN. The magic volume lens: an interactive focus+context technique for volume rendering. In *Proc. of IEEE Visualization*, pp. 367–374, 2005.

S. WANG and A. KAUFMAN. Volume sampled voxelization of geometric primitives. In *Proc. of IEEE Visualization*, pp. 78–84, 1993.

C. WARE. *Information Visualization*. Morgan Kaufmann, 2000.

S. K. WARFIELD, K. H. ZOU, and W. M. WELLS III. Validation of image segmentation and expert quality with an expectation-maximization algorithm. In *Proc. of Medical Image Computing and Computer-Assisted Intervention (MICCAI)*, volume 2489 of *Lecture Notes in Computer Science*, pp. 298–306, 2002.

K. WASSER, S. K. KLEIN, C. FINK, H. JUNKERMANN, H. P. SINN, I. ZUNA, M. V. KNOPP, and S. DELORME. Evaluation of neoadjuvant chemotherapeutic response of breast cancer using dynamic MRI with high temporal resolution. *European Journal of Radiology*, 13(1):80–87, 2003.

K. WATERS and D. TERZOPOULOS. A physical model of facial tissue and muscle articulation. In *Proc. of Visualization in Biomedical Computing*, pp. 77–82, 1990.

S. L. WAXBERG, K. H. GOODELL, D. V. AVGERINOS, S. D. SCHWAITZBERG, and C. G. L. CAO. Evaluation of physcial versus virtual surgical training simulators. In *Proc. of the Human Factors and Ergonomics Society*, pp. 1675–1679, 2004.

S. WEBER, M. KLEIN, A. HEIN, T. KRUEGER, T. LÜTH, and J. BIER. The navigated image viewer—evaluation in maxillofacial surgery. In *Proc. of Medical Image Computing and Computer-Assisted Intervention (MICCAI)*, volume 2878 of *Lecture Notes in Computer Science*, pp. 762–769, 2003.

R. WEGENKITTL, A. VILANOVA, B. HEGEDÜS, D. WAGNER, M. FREUND, and E. GRÖLLER. Mastering interactive virtual bronchioscopy on a low-end PC. In *Proc. of IEEE Visualization*, pp. 461–465, 2000.

J. WEICKERT. A review of nonlinear diffusion filtering. In *Scale-Space Theory in Computer Vision*, volume 1252 of *Lecture Notes in Computer Science*, pp. 3–28, 1997.

J. WEICKERT. "Tensor-Field Interpolation with PDEs," chapter in *Visualization and Processing of Tensor Fields*, Springer, 2005.

D. WEISKOPF, K. ENGEL, and T. ERTL. Interactive clipping techniques for texture-based volume visualization and volume shading. *IEEE Transactions on Visualization and Computer Graphics*, 9(3):298–312, March 2003.

D. WEISKOPF, U. KRAUS, and H. RUDER. Searchlight and doppler effects in the visualization of special relativity: a corrected derivation of the transformation of radiance. *ACM Transactions on Graphics*, 18(3): 278–292, 1999.

W. M. WELLS, III, P. VIOLA, H. ATSUMI, S. NAKAJIMA, and R. KIKINIS. Multi-modal volume registration by maximization of mutual information. *Medical Image Analysis*, 1:35–51, 1996.

J. WERNECKE. Inventor Mentor. Addison-Wesley, 1994.

R. WESTERMANN and T. ERTL. Effciently using graphics hardware in volume rendering applications. In *Proc. of ACM SIGGRAPH*, pp. 169–177, 1998.

R. WESTERMANN and B. SEVENICH. Accelerated volume ray casting using texture mapping. In *Proc. of IEEE Visualization*, pp. 271–278, 2001.

C.-F. WESTIN, S. E. MAIER, B. KHIDHIR, P. EVERETT, F. A. JOLESZ, and R. KIKINIS. Image processing for diffusion tensor MRI. In *Proc. of Medical Image Computing and Computer-Assisted Intervention (MICCAI)*, volume 1679 of *Lecture Notes in Computer Science*, pp. 441–452, 1999.

C.-F. WESTIN, S. E. MAIER, H. MAMATA, A. NABAVI, F. A. JOLESZ, and R. KIKINIS. Processing and visualization for diffusion tensor MRI. *Medical Image Analysis*, 6(2):93–108, June 2002.

L. WESTOVER. Interactive volume rendering. In *Proc. of Chapel Hill Workshop on Volume Visualization*, pp. 9–16, 1989.

L. WESTOVER. Footprint evaluation for volume rendering. In *Proc. of ACM SIGGRAPH*, pp. 367–376, 1990.

L. WESTOVER. *SPLATTING: A Parallel Feed-Forward Volume Rendering Algorithm*. Ph.D. thesis, University of North Carolina at Chapel Hill, 1991.

J. C. WHELAN and M. VISVALINGAM. Formulated silhouettes for sketching terrain. In *Theory and Practice of Computer Graphics*, pp. 90–96, 2003.

J. WIENER, K. J. SCHILLING, C. ADAMI, and N. A. OBUCHOWSKI. Assessment of suspected breast cancer by MRI: a prospective clinical trial using a combined kinetic and morphologic analysis. *American Journal of Radiology*, 1:878–886, 3 2005.

G. J. WIET and J. BRYAN. Virtual temporal bone dissection. In *Proc. of Medicine Meets Virtual Reality*, pp. 378–384, 2000.

J. WILHELMS and A. VAN GELDER. Octrees for faster isosurface generation. *ACM Transactions on Graphics*, 11(3):201–227, 1992.

J. WILHELMS and A. VAN GELDERN. A coherent projection approach for direct volume rendering. In *Proc. of ACM SIGGRAPH*, pp. 275–284, 1991.

O. WILSON, A. VAN GELDER, and J. WILHELMS. *Direct Volume Rendering via 3D Textures*. Technical Report UCSC-CRL-94-19, University of California, Santa Cruz, School of Engineering, 1994.

O. WINK, W. J. NIESSEN, and M. A. VIERGEVER. Fast delineation and visualization of vessels in 3D angiographic images. *IEEE Transactions on Medical Imaging*, 19(4): 337–346, 2000.

C. WITTENBRINK, T. MALZBENDER, and M. GOSS. Opacity-weighted color interpolation for volume sampling. In *Proc. of IEEE/ACM Symposium on Volume Visualization*, pp. 135–142, 1998.

I. WOLF, M. VETTER, I. WEGNER, T. BÖTTGER, M. NOLDEN, M. SCHÖBINGER, M. HASTENTEUFEL, T. KUNERT, and H.-P. MEINZER. The medical imaging interaction toolkit (MITK). *Medical Image Analysis*, 9(6):594–604, 2005.

I. WOLF, M. VETTER, I. WEGNER, M. NOLDEN, T. BÖTTGER, M. HASTENTEUFEL, M. SCHÖBINGER, T. KUNERT, and H.-P. MEINZER. The medical imaging interaction toolkit (MITK)—a toolkit facilitating the creation of interactive software by extending VTK and ITK. In *Proc. of SPIE Medical Imaging*, volume 5367, pp. 16–27, 2004.

M. WOO, J. NEIDER, and T. DAVIS. *OpenGL Programming Guide, 2nd ed.* Reading, MA: Addison Wesley, 1997.

S. WOOP, J. SCHMITTLER, and P. SLUSALLEK. RPU: a programmable ray processing unit for realtime ray tracing. *Proc. of ACM SIGGRAPH*, 24(3), 2005.

D. WORMANNS. Radiologic measurements as method for assessment of the therapy response of solid tumors. *Radiologie*, 5(3):261–272, 2005.

M. T. WU, H. B. PAN, A. A. CHIANG, H. K. HSU, H. C. CHANG, N. J. PENG, P. H. LAI, H. L. LIANG, and C. F. YANG. Prediction of postoperative lung function in patients with lung cancer: comparison of quantitative CT with perfusion scintigraphy. *American Journal of Roentgenology*, 178(3):667–672, 2002.

Y. WU, V. BHATIA, H. C. LAUER, and L. SEILER. Shear-image order ray casting volume rendering. In *Proc. of ACM Symposium on Interactive 3D Graphics*, pp. 152–162, 2003.

Z. WU and R. LEAHY. An optimal graph theoretic approach to data clustering: theory and its application to image segmentation. *IEEE Transactions on Pattern Analysis and Machine Intelligence*, 15(11):1101–1113, 1993.

B. C. WÜNSCHE. Advanced texturing techniques for the effective visualization of neuroanatomy from diffusion tensor imaging data. In *Proc. of the Second Asia-Pacific Bioinformatics Conference*, pp. 303–308, 2004a.

B. C. WÜNSCHE. *A Toolkit for the Visualization of Tensor Fields in Biomedical Finite Element Models*. Ph.D. thesis, Department of Computer Science, University of Auckland, 2004b.

G. WYVILL, C. MCPEETERS, and B. WYVILL. Datastructures for soft objects. *The Visual Computer*, 2(4):227–234, 1986.

J. XIA and A. VARSHNEY. Dynamic view-dependent simplification for polygonal models. In *Proc. of IEEE Visualization*, pp. 327–334, 1996.

Y. XIE and Q. JI. A new effcient ellipse detection method. In *International Conference on Pattern Recognition*, pp. II: 957–960, 2002.

H. XU, M. X. NGUYEN, X. YUAN, and B. CHEN. Illustrative silhouette rendering for point-based models. In *Proc. of Symposium on Point-Based Graphics*, pp. 13–18, 2004.

R. YAGEL and A. KAUFMAN. Template-based volume viewing. In *Proc. of Eurographics*, pp. 153–167, 1992.

T. YASUDA, Y. HASHIMOTO, S. YOKOI, and J. I. TORIWAKI. Computer system for craniofacial surgery planning based on CT data. *IEEE Transactions on Medical Imaging*, 9(3):270–280, March 1990.

P. J. YIM, P. L. CHOYKE, and R. M. SUMMERS. Grey-scale skeletonization of small vessels in MRA. *IEEE Transactions on Medical Imaging*, 19(6):568–576, 2000.

T. S. YOO. *Insight into Images Principles and Practice for Segmentation, Registration and Image Analysis*. AK Peters, 2004.

E. C. YOUNG. *Vector and Tensor Analyis*. Dekker, 1978.

H. YOUNG, R. BAUM, U. CREMERIUS, K. HERHOLZ, O. HOEKSTRA, A. A. LAMMERTSMA, J. PRUIM, and P. PRICE. Measurement of clinical and subclinical tumour response using [18f]-fluorodeoxyglucose and positron emission tomography: review and 1999 eortc recommendations. *European Journal of Cancer*, 35(13):1773–1782, 1999.

I. R. YOUNG. Significant events in the development of MRI (editorial). *Journal of Magnetic Resonance Imaging*, 19:523–526, 2003.

X. YUAN, M. X. NGUYEN, N. ZHANG, and B. CHEN. Stippling and silhouettes rendering in geometry-image space. In *Proc. of Eurographics Symposium on Rendering*, pp. 193–200, 2005.

S. ZACHOW, E. GLADILIN, R. SADER, and H.-F. ZEILHOFER. Draw and cut: intuitive 3D osteotomy planning on polygonal bone models. In *Proc. of Computer Assisted Radiology and Surgery*, pp. 362–369, 2003a.

S. ZACHOW, E. GLADILIN, A. TREPCZYNSKI, and R. SADER. 3D osteotomy planning in cranio-maxilofacial surgery: experiences and results of surgery planning and volumetric finite-element soft tissue prediction om three clinical cases. In *Proc. of Computer Assisted Radiology and Surgery*, pp. 983–987, 2003b.

S. ZACHOW, H.-C. HEGE, and P. DEUFLHARD. Computer assisted planning in cranio-maxillofacial surgery. *Journal of Computing and Information Technology*, 14(1):53–64, 2006.

C. ZAHLTEN, H. JÜRGENS, and H.-O. PEITGEN. Reconstruction of branching blood vessels from CT data. In *Proc. of Eurographics Workshop on Visualization in Scientific Computing*, pp. 41–52, 1995.

J. ZANDER, T. ISENBERG, S. SCHLECHTWEG, and T. STROTHOTTE. High quality hatching. *Computer Graphics Forum*, 23:421–430, 2004.

D. ZELTZER. "Task-level Graphical Simulation: Abstraction, Representation, and Control," chapter in Making them Move: Mechanics, Control and Animation of Articulated Figures, pp. 3–33. Los Altos, 1990.

X. ZENG, L. STAIB, R. SCHULTZ, and J. DUNCAN. Survey: interpolation methods in medical image processing. *IEEE Transactions on Medical Imaging*, 18(10):100–111, 1999.

H. ZHANG, D. MANOCHA, T. HUDSON, and K. HOFF. Visibility culling using hierarchical occlusion maps. In *Proc. of ACM SIGGRAPH*, pp. 77–88, 1997.

S. ZHANG, C. DEMIRALP, and D. H. LAIDLAW. Visualizing diffusion tensor MRI images using streamtubes and streamsurfaces. *IEEE Transactions on Visualization and Computer Graphics*, 9(4):454–462, October 2003.

Y. ZHANG. A survey of evaluation methods for image segmentation. *Pattern Recognition*, 29:1335–1346, 1996.

Y. ZHANG, R. ROHLING, and D. K. PAI. Direct surface extraction from 3D freehand ultrasound images. In *Proc. of IEEE Visualization*, pp. 45–52, 2002.

J. ZHOU, A. DÖRING, and K. D. TÖNNIES. Distance based enhancement for focal region based volume rendering. In *Proc. of Workshop Bildverarbeitung für die Medizin, Informatik aktuell*, pp. 199–203, 2004.

L. ZHUKOV and A. H. BARR. Oriented tensor reconstruction from diffusion tensor MRI. In *Proc. of IEEE Visualization*, pp. 387–393, 2002.

K. ZUIDERVELD. *Visualization of Multimodality Medical Volume Data using Object-Oriented Methods*. Ph.D. thesis, University Utrecht, 1995.

K. ZUIDERVELD, A. KONING, and M. VIERGEVER. Acceleration of ray-casting using 3D distance transforms. In *Proc. of Visualization in Biomedical Computing*, pp. 324–335, 1992.

M. ZWICKER, H. PFISTER, J. VAN BAAR, and M. GROSS. EWA volume splatting. In *Proc. of IEEE Visualization*, pp. 29–36, 2001.

Index